The Selected Papers of
Elizabeth Cady Stanton and Susan B. Anthony

The Selected Papers of Elizabeth Cady Stanton and Susan B. Anthony

·⟨⟶⟩· VOLUME IV ·⟨⟶⟩·

WHEN CLOWNS MAKE LAWS FOR QUEENS
1880 TO 1887

Ann D. Gordon, EDITOR

Krystal Frazier, EDITORIAL ASSISTANT
Lesley L. Doig, EDITORIAL ASSISTANT
Emily Westkaemper, EDITORIAL ASSISTANT
Robin Chapdelaine, EDITORIAL ASSISTANT

RUTGERS UNIVERSITY PRESS
NEW BRUNSWICK, NEW JERSEY

Library of Congress Cataloging-in-Publication Data

Stanton, Elizabeth Cady, 1815–1902.
 [Selections. 1997]
 The selected papers of Elizabeth Cady Stanton and Susan B. Anthony /
Ann D. Gordon, editor.
  p. cm.
 Includes bibliographical references and index.
 Contents: v. 4. When clowns make laws for queens, 1880 to 1887
 ISBN 0-8135-2320-6 (alk. paper)
 1. Feminists—United States—Archives. 2. Suffragists—United
States—Archives. 3. Stanton, Elizabeth Cady, 1815–1902—
Archives. 4. Anthony, Susan B. (Susan Brownell), 1820–1906—
Archives. 5. Feminism—United States—History—19th
century—Sources. 6. Women—Suffrage—United States—History—
19th century—Sources. I. Anthony, Susan B. (Susan Brownell), 1820–
1906. II. Gordon, Ann D. (Ann Dexter) III. Miller, Tamara
Gaskell. IV. Title.
HQ1410.A25 1997
016.30542—dc21   97-5666
                    CIP

British Cataloging-in-Publication information is available from the British Library.

TEXT DESIGN: Judith Martin Waterman of Martin-Waterman Associates, Ltd.
Manufactured in the United States of America

≈

Publication of this volume was assisted by a grant from the National
Historical Publications and Records Commission.

≈

Frontispiece photograph of Elizabeth Cady Stanton, n.d., (LC-USZ62-28195,
Prints and Photographs Division, Library of Congress), and Susan B. An-
thony, c. 1886 (courtesy of Lisa Unger Baskin), both by Aaron Veeder,
Albany, New York.

To the memory
of
Shirley Anita St. Hill Chisholm
1924–2005
Unbought and unbossed

Contents

Illustrations   xvi

Preface   xvii

Acknowledgments   xviii

Introduction   xx

Editorial Practice   xxviii

Abbreviations   xxxiv

1. 23 September 1880 — Article by ECS: The Politics of Reformers   *1*

2. 8 October 1880 — SBA to Matilda Joslyn Gage   *4*

3. 24 October 1880 — SBA to Harriet Hanson Robinson   *6*

4. 25 October 1880 — SBA to Amelia Jenks Bloomer   *12*

5. 2 November 1880 — ECS to Theodore W. Stanton   *14*

6. c. 6 November 1880 — SBA to Jane Snow Spofford   *15*

7. 14 November 1880 — ECS to Friend   *16*

8. 27 November 1880 — SBA to Rutherford B. Hayes   *18*

9. 30 November 1880 — SBA to Mary Tenney Gray   *20*

10. 30 November 1880 — SBA to Amelia Jenks Bloomer   *23*

11. 3 December 1880 — SBA to Ellen C. Sargent   *24*

12. 5 December 1880 — ECS to Edward M. Davis   *27*

13. 9 December 1880 — ECS to Amelia Jenks Bloomer   *29*

14. 13 December 1880 — ECS to Amelia Jenks Bloomer   *31*

15. 22 December 1880 — Clarina Howard Nichols to SBA   *32*

16. after 22 December 1880 — SBA to Clarina Howard Nichols   *33*

17. 16 January 1881 — Interview with SBA   *34*

18. 17 January 1881 — SBA to Lucy Webb Hayes   *35*

19. 18 January 1881 — Memorial Service for Lucretia Coffin Mott   *36*

20. January 1881 — ECS to Editor, *National Citizen and Ballot Box*   *39*

21. 2 February 1881 — ECS to Theodore D. Weld   *46*

22. 8 February 1881 — ECS to Rachel G. Foster   *48*

23. ❧ 14 February 1881   SBA to Clara Barton   *49*

24. ❧ 25 February 1881   SBA to Rachel G. and Julia T. Foster   *51*

25. ❧ 28 February 1881   ECS to Harriot E. Stanton   *52*

26. ❧ 20 March 1881   SBA to Elizabeth Boynton Harbert   *53*

27. ❧ 20 March 1881   ECS to Frederic A. Hinckley   *54*

28. ❧ 7 April 1881   SBA to Harriet Hanson Robinson   *56*

29. ❧ 15 April 1881   SBA to Barbara Binks Thompson   *59*

30. ❧ 20 April 1881   ECS to Marguerite M. Berry   *61*

31. ❧ 21 April 1881   ECS to Theodore W. Stanton   *63*

32. ❧ 29 April 1881   Harriet Hanson Robinson to SBA   *64*

33. ❧ 13 May 1881   SBA to Harriet Hanson Robinson   *66*

34. ❧ 26 May 1881   Mary L. Booth to SBA   *67*

35. ❧ 27 May 1881   Meeting of National Woman Suffrage Association   *68*

36. ❧ 27 May 1881   Address by ECS to Free Religious Association   *72*

37. ❧ 31 May 1881   Speech by ECS in Providence, Rhode Island   *89*

38. ❧ 5 June 1881   ECS to Elizabeth Smith Miller   *93*

39. ❧ 9 June 1881   Lecture by SBA in Concord, New Hampshire   *95*

40. ❧ 21 June 1881   Sarah Pugh to ECS   *98*

41. ❧ 9 July 1881   SBA to Lillie Devereux Blake   *99*

42. ❧ 30 July 1881   ECS to Amelia Jenks Bloomer   *101*

43. ❧ 4 August 1881   SBA to Amelia Jenks Bloomer   *102*

44. ❧ 18 August 1881   SBA to Barbara Binks Thompson   *104*

45. ❧ 24 August 1881   SBA to Elizabeth Wadsworth Anthony   *107*

46. ❧ 10 September 1881   John P. St. John to SBA   *110*

47. ❧ 20 September 1881   SBA to Clara Barton   *112*

48. ❧ 7 October 1881   ECS to Marguerite Berry Stanton   *114*

49. ❧ 13 October 1881   SBA to Clara Barton   *115*

50. ❧ 26 October 1881   SBA to Rachel G. Foster   *116*

51. ❧ 26 October 1881   ECS to Harriet Hanson Robinson   *118*

52. ❧ 1 December 1881   SBA to Laura Carter Holloway   *120*

53. ❧ 6 December 1881   SBA to J. Warren Keifer   *121*

54. 〜 after 9 December 1881   ECS to Editor, New York *Sun*   *122*

55. 〜 13 December 1881   Franklin G. Adams to SBA   *125*

56. 〜 18 December 1881   SBA to Franklin G. Adams   *127*

57. 〜 3 January 1882   SBA to George F. Hoar   *128*

58. 〜 7 January 1882   Wendell Phillips to SBA   *129*

59. 〜 c. 8 January 1882   SBA to Wendell Phillips   *132*

60. 〜 12 January 1882   ECS and SBA to George F. Hoar   *133*

61. 〜 17 & 21 January 1882   Executive Sessions of National Woman Suffrage Association   *134*

62. 〜 20 January 1882   Resolutions of National Woman Suffrage Association   *140*

63. 〜 25 January 1882   Executive Session of National Woman Suffrage Association   *142*

64. 〜 29 January 1882   ECS to Olympia Brown   *145*

65. 〜 29 January 1882   ECS to Frederick Douglass   *147*

66. 〜 30 January 1882   ECS to Frederic A. Hinckley   *148*

67. 〜 31 January 1882   ECS to Harriette Robinson Shattuck   *149*

68. 〜 31 January 1882   Frederick Douglass to ECS   *150*

69. 〜 4 February 1882   SBA to Elizabeth Boynton Harbert   *150*

70. 〜 4 February 1882   ECS to Frederick Douglass   *152*

71. 〜 before 15 February 1882   SBA to Julius C. Burrows   *153*

72. 〜 21 February 1882   SBA to George F. Hoar   *154*

73. 〜 25 February 1882   Thomas B. Reed to SBA   *155*

74. 〜 c. 4 March 1882   SBA to Harriet Hanson Robinson, with enclosure   *156*

75. 〜 8 March 1882   SBA to Elizabeth Boynton Harbert   *161*

76. 〜 5 April 1882   SBA to Rachel G. Foster   *163*

77. 〜 3 May 1882   ECS to Elizabeth Cady Stanton, Jr.   *164*

78. 〜 10 May 1882   SBA to Elizabeth Boynton Harbert   *166*

79. 〜 16 June 1882   ECS to Elizabeth Cady Stanton, Jr.   *168*

80. 〜 19 June 1882   Henry B. Anthony to SBA   *169*

81. 〜 8 July 1882   ECS to SBA   *169*

82. 〜 16 July 1882   ECS to Mary Post Hallowell   *170*

83. 〜 1 September 1882   ECS to National Woman Suffrage Association   *173*

84. ⋙ after 2 September 1882   SBA to Clarina Howard Nichols   *175*

85. ⋙ 13 September 1882   Remarks by SBA to American Woman
Suffrage Association   *176*

86. ⋙ 23 September 1882   Wendell Phillips to SBA   *178*

87. ⋙ c. 30 September 1882   SBA to Rachel G. Foster   *180*

88. ⋙ 7 October 1882   Ellen Wright Garrison to SBA   *181*

89. ⋙ 13 October 1882   Debate by SBA in Omaha   *183*

90. ⋙ 29 October 1882   Priscilla Bright McLaren to ECS   *191*

91. ⋙ 3 November 1882   Speech by ECS in Glasgow   *194*

92. ⋙ 4 November 1882   ECS to Harriot E. Stanton   *196*

93. ⋙ 14 November 1882   Priscilla Bright McLaren to ECS   *199*

94. ⋙ c. 15 November 1882   Interview with SBA   *201*

95. ⋙ 16 November 1882   ECS to Elizabeth Pease Nichol   *202*

96. ⋙ 16 November 1882   Katharine Lucas Thomasson to
ECS   *203*

97. ⋙ 7 December 1882   SBA to Harriet Hanson Robinson   *204*

98. ⋙ 9 December 1882   SBA to Lillie Devereux Blake   *207*

99. ⋙ 2 January 1883   SBA to Jane Cannon Swisshelm   *210*

100. ⋙ 10 January 1883   ECS to Elizabeth Pease Nichol   *212*

101. ⋙ 23 January 1883   SBA to Benjamin F. Butler   *213*

102. ⋙ 23 January 1883   Benjamin F. Butler to SBA   *214*

103. ⋙ 30 January 1883   ECS to Anna M. Priestman   *215*

104. ⋙ 6 February 1883   SBA to Lillie Devereux Blake   *217*

105. ⋙ 6 February 1883   ECS to Elizabeth Smith Miller   *218*

106. ⋙ 13 February 1883   Frances P. Cobbe to ECS   *220*

107. ⋙ 22 February 1883   Interview with SBA   *222*

108. ⋙ 15 March 1883   Article by ECS on SBA in London   *224*

109. ⋙ 1 April 1883   SBA to Daniel R. Anthony   *228*

110. ⋙ 11 May 1883   SBA to Daniel R. Anthony   *232*

111. ⋙ 14–25 May 1883   Diary of SBA   *236*

112. ⋙ 26 May 1883   SBA to Mary S. Anthony   *243*

113. ⋙ 26–28 May 1883   Diary of SBA   *243*

114. ⋙ 25 June 1883   Speech by ECS: On the Position of
Woman in America   *245*

115. ⋙ 2 July 1883   Ursula Mellor Bright to ECS   *272*

116. ⋙ 4–8 July 1883   Diary of SBA   *273*

117. ⇒ 10 July 1883 — ECS to Harriet Cady Eaton *276*

118. ⇒ 11-16 July 1883 — Diary of SBA *279*

119. ⇒ 17 July 1883 — ECS to SBA *281*

120. ⇒ 17 July 1883 — Priscilla Bright McLaren to ECS *282*

121. ⇒ 17–18 July 1883 — Diary of SBA *283*

122. ⇒ 19 July 1883 — SBA to Rachel G. Foster *284*

123. ⇒ 19–20 July 1883 — Diary of SBA *285*

124. ⇒ 3 September 1883 — SBA to H. Louise Mosher *286*

125. ⇒ 27–29 October 1883 — Diary of SBA *290*

126. ⇒ 30 October 1883 — ECS to Anna M. and Mary Priestman and Margaret Priestman Tanner *291*

127. ⇒ 30 October 1883 — Diary of SBA *293*

128. ⇒ 31 October 1883 — Lydia E. Becker to ECS *294*

129. ⇒ 31 October–6 November 1883 — Diary of SBA *295*

130. ⇒ 7 November 1883 — ECS to William H. Blatch, Jr. *296*

131. ⇒ 7–17 November 1883 — Diary of SBA *297*

132. ⇒ 18 November 1883 — William F. Channing to ECS *301*

133. ⇒ 4 December 1883 — Remarks by SBA to American Anti-Slavery Society *302*

134. ⇒ 9 December 1883 — SBA to Elizabeth Boynton Harbert *305*

135. ⇒ 9 December 1883 — ECS to Elizabeth Boynton Harbert *309*

136. ⇒ 17 December 1883 — SBA to Mary B. Clay *312*

137. ⇒ 19–24 December 1883 — Diary of SBA *315*

138. ⇒ 25 December 1883 — SBA to Elizabeth Boynton Harbert *318*

139. ⇒ 25–26 December 1883 — Diary of SBA *319*

140. ⇒ 29 December 1883 — SBA to Editor, *Cincinnati Commercial Gazette* *321*

141. ⇒ 19 January 1884 — Luke P. Poland to SBA *322*

142. ⇒ 27 January 1884 — SBA to ECS *323*

143. ⇒ 5 February 1884 — Jane Cobden to SBA *328*

144. ⇒ 8 February 1884 — ECS to Mary England *330*

145. ⇒ 14 February 1884 — Millicent Garrett Fawcett to SBA *331*

146. ⇒ 15 February 1884 — Lydia E. Becker to SBA *332*

147. ⇒ 17 February 1884 — SBA to William Lloyd Garrison, Jr. *333*

148. ⇒ 17 February 1884 — Hubertine Auclert to SBA *335*

149. ❧ 19 February 1884   Léon Richer to SBA   *337*

150. ❧ 20 February 1884   Margaret Walker Parker to SBA   *338*

151. ❧ 23 February 1884   ECS to SBA   *339*

152. ❧ 1 March 1884   ECS to National Woman Suffrage Association   *340*

153. ❧ 7 March 1884   Testimony of SBA before Senate Committee on Woman Suffrage   *344*

154. ❧ 18 March 1884   Lucy Stone to SBA   *348*

155. ❧ 20 March 1884   ECS to SBA   *349*

156. ❧ 2 May 1884   SBA to Benjamin F. Butler   *350*

157. ❧ 12 May 1884   SBA to Harriet Hanson Robinson   *350*

158. ❧ 25 May 1884   Benjamin F. Butler to SBA   *352*

159. ❧ 27 May 1884   ECS to Frederick Douglass, with enclosure   *353*

160. ❧ 30 May 1884   Frederick Douglass to ECS   *356*

161. ❧ 12 June 1884   SBA to Edward M. Davis   *358*

162. ❧ 4 July 1884   William F. Channing to ECS   *360*

163. ❧ 30 July 1884   Appeal by ECS and SBA: Stand by the Republican Party   *361*

164. ❧ 12 August 1884   ECS and SBA to Benjamin F. Butler   *367*

165. ❧ 19 August 1884   SBA to Benjamin F. Butler   *368*

166. ❧ 12 October 1884   William F. Channing to ECS   *369*

167. ❧ 16 October 1884   ECS to Benjamin F. Butler   *370*

168. ❧ 23 October 1884   SBA to ECS   *371*

169. ❧ 1 December 1884   SBA to Thomas W. Palmer   *374*

170. ❧ 4 December 1884   Speech by SBA to Rhode Island Woman Suffrage Association   *376*

171. ❧ 12 December 1884   SBA to Thomas W. Palmer   *378*

172. ❧ 21 December 1884   SBA to Elizabeth Boynton Harbert   *379*

173. ❧ 21 December 1884   SBA to ECS   *381*

174. ❧ after 21 December 1884   ECS to SBA   *382*

175. ❧ 25 December 1884   Matilda Hindman to SBA   *383*

176. ❧ 28 December 1884   ECS to Laura Curtis Bullard   *385*

177. ❧ 2 January 1885   Lucy Stone to SBA   *387*

178. ❧ early January 1885   ECS to Editor, "Woman's Realm"   *388*

179. ❧ 20 January 1885   Lucy Stone to SBA   *390*

180. ⇝ 21 January 1885   Meeting of National Woman Suffrage Association *391*

181. ⇝ 25 January 1885   Interview with ECS *402*

182. ⇝ 1 February 1885   SBA to Nelson W. Aldrich *404*

183. ⇝ 10 February 1885   SBA to Elizabeth Buffum Chace *404*

184. ⇝ 8 March 1885   ECS to Marguerite Berry Stanton *405*

185. ⇝ 14 March 1885   SBA to Harriet Hanson Robinson *408*

186. ⇝ 16 April 1885   SBA to Harriet Hanson Robinson *410*

187. ⇝ 24 April 1885   ECS to F. Ellen Burr and Hartford Equal Rights Club, with discussion *411*

188. ⇝ 9 May 1885   ECS to Sara Francis Underwood *416*

189. ⇝ 15 May 1885   SBA to Caroline Thomas Merrick *417*

190. ⇝ 6 June 1885   Speech by SBA to Pennsylvania Yearly Meeting of Progressive Friends *420*

191. ⇝ 23 June 1885   SBA to Amelia Jenks Bloomer *429*

192. ⇝ 10 July 1885   SBA to Lillie Devereux Blake *431*

193. ⇝ 17 July 1885   Franklin G. Adams to SBA *432*

194. ⇝ 23 July 1885   Article by ECS: Has Christianity Benefited Woman? *433*

195. ⇝ 1 August 1885   SBA to Amelia Jenks Bloomer *437*

196. ⇝ 6 September 1885   SBA to Lillie Devereux Blake *438*

197. ⇝ 12 September 1885   SBA to Elizabeth Boynton Harbert *440*

198. ⇝ 19 October 1885   ECS to Benjamin F. Underwood *442*

199. ⇝ 27 October 1885   SBA to Lillie Devereux Blake *444*

200. ⇝ 30 October 1885   ECS to Lillie Devereux Blake *445*

201. ⇝ 2 November 1885   ECS to Elizabeth Boynton Harbert *446*

202. ⇝ 7 November 1885   SBA to Mary L. Booth and Anne W. Wright *447*

203. ⇝ 10 November 1885   ECS to Amelia Jenks Bloomer *448*

204. ⇝ 10 November 1885   Antoinette Brown Blackwell to ECS *450*

205. ⇝ 12 November 1885   Speech by ECS: The Pleasures of Age *451*

206. ⇝ 15 November 1885   ECS to Margaret Stanton Lawrence *463*

207. ⇝ 16 November 1885   SBA to Grover Cleveland *465*

208. ⇝ 18 November 1885   SBA to Lillie Devereux Blake *465*

209. ⇝ after 13 December 1885   ECS to Ellen Dana Conway *468*

210. ⇝ 29 December 1885   ECS to Antoinette Brown Blackwell *470*

211. ⇥ 31 January 1886   SBA to Marietta Holley   *471*

212. ⇥ 15 February 1886   ECS to National Woman Suffrage Association   *473*

213. ⇥ 17–20 February 1886   Executive Sessions and Executive Committee of National Woman Suffrage Association   *476*

214. ⇥ 19 February 1886   Remarks by SBA to National Woman Suffrage Association   *490*

215. ⇥ 3 March 1886   SBA to Lillie Devereux Blake   *492*

216. ⇥ before 11 March 1886   ECS to Benjamin F. Underwood   *494*

217. ⇥ 16 March 1886   SBA to Lillie Devereux Blake   *495*

218. ⇥ before 20 March 1886   ECS to F. Ellen Burr and Hartford Equal Rights Club   *496*

219. ⇥ before 25 March 1886   ECS to Benjamin F. Underwood   *498*

220. ⇥ 19 April 1886   John G. MacConnell to ECS   *499*

221. ⇥ before 27 April 1886   ECS to SBA   *501*

222. ⇥ 27 April 1886   SBA to Matilda Joslyn Gage   *503*

223. ⇥ 27 April 1886   ECS to Antoinette Brown Blackwell   *504*

224. ⇥ 23 May 1886   SBA to Harriet Taylor Upton   *505*

225. ⇥ 3 June 1886   SBA to Elizabeth Boynton Harbert   *506*

226. ⇥ 13 August 1886   SBA to John W. Weinheimer   *508*

227. ⇥ 19 August 1886   Article by ECS: The Woman's Bible   *510*

228. ⇥ 27 August 1886   ECS to Harriet Hanson Robinson   *512*

229. ⇥ 2 September 1886   Elizabeth Smith Miller to ECS   *513*

230. ⇥ 13 September 1886   ECS to Elizabeth Boynton Harbert   *513*

231. ⇥ 16 September 1886   Appeal by ECS to governors of thirteen colonial states   *515*

232. ⇥ 26 September 1886   Mary Jane Tarr Channing to ECS   *518*

233. ⇥ 30 September 1886   ECS to Harriet Hanson Robinson   *519*

234. ⇥ before 19 October 1886   SBA to Elizabeth Boynton Harbert   *521*

235. ⇥ 20 October 1886   Remarks by SBA to Luncheon in Wichita   *522*

236. ⇥ 25 October 1886   Antoinette Brown Blackwell to ECS   *524*

237. ⇥ 12 November 1886   SBA to Richard W. Guenther   *524*

238. ⇥ 12 November 1886   ECS to Victoria Woodhull Martin   *525*

239. ⇥ 13 November 1886   Interview with SBA   *526*

240. ⇝ 15 November 1886   ECS to Sara Francis Underwood   *528*

241. ⇝ 15 November 1886   Caroline Coulomb de Barrau to ECS   *530*

242. ⇝ 1 December 1886   SBA to Elizabeth Boynton Harbert   *531*

243. ⇝ 2 December 1886   Speech by SBA in Madison, Wisconsin   *533*

244. ⇝ 3 December 1886   SBA to Jane Snow Spofford   *534*

245. ⇝ 10 December 1886   SBA to Elizabeth Boynton Harbert   *535*

246. ⇝ 30 December 1886   SBA to Caroline Healey Dall   *536*

247. ⇝ 8 January 1887   ECS to SBA   *537*

248. ⇝ after 14 January 1887   ECS to Theodore W. Stanton   *541*

249. ⇝ 15 January 1887   SBA to Rachel G. Foster   *544*

250. ⇝ 25 January 1887   Henry W. Blair to SBA   *545*

251. ⇝ 26 January 1887   Interview with SBA   *546*

252. ⇝ 27 January 1887   Resolutions of National Woman Suffrage Association   *548*

253. ⇝ 27 January 1887   Remarks by SBA to National Woman Suffrage Association   *553*

254. ⇝ after 28 January 1887   Eliza Roxey Snow et al. to SBA   *554*

255. ⇝ 29 January 1887   SBA to Richard W. Blue   *557*

    Appendix   558

    Index   563

ILLUSTRATIONS

Cameo of Susan B. Anthony

Margaret Bright Lucas and Elizabeth Cady Stanton

Henry Brewster Stanton

Nora S. Blatch

Priscilla Bright McLaren

Rachel G. Foster

"The Ladies' Battle"

John Daugherty White

George Frisbie Hoar

Thomas Witherell Palmer

Joseph Emerson Brown

Francis Marion Cockrell

Harriet Hanson Robinson

Elizabeth Avery Meriwether

Clara Bewick Colby

May Wright Thompson Sewall

Page from speech on the position of woman in America

Frederick Douglass and Helen Pitts Douglass

❧ PREFACE

THIS IS THE FOURTH IN A SERIES of volumes publishing selected papers of Elizabeth Cady Stanton (1815–1902) and Susan B. Anthony (1820–1906). Like the earlier volumes, this one builds upon the work of Patricia G. Holland, Ann D. Gordon, Gail Malmgreen, and Kathleen McDonough in preparing the microfilm edition, *Papers of Elizabeth Cady Stanton and Susan B. Anthony* (1991). The underlying search for the papers of Stanton and Anthony is described in detail in the *The Papers of Elizabeth Cady Stanton and Susan B. Anthony: Guide and Index to the Microfilm Edition* (1992).

This series brings the most important documents of that comprehensive collection into print. The *Selected Papers* focuses on the public careers of two co-workers in the cause of woman suffrage, beginning with the start of their activism in the 1840s and pursuing the story of their ideas, tactics, reputations, and impact until the end of their lives in the twentieth century. Volume four draws on the papers dating from 1880 to 1887; it documents their continued advocacy of "national protection for national citizens" through a federal amendment for woman suffrage and pressure on Congress to bring their amendment to a vote, their work on the multi-volume *History of Woman Suffrage*, and their collaboration with woman suffragists in Great Britain.

✌ ACKNOWLEDGMENTS

I T IS A PLEASURE TO ACKNOWLEDGE and thank the people who made this volume possible. The title page credits the people whose work is most evident in the pages of this volume. Many more people contributed their time and talents to the completion of specific tasks. Two transient assistant editors, Harriet E. Sigerman and Peter Mickulas, helped briefly with transcription and research. Timely help was provided by graduate students at Rutgers, Leigh-Anne Francis, Jennifer Manion, Laurie Marhoefer, Damian Miller, Sara Rzeszutek, Margaret Sumner, and Terri Youngwha. Kara V. Donaldson spent four months as a volunteer on the staff after she completed her doctorate in English literature. Lauren Toth and Kathryn Brower came to us as undergraduate interns.

We acknowledge in the notes the archivists, librarians, and local historians across the country who answered our queries about people, places, and sources. In addition, we want to thank Teresa Dearing of the Dansville Public Library in New York and Kathleen Neeley of the Spencer Research Library at the University of Kansas. In Cambridge, Massachusetts, Andrea Constantine Hawkes checked transcriptions against original manuscripts. Jennifer Born read newspapers for us in Indianapolis, and Ann Hambrecht performed the same service in Cincinnati. A special thanks is owed to Elizabeth C. Bouvier, Head of Archives, Supreme Judicial Court of Massachusetts, Archives and Records Preservation, for her assistance with the Eddy Will Case.

Perplexing problems in research for this volume became questions for scholars around the globe, and for their willingness to dig into memory and research files, we thank Bonnie S. Anderson, Alastair Bellany, Charles Capper, Phyllis Cole, Patricia Crawford, Gillis J. Harp, Robert Hudspeth, William Leach, T. Jackson Lears, Phyllis Mack, Clare Midgley, Sally Mitchell, Jill Norgren, Jane Rendall, Richard Vernon, Andrew Wernick, and T. R. Wright.

We extend our gratitude to the owners of manuscripts who allowed us to publish items from their collections: The Huntington Library, San Marino, California; Ella Strong Denison Library, Scripps College,

Claremont Colleges; Bernhard Knollenberg Collection, Manuscripts and Archives, Yale University Library; Special Collections Research Center, Morris Library, Southern Illinois University Carbondale; Iowa Masonic Library; Library and Archives Division, Kansas State Historical Society, Topeka; The Filson Historical Society; The Historic New Orleans Collection; Schlesinger Library, Radcliffe Institute for Advanced Study, Harvard University; Massachusetts Historical Society; Sophia Smith Collection, Smith College; Houghton Library, Harvard University; Clements Library, University of Michigan; Minnesota Historical Society; Missouri Historical Society; Princeton University Library; Special Collections and University Archives, Rutgers University Libraries; Brooklyn Public Library; Jefferson County Historical Society, New York; Seneca Falls Historical Society, New York; Department of Rare Books and Special Collections, University of Rochester; Special Collections Research Center, Syracuse University Library; Rare Book and Manuscript Library, Columbia University; Special Collections, Vassar College Libraries; Rutherford B. Hayes Presidential Center; Haverford College Library; Friends Historical Library of Swarthmore College; Henry Simms; Washington State Historical Society; National Museum of American History, Smithsonian Institution; Wisconsin Historical Society; and Richard Clark of C. & J. Clark Ltd.

This volume was produced with major financial support from Rutgers, the State University of New Jersey; the Research Division of the National Endowment for the Humanities; the National Historical Publications and Records Commission; and Patricia G. Holland. We have also received generous gifts from the following individuals: Nancy Corson, Carolyn De Swarte Gifford, Patricia J. Gordon, David W. Hirst, Janice K. Hobbs, William L. Holland, Mary M. Huth, Esther Katz, Kathi L. Kern, Susan and Lee Lane, John E. Little, Margaret S. Lyons, Gail Malmgreen, Barbara Marhoefer, Delia Moon, Carol Nadell, Jill Norgren, Leslie S. Rowland, Shelah Kane Scott, Stacy Kinlock Sewell, Fredrick E. Sherman, Jeanne Montgomery Smith, Allison Sneider, Ruthann Sneider, Claire Stern, and Judith Wellman.

Thanks are also due to colleagues at Rutgers: to members of the Department of History, to Mary DeMeo, to the staff of the Rutgers University Press, and to Barry Qualls.

≋   A. D. G.

❧ Introduction

"**N**ATIONAL PROTECTION FOR NATIONAL CITIZENS," the definition given in 1878 to their campaign for a constitutional amendment, continued to define the political objective of Elizabeth Cady Stanton and Susan B. Anthony through the 1880s. Their wing of the movement for woman suffrage sought federal action to override state constitutions that granted voting rights only to males. When their National Woman Suffrage Association launched its campaign, Stanton instructed members of the U.S. Senate that "the primal rights of all citizens should be regulated by the national government, and complete equality in civil and political rights everywhere secured."[1]

Over the years documented in this volume, September 1880 through January 1887, Stanton and Anthony grew frustrated in their effort to win passage of a constitutional amendment guaranteeing woman suffrage. Congressional allies remained faithful, and popular support for the cause grew, but those who resisted woman suffrage increased their political power and found cultural acceptance for rejecting the premises that women were individuals and should be treated equally with men. Suffragists were encouraged by finding allies of the National association willing to introduce their constitutional amendment in each Congress. Responding to suffragists' pressure, the Senate created a Select Committee on Woman Suffrage, and, though only for the length of the Forty-seventh Congress, the House did likewise. Three times in the Senate and once in the House, committees reported in favor of the amendment. This apparent progress toward a constitutional amendment attracted wide support from women. Even members of the rival American Woman Suffrage Association joined in petitioning Congress, and just before the amendment came to a vote in the Senate in 1887, petitions arrived from the Woman's Christian Temperance Union, the nation's largest, but conservative, organization of women.

---

[1] Ann D. Gordon, ed., *National Protection for National Citizens, 1873 to 1880*, vol. 3 of *The Selected Papers of Elizabeth Cady Stanton and Susan B. Anthony* (New Brunswick, N.J., 2003), 355. Cited hereafter as *Papers*.

Although Susan B. Anthony could exclaim, at the end of 1886, that she was never "more full of hope and good work,"[2] less encouraging news about progress abounded. In Congress, members and senators spent more time debating whether to disfranchise women in the territories than they did weighing whether to enfranchise women who lacked the right. Across the Atlantic, Great Britain's Parliament voted to exclude women from the larger franchise provided in the Reform Bill of 1884. Between 1880 and 1887, despite attempts in most of the northern states to gain suffrage, only Washington Territory joined Wyoming and Utah in granting full suffrage to women. Then matters moved backwards: women in Washington lost their voting rights by a judicial ruling.

Indeed, progress took place against a background of unbridled opposition to the goal itself and strong resistance to its achievement through federal action. With the end of Reconstruction had come tight political contests that made even idealistic men fearful of an unpredictable experiment like the enfranchisement of women. During the presidential campaign of 1880, Susan B. Anthony chastised the Republican candidate, James Garfield, for standing on a platform that surrendered what Americans gained through the Civil War—"<u>Supremacy</u> of the United States government in the protection of citizens in their right to vote."[3] The revival of the Democratic party, still the party of states' rights, and its success in national elections pulled the Republican party toward the political center and away from its commitment to federal guarantees of rights. Democrats held a majority in the House of Representatives for five of the seven congressional sessions between 1880 and 1887. Republicans gained a majority in the Senate only at the end of 1883 and struggled to keep it. In this environment, the federal amendment was blocked by parliamentary maneuvers to avoid debate, mocked in committee reports, and finally rejected when it reached the floor of the Senate in January 1887. In that same month, at the conclusion of this volume, the House and Senate approved laws to strip the women in Utah Territory of their existing right to vote.

Elizabeth Cady Stanton dubbed these the times "when clowns make laws for queens,"[4] in a speech delivered in Providence, Rhode Island,

[2] See document number 244 within.   [3] *Papers*, 3:573.
[4] See document number 37 within.

in 1881. With such unforgiving language, she engaged the insults hurled at woman suffragists. Men were not only demonstrating their political power by rejecting woman suffrage, they were, from prestigious platforms, expounding a culture that required male-only government. The editor of a midwestern newspaper, who debated Susan B. Anthony in Omaha in 1882, interrupted her to dispute her reference to man's purposeful monopoly of votes: "That monopoly was created by a higher power. It is a monopoly created by the Lord, who made man the protector and bread winner."[5] In Morgan Dix's Lenten lectures at New York's Trinity Chapel in 1883, he denounced women's quest for votes as a "wrestling match with man" by which a woman laid "her honor in the dust."[6] Startled by the clergyman's contempt, the *New York Times* called this "one of the roundest beratings that the woman's rights movement has received, from the pulpit at least, since the movement sprang into being."[7] Politicians spun frightening fantasies about returning home "to be received in the masculine embrace of some female ward politician" rather than "to the earnest, loving look and touch of a true woman."[8] Others raised the specter of polluted purity: "Who will marshal and parade the women of this country among the men, black and white and red, good and bad, put the ballot in their hands, and have them crowd up to the polls to cast their votes?" asked a senator during debate in 1886. "And who after that would ever feel that he would like to lay his hand upon that woman or call her sister or mother?"[9]

Nothing lessened Stanton's frustration. In 1887, with a sneer at the pretense that men represented women, she wrote, "Our representatives are simply playing with us, as a cat does with a mouse, to sacrifice

---

5 See document number 89 within.

6 Quotation from Rochester *Democrat and Chronicle*, n.d., in Susan B. Anthony scrapbook 10, Rare Books Division, Library of Congress. The newspaper reported the publication of Dix's lectures in pamphlet form under the title *Lectures on the Calling of a Christian Woman, and Her Training to Fulfil It. Delivered during the Season of Lent, A.D. 1883* (New York, 1883).

7 *New York Times*, 17 February 1883.

8 George G. Vest, 25 January 1887, *Congressional Record*, 49th Cong., 2d sess., 986.

9 John T. Morgan, 9 April 1886, *Congressional Record*, 49th Cong., 1st sess., 3325.

us at their pleasure."[10] In the same public letter to members of the National association assembled in Washington, she pressed her coadjutors to study the model of Irish women resorting to violence in their resistance to landlords.

≈

In 1880, Elizabeth Cady Stanton (ECS) turned sixty-five, and Susan B. Anthony (SBA) turned sixty. The pace of their lives changed: ECS soon abandoned the rigors of lecturing, and SBA traveled far less around the United States than she had in the previous decade. But neither woman settled into retirement. They remained leaders of the National Woman Suffrage Association, with meetings to organize, routine business to conduct, lobbying in Washington to oversee, and politicians to cajole and chastise. They published four books together between 1881 and 1886,[11] and ECS launched the project that became the *Woman's Bible* in the next decade. Drawn by the decisions of two Stanton children to live abroad, they also crossed the Atlantic and made new friends among Britain's suffragists.

In the National Woman Suffrage Association, ECS and SBA encouraged the younger women attracted to the cause in this decade to acquire the skills of leadership. To some extent, they succeeded. Helen Mar Gougar of Indiana, once described by ECS as the movement's most effective speaker, proved to be an adept organizer.[12] Clara Bewick Colby, who built her Nebraska monthly, the *Woman's Tribune*, into a national organ affiliated with the National association, also showed skills as a lecturer and organizer. Harriette Robinson Shattuck worked alongside her mother to make the National Woman Suffrage Association of Massachusetts a strong new force in New England. Rachel G.

[10] See document number 247 within.

[11] In addition to three volumes of the *History of Woman Suffrage*, discussed below, they published Elizabeth Cady Stanton and Susan B. Anthony, eds., *National Woman Suffrage Association. Report of the Sixteenth Annual Washington Convention, March 4th, 5th, 6th and 7th 1884, With Reports of the Forty-Eighth Congress* (Rochester, N.Y., 1884), a work of two hundred and twenty pages.

[12] Elizabeth Cady Stanton to Clara Bewick Colby, 5? November 1888, in Patricia G. Holland and Ann D. Gordon, eds., *Papers of Elizabeth Cady Stanton and Susan B. Anthony* (Wilmington, Del., 1991, microfilm), 26:943–46. (Cited hereafter as *Film*.)

Foster of Philadelphia and May Wright Sewall of Indianapolis, both young women willing to work hard, brought office efficiency to the association in their positions as corresponding secretary and chair of the executive committee.

New faces brought new ideas. A significant number of the National association's members also belonged to the Woman's Christian Temperance Union, with the result that the new evangelical element sometimes collided with the old-line freethinkers in the organization. Southern Democrats also joined the association, and the contradiction between their commitment to states' rights and the National's advocacy of national protection for national citizens could lead to arguments.

Time had not softened Lucy Stone's hostility to the National association and its leadership. At the opening of this volume, the National was on course to compete directly for the loyalty of New England's suffragists by holding its annual meeting of 1881 in Boston and then touring the New England states with the message of national protection for national citizens. The National association could penetrate New England, because sentiment was growing that the division between the two suffrage associations had outlived its time. While skirmishes between the leaders continued well into the 1880s, some members of both associations took steps toward reconciliation. The Rhode Island Woman Suffrage Association, for instance, repeatedly invited prominent speakers from both associations to share the platform at their annual meetings.[13] In Boston, William Lloyd Garrison, Jr., who by inheritance identified with the American but by marriage befriended the National, took it upon himself to open communication between SBA and Lucy Stone. When Matilda Hindman, an able organizer for both the National and American since the 1870s, settled in Pittsburgh to edit a column in a local newspaper, she chose her contributors from both associations.[14]

When ECS and SBA drew back from the presidential campaign of 1880, they took up again their project to edit a volume of reminiscences by pioneers in the movement for woman's rights. Once anticipated as a slim volume to be available by the end of the centennial year of 1876, their book swelled into the more ambitious, multi-volume *History of Woman Suffrage*, which traced antebellum agitation, wartime contributions of women, and postwar political work at the national and state capitals. Separate chapters recounted the annual meetings of the American

[13] See, for example, document number 170 within.
[14] See document number 175 within.

Woman Suffrage Association, activism in Great Britain, and progress in the countries of Europe. The *History of Woman Suffrage*, edited by ECS, SBA, and Matilda Joslyn Gage, exploded into three volumes, totaling 2,738 pages, which appeared in 1881, 1882, and 1886.

The editors corresponded with scores of women who contributed to the books, contesting the right of the editors to edit, checking facts, and debating about how much inner history to reveal. Only a small fraction of that vast correspondence survives. If even a few contributors required the constant care and negotiation evident in the correspondence between the editors and Amelia Bloomer and Harriet Robinson—two women who retained their letters—theirs was a managerial nightmare. The absence of correspondence also makes it difficult to establish the division of labor with Matilda Joslyn Gage. Because Gage infrequently worked alongside ECS and SBA, letters among the editors must once have been numerous. Now virtually no correspondence among them survives.[15]

The entire editorial enterprise was disorganized. Some chapters mentioned in letters never found their way into the volumes. Inexperienced in book publishing and naive about the scale of information they solicited from contributors, the three editors repeatedly changed their plans, sometimes while face to face with a printer or bookbinder. Pages already set into type for one volume were set aside for the next, and, adding to the disorder, they left the New York publishing firm of Fowler & Wells between volumes two and three. With money left to her by the Boston philanthropist Eliza Eddy, SBA took over as publisher of the final volume and the second printings of the first two volumes.

In the interval between work on the second and third volumes of the *History*, ECS and SBA went abroad. The Stanton children drew their mother across the Atlantic in May 1882 and set in motion SBA's trip nine months later. In Great Britain, both women were embraced and feted by suffrage leaders. ECS, in particular, was put to work speaking at mass demonstrations that led up to a parliamentary vote on suffrage, and in London, a large meeting was called specifically to hear SBA and ECS speak about progress toward equal rights in the United States. On

---

[15] For a possible reconstruction of the contributions of Matilda Joslyn Gage, see Mary E. Paddock Corey, "Matilda Joslyn Gage: Woman Suffrage Historian, 1852–1898" (Ph.D. diss., University of Rochester, 1995), chapter four.

the eve of their departure together in November 1883, their hosts laid plans for an international correspondence and collaboration among suffragists.

By the end of their trip, both women had gained an appreciation of their own transatlantic significance. The National association invited their new French and British friends to attend the annual Washington convention of 1884. Although a delegate from the suffrage society in Edinburgh was the only representative to make the transatlantic trip, dozens of letters expressing admiration and solidarity were received from France and Great Britain. In 1886, in the pages of the third volume of the *History*, ECS and SBA announced their intention to convene an international celebration in 1888 to mark the fortieth anniversary of the woman's rights convention at Seneca Falls.

꙰

Susan B. Anthony continued to live without a home of her own. When she stopped in Rochester, New York, she was a boarder in the home of her sister Mary, whose house on Madison Street was also home to a rotation of nieces taking advantage of the city's superior facilities for the education of girls. Mary Anthony had retired from her career in the Rochester public schools, and once the last of the nieces graduated from the Rochester Free Academy, she had time to join her sister in suffrage work. Though she chose not to join SBA in England in 1883, she became a presence at the National's conventions in Washington. Her brothers in Kansas saw less of SBA in these years, when she crossed the country less often, but their connections in the state encouraged SBA to make Kansas an important site of her political work.

The hospitality of Jane and Caleb Spofford at their hotel, the Riggs House, in Washington allowed SBA to spend more time in Washington during each session of Congress than she could afford to do in previous years. But it was the Stanton family who hosted her most often in these years. While at work on the *History of Woman Suffrage*, she spent weeks at a time in Tenafly, New Jersey, and she boarded near the Cady house in Johnstown, New York, for several months when the Stantons moved there in 1884. Even in England, SBA found a temporary home with ECS and her daughter, Harriot Blatch.

For a time after ECS retired from the lecture circuit after the 1879–1880 season, it appeared she might settle into her house in Tenafly.

She and SBA spent several months there together in the winter of 1880–1881, and ECS welcomed her son's bride there in June of that year. Less than a year later, she leased the house, moved into her sister's house in Manhattan, and prepared to sail for France. When she returned to New York eighteen months later, she bypassed Tenafly to move with her husband into her family's house in Johnstown, New York. Not until the spring of 1885 did she take possession of her Tenafly house again, but this last stay was a short one: in October 1886 she recrossed the Atlantic to stay with her children until 1888.

Henry Brewster Stanton (1805-1887) died on 14 January 1887, while ECS was in England. According to his obituaries, sons Henry and Robert were with him. The New York *Sun* reported that he worked at the newspaper's offices until a week before his death, and while sick at home, he corrected proofs of a third edition of his *Random Recollections*.[16] Young Henry, known as Kit to his family, and his brother Bob were the only Stanton children living on the East Coast in 1887. Henry Brewster, Jr., (1844-1903) and Robert Livingston (1859-1920) practiced law together in New York City. Two children married and settled abroad, while two others married and moved to the Midwest. Theodore Weld (1851-1925) married Marguerite Marie Berry in Paris in 1881, and a year later, Harriot Eaton (1856-1940) married William Henry Blatch, Jr., an English brewer, in London. In the Midwest were Gerrit Smith (1845-1927), known as Gat, a rancher in Iowa married since 1875, and Margaret Livingston Stanton Lawrence (1852-1930), who settled in Council Bluffs, Iowa, after her marriage in 1878.[17] The oldest of the Stanton children, Daniel Cady (1842-1891), known as Neil, tended to wander. Early in adulthood he practiced law, but later he managed his real estate investments in Iowa and spent considerable time living with his mother. He married in Chicago in 1884, but abandoned his wife and daughter; Frederika Stanton filed for divorce in 1886, and the court ordered Daniel to provide support for his child. Nothing is known of ECS's reaction to this troubling story.

[16] New York *Sun*, 15 January 1887.

[17] In Margaret Lawrence's account in 1885 of her siblings (in the appendix to this volume), she describes one brother as engaged "in the rigid analysis of pig iron in Pittsburg; another is a gentleman of leisure." The latter is almost certainly Daniel, but that leaves Gat embarked upon activity otherwise undocumented.

✌ EDITORIAL PRACTICE

PRINCIPLES OF SELECTION

This volume selects roughly fifteen percent of the documents available for the period from September 1880 through January 1887. Documents are printed in their entirety with two exceptions: entries from diaries are selected from the larger document; ECS's and SBA's contributions to meetings are occasionally excerpted from the fullest coverage available.

The high cost of producing and publishing historical editions creates an editorial imperative to bulldoze most of the trees while leaving an attractive and useful forest in place. The selection of documents to include in each volume often boils down to arbitrary choices between equally valuable items. There are, however, guidelines. Selection is governed first by the mission to document the careers of the two co-workers. Drawn from the papers of two people, the selections must next represent differences in the documentation of each one. Although writings by ECS and SBA have priority, incoming mail is included if it documents the other voice in longstanding friendships with ECS or SBA or supplies unusual evidence about their lives. The dominant stories evident in the documents of any year or era are also retained. In this volume, entries from SBA's diary were included when they provided unique perspective on her experience or best captured the pace of her daily life. The inclusion of discussions in which people other than ECS and SBA participate reflects the editors' conviction that in the battle of ideas waged by these women, exchanges with opponents and allies give critical evidence about political style, intellectual influences, and differences of opinion that the principals might otherwise have failed to mention.

A considerable "selection" of documents for the years of this volume occurred long before the editors began their work. For example, SBA's diaries for the years 1880 to 1882 and 1884 to 1887 all disappeared. More notably, a gaping hole in the historical record is created by the loss of most correspondence with contributors to the *History of Woman Suffrage*. Scores of women contributed to the volumes, and if the surviving correspondence with two of them—Harriet Hanson Robinson and Amelia Jenks Bloomer—is any indication of the care the editors administered to other contributors, hundreds of letters must be lost. Moreover, Matilda Joslyn Gage, who edited the *History* with ECS and SBA but rarely worked alongside of her coeditors, must have communicated with them through letters that have not been found.

ARRANGEMENT

Documents are presented in chronological order according to the date of authorship, oral delivery, or publication of the original text. Documents dated only by month appear at the start of the month unless the context in surrounding documents dictates later placement. Documents that cover a period of time, such as diaries, are placed at the date of the earliest entry, and the longer text is interrupted for the placement of other documents that fall within the same period of time.

If a diary entry appears on the same date as another document, it is assumed that the entry was written at day's end. When two or more documents possess the same date, ECS and SBA authorship takes precedence over incoming mail, and SBA's papers appear before those of ECS unless the context dictates otherwise.

SELECTION OF TEXT

Most documents in this edition survive in a single version. When choices were required, original manuscripts took precedence over later copies, and the recipient's copy of correspondence was used. A speech reported by a stenographer, however, took precedence over the manuscript. The newspaper to which SBA or ECS submitted a text took precedence over newspapers that reprinted it.

When letters survive only in transcripts made by editors and biographers, the earliest transcript was used as the source text. Typescripts by Harriot Stanton Blatch and Theodore Stanton took precedence over their published texts; considerable rewriting occurred between the two.

For the text of meetings and other oral events, the official report, or in its absence, the most comprehensive coverage, is the primary source text. If reports differ widely, composite reports were created. Additions to or substitutions from a second source are set off by angle brackets. The sources are separated by a semicolon in the endnote.

The goal with speeches is to publish a text as close as possible to the version delivered at a particular date, but how to achieve that varies in nearly every case, depending on what has survived. A stenographic report of a speech is usually regarded as the most authoritative text. Stenographers reported several speeches and discussions in this volume; the evidence is clear for documents at 7 March 1884, 20 January and 6 June 1885, and 17 February 1886, and it is likely that stenographers reported the debate at 13 October 1882 and meeting at 4 December 1883. The majority of the speeches are based on a local reporter's own notes. The text of ECS's speech of 27 May 1881 is that published in proceedings of the Free Religious Association; it matches closely a nearly complete manuscript of the speech and may derive directly from the manuscript. For her speech of 12 November 1885, the text is that published by ECS in 1901, the only text published in her lifetime. In one case in this volume (25 June 1883), the speaker's manuscript is the only text of the speech available.

Format

Some features of the documents have been standardized when set into print. The indentation of existing paragraphs was consistently set. The dateline of each letter appears as the first line of text, flush to the right margin, regardless of its placement in the original. The salutation of letters was printed on one line, flush left. Extra space in the dateline or salutation indicates the author's line break. The complimentary close of letters was run into the text itself, regardless of how the author laid it out, and signatures were placed at the right margin beneath the text. The dash is uniformly rendered even though the lengths vary in the originals.

Each document is introduced by an editorial heading or title that connects the document to ECS or SBA, except in cases of meetings at which both women participated and texts to which they both contributed.

Following the text, an unnumbered endnote describes the physical character of the document and the source or owner of the original. The endnote also explicates unusual physical properties of the document and explains the uses made of square brackets in the transcription. In the case of diary entries, this note appears at the end of the series. Numbered notes follow the endnote, except that numbered notes for diary entries follow each entry.

TRANSCRIPTION

The editors strive to prepare for print the most accurate transcription that reproduces the format of the original as nearly as possible. However, the greater the remove from the author, the less literal is the representation.

LETTERS AND DIARIES. The editors retained the author's punctuation, including the absence of customary symbols; emphasis by underlining, although not occasional use of double or triple underlines; spelling and capitalization; mistakes; abbreviations; superscripts; and paragraphing, or its absence. The author's form of dating was retained. Opening or closing quotation marks have been supplied in square brackets when the author neglected to enter them.

Emendations in the original text are marked by symbols to show cancelled text, interlineations, and other corrections and additions. A minimum number of exceptions were allowed when the interlineation obviously resulted from slip of the pen or thought, as when an infinitive was clearly intended but the "to" was added above the line. Strike outs and other erasures are indicated with a line through the text. Interlineations, above or below the line, are framed in up and down arrows. Text from the margin is moved into place with an editorial notation about the original location.

SBA's dashes can usually be distinguished as pauses or full stops, and the distinction is represented by spacing. The em-dash is flush to the words on either side in a pause; extra space is added after the dash at a full stop. SBA made no visible distinction when capitalizing letters "a," "m," and "w," and in haste, often lost the distinction for other letters. When her customary practice could not be found, the editors resorted to standard usage. Haste also affected SBA's ending syllables. Her rendition of "evening" became "evenng" and then something resembling "even^g." A similar evolution occurred with the "ly" ending. These compressions and contractions were ignored and the invisible letters supplied.

When SBA kept her diary in commercial appointment books, the printed date is set in capitals and small capitals to distinguish it from her entry.

Ecs's letters contain a form of implied punctuation; if a comma or period were required and she had reached the right margin of her paper, she omitted the punctuation. Rather than supplying what she left out, extra space was introduced into the text, larger for a full stop.

SPEECHES. One speech by ECS in this volume survives only in manuscript. In order to preserve two very different kinds of evidence in this document, indications of revisions, underlinings, and symbols were moved out of the text into textual notes. This practice allows experts concerned with composition and inscription to recover the writing process, while permitting the general reader to "hear" the speech. Despite the condition of their manuscripts, speakers introduce the necessary punctuation, pronounce the misspelled word, sound emphasis, place interlineations, omit strike outs, and expand abbreviations. In the textual notes, the alterations are listed by paragraph and line numbers, referenced to paragraph numbers printed beside the text. The textual notes employ the same editorial symbols in use elsewhere.

PRINTED TEXTS. In printed texts, obvious typographical errors have been silently corrected. When new words were substituted, the original wording was recorded in a numbered note. The original titles of articles and appeals were retained as part of the text. The practice of typesetters to use small capitals for emphasis and for highlighting the names of speakers has been ignored. To preserve the emphasis, italics have been substituted.

ANNOTATION

In numbered notes, the editors provide the information they think necessary for readers to understand the document. Editorial notes placed either beneath a document's heading or interjected in the transcription provide context for texts excerpted from reports of a meeting.

To incomplete place and datelines, the editors have added, in italic type within square brackets, the best information available to complete the line. The basis for supplying a date is explained in a note.

The numbered notes principally identify references in the text, explain textual complexities, and summarize documents omitted from the edition. People are identified at the first occurrence of their names in the documents. The editors have tried to identify every person and reference, but they have not added notes simply to say "unidentified" or "not located." Biographical notes about people identified in previous volumes of this series do not recapitulate earlier information; if previous volumes contain useful references to the individual, readers are directed to them.

Unless otherwise indicated, documents published in this volume may be found at their date in the microfilm edition of the *Papers of Stanton and Anthony*. A citation to the film (as *Film*, reel number:frame numbers) appears in the endnote only if the document is filmed at a different date. *Film* citations are included for documents mentioned within the numbered notes. An indication that a text is "not in *Film*" signifies that it has been acquired since publication of the microfilm edition.

TEXTUAL DEVICES

[roman text]	Text within square brackets in roman type is identified in the unnumbered endnote.
[roman text?]	The question mark indicates that the editors are uncertain about the text within the square brackets.
[roman date]	Date when a speech was delivered or an article published.
[*italic text*]	Editorial insertion or addition.
[*italic date*]	Date supplied by editors. In most cases, the basis is explained in a numbered note.
⟨text⟩	Authorial interlineation or substitution.
~~text~~	Text cancelled by the author.
~~illegible~~	Text cancelled by author that cannot be recovered.
\<roman\>	Addition to the source text from a second source.

⚜ ABBREVIATIONS

Throughout the volume Elizabeth Cady Stanton is referred to as ECS and Susan B. Anthony as SBA.

In notes only the National Woman Suffrage Association is abbreviated as NWSA and the National-American Woman Suffrage Association as NAWSA.

ABBREVIATIONS USED TO DESCRIBE DOCUMENTS

AL ⚜ Autograph Letter

ALS ⚜ Autograph Letter Signed

AMs ⚜ Autograph Manuscript

ANS ⚜ Autograph Note Signed

LS ⚜ Signed Letter in Hand Other than Author

TL ⚜ Typed Letter

STANDARD REFERENCES, NEWSPAPERS, AND JOURNALS

ACAB ⚜ James Grant Wilson and John Fiske, eds., *Appletons' Cyclopaedia of American Biography*, 6 vols. (New York, 1888–1889)

ACAB Supplement ⚜ James Grant Wilson, ed., *Appletons' Cyclopaedia of American Biography*, (1901; reprint, Detroit, Mich., 1968)

Allen ⚜ Charles Allen, *Reports of Cases Argued and Determined in the Supreme Judicial Court of Massachusetts*, 14 vols. (Boston, 1863–1883)

Allibone ⚜ Samuel Austin Allibone, *A Critical Dictionary of English Literature and British and American Authors*, 3 vols. (Philadelphia, 1854–1871)

Allibone Supplement ⇌ John Foster Kirk, *A Supplement to Allibone's Critical Dictionary of English Literature and British and American Authors*, 2 vols. (Philadelphia, 1891)

American Women ⇌ Frances E. Willard, *American Women: Fifteen Hundred Biographies with over 1,400 Portraits*, 2 vols. (New York, 1897)

ANB ⇌ John A. Garraty and Mark C. Carnes, eds., *American National Biography*, 24 vols. (New York, 1999)

Anthony ⇌ Ida Husted Harper, *Life and Work of Susan B. Anthony*, 3 vols. (1898–1908; reprint, New York, 1969)

Banks, *Biographical Dictionary of British Feminists, 1800–1930* ⇌ Olive Banks, *The Biographical Dictionary of British Feminists*, vol. 1, *1800–1930* (Brighton, England, 1985)

BDAC ⇌ *Biographical Dictionary of the American Congress, 1774–1971* (Washington, D.C., 1971)

Blatchford ⇌ Samuel Blatchford, *Reports of Cases Argued and Determined in the Circuit Court of the United States for the Second Circuit*, 24 vols. (Auburn, N.Y., 1852–1888)

BDGov ⇌ Robert Sobel and John Raimo, eds., *Biographical Dictionary of the Governors of the United States, 1789–1978*, 4 vols. (Westport, Conn., 1978)

BDTerrGov ⇌ Thomas A. McMullin and David Walker, *Biographical Directory of American Territorial Governors* (Westport, Conn., 1984)

Connecticut Reports ⇌ *Connecticut Reports. Cases Argued and Determined in the Supreme Court of Errors of the State of Connecticut*, 150 vols. (Hartford, Conn., 1817–1966)

DAB ⇌ Allen Johnson and Dumas Malone, eds., *Dictionary of American Biography*, 20 vols. (New York, 1928–1936)

DANB ⇌ Rayford W. Logan and Michael R. Winston, eds., *Dictionary of American Negro Biography* (New York, 1982)

DBF ⇌ J. Balteau et al., eds., *Dictionnaire de biographie française* (Paris, 1939–)

DNB ⇌ Leslie Stephen and Sidney Lee, eds., *The Dictionary of National Biography*, 22 vols. (1885–1901; reprint, London, 1973)

Douglass, *Papers* ⚭ Frederick Douglass, *The Frederick Douglass Papers. Series One: Speeches, Debates, and Interviews*, ed. John W. Blassingame et al., 5 vols. (New Haven, 1979–1992)

Eighty Years ⚭ Elizabeth Cady Stanton, *Eighty Years and More: Reminiscences, 1815–1897* (1898; reprint, Boston, 1993)

Film ⚭ Patricia G. Holland and Ann D. Gordon, eds., *Papers of Elizabeth Cady Stanton and Susan B. Anthony* (Wilmington, Del., 1991, microfilm)

Garrison, *Letters* ⚭ William Lloyd Garrison, *The Letters of William Lloyd Garrison*, ed. Walter M. Merrill and Louis Ruchames, 6 vols. (Cambridge, Mass., 1971–1981)

Garrison and Garrison, *Life* ⚭ Wendell Phillips Garrison and Francis Jackson Garrison, *William Lloyd Garrison: The Story of His Life Told By His Children*, 4 vols. (New York, 1885–1889)

History ⚭ Elizabeth Cady Stanton, Susan B. Anthony, Matilda Joslyn Gage et al., *History of Woman Suffrage*, 6 vols. (vols. 1–2, New York, 1881, 1882; vols. 3–4, Rochester, 1886, 1902; vols. 5–6, New York, 1922)

JAH ⚭ *Journal of American History*

Larousse, Grand dictionnaire universel, Deuxième supplement ⚭ Pierre Larousse, *Grand dictionnaire universel du XIX siecle*, 17 vols. in 28 (1866; reprint Nimes, France, 1990–1992)

London Encyclopaedia ⚭ Ben Weinreb and Christopher Hibbert, *The London Encyclopaedia* (Bethesda, Md., 1986)

McPherson, *Hand-Book of Politics* ⚭ Edward McPherson, *A Hand-Book of Politics for 1874, 1882, 1884* (Washington, D.C., 1874–1884)

Massachusetts Reports ⚭ *Cases Argued and Determined in the Supreme Judicial Court of Massachusetts*, 135 vols. (Boston, 1871–)

Mill, *Collected Works* ⚭ John Stuart Mill, *Collected Works of John Stuart Mill*, ed. J. M. Robson, 33 vols. (Toronto, Canada, 1963–1991)

National Party Platforms ⚭ Kirk H. Porter and Donald Bruce Johnson, eds., *National Party Platforms, 1840–1968* (Urbana, Ill., 1970)

NAW ⪜ Edward T. James, Janet Wilson James, and Paul S. Boyer, eds., *Notable American Women, 1607–1950: A Biographical Dictionary*, 3 vols. (Cambridge, Mass., 1971)

NCAB ⪜ *National Cyclopaedia of American Biography*, 63 vols. (New York, 1891–1984)

NCBB ⪜ *National Citizen and Ballot Box* (Syracuse, N.Y.)

Ohio Authors and Books ⪜ William Coyle, ed., *Ohio Authors and Their Books: Biographical Data and Selective Bibliographies for Ohio Authors, Native and Resident, 1796–1950* (Cleveland, Ohio, 1962)

Oxford DNB ⪜ H. C. G. Matthew and Brian Harrison, eds., *Oxford Dictionary of National Biography*, on-line edition (Oxford, England, 2004)

Papers ⪜ Ann D. Gordon, ed., *Selected Papers of Elizabeth Cady Stanton and Susan B. Anthony*, vol. 1, *In the School of Anti-Slavery, 1840 to 1866* (New Brunswick, N.J., 1997); vol. 2, *Against an Aristocracy of Sex, 1866 to 1873* (New Brunswick, N.J., 2000); vol. 3, *National Protection for National Citizens, 1873 to 1880* (New Brunswick, N.J., 2003)

PMHB ⪜ *Pennsylvania Magazine of History and Biography*

Quaker Genealogy ⪜ William Wade Hinshaw, *Encyclopedia of American Quaker Genealogy*, 3 vols. (Ann Arbor, Mich., 1936–1940)

Register of Federal Officers ⪜ *Register of Officers and Agents, Civil, Military, and Naval, in the Service of the United States . . .* (Washington, D.C., 1865–1889)

Report of the Sixteenth Annual Washington Convention, 1884 ⪜ Elizabeth Cady Stanton and Susan B. Anthony, eds. *National Woman Suffrage Association. Report of the Sixteenth Annual Washington Convention, March 4th, 5th, 6th and 7th, 1884, With Reports of the Forty-Eighth Congress* (Rochester, N.Y., 1884)

Rev. ⪜ *Revolution* (New York)

SEAP ⪜ Ernest H. Cherrington, ed., *Standard Encyclopedia of the Alcohol Problem*, 6 vols. (Westerville, Ohio, 1925–1930)

Stanton ⪜ Theodore Stanton and Harriot Stanton Blatch, eds.,

Elizabeth Cady Stanton, as Revealed in Her Letters, Diary and Reminiscences, 2 vols. (1922; reprint, New York, 1969)

Tribune Almanac ⟨ *The Tribune Almanac and Political Register for 1875* (New York, 1875)

TroyFS ⟨ Mrs. A. W. Fairbanks, ed., *Emma Willard and Her Pupils, or Fifty Years of Troy Female Seminary, 1822–1872* (New York, 1898)

TwCBDNA ⟨ Rossiter Johnson, ed., *The Twentieth Century Biographical Dictionary of Notable Americans*, 10 vols. (Boston, 1904)

Wallace ⟨ John William Wallace, *Cases Argued and Adjudged in the Supreme Court of the United States*, 23 vols. (Washington, D.C., 1866–1876)

Washington Territory Reports ⟨ *Reports of Cases Determined in the Supreme Court of the Territory of Washington, 1854–1888*, 3 vols. (1879; reprint, Seattle, Wash., 1906)

Who's Who of British Members of Parliament ⟨ Michael Stenton and Stephen Lees, eds., *Who's Who of British Members of Parliament: A Biographical Dictionary of the House of Commons*, 4 vols. (Atlantic Highlands, N.J., 1976–1981)

Wisconsin Reports ⟨ *Reports of Cases Argued and Determined in the Supreme Court of the State of Wisconsin*, 1st ser., 275 vols. (Chicago, 1853–1957)

Woman's Who's Who 1914 ⟨ John William Leonard, ed., *Woman's Who's Who of America, 1914–1915* (1914; reprint, Detroit, Mich., 1976)

Women Building Chicago ⟨ Rima Lunin Schultz and Adele Hast, eds., *Women Building Chicago, 1790–1990: A Biographical Dictionary* (Bloomington, Ind., 2001)

WWW1 ⟨ *Who Was Who in America*, vol. 1, *1897–1942* (Chicago, 1942)

WWW4 ⟨ *Who Was Who in America*, vol. 4, *1961–1968* (Chicago, 1968)

ARCHIVES AND REPOSITORIES

CSmH ⫽ The Huntington Library, San Marino, Calif.

Ct ⫽ Connecticut State Library, Hartford. Conn.

CtY ⫽ Yale University Libraries, New Haven, Conn.

DLC ⫽ Library of Congress, Manuscript Division (unless otherwise noted), Washington, D.C.

DSI ⫽ Smithsonian Institution, Washington, D.C.

IaCrM ⫽ Iowa Masonic Library, Cedar Rapids

ICarbS ⫽ Southern Illinois University, Morris Library, Carbondale

In ⫽ Indiana State Library, Indianapolis

InU ⫽ Indiana University Archives, Bloomington

KHi ⫽ Kansas State Historical Society, Topeka, Kan.

KyLoF ⫽ Filson Historical Society, Louisville, Ky.

MCR-S ⫽ Schlesinger Library, Radcliffe Institute, Harvard University, Cambridge, Mass.

MHi ⫽ Massachusetts Historical Society, Boston, Mass.

MH-H ⫽ Harvard University, Houghton Library, Cambridge, Mass.

MNS-S ⫽ Sophia Smith Collection, Smith College, Northampton, Mass.

MWiW ⫽ Williams College, Williamstown, Mass.

MiU-C ⫽ University of Michigan, William L. Clements Library, Ann Arbor, Mich.

MnHi ⫽ Minnesota Historical Society, St. Paul

MoSHi ⫽ Missouri Historical Society, St. Louis

NjP ⫽ Princeton University Library, Princeton, N.J.

NjR ⫽ Rutgers University Libraries, New Brunswick, N.J.

NB ⫽ Brooklyn Collection, Brooklyn Public Library, N.Y.

NIC ⫽ Cornell University Library, Ithaca, N.Y.

NJost ⤟ Johnstown Public Library, Johnstown, N.Y.

NNC ⤟ Columbia University, New York, N.Y.

NPV ⤟ Vassar College Library, Poughkeepsie, N.Y.

NRU ⤟ University of Rochester Library, Rochester, N.Y.

NSyU ⤟ Syracuse University Libraries, Syracuse, N.Y.

NWattJHi ⤟ Jefferson County Historical Society, Watertown, N.Y.

OFH ⤟ Rutherford B. Hayes Presidential Center, Fremont, Ohio

PHC ⤟ Haverford College Library, Haverford, Pa.

PSC-Hi ⤟ Friends Historical Library of Swarthmore College, Swarthmore, Pa.

PU ⤟ University of Pennsylvania, Philadelphia, Pa.

UkLQ ⤟ Friends House Library, London, U.K.

WaHi ⤟ Washington State Historical Society, Tacoma

WHi ⤟ Wisconsin Historical Society, Madison, Wis.

Manuscript Collections

Blackwell Papers, DLC ⤟ Blackwell Family Papers

Blackwell Papers, MCR-S ⤟ Blackwell Family Papers

ECS Papers, NjR ⤟ E. C. Stanton Papers, T. Stanton Collection, Special Collections and University Archives

Gage Collection, MCR-S ⤟ Matilda Joslyn Gage Collection

Garrison Papers, MNS-S ⤟ Garrison Family Papers

NAWSA Papers, DLC ⤟ National American Woman Suffrage Association Papers

Rare Books, DLC ⤟ Rare Books Division

SBA Papers, MCR-S ⤟ Susan Brownell Anthony Papers

Smith Papers, NSyU ⤟ Gerrit Smith Papers, Special Collections Research Center

The Selected Papers of
Elizabeth Cady Stanton and Susan B. Anthony

1   **ARTICLE BY ECS**

[23 September 1880]

"THE POLITICS OF REFORMERS."

How Woman Might, Could, Would, or Should Vote, Secondary Questions to whether she has the Right to Vote at all.

In the *Index* of Sept. 2, in an article on "The Politics of Reformers,"[1] the writer lays down many propositions in which all reasonable men and women must agree, such as: "Political parties cannot be based on special reforms"; and "Special reforms can only be carried by adhering to one well-defined purpose."

The one objectionable feature in the article is the comparative estimate of the importance of woman's enfranchisement with other reforms. And here the writer makes two points that demand consideration.

1. He places the civil and political rights of one-half the citizens of this Republic on a par with temperance, greenbacks,[2] and theological abuses,—the inalienable rights of the individual on a par with what he shall drink, what kind of money he shall carry in his pocket, and what religious superstitions he shall defend or deny!

Religion is a blind sentiment, whose vision grows steadily clearer in the wake of science and civilization; temperance is a question of heredity and dietetic; finance, a riddle, a cunningly devised system of legislation, by which nine-tenths of the human family are doomed to endless labor and taxation, that one-tenth may enjoy ease and luxury. But the political rights of woman involve the acceptance or denial of every fundamental principle on which our republican institutions rest.

My right to doubt or believe the Christian religion, to drink wine or refuse it, to accept or decline the silver trade-dollar, are minor questions to my inalienable right to protect my person and property, my life, liberty, and happiness under government, by having a voice in making the laws and choosing the rulers under whom I live. The founders of our Republic said, "No *just government* can be formed without the *consent* of the governed"; but who would have the audacity to say that no just government could be formed without a temperance pledge, a gold basis for our currency, or faith in some theological dogma?

Though all questions of political economy are important in carrying on a government, the primal question is, *Who* constitute the government,—the people, all men and women, or a male aristocracy? And this is the so-called woman question, the most momentous and far-reaching ever under consideration.

2. The writer refers to the oft-repeated assertion that, "if women were enfranchised, their influence would be thrown against the secular nature of our government," in favor of rigid Sunday laws, God in the Constitution, the Bible in our schools, and the exemption of church property from taxation, etc.

It is a legitimate question for women to ask, Who made the laws by which all these abuses exist to-day? Men! Who uphold them by pen and tongue in every pulpit and legislative hall and popular journal in the nation? Men! Who go to Washington year after year, urging a sixteenth amendment recognizing God and the Christian religion in the Constitution?[3] Men! By what process of logical reasoning, then, is it proposed to keep women in political slavery, because it is feared that in freedom they would do precisely what their fathers, husbands, and brothers have already done? Men have been the spiritual guides and teachers of women: they have written, interpreted, and expounded the Bibles, the creeds, the confessions of faith, the catechisms longer and shorter. All women know of the eternal past and future and of the great first cause they have learned from the lips of men. And now, having connived with the priesthood and played upon the religious element in her nature, to her own complete subjection and degradation, in all ages and under all forms of religion alike, would men in the advance-guard of liberal thought in this day perpetuate her spiritual bondage by denying her political liberty? How often in conversation with a husband, when, expressing the most liberal sentiments on religion, suddenly hearing his wife's footsteps, he will say, "But I never talk on this subject with Mary. I think religion is a good thing for women and children. A wholesome fear of something keeps them docile and virtuous. Mary is happy in her faith. I would not unsettle her." To keep woman in ignorance has been the policy in the long past, and we are reaping the evil results to-day. If the husband's love for Mary were not sufficiently strong to rouse him to try and lift *her* out of her superstitions, his duty to *his children* should have impelled him to the effort.

Let liberal men remember that fanatical mothers, all over our land, are insidiously training the minds of the Johns and Josephs in their own false ideas; and these sons will bear the scars, all their lives, of the cruel theologies they are instilling to-day. Woman's influence is not less dangerous because it is permitted no expression at the ballot-box, but infinitely more so; for, by denying her all interest in politics, you intensify her enthusiasm for the Church,—the only outlet, outside the home, now vouchsafed, on which she can expend her forces.

In the education of woman, let thinking men now substitute patriotism, the most exalted of all virtues, for religious devotion. Recognize her duty to the State as well as the Church, and she will readily learn the new lesson,—that the affairs of this life which we can comprehend and control are as sacred and important as those of the life hereafter, of which we can have no positive knowledge whatever.

Over the barren deserts of the past, down to the valleys of darkness and death, woman has ever followed the footsteps of fanatics and bigots, earnestly fanning the fires of persecution by the way, though ever bearing the heaviest burdens of superstition on her own shoulders; and why will she not, by the same eternal law of her being, as readily follow the lead of wise men to the promised land of light and liberty, of religious freedom? where there is no funeral pyre for widows, no sacred crocodiles to feed on the flesh of her newborn children, no car of Juggernaut to grind their bones to powder; where women are not hung for witchcraft, and where no Sir Oracle[4] from sacred altars shall dare to say, "I suffer not a woman to speak in the churches," "Wives be in subjection to your husbands," "As Christ is the head of the Church, so is the man the head of the woman."[5] It will not take much liberalizing to induce the women of this Republic to repudiate all such religions.

≈ *E. C. S.*

≈ Boston *Index*, 23 September 1880.

1. In this article in the *Index*, the journal of the Free Religious Association and National Liberal League, Benjamin F. Underwood answered an editorial

by Matilda Gage in her newspaper, the *National Citizen and Ballot Box*. Gage had argued that woman suffrage was the primal consideration, before all other reforms: without it, "ordinary governmental questions can neither be fairly presented nor justly settled." Suffragists should support only those political candidates who offered encouragement to their cause, regardless of the candidates' views on other questions. Underwood spoke for members of the Liberal League who placed state secularization at the head of all reforms, and he reiterated a belief among many liberals that "the extension of suffrage to woman would strengthen the political power of Orthodoxy, and lead to a revival of restrictive and proscriptive legislation." But he also despaired of unifying reformers around a candidate or party in 1880. "To single out one reform, and to expect that all progressive minds will subordinate to that one every other movement is to expect the impossible."

2. Greenbacks, or paper money, were the emblem of discontent about the distribution of wealth and concentration of capital after the Civil War. The Greenback-Labor party fielded candidates in the 1880 presidential election. For the party's connection to woman suffragists, see *Papers* 3.

3. On the efforts to put Christianity into the Constitution, see Gaines M. Foster, *Moral Reconstruction: Christian Lobbyists and the Federal Legislation of Morality, 1865–1920* (Chapel Hill, N.C., 2002), 27–46, 81–82. The National Liberal League countered this movement.

4. A dogmatical person, from William Shakespeare, *Merchant of Venice*, act 1, sc. 1, lines 94–95.

5. 1 Cor. 11:3 and 14:35; 1 Pet. 3:1; Eph. 5:23–24.

2 ❨ SBA to Matilda Joslyn Gage[1]

Rochester, N.Y., Oct. 8th, 1880.

Dear Mrs. Gage:—

Thanks for the reading of Mr. Reed's comments.[2] I believe men, like women, are what their mother's made them—no better no worse. And I hate the assumption by women that women are purer, better than men. It does well enough for men to throw such "taffy" at women.

Given equality of rights, privileges and opportunities in every respect, the sexes may develop differently and equally. Good women, with financial and political power, will then no more accept marriage with low, obscene men, than men of good morals now choose women of vice and indecency for their life companions. The weaknesses and wickedness of women are to-day very different in kind from those of men, but they exist nevertheless, and I am always amazed at any woman's assertion of superior honesty or virtue for her sex. Women, in politics, will act from self-interest, as their husbands and brothers now do; and it is from the interests of the two halves of the people coming in collision, each with equal chance and power to make, shape and control the conditions of the home, society, church and government, that we hope for something better than now, when the instincts of only one-half—and that not the better nor the worse half, but the equal half—controls.

⇐ *Susan B. Anthony.*

⇐ *NCBB*, October 1880.

1. Matilda Joslyn Gage (1826–1898) of Fayetteville, New York, began to work with ECS and SBA in the 1850s, and in the 1870s, she held top leadership posts in the National and the New York State woman suffrage associations. In 1878 she took over the newspaper the Toledo *Ballot Box*, moved it to Syracuse, and renamed it the *National Citizen and Ballot Box*. She was also one of the authors of the *History of Woman Suffrage*. (*NAW*; *ANB*.)

2. Under the column heading "Miss King Once More," Gage published letters by Samuel Rockwell Reed and Virginia Minor along with this one by SBA about a controversy over the role woman suffragists played in the New York State elections in 1879. The state suffrage association joined the campaign in order to stop the reelection of Governor Lucius Robinson, a Democrat who vetoed a bill to make women eligible to any office under the school laws. Susan A. King, the sister of a late Tammany Democrat and a wealthy woman in her own right, boasted that she bribed voters to defeat Robinson and a local senator, and Gage celebrated her action in editorials. Lucy Stone's *Woman's Journal* condemned King and all who supported her. Reed (1820?–1889), an editor of the *Cincinnati Gazette*, had read an earlier statement by SBA in which she said, "it ill becomes any one of the ruling class, who tax [King's] vast real estate . . . while they deny her the only weapon of defence, to taunt her with dishonesty." Reed pointed out in his short letter that the dispute boiled down to the question, whether women were "too delicate to enter into party organization, and into general political affairs, but to vote only on moral questions." He concluded, "There is none of this Miss Nancyism in the ground Miss Anthony takes." (*History*, 3:417–19, 422–23; *NCBB*, November 1879, April, May, August, October 1880; *Woman's Journal*, 17 July, 21 August 1880; Allibone Supplement; SBA to Catharine F. Stebbins, before August 1880, *Papers*, 3:553–56.)

3   SBA TO HARRIET HANSON ROBINSON[1]

Tenafly N. Jersey,[2] Oct. 24th 1880.

My Dear Friend

Yours of the 18th inst met me here the night of the 21st on my return from Reading Pa.[3] Philadelphia and New York—and I enjoyed its contents—but seriously—it would have been the highest gratification to me to have met Phillips[4] & Channing[5] of the olden friends—and Mr Hinckley[6] & yourself & daughter[7] & the younger friends—could I have done so without bringing a cloud like midnight over Lucy Stone's brow[8]—and now I very much want to see the reports of the meeting— & wish I had had the forethought to have asked you to send me the Worcester papers— Only the N.Y. Herald has had an item of the <u>fact</u> of the Con—and that was ↑only↓ a mention[9]—so we are wholly in the dark about it— If there is no other way—wont you send me the W.J's[10] account of it—as Mrs Stanton nor I take that <u>eminently proper paper</u>— And wont you give us a little of the <u>inside spirit</u> of the Con— Your experience in trying to re-unite the W.S. ranks is precisely that of every other person who has ever attempted it— Mrs Hooker[11] undertook it— & really believed <u>she</u> could accomplish it—but she never got one of them to step on our platform—nor one of us invited to step on theirs— <u>She</u> only got snubbed & dropped by them— So beware lest her fate should be yours— and I have heard that others <u>in</u> New England who have shown a kindly face toward the N.W.S.A. had been made to step down & out of her Ladyships good graces— I have laughed in my sleeves at the <u>national</u> <u>face</u> of the <u>American</u> <u>W.S.A.</u> ever since the Cincinnatti Con. last Nov. ~~and~~ ↑with↓ its less than 20 persons in its business meeting—and its election of officers by <u>Congressional District votes</u>—with only 5 states represented ↑and those↓ by only one person ↑from each↓—save in the case of Ohio & Indiana—[12] What a farce of a system—& then the result—<u>H. B. Blackwell</u>—Pres—<u>Lucy Stone</u>—Chair. Ex. Com—& <u>T. W. Higginson</u>[13] first Vice Pres— Just Lucy Stone with <u>her</u> <u>two</u> <u>adorers</u>—one on each side to shield & pro-tect— <u>It is too rich</u>—for <u>the</u> "<u>only</u> <u>truly</u> <u>National</u> <u>W.S.</u> <u>Association</u>" as she insists hers is— Or,—did I tell you all this before— And then when I passed near her & was ready to speak to her, she turned square round—back to me—and then, when she was passing round the hat— (after making a most ↑urgent↓ appeal for money from everybody) as she saw me, she lifted the hat above my head, & said "I don't want any of your money Miss Antony["]!!— But after my reminding her that a collector had no right to say who should or who should not contribute, she lowered the hat—and as I dropped the half dollar—↑she↓ said— "Well you can be sure you give it to a good cause"!— And the people all around me heard the colloquy— Then friends asked me "why arent you on the platform," "Why dont you speak?"— I, every time, re- plied—"I dont know, ask Lucy Stone."— I just wish you could have witnessed that Cincinnatti scene— They voted to hold their next Annual Con. at Washington in the first week of December next— But I've seen no notice yet— So if they may go to Washington, we surely may go to Boston—

What Hall or Church could we get in Boston— Not the Menonian[14]— I remember that dingy place—in 1855—when Paulina Wright Davis,[15] Mrs E. Oakes Smith[16] Emerson[17] et al—were there in a W.R. Conven- tion— Then what days can we have ↑it↓—so as not to come in collision with the New England Convention[18] for I do not want to ↑do↓ what they did with us in New York—that is, take the very same days & hours that they hold their meeting— Will you, therefore—give me your opinion as to the best hall & the best days— We shall want two days— and we mean to make it the grandest Con. the N.W.S.A ever held— with strongest speakers with their best arguments for National Protection of the Suffrage— So—please tell me exactly what you see the best arrangements for us to make to ensure a success and shant ignore nor reject any one—not even Lucy Stone—

I am Oh—Yes—before ↑I↓ go to ↑the↓ next point—will not you attend our next Wash. Con. the 2^d week in January?—and be one of our speakers?— If you have no friends there—we will pay your board during the Con— Wish we could promise travelling expenses—but cannot—

I am here at work with Mrs Stanton upon our W.S. history—we have Massachusets written down to the rebellion—pretty nearly— Our plan now is to make two volumes—the first reaching to the War & Womens Loyal League movement in 1863 & 64[19]—and the second one,

From the revival of our Woman's Rights Con's in 1866—↑down to the present—↓ You remember we suspended them from 1860—to 1866—now ↑And here will come the tug of the work—for from 1866 began the differences↓ Will you send us what you have written—and let us see it—and take such points, if any there be, as we have missed & add to ours—or perhaps yours may be so entirely unlike ours that we may put yours in as Mrs H. H. Robinsons reminiscences as we have put in Mrs Nichols[20] & Mrs F. D. Gage's—[21] Mrs Gage[22] said you required us to put in whatever you sent, if at all, exactly as you sent it— It may be we should not wish to change a word of it—but we could not promise to put it in as you say—until we see it—

Mrs Elizabeth Thompson[23] last week gave me a liberal check to go toward publishing our history—and we begin, at once, to put copy into our printers hands—hence we must get together all our material very quickly— But very little was done in Mass. & New England before the war—beyond the two Worcester Con's in 1850 & 51—and two or three Cons in Boston & hearing before Con. Con. in 1857—I think it was—[24] What more than these   Whatever else there was done, we would be very glad to know & incorporate—but if we fail to get all noted in our book—whoever shall undertake after us must finish up— Indeed—we have ceased to hope to get from each of the actors, now living, what they can she or he can remember—each seems so tardy to respond— I should think that each one who read Mrs Nichols reminiscences would be so interested as to at once jot down his or her recollections & early experiences & send them on— Your History from the War down—we should like also to see & have— I wish we could promise to pay you & every one who would send us facts—but alas we are doing the work now as a matter of duty & justice to the pioneers of our movement—so little of our true spirit & purpose was understood by the newspaper Editors at that time—↑and there is no expectation of ever getting back even the first cost—↓

With ever so much Love from both Mrs S. & myself & many thanks for your effort to secure to us respectful consideration from Lucy—I am sincerely yours—

            ↢ *Susan B. Anthony*

↢ ALS, on NWSA letterhead for 1880, Robinson-Shattuck Papers, MCR-S.

1. Harriet Jane Hanson Robinson (1825–1911) was the National association's vice president for Massachusetts, a position that placed her in the middle of

conflicts between Lucy Stone and SBA and their respective suffrage associations. She had agreed to host a meeting of the National in Boston in May 1881, and she was also conducting research for what became her book *Massachusetts in the Woman Suffrage Movement* (1881). In Robinson's now missing letters to SBA, she posed many questions about the split in the suffrage movement and recounted her adventures among reformers in Boston. (*NAW*; *ANB*; Claudia L. Bushman, *"A Good Poor Man's Wife": Being a Chronicle of Harriet Hanson Robinson and Her Family in Nineteenth-Century New England* [Hanover, N.H., 1981].)

2. Tenafly, New Jersey, was home to ECS. SBA arrived there early in October, pressed by ECS and Sarah Pugh to stop lecturing and resume work on the *History of Woman Suffrage*. Matilda Gage joined them on November 19. (SBA to Rachel G. Foster, 7 September 1880, *Papers*, 3:570–71; SBA to R. G. Foster, 24 September 1880, and SBA to H. H. Robinson, 19 November 1880, *Film*, 21:409–11, 579–84.)

3. In Reading, SBA substituted for ECS in a lecture at the Grand Opera House on October 18. That is the one known point in this schedule. Robinson had described the thirtieth anniversary of the first National Woman's Rights Convention, a celebration convened by Lucy Stone's Massachusetts Woman Suffrage Association on October 21 and 22 in Worcester, Massachusetts. There, when Robinson read from her history, she faced sharp criticism from several participants. Her work "showed research and care," Stone wrote in the *Woman's Journal*, "though on some minor points she will have to correct it." (*Film*, 21:432; *Woman's Journal*, 30 October 1880.)

4. Wendell Phillips (1811–1884) of Boston was a great abolitionist orator who remained a reformer in the postwar period, noted for his advocacy of labor reform, woman suffrage, and greenbacks. (*ANB*.)

5. William Henry Channing (1810–1884), a Unitarian minister residing in London and an officer of the meeting in 1850, attended the anniversary near the end of a six-month visit to the United States. An early supporter of woman's rights in Boston and Rochester, Channing was considered a good friend by Lucy Stone, ECS, and SBA, and they would, in coming years, fight for his favor. (*ANB*.)

6. Frederic Allen Hinckley (1845–1917), a Unitarian minister who led the Providence Free Religious Society and held office in the Rhode Island Woman Suffrage Association, was a new ally of ECS and SBA. In the *Woman's Journal*, 21 August 1880, he announced his intention to work with the National rather than the American association for a constitutional amendment for woman suffrage. (*WWW1*; Lillie Buffum Chace Wyman and Arthur Crawford Wyman, *Elizabeth Buffum Chace, 1806–1899: Her Life and Its Environment* [Boston, 1914], 2:51–52. See also *Papers 3*.)

7. Harriette Lucy Robinson Shattuck (1850–1937) followed the family trade as a writer and shared her mother's commitment to woman suffrage. (*WWW4*; *New York Times*, 23 March 1937; Bushman, *"Good Poor Man's Wife."*)

8. Lucy Stone (1818–1893) and her husband, Henry Browne Blackwell (1825–1909), known as Harry, shared editorial duties at the Boston *Woman's Journal* and controlled the powerful executive committee of the American Woman Suffrage Association. Stone ignored suggestions that she collaborate with the National association to organize the anniversary celebration. (*NAW*, s.v. "Stone, Lucy"; *ANB*, s.v. "Blackwell, Henry Browne" and "Stone, Lucy"; Antoinette L. B. Blackwell to L. Stone, 5 July 1880, in Carol Lasser and Marlene Deahl Merrill, eds., *Friends and Sisters: Letters between Lucy Stone and Antoinette Brown Blackwell, 1846–93* [Urbana, Ill., 1987], 218–19. See also *Papers* 1–3.)

9. *New York Herald*, 23 October 1880.

10. The *Woman's Journal*, a weekly begun in 1870, was the most successful of the woman suffrage newspapers. Not until January 1880 did the editors consent to name the National Woman Suffrage Association in its pages, and it continued to express Stone's hostility to the association and its leaders.

11. Isabella Beecher Hooker (1822–1907) of Hartford, Connecticut, tried to reconcile the divided suffrage movement in 1869, when Lucy Stone and Henry Blackwell were recruiting her to help found their American association. (*NAW*; *ANB*; Jeanne Boydston, Mary Kelley, and Anne Margolis, *The Limits of Sisterhood: The Beecher Sisters on Women's Rights and Woman's Sphere* [Chapel Hill, N.C., 1988], 184–87, 196–200, 293–95, 304–6. See also *Papers* 2 & 3.)

12. SBA attended the opening session of the American's annual meeting on 4 November 1879 in Cincinnati. She refers to the American association's constitutional provision that assigned votes to state affiliates based on each state's congressional representation regardless of each affiliate's membership. The executive committee could also assign a state's votes to an individual resident of a state if no affiliate existed in that state. The official count of states represented at the annual meeting was eight. (*Cincinnati Daily Gazette*, 5 November 1879; *Woman's Journal*, 15 November 1879; *Constitution of the American Woman Suffrage Association and the History of Its Formation* [Boston, 1881], NAWSA Papers, DLC.)

13. Thomas Wentworth Higginson (1823–1911) of Providence, Rhode Island, was an editorial contributor to the *Woman's Journal*. (*ANB*. See also *Papers* 1–3.)

14. Meionaon Hall, with a seating capacity of nearly one thousand, was beneath the far larger main hall of the Tremont Temple on Tremont Street. SBA attended the woman's rights convention there in September 1855. (Moses King, *King's Hand-Book of Boston*, 5th ed. [Cambridge, Mass., 1883]; *Film*, 8:282–84; *History*, 1:255–58.)

15. Paulina Kellogg Wright Davis (1813–1876) of Providence, Rhode Island, who called the woman's rights convention in 1850, presided at this later convention in 1855. Although she helped to organize the New England Woman Suffrage Association in 1868, Davis left when it became the vehicle for attack-

ing SBA and ECS, and she worked with the National association until her death. (*NAW*; *ANB*. See also *Papers* 1–3.)

16. Elizabeth Oakes Prince Smith (1806–1893), a writer and one of the first American women to earn a living as a lecturer, was active in the woman's rights movement in the early 1850s. (*NAW*; *ANB*.)

17. Ralph Waldo Emerson (1803–1882), essayist and philosopher, addressed the convention in 1855.

18. The New England Woman Suffrage Association of Lucy Stone traditionally held a meeting during anniversary week in Boston. SBA refers to Stone's decision in 1870 to call a meeting of the American association during New York's anniversary week at precisely the time of the National association's annual meeting. The announcement of simultaneous meetings prompted activists across the country to call for a union of the two associations. (*Papers*, 2:307–9.)

19. ECS, SBA, and others founded the Women's Loyal National League in 1863 and organized an immense petition drive urging Congress to pass the Thirteenth Amendment. See *Papers* 1 and *History*, 2:50–88.

20. Clarina Irene Howard Nichols (1810–1885), a journalist and pioneer agitator for woman's rights in Vermont and Kansas, wrote her reminiscences at the request of ECS and SBA for the *History*. Two installments were published in the *National Citizen* in July and August 1879 and thus served as a model for others. Nichols left Kansas to settle near her children in Mendocino County, California, at the end of 1871. (*NAW*; *History*, 1:171–200. See also *Papers* 1–3.)

21. Frances Dana Barker Gage (1808–1884), known to her readers as "Aunt Fanny," described her pioneering work in the woman's rights movement in Ohio in chapters of the *History* previewed in the *National Citizen* in 1879. To that text, the editors later added her report of Sojourner Truth's speech at the Akron convention of 1851. (*NAW*; *ANB*; *NCBB*, September 1879, *Film*, 20:871; *History*, 1:115–19.)

22. That is, Matilda Gage. For earlier discussions about Robinson's insistence that she retain total control of anything she wrote for the *History* and the editors' insistence that they needed the final word on language and length, see *Papers*, 3:468–71.

23. Elizabeth Rowell Thompson (1821–1899) became a noted philanthropist after the death of her husband in 1869. She called on SBA in Washington in the winter of 1879 with an offer to help underwrite publication of the *History of Woman Suffrage*, and at this time, she delivered a check for one thousand dollars. (*NAW*; *ANB*; *NCBB*, November 1880; *History*, 4:vii.)

24. The first and second National Woman's Rights Conventions met in Worcester in October of 1850 and 1851. In addition to the Boston meeting of 1855 already mentioned, New England conventions were held in Boston in June 1854 and May 1859. Women sent many petitions to the constitutional convention of 1853, and T. W. Higginson was granted a hearing in their

behalf. All of these events are treated in the Massachusetts chapter of the first volume of the *History*.

4 ❧ SBA TO AMELIA JENKS BLOOMER[1]

Tenafly N.J. Oct. 25th 1880.

Dear Mrs Bloomer

Here I am, once more, at Mrs Stantons lovely home, settled down to history work with her—

Two things we want of you—a brief chapter of personal reminiscences of your own early days—& early work—and then we want you to write out the Iowa Chapter— You have been in the state from the first agitation— Now—will you do these two things— If you will do Iowa, it shall go into our book as you send it & over your own name—or with credit for it— Mrs Stanton is going to give your "<u>Lily</u>" description of our treatment at the Temp. Con. in Syracuse in 1852—[2] Wasn't that Samuel J. May who came to the Temp. Hotel and told us of the spirit of those priests?— Wont you look it over & add anything you can remember—or, if you choose re-write it—and we will say "Mrs Bloomer thus describes the scene—" We are in luck for once—as Mrs Elizabeth Thompson has given us money to start the publishing of our History— so we now have no excuse for delay, but ourselves— we have both thrown up our Lecturing for the winter—& I am to stop here with Mrs S. I have all of my papers, letters &c sent on to me here this week— This is the third time that I have thus planned to sit down here with Mrs S. until this History was done— was called home to my dear Mother a year ago[3]—and now—though she passed beyond need of her daughter—it seems as if something was gathering to summon me away from this work again—but I hope not—for we both long to have done with this herculean undertaking— Mrs Stanton looked for you & Mr Bloomer over to her home all through the Episcopal Con. in New York—[4] She is very well indeed—all of her men are quarted in the city for the winter—and just she and I and her faithful Amelia[5] are sole occupants of the house— It is delightful here though—as we work on— with such perfect quiet—

I hope you will feel just in the mood of helping us to the things we so much need from your pen—and will write us very soon to that effect— With ever so much Love as ever yours

❧ *Susan B. Anthony*

P.S. Mrs Stanton says tell Mrs Bloomer she was very sorry she did not visit her—& I told her I had already spoken of it—

Mrs S. suggests that you look at Mrs C. I. H. Nichols chapters of her work—and she thinks her style charming—& wishes each early worker would give similar reminiscences—

Mrs S. say tell her—["]I want her to go down to Red Oak & see Maggie[6] & then write me if she is pleased with the match she made—" Mrs S. seems to feel that it is a pretty good one—so far as her talk ↑to me↓ goes— But we <u>talk</u> <u>work</u>—more than marriages— She sends love to you—& so do I—and both send kind regards to Mr Bloomer— Good Bye S. B. A

❧ ALS, on NWSA letterhead for 1880, Amelia Bloomer Papers, Seneca Falls Historical Society.

1. Amelia Jenks Bloomer (1818–1894), formerly of Seneca Falls, New York, settled in Council Bluffs, Iowa, with her husband, Dexter Chamberlain Bloomer (1816?–1900), in 1855. While in New York, she published the *Lily*, a temperance paper to which ECS contributed many articles, and she collaborated with ECS and SBA in the temperance movement. In Iowa, she was among the earliest proponents of woman's rights. (*NAW* and *ANB*, s.v. "Bloomer, Amelia Jenks"; Edward H. Stiles, *Recollections and Sketches of Notable Lawyers and Public Men of Early Iowa* [Des Moines, Iowa, 1916], 893–94; Benjamin F. Gue and Benjamin F. Shambaugh, *Biographies and Portraits of the Progressive Men of Iowa* [Des Moines, Iowa, 1899], 1:452–53. See also *Papers* 1 & 3.)

2. SBA recalls the New York State Temperance Society refusing to receive delegates from the Women's New York State Temperance Society. Samuel Joseph May (1797–1871), well-known abolitionist and the Unitarian minister in Syracuse, New York, was an important figure in the woman's rights movement in New York from 1845 until his death. On this occasion, he not only warned SBA and Amelia Bloomer about the opposition but also helped them organize a rival meeting in a nearby church that attracted most of the delegates to the men's meeting. ECS cited the *Lily* as her source for the account in the *History of Woman Suffrage*, 1:485–88. (*ANB*.)

3. Lucy Read Anthony died in April 1880. For earlier attempts to finish the *History of Woman Suffrage*, see *Papers* 3.

4. The General Convention of the Protestant Episcopal Church opened in New York on 6 October 1880.

5. Amelia Willard (c. 1825–c. 1920) went to work for the Stantons at a young age in Seneca Falls and became the family's housekeeper. Although family members thought her to be only sixteen in 1851, the federal census of 1880 gives her age as fifty-five. She died in Ypsilanti, Michigan, at age ninety-six. (*History*, 3:477n; *Eighty Years*, 203–5; G. Smith Stanton, "How Aged House-keeper Gave Her All To Cause Of Woman Suffrage," unidentified and un-dated clipping, Seneca Falls Historical Society; Federal Census, Tenafly, 1880. See also *Papers* 1–3.)

6. Margaret Livingston Stanton Lawrence (1852–1930) moved to Red Oak, Iowa, after her marriage in 1878 to Frank Eugene Lawrence (1848–1890). Frank Lawrence's parents were acquaintances of the Bloomers in Council Bluffs, and Margaret met him at the Bloomers' house. (Marriage return, New Jersey State Department of Health; Chicago *Inter-Ocean*, 22 June 1878, *Film*, 20:295; Federal Census, Iowa, 1870; *History of Pottawattamie County, Iowa* [Chicago, 1883], pt. 2, p. 37. See also *Papers* 3.)

5 ⮑ ECS TO THEODORE W. STANTON

Tenafly, November 2, 1880.

Dear Theodore:—

I went down to-day to the polling-booth, offered my ballot and argued the case with the inspectors. The republican wagon and horses all decked with flags and evergreens, came for the male part of the household. I told the driver that my legal representatives were all absent, but I would go down and vote. Susan went with me and we had great fun frightening and muddling these old Dutch inspectors.[1] The whole town is agape with my act. A friend says he never saw Tenafly in such excitement. The men have taken sides about equally. This evening, when Susan and I went down for the mail, the post-man said he would give five dollars for that ticket that I proffered; he would have it framed and hung up in his house. I have sent a full description of the affair to the press.[2] But I must say good night. I am tired after holding that ballot so long and arguing with the judges of elections. Good night,

⮑ *Mother.*

⮑ Typed transcript, ECS Papers, NjR.

1. The Dutch settled Bergen County in the seventeenth century and made up a majority of the population until railroads brought outsiders after the Civil

War. Many residents spoke "Jersey Dutch," a language of Flemish and English words that survived into the early twentieth century.

2. Her account appeared in the Chicago *Inter-Ocean*, 13 November 1880; the *National Citizen*, November 1880; and the *Woman's Journal*, 13 November 1880; the first of these is in *Film*. Local papers took note of her attempt to vote but offered no details to their readers. (*Film*, 21:570; *Bergen Index*, 2 November 1880; *Englewood Standard*, 6 November 1880.)

6   SBA TO JANE SNOW SPOFFORD[1]

[*Tenafly, c. 6 November 1880*][2]

I feel exactly as you do about having the convention. I have never for a moment felt ready *not* to hold it. I wrote you under Mrs. Stanton's orders not to tell you how I felt, as that would be sure to influence you. Now I have read her your letter and told her my determination was to go ahead. She won't promise to attend, she never does, but I never fail to take her with me when I am on the spot, as I shall be when the time comes next January. So you may save us each a bedroom away up, no matter how lofty—you know I love the fresh air of the high heavens. Don't give yourself one moment's uneasiness in regard to the convention. I am going to set about it and am bound to make it one of the best, if not the best ever held in Washington, and you shall have Mrs. Stanton too, unless I miss my guess.

  Anthony, 2:526. In *Film* dated November? 1880.

1. Jane H. Snow Spofford (1828–1905) and her husband, Caleb Wheeler Spofford, ran the Riggs House, a hotel at Fifteenth and G streets, Northwest, in Washington, D.C. She was active in city suffrage societies and represented the District of Columbia association at the National's meetings. She became the National association's treasurer in 1879. (Jeremiah Spofford, *A Genealogical Record, Including Two Generations in Female Lines of Families Spelling the Name Spofford, Spafford, Spafard, and Spaford* [Boston, 1888], 247; research by Katherine W. Trickey, Bangor, Me.; *Woman's Journal*, 6 January 1906; *History*, 3:98–99, 260, 4:387, 571, 689, 5:180; city directories, 1877 to 1892. See also *Papers 3*.)

2. Ida Harper introduced this letter in her biography of SBA with references to an earlier exchange: SBA asked Jane Spofford if she thought the Washington convention should be postponed, and Spofford advised against

it. Harper did not provide a date other than late in 1880. By November 6, SBA considered the convention a sure thing and noted that Julia and Rachel Foster had responded to the same question with votes in favor of the meeting. At the end of the month, responsibility for planning the convention passed to Belva Lockwood and Ellen Sheldon in Washington and the Fosters in Philadelphia. (*Anthony*, 2:526; SBA to Rachel G. Foster, 6, 28 November 1880, in *Film*, 21:530–33, 607–8.)

7 ✎ ECS TO FRIEND[1]

Tenafly N.J. Nov 14th [*1880*]

My dear Friend,

I was not surprized on taking up "The Tribune" yesterday morning to find that your dear mother had at last fallen asleep.[2]

Having known her not only in the flush of life, when all her faculties were at their zenith, but in the repose of advanced age, when her powers began to wane her transformation seems ↑to me↓ as beautiful, & natural, as the changing foliage, from the spring time to the autumn, of some grand oak tree I have long loved & watched.

One who has lived eighty eight years, reflecting ever the sober virtues of the true wife & mother, the earnest reformer, the religious teacher, both in the school room & "Friends Meeting," must have ~~illegible~~ ↑exerted↓ a strong influence for good on our young impressible nation. When we remember that every word we utter, every act we perform, in all our waking hours, the very atmosphere, the combination of all our faculties, creates have their constant effect, on every one who comes within the circle of our individual influence & through them are wafted by word, & letter, & thought, to innumerable other circles beyond, when we try to estimate all this, we can in a measure appreciate the elevating influence on a nation of one grand life. And these good words & deeds, & this holy influence are immortality. It is this in humanity that will never die. As long as memory serves us, & we can recall your noble mothers wise opinions on all questions she will live to us though her sweet presence be forever withdrawn. My friendship for two such pure minded women as Lucretia Mott, & Martha C Wright,[3] has ever been to me a constant inspiration, & strengthened my hope for all woman kind, & I rejoice that although remotely, a family link has bound us together,[4] as well as our mutual interest in many of the great reforms of our times   With best regards & sympathy for the different members of the family in their great loss very sincerely yours

❧ *Elizabeth Cady Stanton.*

Miss Anthony went to Providence last Wednesday to fill some engagements for me,[5] as I have a bad cold & am very hoarse or she would join me in words of love & sympathy.

❧ ALS, Mott MSS, PSC-Hi. Endorsed "Red. 11/16 1880".

1. The recipient of this letter was either Edward Morris Davis or his wife, Maria Mott Davis, the members of Lucretia Mott's family best known to ECS. A son-in-law of Mott, Edward Davis (1811–1887), was a noted reformer and the leading figure in Philadelphia's Radical Club and Citizens' Suffrage Association. Maria Davis (1818–1897) was the eldest of the Mott children. (Anna Davis Hallowell, *James and Lucretia Mott: Life and Letters* [Boston, 1884]; *Philadelphia Inquirer*, 28 November 1887; *Friends' Intelligencer* 54 [1897]: 582. See also *Papers* 1–3.)

2. Lucretia Coffin Mott (1793–1880) died on November 11 at Roadside, her home outside Philadelphia, as the *New York Herald* of 12 November 1880, not 13 November, announced. Mott, who met ECS in London in 1840 at the World's Anti-Slavery Convention and signed the call to the woman's rights convention at Seneca Falls in 1848, was a major influence on ECS's religious and political ideas. A member of the Society of Friends, Mott also helped to shape Unitarianism. (*NAW*; *ANB*. See also *Papers* 1–3.)

3. Martha Coffin Pelham Wright (1806–1875) of Auburn, New York, predeceased her older sister, Lucretia Mott. Active in the woman's rights movement since the convention at Seneca Falls in 1848, Wright was the founding president of the New York State Woman Suffrage Association. (*NAW*; *ANB*. See also *Papers* 1–3.)

4. ECS refers to the marriage in 1869 of her niece Flora McMartin (1843–1898) to William Pelham Wright (1842–1902), a son of Martha Coffin Wright. (Wright genealogy, Garrison Papers, MNS-S; Orrin Peer Allen, *Descendants of Nicholas Cady of Watertown, Mass., 1645–1910* [Palmer, Mass., 1910], 174.)

5. SBA spoke in her place to the annual meeting of the Rhode Island Woman Suffrage Association on November 11 and to members of the Providence Free Religious Society on November 14. See *Film*, 21:545–57, 576.

·⟨⟨══════⟩⟨══════⟩⟩·

8 ≫ SBA TO RUTHERFORD B. HAYES[1]

Rochester[2] Nov. 27th 1880.

To the President   My Dear Sir

Will you not in your forthcoming message to Congress recommend the passage of the 16th amendment proposition?— bills are in both houses—[3] Hundreds of thousands of women's petitions for <u>national</u> protection in their citizens right to vote, have been poured into Congress during the past fifteen years—and are now piled away in the vaults of the Capitol.

In Dec. 1865, we petitioned Congress not to put "<u>male</u>" in the 14th amendment,[4] in 1867 & 8, to put "<u>sex</u>" in the 15th—[5] Failing in both those appeals—in 1869—we petitioned for a 16th am't, that should prohibit the disfranchising ↑of↓ citizens on account of sex.[6] In 1871, 72, 73 & 74, we petitioned for a "Declaratory act"[7] and got an unanswerable ↑minority↓ favorable report from Benj. F. Butler,[8] showing that women citizens should be protected under the 14th am't. The Supreme Court deciding against our demand,[9] we again petitioned for a 16th am't,[10] from 1876 to the present—securing an admirable minority report from Senator Hoar[11]—in the last Congress—and the presentation of bills in both houses at the first session of this Congress—together with a promise from leading ↑men↓ in both Houses to have a <u>special</u> Committee appointed to take charge of our demands for ~~Woman's~~ ↑national↓ protection ~~in~~ ↑of↓ ~~her~~ ↑woman's↓ right to vote.[12]

And yet with all of this persistent work upon Congress, with our annual Conventions in Washington for the last 12 years, with our frequent hearings before Committees of both Houses, and with all of the meetings and Conventions throughout all the states of the North— with all the "rub-a-dub of agitation"[13] we women have kept up for the past thrirty two years—no president has ever mentioned even the fact of our demand for woman's right to a voice in the government to be secured by the National Constitution, precisely as is the negro's right.

And, now, I pray you, in the name of the millions of women who want to vote on ↑the↓ temperance question, if none other, and of the multitudes who want to vote on all questions, and more especially in the name of the National Woman Suffrage Association, which through all these fifteen years has besieged Congress for protection for women,— I pray you, suffer not this last opportunity to speak with Presidential position and power, to pass without your full and ↑earnest↓ recognition of the justice of our demand—and the duty of Congress to take the steps necessary to secure perfect equality of rights, privileges and immunities to the women citizens of the United States, in every state and territory of the Union.

Do this, and ↑you↓ shall make your administration more illustrious, more marked than that of any of your predecessors—not excepting even that of Lincoln[14]—as the freedom of eight—yes <u>ten millions</u> of women from the <u>political slavery</u> that has bound ~~her~~ all of womankind from generation to generation, is greater than breaking the chains of four millions chattel slaves— In the hope that ↑you↓ will speak this grand word for equal rights for women— I am most respectfully yours

⥤ *Susan B. Anthony*

⥤ ALS, on NWSA letterhead for 1880, Rutherford B. Hayes Papers, OFH. Was enclosed in SBA to Lucy Webb Hayes, 26 November 1880.

1. Rutherford Birchard Hayes (1822–1893) became the nineteenth president of the United States in March 1877. James A. Garfield had just won the election to replace Hayes in 1881.

2. SBA wrote from Tenafly.

3. Thomas W. Ferry introduced Senate Resolution No. 65 on 19 January 1880, and George B. Loring introduced House Resolution No. 175 on 20 January 1880. The resolutions were referred to the judiciary committees. (*Congressional Record*, 46th Cong., 2d sess., 380, 418.)

4. See *Papers*, 1:566–67.

5. See *Papers*, 2:188–90.

6. See petitions at 2 and 18 January 1869, *Film*, 13:254–59, 278–79.

7. See, for example, the petition to Congress for a declaratory act, at 21 December 1871, *Film*, 15:841–44.

8. Benjamin Franklin Butler (1818–1893) of Massachusetts served as a Republican in the House of Representatives from 1866 until 1875 and again for one term in 1877. In a minority report from the House Judiciary Committee in 1871, he and William Loughridge urged Congress to declare that "the right of suffrage is one of the inalienable rights of citizens . . . included in the 'privileges of citizens of the United States,' which are guaranteed by section 1 of article 14 of the amendments," and that women could vote for members of Congress. (*BDAC*; House Committee on the Judiciary, *Victoria Woodhull*.

Views of the Minority, 41st Cong., 3d sess., H. Rept. 22, Pt. 2, Serial 1464. See also *Papers* 2 & 3.)

9. Minor v. Happersett, 21 Wallace 162 (1875).

10. See *Papers*, 3:269.

11. George Frisbie Hoar (1826–1904) of Massachusetts served as a Republican in the House of Representatives from March 1869 to March 1877, when he took his seat in the Senate. His report favored woman suffrage but said nothing in favor of a federal amendment. (*BDAC*; Senate Committee on Privileges and Elections, *Views of the Minority*, 45th Cong., 3d sess., 1 February 1879, S. Rept. 523, pt. 2.)

12. In the House, a resolution asking for a Committee on the Rights of Women Citizens was introduced in April 1879 and referred to the Committee on Rules. On 27 March 1880, the rules committee reported a resolution to appoint such a special committee, and it was placed on the calendar. In the Senate on 16 February 1880, Joseph E. McDonald proposed creating a committee of the same name. (*History*, 3:142; *Congressional Record*, 46th Cong., 2d sess., 913, 1903.)

13. The phrase originated in an exchange between Daniel Webster and Wendell Phillips in 1852: when Webster dismissed the rub-a-dub of the abolitionist press, Phillips embraced the phrase, referring to "a 'rub-a-dub of agitation,' as ours is contemptuously styled." (Wendell Phillips, *Speeches, Lectures, and Letters* [1863; reprint, Boston, 1891], 36.)

14. Abraham Lincoln (1809–1865), sixteenth president of the United States, issued the Emancipation Proclamation during the Civil War.

9 ❧ SBA TO MARY TENNEY GRAY[1]

Tenafly N.J. Nov. 30th 1880.

My Dear Mrs Gray

In returning from New York to night, I met dear Mrs Taylor[2] of Wyandotte, who told me you now lived in that City— I gave her my wish that the women of Kansas should now make a testimonial to dear Mrs C. I. H. Nichols—in this wise—make up a purse of $150. to pay for a steel engraving—(& 2000 copies of it for our first edition)—of Mrs Nichols to go into our <u>history</u> of Woman Suffrage— Mrs N. is not able to pay for the plate & 2000 copies herself—and ↑the↓ sum given me to print the history, is not large enough to do more than pay the bare printing— So that the persons whose pictures are put into our history will have to pay the cost thereof— If you cant raise the $150— get as near to it as you can—for I want Mrs Nichols sweet face to go down to posterity in our book together with ↑that of↓ dear Lucretia Mott, Mrs Stanton, Mrs Rose—& the rest of the early workers— I hope you have taken the "National Citizen & Ballot Box,["] published ↑by↓ Mrs M. Joslyn Gage, Syracuse N.Y—price $1. a year—and read all of Mrs Nichol's reminiscences of Kansas— If none of you take ↑it↓—don't fail to send on your dollar, at once—so you can see from time to time how we get on with the history.

And wont you good friends of Mrs Nichols & of our cause, put on your thinking caps and recall every funny incident you can, and write everything down and send to me—to help us in history

I met Gov. Crawford[3] in New York, and he thought Gen. Adams[4] of the state Historical Society would see that money was raised for the engraving of Mrs Nichols— And I should think Gov. Robinson[5] would contribute— Will you look over the ground & tell me what can be done— I am spending the winter with Mrs Stanton, working on our history, which is now in progress— Mrs S. is correcting proof this evening— Thus you will see that I want to know immediately what you women of Kansas—& men too—will do to help us to have Mrs Nichols picture in it—

I sent ever so much love by Mrs Taylor to you and to Dr & Mrs Root[6]—& to the Judge & to "bairns"— Sincerely yours

⇒ *Susan B. Anthony*

⇒ ALS, on NWSA letterhead for 1880, Papers of SBA, NPV.

1. Mary Tenney Gray (1833–1904) taught school in Binghamton, New York, before her marriage to Barzillai Gray (1824–1918) in 1859 and their move to Kansas. As a result of SBA's insistence in 1854 that women be placed on committees of the New York State Teachers' Association, Mary Tenney was named to the board of editors of the *New York Teacher*. She helped with the Kansas amendment campaign in 1867 and earned a regional reputation for her efforts to organize women into clubs and philanthropic societies. The Grays had just moved to Wyandotte at this date, after many years living in Leavenworth and time in Topeka while Barzillai Gray, formerly a judge on the First District Court of Kansas, was secretary to Governor George T. Anthony. The Grays had three children: Jessie M. (c. 1863–?), later Caswell; Lawrence T. (c. 1865–?); and Mary Theodosia (1866–1949), later Harriman. (*American Women*; Perl W. Morgan, ed., *History of Wyandotte County, Kansas, and Its People* [Chicago, 1911], 1:262–64; *New York Teacher* 2 [September 1854]: 266, and 5 [September 1856]: 560, in *Film*, 7:1063ff, 8:491ff; *History*, 2:258n; *United*

States Biographical Dictionary: Kansas Volume [Chicago, 1879], 707; *Kansas City Times*, 26 December 1918, Vertical files, KHi; assistance from Brooke M. Black, Huntington Library.)

2. Rachel Ann Broadhead Taylor (c. 1829–1913), a New Yorker who moved to Kansas in 1858, was the widow of Richard Baxter Taylor, editor and publisher of the *Wyandotte Gazette*. (*U.S. Biographical Dictionary: Kansas*, 315–16; *Kansas City Gazette Globe*, 29 May 1913, Vertical files, KHi.)

3. Samuel Johnson Crawford (1835–1913) was governor of Kansas from 1865 to 1868. As the state's agent to pursue claims against the federal government since 1877, he was often on the East Coast. (*ANB.*)

4. Franklin George Adams (1824–1899) was known as "Judge" Adams, not "General," for serving as probate judge of Atchison County in 1858. SBA met him in 1865, when he was editor of the *Atchison Free Press* and her host on a lecture tour. In 1875, he, along with Daniel Read Anthony and others, founded the Kansas State Historical Society, where he held the posts of librarian, secretary, and director. Crawford wrote to Adams a few days after talking to SBA to say that "[a] debt of gratitude is unquestionably due to Mrs N. for those early services in shaping the foundation of our political system." (Alfred Theodore Andreas, *History of the State of Kansas, Containing a Full Account of Its Growth* [Chicago, 1883], 283–85, 554; *NCAB*, 6:498; *WWW1*; *Topeka Daily Capital*, 3 December 1899, SBA scrapbook 31, Rare Books, DLC; *Papers*, 1:552; S. A. Crawford to F. G. Adams, 9 November 1880, Records of the Kansas State Historical Society, Correspondence Received, Department of Archives, KHi.)

5. Charles Robinson (1818–1894), the first governor of Kansas and a leader in the State Impartial Suffrage Association, joined ECS in 1867 to campaign for the woman suffrage amendment to the state constitution. (*ANB.* See also *Papers* 2.)

6. Joseph Pomeroy Root (1826–1885), a physician and politician, settled in Wyandotte, Kansas, in 1857 with his wife, Frances Evaline Alden Root (1827–1900). He won election as lieutenant governor in 1861 and served on the executive committee of the Impartial Suffrage Association during the state amendment campaign of 1867. (*ANB*, s.v. "Root, Joseph Pomeroy"; obituaries, Kansas Biographical Scrapbooks, KHi.)

10 ✒ **SBA to Amelia Jenks Bloomer**

Tenafly N.J. Nov. 30th 1880.

My Dear Mrs Bloomer

Your several letters with incidents have arrived—and Mrs Stanton has worked you out a nice chapter of reminiscences—[1] Now your picture should go at front of your chapter of reminiscences— But here is where we are— Mrs Thompson's gift will not <u>cover</u> the cost of single picture—nothing but the bare stereotype—so that we are driven to the alternative of putting in the History only such pictures as the women themselves, or some of their friends, will pay for— And I have just returned from New York to night— I found that the very lowest figure is $100. for a <u>steel plate</u> engraving—and we have decided on <u>steel engravings</u>.— Mrs Motts children will of course pay for hers—Mrs Stanton for hers &c &c—but dear Mrs Nichols—cannot—and I have just written to her <u>Kansas friends</u>—to make up a testimonial to her—for we ought to have her picture—then I have written to a very dear friend of Mrs Rose's[2] to get him to pay for hers—and so on & so on— Now will you send on the $100— to pay for putting your picture into the history— <u>Yours should</u> go into the first volume, hence we must know at once—as the engraver is already at work on Mrs Stanton's—

I have been in hopes Mrs Thompson would contribute to do all of this—but have given it up entirely—

I have to the <u>engraver cash down</u> as fast as the engravings are done—and he & his work have nothing to do with Fowler & Wells—[3] Well let me know what you will do in the matter— And if you decide to send on the amount—send also one or two of your <u>best</u> photographs— <u>I have one here</u>—that you sent four years ago—but the artist likes to have two or three different ones—and to be told <u>which one is best</u>

as—no 1—has the best eyes

no 2—the best hair

no—3—the best mouth—

That is, he wants to make the engraving the best possible of each point of the face— Hoping to hear from you very soon—Sincerely yours

✒ *Susan B. Anthony*

❧ ALS, on NWSA letterhead for 1880, Amelia Bloomer Papers, Seneca Falls
Historical Society.

1. When Bloomer agreed earlier this month to provide material for her
reminiscences and the chapter on Iowa, SBA gave her further advice. Of her
own story, she said, "Put it together just as it comes easiest to you—only
short—" Of Iowa, SBA advised her, "Don't try to work out the rhetoric—Mrs
Stanton will do that—only get the important points & facts, & incidents—
together in order & concisely told—" (SBA to A. J. Bloomer, 4 November
1880, *Film*, 21:525–28.)

2. Ernestine Louise Siismondi Potowski Rose (1810–1892), born in Poland
and married in England, moved to New York in the 1830s. She was one of the
first women to petition for reform in the laws regarding married women's
property. (*NAW*; *ANB*. See also *Papers* 1–3.)

3. After talks with D. Appleton & Company collapsed in 1877, SBA arranged to have the *History* published by the New York firm of Fowler &
Wells, specialists in books on phrenology and reform.

11 ❧ SBA TO ELLEN C. SARGENT[1]

Tenafly N.J. Dec 3[d] 1880.

My Dear Ella

Your good letter here to night— I don't see what I can do for you—
only to refer you to Mrs Stantons description of Mrs Mott in "Eminent
Women of the Age"—first[2]—and then to the article in the N.C. & B.B.
for this month—which will be out about the 10th and that will not reach
you before the 15th or 20th—so I fear will not be in season—[3] I enclose
a little description of the funeral—sent us by Miss Rachel Foster—[4]

Mrs Mott fought a tripple battle—1st in the religious society[↑]—
Quaker—[↓] of which she was a member— She being Hicksite[5]—Unitarian—she was persecuted—or ostracised by many of her old & best
friends— When in England at the Worlds Anti Slavery Convention—
in 1840—& at a great dinner given to the American delegates—given by
Samuel Guerney, the brother of Elizabeth Fry—Mrs Mott was among
the guests—[6] Mrs Fry and nearly all of the English Quakers were
Orthodox Quakers—and Mrs Fry, while she was very sociable with all
the other delegates—took special pains to avoid Mrs Mott— Mrs
Stanton was present—& had told me about it—and the other day,

walking the streets of Boston, Wendell Phillips told it to Edward M. Davis— Mrs Fry—through the whole time managed always to be in the house, when Mrs Mott was in the garden and when Mrs Mott went into the garden, Mrs Fry would pass into the house— Studiously avoiding meeting Mrs Mott— Then—2[d] Anti Slavery—& for her work for that she was almost turned out of her society—the Hicksites— Then for her Woman's Rights—she again lost the favor of many of her oldest & best friends— But through it all—she was ever sweet-tempered and self-poised—

But you must write out of your own soul's feeling—you saw Mrs Mott that Centennial summer[7]—& I am so glad you did—& Lizzie too & George[8]—the memory of her beautiful face will always be a benediction to you—

I am so glad you dear Mother & Father[9] are working up California W.S. facts & doings for our history—

With ever so much Love to you & to each & all— I can see you now—10.15—Oclock—in that great nice room—your Mother pictured out so clearly to Mrs Stanton— We enjoyed that recital ever & ever so much— Good night—

⇒ *Susan B Anthony*

⇒ ALS, on NWSA letterhead for 1880, SBA Papers, NRU.

1. Ellen, or Ella, Clark Sargent (1854–1908), later Montgomery, was the eldest child of former California senator Aaron A. Sargent and his wife Ellen. After many years living in Washington, D.C., she had returned to San Francisco with her parents at the end of her father's term in the Senate in 1879. The family lived at 208 San Jose Avenue. (Edwin Everett Sargent, comp., *Sargent Record: William Sargent of Ipswich, Newbury, Hampton, Salisbury and Amesbury, New England, U.S.* [St. Johnsbury, Vt., 1899], 218; unpublished paper by Paula Lichtenberg, San Francisco; *NCAB*, 31:311; city directory, 1880–1881.)

2. Within ECS, "The Woman's Rights Movement and Its Champions in the United States," in James Parton et al., *Eminent Women of the Age* [Hartford, Conn., 1868], 362–404, in *Film*, 13:193ff.

3. Under the heading "The History of Woman Suffrage, Chapter VII, Lucretia Mott," the *National Citizen* published a biography and tribute to Mott. Though unsigned, it was attributed elsewhere in the issue of December 1880 to ECS and Matilda Gage. The article continued in the issue of February 1881. Both in *Film*, 21:727–28, 864–67.

4. She may have sent a clipping from the *Philadelphia Times*—an account reprinted in *NCBB*, December 1880, and *History*, 1:835.

5. Hicksite Friends distinguished themselves from Orthodox Friends by their greater reliance on individual perceptions of godliness than on the Bible and ministerial leadership.

6. Samuel Gurney (1786–1856), a wealthy London banker and member of the Society of Friends, entertained the American delegates to the World's Anti-Slavery Convention on 29 June 1840, and his sister, Elizabeth Gurney Fry (1780–1845), a distinguished prison reformer, was among the guests. Throughout Lucretia Mott's time in England that year, the Friends made no secret of their conviction that she was a heretic, and the charge was made that the exclusion of women from the convention was the work of Friends determined to bar Mott. The scene reported here, and recounted further in the next letter, expresses ECS's dramatic reconstruction of events. She would rewrite it for the obituary of Mott in the *National Citizen*, the memorial of Mott in the *History of Woman Suffrage*, and her own reminiscences in *Eighty Years*. (*DNB*; William Howitt to L. C. Mott, 27 June 1840, *History*, 1:434; Lucretia Mott, *Slavery and "The Woman Question": Lucretia Mott's Diary of Her Visit to Great Britain to Attend the World's Anti-Slavery Convention of 1840*, ed. Frederick B. Tolles [Haverford, Pa., 1952], 31, 32, 46, 47, 49, 50–51; William L. Garrison to Helen B. Garrison, 3 July 1840, Garrison, *Letters*, 2:661; *Selected Letters of Lucretia Coffin Mott*, ed. Beverly Wilson Palmer [Urbana, Ill., 2002], 80n; *NCBB*, February 1881, *Film*, 21:864–67; *History*, 1:422–24; *Eighty Years*, 83–84.)

7. In the summer of 1876 during centennial celebrations of the Declaration of Independence, the Sargent family visited Philadelphia and called several times at the National Woman Suffrage Association's Centennial Headquarters, where Lucretia Mott often greeted callers. (SBA diary, 12, 15, 18, 19 June 1876, *Film*, 18:516ff.)

8. The two younger Sargent children, these were Elizabeth (1857–1900) and George Clark (1860–1930).

9. Ellen Clark Sargent (1826–1911), an early advocate of woman suffrage in California, was for many years treasurer of the National Woman Suffrage Association and one of its most active members in Washington. Aaron Augustus Sargent (1827–1887), the Senate's chief promoter of woman's rights, introduced a constitutional amendment for woman suffrage in 1878. Their contributions to the *History of Woman Suffrage* are not acknowledged. (*BDAC*; Sargent, *Sargent Record*, 218; unpublished paper by Paula Lichtenberg, San Francisco. See also *Papers* 2 & 3.)

12 ❧ ECS TO EDWARD M. DAVIS

Tenafly N.J.   Dec 5th [*1880*]

My dear Friend

Yes I do remember how studiously Elizabeth Fry avoided Lucretia on several occasions when we all met & I remember too on some of these occasions she felt moved to pray, & knelt down & prayed most pointedly in Lucretia's presence for those who had wandered from the faith of the society who had exalted their reason above the teaching of the spirit not that these were her exact words, but the idea   I stayed more or less in my three months travels with "Friends," & they never would mention Lucretias name except with a sigh   To my enthusiastic praise they were simply reproachfully silent, always looking sad & mournful as if they regarded her as a calamity to that Society   John Scoble, Birney, Henry, & myself made the tour of England Scotland & Ireland together.[1] Everywhere John Scoble denounced her & George Thompson[2]   One night at Mr Wigham's[3] in Edinboro Thompson & Scoble met & what an intellectual fisty cuffing & row they had about Lucretia among other things. Scoble exaperated me so in his talk about her & woman's rights, that at last I told Henry I would not travel with Scoble another hour. I went straight to London & stayed there above ten days. In all my life I never did desire so to ring a man's neck as I did his, & I never enjoyed anything more than his agonizing sea sickness crossing the channel, & Mr Birney to console him told him Lord Nelson[4] was always seasick, but he did not dispose of all his bile that awful night   he was as <u>bitter</u> as ever next day on the independence of American women. The next Citizen will contain my sketch of your dear mother, the outline of what we should put in the History. I intend in the middle of the sketch as it will appear to put many of my personal reminiscence & conversations with her, for wherever our party went I took possession of Lucretia much to Henry's vexation, as we were just then married. I was completely fascinated with her, & what a blessing that meeting was to me just in the turning point of my religious faith. I am glad that you talk of getting up a life of her by the family.[5] I think it would be interesting to collect at the end of the sketch all that the press & the pulpit have said, as you could not yourselves pay such generous praises.

The plan of my sketch in opening was suggested to me by Robert Collyer's sermon.[6] You remember he notes the great events of history in the century in which she was born. I more appropriately have noted the great women of that time, & I make one point to which no other pen has referred the disgrace & humiliation of disfranchising such a woman. Send us the picture Maria & yourself would prefer in the History. If Maria would like to have me help her select, & arrange material when she is all ready I will gladly do so. With best regards for both sincerely yours

⤠ *Elizabeth Cady Stanton*

One thing more I wish you would ask Robert Purvis wife[7] for me if she can rake up any brave deeds of women in the early History of Pa. In the opening of the Penn chapter, we want some record of the women   If she can find half a dozen dotting[8] along that have done or said something worthy of mention, let us have the names & facts. I wish you could put Roberts wife & Rachel Foster in communication. We must have the Penn chapter within this month as a dozen printers are on our heels.

⤠ ALS, Mott MSS, PSC-Hi.

1. John Scoble (c. 1810–c. 1868), a British clergyman and early worker in the transatlantic antislavery movement, joined Henry Stanton and James Gillespie Birney (1792–1857), a former slaveholder and the Liberty party candidate for president in 1840, in a tour of the British Isles. Their tour was sponsored by the British and Foreign Anti-Slavery Society, a conservative group opposed to William Lloyd Garrison's American Anti-Slavery Society. ECS's dislike for Scoble was no secret: her hosts in Dublin described her "hearty well grounded horror of Scoble." However, the details of the story below are inventive, and they underwent a later transformation in her reminiscences. Scoble did indeed get sick on a passage from England to Ireland, but he was traveling alone with Birney. ECS did return to London alone for a time in August but not to avoid Scoble, and after her sojourn in London, she returned to the tour when Scoble resumed his travels with Henry Stanton. (*ANB*; Garrison, *Letters*, 3:389n; Richard D. Webb to Elizabeth Pease, 4 November 1840, in Clare Taylor, ed., *British and American Abolitionists: An Episode in Transatlantic Understanding* [Edinburgh, Scotland, 1974], 119–20; H. B. Stanton to J. G. Birney, 15 August 1840, and J. G. Birney to Lewis Tappan, 29 August 1840, in

Letters of James Gillespie Birney, 1831–1857, ed. Dwight L. Dumond [New York, 1938], 2:594–95, 596–97; H. B. Stanton to Gerrit Smith, 22 September 1840, Smith Papers, NSyU; J. Scoble to J. H. Tredgold, 30 October 1840, in Annie Heloise Abel and Frank J. Klingberg, eds., *A Side-Light on Anglo-American Relations, 1839–1858* [Lancaster, Pa., 1927], 75; *Eighty Years*, 103–4.)

2. George Thompson (1804–1878), a British antislavery orator with close ties to the Garrisonian wing of abolitionists, had fierce disagreements on many points with the more conservative John Scoble. (*DNB*.)

3. John Wigham, Jr. (1782–1862), a Quaker manufacturer with many interests in reform, hosted the Stantons in Edinburgh in October 1840. (Garrison, *Letters*, 3:443n, 4:36n.)

4. Horatio, viscount Nelson (1758–1805), a celebrated British naval admiral.

5. Anna Davis Hallowell, ed., *James and Lucretia Mott. Life and Letters* (Boston, 1884).

6. Robert Collyer (1823–1912) was pastor of the Unitarian Church of the Messiah in New York City, where he settled in 1879 after many years in Chicago. To Lucretia Mott he owed his conversion to Unitarianism in the 1850s, and he paid tribute to her at his church in the evening of November 21. His lecture was published in the *New York Tribune*, 22 November 1880. (*DAB*.)

7. Robert Purvis (1810–1898) of Philadelphia, a prominent African-American abolitionist and one of the few who argued that the rights of his daughters were as important as those of his sons, was a member with Davis of the Citizens' Suffrage Association and a regular participant in meetings of the National Woman Suffrage Association. After the death of his first wife, Harriet Forten Purvis, in 1875, he married Tacy Townsend (c. 1827–1900), a Philadelphia Quaker and author of two children's books, *Abi Meredith* (1878) and *Hagar; the Singing Maiden, with Other Stories and Rhymes* (1881). Although included in dictionaries of African-American writers, Tacy Purvis was a white woman. (*DANB*; *ANB*; *Friends' Intelligencer* 57 [1900]: 759; Federal Census, 1880; *Washington Post*, 26 January 1884.)

8. Perhaps ECS meant "doting," in the sense of a mind weakened with age.

13   *⟫*   **ECS TO AMELIA JENKS BLOOMER**

[*Tenafly,*] December 9th [*1880*]

My dear Mrs Bloomer

If you can make a spicy interesting chapter of Iowa, condensed in a style that you would feel proud of in the History over your own name all well, as this is a labor of love all round & there is no pay extract all the fame you can out of it by making your chapter in style, conciseness, interest, wit & pathos the most brilliant star in the book   We do not want speeches & resolutions, unless it be a few brilliant extracts, or a resolution that contains enough gunpowder to blow all the editors & legislators of Iowa into their right minds.[1] We do not care about the differences & divisions but the successive steps year by year in progress[2] Your experience in getting bushels of chaff with a kernel of wheat therein is exactly ours. Once in awhile newspapers say witty things, give us them   You need not be as solemn as an owl, let us have a little something to laugh at occasionally. Whatever man has said or done ought for us let us mention him & thus make our champions immortal. Your reminiscences cover 15 pages can you put Iowa in the same. I shall try to see that you have the full honor for "The Lily"   Did Mrs Bull[3] ever answer you. I should have written you sooner but I have been so tired writing History all day that I have had no time for letters. So as not to offend the dear women that send you such voluminous trash as you describe, try & use a little of what they send you. Some women have sent us a minute history of ↑their↓ lives from birth to the present hour, all they have thought   done & said & nothing of the public work or change in the laws & public sentiment   If you could see Mrs Gage Susan & myself worrying over manuscripts, contending over dates, facts, philosophy, what is, & what is not pertinent, you would have no faith in the final appearance of the 1. Vol. promised for Christmas. If 400 pages were not in type I should have no hope myself   in haste

⋘   *E. C S.*

⋘ ALS, Autographed Letter Collection, IaCrM.

1. SBA explained to Bloomer on the same day that the second volume would not contain the many speeches and resolutions included in the first volume, "except some new or startling points—as they come up—" (SBA to A. J. Bloomer, 9 December 1880, *Film*, 21:650–52.)

2. To write the history of woman suffrage in Iowa, Bloomer needed to revisit some of the most cantankerous disagreements resulting from the division between the National and the American suffrage associations after 1869 and especially an effort to label some suffragists as free lovers aligned with Victoria Woodhull. SBA took up Bloomer's now missing question a few days later to say, "We propose to make as <u>little</u> of the differences that occur all along the line of the 30 years warfare—as truth will allow—" (Louise Noun,

"Annie Savery: A Voice for Women's Rights," *Annals of Iowa* 44 [1977]: 3–30; Louise Rosenfeld Noun with Rachel E. Bohlmann, *Leader and Pariah: Annie Savery and the Campaign for Women's Rights in Iowa, 1868–1891* [Iowa City, Iowa, 2002]; SBA to A. J. Bloomer, 12 December 1880, *Film*, 21:662–65.)

3. Mary Sherwood Bascom Bull (1835–1881), who grew up in Seneca Falls, New York, and attended the woman's rights convention of 1848 with her father, published an article, "Woman's Rights and Other 'Reforms' in Seneca Falls," in the summer of 1880. She ridiculed the appearance of Bloomer and ECS in their bloomer costumes and made light of reformers' motives. Amelia Bloomer sent a copy to ECS for comment. (Edward Doubleday Harris, *A Genealogical Record of Thomas Bascom, and His Descendants* [Boston, 1870], 62; Mary Bull, "'Woman's Rights and Other Reforms in Seneca Falls': A Contemporary View," ed. Robert Riegel, *New York History* 46 [January 1965]: 41–59; *Papers*, 3:550–52.)

14 ∽ ECS TO AMELIA JENKS BLOOMER

[Tenafly, 13 December 1880]

I would make a pleasant chapter of the progressive steps in the state, but give nothing of the petty warfare. Our little dissensions are of little account in the grand onward march. Give a fair list of the names of the women who have helped to roll the ball. Considering the slavery of woman they have all behaved [*continued in margins*] as well as could be expected

∽ E. C. S.

∽ ANS on postal card, Amelia Bloomer Papers, Seneca Falls Historical Society. Postmarked at Tenafly; addressed to Council Bluffs, Iowa.

·⊂══════⟫⟨⟪══════⊃·

15 ⤳ CLARINA HOWARD NICHOLS TO SBA

[*Pomo, Calif.*,] Dec 22 1880

Dear Susan

I omitted one topic in my last expecting before this to have sent another package for which I wanted an Aug '79 no of the Citizen I thought I could get of a Subscriber in the town, but <u>it</u> had been sent on a mission. So I write to say that I want to <u>suppress</u> <u>my</u> <u>mention</u> of <u>Judge Kingman's</u> <u>opposition.</u>[1] I had been feeling uncomfortable about it as I recollected him as the only opponent named individually & tho' his sarcastic humor was the concentrated influence that counted most for the opposition <u>then</u>, he, it seems, has progres[d] and I feel is entitled to the forbearance of which age ~~and providence (being out of judicial office)~~ ↑& much good service for the State & Society↓ and above all, womanly consideration for an opponent shorn of power—entitle him I can change the paragraph with little trouble ↑to the printer↓ when I get the proof. But lest I should not live to correct it <u>myself</u>, I write to ask <u>you</u> to see that Judge Kingmans <u>name</u> is left out in the mention of the opposition as "<u>leading</u>" it & again as a "bitter opponent." I do not remember whether the expressions are in the same or separate paragraphs. A letter from Judge Adams on this point came to hand last mail. I am no spiritualist but here as in many instances in my life my mind has been haunted by some fact, feeling, or incident—and lo! an expression of similar feelings have come to ↑me↓ penned about the same time from some friend interested in me or the subject upon which both were impressed. It is storming & has been for a week & I suffer as I always do on such occasions. Will get the pictures to you soon as sunshine helps A. O.[2] to take copy—which I will put up with the daguerreotype— In great haste & much love

⤳ *C I H Nichols*

⤳ ALS, SBA Papers, MCR-S.

1. Nichols wanted to revise her reminiscences of the Kansas constitutional convention of 1859 as they appeared in the *National Citizen*, August 1879, before publication of the *History*. She had not, as she thought, used the words

"bitter opponent" in that text, but she did write that "[t]he head and front of the opposition was Judge Kingman, Chairman of the Judiciary Committee to which with Committee on Elections my petition was referred. He wrote the Report against granting our demand." She continued, "but for Judge Kingman," woman suffrage would have gained a majority in the convention, and it was Kingman who sought to preserve the common law rights of husbands to personal services. The passages were not rewritten for the *History of Woman Suffrage*, 1:192–94. Nichols described Kingman as a man of "bitter prejudices" in an article for the *Woman's Journal*, 16 August 1879. Samuel Austin Kingman (1818–1904), a Republican lawyer, went on to serve on the state supreme court and as the first president of the Kansas State Historical Society. (*NCAB*, 13:76; Frank W. Blackmar, ed., *Kansas: A Cyclopedia of State History, Embracing Events, Institutions, Industries, Counties, Cities, Towns, Prominent Persons, Etc.*, [Chicago, 1912], 2:74–75.)

2. Aurelius Ormando Carpenter (1836–1919), the son of her first marriage, was a photographer as well as a farmer and publisher of a newspaper in Ukiah, California. (*History of Mendocino County, California: Comprising Its Geography, Geology, and Topography* [1880; reprint, N.p., 1967], 632–34, 686; family notes, Clarina I. H. Nichols Papers, MCR-S.)

16   SBA TO CLARINA HOWARD NICHOLS

[Tenafly, after 22 December 1880]

History ought to be true, and the men and women who at the time enjoyed the glory of opposing us ought to be known to posterity even if it is to their children's sorrow; just as those who suffered the torments of ridicule and hatred then, now enjoy the rewards, and their children and grandchildren glory in their ancestors. Robert Dale Owen's daughter,[1] in writing up the Indiana Constitutional Convention and her father's opponents, withheld their names from sympathy for their children. I have told her, that as she now rejoices in what was then considered her father's reproach, so she should let the children of those men hang their heads now for what then was their father's pride. Isn't that fair? Garrison[2] used to say, "Where there is a sin, there must be a sinner." When people understand that their descendants and all Israel will know of their deeds, a hundred years hence, maybe they will learn to be and do better.

I am a genuine believer in the doctrine of letting the seed bear its fruit on the sower's own ground. For us not to give the names of our opponents, but only of those who were wise and good, not only would not be true history, but would rob the book of one-half its interest. If all persons felt that their children must suffer for their wrong-doings, they would be more cautious, but the belief that all their ill record is to be hidden out of sight helps them to go on reckless of truth and justice. It is not in malice or with a desire to make any one suffer, but to be true to history that every name should stand and be judged as the facts merit.

⪻ *Anthony*, 2:529–30.

1. Rosamond Dale Owen (1846–1937), later Oliphant and Templeton, was the younger daughter of Robert Dale Owen (1801–1877) and Mary Jane Robinson Owen (1813–1871). Her father was an early proponent of women's property rights and liberal divorce both as a co-worker of Frances Wright and as a young politician in Indiana. Her mother, who met Owen at Wright's lectures in New York, was active in the American Equal Rights Association. In "Robert Dale Owen and Mary Robinson," written for the *History of Woman Suffrage*, she indeed omitted the names of her father's opponents whose remarks she quoted in the essay. (Donald E. Thompson, comp., *Indiana Authors and Their Books, 1917–1966* [Crawfordsville, Ind., 1974], s.v. "Templeton, Rosamond Dale Owen"; Anne Taylor, *Laurence Oliphant* [New York, 1982], 242–47, 253–56; *ANB*, s.v. "Owen, Robert Dale"; Richard William Leopold, *Robert Dale Owen: A Biography* [New York, 1969]; *History*, 1:293–306.)

2. William Lloyd Garrison (1805–1879) was the leading voice for the immediate emancipation of slaves. (*ANB*.)

17 ⪼ INTERVIEW WITH SBA IN WASHINGTON, DISTRICT OF COLUMBIA

[*16 January 1881*]

"The immediate object of our Convention," said Miss Anthony to a *Tribune* correspondent, "is to secure the passage of a measure in both houses of Congress authorizing the appointment of special committees to take under consideration the question of woman suffrage. We have such a committee in the House already,[1] but it will do nothing, and we want a new one. We have assurances from leading members of both houses that they will assist us. They have committees for the Indians and for the freedmen; why not for women? It seems a great undertaking for a few women without money or political influence to come here and attempt to gain recognition in competition with so many and such immense interests as find advocacy before Congress. We have been working a long time, but we are not discouraged."

⫸ *New York Tribune*, 17 January 1881.

    1. This was inaccurate. The resolution in favor of a committee was still on the calendar. See above at 27 November 1880.

18 ⫸ SBA TO LUCY WEBB HAYES[1]

Riggs House   Washington Jan. 17, 1881

My Dear Mrs Hays

    We very much wish you to attend our Memorial service to our venerated friend Lucretia Mott, to be held in Lincoln Hall[2] tomorrow, Tuesday, A.M. at 10 Oclock.

    Elizabeth Cady Stanton is to deliver the Eulogy—

    Miss Phebe Couzins[3] called to extend the invitation to you in person this A.M. but failed to see you—

    Will you my dear friend—as the champion of all true womanhood—and especially of the noble one ~~we are~~ ↑whose↓ memory we are to honor be present with us tomorrow morning—and if agreeable to you—we shall be very happy to have you sit upon the platform. Very Truly Yours

⫸ *Susan B. Anthony*

⫸ ALS, Lucy Webb Hayes Collection, OFH.

    1. Lucy Ware Webb Hayes (1831–1889), wife of the president, was a college graduate with many of the same interests as the women active in reform movements, especially temperance. She often received leaders of women's groups at the White House. (*ANB*; *NAW*. See also *Papers 3*.)

    2. Built in 1867 at the corner of Ninth and D streets, Northwest, Lincoln Hall held Washington's largest auditorium with seating for thirteen hundred.

    3. Phoebe Wilson Couzins (1839–1913) of St. Louis was on hand for the founding of the National Woman Suffrage Association in 1869, took part in most of its meetings over the next decade, and at this date, served on its executive committee. The first woman to enter the law school of Washington

University, Couzins worked primarily as a lecturer after her graduation in 1871. (*NAW*; *ANB*. See also *Papers* 3.)

19 ❧ MEMORIAL SERVICE FOR LUCRETIA COFFIN MOTT

EDITORIAL NOTE: The Washington convention of the National Woman Suffrage Association opened in Lincoln Hall with the memorial service for Lucretia Mott. "The decorations of the stage," the *Washington Post* reported, "which have seldom been surpassed in point of beauty and tastefulness of arrangement, formed a fitting setting for the notable assemblage of women." First Lady Lucy Hayes sat near the front of the packed hall, while Frederick Douglass, Robert Purvis, former Kansas senator Samuel C. Pomeroy, and Richard J. Hinton joined members of the association on the stage.

[18 January 1881]

Presently Miss Phoebe W. Couzins arose, and stepping to the front of the stage, said gently, "In accordance with the custom of Mrs. Mott and the time-honored practice of the Quakers, I ask you to unite in an invocation to the spirit."

She bowed her head. The audience followed her example. For several minutes the solemn silence of devotion pervaded the hall. When Miss Couzins had taken her seat the quartette choir of St. Augustine's church (colored), which was seated on the platform, sang sweetly an appropriate selection.[1] Then the venerable Mrs. Elizabeth Cady Stanton, whose portly form and lovely white hair has been the central figure in these annual conventions for years, came forward and, adjusting her spectacles, placed her manuscript on the desk and commenced to read in a low but distinct voice. She began: "On the 3d day of January, 1793, there was born on the Island of Nantucket the most remarkable woman of her time." The first part of the eulogy was biographical in its character, and a tone of quiet appreciation pervaded it throughout. The tribute paid to her as a wife and mother was especially beautiful, and the contrast, which ran through a number of antithetical sentences between Mrs. Mott and her husband, James Mott,[2] showed a power of analysis and a conception of character which was striking. The speaker said that Mr. Mott loved quiet, but she loved nothing better than talking. This statement sent a gentle ripple of laughter over the audience. She described her home in Philadelphia, the headquarters of the reformers and the refuge of runaway slaves. Here came women and men of distinction from this and foreign lands, and while Mrs. Mott attended to her household duties, discussions of great topics were had which Mrs. Mott, pausing in her work, joined. Sagacity, the speaker thought, was her chief characteristic, or, rather it might be called a wise diplomacy. In June, 1840, the speaker met Mrs. Mott for the first time in London, and found her to be the greatest wonder of the world—a woman who thought and had opinions of her own. She was a woman emancipated from all man-made creeds, and not afraid to question anything. It was like meeting a creature from a higher sphere to meet one who dared to recognize the judgment of a woman's mind. In closing the speaker referred to the numerous tributes that had been paid to the life and character of Mrs. Mott in the public press, and the vast strides that public opinion had made since Mrs. Mott first appeared before the public. But amid all this no mention has been made of her political degradation, which she so deeply deplored during her life. When the Nation mourns the grandest of her sex, no tear is shed, no mention is made of her disfranchisement.

When Mrs. Stanton had taken her seat Fred Douglass[3] arose and said that he had listened with interest to the fine analysis of the life and services of Lucretia Mott. He was almost unwilling to have his voice heard after what had been said. He was there to show by his presence his profound respect and earnest love for Lucretia Mott. He recognized none whose services in behalf of his race were equal to hers. Her silence even in that cause was more than the speech of others. He said that he had no words for this occasion and took his seat.

Miss Susan B. Anthony with tears in her eyes arose and said: "I am sure if Frederick Douglass cannot speak I cannot. Next to the feeling that we have the love and confidence of the great creator is to have the love and confidence of a grand human being. Such was Lucretia Mott, and such was my lot. I say to you I cannot speak." The speaker whose voice had become choked with emotion sat down and buried her face in her handkerchief.

Dr. Purvis[4] said that at the request of a number of citizens of Washington, he wished to present the floral harp to Mr. Edward M. Davis, the son-in-law of Mrs. Mott. He then read a brief tribute to the memory of the deceased.

Mr. Davis, who is a middle-aged gentleman, had a seat on the platform, and received the floral gift with appropriate words of thanks. He said that he would follow the example of Mrs. Mott, who seldom retained a gift long, and present it to Mrs. Spofford, the treasurer of the association.

⪼ *Washington Post*, 19 January 1881.

1. The choir of St. Augustine's Church, an African-American Catholic church on Fifteenth Street, was thought to be the best in Washington, and it drew Protestants and whites, politicians and tourists, to the church's services. (Morris J. MacGregor, *The Emergence of a Black Catholic Community: St. Augustine's in Washington* [Washington, D.C., 1999], 88–89, 98–99.)

2. James Mott (1788–1868) was his wife's partner in reform. A passage about the Motts' marriage is found in the *National Citizen*, February 1881, within the second part of "The History of Woman Suffrage, Chapter VII, Lucretia Mott." Elsewhere ECS's memorial address draws on the article published in December. With significant modification and rearrangement of material, the two articles became chapter eleven of the *History*. All three texts are in *Film*, 21:727–28, 786–98, 864–67.

3. Frederick Douglass (1818–1895), former slave, abolitionist, and early supporter of woman suffrage, moved from Rochester, New York, to Washington in 1872. During the Hayes administration, he served as federal marshal of the District of Columbia, but he lost that post after the inauguration of James A. Garfield in March 1881. (*DANB*; *ANB*. See also *Papers* 1–3.)

4. Charles Burleigh Purvis (1842–1929) of Washington was a professor at the medical school of Howard University. The son of two pioneer abolitionists in Philadelphia, he had known Lucretia Mott and her family through his entire life. There are other reports that Robert Purvis, rather than Charles, spoke at this point in the ceremony. According to the *Evening Star*, Robert recalled the founding of the American Anti-Slavery Society in 1833. The large harp, "formed of beautiful red and white flowers," stood on a table during the memorial service. It was furnished by James Wormley, the African-American proprietor of Wormley's Hotel in Washington. (*DANB*; *ANB*; *Washington Post*, 19 January 1881, and Washington *Evening Star*, 18 January 1881, *Film*, 21:777, 780–81.)

20 ⟿ ECS to the Editor, *National Citizen and Ballot Box*

[*January 1881*]

Ed. National Citizen:—

Can it be that we have held thirteen successive annual conventions at the Capitol,[1] with as many hearings before committees, and innumerable petitions pigeon-holed in the national archives, and yet have no Standing Committee to hear and consider the interests of women, of one-half the people of the United States? Committees on Territories, Commerce, Railroads, Finance, Banks, Claims, Grievances, Indians, but none for women! It may take us another thirteen years to secure full justice, but it will be accomplished without the assistance of Mr. Davis of Virginia,[2] who referred it to the Committee on Rules, or of Mr. Conkling of New York,[3] who killed Senator McDonald's[4] motion for a Standing Committee with such a plausible substitute that even the very elect were deceived, and half our friends in the gallery clapped the New York Senator's ridicule and irony. When some of our friends saw that Senators McDonald and Conkling voted together, they said, "there, we told you so! Conkling is favorable to our demands," without stopping to see that they proposed opposite measures, and alike voted "no," on the Virginia Senator's motion to refer the whole subject back to the "committee on rules." As if the arbitrary rule of a "male dynasty" were not the very thing against which we are protesting. Of all places to send us the most objectionable was the "committee on rules." Women hate rules. Aside from the ungracious behavior of the New York Senator, we had every reason to congratulate ourselves at our hospitable reception at Washington. The convention was a complete success, in crowded houses at every session, in an admission fee of ten cents, remarkably good speaking, a few resolutions that passed into history without a ripple,[5] and no heart burnings behind the scenes. Edward M. Davis, Frederick Douglass and Robert Purvis, stood by us as faithful coadjutors should, pulling out their well stuffed pocket-books every time the hat went round, which gave the Treasurer a feeling of satisfaction that our association would begin the New Year with no debts of honor unpaid.

The number of new faces on our platform was a most encouraging feature of this convention. Mrs. Martha McClellan Brown[6] of Pittsburgh, is a woman of stately and beautiful presence and a fine speaker, her voice is full and clear and her style impressive. She spoke several times and with marked effect. Mrs. Emily Thornton Charles,[7] gave a short poem of great wit and beauty, with good elocutionary power. Miss Jessie Waite[8] of Chicago, just in her teens, made a beautiful appeal to girls to enroll themselves in this grand work for woman's freedom. Her mother, Mrs. Catharine V. Waite,[9] gave an admirable report of all that had been accomplished in Illinois. She presented several members of the convention with a copy of Judge Charles B. Waite's great work just published, "History of the Christian Religion to the year two hundred." We advise all women who desire to know how much reliance they can place on their teachers of theology to study this work. And this is the more important for women, because the great block in the way of their progress in all nations and under all forms of religion today, is the dogmas and superstitions of their faith. Among the list of new comers we must not forget to mention Miss Rachel Foster[10] of Philadelphia, who not only aims to speak well but is ambitious to fill the place of Susan B. Anthony in executive ability, and generous devotion to all those trying business matters, that most of us would fain escape; and she has already proved herself a worthy successor of our indomitable financier.

Mrs. May Wright Sewall[11] of Indianapolis, made her first appearance in a Washington convention, and was listened to with marked attention. She is one of the most ready extemporaneous speakers we have ever had on our platform, and a very pleasing woman withal. Her bravery and self-control is beyond praise; coming as she did with a broken arm, the accident having occurred only the day before she left home. Yet because she had promised to come she took the risk of that long journey, disabled as she was. However, she found willing hands at every point to supply her needs. One thing about her I especially admired, in all our social gatherings and on the platform she never made the slightest reference to herself, or the accident from which she was suffering. It is so much the fashion to begin a speech with apologies and confessions of inability, that it is a great relief when a speaker without any preliminaries lights at once on the central idea of the subject in hand. Mrs. Sewall evidently felt a proper pride in her State that can boast of a Republican Governor and his wife[12] pledged to woman suffrage, and a Democratic Senator ready to champion our cause at the National Capitol. Governor Porter's liberal message to the legislature, and Senator McDonald's motion for a standing committee on woman suffrage, must inspire the women of Indiana with new hope and courage.

After the close of the convention a number of us passed a pleasant hour with Mrs. Hayes at the White House. I heard but one opinion expressed of her, "an agreeable, good common sense woman, in whom we may all feel a proper pride."

She has kept the White House morally clean and free from all gossip and reproach, and will be always held in affectionate remembrance by the women of our nation. Mrs. Hayes' manners are free from all affectation, airs and graces; she is simple, frank and cordial. She took the younger members of the party all over the house, showing them just what she knew they would like to see. I really wish all our young American women who are imitating the mock dignity of snobs, the airs and attitudes of a French dancing master, could make Mrs. Hayes a study.[13] Mrs. Spofford of the Riggs House, is another woman of the same type, who adds one more charm to me, in that she is a pronounced woman suffragist. I did not ask Mrs. Hayes her views on our question thinking it was not quite fair or polite under the circumstances, to compel her to express an opinion; that she volunteered none, led us to infer that she had not yet investigated the subject.

We had a crowded reception and fine supper at the Riggs House, on which occasion I had the honor of presenting the beautiful life size photograph of Lucretia Mott to Howard University, after reading the following letter from Edward M. Davis:[14]

<Riggs House, Washington, Jan. 20, 1880.

To the President of the Woman's National Suffrage Association, Elizabeth Cady Stanton:
Dear Madam: I want to do something to show my gratitude for the beautiful floral tribute of the colored people of the District to the memory of my dear mother. Will you,

therefore, present in my name and the name of Mrs. Mott's children, the photograph of Mrs. Mott which was on the stage at our convention to the institution that admits within its doors any and all, without regard to color, sex, or previous condition—the Howard University, which I know includes also all nationalities. To such an institution it seems that this picture should be presented.

With sincere regret that I cannot be present at the reception this evening to you and Miss Anthony, I am gratefully yours,

EDWARD M. DAVIS>

In acknowledging the beautiful gift, Dr. Patton,[15] President of the institution, made a touching and eloquent speech. For some time we were under the impression that Dr. Patton was the same clergyman who drove Dr. David Swing from his pulpit for heresy,[16] and you may imagine our hesitation in asking him to receive from a company of heretics, the picture of one so liberal, henceforth to look down from the walls of an institution of which he was President. When he offered me his arm to walk out to supper I was sorely troubled lest, as our guest, something might be said or done to embarrass him. As he stepped to the table to secure some viands for me, May Wright Sewall whispered in my ear, "He is not the man. I cut the Gordian knot by frankly asking him, and thus relieved the general embarrassment."

The generous hospitality of Mr.[17] and Mrs. Spofford to many members of the convention, is another encouraging feature of the growing interest in our movement. Everybody remarked on the striking difference between the Boston convention with its empty seats, cold atmosphere, no fee at the door, conducted by Mr. Blackwell,[18]—and the National convention with its packed audiences, sustained enthusiasm, catholic platform, ten cents admission to every session, conducted by women. It is evident our New England friends must after all learn of the Nationals how to get up rousing conventions. To eliminate from a meeting all spontaneity[19] is certain death. To suspend the motto "I am holier than thou!" over the platform may awe the multitude, but it makes Pharisees of those who place it there.[20]

  Elizabeth Cady Stanton.

❧ *NCBB*, February 1881; Washington *National Republican*, 21 January 1881.

1. The National Woman Suffrage Association numbered its conventions at the capital from January 1869, although that first convention, predating the National's founding, was called by the Universal Franchise Association based in Washington.

2. Henry Gassaway Davis (1823–1916), a Democrat from West Virginia, not Virginia, served in the Senate from 1871 to 1883. (*BDAC*.)

3. Roscoe Conkling (1829–1888), the colorful leader of New York's Republican party and a consistent opponent of woman suffrage, served in the Senate from 1867 to 1881. He resigned in May 1881 to protest federal appointments in New York and failed to win reelection to his seat. (*BDAC*. See also *Papers* 2 & 3.)

4. Joseph Ewing McDonald (1819–1891), Democrat of Indiana and an ally of the National association in passing the bill that allowed women to practice law before the Supreme Court, served one term in the Senate. He would leave at the end of the Forty-sixth Congress in March. ECS refers to his request on January 20 that the Senate give unanimous consent to his resolution in favor of a committee on the rights of women. Roscoe Conkling objected, and oozing sarcasm, he observed that McDonald's request for a standing committee boded ill for women's rights, as it implied a perpetual wait for suffrage; a special committee, instructed "that before the sun goes down on the last day of this session it is to take final, serious, intelligent action for which it is to be responsible," would better express McDonald's hopes for the cause. Henry Davis opposed any new committee and moved that the resolution be referred to the Committee on Rules. Both Conkling and McDonald voted against the Davis motion, which passed by a vote of twenty-six to twenty-three. (*BDAC*; *Papers*, 3:436–37n, 525, 526n; *Congressional Record*, 46th Cong., 3d sess., 774–75.)

5. See *Film*, 21:778, 782. The resolutions reiterated the National's contention that "we are a nation and not a confederacy of states. We are all citizens first of the United States and second of the states wherein we reside; hence the right of self government should be guaranteed by the national constitution to all citizens." They also decried the exemption of church property from taxation as "a union of Church and State, an old monarchical idea opposed to the secular nature of our Government."

6. Martha McClellan Brown (1838–1916) was an experienced lecturer, prominent in the order of Good Templars, and a member of the executive committee of the Prohibition party. While her husband continued to live in Pittsburgh, she moved to New York City to develop the National Prohibition Alliance and encourage greater cooperation between prohibitionists and political parties. (*NAW*; *SEAP*.)

7. Emily Thornton Charles (c. 1840–?) was a journalist and poet from Indiana who moved to Washington in 1880 or 1881. A reporter described her poem, "Woman's Sphere," as "a vision of the inception, the struggle, the

approaching triumph of the cause. . . ." A widow at age twenty-four, with two children to support, she wrote for newspapers in Indianapolis and published her first book of poems in 1876. She included "Woman's Sphere" in her second book, *Lyrical Poems, Songs, Pastorals, Roundelays, War Poems, Madrigals* (1886). In Washington, she became editor of the *Washington World and Citizen-Soldier* and also founded a small press, specializing in works by veterans. Although several sources give her birthdate as 1845, the census takers who found her in both Indianapolis and Washington on different days in 1880 recorded her age as forty years. (*American Women*; R. E. Banta, comp., *Indiana Authors and Their Books, 1816-1916* [Crawfordsville, Ind., 1949]; *History*, 3:190n; Washington *National Republican*, 20 January 1881, *Film*, 21:784; city directories, 1881 to 1893; Federal Census, District of Columbia, 1880, and Indiana, 1880.)

8. Jessie Fremont Waite (1856–?), the eldest daughter of the Illinois suffragists Charles B. and Catharine Van Valkenburg Waite, first attended a Washington convention in 1880. Later in life, as Jessie Waite Wright, she presided over the District of Columbia Woman Suffrage Association from 1906 to 1908. (*Women Building Chicago*, s.v. "Waite, Catharine Van Valkenburg"; Patricia R. McMillen, "Catharine Van Valkenburg Waite," *Bar None: 125 Years of Women Lawyers in Illinois*, ed. Gwen Hoerr McNamee [Chicago, 1998], 47–50; *History*, 3:151, 161, 190, 254, 6:105.)

9. Catherine Van Valkenburg Waite (1829–1913), educator and publisher, and Charles Burlingame Waite (1824–1909), former federal judge and author, were founding members of the Illinois Woman Suffrage Association. In 1871, they initiated one of the legal cases to test whether women could claim their voting rights under the Fourteenth Amendment. Catherine Waite's publishing firm had just released Charles Waite, *History of the Christian Religion, to the Year Two Hundred* (1881)—a book that is still in print. In 1885, Catherine Waite enrolled in Chicago's Union College of Law, graduated one year later, and began a new career. (*NAW* and *ANB*, s.v. "Waite, Catherine Van Valkenburg"; *WWW1*, s.v. "Waite, Charles Burlingame"; *United States Biographical Dictionary: Illinois Volume* [Chicago, 1876], 298–99. See also *Papers 2*.)

10. Rachel G. Foster (1858–1919), later Avery, was a relative newcomer to the National association, but her responsibilities were growing rapidly, especially while SBA worked on the *History*. The Citizens' Suffrage Association of Philadelphia sent Rachel and her sister, Julia, to the Washington convention in January 1879, and the two young women were immediately recognized for their efficiency, willingness to work, and independent wealth. Delegates to the annual meeting in 1880, however, rejected an attempt to make Rachel Foster the corresponding secretary in the place of Sara Andrews Spencer. She assumed the post at the annual meeting in 1881. (*NAW* and *ANB*, s.v. "Avery, Rachel G. Foster.")

11. May Eliza Wright Thompson Sewall (1844–1920) was a cofounder of the

Indianapolis Equal Suffrage Society in 1878, and in 1880, she became a member of the National association's executive committee. A widow and a schoolteacher, she married Theodore Lovett Sewall on 30 October 1880 and with him established the Girls' Classical School of Indianapolis. (*NAW*; *ANB*.)

12. Albert Gallatin Porter (1824–1897) took office as Republican governor of Indiana on 10 January 1881, five days after his marriage—his second—to Cornelia Stone (?–1886) in New York. In his inaugural address, Porter drew the attention of legislators to the plan of the Indianapolis Equal Suffrage Society to work in the coming months with the legislature to secure woman suffrage. (*DAB*; records of Crown Hill Cemetery, Indianapolis; *New York Times*, 11 January 1881; Charles Kettleborough, *Constitution Making in Indiana: A Source Book of Constitutional Documents with Historical Introduction and Critical Notes* [Indianapolis, 1916], 2:193–94; *History*, 3:537.)

13. See ECS diary of 25 January 1881 for a similar description of Mrs. Hayes, *Stanton*, 2:182.

14. The text of Davis's letter published here is that provided immediately after the event in the Washington *National Republican*'s report of this reception on January 20. The text in the *National Citizen* had undergone revision.

15. William Weston Patton (1821–1889), a Congregational minister, became president of Howard University in 1877 and served until his death. (*NCAB*, 10:165.)

16. Francis Landey Patton (1843–1932), a young professor at Chicago's Seminary of the Northwest, brought charges of heresy against David Swing (1830–1894), the minister of the city's Presbyterian Westminster Church in 1874 for departing from the Westminister Confession of Faith. The Chicago Presbytery supported Swing, but he left the church in order to avoid further trials on appeal, and he became one of Chicago's most popular preachers at an independent church in the Central Music Hall. Patton went on to become president of Princeton University. (*DAB*, s.v. "Patton, Francis Landey"; *ANB*, s.v. "Swing, David"; William R. Hutchison, "Disapproval of Chicago: The Symbolic Trial of David Swing," *JAH* 59 [June 1972]: 30–47.)

17. Caleb Wheeler Spofford (1823–1901) became a proprietor of the Riggs House about 1877 and the sole owner a year later. By 1892, the Spoffords had moved out of the hotel, which was then managed by the Riggs House Company. (Spofford, *Genealogical Record of Spofford Families*, 247; city directories, 1877 to 1892; SBA diary, 11 February 1901, *Film*, 41:649ff.)

18. The eleventh annual meeting of the American Woman Suffrage Association took place in Lincoln Hall on 15 and 16 December 1880 with Henry Blackwell presiding. The *National Republican* explained that "this association is supposed to represent the dignity . . . of the woman suffrage movement, even if it does not claim the rushing enthusiasm which marks the progress of the sister wing of the party." It also remarked upon "a noticeable absence of the long-haired brethren and the pantalooned sisters." (Washington *National Republican*, 16, 17 December 1880, SBA scrapbook 9, Rare Books, DLC.)

19. The *National Citizen* printed "spirituality"; on the misreading, see letter below at 7 April 1881.

20. An allusion to the description in Matt. 23 of the sectarian Pharisees, especially verse 28: "ye also outwardly appear righteous unto men, but within ye are full of hypocrisy and iniquity."

21   ECS TO THEODORE D. WELD[1]

Tenafly N.J.   Feb 2nd 1881

Theodore Weld   Dear Friend,

Allow me at this late day to thank you for the pamphlet you sent me of Angelina & Sarah's[2] beautiful tributes. The thought has just struck me to ask you, over your own or your daughter's[3] name to prepare a sketch of each for our forthcoming history of the woman suffrage movement. We shall have two volumns, royal octavo of 800 pages each. With the threads of history we shall interweave reminiscences & sketches. Robert Dale Owen's daughter has written a charming sketch of her mother & father's work towards liberalizing the laws for women in Indiana. I have this moment finished reading the whole pamphlet, & really I feel that Angelina was one of the grandest women of the century. She looms upon me at this moment as never before. A sketch of her must go into our History. The question for you to decide is <u>how</u>. Will you do it or cause it to be done for us; or shall I write one from the pamphlet before me?[4] Though we seldom meet or hear of each other yet I feel an interest in all that concerns you, & more than ever now as I have been refreshing my mind with the antislavery struggle & the part women took in it. I have just spent several days with Robert Purvis in Philadelphia[5] & talked over those eventful times when Penn Hall[6] was burned & he was so active in helping runaway slaves. We have just had a very enthusiastic convention in Washington & devoted one session to a memorial service to Lucretia Mott. I am now writing a sketch of her. Where are your children & what are they doing & saying? Henry is well   looks about fifty, scarcely any gray hairs in his head   He is practicing law & writing for "The Sun"   My sons are all in business doing well, one of my daughters is married & lives in Iowa, & the other is in Germany, a girl of rare genius as a speaker, & writer, & a faithful conscientious student. I am alone here with Miss Anthony for the winter buried in manuscripts   Let me hear from you soon. With best regards sincerely yours

⇝ *Elizabeth Cady Stanton*

⇝ ALS, Weld-Grimké Papers, MiU-C.

1. Theodore Dwight Weld (1803–1895) worked closely with Henry B. Stanton in the antislavery movement. After his marriage to Angelina Grimké, the Welds founded a school, to which many abolitionists, including the Stantons, sent their children. (*ANB*. See also *Papers* 1.)

2. Sarah Moore Grimké (1792–1873) and Angelina Emily Grimké Weld (1805–1879), the daughters of slaveholders, became abolitionists and early advocates of woman's rights. When Theodore Weld published *In Memory. Angelina Grimké Weld. Born in Charleston, South Carolina, February 20, 1805. Died in Hyde Park, Massachusetts, October 26, 1879* (1880), he appended a brief biography of Sarah Grimké. (*NAW; ANB*.)

3. Sarah Grimké Weld Hamilton (1844–?), the youngest of Weld's children, was the wife of the Unitarian minister William Hamilton. His sons were Charles Stuart Weld (1839–1901), also known as Charles Stuart Faucheraud Weld, who became a writer and teacher after his graduation from Harvard College, and Theodore Grimké Weld (1841–?), who suffered from mental imbalance most of his life. (Garrison, *Letters*, 5:144n, 6:372n; Benjamin P. Thomas, *Theodore Weld: Crusader for Freedom* [New Brunswick, N.J., 1950], passim; Gerda Lerner, *The Grimké Sisters from South Carolina: Pioneers for Woman's Rights and Abolition* [New York, 1971], passim; Robert H. Abzug, *Passionate Liberator: Theodore Dwight Weld and the Dilemma of Reform* [New York, 1980], passim.)

4. A memoir of the Grimké sisters, incorporating portions of Theodore Weld's tribute, is in *History*, 1:392–406.

5. En route home from Washington, ECS also addressed a joint session of the general assembly in Delaware and visited Lucretia Mott's children outside Philadelphia. (*Film*, 21:800–801; *Memorial of Sarah Pugh. A Tribute of Respect from Her Cousins* [Philadelphia, 1888], 134–35.)

6. A mob attacked Pennsylvania Hall in Philadelphia on 17 May 1838, while the Anti-Slavery Convention of American Women met inside. In the evening, when the hall was empty, the mob returned to burn the building down. Robert Purvis helped to finance the building, and his late wife, Harriet Forten Purvis, a member of the Philadelphia Female Anti-Slavery Society, attended the meeting. The story is told in *History*, 1:326–27. (Pennsylvania Hall Association, *History of Pennsylvania Hall, which Was Destroyed by a Mob, on the 17th of May, 1838* [Philadelphia, 1838]; Dorothy Sterling, ed., *We Are Your Sisters: Black Women in the Nineteenth Century* [New York, 1984], 121.)

·(⸺⸺)·

22 ～ ECS TO RACHEL G. FOSTER

[*Tenafly,*] Feb. 8 [*1881*]

Dear Rachel,

I have received your two messages & hasten to relieve your little soul by saying that I did write a hasty letter with a <u>birds eye view</u> of the con. & made honorable mention of our secretary.[1] I trust Phoebe is ready to fill Susan's appointments as it is very important for Susan to remain here[2]   Keep on with your elocution & may a splendid orator too, & then you can fill every niche   I have great hopes hanging on you Phebe May Wright[3] & Jessie Waite & Julia[4] to [push?] you in every niche you can fill   With kind regards to all. I have laughed to myself thinking that I never knew who you were until I identified your Mother[5] that evening at your house   I did not know her the day she called at Miss Thompsons[6]   supposed it was the first time I ever saw her, just think of it, & how surprized I was when the fact dawned on me. Susan is writing names & dates for Phebe, the moment she gets them she better start so as to have a day to rest   Tell her to take care of herself & rest all she can. sincerely yours

～ *Elizabeth Cady Stanton*

～ ALS, Papers of ECS, NPV. Square brackets surround uncertain word.

1. Above at January 1881.

2. Phoebe Couzins fulfilled SBA's engagements over several weeks, including lectures in Pennsylvania, Delaware, and Indiana. (SBA to R. G. Foster, 13 February, 1 March 1881, *Film*, 21:840, 868–69.)

3. That is, May Wright Sewall.

4. Julia T. Foster (c. 1849?–1890), Rachel's older sister, took an interest in the woman suffrage movement and helped out with the work of the National association. (Federal Census, Pittsburgh, 1870; *Anthony*, 2:701; SBA to R. G. F. Avery, 18 November 1890, *Film*, 28:737–41.)

5. Julia Manual Foster (c. 1830–1885) was the wealthy widow of J. Heron Foster, publisher of the Pittsburgh *Daily Dispatch*. Sometime after 1870, she moved to Philadelphia with her daughters. ECS had known her in Johnstown, New York, when they were growing up. According to a later, less genial reference to this prior connection, ECS said she was a servant in the Cady

household. (Federal Census, Pittsburgh, 1870, and Philadelphia, 1880; Samuel W. Durant, *History of Allegheny Co., Pennsylvania* [Philadelphia, 1876], 127, 128, 138; Adelaide Mellier Nevin, *The Social Mirror; A Character Sketch of the Women of Pittsburg and Vicinity* [Pittsburgh, Pa., 1888], 30; ECS to Clara B. Colby, c. 5 February 1896, *Film*, 35:541–50.)

6. Anna Thomson (1806–1885) and her sister, Mary Adeline Thomson (1812?–1895), known as Adeline, lived at 114 North Eleventh Street in Philadelphia. Friends first of SBA, since their meeting at a woman's rights convention in 1854, the sisters often hosted ECS and SBA in the city. Adeline was the more active reformer; she represented Pennsylvania at the founding of the National association in 1869 and served on the executive committee in the 1870s. (*Friends' Intelligencer* 42 [1885]: 697, 52 [1895]: 109; *Woman's Journal*, 9 March 1895; *Anthony*, 1:122, 327n, 2:264, 814; *History*, 3:468n; with assistance of the Estate of J. Edgar Thomson, Philadelphia.)

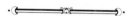

23 ⇝ SBA TO CLARA BARTON[1]

Tenafly N.J. Feb. 14/81

My very Dear Friend—

We are drudging away at our Woman Suffrage History—and now come to our <u>want</u> of a <u>graphic</u> <u>summing</u> <u>up</u> of the wonderful work our women did in the Hospital, Field, on the march—at <u>home</u> making Jellies & bandages— Now <u>can't</u> <u>you</u> do this for us—in what will make 10. 20. 30 50 pages—giving the <u>names</u> of leading women—also ~~are~~ ↑the↓ number of those who actually shouldered the musket—

What we want, is, to open our 2<u>d</u> <u>Volume</u> with this <u>grand</u> <u>work</u> of women to save <u>the Liberty</u>— <u>Both</u> <u>through</u> <u>the</u> Army—and the <u>Loyal Womens</u> Leagues with their 300,000 petition for Emancipation— Sarificing everything—holding woman's own <u>claim</u> <u>for</u> <u>rights</u> in abeyance even—and then after all this herculean work—<u>we</u> <u>shall</u> charge back on man his ingratitude & injustice in <u>denying</u> <u>to</u> <u>women</u> their <u>equal</u> <u>share</u> in the <u>new</u> powers—the new guarantees for freedom & the franchise— They fought for national supremacy <u>over</u> the states to enslave & disfranchise—and then refused to excercise that new power in behalf of half the people— It was—and is—the crime of the ages— What we want you to do—is to put woman's heroism in the war—into your most graphic & telling sentences— Can you do it?— Will you do it?— We would like you to do it—& let us put it into our book as a contribution from the Maj. Gen'l of the Soldier ↑Women↓ friends & helpes—

If it is impossible (which I hope it is not) for you to do this—who do you could & would?—or could you furnish ↑us↓ with the data—?

How are you this terrible winter?— I hope growing stronger & stronger   When you the Doctor[2]—the <u>Senior</u>—I specially mean—give my regards to him— Tell him I haven't forgotten <u>where</u> I am to go when I get broken down!!— But my chance of enjoying the quiet retreat doesnt seem very great now—there is too much work to do— But I would love see him & his family one & all—and ever & ever so much your own dear self— When will my time come to throw off all feeling of responsibility for our W.S. movement?— Sincerely & Affectionately—

         ✍ *Susan B. Anthony*

PS—We are working for dear life to get our first Volume out by the first of May!!—but alas, alas, I fear we shan't— It is to be Royal Octavo—of 6 or 7 hundred pages— When we come to the 2^d Vol—we would like to your picture to place at head of your contribution—[3]

In the first Volume—we shall have the pictures, steel Engravings, of Mrs Mott, Stanton—& the <u>pioneers</u> of our movement— S. B A

✍ ALS, Clara Barton Papers, DLC. Envelope addressed to "Maj. Gen'l Clara Barton" at Dansville, N.Y. Endorsed "Ansd from Wash March 15 1881."

1. Clara Barton (1821–1912), noted for her aid to soldiers during and after the Civil War, was on a mission to persuade the United States government to sign the Treaty of Geneva and join the International Red Cross. Stymied by the administration of Rutherford B. Hayes, she was ready to resume talks with the Garfield administration. Although often in Washington, she maintained a residence in Dansville, New York. SBA's use of the title "Major General" for Barton may be a private joke or a reference to the honors she garnered from veterans of the Union army. (*NAW*; *ANB*; Foster Rhea Dulles, *The American Red Cross: A History* [New York, 1950], 12–15.)

2. James Caleb Jackson (1811–1895) was an early abolitionist and journalist and the head physician at the Dansville Water-Cure. (*ANB*.)

3. The chapter "Woman's Patriotism in the War" opens the second volume of the *History* and includes Barton's picture. Barton wrote the chapter's section on her own life and work, using as the basis an entry she submitted to SBA for *Johnson's Cyclopaedia* in 1876. (SBA to C. Barton, 13 September 1876, 24 June 1881, *Film*, 18:1022–25, 21:1116–18; *Papers*, 3:259–61, 262–64; American National Red Cross, Clara Barton Chapter No. 1, *Clara Barton and*

Dansville. Together with Supplementary Materials [Dansville, N.Y., 1966], 289.)

24 ⤳ SBA TO RACHEL G. FOSTER AND JULIA T. FOSTER

Tenafly N.J. Feb. 25/81

Personal Private

My Dear Girls   Rachel & Julia

I am not going to accept your most generous proposition to <u>sink</u> a $1000— <u>in History</u>—but I want to loan of you from time to time a $1,000— and give you as security a <u>4 per cent</u> $1000. Government Bond—which I should send to you now—only that it is at <u>home</u>—& I cannot get without my sister's[1] knowing it—and I do not wish to give her the anxiety she would have—if she knew I were going to encroach upon my own money— I shall <u>give you notes</u> from time to time—if you decide to make me the loan—so that in case of my death—before I get the Bond made over to you—you will have <u>legal</u> claim on my little estate left—

If you can thus help me to get this first volume out, without my letting any of my friends know that I am advancing money on it[2]—you will do me a great favor—by saving me from <u>troubling</u> my one & only sister—who has care enough for me—without this added—   sincerely yours

⤳ *Susan B. Anthony*

⤳ ALS, SBA Papers, DLC.

1. Mary Stafford Anthony (1827–1907), the youngest of the Anthony sisters, taught school in Rochester and lived in the house on Madison Street which had belonged to her parents. (Charles L. Anthony, comp., *Genealogy of the Anthony Family from 1495–1904* [Sterling, Ill., 1904], 173; Rochester *Post Express*, 6 February 1907.)

2. ECS, SBA, and Matilda Gage signed a partnership agreement on 15 November 1876 that spelled out a division of labor and some financial arrangements for work on the *History of Woman Suffrage*. Many of its terms were out of date by 1881—such as the expectation of commercial sales, left over from their early negotiations with D. Appleton & Co.—but it is not known whether the editors had revised it. Although the agreement stipulated that none of the editors could make promise of payment for any aspect of the work without the

consent of all, it did not require the same consent if an editor advanced money toward publication. It simply provided that the person would be repaid from future profits. Neither Matilda Gage nor ECS put money in the project. (*Film*, 18:1081–84.)

25 ✎ ECS to Harriot E. Stanton

Tenafly, February 28, 1881.

My precious Child:

I rejoice in your good fortune to be able to visit Italy and see Rome. As a preparation for that journey and a prevention of the Roman fever[1] eat oranges and drink lemonade. You remember Libbie Baldwin[2] nearly died of it, and she would not eat oranges or drink lemonade, while Mr. Baldwin did continually. Now, begin at once with oranges. Mr. Channing[3] says anyone who will drink plenty of water and eat plenty of fruit will ward off many diseases.

I have had a delightful visit from Mr. Channing. We sat in the parlor and talked hour after hour on the dual humanity; what we are to each other and what we can, would and should give to each other in freedom; the glory of fullness of love and friendship and all that we lose under the present restraints. Susan attacked Mr. Channing the next morning in her blunt way, calling a spade a spade, permitting no mysticism, pinning him down most mercilessly with some plain questions.[4] I went to his relief and silenced Susan's guns. But he was bound to answer the questions and he did.

You complain that my letters are dwindling in number and hint that I may be purposely following your example. No, No, I am no Pharisee in love. But I too am very busy. I write, write, write until I am sick of the sight of a pen. You see, I have all the family letters to write and that makes a great many, and there is no end to the business letters this book involves. I suppose you and Theodore will be profuse in criticism. But if you knew what a labor this is we are performing, you would praise rather than blame. Good night, my sweet one,

✎ *Mother.*

✎ Typed transcript, ECS Papers, NjR.

1. Roman fever is malaria, a disease not yet traced back, in 1881, to transmission by mosquitoes.

2. Elizabeth McMartin Baldwin (1846–1941) or, according to one source, Elizabeth Cady McMartin Baldwin, was a niece of ECS. She married Charles Hume Baldwin (1839–1899), formerly the Presbyterian minister in Johnstown, New York. The Baldwins spent a year in Europe after their marriage in 1874, when Charles's poor health prevented his working. (*Portrait and Biographical Record of Jasper, Marshall and Grundy Counties, Iowa* [Chicago, 1894], 272; *Class of Sixty-Three, Williams College, Fortieth Year Report*, from college archives, MWiW; genealogical notes courtesy of Barbara McMartin, Canada Lake, N.Y., and Barbara Wood McMartin, Beaman, Iowa.)

3. William Francis Channing (1820–1901) of Providence, Rhode Island, was a medical doctor, trained at the University of Pennsylvania, but he devoted his time to invention and reform. He had befriended ECS and SBA since the days when he wrote for their newspaper, the *Revolution*. (*DAB*; alumni files, University Archives and Records Center, PU. See also *Papers* 2.)

4. This paragraph also appears as an entry in ECS's diary at 22 February 1881, *Stanton*, 2:183.

26 ⇝ SBA to Elizabeth Boynton Harbert[1]

[*Tenafly*,] Sunday P.M. March 20/81

My Dear Mrs Harbert

Fearing that the N.C. might not reach you in time for this weeks W.K. I enclose this proof slip of the Call for our May Anniversary—which I trust you will duly credit to the N.C.—as it is material—[2]

We decided <u>not</u> to announce our intention to make the tour of Cons. until next month—and so not confuse or detract from the <u>National Anniversary</u>—[3] But every one of the Ex. Com. thus far heard from highly approves of the N.W.S.A. carrying its Citizenship & Suffrage Synonomous Gospel into the Hub and thence out on the several spokes of its wheel— I do not see why the N.W.S.A.'s going into New England cities should provoke animosities, any more than the American Associan's going into New York Washington, or any city outside of New England!!!—

I am glad you will be at Boston with us—and since it is impossible for us ever to get our whole ex. Com. together at one place & time—we must henceforth <u>officially</u> appoint a <u>Sub-Committee</u>—to do & decide—as hitherto—those who could get together have done unofficially—for instance the N.E. tour—was thought of—& decided upon by four of us—Stanton, Gage, Foster & Anthony—and at once letters despatched to the other members to secure their votes pro or con— So you see it wasn't a <u>very</u> autocratic proceeding—after all—[4] Good Bye My dear— I hope you are getting on finely—as the I.O's Woman's Kingdom indicates— I read it all aloud last evening— Affectionately

⤝ *Susan B. Anthony*

Ms Gage & Mrs Stanton—& dear <u>Miss</u> Thomson of Philadelphia,[5] who is visiting us over Sunday—all send love— We are in the last agonies of going to press with history—will tell you of your chapter the minute we can read it—but I am quite sure it will need to be cut down shorter—[6]

⤝ ALS, Box 2, Elizabeth Harbert Collection, CSmH.

1. Elizabeth Morrison Boynton Harbert (1843–1925) edited the "Woman's Kingdom," a weekly column in the Chicago *Inter-Ocean*, a major Republican newspaper in the Midwest. She was also a leader of the Illinois Woman Suffrage Association and a former member of the National's executive committee. (*American Women*; *NCAB*, 18:232; *Women Building Chicago*.)

2. Enclosure missing. The call appeared in the "Woman's Kingdom," Chicago *Inter-Ocean*, 26 March 1881, with credit given to the *National Citizen*.

3. Planning was underway to tour the New England states after the National's annual meeting, taking along the best of the speakers who made the trip to Boston.

4. At the meeting in Boston in May, it was decided that "a quorum of the executive committee shall consist of nine" and that officers of the association were voting members of the committee. (*NCBB*, June 1881, *Film*, 21:997–1010.)

5. That is, Adeline Thomson.

6. A reference to the chapter on Illinois for the *History of Woman Suffrage*.

27 ⤜ **ECS to Frederic A. Hinckley**

Tenafly N.J. March 20th 1881

Dear Mr Hinckley,

Four members of our executive committee in solemn council this morning after an exhaustive consideration of the whole situation, resolved to send no special invitation to the Lucy Stone clique, to attend our convention, for the following reasons.

1st With all our own speakers we shall have no place for them, & we prefer to give a New England audience our national view of Congressional action, to theirs of state action.

2nd They have in public & private so frequently signified their hostility, to us & our measures individually & collectively, so pertinaciously & vindictively maligned & persecuted us, that we have no respect for their opinions, & no confidence in their veracity, & therefore could not honestly ask them to our platform, although if they should come of their own accord we would not push them off.

3rd Our call will read "All persons interested in this great reform are invited"[1] an invitation sufficiently broad for all those who feel friendly, & for those who do not no invitation would avail.

4th A proper self respect under the circumstances restrains us from making any advances to some half dozen of those persons & Mrs Livermore[2] among them.

While we are too magnanimous to exclude any one in favor of our principles & should receive all who come courteously, we cannot give them an opportunity to say no   especially as we do not need their services. You & Anna Garlin Spencer[3] ↑& Mrs Robinson↓ to speak Dr & Mrs Channing[4] Mr Cabot[5] Mrs Chace[6] & many other New England friends to sit on our platform, the Puritan element will be well represented. I will consider the last proposition in your letter a few days before writing. We are in the last agonies with our History, as soon as that is finished I will see what I can do. With kind regards for Mrs Hinckley[7] & yourself sincerely yours

⟿ *Elizabeth Cady Stanton.*

⟿ ALS, Charles Roberts Autograph Letters Collection, PHC.

1. *NCBB*, March 1881, *Film*, 21:872.

2. Mary Ashton Rice Livermore (1820–1905) was a very popular lecturer and former editor of the *Woman's Journal.* (*NAW; ANB.*)

3. Anna Carpenter Garlin Spencer (1851–1931) lived in Providence, Rhode Island, where she belonged to the state suffrage association and attended Frederic Hinckley's Free Religious Society. She spoke at the National's meeting in Boston in May 1881. (*ANB; NAW; NCBB,* June 1881, *Film,* 21:997–1010.)

4. Mary Jane Tarr Channing (1828–1897) was the second wife of William F. Channing and for fifteen years an officer of the National association, as vice

president from Rhode Island and later executive committee member from California. (Genealogical files, Grace Ellery Channing Stetson Collection, MCR-S.)

5. Frederick Samuel Cabot (1822–1888) founded the Mill Owners' Mutual Fire Insurance Company in Boston and served as its secretary, but his passion for reform dated back to his residence at Brook Farm in the 1840s. A regular writer for the *Revolution*, he covered topics ranging from the connection between physiology and dress reform to the need for a new political party representing the interests of labor. (L. Vernon Briggs, *History and Genealogy of the Cabot Family, 1475–1927* [Boston, 1927], 2:650–51; Marianne Dwight Orvis, *Letters from Brook Farm, 1844–1847*, ed. Amy L. Reed [1928; reprint, Philadelphia, 1972], passim.)

6. Elizabeth Buffum Chace (1803–1899) was the president of the Rhode Island Woman Suffrage Association and a noted reformer and early supporter of William Lloyd Garrison. Her invitations to ECS and SBA to speak in Providence in 1879 and 1880 encouraged them to think she would attend their meetings, but there is no indication that Chace joined them either in Boston or at their subsequent meeting in Providence. (*NAW*; *ANB*; *Papers*, 3:480–81.)

7. Elizabeth Shepard Carter Hinckley (c. 1848–?) married Frederic Hinckley in 1869 and moved with him to Providence, Rhode Island, in 1878. In 1880, with two young children at home, she held office in the state suffrage association, and in 1881, she served on the executive committee of the National association. (*WWW1*, s.v., "Hinckley, Frederic Allen"; *NCAB*, 41:519; Federal Census, 1880; *History*, 3:347n, 4:910n.)

28 ❧ SBA TO HARRIET HANSON ROBINSON

Tenafly N.J. April 7/81

My Dear Mrs Robinson

I have been wondering and wondering why ↑you↓ had thrown me overboard for all these weeks of your silence—and now comes your letter telling me that it ↑is↓ <u>myself</u> who is at fault— Well—Well—I could have "sworn in court" that I had written you since receiving the letter to which you allude & which was duly pondered and in <u>thought</u> <u>answered promptly</u>—[1]

Now didn't I write you that I had negotiated with Tremont Temple for the 26 & 27—May—& given up the lower hall?— Then didnt I write you that Miss Foster would go on to Boston a week or more in advance and consult with you and Mrs Shattuck as to the[2] of last fixings?— And now—I want to say that it is our wish to confer with you on all the practical details—because every locality has certain ways of doing the same things—and <u>you know Boston ways</u>— But when it comes to principles—and facts—and way of stating them—we of the N.W.S.A. as Harriot K. Hunt[3] used to say—(but as the Printers didn't let Mrs Stanton say in her little turn on H. B. B's Washington platform)— ~~"Spontaneity"~~—<u>believe in</u> "<u>Spontaneity</u>"[4]—that is, letting you & every other one of us—say her say in her own way— I guess you will have no occasion to be ashamed of us—or rather of your having turned a kindly side to us of the N.W.↑S.↓A.!!

You shall be one of our preliminary meeting as <u>Vice. Pres.</u> ↑for Mass.↓—and <u>shall help us to make</u> and <u>shape</u> our <u>official</u> <u>utterances as grand as possible</u>—for I want this May Con. to overtop every Con. ever yet hold—in the depth, breadth and wisdom of our Resolutions— Then I <u>want</u> our <u>practical work</u> to be definitely set forth—and so evidently the only <u>best</u> thing to do—that everybody will second it in word—& help us to carry it out— And I want you to have your thought on our next step—for <u>the National work</u>—not Mass. or N.Y.—but all the states—

Then about your & Mrs Shattucks names not being in the call—[5] I could have <u>sworn</u> <u>they</u> <u>were</u>—I <u>know</u> they were in some of the manu-script copies—I <u>know</u> Mrs Gage & Stanton & I talked about both of your names going in— It is inexplicable any way—surely, surely, not <u>intentionally</u> <u>left out</u>— They shall be in the April & May numbers—

Didn't I write you, too, that we we were going to hold a series of Conventions through New England?— Of cours I have done nothing— if not all— Well we have responses ↑from↓ & fixed upon—Dover, Concord, Keene, N.H.—Hartford, New Haven—Ct—and Providence— Can you help us to somebody in Lowell—Lawrence—or any of the larger towns of Massachusetts— Or are there any of them that you could arrange Con's for us— Mrs Stanton, Gage, Olympia Brown,[6] Mrs Blake[7]—Mrs Hooker—Mrs Meriwether[8] of Memphis Ten. & the Miss, Fosters—will go with us—and perhaps, if we dont frighten you away from us at our Boston meeting—you will go to some of them with us— We shall devote most of June to New England— It is to be Mrs Stantons & my <u>pleasure</u> <u>excursion</u> for the summer—the vacation be-tween Vol. 1st and Vol. 2d of History—

The last Chapter of the main book went to printer yesterday— We are now getting the Appendix ready— Our printers promise us to have it done—so we can have some at our May meeting— Your Massachusetts will probably be very much fuller than ours—then ours only goes down to 1861—while yours doubtly is mainly since that—so yours will complement our Mass. Chapter— Our book will be fully 700 pages— with 12 steel engravings—of the "<u>Sinners</u>" of our movement—or at least those who fellowshipped with such—as they said of Him of Old—

What do you think we ought to do about advertising in Boston? The Commonwealth[9] & Index? Wonder if the W.J. would publish our call for the cash?— They have always, <u>heretofore</u> refused to do so— Wouldn't even publish our 16th Amendment petition & appeal—sent the $5. back—that was in 1876—or 77—[10]

Tell everybody our platform is broad & free in the true sense—we of course invite those we choose to make the <u>set</u> <u>addresses</u>—but in the discussions on the resolutions & plan of work—&c. &c. we shall welcome all—<u>even</u> the proscriptive of all proscriptives—Lucy Stone— to discuss principles and measures with us— We never drove any ↑of them↓ off our platform—and shant begin doing so now— I will tell Miss Foster to ~~send~~ write you about advertising in Boston—

We will make The Parker House our Head Quaters—[11] I want to visit you—but during the Con—you'd better let me stay with the rest at Parkers—and Beside—I must have time to go & see quite a number of friends while in Boston— Love to Mrs Shattuck—& tell we do want her & her mother to speak—20 or 30 minutes each— Sincerely yours—

⮜   Susan B. Anthony

⮜   ALS, Robinson-Shattuck Papers, MCR-S.

1. SBA had indeed told Robinson about renegotiating the dates and location of the annual meeting in a letter of March 1, but the decision to send Rachel and Julia Foster to Boston in advance of the meeting is not mentioned in earlier letters. Tremont Temple was not available for the two dates SBA preferred, and no one she consulted thought it wise to open in Meionaon Hall and move the next day to Tremont Temple, as Robinson proposed. (<i>Film</i>, 21:870–71.)

2. SBA lost track of her noun when turning the page.

3. Harriot Kezia Hunt (1805–1875) practiced medicine in Boston, where her annual protests against paying her property taxes were legendary. (<i>NAW</i>; <i>ANB</i>.)

4. SBA refers to the printer's error in the penultimate sentence of ECS's letter about the Washington convention, above at January 1881.

5. SBA refers to the list of possible speakers within the call published in the *National Citizen* in March. The text published in April included the names of Robinson and Shattuck. The later call also announced the dates and locations for the series of additional meetings in New England. (*Film*, 21:872, 892.)

6. Olympia Brown (1835–1926), an ordained Universalist minister, was pastor of the church in Racine, Wisconsin. She served on the executive committee of the National Woman Suffrage Association. (*NAW*; *ANB*. See also *Papers* 2 & 3.)

7. Lillie Devereux Blake (1833–1913), a writer and the leading spirit in the New York City suffrage society, became president of the state association in 1879. Over the next decade, she made it one of the most active and sophisticated state societies in the country. (*NAW*; *ANB*. See also *Papers* 2 & 3.)

8. Elizabeth Avery Meriwether (1824–1917) of Tennessee became a featured speaker at meetings of the National association after 1879, although her commitment to states' rights often collided with the National's federalism. She was the author of romanticized tales about slavery and the Old South and the wife of a Ku Klux Klansman. Meriwether took a particular interest in women's economic and legal rights, and as a taxpaying owner of property, she succeeded in voting in a local election in 1871. (Kathleen Christine Berkeley, "Elizabeth Avery Meriwether, 'An Advocate for her Sex': Feminism and Conservatism in the Post-Civil War South," *Tennessee Historical Quarterly* 43 [Winter 1984]: 390–407; *History*, 3:153–54, 180n, 181n, 184n, 193, 822. See also *Papers* 3.)

9. The Boston *Commonwealth* was a weekly paper that began in 1862 as the organ of the Emancipation League and continued into the 1890s with a more general interest in reform under the editorship of Charles W. Slack.

10. On this flap, see *Papers*, 3:337, 339n.

11. At School and Tremont streets, the Parker House, founded in 1856, was one of Boston's best-known hotels.

29 ∾ SBA to Barbara Binks Thompson[1]

Tenafly, N.J. April 15th 1881

My Dear Mrs Thompson

Yours of the 22^d ult—with its stamp still on it—lies waiting attention— Yes the tendency of women's clubs everywhere is to run into literary & scietific questions—they are pleasanter, than <u>growling</u> for <u>Suffrage</u>—and not half as <u>important</u>— So I hope you will do all you can to make the women feel that the vital point is to <u>study</u> <u>Suffrage</u>— And now the conversion of <u>every</u> <u>voter</u> is the <u>practical business</u> of the women of Nebraska[2]   The best work the town & county W.S. societies can do is to raise money to subscribe for National Citizens enough to put a copy in every family in the whole state—that quiet way of educating the people—is the true one— Tell the societies to meet in the afternoon—and the women take their knitting or sewing work if they want to—& then have <u>one</u> <u>read</u> <u>aloud</u> some good speech— But you want active Missionary Committees to go round & visit every family, in every township—and carry tracts and papers—for them to read—& then call again & talk with them after they have read— I stopped with Mrs Colby[3] at Beatrice—and a right splendid woman she is— I hope you can get your state well organized—so as to make a thorough canvass of it—first quietly with your own women talking in school districts—& carrying the documents— In the winter of <u>1855</u>— I went into 54 out of the 60 counties of New York State—& organized county societies[4]—and really that is what you ought to have done in Nebraska—<u>hold</u> a county convention—at the county seat of every county— with one or two speakers—& thus find out a few people ⸀in⸕ every county who will help you— Yes—try and get a column in every one of the Nebraska papers—& get your men & women to write for them— If the men editors would only <u>help</u>—but as a rule they are simply silent— I see this is the very day of your monthly meeting— It is a shame I have [*in margin of first page*] failed to answer in time for it— Yours Truly

∽   *Susan B. Anthony*

∽ ALS, on NWSA letterhead for 1880–1881, Woman Suffrage Collection, WaHi.

1. Barbara J. Binks Thompson (c. 1826–1913) was the secretary of the Thayer County Woman Suffrage Association in Hebron, Nebraska. Born in England and married in Wisconsin, she moved to Hebron in 1872 with her husband, Thomas J. Thompson, and two children. Thomas Thompson, also born in England and at one time a shoemaker, conducted at least two businesses in Hebron, selling shoes in one location and books and stationery in another. He also served as postmaster with his wife as his deputy. Barbara Thompson met ECS and SBA when they lectured in Hebron, and in 1879, she was among those who organized the county association with ECS's help. She stayed in touch: her papers contain eleven letters from SBA and one from ECS written between 1878 and 1882. The Thompsons left Nebraska in 1883 to join their son Walter in Tacoma, Washington, where Barbara Thompson led the

town's first suffrage association and represented Washington Territory on the National's executive committee. (Federal Census, 1880; *History*, 3:686, 693, 957; *History of the State of Nebraska; Containing a Full Account of Its Growth from an Uninhabited Territory to a Wealthy and Important State* [Chicago, 1882], 1449–50; Herbert Hunt, *Tacoma: Its History and Its Builders, A Half Century of Activity* [Chicago, 1916], 3:474–77; *Tacoma Daily Ledger*, 3 July 1913; with the assistance of Robert L. Schuler, Tacoma Public Library.)

2. At the end of February 1881, both houses of the Nebraska legislature adopted by the requisite three-fifths vote a joint resolution to submit the question of woman suffrage to the voters in November 1882. A small band of women began to petition and lobby for that goal early in 1880, and the election of editor and suffragist Erasmus M. Correll to the state assembly in the fall of 1880 provided them with political leadership. Just before Correll introduced the resolution, activists organized the Nebraska Woman Suffrage Association. Their president Harriet S. Brooks and vice president Clara B. Colby stayed in the capital to lobby. With their resolution adopted, Nebraska's suffragists faced a daunting challenge of organization before the election. Correll launched the monthly *Western Woman's Journal* in April 1881. Clara Colby was named state organizer in March, charged with lecturing and starting local societies, and a new woman's column by Harriet Brooks in the *Omaha Republican* provided a rallying point for activists statewide. (*History*, 3:682–94; reports of H. S. Brooks and C. B. Colby to National Woman Suffrage Association, May 1881, in *Film*, 21:997–1010; *Woman's Journal*, 12 February, 5 March 1881; Thomas Chalmer Coulter, "A History of Woman Suffrage in Nebraska, 1856–1920" [Ph.D. diss., Ohio State University, 1967], 34–39; Dennis Anthony Fus, "Persuasion on the Plains: The Woman Suffrage Movement in Nebraska" [Ph.D. diss., Indiana University, 1972], 17–29.)

3. Clara Dorothy Bewick Colby (1846–1916), later editor of the *Woman's Tribune*, moved to Beatrice, Nebraska, in 1871, and took a leading role in building a suffrage movement in the state. She hosted SBA in the fall of 1877. (*NAW*; *ANB*; *Papers*, 3:333–35.)

4. On this tour, see *Papers*, 1:273–77, 280–82, 283–85, 288–89, 291–97, 301–3.

30 ~ ECS TO MARGUERITE M. BERRY[1]

Tenafly N.J. April 20th [*1881*]

My dear Margaret,

I am very happy to learn from Theodore that he has at last found some charming girl at whose shrine he can faithfully & lovingly worship.

I can assure you his family will receive the one he loves with open arms & warm hearts. Making all due allowance for Theodores partiality we are quite prepared from his description to make an idol of you at once. Your name "Margaret" awakens at once in my heart the tenderest memories. My angel Mothers name was Margaret,[2] one of my own good sisters[3] too, & my first born daughter. After I had had four sons & feared I never should have a girl came sweet little Maggie, but alas! on a warm October day a youth coaxed her away, & I have had no daughters at home since, for Theodore pursuaded Hattie to go to Europe with him. So I am counting on all the pretty girls my boys will bring to fill their places. I cannot tell you how impatient we all are to see you. Theodores old nurse is unable to express her delight, & is quite resolved to return with you to France. I think you will find much to surprize & amuse you in our young civilization, but there is no Paris this side of the Atlantic! We have grand rivers, magnificent lakes mountains falls, & vast prairies where you can travel days on a level over the beautiful grass & flowers, not a hill or tree to be seen, a boundless solitude, like the ocean. I can hardly realize that I am writing to Theodores future wife. You will seem a myth to me until I can clasp you in my arms. Please send your photograph, we are all so impatient to see your face. I hope no accident by sea or land may detain you. You will find a large circle of family friends ready to greet you on your arrival. Theodore has not told me whether you can speak English. I hope so, as I cannot speak French, & I should dislike to have all the tender expressions of a mothers love translated by another when intended for your ear alone. With best regards for your family from Mr Stanton & myself, & love for you dear Margaret, sincerely

❧ *Mother*

❧ ALS, Scrapbook 2, Papers of ECS, NPV.

1. Marguerite Marie Berry (1857–1951) married Theodore Stanton on 19 May 1881 in Paris. American newspapers reported that he met Marguerite in 1880 through the family of Emilie de Barrau, a university graduate with whom he had corresponded since 1878. The Berry and de Barrau families raised their children together and shared a house in Paris. Marguerite's family also owned an estate in the south of France. Harriot Stanton attended the marriage ceremonies, and on her return to Berlin no doubt informed the description offered by Theodore's ex-fiancée, Clara White: the couple were married "at the Mayor's office, and the Legation; some clergymen also helped join this

much-married pair." The couple sailed for the United States on May 21. (Wedding announcement, 19 May 1881, *Film*, 21:976; Harriot Stanton Blatch and Alma Lutz, *Challenging Years: The Memoirs of Harriot Stanton Blatch* [New York, 1940], 55–58; genealogical notes of Robert and Francis Stanton, Mazamet, France; *New York Times*, 2 June 1881; Clara White to Grandma, 26 May 1881, Andrew D. White Papers, NIC.)

2. Margaret Livingston Cady (1785–1871).

3. Margaret Chinn Cady McMartin (1817–1902), ECS's next younger sister, settled on a farm in Iowa but spent time each year in Johnstown, New York. (Allen, *Descendants of Nicholas Cady*, 174; *TroyFS*; *Jasper, Marshall and Grundy Counties, Iowa*, 371–72; genealogical notes courtesy of Barbara McMartin, Canada Lake, N.Y., and Barbara Wood McMartin, Beaman, Iowa.)

31 ⇝ ECS to Theodore W. Stanton

Tenafly, April 21, 1881.

Dear Theodore:—

In marrying, there is everything in starting right. Be scrupulously refined and delicate. Be reverent and worshipful always towards your wife; never joke, or ridicule, nor use badinage with her. In all encounters of fun and repartee, you must always defend her. Never argue or dispute with her; nothing wears her out so soon as contention. Study self-control at all times. Mr. Channing, son of the famous doctor,[1] says the next form of religion will be the worship of one another. I want you to cultivate a reverence and devotion for women; be ready to help all women in trying circumstances. Every man should remember that his mother, wife and sister are women, and to treat other women as he wishes those treated whom he loves. How much safer we should feel if there was a true code of honor among all men binding them to be protectors of all women. Now, in starting in life, make the character for yourself to always speak kindly and tenderly of women; never join in that common coarse sneering way of berating "the sex." Weak and frivolous women have been made so by false education, customs and conventionalisms; think of all the disadvantages they have had to contend with. You will see enough of this as you read our History page by page to make any just man indignant. Do not feel that your courtship ends with marriage; but make it your pride to have your wife more and more in love with you every-day. Men and women can do a great deal to elevate and intensify each others lives and quite as much to enfeeble and degrade each other. Do not be self-willed about trifles; leave your wife free to go ahead and do as she pleases in ten thousand little things. Men by constantly interfering saying Go here go there, Say this say that, think this think that, drill all spontaneity out of women until the mass of them look and act as if they were not certain of anything. A husband has the making of his happiness or his misery in his own hands. He should start right. By his wisdom and truthfulness, he can inspire his wife with confidence and respect. There is nothing in our constant companions that we discover so quickly as the slightest deception. Lovingly,

                   ❧ *Mother.*

❧ Typed transcript, ECS Papers, NjR. Variant in ECS's diary at 6 August 1881, *Stanton*, 2:186.

    1. William F. Channing was the son of William Ellery Channing (1780–1842), a renowned Unitarian minister of Boston. (*ANB.*)

32 ❧ HARRIET HANSON ROBINSON TO SBA

Malden, [*Mass.*] April 29 1881.

Dear Susan B.

I dont know whether or not I owe you a letter and its no matter if I dont, if I have anything to say—is it?[1] Your secretary[2] has straightened matters and we (Mrs Shattuck & I) are in correspondence with her. I have been to see about accomodations for your party, but have nothing to write definately. I have seen Mr Parker himself,[3] and he wants me to come ~~and see him~~ again, one week before you expect to come ↑to Boston↓. You can get good rooms there for about 1.00 a day, two in a room, or more, if one occupies a room. These cheap rooms are pretty high up (elevator). A parlor will be thrown in. How many will come and for how long do you want the rooms. This I must know as accurate as possible. The food will be extra. I will see about that later. You will find cheaper places than Parkers—pay for what you eat. Parker asked about that—I said "Oh I suppose they'l be invited round."

Every thing looks well for your successful trip to New England. You can come with a great deal of courage, for you have many friends here. Things are different from what they were ten years ago. There ~~are~~ ↑is↓ more than one who dares to speak out at the right time, and ~~defend~~ ask for a new order of things. I have a little <u>coup</u> de <u>etat</u> in mind, if it succeeds you will you will be the first to hear of it. A word of caution: You know that we have all sorts of platforms here in anniversary week, and it is well to know what sort of people are those manage them. If the ↑National↓ womans rights people ↑should↓ appear upon some of them it would hurt our cause in the estimation of the general public. I do not presume to dictate but it is well to know who people are. You, good speakers, will have plenty of invitations to speak, and I hope you will do so. Only take a little care in selecting platforms. We may believe in a great many things but it is not wise to lower the cause we all think the greatest—for the sake of helping side issues. Boston is a funny place. Everything has an annual meeting in Anniversary week and every body comes to air his or her isms.

↙ AL draft or copy, on NWSA letterhead for 1880, year corrected, Robinson-Shattuck Papers, MCR-S.

1. It is not certain that Harriet Robinson mailed this warning about associating with the wrong sort of reformers while in Boston, though it is evident, in SBA's reply below, that she raised the topic before May 8. But judging by SBA's letter to Robinson and Harriette Shattuck on May 11, Robinson had written more specifically to steer SBA and others away from the meeting of the Institute of Heredity. (*Film*, 21:950–53.)

2. That is, Rachel Foster.

3. Harvey D. Parker (1805–1884) founded the Parker House. (James W. Spring, *Boston and the Parker House: A Chronicle of Those Who Have Lived on That Historic Spot Where the New Parker House Now Stands in Boston* [Boston, 1927].)

33 ∾ SBA TO HARRIET HANSON ROBINSON

Tenafly N.J. May 13/81

My Dear Mrs Robinson

Mrs Shattuck's letter of the 6th and yours of the 8th and 9th are all received here—via Rochester—hence late— Your Winthrop House looks pleasant—especially on the cash side—[1] I have sent your word of it to Mrs Gage— I should incline to all go there—if you can get a good <u>parlor floor</u> room for Mrs Stanton—<u>she</u> <u>cannot</u> go up over two flights of stairs—& would prefer only one— I fear it will be too late for the N.C. notice—still it may not— The Fosters will soon learn whether the house is all "<u>O.K.</u>"—

It is really a great task that you and Mrs Shattuck have undertaken for us of the N.W.S.A— I note all you say on the 8th as to Heredity &c. &c. and every word of it is in line with my action and my advice to Mrs Gage & Mrs Stanton—[2] I have never <u>given</u> <u>even</u> <u>my</u> <u>name</u> to his list— I never have & never shall enlist in any <u>resultant</u> <u>movement</u>—until I get the "<u>Cause</u>" battle fought to a glorious victory— It is worse than useless to go into any of the <u>man</u> organizations—it is humiliation for not one, even of the most liberal <u>fully</u> recognize women's equality—they all go on the premise of man's superiority and <u>all</u> I should go into one of them for would be to <u>fight</u> <u>the</u> <u>actors</u>—but I shant do that in any so called <u>liberal</u> societies— I have done my part of breaking down walls in the Temperance & Educational—and if I wanted to re-enlist in such work—I should go right into the most conservative societies— I have no patience to fight for equal rights with Unitarians & Free Religionists—

I think we should all help woman a great deal more—if we could only remember that we can do nothing go nowhere in any organization <u>with</u> men—except to surrender our reason & instinct to them in the work— and that I will ↑not↓ do—even to the very noblest & best & most unselfish of men—for not one of the sex—even the "Male God" <u>can</u> understand the <u>feelings</u> of subjected womanhood—therefore I trust & believe in <u>woman's head & heart</u>-guidings in our movement for emancipation— But enough— I shall go on to the Winthrop House—if that shall be the one fixed upon—on Saturday the 21st—or Monday the 23[d] at farthest[3]—and be there with the Fosters & you to see & ↑be↓ seen— hear & be heard—in all the preliminaries— With ever so many thanks— I am sincerely yours—

⇝ *Susan B. Anthony*

⇝ ALS, Robinson-Shattuck Papers, MCR-S.

1. At 84 Bowdoin Street.

2. Loring Moody (c. 1814–1883) announced the formation of the Institute of Heredity in 1880 and invited various reformers to become members. ECS had enrolled her name, although she also told Moody that his ideal of scientific motherhood required "the education, elevation, & enfranchisement of woman." Matilda Gage, ECS, Lucinda Chandler, and James C. Jackson were some of the people named as vice presidents and directors of the institute, and on 25 May 1881, ECS addressed its meeting in Boston, despite SBA's warning. An old friend of Parker Pillsbury, Moody served as general agent of the Massachusetts Anti-Slavery Society at the time of the war and thereafter as secretary of the Society for the Prevention of Cruelty to Animals. (Parker Pillsbury, *Acts of the Anti-Slavery Apostles* [Concord, N.H., 1883], 488–90; Loring Moody, *Heredity. Its Relations to Human Development. Correspondence between Elizabeth Thompson and Loring Moody* [Boston and New York, 1882]; *Herald of Health* 66 [May 1881]: 106–7; Taylor Stoehr, *Free Love in America: A Documentary History* [New York, 1979], 563–73; ECS to L. Moody, 24 October 1880, and *NCBB*, June 1881, *Film*, 21:455–57, 1046–48.)

3. SBA decided to go to Boston on May 21 rather than accompany ECS to Providence, Rhode Island, where she spoke to the Free Religious Society on May 22.

34 ⇝ Mary L. Booth[1] to SBA

[*New York*] May 26, 1881.

My Dear Miss Anthony:—Pray accept my cordial thanks for your friendly letter, and for the handsome volume which reached me this morning.[2]

I have only had time thus far for the most cursory glance at its contents, the reading of which I anticipate with much pleasure; this has sufficed however to show the magnitude of the work, and the toil and industry involved in its preparation.

I am heartily glad that the history of this most important movement has been written by the veritable pioneers therein. This record will be of great value, not only for its present interest, but as documentary proof for future writers who, when the golden age arrives in which men and women shall be really free and equal, will wish to retrace the steps by which this result has been obtained. The day is sure to come, sooner or later, when it will be wondered that any woman could have been indifferent to the wrongs of her sex as they existed at the time when you and your valiant co-workers took the field, and when you will receive the honors that are your due.

I congratulate you on the successful accomplishment of this part of your mammoth work, and wish it a signal success. I shall be glad to contribute to this as far as is in my power. Unfortunately, in the Bazar, we have no department of book reviews, and very seldom speak even of any of our own publications. This will make it impossible to give it the notice therein which you desire; though I shall doubtless be able to aid through other channels. Yours cordially,

✑ *Mary L. Booth.*

✑ *NCBB*, August 1881.

1. Mary Louise Booth (1831–1889), who published the *History of the City of New York* in 1859, edited *Harper's Bazar*, a weekly magazine published in New York. Her friendship with SBA went back to their collaboration to reform the New York State Teachers' Association. (*NAW*; *ANB*; *Papers*, 1:372–77.)

2. On May 17, Fowler & Wells began to mail out unbound sheets of volume one of the *History of Woman Suffrage* for reviewers at newspapers in Boston and Chicago, and bound volumes were ready by May 20 for reviewers in New York. (SBA to Elizabeth B. Harbert, 17 May 1881; SBA to Harriet H. Robinson, 18 May 1881; SBA to Julia T. Foster, 20 May 1881; and SBA to Friend, 21 May 1881; all in *Film*, 21:963–64, 970–75, 980–81, 984–85.)

35 ✒ MEETING OF THE NATIONAL WOMAN SUFFRAGE ASSOCIATION

EDITORIAL NOTE: The National association's thirteenth annual meeting opened in the morning of May 26 at the Tremont Temple in Boston. After Harriet Robinson welcomed the delegates and guests, ECS and SBA explained the National association's mission and then yielded to speakers from other parts of the country, who spoke into the evening. On the morning of May 27, Isabella Hooker presided while ECS spoke to the Free Religious Association.

[27 May 1881]

SECOND DAY'S SESSION.

The morning session was presided over by Isabella Beecher Hooker. Prayer was offered by Rev. Ada C. Bowles,[1] of Cambridge.

Miss Anthony, from the committee, then presented the following resolutions, which were adopted without discussion:—

Whereas, The Republican idea is self-government, and the ballot the power by which this right is exercised, and whereas, it is a national principle that all matters of common interest should be under the control of the general government, and whereas, all persons born in the United States are declared by the fourteenth amendment to be citizens of the United States,

Resolved, That the right of suffrage, which underlies all other rights, should be based on citizenship, and that all citizens, without distinction of sex, should be protected by the national government in the exercise of this right.

Whereas, The right of suffrage for woman can be secured by an act of Congress, or ratified by the several state legislatures, in a more speedy and direct manner than by the popular vote of the ignorant masses,

Resolved, That it is the duty of Congress to submit a proposition for a sixteenth amendment to the national Constitution that shall prohibit the several states from disfranchising any citizens on account of sex, and thus place this vital question of citizenship where it may be adjusted by the most educated and responsible men in the nation.

Whereas, In the revision of a state constitution the state is for the time being resolved into its original elements, and all the people have the right to vote for the fundamental laws that are to govern them,[2]

Resolved, That in submitting the proposed woman suffrage amendments in the states of Oregon,[3] Nebraska and Indiana[4] to the people, women clearly have the right to vote on the question, and should be secured in the exercise of this right by state action,

Resolved, That it is the duty of the women of Texas to avail themselves of their acknowledged right to vote, recently secured by their new constitution, and to make it the banner state on all moral questions.[5]

The following resolution was offered by Harriet H. Robinson, of Massachusetts:

Whereas, We believe that it is not safe to trust the great question of woman's political rights solely to the legislature, or to the voters of the state, therefore

Resolved, That it is the duty of the women of Massachusetts to organize an active work, to secure a sixteenth amendment to the United States Constitution.

The following resolution was offered by Catharine A. F. Stebbins,[6] of Mich.:—

Resolved, That we should fail to give expression to our great love and honor for some of the earliest workers, did we not remember to record, as we remember in our hearts, the grand testimonies of Angelina Grimke Weld and Lydia Maria Child.[7]

Their memories are fragrant with the incense of love, good deeds, and high aspiration for humanity, and we believe the love to be immortal that still links us to them and to their tasks.

❧ *NCBB,* June 1881.

1. Ada Chastina Burpee Bowles (1836–1928) was ordained as a Universalist minister in 1875. Since her marriage in 1858 or 1859, she had lived in Massachusetts, Pennsylvania, Iowa, and California, before returning to Massachusetts in 1880. She allied herself early with the American association and contributed often to the *Woman's Journal,* but she nonetheless delivered prayers to open several sessions of the National's meeting in Boston. (E. R. Hanson, *Our Woman Workers: Biographical Sketches of Women Eminent in the Universalist Church for Literary, Philanthropic and Christian Work,* 2d ed. [Chicago, 1882], 478–81; Catherine F. Hitchings, "Universalist and Unitarian Women," *Journal of the Universalist Historical Society* 10 [1975]: 27–28; *American Women; History,* 2:821, 4:61, 128, 414, 425, 910.)

2. In advance of New York's constitutional convention of 1867, the state equal rights association adopted this view that a state constitution "must originate with and be assented to by a majority of the people, including as well those whom it disfranchises as those whom it invests with suffrage." Advocates of this position, including members of the legislature, pointed to the provisions for electing delegates to New York's constitutional conventions in 1801 and 1821 that allowed disenfranchised men to vote. (*Papers,* 2:3–4, 12n, 24, 27–28, 42, 44n; Charles Z. Lincoln, *The Constitutional History of New York* [1906]; reprint, Buffalo, N.Y., 1994], 2:298–300, 311–12.)

3. In Oregon, proposals for a woman suffrage amendment were introduced into the senate and the house of representatives on 27 September 1880.

Senators approved the amendment on October 8 by a vote of twenty-one to nine. In the house, a majority approved the amendment on October 6 but with less than the thirty-one votes required for passage. On a motion to reconsider, the house later passed the amendment, thirty-two to twenty-five. Like many state constitutions, Oregon's required that amendments be passed by two successive legislatures before the measure went to the voters in a referendum. The amendment would next come before the legislature of 1882. (*History*, 3:776–79; *New Northwest*, 30 September, 14, 21 October 1880.)

4. The Indiana legislature in special session approved a constitutional amendment to enfranchise women. The measure passed the house on April 7 by a vote of sixty-two to twenty-four. Voting the next day, the senate passed it twenty-seven to eighteen. The state constitution required approval by two successive legislatures, and suffragists were gearing up to ensure that their supporters won election in the fall of 1882. (*History*, 3:540–44; L. Alene Sloan, "Some Aspects of the Woman Suffrage Movement in Indiana" [Ph.D. diss., Ball State University, 1982], 79–99; Kettleborough, *Constitution Making in Indiana*, 2:194–96; Ray E. Boomhower, *"But I Do Clamor": May Wright Sewall, A Life, 1844–1920* [Zionsville, Ind., 2001], 39–47.)

5. The news that women in Texas had a right to vote circulated in the North in December 1880. According to an editorial in the *New York Herald*, reprinted in the *Woman's Journal*, the state legislature adopted as a statute the language about qualified voters in the state's constitution of 1876. There, in article VI, a list of persons barred from voting omitted women, and "[e]very male person" not in one of the prohibited categories was a qualified voter. At the same time, the legislature adopted a statute about "the construction of all civil statutes," saying that "[t]he masculine gender shall include the feminine and the neuter." When applied to the new statute about voters, the argument went, this interpretive guideline applied and allowed women to vote. "It was probably done inadvertently," the *Herald*'s editorial admitted; "nevertheless it is now the law." (*Woman's Journal*, 8 January 1881, 27 August 1881; *NCBB*, January 1881.)

6. Catharine Ann Fish Stebbins (1823–1904), a participant in the woman's rights conventions of 1848, lived in Detroit, where she was an activist in city and state suffrage associations as well as the National Woman Suffrage Association. (*American Women*; *History*, 3:47–48, 523–25; research by Jean M. Czerkas, Rochester, N.Y. See also *Papers* 2 & 3.)

7. A footnote here in the *National Citizen* read, "Who have passed away since our last spring meeting." Lydia Maria Francis Child (1802–1880) died on October 20. A professional writer and early editor for the American Anti-Slavery Society, Child also wrote the influential *History of the Condition of Women, in Various Ages and Nations* (1835). (*NAW*; *ANB*.)

·❮━━━━━❯·

36 ❧ ADDRESS OF ECS TO THE FREE RELIGIOUS ASSOCIATION, BOSTON

EDITORIAL NOTE: ECS's decision to visit Boston during anniversary week led several groups to extend her invitations to address their annual meetings. On 25 May 1881, she spoke to the Moral Education Association and to the Institute of Heredity. On the morning of May 27, she addressed the fourteenth annual meeting of the Free Religious Association at Parker Memorial Hall. There she was introduced as "a good friend to the Free Religious Association for many years" but a newcomer to its platform. Since its founding in 1867, the association provided a forum for the scientific study of religion and development of what members called a "pure religion" that transcended the dogma of the world's religions. In an address that she previewed for Frederic Hinckley's Free Religious Society of Providence on May 22, ECS questioned whether her audience of ministers and intellectuals appreciated the import of women's critique of Christian theology for their own search for a Religion of Humanity. She urged them to center their vision of pure religion on "a reconciliation and communion" of the sexes. Around this core message, ECS incorporated parts of her lectures on women and the Bible, and for historical examples of women's mistreatment by the church, she borrowed heavily from Matilda Gage's work on "Woman, Church, and State," just published in the *History of Woman Suffrage*. The text below is that published by the *Index* as proceedings of the annual meeting. It has been compared to ECS's nearly complete manuscript. (*Film,* 21:986-88, 990-91; Sidney Warren, *American Freethought, 1860-1914* [New York, 1943], 96-116.)

[27 May 1881]

My text for this address will be found in Gen. i, 27—"So God created man in his own image: in the image of God created he him; male and female created he them."

If language has any meaning, here is a plain declaration of the existence of the feminine element in the Godhead, equal in power and glory with the masculine. The Heavenly Mother and Father! "God created man in his *own image, male* and *female*." Thus Scripture, as well as science and philosophy, declares the eternity and equality of sex,—the philosophical fact, without which there could have been no perpetuation of creation, no growth or development in the animal, vegetable, or mineral kingdoms, no awakening nor progressing in the world of thought. The masculine and feminine elements, exactly equal and balancing each other, are as essential to the maintenance of the equilibrium of the universe as the positive and negative electricity, the north and south magnetism, the centripetal and centrifugal forces, the laws of attraction which bind together all we know of this planet whereon we dwell and of the system in which we revolve.

Thus, the Old Testament, "in the beginning," proclaims the simultaneous creation of man and woman, the eternity and equality of sex; and the New Testament echoes back through the centuries the individual sovereignty of woman, growing out of this natural fact. Paul, in speaking of equality as the very soul and essence of Christianity, said, "There is neither Jew nor Greek, there is neither bond nor free, there is neither male nor female; for ye are all one in Christ Jesus."[1] With this recognition of the feminine element in the Godhead in the Old Testament, and this declaration of the equality of the sexes in the New, we may well wonder at the contemptible status woman occupies in the Christian Church of to-day.

But the fact that it is so only shows that the passing generations are far more influenced by precedents and authorities, no matter how monstrous and absurd, than by their own common-sense, reason, and the noblest sentiments of the human soul. The Church builds all its opinions of woman's degradation and subordination on the Scriptures; and yet the first chapter of Genesis declares the simultaneous creation of man and woman, their equal dominion over everything on the earth, their divine origin and destiny. Yet Adam Clark[2] in his Commentaries takes no note of these grand declarations, but draws his conclusions of woman's true position from the allegory in the second chapter, and teaches the rightful subordination of woman, over and over, from Genesis to Revelation. The most grievous wounds that could have been inflicted on woman have come through the teaching of the Church that she was not created with man, that she was an inferior, an afterthought, made for him, but he not for her; a being of secondary importance, a lower caste, of feebler intellect and of more depraved tendencies, cursed of Heaven, and unworthy the companionship of holy men. All the provisions of the canon law and decisions of ecclesiastical courts, based on these ideas, have not only degraded woman, but deeply injured and retarded civilization.

The Church, looking upon woman as under a curse, considered man as God's divinely appointed agent for its enforcement, and that the restrictions she suffered under Christianity were but parts of a just punishment for having caused the fall of man. To this end, the scientific facts of creation are falsified and perverted, and the opinion seriously expressed by learned divines that the creation of woman was no part of the great original plan: whereas facts and philosophy alike prove that the masculine and feminine elements must have existed from the beginning; that man never was perfect, and therefore never fell; that the race, through a process of evolution, is gradually coming up from ignorance, superstition, slavery, and animalism to a degree of morality and intelligence unknown before. But, all along through these dark ages, these slowly changing centuries, the most grievous burdens have fallen on woman. To degrade her more completely, learned councils of bishops have decided that she had no soul.[3] Catholic and Protestant countries alike agreed in holding woman as the chief accessory of the devil. The terrible persecutions for witchcraft fell chiefly on her, in which even such men as Luther, John Wesley, Richard Baxter, Cotton Mather, and Sir Matthew Hale[4] believed, and stimulated the persecution. The victims were chiefly women; the young and beautiful, the old and feeble, alike were sacrificed, hundreds in the same hour burning in the town square; while scarce one wizard to a hundred or thousand witches was ever sacrificed. While the practice of medicine among the lower classes was almost entirely in the hands of women at one time, their skill in healing and their scientific knowledge were attributed to diabolical agency.[5] It was a maxim of Luther's that "no gown or garment worse becomes a woman than that she shall be wise."[6] Charles Kingsley,[7] in a letter to John Stuart Mill, says there will never be a good world for woman until the last vestige of canon law and all the legislation for woman, and the monastic ideas that have grown out of it, are civilized off the face of the earth. "Though Puritanism was first dominant here in New England, it brought no element of toleration for women," says Lydia Maria Child, in her *History of Woman*.[8] "Under the Commonwealth, society assumed a new and stern aspect. Women were in disgrace. It was everywhere reiterated from the pulpit that woman caused man's expulsion from Paradise, and ought to be shunned by Christianity, as one of the greatest temptations of Satan. Man, said they, is conceived in sin and brought forth in iniquity;[9] it was his complacency to woman that first caused his debasement; let him not therefore glory in his shame, let him not worship the fountain of his corruption. Learning and accomplishments were alike discouraged, and women confined to a knowledge of cooking, family medicines, and the unintelligible theological discussions of the day."

Canon law had its largest growth through the pious fictions of woman's created inferiority; and its whole tendency has been to separate man and woman into a holy or divine sex and an unholy or impious sex, creating antagonism between those whose interests are by nature one. All the evils that have resulted from dignifying one sex and degrading the other may be traced to this central error, a belief in a trinity of *masculine* gods from which the *feminine* element is wholly eliminated.

We find the same discrepancies between the liberal universal principles, enunciated in all religions, and the practices of the churches, that we find between the spirit of our Constitutions and the practices of governments. Both alike declare justice, liberty, and equality for humanity, but by their creeds and codes make the people slaves and pariahs. Man is godlike in his perception of truth, but blind and faithless in its application. There are moments when prophets and seers, statesmen and scholars, seem to rise above their ordinary conditions and surroundings into an atmosphere where, with more extended vision, they catch glimpses of eternal principles, and their utterances from these divine heights find a ready response in every true soul,— principles that, like the north star, always point the same way, guiding those who will watch and follow to liberty and peace. It is this fine, almost imperceptible cobweb of truth, binding society together, that will make the religion, the government, and social life of the future peaceful, satisfactory, and enduring. It is thus, in his inspired moments, that man has given his highest, truest perception of exalted womanhood, making her a divinity to be loved, honored, and worshipped, while in his creeds and codes she is the most degraded of his subjects. While exhausting his genius to dignify the ideal woman, he has summoned all the powers of Church and State to degrade the real woman.

The most demoralizing doctrine taught by the Church of to-day is that woman brought sin and death into the world. A curious old blackletter volume, published in London in 1632, entitled *The Lawes and Resolutions of Woman's Rights*, says, "The reason why women have no control in Parliament, why they make no laws, consent to none, abrogate none, is their Original Sin."[10] To this idea, we may trace all the humiliations and deprivations, political, religious, social, that have been visited upon woman as the result of the degradation of her sex. It is for the women who fill the churches to-day to abjure this doctrine of "Original Sin," and to preach the equality of sex in dignity and power, a simultaneous creation, eternal in the Godhead.

What we call God is the infinite ideal of humanity. The preposterous, ridiculous absurdity of supposing God so defined to be of the male sex, and of calling God *him* only, does not need a word to make it apparent. This ideal[11] which we all reverence, and for which we yearn, necessarily enfolds in one the attributes which, separated in our human race, express themselves in manhood and womanhood. Thence come our limitations, our mortality in this state of being. In God's perfect form, the creative attributes, separated in us, together flow out as life, energy, production, power. Our probation here is to reconcile and combine the fractional life of man and woman into complete unions: then shall we become like gods, knowing all truth. In proportion as man and woman learn to put their lives together spiritually and harmoniously, the divine order of society becomes possible, and the spiritual world will unfold to this twofold consciousness. Men and women naturally antagonize and misunderstand each other until and except as they harmonize by love. To render this harmony universal and integral is the great work to be done. No amount of wisdom divorced from love will enable the sexes to understand each other. The horrible selfishness of the disintegrated society in which we live could not continue, if man and woman ceased to be rivals. The desolation caused by pent-up passion would cease, if we began life with co-education made the central point, the foundation, of all culture; and if we proceeded thence in a social order in which the positive and negative magnetism would all the time be finding its equilibrium. In such natural, normal relations, life would not become tame on the one side, nor would the animal propensities run riot on the other. The body would be the obedient servant of the soul! There would be a continual flow and interflow of moral, spiritual, and intellectual forces; and the natural law of relation would be found, when men and women would think to-gether as one.

Now, the first step to this grand result is to equalize these great moral forces; and instead of making sex a crime, marriage a defilement, maternity a curse, and womanhood the sport of devils, the *victim* in all ages alike, under canon and civil law, under all forms of religion and government, let us proclaim the eternity and equality of sex in the Godhead, and in the whole universe of mind and matter. Let this be the cornerstone of the Religion of Humanity.[12] If the Free Religious move-ment is to be successful, it is to be made so through the recognition and elevation of woman. The Catholic Church with a wonderful adaptabil-ity gave her children the mother of Jesus for an object of worship.[13] Without intending it, she has given us a feeble apotheosis of woman. Art is deeply indebted to Rome for this beneficent gift to her inspired sons. The genius of Raphael[14] dwelt fondly on the Queen of Heaven, Mary, our Mother. Swedenborg[15] also meets this hunger of the heart by giving us a divine man, in whom wisdom and love represent the mascu-line and feminine principles. He always speaks of God as the Divine Marriage. Much that is plaintive in music, sad in poetry, and pathetic in art is the expression of the soul's instinctive sigh for a divine mother. We shall give a new impulse to religious thought and civilization, when we uplift the veil that hides the heavenly Mother's face, and with loving lips pray after this manner, "Our Father and Mother who art in heaven, hallowed be thy name."[16] Here is the reason above all others of the enduring power of the Catholic religion. In speaking of it, Lord Macaulay[17] says that the Roman Catholic Church is older than any civilized gov-ernment on the globe. It is the only institution left standing which carries the mind back to the time when the smoke of sacrifice rose from the Pantheon, and when tigers and camel-leopards bounded in the Flavian Amphitheatre. The proudest royal houses are but of yesterday, compared with the line of the supreme Pontiffs, traced back in unbro-ken series, from the Pope who crowned Napoleon[18] in the nineteenth century to the Pope who crowned Pepin in the eighth; and far beyond stretches the august dynasty, until it fades into the twilight of fable! She saw the commencement of all the governments on the globe, and of all the ecclesiastical establishments now existing; and there is no assur-ance that she is not destined to see the end of them all. Lord Macaulay, in accounting for her astonishing longevity as compared with other institutions, turns with felicitous insight to female influence as one of the principal causes.

In her system, he says, she assigns to devout women spiritual functions, dignities, and even magistracies. In England, if a pious and benevolent woman enter the cells of a prison to pray with the most unhappy and degraded of her sex, she does so without any authority from the Church. Indeed, the Protestant Church places the ban of its reprobation on any such irregularity. "At Rome, the Countess of Huntington would have a place in the Calendar as St. Selina,[19] and Mrs. Fry would be Foundress and First Superior of the Blessed Order of Sisters of the Jails."

But even Macaulay overlooks another element of power and permanence in the economy of the Catholic Church. God, as Father and as Son and as Holy Ghost, might inspire reverence and dread only, in hearts that at the shrine of the ever-blessed Mary, Mother of God (God the Mother), would kindle into humble, holy, and lasting love.

Frances Power Cobbe,[20] though deprecating the worship of the Virgin, yet says of it: "The Catholic world has found a great truth,— that love, motherly tenderness and pity is a divine and holy thing, worthy of adoration. . . . What does this wide-spread sentiment regarding this new divinity indicate? It can surely only point to the fact that there was something lacking in the older creed, which, as time went on, became a more and more sensible deficiency, till at last the instinct of the multitude filled it up in this amazing manner."

When Theodore Parker,[21] in his morning prayer on a beautiful summer Sunday, addressed the All-loving as "our Father and our Mother," he struck a chord which will one day vibrate through the heart of universal humanity. It was a thought worth infinitely more than all the creeds of Christendom.

That mild virgin face is omnipresent not only in our homes and cathedrals, but in the gloomiest prisons of the Old World. As you descend into those fearful dungeons of Venice, below the Bridge of Sighs, which in the days of the glory of this strange city no one ever recrossed but on his way to execution or to the tomb,[22] the sweet face of the Virgin Mother guards every turn. As you go down, down from the light of day, deeper and deeper into the oppressive darkness, ever and anon the light of the guide's torch reveals the same mild face, above the door of some cell of torture, some oubliette into whose depths the poor prisoner is forced to leap,—above the conduits for the blood of the victims who perished there,—above all this and from every side looks down the Holy Mother, designed, tradition says, to add intensity to the death agony by its mocking show of pity. Facts were these,[23] realities of awful import; but to me they have a deeper meaning: they seem like prophecies of the day dawning, when the mother soul shall descend with healing in her wings into these abodes of sorrow and suffering, of outrage and oppression, giving light and joy and peace where darkness and despair and death now reign.

In Catholic countries, the Virgin Mary is the avenue through which the religious nature of man is reached. Her name rouses in man the same love and tenderness that the name of Jesus inspires in woman. Dr. William F. Channing says, "A French teacher and companion whom I had in Rome, when a youth of sixteen, told me that, if I should say to an Italian, 'I do not believe in God,' he would shrug his shoulders; if I should say, 'I do not believe in Christ,' he would say, 'What a misfortune'; but if I should say, 'I do not believe in the Virgin Mary,' he would take up stones to throw at me." I do not think this relation of sex to the very substance of religion can be overstated. The old masters represented the trinity by three bearded male heads. To have made the Holy Ghost feminine would have been more in harmony with the Biblical description of the divine family, and with the offices the third person in the Godhead was supposed to fill. The frequent reference to the Holy Ghost as the Comforter seems to imply the presence of the feminine element, its love, tenderness, and mercy. The third person in the Trinity, then, should not have been Christ, but the aggregate of humanity, the whole human race. Religions like the Jewish and the Christian, which make God exclusively male, consign woman logically to the subordinate position assigned her in Mohammedanism. History has perpetuated this tradition. The subjection of woman has existed as an invariable element in Christian civilization. It could not be otherwise with the Godhead represented as a trinity of males. It stood to reason and appealed to fanaticism that the male form was the godlike. Hence, logical intellect and physical force were exalted above the intuition of conscience, the finer sentiments, the more tender affections, and attractive charms. The male religion shaped government and society after its own form. The reason why we have an exclusively male God, and a religion which depreciates and degrades woman, is that our religion is purely emotional, hence *feminoid*, and sustained mainly by women; and, as we naturally deify and aspire to our opposites, woman's God is man. Our Scriptures and creeds are written from the man stand-point, our priesthood are men; and hence God, religion, and the Church, with its ordinances, are not so attractive to men. The existing churches being projected by the emotional side of our nature, not merely by woman, but by the feminoid in man, they are hitherto the product of the infantile or feminoid state of the race. The race has not yet reached its maturity, when governed by reason. It is still governed by its emotions, often by its reverse passions, as hate, fear, greed, rather than by love, attraction, devotion. It will glorify woman, when it comes to its reason. The Positivists,[24] who base everything on reason, whose religion is *masculoid*, point to the church of humanity, which makes woman, and especially the mother, the central figure, the actual Divinity. It remains for us to take the next step, and reunite both in the trinity of Father, Mother, and Child.

Is this practicable? you will ask. It is impracticable to the last degree at this stage of our development; but, as thought precedes action, discussion precedes decision. Now is always the time for those who first perceive a great truth to utter it. Then, it is caught up by one after another, and reiterated, until it becomes familiar to the multitude. This idea of the eternity and equality of sex is a quest after the ideal of God and man; but, as an ideal, it points the direction and path of progress for society and religion. Meanwhile, the social steps must not be de-structive nor arbitrary. We shall grow up to the social changes rather than mechanically contrive them. We are finite and mortal beings, because disintegrated by the cleft of sex. The divine being, the divine type, is the communion of the masculine and feminine attributes, and thence complete, infinite, without limitation. We enter the divine or-der on earth in proportion as we attain the reconciliation and commun-ion of sex in every phase of social life; and that is the divine order which, under far more fluent conditions, we shall enter upon in our next experiment of living. This gives a new meaning and wider scope to the woman movement.

The Church, springing as it did from the emotional element and supported by woman, having a male tyrant for its God, has done its worst to degrade woman; and she has accepted her position as coming from divine authority (though of her own creation), as the Russian peasant identifies the Czar with God, and worships him while suffering from his tyranny. There is no power by which the human soul can be held in such bondage as through the religious emotions, no realm of thought where it is so difficult to displace error with truth as the religious realm. And, so long as we base our religion on the fundamental error of a *"male God,"* it is in vain to struggle for woman's equal status in the Church; and, until her equality is recognized, all talk of establishing a religion of humanity is idle, since one-half of humanity is in social, religious, political subjection to the other. I have often thought that we shall take the first step for woman's freedom and for that of humanity, when we shall have outgrown the popular idea of a male God in the skies or elsewhere: then, we might see and worship God *in* humanity; then, we might love home and deify each other. "If you love not man whom you have seen, how can you love God whom you have not seen?"[25] The highest form of revelation is that of God in man; and yet we place everything, seen and unseen, scriptures, Bibles, sacraments, altars, vestments, symbols, cathedrals, all above humanity in sacredness, dignity, authority. Religion is native to us; but, to exalt the true God, we must dethrone the false. I do not think the idea of King God can long maintain itself in a genuine democracy. You see in Europe how naturally and inevitably the democrats, the nihilists,[26] and the communists are or become infidels. The two ideas of a divine sovereign and a human sovereign go together. They will stand or fall together. They antagonize the idea of Divine Humanity and the individual sovereignty of personal freedom as the basis of public order. Even the Catholic Church is quite different in its actions in this country. Its votaries will not submit to its tyranny here as they do in the old monarchical countries. Why is it possible for France to be a republic? Because her leading minds are infidel. When Russia throws off the superstitions of the Church, she will be a republic. When woman discards its creeds, dogmas, and authorities, she, too, will be free; and a free, enlightened woman is a divine being, the savior of mankind. We would not have man deify and worship a slave. He cannot, if he would.[27] I believe we have reached a point where the world of thought is ready to accept anything which can be proved to be true, whether it is indorsed by the Church or not. That is a great step in advance. People no longer ask, Is this in the Bible, or according to Bible teaching? but, Is it true? Is it according to the nature of things? Not, Does

God's word in a book, not, Does the Church, affirm or deny this? but, Does God's human reason say it? Is it according to logic and mathematics? Then, Can it be proved practically? Does it tend to make us happy? Will it work? Will it pay? These are the questions we ask today: they are the signs and tokens of an extended emancipation, that has come so gradually that we hardly realize it.

The Church still keeps its form, but the substance is not there. If it were not for the intense conservatism of woman, the dogmas and superstitions of the Church would be nowhere. Thanks to the law of progress, woman is awaking to the degradation she has endured in the name of religion, and is interpreting for herself the laws of life. Were the existing ecclesiasticism out of the way, man would naturally deify woman, as men do who are emancipated from the Church. But with the Church as it is, sustained mainly by woman, yet degrading her and deifying absolute, tyrannical force, what could we expect? And here is the reason our popular religion has so little power over man. Women fill our churches: only through their prayers and tears and persuasions can the men be drawn thither. The woman worships the male God and the male Christ as man never can. He is to find his Deity through his opposite. To the inspired sons of earth, the poets, the painters, the prophets, it has been the same at all periods and under all forms of religion and government. All ages alike have bowed down to exceptional women with love and reverence, according them places of power and influence in both State and Church. This ideal womanhood has immortalized itself, too, in marble, and on canvas. Go into the galleries of art, and there you find the graces, the virtues, the beatitudes, music, poetry, painting, philosophy, science, liberty, justice, mercy, the seasons, day with its glorious dawn, and night with its holy mysteries, all represented by woman. Is it not a wonder, then, that, while the ideal woman is thus exalted and glorified, the real woman should be so degraded and humiliated? It is a light matter in the minds of even many advanced thinkers that woman's natural rights are the mere football of popular caprice; but the great fundamental principles of all just government and pure religion, violated in the person of the humblest citizen, must be fraught with danger to all. The spirit of liberty, in whatever form it comes, whether as African, Chinese, Woman, Nihilist, Socialist, Communist, will assert itself and avenge its wrongs. Ariosto[28] tells a pretty story of a fairy, who by some mysterious law of her nature was condemned to appear at certain seasons in the form of a foul and poisonous snake. Those who injured her in the period of her disguise were forever excluded from participation in the blessings which she bestowed in her power. But, to those who in spite of her loathsome aspect pitied and protected her, she afterwards revealed herself in the beautiful and celestial form which was natural to her, accompanied their steps, granted all their wishes, filled their homes with wealth, made them happy in love and victorious in war. Such a spirit is liberty. At times, she takes the form of a hateful reptile. She *grovels*, she hisses, she stings. But woe to those who in disgust shall venture to crush her. And happy are those who, having dared to receive her in her degraded and frightful shape, shall at length be rewarded by her in the time of her beauty and glory.

The world has been slow to understand that all the accumulated wrongs of sex have made the superior class of women, the writers, the thinkers, the artists, the noblest wives and mothers, especially those of great men, with but few exceptions uniformly sad and despairing. All men note the fact, some but to travesty the sour old maid or scolding wife in "Caudle Lectures"[29] and the "Taming of the Shrew."[30] Other men go deeper, and feel in part the insults and humiliations heaped on womanhood, but wonder at the cause. So black is the page of history with crimes against my sex that even a Russian poet makes one of his heroines say, "God has forgotten the nook where he hid the keys of woman's emancipation."[31] The hearts of noble men are responding at last to this infinite sadness, awaking to the agonies of woman's crucifixion, and prophesying the coming transfiguration. Thomas W. Higginson, at the anniversary of the Young Men's Christian Union, in New York City, as long ago as 1858, in an address upon women in Christian civilization,[32] said: "No man can ever speak of the position of woman so mournfully as she has done it for herself. Charlotte Bronte, Caroline Norton,[33] and indeed the majority of intellectual women, from the beginning to the end of their lives, have touched us to sadness, even in mirth; and the mournful memoirs of Mrs. Siddons, looking back upon years when she had been the chief intellectual joy of English society, could only deduce the hope 'that there might be some other world hereafter, where justice would be done to woman.'"

The essayist, E. P. Whipple,[34] in a recent speech before the Papyrus Club, of Boston, said of George Eliot: "The great masculine creators and delineators of human character, Homer, Cervantes, Shakspeare, Goethe, Scott,[35] and the rest, cheer and invigorate us even in the vivid representation of our common humanity in its meanest, most stupid, most criminal forms. Now comes a woman endowed not only with their large discourse of reason, their tolerant views of life, and their intimate knowledge of the most obscure recesses of the human heart and brain, but with a portion of that rich imaginative humor which softens the savageness of the serious side of life by a quick perception of its ludicrous side; and the result of her survey of life is that she depresses the mind, while the men of genius animate it, and that she saddens the heart, while they fill it with hopefulness and joy. I do not intend to solve a problem so complicated as this: but I would say, as some approach to an explanation, that this remarkable woman was born under the wrath and curse of what our modern philosophers call 'heredity.' She inherited the results of man's dealings with woman during a thousand generations of their life together."

The man was master, the woman was an appendage to him. He alternately worshipped and wronged her; he knelt as lover, but commanded as husband; and he established the absurd superstition that she belonged to the "weaker sex," because her brute force was inferior to his.

Now, when the worth of woman is more generally realized; when her substantial equality with man is forcing itself into legislation; when she is fast becoming the co-mate, and not a mere helpmate of man, we may hope that when another George Eliot appears, with equal comprehensiveness of intellect and equal creativeness of imagination, she will teach to our common humanity a gospel of cheer as cordial and humane as that which has ever come from any man of genius since the creation of the world.

I never look a colored man, woman, or child in the face that my soul does not glow with an intense desire to render them some service, to give them some sign of my recognition of their equal humanity, as their just due from every member of the Saxon race for all the wrongs they have suffered at our hands. It seems to me that every true man must have a touch of this same feeling toward woman, in view of all[36] the insults and outrages perpetrated on her by his base creeds and codes and customs. And yet into how many manly faces have I looked in vain for the equal recognition of my unhappy sex.

We see reason sufficient in the outer conditions of human beings for individual liberty and development; but when we consider the inner life, the self-dependence and solitude of every human soul in all the great emergencies of life, we see the need of courage, judgment, independence, skill in the use of every faculty, and sense of mind and body strengthened and developed in woman as well as man. In that solemn solitude of self that links us with the immeasurable and the eternal, as individuals each one stands alone forever. A recent writer says: "I remember once, in crossing the Atlantic, to have gone upon the deck of the ship at midnight, when a dense black cloud enveloped the sky and the great deep was roaring madly under the lashes of demoniac winds. My feeling was not of danger nor fear (which is a base surrender of the immortal soul), but of utter desolation and loneliness: a little speck of life shut in by a tremendous darkness. Again, I remember to have climbed the slopes of one of the Swiss Alps, up beyond the point where vegetation ceases, and the stunted conifers no longer struggle against the unfeeling blasts. Around me lay a huge confusion of rocks, out of which the gigantic ice-peaks shot up into the measureless blue of the heavens; and again my only feeling was the awful solitude!"[37] And yet in the estrangement and antagonism of man and woman there is a solitude which each and every one of us has always carried with him, more inaccessible than the ice cold mountains, more profound than the midnight sea,—the solitude of self!

Our inner being, which we call ourself, no eye nor touch of man nor angel has ever pierced. It is more hidden than the caves of the gnome, the sacred adytum of the oracle, the hidden chamber of Eleusinian mystery:[38] for to it only omniscience is permitted to enter. Such is individual life. Who, I ask you, can take, who dare take on himself the responsibility of deciding the rights, the duties, the limitations of another human soul?

❦ Boston *Index*, 23 June 1881. Also AMs at date in *Film*.

1. The apostle Paul, usually quoted for his strictures on women's activities, also supplied reformers with this apotheosis of human equality. Gal. 3:28.

2. Adam Clarke (1762–1832), an Anglo-Irish Methodist, published *The Holy Bible, with a Commentary and Critical Notes* between 1810 and 1826. (Allibone.) Clarke omitted Gen. 1:27 from his commentary and concentrated on the alternative story of creation in Gen. 2:21–23. Rather than a simultaneous creation, this second account depicts the creation of Eve from the rib of

Adam. Clarke commented that the woman "possess[ed] neither inferiority nor superiority," but she lacked individuality, being a part of man.

3. ECS borrowed much of the historical material in this speech from Matilda Gage, "Woman, Church, and State." This statement about the bishops is found in Gage's text at *History*, 1:757. The next sentence is found at 1:765, and thereafter, ECS paraphrases Gage's discussion of witchcraft at 1:765–68.

4. These were Martin Luther (1483–1546), German reformer and founder of Protestantism; John Wesley (1703–1791), leading figure in English Methodism; Richard Baxter (1615–1691), English Puritan clergyman; Cotton Mather (1663–1728), Congregational clergyman in Massachusetts; and Sir Matthew Hale (1609–1676), English jurist. All five men defended the prosecution and execution of witches. The same list is found in *History*, 1:765; both Gage and ECS were familiar with the chapter on witchcraft in William Lecky, *History of the Rise and Influence of the Spirit of Rationalism in Europe* (1865).

5. On women and medicine, ECS paraphrases Gage, *History*, 1:769.

6. ECS quotes Gage on Martin Luther, *History*, 1:775. A modern translation of the opinion, from notes made of Luther's "Table Talk," reads, "There is no dress that suits a woman or maiden so badly as wanting to be clever." (Susan C. Karant-Nunn and Merry E. Wiesner-Hanks, eds., *Luther on Women: A Sourcebook* [Cambridge, England, 2003], 29.)

7. Charles Kingsley (1819–1875) wrote this sentence in a letter to John Stuart Mill (1806–1873) in 1870, explaining why he had withdrawn from the woman suffrage movement. Mill, a philosopher who sat in Parliament from 1865 to 1868, answered Kingsley on 9 July 1870. ECS quoted Kingsley's words over many years, despite their original purpose as a justification for limiting the role of women in their own emancipation. A clergyman and founder of Christian Socialism, Kingsley aided early efforts of the women's movement aimed at greater economic and educational opportunities, and he supported Mill's work for woman suffrage. When he withdrew support in 1870, he explained that the movement had attracted "foolish women . . . of often questionable morals" who insinuated "sexual questions" into a moral reform. (*Charles Kingsley: His Letters and Memories of His Life*, ed. Frances Grenfell Kingsley [New York, 1877], 416–19; Mill, *Collected Works*, 17:1742–45; Ray Strachey, *The Cause: A Short History of the Women's Movement in Great Britain* [1928; reprint, London, 1978], 49, 60, 87, 118.)

8. ECS quotes Gage, *History*, 1:775, who in turn quotes Lydia Maria Child, *History of the Condition of Women, in Various Ages and Nations* (1835), 2:139–40, in a description of seventeenth-century England.

9. Adapted from Psalms 51:5.

10. ECS paraphrases *History*, 1:755–56, referring to *The Lawes Resolutions of Womens Rights: or, The Lawes Provision for Woemen: A Methodicall Collection of such Statutes and Customes, with the Cases, Opinions, Arguments and points of Learning in the Law, as doe properly concerne Women*, liber 1, sec. 3. On this compilation of law, its probable authorship, and date of composition,

see W. R. Prest, "Law and Women's Rights in Early Modern England," *The Seventeenth Century* 6 (Spring 1991): 169–87.

11. ECS's manuscript reads *ideal*, while the printed text reads *idea*.

12. The ideal of a Religion of Humanity, originating in the social scientific theories of Auguste Comte, replaced faith with human reason and directed worship toward a collective vision of humanity. The term was used by John Stuart Mill, found converts among American Unitarians like Octavious Brooks Forthingham, and provided a common language for the Free Religious Association. See Mill, *Collected Works*, 10:263–368; Linda C. Raeder, *John Stuart Mill and the Religion of Humanity* (Columbia, Mo., 2002); and Frothingham, *The Religion of Humanity* (1873; reprint, Hicksville, N.Y., 1975).

13. With this sentence ECS begins to quote her speech "The Bible and Woman Suffrage." The quotation continues through "hallowed be thy name." See *Papers*, 3:450.

14. Raphael (1483–1520), an Italian painter, was noted for his pictures of the mother of Jesus, notably the *Sistine Madonna* (1513).

15. Emanuel Swedenborg (1688–1772), a Swedish mystic and writer, inspired a large religious society, organized into the Church of the New Jerusalem. He wrote that man and woman were not embodiments of opposing principles but each one a combination of wisdom and love.

16. ECS amends the opening of the Lord's Prayer, Matt. 6:9.

17. ECS pasted onto her manuscript page an unidentified clipping of the text from this reference to the English historian Thomas Babington Macaulay (1800–1859) through that to Theodore Parker below. The same passage, also as a clipping placed on the manuscript page, appeared in the speech she first gave in 1867 and variously titled "The Bible on Woman's Rights" and "The Bible Position of Women," in *Film*, 12:712–51, 45:367–69. She quotes Macaulay's review of Leopold Ranke, *The Ecclesiastical and Political History of the Popes of Rome, during the Sixteenth and Seventeenth Centuries*, first published in the *Edinburgh Review* 72:145 (October 1840): 227–58, and reprinted in *Works of Lord Macaulay. Complete*, ed. Lady Trevelyan (London, 1866) 6:454–89. Quotations at 6:454–55 and 479.

18. Napoléon I, emperor of France (1769–1821), was crowned by Pope Pius VII in 1804. Pépin III, king of the Franks (714?–768) was anointed by Pope Stephen in 754.

19. Selina Hastings, Countess of Huntington (1707–1791) contributed to the spread of Methodism in England, especially among aristocrats. (*DNB*.) The philanthropist Elizabeth Gurney Fry is already identified.

20. Frances Power Cobbe (1822–1904) was an English writer, reformer, and leading figure in the antivivisection movement. ECS quotes sentences from the chapter entitled "Madonna Immacolata," in Cobbe's *Italics. Brief Notes on Politics, People, and Places in Italy, in 1864* (London, 1864), 329–30. (*DNB*; Banks, *Biographical Dictionary of British Feminists, 1800–1930*. With the assistance of Sally Mitchell, Temple University.)

21. Theodore Parker (1810–1860), Boston clergyman, author, Transcendentalist, and reformer, adapted many of his prayers to recognize both a mother and a father.

22. The Bridge of Sighs, or Ponte dei Sospiri, connects the Palace of the Doges with the Prigioni di San Marco. It was made famous in the English-speaking world by Lord Byron, for whom it symbolized the murderous intentions of the doges. In one of many examples, the fourth canto of his *Childe Harold's Pilgrimage* begins: "I stood in Venice, on the Bridge of Sighs; / A palace and a prison on each hand." Where ECS found her description is not known.

23. ECS's manuscript seems to read *these*; the printed text reads *there*.

24. Again, the term Positivists originally described followers of Auguste Comte but broadened to encompass a variety of views that put science and human agency ahead of supernaturalism. ECS points to Comte's Romantic cult of woman, which, she suggests, survived among many of his followers, even though they had pruned and reshaped Comte's ideas in other particulars. See Andrew Wernick, *Auguste Comte and the Religion of Humanity: The Post-Theistic Program of French Social Theory* (Cambridge, England, 2001), especially pp. 147–49.

25. 1 John 4:20.

26. Nihilists were the revolutionaries in Russia, whose direct action and assassinations received heightened international attention after the killing of Czar Alexander II in March 1881.

27. The manuscript reads "He cannot if we would."

28. From this sentence to the end of the paragraph, ECS quotes Thomas Babington Macaulay's review of John Milton, *A Treatise on Christian Doctrine, compiled from the Holy Scriptures alone*, published in the *Edinburgh Review* 42:84 (August 1825): 304–46, and reprinted, as in the earlier reference to Macaulay, in *Works of Lord Macaulay*, 5:1–45. Quotation at 5:31. Ludovico Ariosto (1474–1533) was an Italian poet.

29. Douglas Jerrold, *Mrs. Caudle's Curtain Lectures* (1845) recounts the trials of a man who endures thirty years of insomnia enforced by his wife's scolding.

30. Katharina is the shrew in the title of William Shakespeare, *The Taming of the Shrew*.

31. A newspaper article included in a footnote to Matilda Gage's chapter in *History*, 1:774n, attributed this line to the Russian poet Nikolay Alekseyevich Nekrasov (1821–1877).

32. With this sentence ECS returns to Gage's chapter in the *History* at 1:791–92, taking from it the two extracts that follow and the sentences introducing each one. She pasted the printed page into her manuscript. The first quotation comes from Thomas Wentworth Higginson, "Woman in Christian Civilization," in *The Religious Aspects of the Age, With a Glance at the Church of the Present and the Church of the Future: Being Addresses Delivered at the Anni-*

versary of the Young Men's Christian Union of New York, on the 13th and 14th Days of May, 1858 (New York, 1858), 80.

33. Englishwomen, these are Charlotte Brontë (1816–1855), who wrote the novels *Jane Eyre* (1847), *Shirley* (1849), and *Villette* (1853); Caroline Elizabeth Sarah Sheridan Norton (1808–1877), who wrote poems and novels, but was best known for urging passage of the Infant Custody Act of 1839 and the Marriage and Divorce Act of 1857; and below, Sarah Kemble Siddons (1755–1831), an actress known for her tragic roles.

34. Edwin Percy Whipple (1819–1886), an author, literary critic, and lecturer, eulogized George Eliot at the annual ladies' night of Boston's Papyrus Club on 24 February 1881. (*ANB*.) Gage included this quotation in her chapter in the *History of Woman Suffrage*, 1:791–92; Whipple's essay appeared first in the *Boston Evening Transcript*, 26 February 1881. George Eliot was the penname of the English novelist Mary Ann Evans (1819–1880).

35. These renowned male authors are Homer, the ancient Greek poet; Miguel de Cervantes (1547–1616), Spanish novelist; William Shakespeare (1564–1616), English dramatist; Johann Wolfgang von Goethe (1749–1832), German poet; and Sir Walter Scott (1771–1832), Scottish poet and novelist.

36. The manuscript ends here.

37. Although the quotation marks are closed at this point in the text published by the *Index*, the quotation probably continues. ECS used these final paragraphs to conclude her speech "The Solitude of Self" in 1892, and in that instance, the published texts all close the quotation from a "recent writer" at the phrase "for to it only omniscience is permitted to enter." The final two sentences, alike in both speeches, are printed as ECS's own words. (*Film*, 29:1006–9, 1017–24.)

38. Symbols of the most secret and sacred knowledge, these are the adytum, or innermost chamber of a temple, where oracles were spoken, and the mysteries of Demeter, celebrated at Eleusis in ancient Attica.

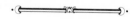

37 ᨠ SPEECH BY ECS TO THE NATIONAL WOMAN SUFFRAGE ASSOCIATION IN PROVIDENCE, RHODE ISLAND

EDITORIAL NOTE: The New England conventions opened on May 30, with a two-day meeting at the First Light Infantry Armory in Providence, Rhode Island. Olympia Brown, Elizabeth Saxon, Elizabeth Meriwether, and Matilda Gage joined SBA and ECS as speakers. For her principal address, ECS revived a lecture she wrote in 1869. From an article entitled "Manhood Suffrage," published in December 1868 (*Papers*, 2:194–99), she had developed her speech against the

Fifteenth Amendment for the winter of 1869 and reworked it in the spring of that year to be an argument for a sixteenth amendment. One imagines that she rediscovered the speech while at work on the *History of Woman Suffrage*: the version she delivered in May 1869 is reproduced at length in the second volume of the *History* (though misdated as the January 1869 text). All the versions are organized around a list of reasons to oppose manhood suffrage. This report of the Providence meeting includes the full list but in skeletal form. The *Providence Evening Press* opted to report more detail but only of the first, second, and last points. ECS returned to Tenafly after this meeting. (*History*, 2:348–55; *Film*, 21:1061.)

[31 May 1881]

Mrs. Elizabeth Cady Stanton, President of the Convention, was the next speaker. She gave six reasons against an exclusively male government.

First, government based on caste or class cannot stand. Thus far, as history shows, all nations that have been built upon this idea have failed. Today, while all men everywhere are rejoicing in new-found liberties, shall women alone be deprived of these rights and privileges? Of all kinds of aristocracy, that of sex is the most odious and unnatural, invading as it does our homes, desecrating our family altars, dividing those whom God has joined together; exalting son above mother, and subjugating everywhere moral power to brute force. But the true statesman can see the free Republic of the future on the ruins of the mighty nations of the past.

Second, we urge the adoption of "The Sixteenth Amendment," because man's government is destructive to civil, religious and political liberty. The male element has thus far held high carnival, crushing out all the diviner elements of human nature, until we know little now of strong manhood and womanhood, of the latter scarcely anything. No one need wonder at the disorganization of society when we remember that man, who represents only half of human nature, has undertaken the absolute control of all sublunary things. To keep her foothold in society, woman must be as near like man as possible—to be his reflection. She must respect his laws, though they ignore her rights. She must believe his theology, though it makes God a minister of vengeance and hypocrisy. The need of this hour is not railroads, specie payments and all these things, but a new era for woman. The present disorganization of society warns us that in the disfranchisement of woman we have let loose the rules of violence and ruin which she only has the power to avert.

Third, we urge the adoption of the sixteenth amendment because in manhood suffrage, an aristocracy of sex, established from Maine to California, woman has reached in this country the lowest depths of degradation. Ignorant and unintelligent men make the laws for our cultured and learned women. This manhood suffrage is an appalling question, and it would be well for thinking women to remember that the most ignorant men are the most hostile to women, since they only know her in slavery and degradation. It is a deliberate insult to woman to be cast down under the iron heel of the peasantry of the Old World and the ignorance of the new.

Not since God called light out of darkness, order out of chaos, was there ever made such a base proposition as manhood suffrage in a republic. But whither is a nation drifting when the highest offices in the gift of the nation are bought and sold in Wall Street, when brains are of less account than bullion, and when clowns make laws for queens. In the Old World women are not degraded as they are in this country. There are women of rank in the Old World aristocracy who have certain privileges above the ignorant masses. The educated woman of this nation feels as much interest in education and the good of the race, and certainly in their own welfare, as any man possibly can, and we learn the same distrust of man's power to legislate for us as he has of a woman's power to legislate for themselves. (Applause.)

Fourth, we urge the adoption of the sixteenth amendment, because the history of American statesmanship does not inspire us with confidence in man's capacity to govern the nation alone with justice and mercy. Priests and politicians from the beginning have hoodwinked the masses with the idea that all the ills of life are blessings in disguise for their good and instruction, and that all the good of life was in the order of Divine Providence. It is not Providence that is opening a sort of Pandora's box, destroying the virtue and honor of the people, but our corrupt rulers, who have demoralized the political sentiment of the whole country. We have a great fight to wage, and this is against Mammon. If things go on as they do, the purse will control the law. Mammon will be mightier than Senators or Representatives. Is it for citizens to sit calmly by, without a cry or protest, and see one thing after another swept away by this yellow stream that beats against Congress, the Legislature and the judiciary, and threatens to undermine them?

Fifth, we urge the sixteenth amendment because the present political ostracism of one-half of humanity is opposed to the teachings of science, philosophy and common sense. All writers recognize woman as the great harmonizing element in the "new era"; yet while eloquent tongues in Italy, Germany, France and England are paying glowing tributes to woman, why is it that the liberal party in this country, whose talk is all of human rights, is so deaf and dumb on the subject of woman, when she is the theme now the world over? Are women of this land less worthy of respect than those of other lands? Nay, Nay! America can boast of many noble women as worthy of respect as Victoria.[1]

Lastly, we must have the sixteenth amendment because the safety and dignity of woman demands her immediate enfranchisement. We cannot to-day take up a paper without reading of outrages by the lower classes upon all classes and ages of women. Such are the practical results of man's dominion. When I hear of these outrages I do not feel so indignant against these lower orders of men as I do against men in high places who dare to express sentiments of contempt for woman. You cannot go so low down into the depths of being that you could find a class of men that would go up into our churches and desecrate its altars and toss about the sacred vessels of the sacrament, because in their infancy they have been taught the sacredness of these things. But where have any sentiments of honor and respect to woman been taught? But as she is the mother of the race, is she not more sacred than churches, or altars, or symbols? Let society do as much to dignify woman as to dignify the priest; teach the masses that there is no office so sacred as motherhood, no communion more sacred than marriage and that it is more sacrilegious to desecrate a young girl than any sacred altar of the church, and we shall see an end to the assaults on women that we hear of every day.

The speaker saw something more in the ballot than a slip of paper dropped into a box once a year to choose a county sheriff. It had a deeper sentiment. It meant liberty. It was throwing aside a badge of degradation and assuming the seal of sovereignty.

In conclusion the speaker said that even now she saw societies on the boundaries of that better land where moral power shall govern brute force, and in the dazzle of that coming glory it was wearisome to parley with carping minds to-day.

Mrs. Stanton's peroration was very eloquent, and was warmly applauded.

⇜ *Providence Daily Journal*, 1 June 1881.

1. Victoria, queen of the United Kingdom of Great Britain and Ireland and empress of India (1819–1901).

38 ⇜ ECS to Elizabeth Smith Miller[1]

Tenafly, N.J., June 5, 1881.

[My] dear Julius:

Your letters and marmalade were awaiting me on my return from Boston. [Ma]ny thanks for the marmalade; it is delicious. I had a grand time in Bos[to]n and Providence. We were received by the Governor at the State House,[2] by [t]he Mayor at the City Hall,[3] at Jordan Marsh's great establishment[4] at Sher[bo]rn Prison,[5] and Susan and I were invited to dine at the Bird Club.[6] At [P]rovidence I visited Dr. Channing and had a charming time. Altogether we [w]ere received right royally in Boston, in spite of persistent efforts to [u]ndermine us. I spoke before the Free Religious Association, following [Ad]ler whom I heard and enjoyed exceedingly.[7]

I expect Susan back soon to move on with our second volume. But that [w]ill not be as much trouble as the first and we shall write it more de[l]iberately. I sent you a copy; did you get it? I want Charley to read the last chapter and tell me if he thinks woman is much indebted to Christianity.[8]

I found Theodore and his wife here, they arrived a few hours in advance of me. They came from Havre in eleven days. Affectionately,

⇜ *Johnson.*

⇜ Typed transcript, ECS Papers, NjR. Letters in square brackets obscured by binding.

1. Elizabeth Smith Miller (1822–1911), the daughter of ECS's cousins Gerrit

and Ann Smith, was a close friend since girlhood and sometime officer of state and national suffrage associations. Since 1851, ECS and Miller had called each other Johnson and Julius after characters in a show by the Christy Minstrels. Julius was the wit, while Mr. or Missur Johnson played the philosopher. Miller was well known for her marmalade: several recipes appeared in her cookbook, *In the Kitchen* (1875), and jars were often sold to benefit good causes. With her husband, Charles Dudley Miller (1818–1896), she moved between New York City and a lakeside house in Geneva, New York. (*NAW*; *ANB*; genealogical scrapbook, Smith Papers, NSyU. See also *Papers* 1–3.)

2. John Davis Long (1838–1915), Republican governor of Massachusetts from 1880 to 1883 and member of the House of Representatives from 1883 to 1889, welcomed sixty delegates at the State House on May 27 with remarks in favor of woman suffrage. (*ANB*; *NCBB*, June 1881, *Film*, 21:1046–48.)

3. Frederick Octavius Prince (1818–1899), Democratic mayor of Boston in 1877 and again from 1879 to 1881, received delegates at City Hall on May 28. As secretary of the Democratic National Convention in Cincinnati in 1880, he assisted representatives of the National association in their quest for a suffrage plank in the party's platform. (Melvin G. Holli and Peter d'A. Jones, eds., *Biographical Dictionary of American Mayors, 1820–1980: Big City Mayors* [Westport, Conn., 1981]; *NCBB*, June 1881; *Papers*, 3:546n.)

4. At Jordan, Marsh & Company, the delegates were shown a new recreation room where fifty young employees of the department store were dancing on their noon break. (*NCBB*, June 1881, *Film*, 21:1046–48.)

5. At the suggestion of Governor Long, Ellen Cheney Johnson conducted this tour of the Massachusetts Reformatory Prison for Women in Sherborn, a well-known model prison under the management of women. (*NCBB*, June 1881.)

6. The Bird Club originated as an informal group of Radical Republicans in Boston who met weekly for dinner to discuss state politics. ECS dined with them in 1870 to debate woman suffrage, and she returned with SBA and Harriet Robinson on 28 May 1881. (*Rev.*, 10 February 1870, *Film*, 2:253; *Boston Times*, 30 January 1870, SBA scrapbook 3, Rare Books, DLC; *NCBB*, June 1881.)

7. Felix Adler (1851–1933), founder of the New York Society for Ethical Culture in 1876, lecturer and social reformer, was president of the Free Religious Association. He delivered his lecture "The Teachers of Ethics as the Successors of the Clergy." (*ANB*; Boston *Index*, 16 June 1881.)

8. Matilda Joslyn Gage, "Woman, Church, and State," *History*, 1:753–99.

·⊂══════⟩·

39 ⊱ LECTURE BY SBA IN REPRESENTATIVES'
HALL, CONCORD, NEW HAMPSHIRE

EDITORIAL NOTE: From Providence, a smaller group of speakers
continued to Portland, Maine, on June 1 and 2, and to meetings in
New Hampshire, at Dover on June 3 and 4, and Concord on June 7
and 8. SBA and Olympia Brown stayed in Concord an extra day in
order to speak to members of the legislature and the public in the
evening of June 9. They rejoined the tour in Keene, New Hampshire,
on June 10, and continued to Connecticut for meetings at Hartford
and New Haven, completing the tour on June 17. (SBA to Speaker,
House of Representatives, 9 June 1881, *Film*, 21:1075.)

[9 June 1881]

A very large and interested audience assembled in Representatives'
Hall, Thursday evening, to listen to addresses by Rev. Olympia Brown
and Miss Susan B. Anthony, upon the subject of Woman Suffrage, the
hall having been granted by the Representatives for that purpose, and
a large number of members were present.

Senator Kaley,[1] of the Milford District, called the meeting to order,
and prayer was offered by Rev. Olympia Brown.

Miss Anthony then read some joint resolutions, which were to be
offered in the House.[2]

<Resolved, That it is the duty of Congress to submit a proposition
for an amendment to the national constitution, prohibiting the several
states from disfranchising United States citizens on account of sex.

Resolved, That the Senate and Assembly of the state of New Hampshire hereby urge the Senators and Representatives in Congress from
this state to use their efforts to secure the proposition of an amendment
to the national constitution which shall guarantee the right to vote to all
citizens of the United States irrespective of sex.

Resolved, That it is the duty of Congress to appoint a standing
committee in each house to whom all petitions on the rights of women
citizens shall be referred, and whose duty it shall be to consider and
report on them.>

EDITORIAL NOTE: Olympia Brown spoke first, answering objections to woman suffrage.

Miss Susan B. Anthony commenced with a criticism of the late Senator Wadleigh's[3] report against the 16th Amendment, in which he said "Women were a dependent class." This was the reason why she wanted the ballot for woman, and she desired that some of the civil positions in the country should be filled by women, as well as the few post-offices of no pecuniary interest to women, and which no man would take.

She called attention to the condition of the negro, and the change which had been wrought in his condition by the ballot. All places in the Government were eligible to negroes, because they were a political power. Negroes were admitted to practice law in the Supreme Court, while Belva A. Lockwood,[4] a graduate of a college, was refused admission. John M. Langston[5] was admitted because of the 14th and 15th Amendments, but a law was passed prohibiting exclusion of lawyers on account of sex, and Belva Lockwood was admitted. She gave her experience in a First of August celebration in Lawrence, Ka., in 1865, before negroes were citizens, and in 1870, when Senator Revels, a negro, was welcomed to that city.[6] It was the right of citizenship and the ballot that wrought the change, and these negroes had held the balance of power in that city from that day to this. She wished that women could be treated as respectfully as the Irishmen, Germans, Bohemians, Swedes, and negroes are for a few days before election.

She wanted the ballot for woman for the purpose of helping society. There were two methods of getting this right—one was, praying the States to strike the word "male" from their Constitutions. After the adoption of the 13th and 14th Amendments, the women suffragists went down to Washington in 1865, with 10,000 petitioners praying that the word "white" should be omitted from the Constitution. Then came the 15th Amendment, and we asked to strike out "sex," and were told it was the negroes' hour, and were turned aside. We then asked that the 16th Amendment should give women the same rights as negroes, and have met with rebuffs thus far. We say it is a great outrage for you to admit all classes of men to citizenship and deny it to us. The speaker elaborated this point at some length, and in a forcible and telling manner. She also gave her experience in Kansas, Michigan, and Colorado, in canvassing for the enfranchisement of woman, where it was voted down by the ignorant, the whiskey ring, etc.[7] We ask you, legislators, to ask your Senators and Representatives in Congress to submit a 16th Amendment to the Legislatures of the States. When you deny me the right of having my opinion counted, you reduce me to the condition of a slave. Citizenship should be homogeneous, and when I am deprived of my rights, the Government should stretch out its arm and restore my right to me. If we can secure a two-thirds vote in Congress to submit the 16th Amendment, something is accomplished. Gentlemen, will you put this question in a position where it can be submitted to the Legislatures of the States, or thrust us back into a helpless condition? She urged members of the Legislature to pass the resolutions submitted, or something like them, and thanked the members present and the audience for the attention given the speakers, and the meeting closed at 9:50 o'clock.

⚒ *Concord Daily Monitor*, 10 June 1881; *NCBB*, June 1881.

1. Timothy Kaley (1817–1882) was the state senator from Milford. An immigrant from Ireland and former millworker in Massachusetts, he moved to New Hampshire in 1860, bought a mill, and entered local politics. After serving in the state's lower house in 1876 and 1877, he won election to the senate in 1881 and 1882. (George A. Ramsdell, *The History of Milford* [Concord, N.H., 1901].)

2. The local newspaper omitted the resolutions she read; they are supplied from the report in the *National Citizen*. The first two resolutions pursued a tactic adopted by the National association in 1878, when it urged women in every state to press their legislators to direct memorials in favor of the amendment to their congressional delegations. (SBA to Elizabeth B. Harbert, 24 October 1877, and *NCBB*, August 1878, *Film*, 19:574–77, 20:313–21; *Papers*, 3:333–35, 337, 411, 414n.)

3. Bainbridge Wadleigh (1831–1891), New Hampshire's Republican senator from 1873 to 1879, chaired the Senate Committee on Privileges and Elections when it issued an infamous but unsigned report against the sixteenth amendment, *Report*, 45th Cong., 2d sess., S. Rept. 523, Serial 1791. The report, submitted on 14 June 1878, reasoned that the amendment would "make several millions of female voters, totally inexperienced in political affairs, . . . and comparatively very few of whom wish to assume the irksome and responsible political duties which this measure thrusts upon them." (*BDAC*. See also *Papers 3*.)

4. Belva Ann Bennett McNall Lockwood (1830–1917), one of the National association's key allies in Washington, practiced law in the District of Columbia. She was admitted to the bar of the Supreme Court on 3 March 1879, after

a long dispute with the court and a successful campaign for federal law directing the court to admit women. (*NAW*; *ANB*. See also *Papers* 2 & 3.)

5. John Mercer Langston (1829–1897) was admitted to the bar of the Supreme Court of the United States in January 1867, a year before he joined the new faculty of law at Howard University. A graduate of Oberlin College, Langston was a prominent African-American leader both before and after the war. (*ANB*; Rayford W. Logan, *Howard University: The First Hundred Years, 1867–1967* [New York, 1969], 62, 66, 72.)

6. A favorite illustration in SBA's speeches, this refers to the celebrations of emancipation in the British West Indies held in Leavenworth (not Lawrence), Kansas, on 1 August 1865, and a visit by Hiram Rhoades Revels in 1870. For earlier accounts, see *Papers*, 1:552, 2:328–29, 3:217–18. Revels (1827?–1901) was a minister of the African Methodist Episcopal Church in Leavenworth when SBA lived there in 1865. A resident of Mississippi after the war, he was elected to the state senate in 1869 and to the United States Senate in 1870. (*ANB*.)

7. In these three states, legislatures approved constitutional amendments to make women voters and submitted them to the electorate—in Kansas in 1867, Michigan in 1874, and Colorado in 1877. Voters rejected the amendments in all three instances. See *Papers* 2 & 3.

40 ⤳ SARAH PUGH[1] TO ECS

[*Philadelphia,*] June 21, 1881.

I have just laid down your "History" over which I have laughed and cried by turns, shouted and shed tears of joy over your victories and could I only send with it my joy and rejoicing that you—the "trio" have been able to do the work so well. Only a few words that I would change, only a few phrases that I would have omitted.

⤳ *NCBB*, August 1881.

1. Sarah Pugh (1800–1884), a close friend of Lucretia Mott and early member of the Philadelphia Female Anti-Slavery Society, was a leader in Philadelphia's suffrage and woman's rights organizations. (*NAW*; *ANB*. See also *Papers* 1–3.)

41 ❧ SBA to Lillie Devereux Blake

Rochester[1] July 9/81

My Dear Mrs Blake

Mrs Gage forwards me yours of June 28—and I note what you say of pictures for Vol. 2^d of History— I did <u>advance</u> the cash for those of Vol. 1—because the most important women were dead or utterly unable to pay for them— The ~~friends~~ ↑children↓ of Mrs Mott & Mrs M. C. Wright—however have each sent me $100— so I am whole on those—but for the others I am still out $700—

I have declared that of the young women whose pictures ~~who~~ go into the 2^d Vol. they are as well able to <u>work</u> out the for them as I am—and hence I shall not sink—or venture another $1200— on engravings—and I am telling each one—I am sorry that we have to come to this—because the women who will pay <u>may</u> be the one's that will do the book the least good—

Dr Lozier[2] must of course represent New York in the 2^d Vol. and she is getting her engraving— Thus you see the matter lies wholly with yourself— You can get just as expensive a picture as you please—& furnish 2000 copies of it— You can go to whomsoever you please, too, to engrave it— I should think you ought to make a good picture

I got your note about History to <u>Mrs Wendt</u>—[3] I immediately ordered a copy sent to her—but do not get an acknowledgment of its receipt— The <u>Tribune</u> did splendidly in view of what we naturally expected—[4]

I hope you & your lovely girls are well & having a good time & that Mr Blake is well again[5]   Sincerely yours

❧ *Susan B Anthony*

How cheering that our President is in hopeful way of recovery—what an appalling week it has been—set me back to 1875 when my brother was shot—[6]

❧ ALS, Lillie Devereux Blake Papers, MoSHi.

1. SBA returned to Rochester "to rest & recruit in spirit, body & clothes—for two weeks—" (SBA to Amelia J. Bloomer, 28 June 1881, *Film*, 21:1125–34.)

2. Clemence Sophia Harned Lozier (1813–1888), a successful physician in New York City, was dean and professor at the New York Medical College and Hospital for Women, which she organized in 1863. She served as president of the National Woman Suffrage Association in 1877. (*NAW*; *ANB*; ECS, "Tribute to Dr. Clemence S. Lozier," 7 June 1888, *Film*, 26:797–800. See also *Papers* 3.)

3. Mathilde F. Wendt of New York City served frequently on the executive committee of the National association. From 1869 to 1872, she coedited *Die Neue Zeit*, a German-language paper advocating woman suffrage. In 1871, she and her husband, Charles E. Wendt, moved to East Fifty-first Street from the German-American community of Hoboken, New Jersey. According to the city directory, she was still employed as an editor in 1881. (Jersey City and Hoboken directories, 1869, 1870; New York City directories, 1871 to 1881; Mari Jo Buhle, *Women and American Socialism, 1870–1920* [Urbana, Ill., 1983], 2–3.)

4. *New York Tribune*, 3 July 1881. After conceding that the woman suffrage movement was "one of the most striking episodes in the social history of the century," the anonymous reviewer praised the editors for work done "with care and good judgment."

5. Lillie Blake's two daughters by her first husband were identified in the census of 1880 by their father's name, when both young women taught in New York City's public schools. Elizabeth Johnson Devereux Umsted (1857–?) married John Beverly Robinson, an architect, in 1885. Katherine Muhlenbergh Devereux Umsted (1858–1950) used the name Blake. Grinfill Blake (c. 1835–1896) married Lillie Blake in 1866. Ill health led to frequent changes in his employment and hard times for his family, and he never recovered fully from the illness he suffered in 1881. (Katherine Devereux Blake and Margaret Louise Wallace, *Champion of Women: The Life of Lillie Devereux Blake* [New York, 1943], passim; *Woman's Who's Who 1914*; city directories 1880, 1881; Federal Census, 1880.)

6. James Abram Garfield (1831–1881) became the twentieth president of the United States in March 1881. On July 2 in Washington, he was shot by Charles Guiteau. He survived for two months. SBA compares it to the attempt to murder Daniel Read Anthony in 1875. (*ANB*; *Papers*, 3:203n.)

42 ≈ ECS TO AMELIA JENKS BLOOMER

Tenafly N.J. July 30th [*1881*]

Dear Mrs Bloomer,

Yours of the 24th received & sent to Miss Anthony. I knew nothing of what she wrote you.[1] When we received & read yours we agreed that it was good & concise & why it was returned to you I do not know unless you requested it   Whatever you would like said of yourself can be put in notes, in fine print as you will see I have mentioned Susan, Mrs Gage, & my home, or in the Appendix as you see we have Margaret Fuller.[2] I hope you will arrange it all yourself & add in notes the sum & substance of what you said of yourself. I had no intention of doing you any wrong in taking your temperance work out of your sketch & putting it in the New York chapter, & preserving the remaining facts in Seneca Falls, but as you felt wronged, it was left out, & now you can reproduce in notes what you choose. Perhaps you better go over it carefully & drop out every superfluous word & paragraph that does not affect the sense. Many sentences in almost every ones writings can be improved by <u>striking out</u>. We have nothing from Nebraska yet, & what you say better remain. As a whole, how do you like the first volumn, what criticism would you make, we want to know what all the friends think & what blunders blunders they see as small changes can be made. I made Mrs Gage write exactly what she wanted said of herself, now you do the same & I can put my initials to the note   It has been my aim & wish that justice should be done, if we have failed it has been an error of the head & not the heart   With kind regards for yourself & Mr Bloomer sincerely yours

≈ *Elizabeth Cady Stanton*

≈ ALS, Amelia Bloomer Papers, Seneca Falls Historical Society.

1. On June 28, SBA mailed the chapter on Iowa back to Bloomer with the recommendation that she "chop out all of the details of things you can & <u>save</u> the story of Iowa work & workers in substance & spirit—" But discussion of the chapter for volume two was colored by the decision to omit her reminiscences

from volume one. In this letter and the next by SBA, that decision is described. The pages intended for Bloomer, in a chapter after the account of the
Seneca Falls convention, were given over to an account of Ernestine Rose. See
also SBA to A. J. Bloomer, 19 December 1880, 7, 29 January, 9 February 1881,
ECS to A. J. Bloomer, 29 January 1881, *Film*, 21:701–3, 753–60, 802–8, 821–
27, 1125–34.

2. Notes on SBA, Matilda Gage, and ECS's home are found in *History*,
1:38, 457–58, 461, 466. Margaret Fuller (1810–1850) was a Transcendalist
writer whose *Woman in the Nineteenth Century* (1845) influenced the woman's
rights movement. To supplement one paragraph about her in the chapter
"Preceding Causes," the editors provided a more detailed biography in the
appendix, *History*, 1:40, 801–2. (*NAW*; *ANB*.)

43   SBA TO AMELIA JENKS BLOOMER

Rochester August 4th 1881

My Dear Mrs Bloomer

Yours of a long time ago was received just as I was summoned to the
sick-bed of our dear friend Phebe H. Jones[1]—at Albany—from which
she passed—or her mortal remains to their last resting place July 29th &
I returned Aug 1st— For all of the fearful array of broken propositions
that you place on your pages—what can I say—but that I am very, very
sorry that we found it impossible to do what I had thought we could &
should do— When I wrote you that every word of your chapter of
reminiscences would go into history exactly as you sent—I didn't
dream they would comprise the history of N.Y. State Temp. work so
largely—as, that if we published yours—it would leave the chapter of
↑[its?]↓ history of N.Y. bald & imperfect— So I <u>myself</u> said to Mrs
Stanton—it won't do to tell the story of that work over twice—& it
surely ought to go in the main chapter—giving the Lily the credit of
reporting it— Then of all of what you call my failures—I am <u>sure</u> of but
<u>one thing</u>—& that is of my <u>wish</u> to have the <u>right</u> done— I surely got
the impression that you would rather <u>not have the rem's</u> in any <u>way</u>
after they had been cut out of as they had been— I am dreadful sorry
for all of my short-comings—but cannot alter the facts now— I have felt
as if I ~~be~~ ↑were indeed,↓ as the prayer book says,[2]—"<u>a miserable</u>

<u>sinner</u>"—ever since receiving your arraignment—but where is the atone-
ment for me, I cant see—

About the promise of <u>verbal corrections</u> I had entirely forgotten—&
when I got your <u>very</u> <u>brief</u> <u>letter</u> desiring the return of the manuscript—
I couldn't for the life of me quite comprehend the cause of its return—
Had you been a little more explicit & reminded me of my "promise"—
I should have tried to comply—but I can assure ↑you↓ Mrs Bloomer—
that in the whirl of getting out that book—working 12 & 14 hours
steadily, every day—Sundays not excepted, for six months & more—I
got to where I couldn't do everything that everybody waited me to, &
<u>as</u> they wanted me to—

Mrs Stanton spoke of your making a letter—of supplying what you
wanted— I tell you—I do not know what to say to you—only this—that
<u>we</u> <u>must</u> <u>decide</u> <u>upon</u> <u>every</u> chapter by whomsoever contributed— I
am really inclined to the belief that <u>my</u> mistake was in saying <u>yours</u> or
<u>anybodys</u> should go in exactly as sent—for not a single persons has
thus gone into the book—I think—

So now—Fix your letter—or chapter of reminiscences—& Iowa—as
you think them right—and let us have them as early as convenient— I
do not dare to say how or what we will do with them— Indeed—
according to your version of me—it wouldn't matter what I should
say— So you will have to trust to our judgement in the matter as
everybody ↑else↓ has to— We <u>refused</u> one persons offer to write up a
state <u>because</u> we <u>wouldnt</u> <u>promise</u> to take it exactly as it was sent— We
shall do the best we know how, ~~and~~ if you send back the m'ss—that is
all I can promise—as I have said, my blunder was in saying you should
have everything as you sent it—when it was impossible for me to know
where or how it would fit in with what we had— I am sorrier than a
dozzen sheets of paper could tell to have been the cause of so much
suffering to you & not a little to myself—but all I can do—is to be more
cautious in my writing— Now don't waste your time nor strength to
tell what has been done wrong—but just what you see can be done to
make amends ~~for them~~—& we will yet try to be "just." Sincerely &
Sorrowfully yours—

~ *Susan B. Anthony*

P.S—I stop at home 8 or 10 days longer—& then return to Tenafly to
bone down to 2^d Volume of History— This is awfully hot weather—

If we had had the "Lily" as we did have the "Una"[3]—we could & should have quoted from it as much or more doubtless than we did from Una— Am glad the Nebraskans had such a good Convention—& of their good prospect of success—[4] Is it true that the Iowa School Law gives women the right to vote on school questions?—as the W.J. reports?—[5]

⚜ ALS, on NWSA letterhead for 1880–1881, Amelia Bloomer Papers, Seneca Falls Historical Society. Square brackets surround an uncertain reading.

1. Phebe Hoag Jones (1812–1881), a longtime activist in the reform community at Albany, died on July 28. SBA reached her side several weeks before her death and cared for her. (SBA speech at funeral, *Film*, 22:38; unidentified clipping, SBA scrapbook 9, Rare Books, DLC. See also *Papers* 1 & 2.)

2. *The Book of Common Prayer*.

3. Paulina Davis published the *Una*, subtitled "A Paper Devoted to the Elevation of Woman," in Providence, Rhode Island, from 1853 to 1854. She moved it to Boston in January 1855, when Caroline Dall became coeditor until the paper ceased publication in October 1855. Reprints from the *Una* are found in *History*, 1:246–54, 388, 501–3, 509, 511–12, 585.

4. The Nebraska Woman Suffrage Association met in Omaha on 7 and 8 July 1881 to plan their campaign for passage of the state constitutional amendment. Amelia Bloomer addressed the gathering. (*Woman's Journal*, 30 July 1881.)

5. In "School Suffrage Law of Iowa," *Woman's Journal*, 30 July 1881, Lucy Stone published a "revised" law that allowed males and females who paid the school tax to vote at school meetings on all questions.

44 ⚞ SBA TO BARBARA BINKS THOMPSON

Rochester August 18, 1881

My Dear Mrs Thompson

I find yours of the 11th inst here at home on the return of myself & sister from a four days absence at Dr J. C. Jacksons Water Cure—at Dansville N.Y.—where we had a feast of fat things,—saw & heard the charming & earnest Frances E. Willard[1] ↑(on Temperance)↓—Pres. of the W.T.C.U.— The brave & loyal Clara Barton ↑on her "Red Cross" Treaty of Nations—↓[2] the daughter of Finland—Selma Borg[3]—on Rusia

& the Nihilists—Dr Jackson himself on "<u>Woman</u>"—in which he went to <u>bed</u>-<u>rock</u> <u>on the question</u>—and by the way—I will give your name to the Doctor to send a copy of it to— And then in turn—when I gave my Bread & Ballot speech to 400 people—in his "Liberty Hall"— representing <u>28 different States</u>—what a <u>seed scattering</u>, <u>broadcast</u>— was there—⁴

I think I remember about Mrs Vermillions⁵ paper—and that I put it together with all ↑the↓ other items I had on Nebraska, into a bundle— & that it is at Tenafly, all safe & waiting my return to work— I am ashamed if I didn't acknowledge the receipt of it— But I can assure ↑you↓ it is a "<u>big job</u>" to answer all the letters I get—<u>even</u> <u>those</u> of <u>most importance</u>—still I always try to do at least a Postal—so she & you must forgive me this time—

It is a most remarkable fact that each person, almost, feels that the cause <u>began</u> <u>with</u> their interest in it— I have just received two letters from London—from different persons—telling of Mrs ~~Livermore~~ Livermore's lecturing there—and that one would never dream from her presentation of the question that there was ever any movement in America prior to her birth into it—in 1869—<u>twenty one years</u> <u>after</u> the first Convention was held at Seneca Falls—July 19 & 20—1848—⁶ And <u>she</u> was <u>not</u> <u>only</u> <u>not one of us</u>—until that <u>late day</u>—but as the wife of a <u>minister</u> & of ~~the~~ ↑an↓ editor of a <u>church</u> paper—decidedly <u>not</u> with us— So if such a late convert can thus impress people—we must not wonder at others who shall come in the <u>state</u> movements—after much good work has been done— Still—<u>In</u> <u>our</u> <u>history</u>—we want to get actual <u>facts</u> <u>about</u> <u>persons</u> & dates & names in their proper order—<u>not</u> the individual's ↑personal↓ <u>feelings</u>—and we <u>try</u>—but oh how difficult—almost impossible—to accomplish—

I shall put this printed slip safely away now—to keep to refer to & be guided by—whatever else comes—

I hope your society⁷ will send Mrs Colby to represent you at our next Washington N.W.S.A. Convention—in January 1882!— She is an attractive & good speaker—& will carry weight with our Congressional Committees— Please accept this ↑as a↓ <u>hint</u>—but <u>don't quote me</u>—as I do not wish to <u>seem</u>, even, to meddle with your state affairs—but if my thought hasn't hit upon the woman you all shall think your best representative one—take the one ↑you think best↓—<u>send to Washington</u> the lone that you feel will help our cause the most there— For if we can get a Standing Committee for Women's claims in Congress—it will help us everywhere— Love to all—sincerely—

⪼ *Susan B. Anthony*

⪼ ALS, on NWSA letterhead for 1881–1882, Woman Suffrage Collection, WaHi.

1. Frances Elizabeth Caroline Willard (1839–1898) became president of the Woman's Christian Temperance Union in 1879. She spoke on temperance in Dansville's Presbyterian church on Sunday, August 14, and held a meeting the next day with sixty women to organize a local temperance union. SBA spoke at the Monday meeting. (*NAW*; *ANB*; *Dansville Advertiser*, 18 August 1881. See also *Papers* 3.)

2. SBA arrived too late to hear Clara Barton's major speech on August 7 about the Treaty of Geneva and the International Society of the Red Cross, and she left Dansville before Barton's meeting on August 22, called to organize the first local chapter of the American Red Cross. Barton established the national society in May 1881, and while awaiting action on the treaty by the secretary of state and the Senate, she organized local branches. (*Dansville Advertiser*, 11, 25 August 1881; *Dansville Express*, 11 August 1881; William E. Barton, *The Life of Clara Barton: Founder of the American Red Cross* [1922; reprint, New York, 1969], 2:147–56.)

3. Selma Josefina Borg (1838–?) of Finland was a musician, lecturer, and translator of Swedish literature into English, who lived in the United States after 1864. Although she settled first in Philadelphia, where she worked with the women's committee for the Centennial of 1876, she lived in Boston by 1880. (Anders Myhrman, "Selma Josefina Borg: Finland-Swedish Musician, Lecturer, and Champion of Women's Rights," *Swedish Pioneer Historical Quarterly*, 30 [1979]: 25–34; Federal Census, Boston, 1880.)

4. Liberty Hall, adjoining the main building of the water-cure, was the platform for a regular program of lectures and entertainment. Its arrangements included space for cots to accommodate the weaker residents. SBA's speech on August 16 was reported in the *Dansville Advertiser*, 18 August 1881. (American Red Cross, *Clara Barton and Dansville*, 82, 86.)

5. A. Martha Vermillion was the original corresponding secretary of the Thayer County Woman Suffrage Association. SBA refers to the "splendid" address she delivered in Hebron, Nebraska, on the Fourth of July 1880. According to a letter to Thompson, 16 December 1880, SBA had given her copy to Matilda Gage for publication in the *National Citizen*. (*History of the State of Nebraska*, 1445; *History*, 3:686–87; *Film*, 21:675–82.)

6. Mary Livermore delivered a lecture, "On the Duties of Women in Regard to the Life of a Nation," in St. George's Hall in London on 17 June 1881. Livermore traced the question of woman suffrage back only to the Civil War

and women's realization that they should have the right to say whether or not the nation went to war. (*Women's Suffrage Journal* 12 [1 July 1881]: 102–3.)

7. That is, the Nebraska Woman Suffrage Association, in which a disagreement about leadership simmered in August 1881. Several members of the executive committee found their president, Harriet S. Brooks, an ineffective leader. Brooks blamed Clara Colby for the criticism. (Fus, "Persuasion on the Plains," 29–32.)

45 *≈* SBA to Elizabeth Wadsworth Anthony[1]

Rochester N.Y. Aug. 24, 1881

My Dear Aunt Eliza

Yours of the 19th inst. is just here with its <u>five dollars</u> to help the History cause along— No, indeed, I do not take a V from any of very best friends and relatives as other than the most kindly sympathy with my efforts to make the world the better in the direction of freedom and equality to woman. Your Postal telling of receipt of History & of your visit to Charles[2] & long illness there did come very soon after I wrote Jessie—and I fully meant to have acknowledged its receipt at once—but we do fail—or I do—of doing so many things I fully intend to do—

Yesterday morning sister Mary & I met at Depot for a half hour Fanny Dickinson[3]—who was on way home after a two months in the "Old Hive" and dear Grand Father[4] used to call the old homestead at Adams— she had gained 10 lbs. averdepois & looked brown & brisk— Said Aunt Ann Eliza was better than she had been in years—that she had spent several weeks at Waukesha Springs in Wisconsin—all the rest were well—

Sister Mary has gone down to the Lake for the day—else should↑e↓ would put in love to you & Uncle John & all the "<u>boys</u>" and their families—[5] She is very well indeed this summer— Our nieces Lucy & Louise[6] are at brother D R's at Leavenworth now—but are to be back to begin school the first Monday in September—

I hope you will know more & more of lifes enjoyments as you near the portals of the beyond— Uncle John now ranks with the few left of his age—and all of us are fast passing into the ranks of the "old folks"—

I stand the <u>oldest</u> of Grand Father's oldest born on one side—& ~~on the~~ ↑on the other side, the↓ oldest of Grand Father Read's youngest born—[7]

Fanny reported ↑the↓ two uncles at Adams[8] very well— Uncle Abram lives with his <u>widowed</u> daughter—Susan Brown—in the old home of Grandfathers—and digs about in the garden &c   She left Cousin Hannah Boyles' Maggie[9] there—to stay till middle of September—

How lonely it seems that I cannot tell you how our dear Mother is!! nor how we miss her all the time—though she was so feeble for many years—yet so long as we had her & could say "<u>Mother</u>"—it kept up the feeling & the <u>fact</u>, too,—of <u>home</u>—to which all the children were drawn as the centre—while, now, there is nothing left here to draw all to this spot, any more than exists at Leavenworth or Fort Scott— Your boys cannot begin to comprehend what a feeling of strength & comfort there is in their <u>possession</u> of <u>father</u> & <u>mother</u>— So long as they live—the children are <u>young folks</u>—no matter how old—and when they are gone—the children become the "<u>old folks</u>" no matter how young—but then, dear Aunt, we used to think our mother & father <u>very</u> <u>old</u>—and needing to be watched over & cared for, too, tenderly—when they reached <u>my</u> <u>age</u>—which is 61½ years— Starting into my ten years after the three score—you see— I hope yet to see you & Uncle John here— but if you cant come east—then I mean to come and see you once more—& have time enough to stay and really see you, too— Give my love to Jessie & to each & all, old & young—especially Uncle John— our father's next younger brother, the one link left of the older members of Grandfather's family   Affectionately your Niece—

∾ Susan B. Anthony

P.S—Dear Aunt on looking over your beautiful letter—that carries me back so to my dear Mother's letters—wakes up all the old and precious memories— I am afraid I haven't done myself justice—that is my feeling of thankfullness that you, my dear Aunt, appreciate my work— my efforts—so much as to make you feel to send me this beautiful and generous present— It comforts & cheers me a great deal more than the bare money will pay or purchase— It ↑is↓ what <u>it</u> <u>represents</u> that gives me so much pleasure—that is—↑it is↓ the <u>fact</u> of <u>your</u> <u>sympathy</u> and sort of <u>sanction</u> of the aim and pursose of my life work— It does me good, too, because, if my dear father & mother can & do look back here—it <u>rejoices</u> <u>their</u> <u>hearts</u> to see <u>you</u> thus holding up their Susan's hands, in her work which they highly approved when in the body—and if they take cognisance of things here now—I doubt not, approve now—even more heartily than then— How we do try to peer into the beyond—try to penetrate the vail that hides it from us— But soon we shall pass on—and then those we leave behind will as vainly long to catch a glimpse of us in our new home.

What a struggle of longings this life is— I do hope your pathway may grow smoother & smoother—and that ↑your↓ grand-daughters will in a measure be able to somewhat make up to you the loss of your one & only daughter Annie—[10] What a stay & a comfort she would have been to you in these last years—but Jessie must try & be all she possibly can— Lovingly— S. B. A.

⬦ ALS, Macpherson Collection, Ella Strong Denison Library, Claremont Colleges.

1. Elizabeth Wadsworth Anthony (1806–1892) was married to John Anthony (1800–1882), a younger brother of SBA's father, and lived in Coleta, Illinois. Their household included their son Joseph Anthony (1829–1887) and three of his children—Jessie (1856–1916?), Joseph, Jr., (1863–?), and Horace G. (1865–?). (Anthony, *Anthony Genealogy*, 198–99; SBA diary, 23 April 1892, *Film*, 29:655ff; Brief Account of Joseph Anthony, Sr., typescript, MNS-S. See also *Papers* 3.)

2. Probably this was her son Charles Anthony (1838–1900), who lived in Minnesota.

3. Frances Dickinson (1856–1945), known as Fanny, was the daughter of another of Daniel Anthony's siblings, Ann Eliza Anthony Dickinson (1814–1886) of Chicago. Her father, Albert Franklin Dickinson, died on 7 March 1881. Fanny was a student at the Woman's Medical College in Chicago. After graduation in 1883, she specialized in opthamalogy and had a distinguished medical career. (F. M. Sperry, comp., *A Group of Distinguished Physicians and Surgeons of Chicago: A Collection of Biographical Sketches of Many of the Eminent Representatives, Past and Present, of the Medical Profession* [Chicago, 1904], 150–53, and obituary in unidentified paper, 24 May 1945, both courtesy of Chicago Historical Society; Anthony, *Anthony Genealogy*, 216; Elinor V. Smith, comp., *Descendants of Nathaniel Dickinson* [N.p., 1978], 233–34; *Friends' Intelligencer* 43 [1886]: 184; *Chicago Tribune*, 9 March 1881.)

4. Humphrey Anthony (1770–1866) of Adams, Massachusetts. SBA's father, Daniel (1794–1862), was his eldest child. (Anthony, *Anthony Genealogy*, 165, 169.)

5. In addition to her sons Joseph and Charles, Eliza Anthony's family included sons Samuel (1830–?), Joshua (1841–?), and Humphrey (1845–?).

Humphrey probably lived with or near his parents in Coleta. (Anthony, *Anthony Genealogy*, 198–99, 201–3.)

6. Lucy Elmina Anthony (1860–1944) was the daughter of Jacob Merritt Anthony of Fort Scott, Kansas. Helen Louise Mosher (1862–?) was the daughter of the late Hannah Anthony Mosher. On break from school in Rochester, they visited their uncle Daniel Read Anthony (1824–1904) in Leavenworth, Kansas. D. R. Anthony, as he was known, was the publisher of the *Leavenworth Daily Times*. (Anthony, *Anthony Genealogy*, 189; *New York Times*, 6 July 1944; Mildred Mosher Chamberlain and Laura McGaffey Clarenbach, comps., *Descendants of Hugh Mosher and Rebecca Maxson through Seven Generations* [Warwick, R.I., 1980], 312, 550; Bertha Bortle Beal Aldridge, *Laphams in America* [Victor, N.Y., 1953], 223; *U.S. Biographical Dictionary: Kansas Volume*, 56–63.)

7. Lucy Read Anthony was the youngest child of Daniel Read (1754–1838). (Read Genealogical Ms., SBA Papers, MCR-S.)

8. These were Humphrey Anthony, Jr. (1818–1896), the youngest of Daniel Anthony's brothers and the father of thirteen children, and Abram Anthony (1806–1894). Abram Anthony lost his wife in 1879 and lived with Susan Anthony Brown (1849–?), one of his nine surviving children. She married Timothy Caleb Brown in 1871 and was left with four small children when her husband died in March 1881. (Anthony, *Anthony Genealogy*, 171, 206–9, 221, 223; Ruth Story Devereux Eddy, *The Eddy Family in America* [Boston, 1930], 380, 581; *Adams Freeman*, 15 September 1894, SBA scrapbook 21, Rare Books, DLC.)

9. Hannah Dickinson Boyles (1838–1920), an older sister of Fanny, lived in Chicago with her husband, Charles Carroll Boyles, a dry goods merchant. Margaret Louise Boyles (1860–1945) was a child of Charles's first marriage. (Anthony, *Anthony Genealogy*, 216–17; Frederick A. Virkus, ed., *The Compendium of American Genealogy* [1930; reprint, Baltimore, 1968], 4:67, s.v. "Boyles, Katherine.")

10. Anna Wadsworth Anthony (1826–1857).

46 ❧ JOHN P. ST. JOHN[1] TO SBA

[*Topeka, Kan.*] Sept. 10th [*1881*].

Miss Susan B. Anthony, Rochester, N.Y.

Your letter of the 21st ult, has been duly received. I have also received the first volume of "The History of Womans Suffrage" for which please accept my sincere thanks; I have not had time to read it as yet, but the cursory examination I have given it, leads me to heartily endorse it. I have for years entertained the opinion that every law-abiding human being in this country, of sound mind and mature years should be entitled to a voice at the ballot-box in the selection of the representatives who control the government, and make the laws that all, irrespective of sex, race or color are bound to obey.

I think you are mistaken about us "having the cart before the horse," in Kansas; we submitted the question of womans suffrage to our people a few years ago and it was then voted down, and it was plain to be seen that so long as we had free whiskey, and the people drunk, womans suffrage would be defeated, but now having adopted prohibition[2] we have full confidence that in a very short time, with a sober people, the native American women of Kansas will, at least so far as the right of suffrage is concerned, be elevated to the exalted position occupied by many of our foreign born male citizens who can scarcely speak the English language.

For several years, under our Kansas laws, women have been entitled to vote at school elections and it is proving so satisfactory to our people that no one for a moment entertains the desire to change the law, unless it would be to enlarge their privileges at the ballot box.[3]

Certainly there is as much justice in giving the wife and mother the right to vote for the protection of the husband or son as there is in extending the right to the saloon keeper to vote for their destruction.

I will talk to the members of Congress from our state, as requested, the first opportunity I have to do so.[4] With my best wishes for the success of the good work in which you are engaged, I am very truly your friend,

⇒ *John P St John*

⇒ TL letterpress, Records of the Governor's Office, Letterpress Volumes, Department of Archives, KHi.

1. John Pierce St. John (1833–1916) was the governor of Kansas from 1879 to 1883 and a leading prohibitionist in the state. He replied to a letter from SBA in which she insisted that by adopting prohibition *before* woman suffrage, Kansas "got 'the cart before the horse.'" (*ANB*; SBA to J. P. St. John, 21 August 1881, *Film*, 22:66–70.)

2. At the general election in November 1880, voters in Kansas approved a constitutional amendment that prohibited the "manufacture and sale of intoxicating liquors." SBA had expressed the hope that the amendment would

discourage immigrants opposed to woman suffrage from settling in the state. (McPherson, *Hand-Book of Politics for 1882*, 74.)

3. The Kansas constitution of 1859 stated that legislation about schools should "make no distinction between males and females." This provision gave rural women the right to vote at school district meetings. In cities, where such meetings were replaced with elections, their rights were more limited. (Kansas const. of 1859, art. II, sec. 23; *History*, 3:706.)

4. SBA explained in her letter the need to poll members of Congress about their views on woman suffrage and also to encourage them to submit the sixteenth amendment to the states.

47   SBA TO CLARA BARTON

Rochester N.Y. Sept. 20, 1881

My Dear Clara Barton

How disappointed my sister and I were last evening to hear read your letter of illness—instead of seeing & hearing you as we expected.[1] Judge Morgan[2] & Dr Robinson[3] both pressed the Red Cross association at once—but the whole matter of relief for Michigan[4] & organization was referred to a committee of which the Mayor[5] & 6 others appointed by him—were to be the members—& when all was thus shelved—I screeched—just to remind those men there were women present & thinking—& perchance thereby cause the Mayor to think put some women the Committee— The feeling seemed to be that to know & do about the Red-Cross, Miss Barton herself must be present— and I want you should get well & if possible make the time <u>before</u> I leave the city, which will be by Oct. 1st so that I can help get some good women into your society—if possible— It was too cruel that you must be cut down & out of being here last night— I shall leave here the 26th & speak at <u>Perry</u> ↑Wyoming Co↓ the 27th & return the 29th Cant you fix a date to speak here say the 30th or 31st—[6] But suit yourself—I can't do much—still I would love to see you Red Cross Launched here before I go back to Tenafly—N. Jersey—to begin work on Vol. 2d of our history—

Hoping you will soon be well—& able to resume your good Samaritan mission I am very sincerely yours

     Susan B. Anthony

⤶ ALS, on NWSA letterhead for 1881–1882, Clara Barton Papers, DLC. Envelope addressed to Dansville, N.Y. Endorsed "Ansd Sept 23."

1. For coverage of this meeting in the common council chambers, called to organize the second local Red Cross society, see Rochester *Democrat and Chronicle*, 20 September 1881. Barton notified the mayor she was too ill to attend, but she urged him to organize a society in her absence. The press made no mention of SBA's intervention or of the presence of women among the "large number of prominent citizens" in attendance.

2. John Shepard Morgan (1847–1888), a former city attorney and a special county judge since 1879, called the meeting to order and explained the purposes of the Red Cross. He was later appointed to the chapter's executive committee. (*Landmarks of Monroe County, New York* [Boston, 1895], 154, 216, 451–52; Federal Census, 1880; research assistance from Jean Czerkas and Timothy O'Connell, Friends of the Mt. Hope Cemetery; Rochester *Democrat and Chronicle*, 2 October 1881.)

3. Charles Edward Robinson (1835?–1920) ministered to the First Presbyterian Church of Rochester from 1878 until 1886. A regular visitor to the water-cure in Dansville, he was privy to Clara Barton's plans for the Red Cross. (Charles Mulford Robinson, *First Church Chronicles, 1815–1915: Centennial History of the First Presbyterian Church, Rochester, New York* [Rochester, N.Y., 1915], 167–75, courtesy of the Presbyterian Historical Society; American Red Cross, *Clara Barton and Dansville*, 368.)

4. Although the decision about a local society was postponed, the gathering raised money to aid the victims of a vast forest fire in Michigan. In her lobbying for an American Red Cross, Barton stressed its value not only in war but also in natural disasters.

5. Cornelius R. Parsons (1842–1901) was elected mayor of Rochester in 1876 and reelected until 1890. (Blake McKelvey, "Civic Medals Awarded Posthumously," *Rochester History* 22 [April 1960]: 15.)

6. Barton spoke in Rochester on October 1, and at the close of her speech, SBA "moved that the people in attendance . . . proceed at once to organize a Red Cross society for Rochester." She was named to the committee to draw up a constitution and by-laws. At a subsequent meeting to complete the organization on October 3, SBA was named to the executive committee. (Rochester *Democrat and Chronicle*, 2, 4 October 1881.)

48 ❧ ECS TO MARGUERITE BERRY STANTON

Tenafly, October 7, 1881.

Dear Marguerite:

You must keep yourself on a high plane in thought as well as action and mould this new life the very best you can. His character and destiny, which you hold in your hands, are infinitely more important than his clothes, which, however, I deem very important too. I can see all my faults and short comings repeated in my children, which oftimes fills me with self-reproach. But I was ignorant of my influence and responsibility. I want my children to profit by my experience. I had had three children before I awoke to the fact of prenatal education and began to consider its importance. Ah! Marguerite, it is a sublime mission to be a true mother. Just as the beautiful flowers and landscapes that adorn our walls grew day by day beneath your skillful brush, so will this new life be attuned to harmony by your thoughts and occupations. Live in the open air as much as possible, in admiration of the glorious scenery about you, and keep yourself in a sweet peaceful frame of mind.

I was very glad to learn that whilst those foolish people arose at five o'clock to hunt the lovely birds to death, you enjoyed your innocent slumbers. Never be laughed out of sleeping. All great people who live to good old age have a <u>genius</u> for sleep. Cultivate it. If you don't want that future boy crowing and laughing and pulling your hair at five o'clock in the morning, stay in bed and sleep yourself until a christian hour. These early risers are always uncomfortable people, keeping everybody on the rack; and we who believe in sleep must assert ourselves and defend our superiority. They always look and act as if they held the vantage ground because they <u>cannot</u> sleep, while we who can sleep when we choose, under all circumstances, and awake when we <u>must,</u> certainly occupy the superior position. Thiers[1] took five little naps a day! Let us exalt the genius of sleep and with the immortal Sancho Panza chant the sentiment, "Blessed is the <u>woman</u> who invented sleep."[2] With love and kisses,

❧ *Mother.*

❧ Typed transcript, ECS Papers, NjR. Variant in ECS's diary of same date, *Stanton*, 2:186–87.

1. Louis-Adolphe Thiers (1797–1877), a French politician and historian, was the first president of the Third Republic from 1871 to 1873. ECS no doubt read François Le Goff, *The Life of Louis Adolphe Thiers*, translated by Theodore Stanton from a manuscript and published in New York in 1879. Though the author described only his famous naps each afternoon, he remarked that "Thiers's way of sleeping has often been spoken of" (275).

2. An adaptation of Charles Jarvis's eighteenth-century translation of Miguel de Cervantes, *Don Quixote de la Mancha*, chap. 68: "blessings on him who invented sleep, the mantle that covers all human thoughts."

49 ❧ SBA to Clara Barton

Rochester N.Y. Oct. 13th 1881

My Dear Friend

I expect to go to New York on Saturday <u>from</u> <u>Albany</u>—go to A. tomorrow— I would love to see you before I go out to Tenafly— Leave word at Fowler & Wells—753 Broadway—where you will be on Sunday— Still there is nothing that can be gained by meeting— The Red Cross is of Monroe County is getting on its feet—& is bound to walk alone— Dr Sarah R. A. Dolley[1]—30 East Avenue—was here yesterday—and said the great need now was news-paper articles from day to day—to keep the people stirred up—& to make them comprehend what the Red Cross means—it takes line upon line to pound anything into the peoples heads doesnt it—

Now—my dear—you really ought to get a N.Y. State Society organized before Congress convenes—but you cannot get the attention of politicians until after the election is over—and then you ought to see President Arthur[2] & get him waked up to recommending the treaty in his Message to the 47th Congress— I see Blaine[3] will probably stay at his Post until December— Oh there are so many things to do & so little money & time to do with— Sincerely yours

❧ *Susan B. Anthony*

❧ ALS, on NWSA letterhead for 1881–1882, Clara Barton Papers, DLC.

1. Sarah Read Adamson Dolley (1829–1909), a physician in Rochester who

was one of the first American women to receive a medical degree, was named to the executive committee of the new Red Cross Society of Monroe County. (*NAW*; Rochester *Democrat and Chronicle*, 4 October 1881.)

2. Chester Alan Arthur (1829–1886) became the twenty-first president of the United States when James A. Garfield died from his bullet wounds on 19 September 1881. Arthur was sworn in in New York City early the next morning. (*ANB*.)

3. James Gillespie Blaine (1830–1893), Republican of Maine, served in the House of Representatives from 1863 to 1876 and in the Senate from 1876 to 1881. Named secretary of state by President Garfield, Blaine stayed in his post until December 1881. In meetings with Barton at the end of October, he promised to prepare language for the president's annual message in support of the Treaty of Geneva. (*ANB*; *BDAC*; American Red Cross, *Clara Barton and Dansville*, 264–65.)

50 ⤙ SBA to Rachel G. Foster

Washington, D.C. Oct. 26th 1881

My Dear Rachel

I called on Senator Jones[1] yesterday—& met a gracious reception— But he told me what I knew before—that the President was over crowded with applicants for office—& must, now while the Senate was in Session, give all such the precedence— So I knew—and yet I felt moved to go to Washington and here I am—but I may yet see some thing to make me feel my longing & its gratification may prove of some of effect—

Mrs Spofford is not yet home from Maine—but both her sisters— Miss Snowe & Mrs Nason[2] are here—and give me best of attention & aid in seeing & doing— Miss Snowe went with me with carriage all yesterday—and today she goes with me to hear Frances Willards Suffrage bomb-shell into the Christian W.C.T. Union Camp[3]—it is expected to make Mrs Wittenmeyer[4] & her like tremble lest <u>Carnal weapons</u> are to be siezed by their hosts

I dont see when I shall leave—but shall stop at Philadelphia a day or so—& will settle the affairs of the nation— Lovingly

⤙ *S. B A*

⤙ ALS, on letterhead of Riggs House, SBA Papers, DLC.

1. John Percival Jones (1829–1912), Republican of Nevada, served in the Senate from 1873 to 1903. President Arthur, a close friend, was living in his house, awaiting repairs and interior decoration of the White House. Despite his discouraging words, Jones did arrange an interview between SBA and the president, probably on November 1. (*BDAC*; *Anthony*, 2:538; Thomas C. Reeves, *The Gentleman Boss: The Life of Chester Alan Arthur* [New York, 1975], 268; American Red Cross, *Clara Barton and Dansville*, 263–64; SBA to Clara Barton, 7 November 1881, and SBA to Harriet H. Robinson 17 November 1881, *Film*, 22:132–33, 143–44.)

2. Maine was home to Jane Snow Spofford's mother. Sophronia C. Snow (1833–1904) and Mary C. Snow Nason (1828–1889) lived at the Riggs House with the Spoffords. Sophronia took an active part in the National Woman Suffrage Association and represented Maine as a delegate and honorary vice president in the 1880s. Mary Nason was a widow whose son attended school in Washington. (Federal Census, 1880; research by Katherine W. Trickey, Bangor, Me.; on-line transcription of gravestones in Locust Grove Cemetery, Hampden, Me., by Mike Desmarais, in possession of editors.)

3. Since its founding in 1874, the Woman's Christian Temperance Union had debated whether to endorse woman suffrage. At the annual meeting of 1881 in Washington, Frances Willard brought to the membership a proposal that the national union encourage and assist state unions whose members wanted to work for equal suffrage. In a vote on October 29, a majority of the members supported the proposal. SBA and Clara Barton went together to the opening session at Foundry Church in the morning of October 26, and they were called to the platform for introductions. Because of SBA's presence on that day and one other, disgruntled union members and some reporters concluded that she had captured the meeting. (Ruth Bordin, *Woman and Temperance: The Quest for Power and Liberty, 1873–1900* [Philadelphia, 1981], 118–19; American Red Cross, *Clara Barton and Dansville*, 263–64; *Washington Post*, 27, 29 October 1881, and SBA to Harriet H. Robinson, 17 November 1881, *Film*, 22:115–16, 143–44. See also *Papers 3*.)

4. Annie Turner Wittenmyer (1827–1900), president of the Woman's Christian Temperance Union from its founding until Frances Willard's election in 1879, favored prayer over politics in the crusade against liquor and resisted efforts by members to change direction. (*NAW*; *ANB*.)

51 ⚘ ECS to Harriet Hanson Robinson

Tenafly N.J. Oct 26th [*1881*]

Dear Mrs Robinson,

Many thanks for your book, which I have read through with a little skipping.[1] Well you have done up Massacheusetts, & as we have already more material than can be crowded into another volumn, I now think we will confine ourselves to the work of the National Association, merely saying that in your work, & the Woman's Journal all the facts of history relating to the American association & the various New England associations are fully recorded & will be preserved for the future historian.

If however you choose over your own name to write a New England or Massacheusetts chapter condensed from your book, with an engraving of yourself, you shall have twenty five pages to say what you choose. I make the offer to you or Mrs Shattuck. Here is an opportunity to immortalize mother or daughter, as our History is going all over Europe. My son Theodore sailed for Europe the last of August & took with him fifty volumns bound in calf to send to the writers in different countries who are preparing something for our second volumn Madame de Barrau[2] my son, & daughter Hattie are all busy translating for our second volumn.[3] I think you better send your book to Madame Caroline de Barrau, rue de Varennes, Paris, France, as she intends to publish an abridgement of our History in French,[4] & your book contains many valuable facts about Mass politics & laws   Susan & I are at work again. I have had a three months seige of intermittent fever & am still week, but am able to work a few hours each day.[5] I am glad that Mrs Shattuck is to make a grand speech in Washington. It does my heart good to see the young women coming on one by one especially when they have grace & beauty enough to please the press of the country. You know the complaint is always that we are all old & cross looking & wear shabby clothes &c &c. With much love for you & yours sincerely

⚘ *Elizabeth Cady Stanton.*

Tell Mrs Shattuck to write her speech <u>now</u> then commit to memory & rehearse as often as possible until Wash. con. & then give it with vim & power & take the con by storm. I hope these young women will not be confined to manuscripts as we old ones are. We must raise up an Anna Dickinson[6] for our cause. Has not Mrs Shattuck the elements in her? Spur her up & let us see what she can do by study & hard work

⇝ ALS, Robinson-Shattuck Papers, MCR-S.

1. Harriet H. Robinson, *Massachusetts in the Woman Suffrage Movement. A General, Political, Legal and Legislative History from 1774, to 1881*, published in 1881.

2. Caroline Françoise Coulomb de Barrau de Muratel (1828–1888) became interested in the education of girls and women while raising her own daughters, for whom she created a school in Paris. She also turned her attention to the conditions facing women in Paris, investigating wages and the migration of girls from the country, studying prostitution, improving women's prisons, and aiding abandoned children. She was active in the international campaign against licensing prostitutes, and she attended the International Congress of Women in Paris in 1878. Theodore Stanton met her in 1880. When not in Paris, where she shared a house with Theodore's in-laws, the Berrys, Caroline de Barrau lived on an estate near Sorèze in the south of France. (*DBF.*)

3. The fact that the editors launched their own research to assemble and translate documents from Europe was not evident when the chapter "Continental Europe" appeared in the third (not the second) volume of the *History*. What ECS here describes as her son helping the editors of the *History* was later described by Theodore Stanton as the start of his edited work *The Woman Question in Europe: A Series of Original Essays*, published in 1884. "I began collecting the materials for this volume in the winter of 1880–'81," he wrote in the preface. When ECS visited Theodore in southern France in 1882, she helped him with his book, entangling the research and translation further. By the time the third volume of the *History* was published in 1886, the chapter on Europe was credited to Theodore Stanton as derived from the *Woman Question in Europe.*

4. Although the French newspaper *Droit des femmes*, 3 September 1882, announced that such a work had been completed, it has not been located.

5. The August number of the *National Citizen* announced that ECS was recovering from a serious illness that would delay completion of the second volume of the *History*. According to SBA's biographer, Ida Harper, this was an "attack of malarial fever." (*Anthony*, 2:537.)

6. Anna Elizabeth Dickinson (1842–1932) was in her youth one of the most successful lecturers in the country on political and cultural subjects. During and after the Civil War, the Republican party employed her to campaign for their candidates. (*NAW; ANB.*)

·◁━━━━━━▷·

52   SBA TO LAURA CARTER HOLLOWAY[1]

Tenafly N. Jersey Dec. 1, 1881

My Dear Mrs Holloway

My eye has just lighted on your most excellent review of our History of Woman Suffrage—and I am reminded of my failure to tell you when it was first received, how grateful I felt to you for it— I often think of you & your spirited pen—and wish both might be given to editing a great <u>Woman's</u> <u>Daily</u> <u>paper</u> ↑in <u>New York</u>,↓— I mean a <u>real</u> <u>live</u> <u>news-paper</u> of everything—like the Times or Tribune—with <u>Equal Rights</u>—civil & <u>political</u>—for woman, <u>its politics</u>—just as the Herald is Democrat & the Tribune Republican— Our papers party politics should be <u>Woman's</u> <u>Rights</u>— With such numbers of women on the New York papers—who are able writers and good editors—it would seem as if such a paper might yet be established— I am sure there are brains enough—if only there were the cash!! I see that Cyrus W. Field[2] has bought the evening Express & will unite it with the Mail— Why cant he ↑be↓ prevailed on to establish his paper on this principle of equal rights to women—and employ the best women writers upon it?—

I am again here with Mrs Stanton at work on our 2^d Volume of History—& the task is simply herculean—such a wilderness of material to cull from and arrange & cut down into the small space we can give it—

Again thanking you—I am very sincerely yours

      Susan B. Anthony

N.B.—Mrs Holloway— Will you not attend our annual Washington Convention on Jan. 18, 19, 20, 1882—and speak from our platform? I wish you would do so—the enemy continually taunt us with having no new faces & voices on our platform— At any rate—I wish you would attend our Convention—that you might see & hear what good meetings we have in Washington— S. B. A.

  ALS, on NWSA letterhead for 1881–1882, Laura C. Holloway Collection, NB.

1. Laura Carter Holloway (1848–1930), later Langford, was a lecturer, author, and journalist. At this date she was an editor at the *Brooklyn Daily Eagle*, and she probably wrote the unsigned review of the *History of Woman Suffrage* in that paper on 20 June 1881. The long and favorable review praised both the book and the movement it documented. Born in Tennessee, she married Junius B. Holloway of Kentucky at a very young age and, while back in Tennessee about 1866, gave birth to one son. She moved to New York before 1870, when she addressed a letter to SBA denying any part in a news story about hostilities between them. In that same year she published *The Ladies of the White House*, a very popular book that she updated frequently for later editions. (Lucian Lamar Knight, comp., *Biographical Dictionary of Southern Authors* [1910; reprint, Detroit, Mich., 1978]; Oscar Fay Adams, *A Dictionary of American Authors* [Boston, 1897]; *History*, 1:49; *Brooklyn Daily Eagle*, 11 July 1930; research by staff of Brooklyn Public Library; Federal Census, 1880, for George Holloway; *Rev.*, 3 March 1870, *Film*, 2:279.)

2. Cyrus West Field (1819–1892), promoter of the first trans-Atlantic telegraph cable, purchased both the New York *Daily Mail* and the *Express* in 1881, merging them into the New York *Mail and Express*. (*ANB*.)

53 ✌ SBA TO J. WARREN KEIFER[1]

Tenafly New Jersey Dec. 6, 1881

Hon. Mr Keifer   Speaker of the House of Representatives
Dear Sir

I do not know what your opinions may be on the question of Woman's Right to vote—but I want to ask you in selecting men for the Committee on Rules, to have a thought on our claim, and choose a majority of them who are intelligent & liberal upon it—

The first point we hope to gain, now, is a "Standing Committee—on the Rights of Women Citizens"— We are driven to ask this, because for the last sixteen years that we have sent up to Congress our petitions & appeals, we have been referred to the <u>Judiciary</u> Committee, in the House—a Committee so over-crowded, always, as to be made an excuse, at least, for failure to give our claims attention. Benj F. Butler, in 1871—gave a minority report in our favor—

Will you not, sir, do all you can to help us to a Standing Committee in the House— I have asked our Committee[2]—Mrs Jones,[3] Miss Snow, and Mrs Lockwood, to call on you and urge you to give our woman suffrage cause this aid— With respect—yours &c

⪌ *Susan B. Anthony*

⪌ ALS, on NWSA letterhead for 1881–1882, J. Warren Keifer Collection, Special Collections Research Center, NSyU.

1. Joseph Warren Keifer (1836–1932), Republican of Ohio, served in the House of Representatives from 1877 to 1885 and again from 1905 to 1911. Republicans regained control of the House in the election of 1880, and Keifer was elected Speaker of the House when the first session of the Forty-seventh Congress opened on 5 December 1881. (*BDAC*.)

2. At the National's meeting in May, the chairman of the executive committee was empowered to invite women from "the East, West and South, to push our work before Congress" for two weeks prior to the association's Washington meeting. (*NCBB*, June 1881, *Film*, 21:997–1010.)

3. Jane Grahame Jones (?–1905) was among the earliest advocates of woman suffrage in Chicago, and she presided over the Illinois Woman Suffrage Association for six years before moving to Europe in 1877. She had returned and was staying this winter in Washington. (*The Book of Chicagoans: A Biographical Dictionary of Leading Living Men of the City of Chicago* [Chicago, 1911], s.v. "Jones, Fernando"; Alfred Theodore Andreas, *History of Chicago, from the Earliest Period to the Present Time* [Chicago, 1885], 2:588–89; *History*, 3:580, 585–86, 589; SBA to Harriet H. Robinson, 6 November 1881, *Film*, 22:125–28. See also *Papers* 2 & 3.)

54 ⪌ ECS TO THE EDITOR, NEW YORK *SUN*

[*Tenafly, after 9 December 1881*]

To the Editor of The Sun—Sir: I find the following in the daily papers:[1]

An old lady in Vermont lately sent to President Arthur a box of butternut candy. He says: "It was delicious. It reached me at dinner time on Thanksgiving Day, and was highly praised by all at the table. I think you will be glad to know that Senator Edmunds,[2] who was present, was so much pleased with it that he copied your address, with the intention of sending for some himself. Thanking you for your good wishes, I am very truly yours,

CHESTER A. ARTHUR."

Several officers of the National Woman Suffrage Association have called on the President, asking his aid in securing their political rights as citizens of the United States.

They specially urged him to recommend in his message a standing committee to look after the political interests of women.

But while he has spoken wisely on so many topics, in taking a statesmanlike survey of the whole habitable globe—of the government of Alaska, of the water supply, the depots, and the Potomac marshes at Washington; of the social customs of Utah, of the civilization and citizenship of savage tribes, of the education of the little Indian boys in Hampton, Carlisle, and Forest Grove—he does not vouchsafe one word in regard to the enfranchisement of the 20,000,000 of his countrywomen.[3]

Ah! Sir, could you have known with what palpitating hearts the leaders of this reform glanced over that message to see if among the headings they could find "A Standing Committee to Look After the Political Interests of Women," you might in a measure appreciate our sore disappointment. Letters also have been written to the President on this point, to which he has deigned no answer; and although "The History of Woman Suffrage," handsomely bound in calf, has been presented to Senator Edmunds, with the compliments of the editors, no letter of thanks has yet been received. And yet how promptly both these honorable gentlemen take note of the lady who sends butternut candy from Vermont.

Can it be that distinguished statesmen in the prime of life, with all their boyish follies and tastes long since outgrown, can prefer butternut candy to the history of all the brave battles their distinguished countrywomen have fought during the last forty years? If so, the wisest move the woman suffrage associations can now make is to suspend all conventions, resolutions, appeals, and petitions, and devote themselves to the dainty compounding of butternut candy.

Perhaps a box placed on the table of each Senator and Congressman might speedily insure woman's enfranchisement.

While rolling the sweet morsel under their tongues and exclaiming, "It is delicious," they might feel willing to place the ballot in the hands that had pulled and twisted the brittle sticks so artistically. However, it is pleasant to note that there are statesmen in Washington who are open to appeals through the intellect rather than the stomach.

Mr. Keifer in his able speech, on taking the chair as Speaker of the House, said:

> This Congress should be, and I profoundly hope it will be, marked peculiarly as a business Congress. It may be true that additional laws are yet necessary to give to every citizen complete protection in the exercise of all political rights.[4]

We have great hope that in Mr. Keifer we shall have a stanch friend; that he should have mentioned the only disfranchised class in his first speech, at the earliest possible moment, is most encouraging.

In the Senate, on Dec. 8, the noble Senator from Massachusetts bravely and boldly rises in his place and offers the long-talked-of resolution for a special committee, to be appointed by the Chair, to whom shall be referred all petitions, bills, and resolutions asking for the extension of suffrage to women and the removal of their disabilities.[5]

If the Committee on Rules do not promptly report on Senator Hoar's resolution, we urge the aforesaid lady in Vermont to send each of those gentlemen a box of her "delicious butternut candy."

↯ *Elizabeth Cady Stanton.*

↯ New York *Sun*, 12 December 1881.

1. New York *Sun*, 9 December 1881.
2. George Franklin Edmunds (1828–1919), Republican of Vermont, entered the Senate in 1866 and served until 1891. He was an outspoken opponent of woman suffrage and woman's rights. (*BDAC.* See also *Papers 3.*)
3. President Arthur's first annual message to Congress, dated 6 December 1881, included all of the topics that ECS lists. See Fred L. Israel, ed., *The State of the Union Messages of the Presidents, 1790–1966* (New York, 1967), 2:1424–52.
4. *Congressional Record*, 47th Cong., 1st sess., 9. Keifer spoke on December 5.
5. George Hoar introduced the resolution on December 7, not 8, seeking a special committee of seven members "to whom shall be referred all petitions, bills, and resolves asking for the extension of suffrage to women or the removal of their legal disabilities," and he asked that it be referred to the Committee on Rules. In the Senate, Democrats lost their majority in the election of 1880, but Republicans and Democrats each held thirty-seven seats. (*Congressional Record*, 47th Cong., 1st sess., 51.)

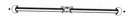

55 ⤳ FRANKLIN G. ADAMS TO SBA

[*Topeka, Kan.*] Dec. 13, [*188*]1.

Miss Susan B. Anthony, Rochester N.Y.

Dear Madam,

For the Kansas ladies contributing to the Mrs. Nichols portrait fund, Hon. John Francis[1] has sent you check for $72.85, the amt. raised, as per the following list:

From	Mrs. S. N. Wood,[2] Elmdale	8.55
"	" John Davis,[3] Junction City	10.00
"	" Hubbs,[4] Kinsley	2.00
"	Col. John Ritchie,[5] Topeka	1.00
"	Mrs. M. T. Gray, Wyandott	40.00
"	Mrs. M. Schmucker,[6] Eldorado	6.00
"	Mrs. Emma C. Wait,[7] Lincoln Center	5.00
		$72.55[8]

This it seems probable is all that will be collected. We are sorry that the sum is not more. Our Hist. Soc'y has contributed the expenses of printing &c.

Hoping that it will be of some satisfaction to Mrs. Nichols to know that she is remembered by some of the people of Kansas I remain Yours Respectfully

⤳ *F. G. Adams.*

⤳ ALS letterpress copy, Records of the Kansas State Historical Society, Letterpress Books, Department of Archives, KHi.

1. John Francis (1837–1918) served as state treasurer of Kansas from 1874 to 1883. He was also treasurer of the Kansas State Historical Society. (With assistance from Lin Fredericksen, Kansas State Historical Society.)

2. Margaret Walker Lyon Wood (c. 1841–1919) arrived in Kansas from Ohio in 1854 with her husband, Samuel Newitt Wood. Samuel Wood, a lawyer who entered politics, introduced the woman suffrage amendment in the state legislature in 1867 and founded the Kansas Impartial Suffrage Association to mobilize support for its passage. (*U.S. Biographical Dictionary: Kansas Volume,*

297–99; Bessie M. Wood, "Col. Samuel N. Wood and Family," *Chase County Historical Sketches* [Emporia, Kan., 1940], 1:424–27; Federal Census, 1880. See also *Papers* 2.)

3. Martha Ann Powell Davis (1828–1900), a sister of the explorer and geologist John Wesley Powell, was born in England and raised in the Midwest. In 1851, she married John Davis, a farmer in Illinois, and in 1872, the couple moved to Junction City, Kansas. John Davis, proprietor and editor of the *Junction City Tribune* as well as farmer, pursued his interests in reform within the Patrons of Husbandry, the Knights of Labor, and later the People's party. (*Kansas City Daily Times*, 4 February 1888, and *Junction City Tribune*, 30 November 1900, in Kansas Biographical Scrapbooks, KHi; *TwCBDNA*; *BDAC*.)

4. Emma M. Leavitt Hubbs (c. 1838–?) was the wife of Charles Leavitt Hubbs, owner of the *Kinsley Republican* and a local politician. She and her husband settled in Kinsley in 1873, after living in Missouri and Minnesota. (*U.S. Biographical Dictionary: Kansas Volume*, 342–43; Federal Census, 1880.)

5. John Ritchie (1817–1887), as a delegate to the constitutional convention of 1859, supported the proposals of Clarina Nichols for woman's rights. In 1867 he served as a vice president of the Kansas Impartial Suffrage Association. (Andreas, *History of Kansas*, 1:575; Joseph G. Gambone, ed., "The Forgotten Feminist of Kansas: The Papers of Clarina I. H. Nichols, 1854–1885," *KHQ* 39 [1973]: 528.)

6. Probably Martha Schmucker (c. 1831–?), the wife of John G. Schmucker, a grain dealer. (Federal Census, 1880.)

7. Adams means to say *Anna*, not *Emma*. Anna Amelia Churchill Wait (1837–1916) organized the Lincoln auxiliary of the National Woman Suffrage Association in November 1879 and edited a suffrage department in the *Lincoln Beacon*, the newspaper that she published with her husband, Walter S. Wait. Described as "for many years the strongest force behind the movement" in Kansas, Anna Wait held office in the National and Kansas associations and wrote the chapter on Kansas for the third volume of the *History of Woman Suffrage*. (*American Women*; Alfred H. Wait, *Anna Amelia Churchill Wait, 1837–1916* [N.p., 1916], in biographical files, KHi; *History*, 3:696–711, 4:638–39, 642.)

8. Adams clearly inscribed the different sums.

·◖━━━━━◗·

56 ⚘ SBA TO FRANKLIN G. ADAMS

Tenafly N.J. Dec 18/81

Dear Friend Mr Adams

The check from Mr Francis came same mail with your letter containing names of the contributors— I have taken a copy of them and will send each a history with the new engraving in, so soon as I can get it done— Mrs Nichol's son[1] at last, has sent me the original daguerotype from the best photographs were all taken— So I have hope of a better picture— I enclose one of the photo's— Wont you show it to Col. Ritchie, or any one who knew Mrs N. and see if he thinks it looks like her?

I will write Mrs Gray at Wyandotte, and get the names of the persons who made up the $40. and send each of them a book too— And as soon as I get the new picture I will send a Leather bound copy or two for your State Library— Could you give me the names of the <u>public Libraries</u> in Kansas—with the proper person to address,—I am making an effort to get the history placed in as many such libraries as possible— Respectfully & Gratefully

⚘ *Susan B. Anthony*

P.S—Suggest any changes in this picture that you think would make it look more like Mrs N.—

⚘ ALS, on NWSA letterhead for 1881–1882, Records of the Kansas State Historical Society, Correspondence Received, Department of Archives, KHi.

1. It is not clear which son sent the picture, as two sons were involved in the decision about which one to use: A. O. Carpenter, already identified, and his half-brother George Bainbridge Nichols (1844–1935), a farmer in California with whom their mother lived. (Family notes, Clarina I. H. Nichols Papers, MCR-S; Federal Census, 1880; C. I. H. Nichols to SBA, 17 December 1880, *Film*, 21:685–88.)

57   ⤳   SBA TO GEORGE F. HOAR

Tenafly N.J. Jan. 3, 1882

Hon. Geo. F. Hoar   Dear   Friend

Accept my many thanks for your protracted effort to get our Senate Committee—[1] I watch the progress with intense interest. It is such an <u>agitation</u> of our question to have it recorded every day in the associated press dispatches—does more to popularize it, than hundreds of lectures,—↑for↓ it speaks to the entire newspaper-reading people every time it comes up in either House— Even if we don't get the Committe, the great work of education will be done— But I hear that Senator <u>Logan</u>[2] says we are sure to get it— How <u>sharp</u> <u>the</u> <u>enemy</u> <u>always</u> <u>is</u>— they see the Com. will be a concession that we have a just claim to carry to Congress—

Did I not send you a copy of our History of Woman Suffrage, Senator?— I really cannot remember—but if I haven't—I want to—so please tell me— I want to raise the money to enable me to put a copy of our history on every members table!! All any one needs is <u>light</u> on the question—

Again thanking you, and hoping for speedy success in getting our Committee in both Houses—I am Very sincerely and gratefully

⤳   *Susan B. Anthony*

⤳ ALS, on NWSA letterhead for 1881–1882, George F. Hoar autograph collection, MHi.

1. Throughout December 1881, Senator Hoar labored to bring his resolution about the committee to the floor of the Senate. On December 13, George Vest of Missouri objected to taking it up; on December 14, Vest and Hoar debated both the need for a committee and the propriety of woman suffrage, but James Beck of Kentucky prevented a vote on the measure. Vest resumed his objections on December 15 and used up the short time allowed for consideration. On December 16, Vest moved to amend Hoar's resolution to refer the matter to the Committee on Revolutionary Claims. In a roll call vote, senators defeated his amendment by a vote of twenty-two to thirty-one. Thomas Bayard of Delaware then took the lead in opposition, moving to refer the resolution to

the Committee on the Judiciary, but again time for the debate expired. On December 19, Beck ran out the clock with a speech against woman suffrage. When senators agreed to consider the resolution on December 20, John Morgan of Alabama spoke at length against woman suffrage, until Bayard moved that the Senate take up other business. There the matter stood until 9 January 1882. (*Congressional Record*, 47th Cong., 1st sess., 76, 120–21, 137, 144–46, 187–88, 229–31.)

2. John Alexander Logan (1826–1886), Republican of Illinois, served one term in the Senate from 1871 to 1877 and returned in 1879 to serve until his death. Logan spoke in the brief time allotted to the question of a committee on December 16. "It is nothing but fair, just, and right that they should have a committee," he told his colleagues. "It is treating them only as other citizens would desire to be treated before a body of this character." (*BDAC*; *Congressional Record*, 47th Cong., 1st sess., 146.)

---

58   WENDELL PHILLIPS TO SBA

Boston 7 Jany '82

My dear Susan

Our friend Mrs Eddy,[1] Francis Jackson's daughter, died a week ago Thursday— She was sick only one week—typhoid pneumonia— Her daughter Lizzy Bacon,[2] who devoted herself to her the last 4 days, sickened & died of same disease <u>yesterday</u>—

At Mrs Eddy's request I made her will some weeks before she died— Her man of business—devoted to her for 25 years—Mr C. R. Ransom[3]—(ex president of one of our Banks) is the Executor. He & I were present & consulted & know all her intentions & wishes from long talks with her in years gone by— She left some $80.000— After leaving about $20000 in legacies, she ordered the remainder divided equally between <u>you</u> & <u>Lucy Stone</u>— There's no question whatever that your portion will <u>now</u> be $40.000—& no doubt that finally it will be $25 or $28000— I advised her (↑in order↓ to avoid all lawyers & court objections) to give this sum to you <u>outright</u>—with no responsibility to <u>any one or any Court</u>—only "<u>requesting you</u> to use it for the <u>advancement</u> of the <u>woman</u> cause"[4]

Let this whole matter be <u>confidential</u> between you & me until it becomes <u>public here</u>—

Now there are three things which in justice to Mrs Eddy's wishes her Executor & I wish you to do

She intended to draw up a paper of instructions to the Executor, which the suddenness of her death probably prevented, tho' a part of it may be put in writing— But from my conversations with her, during the last three months, we know what they were & the paper I inclose for you to sign is merely your giving him, the Executor, full authority to follow out what we know were her wishes & intentions—[5]

1st she intended to distribute her little womanly belongings, dress, jewels, the pictures in her rooms, &c—to certain parties, her daughters,[6] brother[7] &c & we wish to conform to her plans in this matter

2nd she left to relatives & old friends mostly $1000 each putting a bond to that amount in an envelope & marking it with the person's name—the same person to whom her will leaves $1000 for instance;— intending, as she told us that such person should have that bond— Now that bond perhaps is worth a little more than its par value—we wish you, the residuary legatees, to allow Ransom to follow out her plan— It will make hardly any difference to you pecuniarily (tho I know you'd wish her views executed even if it did)—possibly two hundred dollars at the outside—

You may ask why in drawing the will, I did not specify this— Because she was very ill & in great pain & to relieve her mind, I drew as brief & simple a paper as I could in the time I had   It was fortunate I seized the opportunity—as she was not afterwards in so good condition to attend to any business & as she had been, for weeks, planning to have such a will drawn, I felt she would worry & so not be so likely to get well unless I put something on paper & relieved her mind—

3rd Ransom & I think that if she had known that her daughter Bacon would die so soon, & so put double the amount she would ↑otherwise↓ have had, (during her Daughters life) at her disposal—(80.000 instead of $40000) she would have remembered her brother James as she did her other friends with the gift of $1000—so this paper provides that if you have over $10000—you authorize him to pay $500 to James Jackson—

Lucy Stone the other residuary legatee, has signed a paper which is the duplicate of the one I inclose— She knows all the facts of the case & agrees entirely with our views & authorizes Ransom to carry them out—

Now please sign the inclosed have one or two witnesses, & return the paper to me <u>keeping</u> the whole <u>matter private</u> until it comes out naturally here   Yr cordially

⇒ *Wendell Phillips*

⇒ ALS, SBA Papers, DLC. Original shows later emendations by Ida Harper.

1. Eliza F. Jackson Merriam Eddy (1816–1881) died on 29 December 1881 in Boston. She was the oldest child of businessman and philanthropist Francis Jackson (1789–1861) and an early member of the Boston Female Anti-Slavery Society. She married Charles D. Merriam in 1836, and after his death in 1845, she married James Eddy in 1848. (Garrison, *Letters*, 3:186, 592, 5:493; *NCAB*, 2:318; Charles Henry Pope, *Merriam Genealogy in England and America* [Boston, 1906], 150, 250.)

2. Eliza F. Merriam Bacon (1841–1882), the only surviving child of Eliza Eddy's first marriage, was the second wife of Jerome Bacon, of Bedford, Massachusetts. She left a fourteen-year-old son, Francis Warren Bacon. Eddy's will made no provision for Eliza, or Lizzie, Bacon: "As my daughter . . . is already amply provided for & has beside, at my death, more from my father's will I do not make her any gift in this will." Eddy did devise a house on Boston's Hollis Street to her grandson. (Pope, *Merriam Genealogy*, 150, 250; Abram English Brown, *History of the Town of Bedford, Middlesex County, Massachusetts, From Its Earliest Settlement to the Year of Our Lord 1891* [Bedford, Mass., 1891], 50–51, and separately paginated genealogical and biographical section, 3–4; Federal Census, 1880.)

3. Chandler R. Ransom (c. 1816–?), a widower, lived in Cambridge with his daughter. (Federal Census, 1880.)

4. The will of Eliza Eddy, dated 23 December 1881, was filed with the county probate court on 7 January 1882 (Suffolk County Probate Court Docket No. 66836, vol. 534, p. 82, Archives, Supreme Judicial Court, Boston). It directed, as Phillips indicates, that her residual estate "be divided into two equal portions; one of said portions I leave to Miss Susan B. Anthony of Rochester in the State of N York, as her absolute property, and the other portion I leave to Lucy Stone wife of H B Blackwell, as her own absolute & separate property free from any control by him.

"I request said Susan & Lucy to use said fund thus given to further what is called, the Woman's Rights cause. But neither of them is under any legal responsibility to any one or any Court to do so—"

Wendell Phillips and Eliza Eddy settled on this language to differentiate Eddy's will from that of her father, whose bequest to the woman's rights cause was reversed by the Supreme Judicial Court of Massachusetts. In 1858, Francis Jackson created a woman's rights fund of five thousand dollars to be administered by Wendell Phillips. In his will, Jackson directed that this fund become a permanent trust and that one-third of the residue of his estate, after the deaths of his daughter and granddaughter, be added to it. In 1867, the Supreme Judicial Court overturned this part of his will, ruling that the woman's rights movement was not a charity because its purposes were to change and overthrow laws. By her will, Eliza Eddy was making her share of that residual estate available to the movement by other means. She imagined, as Phillips indicates, that Eliza Bacon would continue to enjoy income from her share for many years. (*Papers*, 1:381–83; *History*, 1:743, 3:310–15; Jackson v. Phillips et al., 14 Allen 539 [1867].)

5. Enclosure missing. The consent of SBA and Lucy Stone to these provisions was noted in the executor's final account, 27 April 1885, Suffolk County Probate Court Docket No. 66836, vol. 571, p. 258.

6. Sarah James Eddy (1851–1945) and Amy Eddy (1854–1938), later Harris, were daughters of Eliza Jackson Eddy's second marriage, and lived with their father in Providence, Rhode Island. Sarah, a painter, later became a friend of SBA and painted her portrait. (Eddy, *Eddy Family in America*, 331, 522; Federal Census, Providence, 1880; on-line records of Eddy Family Association, in editor's files.)

7. James Jackson (1817–?) was a businessman in Boston.

59 ᘫ SBA to Wendell Phillips

[*Tenafly, c. 8 January 1882*]

Your most surprising letter reached me last evening. How worthy the daughter of Francis Jackson! How it carries me back to his generous gift of $5,000; to that noble, fatherly man and that quiet, lovely daughter in his home. Never going to Boston during the past fifteen years, I had lost sight of her, though I had not forgotten her by any means. How little thought have I had all these years that she cherished this marvellous trust in me, and now I recognize in her munificent legacy your own faith in me, for such was her confidence in you that I feel sure she would not have thus willed, if you had not fully endorsed her wish. So to you, my dear friend, as to her, my unspeakable gratitude goes out. May I prove worthy the care and disposal of whatever shall come into my hands. Will you, as my friend and Mrs. Eddy's, ever feel free to suggest and advise me as to a wise use thereof? I am very glad it was your privilege to be with her through these years of her loneliness. I am pleased that you and Mr. Ransom propose to appropriate something to her faithful brother James, and most cheerfully do I put my name to the paper you enclose, with the fullest confidence that you would ask of me nothing but right and justice to all parties.

~ *Anthony*, 2:539.

60 ~ ECS AND SBA TO GEORGE F. HOAR

Tenafly N.J. Jan 12th [*1882*]

Hon George F. Hoar, Dear Sir,

Allow me as President of the National Woman Suffrage association, to express to you the gratitude I feel, for the important measure you have just carried through the Senate.[1]

I trust for your credit, as well as our own, the women of the country will prove themselves worthy of whatever rights may be accorded them. Very respectfully

~ *Elizabeth Cady Stanton Pres.*
~ *Susan B. Anthony Vice-Pres. at Large*

~ ECS ALS, George F. Hoar autograph collection, MHi.

1. With five minutes to spare in the morning hour on January 9, the Senate again took up Hoar's resolution for a committee and defeated Thomas Bayard's motion to refer it to the Judiciary Committee in another roll call vote. Time ran out while Benjamin Hill of Georgia spoke against creating any new committees, but senators voted thirty-two to twenty to continue the discussion beyond the allotted time. At the end of Hill's speech, votes were at last cast on the resolution itself, and the Committee on Woman Suffrage was approved by a vote of thirty-five ayes and twenty-three nays. Members of the committee were named on January 11. The three Democrats were newcomers, elected to the Forty-seventh Congress: James Graham Fair (1831–1894) of Nevada, who served one term; James Zachariah George (1826–1897) of Mississippi, who served until his death; and Howell Edmunds Jackson (1832–1895) of Tennessee, who resigned from the Senate in 1886 to become a federal judge. The Republican members, known for their support of woman suffrage, were Henry William Blair (1834–1920) of New Hampshire, who succeeded Bainbridge Wadleigh in 1879; Henry Bowen Anthony (1815–1884) of Rhode Island, who entered the Senate in 1859; Thomas White Ferry (1827–1896) of Michigan, a

senator from 1871 to 1883; and Elbridge Gerry Lapham (1814–1890) of New York, who replaced Roscoe Conkling in 1881 and was named the committee's chairman. Both Anthony and Lapham were cousins of SBA. (*BDAC*; *Congressional Record*, 47th Cong., 1st sess., 267–68, 348. See also *Papers* 2 & 3.)

61 ⤳ Executive Sessions of the National Woman Suffrage Association

[17 & 21 January 1882]

A business meeting of the officers, members and delegates, was held in the Riggs House parlors, January 17, at 2:30 P.M.

Owing to the illness of May Wright Sewall, Chairman of the Executive Committee, rendering her unable to preside, Matilda Joslyn Gage, was appointed by Elizabeth Cady Stanton, President of the Association, to take the chair.

Discussion followed, as to work for the Senate Committee on woman suffrage. That no territory should be admitted as a State unless suffrage to woman be granted by it.[1]

Mrs. Stanton, President of the Association, proposed that each member of the association send petition to the Senate Committee for the removal of political disability.[2]

Advisability of sending out petitions for the Sixteenth Amendment, considered.

Lillie Devereux Blake stated that the whole New York delegation was in favor of woman suffrage, save one, who was opposed to it, but would vote for a committee in the House to consider the question.[3]

May Wright Sewall had written personal letters to every Member, Senator, and had received forty-five replies from members who would vote for suffrage, and thirty-six replies which were favorable.

One man was pledged to move for a Standing Committee on the Sixteenth Amendment. Mr. White,[4] of Kentucky, had made such a motion, which was referred to the Committee on Rules.

A resolution was offered and passed, that a letter, signed by the Executive Officers and Executive Committee of the N.W.S.A., be sent to the Committee on Rules of the House of Representatives, urging immediate action upon Mr. White's resolution, recommending a standing committee upon the rights of women in the House.

A resolution was offered and passed, instructing the delegates present to ascertain the status of the members of the House of Representatives, upon the question of woman suffrage. How many favor their enfranchisement, and who favor appointing a committee to consider the rights of women, so there may be a consideration of the question both by the House and Senate. The result to be reported at the Executive Session the following Saturday. The delegates were then apportioned States, whose Representatives they were to call upon for this purpose.

Ellen M. O'Connor[5] nominated Elizabeth Cady Stanton and Matilda Joslyn Gage, Committee on Resolutions, to be presented and discussed at the convention.

ELECTED ACCORDINGLY.

Susan B. Anthony, Isabella Beecher Hooker and Harriet Robinson, were elected as a Committee on the Associated and City Press.

Jane H. Spofford, Rachel G. Foster and Mrs. Rogers,[6] were elected committee to take charge of the platform and hall during the convention.

Rachel G. Foster, Helen M. Loder,[7] Harriette R. Shattuck and Ellen H. Sheldon,[8] were appointed a Committee on Finance and Memberships.

Matilda Joslyn Gage presented her bill for work done the Association, publishing Treasurer's report, list of officers, printing tracts, &c., in the *National Citizen*, $168.

May Wright Sewall moved that the bill be placed before the usual officers, who act upon bills for the Association for their consideration and action. Passed.

Susan B. Anthony spoke upon the necessity of the Association having a paper, and after some discussion of this question, the meeting adjourned.

[21 January 1882]

An executive session of the Executive Committee and Executive Officers of the Association, was held at the Riggs House, January 21, at 10 o'clock A.M., May Wright Sewall, Chairman of the Executive Committee, in the chair.

Roll of officers called.

Harriet Robinson, of Massachusetts, offered a resolution, extending the time given to the members of the Association, to ascertain the standing of the Representatives in Congress upon the question of granting suffrage to woman, and the appointment of a committee to consider the question of woman's enfranchisement. Passed. Reports to be made in writing to May Wright Sewall, Chairman of the Executive Committee.

Susan B. Anthony offered a resolution in relation to having a report of the convention printed.

A resolution was passed, that a full report should be printed in Helen M. Gougar's[9] paper, "*Our Herald*," published in Lafayette, Ind., and a list of the subscribers for the *National Citizen* be given her for its circulation.[10]

Miss Anthony moved that the usual May anniversary meeting of the Association be omitted this year. Passed.

It was moved and passed that the next convention of the Association be held in September, 1882.

It was moved and passed that the present officers of the Association hold over their positions until the convention in September.

A resolution was offered and passed, that a special committee be appointed to work with the Senate Committee on the rights of women, and the House Committee, when appointed, Jane H. Spofford to be Chairman of the committee, and, with the aid of the Chairman of the Executive Committee, to select other ladies to serve with her, said committee not to entail any expense upon the Association.

A resolution was offered and passed, that general agents be appointed to attend to the work for woman suffrage in the States where constitutional amendments are pending. Clara Bewick Colby, appointed for Nebraska;[11] May Wright Sewall, Indiana;[12] Abigail Scott Duniway,[13] for Oregon.

A resolution was passed, appointing Florence Kelley,[14] of Philadelphia, Pa., Assistant Corresponding Secretary of the Association to aid Rachel G. Foster in her work.

A resolution was passed, that the nomination of a standing committee of the Association, on the nomination of officers, be left in the hands of the Executive Committee, to nominate and arrange a list of officers for action at the meeting in September. One of the Secretaries to be on the committee.

The meeting of the Association adjourned to hold a convention in Philadelphia, Pa., the following week.[15]

⤶ *Ellen H. Sheldon,*
Recording Secretary
National Woman Suffrage Association. Washington, D.C.

A letter just received from Mrs. Gage says: "I take pleasure in presenting the amount due me, $168, to the Association." E. H. S.

⤶ *Our Herald*, n.d., SBA scrapbook 9, Rare Books, DLC.

1. Eight territories awaited statehood: Arizona, Dakota, Idaho, Montana, New Mexico, Utah, Washington, and Wyoming.

2. Individual petitions to Congress requesting the removal of "political disabilities" imposed by state law had been a tactic of the National association since 1877, when Lillie Blake and Matilda Gage started the practice. Woman suffragists took as their model the petitions submitted to Congress for the restoration of rights to rebels after the Civil War. See *Papers*, 3:344n, 375–76, 410, 411, 514.

3. When the House of Representatives voted to create a Committee on Woman Suffrage on 25 February 1882, seventeen of New York's thirty-three representatives voted aye, including five Democrats. However, sixteen members did not vote. In the earlier vote in the Senate, Warner Miller was reported absent, and Elbridge Lapham voted aye. (*Congressional Record*, 47th Cong., 1st sess., 9 January 1882, p. 268, and 25 February 1882, p. 1448.)

4. John Daugherty White (1849–1920), Republican of Kentucky, served in the House of Representatives from 1875 to 1877 and again, after an unsuccessful bid for the Senate, from 1881 to 1885. White did not act alone to gain a committee on suffrage. William D. Kelley of Philadelphia introduced a resolution for a committee on 16 December 1881, and it was referred to the Committee on Rules. White asked the House to consider the resolution on December 21, but Kelley, among others, objected on the grounds that the earlier measure had been referred to committee. (*BDAC*; *Congressional Record*, 47th Cong., 1st sess., 175, 239.)

5. Ellen M. Tarr O'Connor (1830–1913), a sister of Mary Jane Tarr Channing and a close friend of Walt Whitman, was affiliated with the Myrtilla Miner school in Washington. Befriended as a young woman by Paulina Davis, she took part in the New England woman's rights conventions of 1854 and 1855, before her marriage to William Douglas O'Connor. The couple settled in Washington in 1861, and Nelly, as she was known, was a founding member of the Universal Franchise Association in 1867. Active in the local suffrage

movement, she and her daughter attended the annual conventions of the National Woman Suffrage Association. After the death of her husband in 1889, she returned to Rhode Island and married Albert Calder. (Florence Bernstein Freedman, *William Douglas O'Connor: Walt Whitman's Chosen Knight* [Athens, Ohio, 1985], passim; *History*, 1:255, 3:809n.)

6. Caroline Gilkey Rogers (c. 1837–1899) moved from Boston to Lansingburgh, New York, about 1881, probably at the time she married E. F. Rogers, a widower who operated a large custom laundry in Troy. Through the 1880s, she was a key figure in the New York State Woman Suffrage Association, organizing a local society, managing the campaign to elect a woman to the local school board, lobbying the legislature, and addressing most of the state meetings. The National association was quick to recognize her speaking talents. She spoke during the New England tour of 1881, and a year later, she made her first of many appearances at the Washington convention. (*Woman's Journal*, 25 November 1899; *Albany Argus*, 12 March 1884, in SBA scrapbook 10, Rare Books, DLC; *History*, 3:197n, 222n, 258n, 334n, 431n, 437n, 442, 942, 957, 4:19, 38–39, 57, 118, 839, 840, 847–48, 853–54, 855, 939; Arthur James Weise, *Troy's One Hundred Years, 1789–1889* [Troy, N.Y., 1891], 424; Federal Census, New York, 1880.)

7. Helen M. Loder (c. 1833–?) served on the executive committee of the National association from 1878 to 1882, and she frequently represented the New York State Woman Suffrage Association at meetings. She lived in Poughkeepsie with her husband, Frank W. Loder, described as a railroad employee, and several young children. In 1879, she joined the campaign to defeat New York's Governor Lucius Robinson, and the state association named her secretary in 1882, agreeing to pay her for her services. (Federal Census, 1880; *History*, 3:117n, 422n, 4:24, 846n; *Papers*, 3:581; 27 May 1882, Minute Book 1, New York [City & State] Woman Suffrage Papers, NNC.)

8. Ellen Harriet Sheldon (1841–1890), a clerk in the War Department in Washington, had been active in suffrage societies since at least 1874. She also studied medicine at Howard University from 1879 to 1884. (Gloria Moldow, *Women Doctors in Gilded-Age Washington: Race, Gender, and Professionalization* [Urbana, Ill., 1987], 19, 24, 139; *Register of Federal Officers*, 1873, 1876, 1878; Daniel Smith Lamb, comp., *Howard University Medical Department, Washington, D.C.: A Historical, Biographical, and Statistical Souvenir* [Washington, D.C., 1900], with assistance of Clifford L. Muse, Jr., Howard University. See also *Papers* 3.)

9. Helen Mar Jackson Gougar (1843–1907) of Indiana joined the temperance movement in the 1870s and there developed an interest in woman suffrage. She represented Indiana at the National association's mass meeting in Chicago during the Republican National Convention of 1880, and she became increasingly involved in state suffrage activity. She also published *Our Herald* at Lafayette from August 1881 to January 1885, as a voice for both the temper-

ance and woman suffrage movements. The chance to publish the official report of the National's convention was an opportunity to attract readers nationwide. (*NAW*; *ANB*; Robert C. Kriebel, *Where the Saints Have Trod: The Life of Helen Gougar* [West Lafayette, Ind., 1985], 75–76, 98, 100.)

10. Matilda Gage halted the *National Citizen* with the issue of October 1881, explaining that she could not edit both the newspaper and the *History of Woman Suffrage* without risk of severe illness. In private she had talked about halting the paper for a year. With SBA no longer lecturing and selling subscriptions along the way, the *National Citizen* faced a drop in income of seven or eight hundred dollars per year. SBA searched for a new publisher for the paper when she learned about Gage's intentions, "for we of the N.W.S.A. must keep that little flag flying." No one came forward then, and Gage never resumed publication. (*NCBB*, October 1881; SBA to Rachel Foster, 30 October 1880, *Film*, 21:489–92.)

11. Only the decision made at this convention to reschedule the National's annual meeting to Omaha in September hints at undocumented decisions that took the National deeply into the campaign in Nebraska. Leaders in the state sought money, literature, and speakers from both national suffrage associations. The *Woman's Journal* helped to direct national attention and funds to the state, and the American Woman Suffrage Association honored Nebraska in October 1881 by naming state legislator and editor Erasmus Correll as president for the year leading up to the referendum. The American's agent, Margaret Campbell, arrived in the state in May 1882. Meanwhile, Harriet Brooks and Clara Colby reported on state organizing to the National association's meeting in May 1881, and in advance of the Washington convention, May Wright Sewall urged Colby, the National's acting vice president for Nebraska, to attend. Rachel Foster reached Nebraska in June 1882, after raising five thousand dollars to support the National's contributions to the state canvass. In the two months leading up to the election, both associations were represented by lecturers crisscrossing the state. (*Woman's Journal*, 3 December 1881, 7 January, 24 June 1882; SBA to E. M. Correll, 13 December 1881, SBA to Barbara B. Thompson, 3 January, 19 February 1882, and Nebraska accounts in *Report of the Sixteenth Annual Washington Convention, 1884*, pp. 145–46, 149–50, all in *Film* 22:172–73, 235–40, 383–89, 23:573ff.)

12. Suffragists in Indiana still awaited a second legislative vote in favor of the amendment. See above at 27 May 1881.

13. Abigail Jane Scott Duniway (1834–1915) of Portland, Oregon, was the preeminent advocate of woman suffrage in the Pacific Northwest from 1871 until her death. In addition to making frequent lecture tours and lobbying, she published the *New Northwest* from 1871 to 1887. (*NAW*; *ANB*.)

14. Florence Kelley (1859–1932), whose deep family roots in Philadelphia's reform circles led to her acquaintance with Rachel Foster, was at this time a senior at Cornell University and living in Washington to research her senior essay. (*NAW*; *ANB*.)

15. The National Woman Suffrage Association conducted a convention in Philadelphia from January 23 to 25. Many delegates to the Washington meeting stayed for this extra event. (*Film*, 22:304–15.)

62 ↝   RESOLUTIONS ADOPTED BY THE NATIONAL WOMAN SUFFRAGE ASSOCIATION

[20 January 1882]

Resolved, That one pre-eminent duty of the Forty-seventh Congress is to submit a proposition for a Sixteenth amendment to the National Constitution which shall prohibit the several States from disfranchising United States citizens on the ground of sex.

Resolved, That the recent appointment by the Senate of a standing committee on the "Rights and Disabilities of Women" is the first victorious gun for the National Suffrage Association after a persistent bombarding of Congress for the last sixteen years.

Resolved, That the thanks of this association are due to the Hon. George F. Hoar and the thirty-four brave men who followed his lead.

Resolved, That the first duty of this committee is to present a bill for the consideration of the Senate, which shall secure to the women of the Nation the right of self-government.

Resolved, That the second and important duty of this committee is the preparation of a bill prohibiting the admission to the Union of Dakota or any future State containing the invidious word "male" in its Constitution.[1]

Resolved, That a third though minor duty of this committee is the disinterring of all women's rights, petitions of whatever character, from the dust of the Capitol vaults, where they now lie buried, and that they be classified, placed upon record, and presented to Congress.

Resolved, That the recent arguments in the Senate by the Hon. Messrs. Morgan, Bayard, Beck and Vest[2] on the proposition presented by Senator Hoar for a standing committee "on the Rights and Disabilities of Women," are all based on the false idea of the "family unit" and not on the great American idea of individual rights.

Resolved, That as there are propositions now pending to strike the word "male" from the constitutions of Oregon, Nebraska and Indiana and thus secure to women equal political rights, it is the duty of the various suffrage associations to concentrate their efforts for the coming year in these several States.

Resolved, That Senator Morgan's bill to deprive the women of Utah of the right of suffrage because of their social institutions and religious faith originated and maintained by the men of the Territory,[3] is a travesty on common justice. While the wives do not have absolute possession of even one husband, though the husband has many wives, surely the men and not the women, if either, should be deprived of the suffrage for the existence of polygamy in the territory.

⌁ *Washington Post*, 21 January 1882, Scrapbook 52, Robinson-Shattuck Papers, MCR-S.

1. At the start of the first session of the Forty-seventh Congress in December 1881, a number of bills to grant statehood to Dakota Territory were introduced in the House and Senate and referred in each house to the Committee on Territories. See *Congressional Record*, 47th Cong., 1st sess., 6 December 1881, pp. 19–20, 21, 19 December 1881, p. 206. For background on this move to statehood, see Howard Roberts Lamar, *Dakota Territory, 1861–1889: A Study of Frontier Politics* (New Haven, Conn., 1956), and George W. Kingsbury, *History of Dakota Territory* (Chicago, 1915), vol. 2.

2. All Democrats and leading opponents of the Select Committee on Woman Suffrage, these were John Tyler Morgan (1824–1907) of Alabama, who served in the Senate from 1877 until his death; Thomas Francis Bayard (1828–1898) of Delaware, who succeeded his father as senator in 1869 and served until 1885; James Burnie Beck (1822–1890) of Kentucky, who served in the House of Representatives from 1867 until 1875 and in the Senate from 1877 until his death; and George Graham Vest (1830–1904) of Missouri, who served in the Senate from 1879 until his death. Although each of them emphasized different reasons for opposing woman suffrage, all of them shared Vest's view that "the legitimate and proper sphere of woman is the family circle as wife and mother and not as politician and voter." (*BDAC*; *Congressional Record*, 47th Cong., 1st sess., 14, 15, 16, 19, 20 December 1881, pp. 120, 137, 144–46, 188, 229–31.)

3. John Morgan, while mounting a spirited attack on the proposal for a select committee in December, announced his intention to offer a bill to repeal woman suffrage in Utah as the surest way to end Mormon polygamy. When he brought his bill forward on 11 January 1883, he asked that it be referred to the brand new select committee, whose members were named that day. It was a double-barreled insult: Morgan also opposed George Edmunds' pending bill to disenfranchise and remove from office all polygamous voters in Utah. Congress had the authority, he believed, to repeal such territorial legislation

as the act enfranchising women, but it lacked the power to write federal standards for voting, as the Edmunds bill proposed. (*Congressional Record*, 47th Cong., 1st sess., 20 December 1881, 11 January 1882, pp. 229–31, 348; *Resolution*, 11 January 1882, S. Misc. Doc. No. 34, 47th Cong., 1st sess., Serial 1993.)

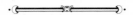

63 ⮞ EXECUTIVE SESSION OF THE NATIONAL WOMAN SUFFRAGE ASSOCIATION

Philadelphia, Jan. 25, 1882,—10:30 A.M.[1]

Present—Mrs. Stanton, Miss Anthony, Mesdames Saxon,[2] Brown, Sewall, Colby, Robinson, Shattuck, Rogers; Misses Adeline Thomson, Rachel Foster and Julia Foster. Mrs. May Wright Sewall, presiding.

Miss Anthony referred to Senator Blair, having told her to watch the Utah bill. Watch the admittance of new States.

Dacota sends forty men to speak before the committee on her claims to be admitted as a State.[3]

The women of Dacota should be told to petition, that when the territory is admitted as a State, it shall only be with the word male omitted from her constitution.

Sarah T. Barnes,[4] of Fargo, Dacota, was an officer of our list.

Small petitions were advisable, and with names of men known to the Congressmen.

Miss Anthony moved that the Chair of the Executive Committee and Corresponding Secretary confer and secure petitions from the Dacota women. Passed.

Mrs. Robinson, of Massachusetts, moved that the same committee be instructed to write to all Suffrage Associations, State and Local, asking that they officially petition Congress not to admit Dacota, with the word male in its constitution. Passed.

Miss Anthony moved that the Corresponding Secretary write to Mrs. Colby, of Nebraska, Mrs. Duniway, of Oregon, and other agents of the National Woman Suffrage Association recently elected, in order that there may be no misunderstanding, and explain how far in any way the National Woman Suffrage Association can be involved. Passed.

Mrs. M. McClellan Brown moved that the Corresponding Secretary write to Mesdames Harbert and Waite, of Chicago, instructing them to take into consideration the propriety of calling a National Woman Suffrage Convention in Chicago, immediately after the National Temperance Conference, to be held in Chicago, March 1 and 2.[5] Passed.

Mrs. Robinson, of Massachusetts, moved that when we meet in Washington next winter, we come together under the name of a Constitutional Congress, under the direction and auspices of the National Woman Suffrage Association. *Lost.*

Mrs. Harriette R. Shattuck moved that the Chair of the Executive Committee and President, consult previous to all conventions, and appoint *five* ladies, members of the Association, as a committee on the press, (they to appoint their chair,) and they are invariably to meet after appointment and attend to their work and then to report to the second executive meeting. Passed.

Mrs. Shattuck moved that *men* be invited to join this Association, and that the invitations to the executive sessions of members be such that men will know that they can attend and vote.[6] Passed.

Miss Rachel G. Foster moved that this motion be appended to the published report of the Washington Convention. Passed.

Miss Rachel Foster, of Pennsylvania, proposed that during each year twice the Chair of the Executive Committee and Corresponding Secretary, issue a circular letter, telling of work done and to be done—this to be sent to each member of the Association and they to be asked for a renewal of their membership and an expression of their opinion. Passed.

Mrs. M. McClellan Brown moved that we raise a committee to present to the next executive session to be held in Washington, 1883, an addition to the constitution providing for a satisfactory basis of representation in the National Woman Suffrage Association. Passed.

Committee appointed—Chairman, Mrs. M. McClellan Brown, Mrs. Harriette R. Shattuck and Miss Anthony.

Adjourned.

⇝ *J. L. Foster,*
Assistant Recording Secretary, N.W.S.A.

⇝ *Our Herald,* n.d., scrapbook 52, Robinson-Shattuck Papers, MCR-S.

1. The meeting was held at the home of Adeline Thomson, 114 North Eleventh Street in Philadelphia.

2. Elizabeth Lyle Saxon (1832–1915), a southern writer who settled in New Orleans after the war and helped to launch that city's suffrage movement, moved north late in 1879 and became a popular speaker for the National association. She was prominent in the National's efforts to influence the presidential campaign of 1880, and she accompanied SBA through New England in 1881. In 1882 she also worked as an organizer for the Woman's Christian Temperance Union. (*NCAB*, 16:207; *American Women*; Carmen Lindig, *The Path from the Parlor: Louisiana Women, 1879–1920* [Lafayette, La., 1986], 43–44. See also *Papers* 3.)

3. On the several delegations from Dakota Territory sent to Washington to lobby this winter, see Kingsbury, *History of Dakota Territory*, 2:1638–43. Petitions against Dakota statehood without woman suffrage are noted in *Congressional Record*, 47th Cong., 1st sess., 13 February 1882, p. 1076, 21 March 1882, p. 2140, 17 April 1882, p. 2934. None is from women in the territory.

4. Sarah Jane Allen Barnes (c. 1831–1906) may have no longer lived in Dakota Territory. The second wife of Alanson H. Barnes, she moved to Dakota when President Grant appointed her husband to the bench of the territorial court in 1873. President Hayes reappointed him in 1877. Soon after A. H. Barnes left the bench in 1881, the couple returned to Delavan, Wisconsin. Barnes was, however, named to lead a northern Dakota delegation to Washington in January 1882. (Judicial Conference of the United States. Bicentennial Committee, *Judges of the United States*, 2d ed. [Washington, D.C., 1983]; Federal Census, 1880; guide to the Lucien A. Barnes Family Papers, 1882–1955, Institute for Regional Studies, North Dakota State University; Wisconsin Death Index; Kingsbury, *History of Dakota Territory*, 2:1639.)

5. This conference of the National Prohibition Alliance was postponed until 23 August 1882. Then, at Chicago's Farwell Hall, delegates from sixteen states adopted a platform for a Prohibition Home Protection party. Most of the women in attendance came from the Woman's Christian Temperance Union, but Phoebe Couzins valiantly defended the positions of the National Woman Suffrage Association. Where the platform remanded woman suffrage to the states, she argued for a federal amendment, and she warned the delegates, "there never could be general prohibition unless the women were allowed to vote." (*Chicago Tribune*, 24, 25 August 1882; SBA to Elizabeth B. Harbert, 19 March 1882, *Film*, 22:430–33.)

6. Nothing in the National association's constitution prevented either the membership or the leadership of men, but unlike the American association, where men frequently held the office of president, no man held high office in the National association. Two days before this meeting, a friend of longstanding in Washington, Richard J. Hinton, published an editorial on the absence of men at the National's meetings. "It is somewhat singular," he wrote, "that the leaders of the woman's suffrage movement should not see the dangerous criticism that can be and is being made to a policy which deliberately excludes

men as advocates of the woman's cause." The presence of men, he reasoned, would temper the rhetorical assaults on the political rights of unworthy men and emphasize the human need for suffrage. (Constitution of the National Woman Suffrage Association, as amended in 1881, *Film*, 22:165; *Papers*, 2:242–43n; Washington *Sunday Gazette*, 23 January 1882, SBA scrapbook 9, Rare Books, DLC.)

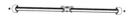

64 ❧ ECS to Olympia Brown

Tenafly Jan 29th [*1882*]

Dear Olympia

We are waiting for your Kansas contribution which we liked but as you said it must be revised before going into History we thought best to have you do it. If you have not time to polish it up a little send it back as it is & I will do what seems necessary.[1] We had two grand conventions of three days each in Washington & Philadelphia. They were successful every way, in numbers speeches & finances   We had two hearings before the or rather <u>our</u> Standing Committee.[2] The prospect is we shall have one in the House also soon   I presented each of the members a copy of our History before beginning my speech. We had two hours two consecutive days, & the southern democrats even were charmed with "our gentle voices & pursuasive arguments."

Send on your chapter on Women in the Ministry as soon as possible as everybody lags & the printers are calling for copy.[3] We have decided on three volumns as we have so much material   so much that must be preserved. Where is your photo for engraver? Be sure & make the artist do you justice, & give us your best expression, if it is possible to catch it. We wish posterity to know that we were a remarkably fine looking body of women!! Did we send you Rev William Henry Channing's review of Vol. 1?[4] We have had it struck off in tract form, it is so good & will send you if we have not already   We do so many things that we do not always know what we have done   Who is there in Wisconsin that would write up what has been done in that state? We are so impatient to finish the work that we want to get all the help on the several states we can. Susan & I are well & are now making up for loss time at the conventions. Another convention comes off at New York this week Wednesday & Thursday, under the auspices of the state society.[5] With kind regards for Mr Willis[6] & yourself & the children Sincerely yours

❧ *Elizabeth Cady Stanton.*

❧ ALS, Olympia Brown Papers, MCR-S.

1. Brown's contribution to the chapter on the Kansas amendment campaign of 1867, dated 16 March 1882, appears in *History*, 2:259–61.

2. For the hearings on 20 and 21 January, see *Film*, 22:292–94. ECS spoke on the second day.

3. The *History of Woman Suffrage* does not contain a chapter on women and the ministry. Referring to this chapter a year earlier, SBA suggested that Brown assemble information about each denomination's practices with respect to women's ordination. At that time SBA thought Matilda Gage's chapter on the church would not fit into volume one, and with a hint about tensions among the *History*'s editors, she promised Brown that hers would appear in volume two rather than Gage's. (SBA to O. Brown, 26 February 1881, *Film*, 21:853–56.)

4. William H. Channing reviewed the *History of Woman Suffrage* for the London *Enquirer*, 5 November 1881, and sent copies to ECS and SBA later that month. His lengthy essay struck SBA as "such a splendid encomium on the principles & the persons of our movement" that she arranged for its publication as a pamphlet, *The History of Woman Suffrage. Review by Rev. William Henry Channing* (1881). She included in it a brief review from Lydia Becker's *Women's Suffrage Journal* 12 [1 September 1881]: 139. (W. H. Channing to ECS, 23 November 1881, SBA to Harriet H. Robinson, 18 December 1881, *Film*, 22:146–49, 182–87.)

5. Many of the speakers at the meetings in Washington and Philadelphia proceeded to New York City for the annual meeting of the New York State Woman Suffrage Association on February 1 and 2. (*Film*, 22:352–56.)

6. John Henry Willis (1825–1893) married Olympia Brown in 1873. When the family moved to Wisconsin in 1878, he reestablished himself in business, eventually to become a partner in a publishing company. The Willis children were Henry Parker Willis (1874–1937), who became an economist, and Gwendolen Brown Willis (1876–1969), who taught classics. (*Portrait and Biographical Album of Racine and Kenosha Counties, Wisconsin* [Chicago, 1892], 702–3; *DAB*, s.v. "Willis, Henry Parker"; *Woman's Who's Who 1914*, s.v. "Willis, Gwendolen Brown"; Charlotte Coté, *Olympia Brown: The Battle for Equality* [Racine, Wis., 1988], 115, 152, 174.)

65 ~ ECS TO FREDERICK DOUGLASS

Tenafly N.J. Jan 29th [*1882*]

Dear Douglass

Is there any truth in the enclosed statement, if so, we wish to record it in History[1]   I was sorry that I could not see more of you in Washington.[2] We had a good convention of three days both in your City & at Phila. & two hearings before <u>our</u> Standing Committee, all well rounded out with receptions & dinners. I think we are making some progress, but it is a sore tax on human patience to be forty years going through this moral wilderness with no one to give us manna, & no pillar of light to lead the way, & no Moses in direct communication with the ruler of the universe   But all this could be endured if we only had a golden calf whose ears & tail & legs could be thrown into the United ↑states↓ mint by piecemeal to supply us with the sinews of war.[3] But alas on the distant horizon we see no coming calf, to say nothing of rich women who will share their abundance with us instead of giving bequests to Harvard Yale & Princeton, to educate theological strip- lings for the ministry. With kind regards for yourself & family[4] Sin- cerely yours

~ *Elizabeth Cady Stanton.*

~ ALS, Frederick Douglass Papers, DLC.

1. Enclosure missing. It was a draft of the chapter on Reconstruction in the second volume of the *History*. There, as published, the editors credited Anna Dickinson, Theodore Tilton, and Frederick Douglass with first proposing the Fifteenth Amendment, while they attended the Southern Loyalists' Conven- tion in Philadelphia in September 1866. (*History*, 2:327–32.)

2. Douglass occupied a seat on the stage with officers of the National association for a portion of the Washington convention. (*Film*, 22:280.)

3. From Exodus, ECS borrows the images of God feeding the Israelites with manna (Exod. 16:1–35) and lighting their way with a divine pillar of fire (13:21), and of Aaron melting jewelry to cast a statue of a golden calf (32:2–4). Unlike ECS, God and Moses regarded the golden calf as an undesirable reversion to pagan worship.

4. His family included his wife, Anna Murray Douglass (1813?–1882), who

died in August of this year after a stroke, and four children, all married with children of their own: Rosetta Douglass Sprague (1839–1906), Lewis Henry (1840–1908), Frederick, Jr. (1842–1892), and Charles Remond (1844–1920). (Rosetta Douglass Sprague, "Anna Murray-Douglass—My Mother As I Recall Her," *Journal of Negro History* 8 [January 1923]: 93–101; Douglass, *Papers*, 4:232–33n, 279n, 5:490n; William S. McFeely, *Frederick Douglass* [New York, 1991], passim.)

66 ❧ ECS to Frederic A. Hinckley

Tenafly N.J.   Jan 30th [*1882*]

My dear Mr Hinckley,

Can you & Mrs Chace pledge us to write up what has been done in Rhode Island. If you can do see her as soon as possible. Perhaps she would like the honor of writing the chapter under her own name with her engraving & thus be immortalized. We have written Mrs Chace several times but she does not answer.[1] Now we must know as soon as possible, for if she cannot do it we must secure some one else & who shall it be? If we cannot get a woman we must accept the services of a "white male" how humiliating!! Did you reach home in safety after the good services you did on our platform?[2] I hope our little manager Rachel Foster paid your expenses, after your good work of love. We wound up with a grand dinner at the elegant home of a Friend in Germantown who told me quite confidentially that henceforth our cause should be generously remember in his annual reform donations.[3] You may imagine our good Susan & myself buried in manuscripts. If we could only get some one in each state to write what has ↑been↓ done in their several localities we could see our way out of this labyrinth. Excuse this gouge on page two   I did not see it in beginning. With kind regards for Mrs Hinckley & yourself sincerely yours

❧ *Elizabeth Cady Stanton*

❧ ALS, coll. no. 325, Charles Roberts Autograph Letters Collection, PHC. Corner of page two cut away.

1. For an earlier invitation to Elizabeth Chace, see *Papers*, 3:482.
2. Hinckley delivered a speech entitled "Our Demand in the Light of

Evolution" at both the Washington and Philadelphia meetings. (*Film*, 22:262–79, 282–89, 304.)

   3. Robert Pearsall Smith (1827–1898) and his wife, Hannah Whitall Smith (1832–1911), hosted a luncheon at their house in Germantown for many of the speakers at the National's convention in Philadelphia. Robert Smith was subsequently the largest donor to the Nebraska amendment campaign. Hannah Smith, already known as an evangelist and an important figure in the temperance union, made her first speech on woman suffrage at the convention in Philadelphia. (*NAW* and *ANB*, s.v. "Smith, Hannah Whitall"; Barbara Strachey, *Remarkable Relations: The Story of the Pearsall Smith Family* [London, 1981], 54–57, 73; Meg A. Meneghel, "Becoming a 'Heretic': Hannah Whitall Smith, Quakerism, and the Nineteenth-Century Holiness Movement" [Ph.D. diss., Indiana University, 2000], 231–39; *Report of the Sixteenth Annual Washington Convention, 1884*, p. 145, *Film*, 23:573ff.)

67 ❧ ECS TO HARRIETTE ROBINSON SHATTUCK

[*Tenafly, 31 January 1882*]

   Yes! your proposition is excellent, charming, just the thing.[1] It would indeed make an interesting chapter & no doubt please our hostess as you could make a most lovely domestic picture, the dinner, the drive out   the generalship of Hannah Smith in marshalling us all, the experiences, so touching & pathetic, those not given must be written up & all filled out. It was indeed a day not soon to be forgotten. Susan wants your pretty face too in the History & so do I. I cannot tell you how thankful I feel for all you young women. I hope nothing will cool your enthusiasm until all is accomplished.

❧ AN on postal card, Scrapbook 104, Robinson-Shattuck Papers, MCR-S. Postmarked at Tenafly; addressed to Malden, Mass.

   1. ECS refers to the luncheon hosted by the Smiths in Germantown, noted above at January 30, and Harriette Shattuck's suggestion that she write about it. Hannah Smith had insisted that her guests not engage in private conversation but instead take turns relating the experiences that brought them to the cause of woman suffrage. Stanton was very moved by the event and had indicated an interest in writing up some of the stories she heard. Shattuck's unsigned description of the event is in *History*, 3:230–31. See also ECS to Harriet H. Robinson, 29 January 1882, *Film*, 22:330–34.

68 ❧ FREDERICK DOUGLASS TO ECS

Washington, D.C., Jan. 31, 1882.

Dear Mrs. Stanton:—. . . Mrs. Gage's version of the origin of the 15th Amendment is in substance true. To dear Anna E. Dickinson and brave Theodore Tilton[1] belongs the credit of forcing that amendment upon the Nation at the right moment and in the right way to make it successful. I have given Miss Dickinson the credit you award her in my "Life and Times," and have made myself one of your earliest converts in the same.[2] Very truly yours,

❧ *Fred'k. Douglass.*

❧ *History*, 2:328. Ellipses in original.

1. Theodore Tilton (1835–1907) was a well-respected editor, lecturer, and reformer and a close friend of ECS and SBA during and after the Civil War. His success came to a dramatic end when Henry Ward Beecher prevailed in the hearings and trials that investigated charges of Beecher's affair with Tilton's wife. He moved to Europe in 1883 and stayed until his death. (*ANB*. See also *Papers* 1–3.)

2. In *Life and Times of Frederick Douglass, Written by Himself* (1881), Douglass named Anna Dickinson and Theodore Tilton as "the chief speakers and advocates of suffrage" for the freedmen at the Southern Loyalists' Convention in Philadelphia in September 1866 (405). He also described an encounter with ECS, "when she was yet a young lady, and an earnest abolitionist," in which she made the case for woman suffrage with "those arguments which she has so often and effectively used since, and which no man has yet successfully refuted" (480–81).

69 ❧ SBA TO ELIZABETH BOYNTON HARBERT

Tenafly N.J. Feb. 4/82

My Dear Lizzie B. H.

What a shame that I didn't send you the Wash. Phila. & New York papers with reports of the Conventions— I was never so heedless before—it seems to me—they were each & all surpassingly excellent—

everybody saying it ↑of↓ each—it was better than any one ever held there before—

Do you ring out the <u>toc↑x↓sin</u>—(I cant spell it) to the Women of the Nation & especially of the Territory of Dacotah—to send in remonstrances to Congress against the Admission of Dacotah or any <u>new</u> state with the word <u>male</u> in its Constitution—& tell the women every where to write letters to their members of Congress—& especially to Mr <u>Burows</u>[1] of Mich—the Chair. of Ex. Com. of the House—asking that no ↑more↓ states shall be admitted <u>as male oligarchies</u>—

What a siege you have had with that pest—Scarlet Fever—but how thankful that no more of the darlings suffered from it—[2] I was very sorry not to have you with us all the rounds— <u>What we always lack</u> at our <u>Con's</u>—is good <u>enterprising</u> newspaper Correspondents with the ~~State~~ press of all the different states— We <u>lose vastly</u> from such lack too—

You—as Chairman of Press Com.[3] for N.W.S.A—did not report at last May meeting at Boston— Will you not work to do so at our next anniversary at Omaha—early in September— If you could get the entire number & names of papers—& ~~names~~ ↑editors↓—of <u>Women's columns</u>—& women's papers in the nation—what an encouragement it would be to each & all

Now you haven't sent us <u>the photograph</u> yet—that you want us to engrave from! Have you?—just the head shoulders—Cabinet size—and about <u>three quarters</u> profile—not a full front—nor yet an entire profile—about half way between—

Mrs Gougar & Mrs Colby & Mrs Sewall did the West splendid credit—

✒ S. B. A—

✒ ALS, Box 2, Elizabeth Harbert Collection, CSmH.

1. Julius Caesar Burrows (1837–1915), Republican of Michigan, chaired the House Committee on Territories. He first entered the House in 1873, lost his bid for reelection in 1874, returned in 1879, lost again in 1882, and returned once more to serve from 1885 to 1895, when he entered the Senate. (*BDAC*.)

2. The children were Arthur Boynton Harbert (1871–1900), Corinne Boynton Harbert (1873–1958), and Elizabeth Boynton Harbert (1875–1949). (Guide to William S. Harbert Papers, Indiana Historical Society; assistance from William P. Frank, the Huntington Library; on-line genealogy of the Soesbe family, in editor's files.)

3. For Harbert's appointment to this committee, see *Indianapolis Sentinel*, 26 May 1880, *Film*, 21:189.

70 ❧ ECS TO FREDERICK DOUGLASS

Tenafly N.J.   Feb 4th [*1882*]

My dear Friend   Frederick Douglass

If you have the facts & dates verified in your book just published, in regard to Anna Dickinson   Theodore Tilton & yourself in counsel please send me a copy. I believe I sent you a copy of our History   if not I will, & you must give me yours; a fair exchange   Yours is no doubt superior in interest, but mine will be in size, three volumns! & you shall have all for yours   Please turn the leaf down that I may find the fact at once. Do you remember where you three sat together   give me a little tableaux of the scene, as I wish to adorn our history with pleasing glimpses behind the scenes. Can you recall the conversation?

Tell me what you can as soon as possible as a chapter waits for this fact.[1] Poor Theodore & Anna have been so berated of late that I want to give them their full meed of praise.[2] With kind regards as ever yours sincerely

❧ *Elizabeth Cady Stanton.*

❧ ALS, Frederick Douglass Papers, DLC.

1. Frederick Douglass's reply to this letter and pages from his *Life and Times* were added to the chapter on Reconstruction, *History*, 2:328–32.

2. Dickinson's new career in the theater, as playwright and actress, was not a success, especially in the view of hostile critics who tracked her efforts in the New York press. (Giraud Chester, *Embattled Maiden: The Life of Anna Dickinson* [New York, 1951], 215–34.)

71 ⤳ SBA TO JULIUS C. BURROWS

[*Tenafly, before 15 February 1882*]

I see your committee is about to report in favor of the admission of Dakota, with a proviso that there shall be no discrimination against citizens on account of "race or color."[1] I beg you to add "sex." Won't you read this request to your committee and urge upon them the duty at this hour to establish equality of right for women in that new State? I wish it were possible for even the best of men to comprehend the humiliation, the degradation, which woman suffers because of her disfranchisement, because her judgment on all questions pertaining to the conditions of society is ignored—is not counted in the gathering up of public sentiment to crystallize into law.

↠ *New York Tribune*, 16 February 1882.

1. The *New York Tribune*, 13 February 1882, leaked the text of a new bill for Dakota statehood drawn up by the House Committee on Territories. Instructions within the bill required that the future state constitution "be republican in form, and make no distinction in civil or political rights on account of race or color, except Indians not taxed." According to the *Tribune* on February 16, Burrows received this letter from SBA on February 15, and later that day he received a protest on the same subject from the National Woman Suffrage Association. Without changing his text, Burrows introduced the bill on the floor of the House on February 16. (*New York Tribune*, 16 February 1882, *Film*, 22:377; 47th Cong., 1st sess., A Bill to Enable the People of the Territory of Dakota to Form a Constitution and State Government, H.R. 4456; *Congressional Record*, 47th Cong., 1st sess., 1220.)

72   SBA TO GEORGE F. HOAR

Tenafly New Jersey   Feb. 21, 1882

Dear Friend

I did not mean to leave Washington without seeing you and thanking you for your perseverance in securing the Committee on Woman Suffrage in the Senate— But failing in my intentions—then & there— I do my next best—write my gratitude—which is most sincerely yours— for every good word & work you have done for woman's enfranchisement

I received your note of a month ago, saying you had received the copy of our history of woman suffrage— I am hoping to see a report from our W.S. Committee in favor of a 16th am't proposition—and the Senate brought to a discussion & vote upon it— Mr Burrows—in his answer to my request that his Com. should add "or sex"—to their report on Dacota—says "the question is of such grave importance, that it should be submitted to <u>people</u> of the <u>territory</u>"—[1] Now that is just the tribunal, we who have studied this question for thirty years—wish to be rescued from!!— The men—the miners, the ranchmen, the tradesmen, the speculators, who make up the <u>electors</u>—<u>the people</u>—have never <u>thought</u> on <u>this</u> or any question of fundamental principle—and hence will surely vote <u>no</u>!— as a rule <u>no</u> <u>man</u>, or woman, believes in suffrage for women—except he has seriously studied the question— and hence all the submissions of W.S. to <u>the</u> people—have been failures—& will continue to be—until it is made a <u>party</u> <u>measure</u>—

Now—pardon me for this ↑long↓ statement—but it is to appeal to you to again aid us by insisting that Dacota shall make no distinction among her citizens on account of color, race, <u>or sex</u>— If the insistance should lose the admission this year, no harm would come of it—but a great deal of good—[2]

I have urged this upon our Com. but I want every friend of W.S. in the Senate to be on the watch to help in establishing this precedent— that no <u>more</u> <u>states</u> <u>shall</u> come into the Union, except on the basis of perfect equality of rights to women—civil & political   With great respect & many thanks

  Susan B. Anthony

⚮ ALS, George F. Hoar autograph collection, MHi.

1. The *New York Tribune*, 16 February 1882, reported nearly identical words in a paraphrase of Burrows' reply to SBA. It may be that he replied through the press rather than by letter and that SBA quotes the *Tribune*. (*Film*, 22:377.)

2. The bills for Dakota statehood did not come up for consideration during this session of Congress.

73 ⚮ Thomas B. Reed[1] to SBA

Washington, D.C., 25 February 1882.

My dear Madam:

I did not at once answer your letter of the 21st because I hoped to be able to send you the information which I now give you that the House to-day voted to give you the Select Committee asked for.[2]

I have delayed action because it seemed to me to be the better course having success in view   Very truly

⚮ *T B Reed*

⚮ ALS, on letterhead of House of Representatives, HM 10580, Ida Harper Collection, CSmH.

1. Thomas Brackett Reed (1839–1902), Republican of Maine, served in the House of Representatives from 1877 to 1899. In 1889 he was elected speaker of the House. (*BDAC*.)

2. On this date, Reed reported from the House Committee on Rules in favor of appointing nine members to a Select Committee on Woman Suffrage. When opponents of the measure maneuvered to prevent a vote on the resolution, Speaker Warren Keifer checked their moves, and the members agreed to establish the committee, by a vote of one hundred and fifteen ayes, eighty-four nays, and ninety-three not voting. Members of the new committee were named on March 13. (*Congressional Record*, 47th Cong., 1st sess., 1447–48, 1836.)

74 ❧ SBA TO HARRIET HANSON ROBINSON, WITH ENCLOSURE

[*Tenafly, c. 4 March 1882*][1]

Our advice to all the <u>state societies</u>—at the time of Lucy's secession—was to <u>vote themselves independent</u>—and leave themselves free to act with each & all societies—state or national— And wherever they voted themselves auxilliary to the American—it was done by a very <u>small vote</u>—& in nearly every instance by a trick—a <u>coup de tah</u> (how do you spell)—[2] But nobody outside of Lucy & Harry care a flip—or know any reason for the existence of the American— they all like good Conventions & speakers—& whoever gets up a Con. in Indiana, Nebraska—anywhere will get a cordial welcome—just the National did at Boston—the rank & file of New England people dont care nor know why nor wherefore— You see Mrs Stanton & I have <u>personally helped</u> the women all over the West—organize their societies— they know us & believe in us—and they wont wont be parties to any war on the National society—because they know we are of that—nor will they make war on the Woman's Journal people—or anybody who is for suffrage—because they are not so narrow & petty as some of the <u>Hubbites</u>— What they all want is to get suffrage— I note Lucys last Editorial[3]—their meetings have always kept clear of the <u>Free Love</u> &c— It is just the mean insinuating flings they have been guilty of putting in their paper & in their resolutions—all along the past fifteen years— the difference is—that then <u>you</u> were like the rest of the people—if you read them—you didn't know what or who they meant— <u>Now</u> all our friends in the west never dream Lucy writes that sentence <u>at</u> Stanton & Anthony & all who belong to the National—hence—in a great measure ↑all↓ such stuff of hers—is <u>wasted powder</u>— But keep at me—& make me explain to you all you wish—for now youre foot is in—you must be fortified at every point— You must not think I want to discourage you—not a bit of it—but you know a mother shrinks from seeing her children burned in the same place she was— Lovingly yours

❧ *Susan B. Anthony*

⤜ ALS incomplete, on NWSA letterhead for 1881–1882, Robinson-Shattuck Papers, MCR-S. In *Film* at May? 1882.

ENCLOSURE

AUXILLIARY SOCIETIES OF THE N.W.S.

The Universal Franchise Association—		Washington D.C.
" Citizens Suffrage Society—		Philadelphia—Penn
" Pittsburg " "		Pittsburg— "
" Vineland— "		~~New Jersey~~ ↑Vineland↓ N.J.
" New York State Society—		N.Y.
Connecticut		Ct—
" Rhode Island—	sends delegate & lacks only <u>one</u> <u>vote</u>—	R.I.
" Mass. N.W.S.A.		Boston—Mas
" Toledo & South Newberry—	The only two <u>live</u> societies in—	Ohio
" Indiana State Society—	sends delegates to N.W.S.A.	
The Equal Rights of Indianapolis—	& ever so many local societies—are Independent in name—↑but really auxilliary↓	Ind
Illinois ↑State↓	is auxilliar—[4]	Ill.
Kentucky—	ditto—The Clay Family[5] are it and they belong to us— were at Chicago mass meeting—& <u>Mary</u> B. Clay—tried to be at our late Wash Con—	
↑The↓ Michigan society	was always independent—but live locals all go with us Franklin Manistee, Grand Traverse Grand Rapids—&c &c—so we have Mich—	Mich—
Wisconsin State—	always steadfast to us—	Wis—
Minnesota—	ditto—loyal—	Minn
Nebraska—	as you heard Mrs Colby say <u>is</u> & feel that it is—but never voted it—	Neb—
Kansas—	↑Leavenworth—Fort Scott—↓ Lincoln Centre, Manhattan, Junction City—	Kan

Iowa—	formed independent—carried by one woman in 1879—& by one or two votes to American[6]—but has always sent delegates to National—	
St Louis N.W.S.	Mrs Minor[7] Pres. is ours—& all the live local societies—Oregon—Holt Co—Macon—&c—Springfield	Mo
Colorado—	Independent—but with us—	Col—
Nevada—	not much organized but locals with—	Nevada
California—	all with us—& legally auxilliary—	Cal
Oregon—	ditto—	Oregon
Washington Territory—	ditto	
Wyoming & Utah—	ditto—	
What there is in Tenn—& La—	ditto—Mrs Meriwether—Mrs Saxon	
And at Keene & Dover N.H.	the societies are with us	N.H.
Rockland, &		Maine

[*in margin of enclosure's first page*] When I get out of this History—I will try a race with anybody on which has the most auxilliaries if they want to.

⪻ AMs, on NWSA letterhead for 1881–1882, Robinson-Shattuck Papers, MCR-S.

1. Dated by reference to article in *Woman's Journal*. Although SBA writes below that Lucy Stone mentioned free love in connection with the National association, her description matches an editorial by Henry Blackwell in the issue of 4 March 1882.

2. Harriet Robinson and Harriette Shattuck brought the wrath of Lucy Stone upon themselves when they organized the National Woman Suffrage Association of Massachusetts in January 1882. Although T. W. Higginson advised her to ignore the new group, Stone chose to fight it. Contention over state auxiliaries to the American and National associations was one source of conflict. As SBA explained in a later letter, Stone waged "a new & ruthless war on us of the National—through Mrs Shattuck & the new society formed in Boston by her— Lucy claims that the National has no auxiliaries—that all the state societies belong to the American!!" In other phases of the conflict, editorials in the *Woman's Journal* questioned the need for a new suffrage society in the state, and privately, Stone attacked the character of ECS, SBA, and anyone associated with them. Her manuscript history of the split in 1869

and subsequent offenses of ECS and SBA bears the date of 4 February 1882: "It seemed," she concluded, "that if there was an indiscreet thing, these two ladies found and did it." The offending behaviors in that document—befriending George F. Train and Victoria Woodhull, endorsing free love, allowing polygamous Mormon women to speak at meetings, dallying with any political party willing to support suffrage, and more—found their way into letters to Robinson's allies. "[A]s men are known by the company they keep," she wrote Robinson's friend M. R. Brown, "so are societies, and those who compose them. I think your children would rather read in the history, that their mother did not cast in her lot with those who did use such methods." When she told friends and strangers that Robinson and her daughter should be asked at their meetings to denounce free love, Sidney Shattuck felt compelled to visit the offices of the *Woman's Journal* to avenge his wife's honor. (Bushman, *"Good Poor Man's Wife"*, 160–61, 169; L. Stone, statement about divisions, 4 February 1882, and T. W. Higginson to L. Stone, 18 February 1882, NAWSA Papers, DLC; *Woman's Journal*, 11, 25 February, 4 March 1882; L. Stone to M. R. Brown, 25 April 1882, and other copies of correspondence kept by H. H. Robinson, folder 59, Robinson-Shattuck Papers, MCR-S; SBA to H. H. Robinson, 21, 24 February 1882, SBA to Elizabeth B. Harbert, 23 May 1882, *Film*, 22:396–402, 406–9, 502–3.)

3. Arguing that the American's Massachusetts Woman Suffrage Association needed no competition in New England, Henry Blackwell wrote in the *Woman's Journal*, 4 March 1882: "The unfortunate affiliations with erratic and immoral movements which in some other States have retarded the cause, have never soiled the work in Massachusetts. No shadow or taint has been allowed to fall upon our banner. . . . The anti-man and free love crazes have never found foothold in Massachusetts woman suffrage meetings." One person who did not miss his meaning was the journalist Anne E. McDowell of Philadelphia. In her column in the Philadelphia *Sunday Republic*, she reprinted the offending paragraph, condemned Blackwell for "an exceeding Pharisaical manner," and named ECS and SBA as the targets against whom Blackwell and Lucy Stone aimed their "poisoned little arrows" in an attempt "to elevate their own labors in the opinion of the public by casting contumely on other workers." (*Sunday Republic*, 16 April 1882, in SBA scrapbook 9, Rare Books, DLC.)

4. Less certain of this judgment in May, SBA asked Elizabeth Harbert if the state society was "officially auxilliary to the National," and if not, "I wish you would vote it so!!" (SBA to E. B. Harbert, 23 May 1882.)

5. Women in the family of Cassius M. Clay, Kentucky's famous opponent of slavery, began to work for woman suffrage in 1879. Mary Jane Warfield Clay (1815–1900), Clay's ex-wife, hosted SBA on her farm in Kentucky. Her two younger daughters, Laura Clay (1849–1941) and Anne Warfield Clay (1859–1945), later Crenshaw, worked locally. Annie Clay was writing a woman suffrage column for the Lexington *Kentucky Gazette*. Mary Barr Clay (1839–

1924) attended the National association's meeting in St. Louis in 1879, while she lived in Kentucky. In 1880, she began to spend at least a part of each year in Ann Arbor, Michigan, where she assumed leadership in the state suffrage association. She also contributed the report on Kentucky to the *History of Woman Suffrage*. Clay's marriage to John Frank Herrick ended in divorce in 1872, and she resumed using her maiden name. Sarah Lewis Clay Bennett (1841–1935), known as Sallie, was the second of the Clay sisters and active with her older sister in the local and national suffrage movements. She lived in Richmond, Kentucky, and edited a suffrage column in the Richmond *Kentucky Register*. (*ANB*, s.v. "Clay, Cassius Marcellus"; *American Women*, s.v. "Clay, Mary Barr"; *History*, 3:818–22; Paul E. Fuller, *Laura Clay and the Woman's Rights Movement* [Lexington, Ky., 1975], 13–18, 22–23, 30; H. Edward Richardson, *Cassius Marcellus Clay: Firebrand of Freedom* [Lexington Ky., 1976], 31n, with assistance of the Filson Club, Lexington, Ky. See also *Papers*, 3:477–80.)

6. A sanitized report of this meeting of the Iowa association, at which it also proved difficult to elect new officers, was published in the *Woman's Journal*, 11 October 1879. The resolution of affiliation read: "*Whereas*, This Society is in unity with the methods of work of the American Woman Suffrage Association; has had its delegates received by that body at its various annual meetings, and has accepted the benefits accruing from working under its auspices: and

"*Whereas*, A large number of the members of this Society have believed and do believe that we are auxiliary to the same; therefore, to remove all doubt on the subject (if such doubt exists), the early records of our Society being lost,

"*Resolved*, That we declare ourselves auxiliary to said American Woman Suffrage Association."

7. Virginia Louisa Minor Minor (1824–1894) helped form the Woman Suffrage Association of Missouri in May 1867 and served as its first president. She resigned in 1871 to protest its decision to affiliate with the American Woman Suffrage Association, and in 1879, she became president of a branch of the National association in St. Louis. With her husband Francis Minor, she developed the legal argument in 1869 that the Constitution guaranteed women's right to vote, and she proceeded to test the law. In *Minor v. Happersett* (1875), the Supreme Court of the United States affirmed the right of states to bar citizens from voting. (*NAW*; *ANB*. See also *Papers* 2 & 3.)

75   SBA TO ELIZABETH BOYNTON HARBERT

Tenafly N.J. March 8/82

My Dear Lizzie B. H.

I hope all the darling "bairns" are well over all their ailments of the winter—

May Wright Sewalls chapter—Indiana—is now in printers hands— & after that is cast—yours—Illinois—shall go— Dont you want to add anything of this years work?— Mrs Stanton—asks <u>who</u> the <u>woman</u> was that turned the heads of the Illinois Con. Con.[1]

Have I written you & asked you to write out your reasons why we ~~ask~~ ↑go to↓ Congress, ~~to~~ instead of the State Legislatures— Mrs Hooker Mrs Gage—Mrs Stanton & myself have sent ours on to the— <u>our</u> Senate Com. at Washington and Mrs Sewall writes that she has hers in her <u>this</u> week's Times—but it hasn't arrived yet—[2] When you see hers—wont you write yours & put in Inter Ocean—unless hers <u>is</u> <u>yours</u>—& so publish it— That was the question the Com. asked us— "Why do you ask Congress? Why dont you go to your respective States?["] And that question we must, among us all, make as clear as the noon-day sun— For in its clear understanding lies our hope of getting our Committees in Congress to move— But if we don't make them see our reason before—the Nebraska election next November will give us ~~an~~ ↑another↓ exposition of the <u>imposibility</u> of getting suffrage by going to the popular vote of the states— For although everything promises so well in Nebraska <u>now</u>—with the editors, ministers, lawyers—&c—&c—the balance of voters that will decide the question against neither talk before audience or write in newspapers— I hope for Nebraska—but it is as they say—all against hope—not a single fact in history lies back of it—

I long to hear from you once more—That you are well & all of yours ditto— Lovingly yours

         Susan B. Anthony

P.S.—We are pushing our 2^d Vol.— Mrs Stanton's daughter Harriet is home from Paris for a few months—and at work on the history with us[3]—and Mrs Gage is hard at work on the Trials for Voting[4]—& Centennial Year—chapters—and we hope by the first of April to see our work well in the hands of the printers— Did I tell you that it has grown so immensely on our hands—that we have decided to make a 3^d Volume—putting our National work into Vol. 2 and the states, England & European—chapters into a 3^d Vol— That is—that is the way it looks as if we should be compelled to do to give the states the showing they deserve & must have at our hands— Our first Chapter—Women in the Civil War—covers 100 pages—of Vol. 2^d—& our National battle on constitutional grounds has been a grand one—& makes a thrilling history—all this is sub rosa—

[*in margin of first page*] So, if when you get proof of your chapter want to put in points—or add something at its close—you can do so—

⪦ ALS, Box 2, Elizabeth Harbert Collection, CSmH.

1. See *History*, 3:570–71 for this incident at Springfield, Illinois, in February 1870, when an unnamed woman from Michigan delivered two lectures against woman suffrage and caused delegates to the state constitutional convention to strike out a proposed woman suffrage amendment.

2. May Sewall edited a column in the *Indianapolis Times* from 1882 to 1885.

3. According to Harriot Stanton's later account, she received "a summons" late in the fall of 1881 to return home from Europe to "lend a hand . . . in completing the second volume of the *History of Woman Suffrage*. It was quite definitely stated that I would be expected by February 1882." Once home, she continued, she assumed sole responsibility for the volume's chapter on the American Woman Suffrage Association. Harriot described the summons as a disappointment and the work as "a dog's life." (Blatch and Lutz, *Challenging Years*, 61–63.)

4. "Trials and Decisions," *History*, 2:586–755, reviews the legal challenges made by women to establish their equal rights under the Fourteenth Amendment. Faced with the crush of material intended for the second volume, the editors removed some details of the cases and referred readers to the state chapters in the forthcoming, third volume. Later, the crush of material in that volume forced out the missing details entirely.

76 ❧ SBA TO RACHEL G. FOSTER

Tenafly N.J. April 5, 1882

Dear Rachel

How splendid— What a nice hit you did make on the Governor—[1] Yes—I think <u>our</u> <u>money</u> put into spreading that speech & discussion far better—than into <u>Bible</u> expositions— This will help even the most bigoted out of their opposition faster than <u>Bible</u> persuasions!! So I fully agree with you to go ahead on that line—& strike off enough to scatter all over Nebraska—just get the names of every Post Maste[r] in the state—& send a package to him or her—& have a whole sermon of what you want the P.M. to do with the contents—printed on the wrapper— By that stroke—you will send the N.W.S.A.—into every nook & cranny of Nebraska—and those <u>country</u> Post Masters will, as a <u>rule</u>—scatter the tracts as requested— I say go ahead & do it—

Did I tell you there was a <u>horrible</u> Son-in-law—trying to break dear Mrs Eddy's <u>Will</u>?[2]—that Ben. Butler is retained to fight him—that Mr Phillips writes there is no possibility of his—the son-in-law—succeeding in breaking it?—that he knows he cant—but that he hopes to extort money out of <u>Lucy & me</u>— Hence I have to wait & hope for the $4,000. even—that Mr P. wrote was coming immediately—

How I wish you were made of <u>iron</u>—so you couldn't tire out— I fear all the time—you will put on that <u>added ounce</u>—that breaks even the Camel's back— You understand <u>just</u> <u>how</u> to make agitation—& that is the <u>secret</u> of successful work— When will you be ready to go to Washington— I suppose the Com's will grant us the hearing at any time we shall decide upon— Lovingly—

❧ *S. B. A*

❧ ALS, on NWSA letterhead for 1881–1882, Anthony-Avery Papers, NRU. Letter in square brackets worn away at margin.

1. Governor John Wesley Hoyt of Wyoming Territory spoke on 3 April 1882 in a lecture series at Philadelphia's Association Hall organized by Rachel Foster. A strong believer in woman suffrage, Hoyt spoke often about its success in Wyoming, and he took part in the National association's meeting in

Philadelphia in January. As SBA advised in this letter, Foster published *Address of Gov. John W. Hoyt, of Wyoming Territory, upon Woman Suffrage in Wyoming: Delivered at Association Hall, Philadelphia, April 3, 1882* (1882), and distributed it in Nebraska. Later in the year, two other editions were published, by Fowler & Wells in New York and by the Central Committee of the National Society for Women's Suffrage in London. Hoyt (1831–1912) was appointed territorial governor of Wyoming by President Hayes in 1878. He and many residents of the territory sought his reappointment in 1882, and their efforts may account for his presence on the East Coast. President Arthur refused to reappoint him, and Hoyt left office in August 1882. (*History*, 3:474; *BDTerrGov*; *DAB*.)

2. When the Suffolk County Probate Court proved the will of Eliza Eddy on 23 January 1882, her son-in-law, Jerome Augustus Bacon, acting for his minor son, Francis, served notice that he would appeal the court's decision. On 21 February, he offered as reasons for an appeal that Eddy was not of sound mind when she wrote the will; that Chandler Ransom, Wendell Phillips, and "other persons confederating with them" unduly influenced Eddy; and that witnesses to the will did not sign in Eddy's presence. Bacon (1827–1904) married Eliza Merriam as his second of three wives. He lived in Bedford, Massachusetts, a town founded by members of his family and in which his father had been a major shoe manufacturer. Like other family members, he chose his own niche in manufacturing, eventually selecting paper as his specialty. To rationalize his acquisition of small companies in the business, he organized the Bacon Paper Company in 1881. (Suffolk County Probate Court Docket No. 66836, Archives, Supreme Judicial Court, Boston; Brown, *History of the Town of Bedford, Mass.*, 50–51, 59, and separately paginated genealogical and biographical section, 3–4; Federal Census, 1880.)

77 ❧ ECS TO ELIZABETH CADY STANTON, JR.[1]

New York[2] May 3rd [*1882*]

My precious baby,

You have no idea what a commotion the announcement that "Elizabeth Cady Stanton" had planted her little foot on French soil created in our household this morning. "Vive Elizabeth" rang from garret to celler. You have no idea my pretty one how we have longed & watched for your arrival, we have expected to hear of you every day for six weeks, & began to fear that you were a myth. But you have come at last & we are all so delighted that you belong to the superior sex. Your own

Victor Hugo[3] says this 19th century belongs to woman, now you must help to make the women grand & worthy of this glorious century.

> "I suppose
> "you have ten little fingers & toes,
> "two eyes a mouth, ears & a nose,
> "& spend most of your time in repose.[4]

In about six weeks I shall see you, so sleep, eat, & grow white & pretty as fast as possible, that you may fill my heart with joy   I shall use my influence with your mother to see that you have a free & happy life, that you are always tenderly treated   <u>Sub rosa</u>. I do not believe in the old fashioned doctrine "that children are to accept injustice & caprice from parents with pious resignation because forsooth they owe them the boon of existence. That children never can discharge the debt of gratitude they owe their parents." I think the duty is on the other side, that parents owe a debt to their children they never can pay for bringing them into a world of so much trial & discord. But we will talk these matters all over when we meet in good old Saxon. I am so glad you do not talk French, as I understand the baby language thoroughly & can sing you many songs from the opera of lullaby. I shall look at all the babies in the street now with new interest, & think of mine   Another little girl arrived in another branch of our family the 27th of April just one week before you   Zelma Wilkeson out in Washington Territory.[5] Perhaps sometime when you visit America you will meet her. We sent half a dozen dispatches about you this morning. Your uncle Daniel intends to send you an American carriage, so that you can ride all round the grounds at Jacournassy,[6] among the trees & flowers   How many things you will have to see & learn in this great world. I laugh to think how busy those little hands will be when you commence your investigations of all material things. I shall tell you of ~~all~~ the amusing things your Father did when he was a wee fellow. There will be no end to all the nice chats we shall have, when we once put our heads together. Good night my pretty one, with love [*in margins of first page*] & kisses from your happy

❧   grandmother.

You must keep this epistle for my little namesake until she can read it

❧ ALS, ECS Papers, DLC.

1. Elizabeth Cady Stanton, Jr., the daughter of Theodore and Marguerite Stanton, was born in Paris on this date. Known into adulthood as Lizette or Lisette, she married Pierre Auriol in 1904, gave birth to a daughter in 1905, and died after a long illness in 1909. (Genealogical notes of Robert and Francis Stanton, Mazamet, France; *Woman's Journal*, 29 February 1910.)

2. ECS was staying with her sister Tryphena Bayard in New York. After deciding to accompany Harriot Stanton to Europe, she and SBA left Tenafly about April 20, when tenants to whom ECS granted a three-year lease moved into the house. ECS sailed for Bordeaux on May 27. (SBA to Frederic A. Hinckley, 10 April 1882, *Film*, 22:469–70; *Eighty Years*, 336–38.)

3. Victor-Marie Hugo (1802–1885), French novelist and political writer. The quotation, used widely by American women in the nineteenth century, is a loose translation of a phrase in Hugo's funeral oration on 26 July 1853 for Louise Julien, who died in exile on the Isle of Jersey: "Le dix-huitième siècle a proclamé le droit de l'homme; le dix-neuvième proclamera le droit de la femme," in Victor Hugo, *Oeuvres politiques complètes. Oeuvres diverses*, ed. Francis Bouvet (Paris, 1964), 523–25.

4. ECS may be remembering the children's poem "Do You Guess It Is I?" by Eliza Lee Follen. The fourth stanza reads: "I have ten fingers too, / And just so many toes; / Two eyes to see through, / And but one little nose."

5. Zelma Wilkeson (1882–1967), later Lane, was the granddaughter of Catherine Cady Wilkeson and the daughter of Samuel Wilkeson III and his wife Isabel Tilton Evans Wilkeson. (Hunt, *Tacoma: Its History and Its Builders*, 1:241, 2:583–84; Federal Census, Tacoma, 1880; research provided by Patricia McAndrew, Bethlehem, Pa.)

6. Theodore Stanton and the Berry family lived at this country house in Tarn when not in Paris. ECS always gave the address as Jacournassy near Sorèze.

78 ⤚ SBA TO ELIZABETH BOYNTON HARBERT

39—West 26th street Millers Hotel[1]   New York May 10, 1882

Dear Mrs H.

Here I am at a hotel—Mrs Stanton at her sisters[2] & to sail the 27th— and we are in the last agonies of Vol. II. find that it must end at close of the first century 1875—and that our Vol. III. must open with the Centennial Celebration—& all the work from that to 1882—then will ↑the↓ Mass. Chap. Ct. & the other New England states—New York, Penn—Ohio, Ind. Mich. Ill. &c. &c— So push your chap through the

Inter Ocean as rapidly as possible & get it all O.K. and ready to send on to me—for there will be no "let up"—but Vol. III. will be pushed right on—even now the Centennial Chap. is in type—as we expected to get it into Vol. II.— Oh! to see the end of it all!! Then we cant have an <u>Index</u> to to ~~Vol. II & I~~ Vols. I. & II. until Vol. III. is done—so you see there is no escape for us—but to hurry that—[3]

———

I enclose the resolution presented in the Senate May 2, by the Chairman of our Com—[4] I have written every member of it—urging their favorable & immediate report to the Senate—and shall write Mr Camp[5]—the Chair of the House Com. urging him to push it—and I wish you could quietly inspire scores of women to write the different members of both the Committees—urging them to report a 16th am't proposition— Oh—how I long to be free to go at the work waiting to be done <u>now</u>—

S. B. A

P.S—I send <u>this</u> to you because your paper has the widest circulation— & May Wright & Mrs Gougar & all can copy from you—

ALS, on NWSA letterhead for 1881–1882, Box 2, Elizabeth Harbert Collection, CSmH.

1. This was the address of Eli Peck Miller's Home of Health Water-Cure, where SBA had stayed on earlier visits to New York. See *Papers*, 3:78.

2. Tryphena Cady Bayard (1804–1891), the eldest Cady daughter, lived at 8 West Fortieth Street with her husband, Edward Bayard. (Allen, *Descendants of Nicholas Cady*, 173; Gravestones, Johnstown, N.Y.; genealogical files, notes from Presbyterian Church Records, NJost; city directory, 1882.)

3. After this paragraph SBA drew two parallel lines on her page to indicate a change of topic.

4. Enclosure missing. It was Senate Resolution No. 60, introduced by Elbridge Lapham, for a constitutional amendment to guarantee that "[t]he right of citizens of the United States to vote shall not be denied or abridged by the United States or by any State on account of sex." The Senate referred it to the Committee on Woman Suffrage. (47th Cong., 1st sess., Joint Resolution, S.R. 60; *Congressional Record*, 47th Cong., 1st sess., 4508.)

5. John Henry Camp (1840–1892), a Republican from New York, served in the House of Representatives from 1879 to 1883. John White, for the Select Committee on Woman Suffrage, introduced a joint resolution for woman suffrage in the House on 10 July 1882. (*BDAC*; 47th Cong., 1st. sess., Joint Resolution, H.R. 255.)

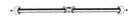

79 ⪼ ECS TO ELIZABETH CADY STANTON, JR.

Toulouse [*France*][1] June 16th [*1882*]

My dear Elizabeth,

I send you a little souvenir by your Father, a dozen silver spoons, given to me as a bride forty two years ago. As my initials are yours, they are marked ready for you to use when you begin housekeeping in the good time coming. All the good & great people who have enjoyed our hospitality have sipped their chocolate coffee & tea from these spoons. Your mother when she was in America, ate currants (of which she was very fond) & "Yankee ice cream" as she called it with these spoons. Thus many pleasant associations will always gather round them for you. More than all there will be the interesting fact than with them you can eat your own bread & milk & look at your little phiz in the convex surface. Bye & bye you will enjoy thinking of your grandmother's wedding day when all the shining silver presents were displayed to admiring eyes, & the little spoons in their midst. I hope I may live to welcome you to America on your wedding trip & show you the spot where your Father was born[2] & introduce you to all your aunts uncles who now rejoice so much in your advent. I hope you will please me as much as your dear Mother did, & be like her a good strong common sense woman   Well as your Father starts in a few hours I must do up the little spoons in a box for you & with much love & many kisses say good night   your affectionate grandmother

⪼ *Elizabeth Cady Stanton*

⪼ ALS, ECS Papers, DLC.

1. From Bordeaux ECS traveled by train to Toulouse, where she and Harriot moved into the Convent de la Sagesse while Harriot studied mathematics at the University of Toulouse and perfected her French at the convent. (*Eighty Years*, 338–43, 345–48; Ellen Carol DuBois, *Harriot Stanton Blatch and the Winning of Woman Suffrage* [New Haven, Conn., 1997], 51–52.)

2. Theodore Stanton was born in Seneca Falls, New York, on 10 February 1851.

80 ⚘ HENRY B. ANTHONY TO SBA

Washington June 19, '82.

My Dear Cousin,

I send you some copies of the "little" majority report of the Committee on Woman Suffrage.[1] I do not suppose you want any of the "old" minority reports. I don't know why it is that you women call every thing that you like <u>little</u> and everything that you dislike <u>old</u>. But so it is. These reports are franked in blank, and will pass through the mails to any person to whom you may choose to address them. Faithfully Yours,

⚘ *H B Anthony*

⚘ LS, on letterhead of Senate, HM 10583, Ida Harper Collection, CSmH.

1. Senate, Select Committee on Woman Suffrage, *Report*, 47th Cong., 1st sess., S. Rept. 686, Serial 2007. The Committee on Woman Suffrage reported on Senate Resolution No. 60 on June 5. The majority report, incorporating a history of the demand for woman suffrage gleaned from the *History of Woman Suffrage*, was signed by Elbridge Lapham, Thomas Ferry, and Henry Blair, with a separate statement by Henry Anthony, concurring with their recommendation that the amendment be sent to the states. In *Views of the Minority*, 47th Cong., 1st sess., S. Rept. 686, Pt. 2, Serial 2007, Senators J. Z. George, Howell Jackson, and James Fair insisted that federal action on a matter of the qualification of voters in the states would cause "a reversal of the theories on which our free institutions are based."

81 ⚘ ECS TO SBA

Jacournassy, near Sorrez, France, July 8, 1882.[1]

[D]earest beloved sister in the Lord:

This is a wild region and the scenery magnificent. The house is a new [on?]e, large and beautifully situated in full view of the Pyranees.

Professor Joly,[2] a man of letters, who has just retired from the

[To]ulouse University, has written a most glowing review of our History and [p]ublished it in three numbers of one of the liberal newspapers of that city. [Yo]u have no idea of his enthusiasm for our movement and for me as one of [i]ts representative. When I bade him good bye in the presence of the children, [he] asked if he might kiss me, which is quite French. Here even men kiss [ea]ch other. And so we kissed! Pray do not let this reach the ears of that [o]ld-fashioned friend of ours, for I suppose she would hold that even [a]n old man of seventy and a woman of sixty-seven should not look at each [o]ther with feelings of regard. So, Susan, let this indiscretion be known [to?] you alone. Lovingly,

❧ *Elizabeth Cady Stanton.*

❧ Typed transcript, ECS Papers, NjR. Square brackets surround letters obscured by binding.

1. ECS spent at least a month visiting Theodore Stanton and his family at their home, Jacournassy, near the town of Sorèze before returning to Toulouse on August 20. (*Eighty Years*, 343–45.)
2. Nicolas Joly (1812–1885), a medical doctor and experimental physiologist, became a professor at Toulouse University in 1873 and retired in 1878. He published frequently on many zoological and anthropological topics but was best known for his research on spontaneous generation. (Larousse, *Grand dictionnaire universel, Deuxième supplément*, 1461.)

82 ❧ ECS TO MARY POST HALLOWELL[1]

à Jacournassy, par Sorèze   Tarn France July 16th [*1882*]

My dear Mrs Hallowell,

The sudden death of your noble husband filled me with surprize & sadness. When I last saw him he looked so well & strong that I thought he had a long life before him. And if we measure time by good deeds he has had a long life of usefulness & heroism, in constant protest against the wrongs & oppressions of this generation. Though not a writer or speaker, he has stood like a granite pillar in all the reforms sustaining the weak & the weary, a sure support, ever in the in the right place, for all to lean upon. Mid the inevitable discord & friction in all organizations, he was ever a proud example of justice & charity doing his best to promote harmony & good feeling. His honest benevolent face, & his impurturbable cheerfulness & good will made the atmosphere of your home a haven of rest indeed. And so well my dear friend did you mirror the same virtues, that it was not easily seen who was the light, or who the reflection.

How many of us will remember with pleasure the generous hospitality ~~illegible~~ ↑of↓ William & Mary Hallowell & the long midnight talks we we all enjoyed so much, by that cosy fireside in the little cottage on the hill.[2] Though his lips are closed now, yet he still speaks to us by his calm consistent life, whose noble deeds & words, those who knew him best, will ever recall with satisfaction. However cheerful our views of death may be, the vacant places that none can fill, must make a sad void in our hearts, & deeply do I sympathize with you in your solitude. Having no assurance of what lies beyond our vision, what consolation can I offer? Only this, that the life just ended was given to a noble purpose, & the world is better for his labors. His efforts have added much to the sum of human happiness, & for him we have nothing to regret but his absence, for you time only can heal your wounds. How many have dropped out of your pleasant family circle since I visited you two years ago. Good Mr Willis[3] gone & Catharine, so kind & self sacrificing. I have the little red pin cushion she gave me at parting. I can recall her look of quiet satisfaction as I narrated the amusing incidents of my lecture trips, & how heartily your good William laughed. Well! we have much ~~in life~~ to laugh at but what a tragedy after all life is. I rejoice that you have our best beloved Susan, that practical saint with you now, with her great sympathetic heart. None so sweet & tender in such an hour as she. God bless her & you. Farewell I think I shall return in October, as I am quite homesick some times, & must help finish up our History. The stagnation & intellectual apathy of the vast majority of the people here, & the hopeless slavery of the working classes makes me almost despair for the freedom of mankind. The church & the army are a terrible tax on the people. The first thing that strikes an American in a foreign city is the soldiers at every turn & the priests in long black gowns & large black hats, & the reverence of the people for both. I rejoice every day that I was born in America. With us there is progress enterprize & hope for the uplifting of all. Remember me kindly to our friend Mrs Willis, for her too I would express warm sympathy. And I must not forget your excellent mother.[4] I never mention the name of Amy Post without a feeling of reverence. Tell her I am writing in full view of the Pyrenees fanned by the gentle breezes of the Mediterranean & should be glad to hear from you all, what you are doing, thinking, proposing. With sincere love yours ever

≈ *Elizabeth Cady Stanton*

≈ ALS, Mss. Collection, NRU.

1. Mary H. Post Hallowell (1823–1913), from an extended family of reformers in Rochester, took part in the woman's rights conventions of 1848 at Seneca Falls and Rochester. Like other women in her family, she attempted to vote in 1872, and she held office in the National Woman Suffrage Association in 1878. Her husband, William R. Hallowell (1816–1882), a dealer in wool and animal skins in Rochester, died on June 14. SBA called him "one of my dearest friends," and when word of his death reached her in Philadelphia, she rushed home to be with Mary Hallowell. (*Quaker Genealogy*, 3:434; William F. Peck, *History of Rochester and Monroe County, New York, from the Earliest Historical Times to the Beginning of 1907* [New York, 1908], 2:1243–44; research by Judith Wellman; SBA to Harriet H. Robinson, 19 June 1882, *Film*, 22:543–45. See also *Papers* 1–3.)

2. ECS apparently refers to the Hallowell's house at 51 Plymouth Avenue. (With the assistance of Nancy Martin, University of Rochester.)

3. Edmund P. Willis (1817–1882), a business partner in a drug company with Isaac Post, died on April 14. Catharine Willis (1822–1882), a sister of his, had lived with Edmund and his wife, Sarah L. Kirby Hallowell Willis (1818–1914), until her death on March 15. Sarah Willis attended the conventions at Seneca Falls and Rochester in 1848 and attempted to vote in 1872. At the time of SBA's trial in 1873, she helped to found the Women Taxpayers' Association to protest taxation without representation. (*Quaker Genealogy*, 3:483, 489, 507; Peck, *History of Rochester and Monroe County, N.Y.*, 2:1342; research by Judith Wellman; Federal Census, 1880.)

4. Amy Kirby Post (1802–1889), Mary Hallowell's stepmother and an early abolitionist and advocate of woman's rights, was at the center of reform in Rochester both before and after the war. Her husband, Isaac Post, died in 1872. (*NAW*; *ANB*. See also *Papers* 1–3.)

83 ⚙ ECS TO THE NATIONAL WOMAN SUFFRAGE ASSOCIATION

Toulouse, France, Sept. 1, 1882.[1]

To the National Woman Suffrage Association in convention assembled: Dear Friends—People never appreciate the magnitude and importance of any step in progress at the time it is taken, nor the full moral worth of those characters who inspire it, hence it will be in keeping with the whole history of reform from the beginning of woman's enfranchisement if in Nebraska it should to many minds seem puerile and premature, and its advocates fanatical and unreasonable. Nevertheless, the proposition speaks for itself. A constitutional amendment to crown one half the people of a great state with all their civil and political rights, is the most vital question the citizens of Nebraska have ever been called on to consider, and the fact cannot be gainsaid, that some of the purest and ablest women America can boast are now in the state advocating the measure.

For the last two months I have been assisting my son in the compilation of a work soon to be published in America, under the title "Woman in Europe," in which distinguished women in different nations have each contributed a sketch of the progress made in their condition in the various countries. One interesting and significant fact, as shown in this work is that in the very years *we* began to agitate the question of equal rights, there was a *simultaneous movement* by women for various privileges, industrial, social, educational, civil and political, throughout the civilized world.[2] And this without the slightest concert of action, or knowledge of each other's existence, showing that the time had come in the natural evolution of the species, in the order of human development, for woman to assert her rights and demand the recognition of the feminine element in all the vital interests of life.

To battle against the palpable fact in philosophy and the accumulated facts in achievement that can be seen on all sides in woman's work for the last forty years, from slavery to equality, is as vain as to battle against the law of gravitation.

We shall as surely reach the goal we proposed when we started, as that the rich prairies of Nebraska will ere long feed and educate millions of brave men and women, gathering there from every nation on the globe.

Every consideration for the improvement of your home life, for the morality of your towns and cities, for the elevation of your schools and colleges and for the loftiest motives of patriotism, should move you, men of Nebraska, to vote for this amendment. Galton in his great work on Heredity[3] says: "We are in crying want for a greater fund of ability in all stations in life, for neither the classes of statesmen, philosophers, artisans nor laborers, are up to the modern complexity of their several professions. An extended civilization like ours comprises more interests than the ordinary statesmen, or philosophers of our race are capable of dealing with, and it exacts more intelligent work than our ordinary artisans and laborers are capable of performing. Our race is overweighted and appears likely to be drudged into degeneracy by demands that exceed its powers. If its average ability were raised a grade or two, our new classes would conduct the complex affairs of state at home and abroad as easily as our best business men now do their own private trades and professions. The needs of centralization, communication and culture, call for more brains and mental stamina than the average of our race possess."

Does it need a prophet to tell us where to begin? Does not the physical and intellectual condition of the women of a nation decide capacity and power of the men? If we would give our sons the help and inspiration of women's thought and interest in the complex questions of our generation, we must first give her the power that political responsibility secures. With the ballot in her own right hand, she would feel a new sense of dignity and command among men a respect they have never felt before. Nebraska now has the opportunity of making this grand experiment, of securing justice, liberty, equality for the first time in the world's history, to woman, and through her education and enfranchisement, of lifting man to that higher plane of thought, where he may be able wisely to meet all the emergencies of the period in which he is now called on to act. Let every man in Nebraska now do his duty that when the sun goes down on the 8th of November, the glad news may be sent round the world, that at last one state in the American republic has fully accorded the sacred right of self government to all her citizens, black and white, men and women. With sincere hope for this victory, Cordially yours,

⚞ *Elizabeth Cady Stanton.*

⚞ *Omaha Republican,* 27 September 1882.

1. ECS, still president of the National Woman Suffrage Association, wrote this letter for its annual meeting that opened in Omaha on September 26. Read aloud at the opening session, the letter appeared in the newspaper the next day as a part of the proceedings.

2. Examples in the *Woman Question in Europe* include England, Germany, France, and Italy.

3. Francis Galton (1822–1911), a cousin of Charles Darwin and a scientist in his own right, founded the science of heredity. ECS shifts the order of sentences in a statement from Galton's *Hereditary Genius: An Inquiry into Its Laws and Consequences* (London, 1869), 345. Either ECS or a typesetter also dropped from the sentences the capital letters that indicated Galton's categories of human genius as deviations from an average established for each race. The letters "F" and "G" represented the two highest classes of genius. The original reads: "If its average ability were raised a grade or two, our new classes F and G would conduct the complex affairs of the state at home and abroad as easily as our present F and G, when in the position of country squires, are able to manage the affairs of their establishments and tenantry."

84 ⚞ SBA TO CLARINA HOWARD NICHOLS

[*En route to Omaha, Neb., after 2 September 1882*][1]

Only think, I shall not have a white-haired woman on the platform with me, and shall be alone there of all the pioneer workers. Always with the 'old guard' I had perfect confidence that the wise and right thing would be said. What a platform ours then was of self-reliant, strong women! I felt sure of you all, and since you earliest ones have not been with us, Mrs. Stanton's presence has ever made me feel that we should get the true and brave word spoken. Now that she is not to be there, I can not quite feel certain that our younger sisters will be equal to the emergency, yet they are each and all valiant, earnest and talented, and will soon be left to manage the ship without even me.

⚞ *Anthony,* 2:544.

1. Ida Harper, who published this letter without a date, described it as written en route to Nebraska. SBA left Rochester on September 2.

85 ⪼   REMARKS BY SBA TO THE AMERICAN WOMAN
SUFFRAGE ASSOCIATION

EDITORIAL NOTE: SBA arrived in Omaha, Nebraska, from Leavenworth, Kansas, on 12 September 1882, the opening day of the American Woman Suffrage Association's annual meeting in the Baptist Church. On the next day, Erasmus Correll, president of the association, invited SBA to open a session with a few remarks. According to the *Omaha Republican*, "[t]he clapping of hands showed how much Miss Anthony is reverenced and how popular she is among the people of America." (*Woman's Journal*, 23 September 1882.)

[13 September 1882]

Miss Anthony said: I feel at home on every woman suffrage platform and am most glad to speak to you today. This is the third campaign in which my friend Lucy Stone and myself have shared. In three different states, Michigan, Kansas and Colorado, has the question of woman suffrage been placed before the voters.[1] Though it failed in each state, yet the time is fast approaching when the question will meet success in all these states. We have come into the state to organize every city, town, hamlet and school district for the campaign. Every vicinity needs its missionary and its tracts. Speakers must be sent into every part of the state, and agitate, organize, enthuse, and the amendment *must* carry.[2] Perhaps one of the biggest straws which showed which way the political wind is blowing is that the Tippecanoe club of Indianapolis,[3] the oldest political club in the country, invited Miss E. Haggart[4] and other prominent woman suffragists[5] of Indiana to address them upon the subject. After listening to them Miss Anthony was also invited to speak and heartily endorsed her sentiments, Dr. R. T. Brown,[6] its president, saying that every member would vote in favor of woman suffrage, which amendment is now pending before Indiana. Our cause is surely gaining when Indiana, Oregon and Nebraska have all constitutional amendments pending, and the republicans of Iowa and Kansas have both endorsed the measure and want to see it submitted to the popular vote.[7] Surely, surely, we are of some importance when the republican party bids for us and our influence. Our star is in the ascendant. Nebraska must not throw away her chance to be the *first* state to adopt woman suffrage. If she does slight the honor, Kansas or Indiana will win it. Why should Nebraska not be first in suffrage, as she is ahead on nearly every other national issue? Miss Anthony's speech received most enthusiastic applause.

⇜ *Omaha Republican*, 14 September 1882, SBA scrapbook 9, Rare Books, DLC.

1. Voters in these three states defeated amendments to their state constitutions that would have enfranchised women—Kansas in 1867, Michigan in 1874, Colorado in 1877.

2. SBA, Lucy Stone, and Henry Blackwell were among the many speakers slated to canvass Nebraska through September and October in collaboration with the state suffrage association. According to the *Woman's Journal*, one hundred local groups existed in Nebraska by July 1882, and the number climbed to one hundred and fifty by September. In private, however, both Stone and Blackwell admitted that they saw little hope of success; "We would not have staid," Stone told her daughter, "if we had known how it was." (*Woman's Journal*, 15 July, 2 September 1882; H. B. Blackwell to Alice S. Blackwell, 24 September 1882, and L. Stone to A. S. Blackwell, 24 September 1882, in Leslie Wheeler, ed., *Loving Warriors: Selected Letters of Lucy Stone and Henry B. Blackwell, 1853–1893* [New York, 1981], 282–84.)

3. Stopping in Indianapolis on her way west, SBA attended a meeting of the Republican Tippecanoe Club on September 6. According to the press, May Sewall, not Mary Haggart, was the guest speaker at the meeting, and she introduced SBA to make a few remarks. The members expressed the hope in a resolution that they would "live a sufficient length of time to witness the day and hour when virtue, temperance and the right will be aided by female votes." (*Indianapolis Journal*, 7 September 1882, and *Indianapolis Sentinel*, 7 September 1882, not in *Film*.)

4. Mary E. Rothwell Haggart (1843–1904) had been active in Indiana's suffrage movement since 1869, and in 1878 and 1879, she published a weekly *Woman's Tribune* in Indianapolis. But it was her skill as a speaker that proved most valuable to the movement. During the 1880s, she held office in both the National and the American suffrage associations. She was present at the American's annual meeting. (*A Biographical History of Eminent and Self-Made Men of the State of Indiana* [Cincinnati, Ohio, 1880], vol. 1, 7th congressional district, pp. 66–68; *Woman's Journal*, 3 July 1880, 3 September 1904; *History*, 2:860, 3:142, 175, 535–44, 551, 4:409, 411, 422–23, 428; *Papers*, 3:473–77.)

5. The *Republican* reported this word as "suffrages."

6. Ryland Thomas Brown (1807–1890) of Indianapolis was credited by May Wright Sewall with "the longest record as an advocate of suffrage to be found in" Indiana. His decision in 1877 to resign from the faculty of the Indiana Medical College when the trustees decided to exclude women earned him additional fame. SBA refers to the campaign to elect legislators who would support the suffrage amendment in Indiana on its second vote. The state Republican party endorsed the amendment in August 1882, but the election turned on an amendment to prohibit the manufacture and sale of intoxicating liquor. Supported by many of the supporters of suffrage, including Helen Gougar, Mary Haggart, R. T. Brown, and the state Republicans, this second, unpopular amendment provided the Democratic party with a cause and financial backing to gain majorities in both houses of the legislature. In 1883, the Democratic leadership refused to vote on either the prohibition or the suffrage amendment. (Thompson, *Indiana Authors and Their Books*; *History*, 2:853, 3:541–44, 550; Sloan, "Some Aspects of Woman Suffrage," 92–99; Kettleborough, *Constitution Making in Indiana*, 2:207–9, 211–34.)

7. The Republican party in Kansas adopted as part of its platform in 1882 a pledge to ask the legislature "to submit such an amendment to the constitution of the State as will secure to women the right of suffrage." Republicans in Iowa had not endorsed woman suffrage for several years. SBA may recall the party's support in 1874. Republicans in Nebraska, however, did not endorse the amendment at their convention in September 1882. (*New York Tribune*, 11 August 1882; "Iowa Republican State Platforms from Birth of the Party, 1856 to 1890," with the assistance of Sharon Avery, State Historical Society of Iowa, Des Moines; McPherson, *Hand-Book of Politics for 1874*, 233; *Papers*, 3:146, 147n.)

86 ≽ WENDELL PHILLIPS TO SBA

Sept 23rd '82

Dear Susan

I have the great pleasure of telling you that the suit against the will of M[rs] Eddy is <u>withdrawn</u>.[1]

The contest might have delayed your reception of the money for years—& had you died ↑meanwhile↓ possibly Lucy w[d] have taken the whole, or your heirs, or Bacon, (the son in law,)— I have not the will by me now & cant say which w[d] have succeeded to you—

This result is mainly due to the Executor M[r] Ransom, who has left no stone unturned & exercised wonderful ingenuity in securing this

result—(tho we did employ Butler as a big dog & he no doubt frightened them—)

There will be about $20,000 coming to you to use as you deem best
for the W.R. cause—

Now the Executor is willing to anticipate matters if you wish it— He
is not <u>obliged</u> to pay for <u>more than a year</u> still— But he will pay <u>at once</u>
over to you, if you'll give him a bond to refund if any thing occurs
<u>previous to that time</u> This I advise you to do, as it will close up all
doubt & save all questions <u>in case of your death</u>, &c &c—↑you & your
heirs take & keep the money↓

Mr Ransom will probably come out to see you at Rochester & settle
with you personally if you are to be at home now or [*in margin of first
page*] soon— Yours with congratulations

➢ *Wendell Phillips*

➢ ALS, SBA Papers, DLC.

1. Phillips was premature in his expectation that the will could be settled
and the money paid to Lucy Stone and SBA. He rested his hopes on the
decision of the Supreme Judicial Court for Suffolk County on 20 September
1882 to approve the Probate Court's earlier decision allowing the will of Eliza
Eddy. A month later, Ransom presented to the court an inventory of Eddy's
real and personal estate valued at nearly $80,000. He had already conveyed to
Francis Bacon the Hollis Street property, worth $11,900, left him by his
grandmother. Still confident, Phillips wrote to Ransom in November 1882, "I
devoutly hope Bacon will be frightened off & give you no further trouble."
Then, on 9 December 1882, Jerome Bacon returned to the fray, filing a
complaint, with other executors of Lizzie Bacon's estate, against Ransom and
the principal heirs of Eliza Eddy's estate. In this complaint, he challenged the
gift to Stone and SBA as a violation of the court's decision about Francis
Jackson's will, holding that the cause of woman's rights was not a charity, and
he laid claim to one-third of Eddy's residual estate for the estate of her
daughter. (Suffolk County Probate Court, Docket No. 66836, vol. 541, p. 182;
Decree, Supreme Judicial Court for Suffolk County, Docket No. 430 in Equity, 20 September 1882; and Bacon et al. v. Ransom et al., Bill of Complaint,
Supreme Judicial Court for the Commonwealth of Massachusetts, Docket No.
324 in Equity; all three in Archives, Supreme Judicial Court, Boston; W.
Phillips to C. R. Ranson, 13 November 1882, SBA Papers, DLC.)

87 ❧ SBA TO RACHEL G. FOSTER

at Lincoln Depot—[*Neb., c. 30 September 1882*][1]

My Dear Rachel

There is a deep feeling against our National's <u>taking</u> ~~the~~ ↑my↓ Lincoln meeting the 4th wholly <u>out</u> of ↑the↓ <u>Local</u> <u>Society</u> ↑hands↓—giving
it no right to aid in getting it up—& no share in the receipts ~~of~~ ↑from↓
the reserved seats— Now I hope you will, at once, write Dr Painter[2] &
throw on their local society the responsibility of working up the audience—& tell her you will give her—the local society one half of the <u>net</u>
proceeds of the meeting— I have not interfered a lisp—only <u>listened</u>—
& told all that I was entirely in your hands to be done with as you
should decide— Still I do think it very poor ↑in↓ policy & principle for
us to give any city <u>no part</u> or <u>lot</u> in our meetings— And while to do so
here in Lincoln wont probably prevent my having an audience—it will
make all the people here feel <u>less interest</u> in my meeting—and most
decidedly cool toward me personally—and I had rather give them the
<u>whole</u> of the receipts than to have the feeling toward me thus chilled—
Still—as I have said I will try not to interfere with your plans—but it
will be hard work for me not to— I think the original proposition that
I made to Mrs Painter would be the "<u>fair play</u>" one— Lovingly—

❧ *S. B. A.*

❧ ALS, Anthony-Avery Papers, NRU.

1. This date is highly speculative. SBA began her canvass in Nebraska on
September 30, after the National association's rousing launch of the campaign
in Lincoln on September 28 and 29. Thereafter, like other speakers assisting
the state suffrage society, SBA followed a tight schedule of daily engagements
through November 6, the eve of the election. SBA caught the train from
Lincoln's elegant depot on this day, in order to head south to her engagements
along the Beatrice branch of the Burlington and Missouri River Railroad in
Crete (October 2), Wilber (the third), and Beatrice (the fourth). Meanwhile
Rachel Foster returned to Omaha, her base during the campaign. The letter's
content suggests also that it was written early in the canvass, before proce-
dures were fixed. However, SBA's reference to her lecture in Lincoln on the
fourth makes no sense: she had no lecture scheduled there in October on any

day. Her lecture in Beatrice on October 4 was announced as early as September 30. During her travels to keep her later appointments, SBA would likely have returned to the Lincoln depot between engagements on October 7 (Falls City) and 10 (Schuyler), and on or about October 12 (en route from Seward to Omaha). There is a chance that a lecture by SBA was once scheduled for November 4, but when that day came, she spoke in Tecumseh. (*Film*, 22:656–59; *Omaha Bee*, 30 September 1882.)

2. Hettie Kersey Painter (1820–1889) practiced medicine in Lincoln, where she also founded the Lincoln Infirmary and started a meeting of the Society of Friends. Born near Philadelphia, she married there in 1840, raised two sons, and studied at Penn Medical University. After her graduation in 1860, she became a battlefield doctor with the Fifth Army Corps, and at war's end, she worked in military hospitals in and near Washington, D.C., until 1868. Before moving to Lincoln, where her husband published a journal for farmers, Painter practiced in Cheyenne, Wyoming, and Salt Lake City, Utah, while living with her sons. (Harold J. Abrahams, *Extinct Medical Schools of Nineteenth-Century Philadelphia* [Philadelphia, 1966], 226; *History of the State of Nebraska*, 1075; *History*, 3:222n, 693; *Friends' Intelligencer* 48 [1889]: 521.)

88 ⁂ ELLEN WRIGHT GARRISON[1] TO SBA

Auburn N.Y. October 7th 1882—

Dear Susan:

It was very kind of you to send us your 2[d] Vol. & we keep it in a conspicuous place, upon our table— We were glad to receive your long letter, & much interested in your account of Lucy & H B B— Why do you care any more to be on close terms with Lucy?— Perhaps she will come around, of her own accord someday, & if not, I'm sure it needn't affect you—[2]

As to using my name, among the Vice Pres[ts]—You know Susan it isn't <u>my</u> name, neither is it my nature to do public work worthy of it— I wish I could—but I object to <u>loaning out</u> the name, when I am a mere figurehead myself— The name should represent the individual & I dont think it should be used for the sound, only— I am much better fitted to be Mrs. John Smith, than to bear the resplendent title that has fallen to my lot— I am just as much interested in the questions, in regard to which I take no public part, & have the success of The Cause as much at heart as if I were out in The Field, but I must keep in my corner, & raise up children, who perhaps will do better service for the world—

We are enjoying a delightful quiet visit here, but Auburn is greatly changed within 18 years— Does it seem as long as that, since you wrote your distinguished autograph, upon our Marriage Certificate?[3] The dear old house is not only wiped out, but every tree cut down, & the whole yard lowered several feet, making such an alteration in the place that there isn't the slightest suggestion of our house about it—

The people are changed, just as much— There really isn't a single family, except the Wises,[4] that I care to call upon— Still there is an atmosphere of home which belongs neither to people nor places, which I breathe in, here, & nowhere else, & so I like to come, occasionally— Tomorrow we return to business & duties & put idleness far away again— I hope next time you are in Boston, you will see our fast growing up family— Goodbye—with love Affy

～ *Ellen W. Garrison*

～ ALS, Garrison Papers, MNS-S.

1. Ellen Wright Garrison (1840–1931) wrote from the city where she grew up as the second daughter of Martha Coffin Wright and David Wright and where her father now lived with another daughter, Eliza Wright Osborne. Ellen and her husband, William Lloyd Garrison, Jr., (1838–1909), a business-man, lived near Boston. (Wright genealogical files, Garrison Papers, MNS-S; *New York Times*, 13 September 1909; Federal Census, Auburn, 1880. See also *Papers* 1–3.)

2. The Garrisons each answered SBA's now missing letter of September 17, sent from Omaha at the close of the American association's annual meeting, but neither of them recounted why SBA came into conflict with Lucy Stone. In his reply, enclosing a check to help with campaign expenses, William said he was "pained at your account of your meeting with Lucy Stone and shall take an early opportunity to ask her why she will not be reconciled." There is evidence that difficulties arose over combining the resources of two national associations during the Nebraska canvass. Stone took pains to explain to readers of the *Woman's Journal* that the American's speakers "put themselves at the disposal of the Nebraska Woman Suffrage Society" and worked "under the auspices of the State Association." She herself worked out of an office in Lincoln that she described as a joint headquarters of the state and American associations. Meanwhile, according to Stone, Rachel Foster worked alone in Omaha at the National's headquarters spending the National's funds on the National's speakers. While she thus signaled that funds raised by the Ameri-can would be kept separate, she misspoke about the Omaha office. It too was

a joint venture, managed by a committee of three people appointed by the state society and two named by the National association. (W. L. Garrison, Jr., to SBA, 7 October 1882, *Film*, 22:668–69; *Woman's Journal*, 8 April, 21 October, 2 December 1882; *Our Herald*, n.d., *Film*, 22:637–43; Unknown to Ada M. Bittenbender, 26 September 1882, scrapbook 4, Grace Julian Clarke Papers, Indiana Division, In.)

3. SBA attended Ellen's wedding on 14 September 1864. (*Anthony*, 1:241.)

4. This was probably William G. Wise (c. 1821–?) and his wife Anne. Wise was the treasurer of a woolen mill in Auburn, a friend of the Wrights, and a supporter of Auburn resident Harriet Tubman. (Federal Census, 1880; Jean M. Humez, *Harriet Tubman: The Life and the Life Stories* [Madison, Wis., 2003], 307–8, 373.)

89 ⇝ Debate by SBA in Omaha, Nebraska

EDITORIAL NOTE: Edward Rosewater, editor of the *Omaha Bee*, challenged SBA to a debate at the start of the campaign in Nebraska; he "had been around the platform all evening urging arrangements for a joint debate," SBA told the National association's annual meeting in September. After their debate, Rosewater complained that because SBA challenged him, he should have had the right of opening and closing the debate. "She was allowed to impose on the public as the challenged party," he wrote in the *Omaha Bee*, "although she was the challenger, and her demand was complied with although it gave her undue advantage." If he sounded like the loser, Lillie Blake had no doubt that SBA lost the contest: it "was not successful for our side," she wrote later. "Mr. Rosenwater [*sic*] was ready and unscrupulous in his statements, and Miss Anthony was never a quick debater. Besides, the audience was much more with him than with her." The event, in Boyd's Opera House, attracted an enormous crowd that "filled every seat, packed the aisles and occupied every inch of standing room. . . . [F]ully two thousand people were denied admission and returned home." Phoebe Couzins presided. SBA opened with her well-known lecture "Woman Wants Bread, Not the Ballot." Rosewater replied with a description of the inauguration of James Garfield and drew from it the lesson that the president's wife and mother "ranked higher in the estimation of mankind than any woman that would sit in the United States senate." From there he argued that suffrage was not an inherent right; that taxation was not a basis for participating in government, but simply a charge for state protection of property; that men in Nebraska represented women well as evidenced by the state's married women's property law and good wages for women. SBA had the right of rebuttal. (*Film*, 22:637–43; *Omaha Bee*, undated clipping, SBA scrapbook 9, Rare Books, DLC; Blake and Wallace, *Champion of Women*, 144.)

[13 October 1882]

In replying to Mr. Rosewater[1] Miss Anthony said: Mr. Rosewater has gone over the same grounds and the same objections that have been urged against the extension of the suffrage for the past thirty years. All these objections have been fully answered and it would be impossible for me to go over the ground again even in the briefest possible manner. I want to ask you right at the beginning, suppose all these difficulties do stand in the way of woman's enfranchisement, is it not woman's place in this world to do her duty to help to make the world better? I admit that to be loved and petted is a very good idea but we must remember that the majority of men are not of the kind that James A. Garfield was, about whom Mr. Rosewater has spoken so eloquently. We must re- member that the number of male criminals greatly exceeds those of female criminals in and out of prison, and the majority of the males have wives and children who have to suffer in consequence of the men's wrong doing. We are not speaking for women who have husbands like James A. Garfield nor for women who have good fathers, sons and brothers to protect them. We ask the ballot for those women who have bad husbands or no husbands at all. These are the women who need the power of protection in their own hands. The wheel of fortune turns very suddenly in this world, the rich of to-day may be the poor of to- morrow. The most fortunately situated woman to-day may to-morrow be left without husband or father and entirely dependent on the tender mercy of the world. If it is true that so many bad women escape from punishment that shows the necessity of having woman legislators, women as judges on the bench.[2] We do not want favoritism. What we want is justice. We do not ask that women who commit crimes shall go scot free. The rule is women are punished more surely and more truly for some offenses than men are. You know there are two moral codes, one code for man which allows not only freedom but license in what is called the pet vices, but there is another and a higher code for woman. She must not only be spotless but like Caesar's wife above suspicion.[3] Put the ballot in the hands of woman to-day and you will see that the laws will be executed, and the woman who violates them will be punished equally with the man. She will hold man to as high a moral standard as he now holds her.

I will tell you an incident about Wyoming. Not long ago I took up The New York World and saw a letter from Wyoming in which the writer said not a decent man in that territory but what wanted the ballot taken away from the women.[4] Now I have been in Wyoming and I have seen the women vote and sit in the jury box. They were the very best women. Well, I wrote Mr. Hayford,[5] the editor of a Laramie paper, asking him to tell me who wrote that letter. Mr. Hayford in reply said so far from being true it is quite the reverse, every decent man did wish the women to have the suffrage, and the man who wrote that letter had dragged the ball and chains through the streets of Cheyenne by a verdict from a jury which was composed of one-half women. I can assure you nobody is sick of suffrage in Wyoming Territory but bad men.

In the Colorado campaign in 1877 Miss Hindman[6] spent months and months in the campaign there and she got signatures of best representative men and women[7] to a paper saying that woman suffrage was a success. There were the names of ministers, lawyers, merchants and the best business men. It is false, and the assertion of the enemy, that only bad women voted in Wyoming. There was just as large a ratio of women voted as men.

I was over in your sister state in Iowa in 1871. I spoke in Sioux City.[8] On my arrival in the town just before the lecture I was told that on the evening previous the good wives of the city had turned out en masse and set fire to a building that contained a dozen of the demi monde that their husbands had brought up from St. Louis. In my lecture I expanded upon this incident. Six years afterwards I was in the city of Sioux and happening to take up a paper the very first article I struck was a complaint against one Mme. Shaw, for keeping a house of ill fame. That grand jury was out thirteen hours and a half and when they came in the verdict was no cause for complaint to bring in a bill of indictment. And this Mme. Shaw was the very woman whose house was burned down by the good wives of that city six years before. Women of Nebraska, do you think if those good wives had been on that grand jury that such a verdict of no cause could have been brought in?

Now, I want women on the juries, and until the women are willing to leave their sofas, and take off their kid gloves and come down to every-day life to make the world better, there is very little hope for mankind. No, my friends, we do not shirk any duty in life. I want women judges on the bench and women as lawyers. Wherever woman goes as a criminal, as a violator of the law, or as an idiot and an unfortunate; wherever a woman goes to be cared for, there I want the best women to go to protect them. Yes, I want women on the police force. (Loud laughter.) In the city of New York poor, unfortunate, drunken and degraded women are arrested by the police and dragged to the station house, where there are no women to protect them, but all are men, and not always men of the highest morals either. It is horrible to put a woman into a jail where she has no women to protect her. It is a horrible thing to put a woman in a state prison or lunatic asylum. I say it is horrible to place them among men alone with no good, brave women to care for them.

Now, about this everlasting objection that women cannot fight in defense of their country.[9]

At the constitutional convention of which Horace Greeley[10] was a member and chairman of the committee on suffrage, at the close of Mrs. Stanton's address, Mr. Greeley arose and said, "Miss Anthony, the ballot and bullet go together. If you have the vote, are you ready to fight?" I said, "Yes, Mr. Greeley, exactly as you fought in the late rebellion, at the point of the goose quill," and as Horace Greeley and possibly Mr. Rosewater fought.

There were plenty of women who paid money for substitutes in the war. They also played a prominent part in the soldiers aid societies. They show a deal of heroism in relieving the boys in blue. Not only that there were hundreds and thousands of women who marched in the rear of the army and who went about picking up the wounded and minister-ing to the dying, and writing letters home to the mothers and friends. And I insist that women aided the war as much in mitigating its horrors as the men did in firing bullets. It is not fair to say women are not ready to fight. They are the best fighters in the world. (Laughter.) Over five hundred women enlisted in the army of the rebellion,[11] but in order to do so they had to disguise themselves in men's clothes, and many of them fought on the field, and they fought as valiantly as the men, but the moment their sex was discovered they were dismissed from the service, and shame be it to the American government they never received a dollar's pay. It is very fine to say the women are not willing and ready to fight when the moment they try to enlist in the army they are punished for so doing. Not only did the government refuse to pay those women who fought but the women who followed in the wake of the army and did such good service got nothing but their transportation. The services rendered by Mother Bickerdyke[12] were never rewarded. She was the woman, you remember, who followed Gen. Sherman[13] in his march to the sea. The last I heard of her she was going out washing by the day. Shame on the ingratitude of the republican party to treat these women in this manner, simply because they are disfranchised and have no political power. Besides all men do not fight. Men over forty-five are not required to enlist in the army while they can vote. All can vote except idiots, lunatics, criminals and women. No woman's opinion is counted in the gathering of public sentiment to crystalize it into law. Don't you know it is a badge of disgrace for a man to be disfranchised. While there are plenty of men, from a workingman to a congressman, who will sell their vote for a dollar, for five dollars, or for five thousand dollars. Where is the man under the American· flag, native or foreign, so low that he would sell his right to vote. That man would be pronounced worse than an idiot. You remember in the rebellion the only punishment meted out to those that laid the knife at the throat of the nation was disfranchisement.[14] The punishment was considered so fearful that congress stood ready to grant the removal of the political disabilities of all who asked it. In New York men who served five or seven years in prison are henceforth disfranchised. But if the prisoner has a single friend he will petition the governor and get that sentence commuted, in order that when he comes out he will not have the mark of Cain[15] branded on him, and the mark of Cain on the forehead of any man is disfranchisement. Do you believe that while disfranchisement is such a terrible disgrace, and such a terrible curse to man, that we women can possibly be persuaded that it is of no value to us? I believe in the principle of liberty for all. (Loud applause.)

Miss Couzins at this juncture rose and reminded Miss Anthony that Mr. Rosewater some years ago, in his paper, had called the men who were employed by the Union Pacific railroad the brass- collared brigade.[16] Now he champions the greatest monopoly on earth. (Laughter and applause.)

Miss Anthony resuming, said: I want to say to you all that all men, republicans, democrats, greenbackers and anti-monopolists,[17] have conspired together to make the laws and do the governing of the nation, and to rule over women without our consent, and have they not legislated that all husbands shall be the sole owners of the joint earnings of the marriage co-partnership. The women only work for their board and clothes, and the husband is bound by law to maintain them.

I was asked to work for the greenbackers and I said to them all you men conspire together to legislate into your own hands the earnings of all the married women and to pay unmarried women one-half as much money as you do men for the same work. All men are conspirators as against woman, and now you feel that some other men have gotten too large a share of the stealings, and you come to us, from whom everything has been taken and ask us to help you to clutch from the monopolists among yourselves what you think is your just share of the steals. You do not propose in your resolutions to make restitution to the women, from whom you have stolen all things. This is a grand monopoly on the part of the men.

Time being called, Miss Anthony sat down amid loud applause from the audience.

Mr. Rosewater said he would like to refute one or two statements Miss Anthony had made. One is, I am not like Horace Greeley, I did not stay at home as Miss Anthony states, I was down there in the war two years, and the other is that man has monopoly of votes in the government. That monopoly was created by a higher power. It is a monopoly created by the Lord, who made man the protector and bread winner for woman and the family, while the sacred function of rearing the family belongs to woman. Miss Anthony says there are three millions of women earning money enough for their own support,[18] so there must be at least ten million women in America who are dependent for their support on their fathers and husbands.

Miss A.—There are only seven millions.

Mr. R.—Very well; this is a grand monopoly which we should certainly like to enjoy. But we do our duty cheerfully like men. We don't go about whining, grumbling and growling about man's serfdom to women. There is many a man who goes on drudging in the factory or workshop, digging in the streets or in the mine, and when he comes home worn out and broken down with toil he is met at the threshold by a woman with a lightning tongue who makes his home a perfect hell.

There is no comfort nor peace for him, so he goes out and seeks comfort in the companionship he finds in the saloons or billiard halls. It is all nonsense about man's monopoly; you are all doing pretty well.

With few exceptions the women of America are much more comfortable and better clothed and fed than the men. Until woman can bear the hardships and burdens man is compelled to bear, as father and husband in every stage of life, it is unreasonable for woman to ask that she shall control our government. (Loud applause.)

⇜ *Omaha Bee*, 18 October 1882.

1. Edward Rosewater (1841–1906) moved to Omaha in 1863, after service during the war as a telegrapher, principally in the War Department. Telegraphy brought him west, but he developed an interest in journalism and founded the *Omaha Bee* in 1871 to advance his own candidacy for the state legislature. The *Bee* would become one of the Midwest's major Republican papers. (*ANB*.)

2. When time was called on Rosewater, he was talking about "the vices and crimes of women" and a tendency to punish women less severely than men who committed the same crime.

3. The phrase originated in the story of Julius Caesar's decision to divorce his wife when she was suspected of adultery, although he thought her not guilty.

4. The letter to which SBA refers appeared in the New York *World* in late July or early August 1878, at a time when a number of disgruntled residents and former residents of the territory began a nationwide campaign against woman suffrage in Wyoming. As reported in the *Woman's Journal*, 10 August 1878, the writer claimed he had not seen "a single respectable woman at the polls. On the contrary, they were all of the lowest description." The controversy about woman suffrage in Wyoming continued into early 1879. The editors of the *Woman's Journal* published a compilation of statements in the argument as *Nine Years' Experience of Woman Suffrage in Wyoming* (1879). In his speech, Rosewater read a similar letter against woman suffrage, accusing women in Wyoming of selling their votes and contributing to the general corruption in territorial government.

5. James Henry Hayford (1828–1902) launched the *Laramie Sentinel* in 1869. His name appears in this report of SBA's speech as Haywood. Hayford assured SBA that his friends in Cheyenne knew the author to be a "worthless, drunken dead-beat, who worked out a ten days' sentence on the streets of that city with a ball and chain to his leg." (T. A. Larson, *History of Wyoming*, 2d ed. [Lincoln, Neb., 1978], 116n; *History*, 3:745–46; J. H. Hayford to SBA, August 1878, *Film*, 20:380.)

6. Matilda Hindman (?–1905) grew up in Washington County in western Pennsylvania, graduated from Mt. Union College in Ohio, and taught school

before turning to full-time work for woman suffrage. After organizing her home state in preparation for the constitutional convention of 1872 and 1873, she went to Michigan in 1874 as an agent of the New England Woman Suffrage Association, to Iowa in 1875 and 1876 in the employ of the state association, to Massachusetts in 1876, to Colorado in 1877 and 1878, and to Nebraska in 1882. (*Woman's Journal*, 26 August 1876, 6 December 1879, 1 April 1905; *History*, 2:819, 832, 849, 857, 3:241, 458–59, 461, 469, 522, 615, 622, 624–25, 719, 4:24, 61–62, 628, 970; Henry Blackwell to Lucy Stone, 26 August 1890, in Wheeler, *Loving Warriors*, 335.)

SBA misdates Hindman's report on woman suffrage in Wyoming. Hindman observed the election in November 1878 and reported on it for a Denver paper in an article that gained attention as far away as London and was reprinted in the pamphlet *Nine Years' Experience of Woman Suffrage in Wyoming* (1879). Proximity to Wyoming, however, made its experiment with woman suffrage a theme of Colorado's amendment campaign of 1877. The state suffrage association solicited letters from supporters in Wyoming, invited J. H. Hayford to speak, and distributed Hayford's speech. Among antisuffragists, Wyoming also illustrated the dangers of woman suffrage: the editor of the Pueblo *Chieftain* decried prostitutes' increased political power in the territory. (*Woman's Journal*, 22 January 1876, 20 January 1877; Pueblo *Chieftain*, 9 October 1877; J. H. Hayford, *Woman Suffrage in Wyoming: An Address Delivered by Dr. J. H. Hayford before the Colorado Woman Suffrage Association, Maennerchor Hall, Denver, January 14, 1876* [N.p., n.d.]; *History*, 3:716; Billie Barnes Jensen, "Colorado Woman Suffrage Campaigns of the 1870s," *Journal of the West* 12 [April 1973]: 254–71.)

7. The text reads: "she got of the signatures of best representative men and women".

8. On this oft-told tale, see *Papers*, 3:167, 174n, 301.

9. Rosewater had said: "Those who cannot defend the flag and compel obedience to our laws have no right to make laws they cannot enforce, nor force upon us war which they cannot fight out."

10. Horace Greeley (1811–1872), editor of the *New York Tribune* and presidential candidate in 1872, was, as SBA notes, a delegate to the New York constitutional convention of 1867 and the chairman of its committee on suffrage. While working hard to give African-American men equal suffrage in New York, Greeley put comparable effort into stopping suffrage for women. For contemporary accounts of his encounter with ECS and SBA, see *Papers*, 2:75–76 and *Film*, 12:259–63. SBA tells the story as it was told in the *History of Woman Suffrage*, 2:284. (*ANB*.)

11. Modern estimates of the number of women serving as soldiers in the Civil War confirm SBA's figure. See Elizabeth D. Leonard, *All the Daring of the Soldier: Women of the Civil War Armies* (New York, 1999), 165, 310.

12. Mary Ann Ball Bickerdyke (1817–1901) gained fame during the Civil War for her trips to the front to evacuate wounded soldiers. Her postwar endeavors

were less successful, though she retained her commitment to veterans. By this date she lived in San Francisco, where, at various times, she worked for charitable organizations and the San Francisco Mint. Congress finally voted her a pension in 1886. (*NAW*; *ANB*.)

13. William Tecumseh Sherman (1820–1891).

14. See Jonathan Truman Dorris, *Pardon and Amnesty under Lincoln and Johnson: The Restoration of the Confederates to Their Rights and Privileges, 1861–1898* (Chapel Hill, N.C., 1953).

15. A sign of infamy, from Gen. 4:15. God's mark on Cain showed that Cain remained under divine protection despite the crime of fratricide, but in common usage the phrase signified a stigma.

16. Brass-collar is a term for railroad officials, but it also describes a person of staunch political loyalty. Couzins may allude to Rosewater's crusades against the corruption of Nebraska politics by the monopoly of the Union Pacific Railroad.

17. The Greenback party first nominated national candidates in 1876. Antimonopolism was one of its tenets of economic reform. Not until 1884 did a distinct Anti-Monopoly party compete in national elections. SBA spoke to a local Greenback convention in Rochester in August 1878, and she addressed the party nominating convention in Chicago in June 1880. (*Papers*, 3:402–3; *Film*, 21:285–93.)

18. SBA said this in her opening argument.

90 ❧ PRISCILLA BRIGHT McLAREN[1] TO ECS

Newington House Edinburgh [Scotland] Oct 29th 1882

My dear Mrs Stanton

I telegraphed to you yesterday on hearing that you were at Basingstoke,[2] asking if you wld do us the honour and give us the pleasure of being present at our Women's Suffrage Demonstration which is to be held at Glasgow on the 3rd of November—[3] If we hear that you can come we will have a room ready for you either at the house of some friend or at a Hotel whichever wld be most comfortable for you— We shld be delighted if you could speak at our meeting just to say even a few words, for the arrangements are so far made now that we could not ask you to speak much, but perhaps next day at the Conference you could instruct us ↑further↓ by your own experience in noble work.

I fear you have not received any note from me thanking you for having so kindly & unexpectedly remembered me by presenting me with a copy of the History of Womens Suffrage in your land. We have done much here, but our struggles have not been equal to yours— It is a grand history of the ability faith and courage of a noble band of women. I sometimes think your women are grander than ours—but I shld rather say you have had grander opportunities for developing the powers God has given you— Our C.D. cause[4] has cost much and we can recognise prophetic power in some of our workers—especially in dear Mrs Butler—[5] I expect my sister Mrs Lucas[6] 7 Charlotte St. Bedford Square London will be coming to Glasgow and it might be nice for you to come in her company as she has been in America and is quite at home with all who come from America   I will not add more now, quite hoping to meet you soon— Believe me, dear Mrs Stanton Gratefully & affectionately your friend

∜ *Priscilla McLaren*

I hope my telegram reached you—I could not decypher the first letter of the name of the gentleman with whom you are staying

∜ ALS on stationary imprinted with address, Scrapbook 2, Papers of ECS, NPV.

1. Priscilla Bright McLaren (1815–1906) was the sister of two members of Parliament (John and Jacob Bright), mother of another member (Charles McLaren), wife of a retired member (Duncan McLaren), and a formidable politician in her own right. The women in the Bright family constituted a powerful and talented network of reformers, working in campaigns to repeal the Contagious Diseases Acts, establish temperance, rewrite married women's property law, and enfranchise women. McLaren was president of the Edinburgh National Society for Women's Suffrage. She and her husband moved into Newington House, at the edge of Edinburgh, in 1852. (*Oxford DNB*; J. Travis Mills, *John Bright and the Quakers* [London, 1935], 1: 244–45, 274–83; *Times* [London], 7 November 1906; *Woman's Journal*, 1 December 1906; Sandra Stanley Holton, "From Anti-Slavery to Suffrage Militancy: The Bright Circle, Elizabeth Cady Stanton and the British Women's Movement," in *Suffrage and Beyond: International Feminist Perspectives*, eds. Caroline Daley and Melanie Nolan [New York, 1994], 213–33; Sandra Stanley Holton, *Suffrage Days: Stories from the Women's Suffrage Movement* [London, 1996], passim.)

2. When ECS and Harriot Stanton left France in mid-October, they traveled to Basingstoke, southwest of London, to meet the family of William Henry Blatch, Jr., and make plans for a wedding. Harriot met Harry Blatch, as he was known, on board ship while sailing to New York in the winter of 1882. When Harry visited Harriot in Toulouse in the summer or fall of 1882,

promises were made to visit his family as soon as mother and daughter reached England. Blatch (1851–1915) was employed in his family's breweries. (Blatch and Lutz, *Challenging Years*, 64–65; DuBois, *Harriot Stanton Blatch*, 48, 52; *New York Times*, 3 August 1915.)

3. This was the Scottish National Demonstration of Women, the eighth in a series of mass demonstrations in major cities that began in Manchester in February 1880 to reinforce the petitions sent to Parliament in advance of a resolution favoring woman suffrage to be introduced in 1883. In Scotland, an additional aim of the demonstration was to mobilize women to exercise their newly won municipal suffrage. Though tax-paying women in England were restored to their right of municipal suffrage in 1869, Scottish women did not gain the right until 1881 and 1882, in two laws that covered different kinds of towns. (*Women's Suffrage Journal* 13 [1 September 1882]: 131, [2 October 1882]: 145, 147; *History*, 3:867–69, 871–72; Helen Blackburn, *Women's Suffrage: A Record of the Women's Suffrage Movement in the British Isles, with Biographical Sketches of Miss Becker* [1902; reprint, New York, 1970], 152–54; Leah Leneman, *A Guid Cause: The Women's Suffrage Movement in Scotland*, rev. ed. [Edinburgh, Scotland, 1995], 26–27, 223n.)

4. By its Contagious Diseases Acts, the government in Britain licensed and regulated prostitution, and a proposal in 1869 to expand the reach of the laws sparked a large protest movement and the founding of the Ladies' National Association for Repeal, led by Josephine Butler and joined by many of Britain's advocates of woman suffrage. McLaren might view the Ladies' National Association as a vehicle for accelerating political activism among women, or she might consider it a competing activity that slowed the growth of the suffrage movement. (Blackburn, *Women's Suffrage in the British Isles*, 118–21; Strachey, *The Cause*, 187–204, 266–72; Barbara Caine, "John Stuart Mill and the English Women's Movement," *Historical Studies* 18 [April 1978]: 52–67; Holton, "From Anti-Slavery to Suffrage Militancy: The Bright Circle," 222–24; Holton, *Suffrage Days*, 37–39.)

5. Josephine Elizabeth Grey Butler (1828–1906) led the campaign to repeal the Contagious Diseases Acts, not only in Britain but also on the Continent, where similar legislation originated. (*DNB*; Banks, *Biographical Dictionary of British Feminists, 1800–1930*.)

6. Margaret Bright Lucas (1818–1890) was a younger sister of John Bright and Priscilla McLaren and the widow of Samuel Lucas, an editor aligned with the parliamentary radicals. She had visited the United States in 1870. Active in reforms since childhood, Lucas supported woman suffrage, worked to repeal the Contagious Diseases Acts, and presided over the British Women's Temperance Association. (*DNB*; *SEAP*; *Women's Suffrage Journal* 21 [1 March 1890]: 33; Holton, "From Anti-Slavery to Suffrage Militancy: The Bright Circle.")

·⫰———————⫱·

91 ⤳ SPEECH BY ECS TO THE SCOTTISH NATIONAL
DEMONSTRATION OF WOMEN AT GLASGOW

EDITORIAL NOTE: Five thousand people, most of them women, filled
St. Andrew's Hall in Glasgow on 3 November 1882 for the Scottish
National Demonstration of Women. A small number of men occupied a section of the balcony reserved for their use. Priscilla McLaren
presided and headed the roster of fourteen speakers. ECS, with "just
a slight touch of the Yankee intonation in her speech," according to
one observer, spoke for seventeen minutes. This report of her speech
lacks at least one topic she treated: "The most telling part," a reporter remarked, "was the reminiscence of the world's convention
on slavery, held in London forty years ago." Though missing from
this report, those recollections appeared in other speeches ECS
delivered in Britain, including the lecture below at 25 June 1883.
(*Women's Suffrage Journal* 13 [1 December 1882]: 182–89, *Film*,
22:700–707; *Eighty Years*, 353.)

[3 November 1882]

Mrs. Cady Stanton an American lady—I can assure you I appreciate
the honor that has been conferred upon me in being permitted to
celebrate with you this grand event of the crowning of thousands of
Scottish women with the great right of franchise. (Applause.) It was
here in Scotland where was fought over and over again the great battle
of freedom: here where your own glorious poet Robert Burns[1] sang the
glad songs of equality for humanity that have gone around the world;
here where your grand novelist Sir Walter Scott[2] drew his heroines,
grand, brave, self-asserting, for I believe the pen of Scott never drew
[a] weak woman; here too where your great divine Chalmers[3] so eloquently defended the rights of individual conscience and judgment;
and it is fitting that here at last the right of the franchise should be
conferred on your women. (Applause.) And what is this right of suffrage—
a right so laughed and scorned at by those who do not appreciate its
blessing and its power. The right of suffrage gives you a voice in the
regulation of your homes, of your streets, of your schools, of your
religion, of your politics. It is vain to talk of the home being woman's

sphere so long as she has not a word to say in regard to the laws that govern that home. I was very much pleased with the remarks of the speaker who preceded me[4] in her rebuke of your members of Parliament and the House of Commons. But, remember, my friends, behind every one of our legislators there stands a woman. And what has been the influence of the women in high places in this great reform. They have whispered into the ears of our legislators, our statesmen, our philosophers that they had all the rights they want. Our trouble has not been with the men—they have been open to reason—our trouble has been with the women themselves. (Applause.) It is the saddest sight to me to see a woman well clothed, fed, and sheltered, in the midst of most fortunate surroundings, robed and mantled, all complacency about herself, and saying "I have all the rights I want." O, selfish one! I ask you to look over your garden gate, where all its beauty, fragrance, and peace, unto the wilderness beyond, where the immortal flowers are fading fast, with no kind hands to lift their drooping heads or any kind hearts to speak to them words of peace and love. (Applause.) Remember, mothers of Glasgow, our jails and prisons are regulated by law, and what a power you have in your hands in trying to build up higher and better towns and cities in your midst.[5] Remember man is the representative of justice, woman of mercy, and we need these two grand elements everywhere hand in hand walking up and down the highways of life. (Applause.) It has sometimes been said that this movement of ours is antagonistic to men. My friends, how can that be? The women on all our platforms have sons as well as daughters, and think you a mother would do aught to take from the dignity, the honor, the glory, and the praise of her sons? (Applause.)

⤟ Unidentified and undated clipping, reprinted from *North British Daily Mail*, 4 November 1882, ECS Papers, DLC. Square brackets surround letter torn from margin.

1. Robert Burns (1759–1796) was Scotland's national poet, with a large audience in the English-speaking world.
2. Sir Walter Scott (1771–1832), Scottish novelist, published popular historical novels, beginning with *Waverly* (1814).
3. Thomas Chalmers (1780–1847), Scottish theologian and professor of moral philosophy, founded the Free Church of Scotland.
4. Laura Elizabeth Pochin McLaren (1854–1933) preceded ECS as a speaker. The daughter of Henry Davis Pochin, an industrialist and former radical

member of Parliament, and Agnes Heap Pochin, an early advocate of woman suffrage, she married Charles McLaren in 1877 and lived at Barn Elms, southwest of London on the River Thames. (*Oxford DNB.*)

5. For examples of women's philanthropic activism in Scotland, see Esther Breitenbach and Eleanor Gordon, eds., *Out of Bounds: Women in Scottish Society, 1800–1945* (Edinburgh, Scotland, 1992).

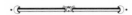

92 ⤙ ECS to Harriot E. Stanton

Glasgow, Saturday Morning, [*4 November*] 1882.[1]

Dearly Beloved:

I had a delightful journey hither, looking at the beautiful scenery, reading, thinking of you and exercising my rare genius for sleep. Having the car entirely to myself, I stretched out full length and had two royal naps. Fortunately, a pretty little quakeress came into the car at the last station before reaching Glasgow, so that I was roused from my slumbers by the gentle hand of woman and not by a bearded Scotchman as would otherwise have been the case. Rooms were ready for you and me at the best hotel. Young Mrs. M'Laren and her husband,[2] who is a member of the House of Commons, are at the same hotel. Mrs. M'Laren the Elder[3] is at the Temperance Hotel, the poorest in the place. I suppose they thought my temperance opinions were not sufficiently strong to lead me to prefer a small hotel built on sound principles to a good one on more worldly basis, a rational conclusion for which I am truly thankful.

I send you a Report of the meeting. It was indeed a grand affair, as far as the size of the audience went; but in our country, we should not have considered the speaking up to the occasion. As you will wish to know how I did, I have only to say that I was much complimented as having made the best speech of the evening; but it was by no means up to what I have often done. However, it was given smoothly and without notes. A Scotch lady[4] and one from Ireland[5] spoke lauding their respective countries and firing bombshells into English policy, to which the audience responded with wild enthusiasm. I was astonished, for even in America you never hear such wholesale criticisms of England. When Mrs. Craigin said, "England never conquered Scotland but we gave them a King," the audience just shouted, rose to their feet and waved their handkerchiefs all over the house, all those on the platform rising and waving until arms ached. I waved with the rest.

After the meeting, we all went to Mrs. McGregor's[6] where we had a grand supper. I was escorted by Professor Cairn[7] of the University. On my left sat Professor Lindsley,[8] an intimate friend of Robertson Smith, who has just been expelled from the University for heresy. I had a nice chat with the two professors. As the meeting did not adjourn until near eleven, we did not reach the hotel, after this supper, until near two. We had music and recitations by the same Irish lady who spoke at the meeting. She again dressed down the English mercilessly.
Later.

I am now in Edinburgh, at the home of Mr. M'Laren,[9] who has been sixteen years in parliament. Mrs. M'Laren is a sister of John Bright. Her sister, Mrs. Lucas, the latter's daughter,[10] and young Mr. M'Laren and wife are of the party. As soon as we arrived, at four o'clock, we took an open carriage and drove all round the beautiful city and feasted our eyes on these magnificent mountains. Mrs. M'Laren's place is near Holyrood Castle, and we see the Saulsbury craggs from the windows.[11]

Lydia Becker,[12] whom you ask about, is the prototype of our precious Susan and is to the movement in this country just what Susan is in America.

I am writing with a miserable pen, a mere stick, and lest it should disturb my placid temper, I must say good night. With love and kisses my precious one,

≫ Mother.

≫ Typed transcript, ECS Papers, NjR.

1. This was the day following the mass demonstration. In *Eighty Years,* 354–55, ECS claims she reached Edinburgh with the McLaren family in time to attend Sunday meeting of the Society of Friends.

2. Charles Benjamin Bright McLaren (1850–1934), a barrister and a strong supporter of woman suffrage, sat in Parliament for Stafford from 1880 to 1886. He was returned in 1892 for Bosworth and sat until 1910. (*DNB; Who's Who of British Members of Parliament,* vol. 2.)

3. That is, Priscilla McLaren.

4. Jessie Hannah Craigen (1834?–1899) drew upon a childhood in the theater to become a rousing speaker. As an organizer for the Ladies' National Association and the temperance and woman suffrage movements, Craigen displayed an

especial rapport with workingclass men and women. Members of the Bright family were, at this date, her chief sponsors and supporters. (*Oxford DNB*; *Englishwoman's Review* 31 [15 January 1900]: 65–66; Sandra Stanley Holton, "Silk Dresses and Lavender Kid Gloves: The Wayward Career of Jessie Craigen, Working Suffragist," *Women's History Review* 5 [1996]: 129–50.)

5. Isabella Maria Susan Tod (1836–1896) of Belfast worked closely with the women in England and Scotland. She joined the campaign to repeal the Contagious Diseases Acts, helped to found the Belfast Women's Temperance Association, and formed the Northern Ireland Society for Women's Suffrage. In addition to working for parliamentary suffrage, she mounted a long campaign to extend municipal suffrage to women in Ireland. An opponent of Gladstone's Home Rule bill in 1886, Tod devoted the last decade of her life to advocating Ireland's union with Britain. ECS and SBA saw her on numerous occasions in 1883, and SBA visited her in Ireland. (Maria Luddy, "Isabella M S Tod (1836–1896)," in *Women, Power and Consciousness in 19th-Century Ireland*, eds. Mary Cullen and Maria Luddy [Dublin, 1995], 197–230; SBA diary, 5, 18 July, 2–7 September, 7, 9 October 1883, *Film*, 22:814ff.)

6. Elizabeth Robertson McGrigor, not McGregor, and her husband, Alexander Bennett McGrigor (1827–1891), both attended the mass demonstration for woman suffrage. A. B. McGrigor succeeded to his family's estate of Cairnoch in 1853, when he also became head of the family's law firm in Glasgow. (Edward Walford, *The County Families of the United Kingdom* [London, 1872]; research assistance from Christine Henderson, Mitchell Library, Glasgow.)

7. Edward Caird (1835–1908), not Cairn, was professor of moral philosophy at Glasgow University from 1866 and 1893 and an active member of the city's women's suffrage society. He helped to organize the mass demonstration. (Elspeth King, "The Scottish Women's Suffrage Movement," in Breitenbach and Gordon, *Out of Bounds*, 130.)

8. Thomas Martin Lindsay (1843–1914), not Lindsley, taught church history at the theological school of the Free Church of Scotland in Glasgow. He and his wife were active in the local suffrage society. William Robertson Smith (1846–1894) was a leading scholar of the Old Testament and Lindsay's lifelong friend. When the general assembly of the Free Church tried Smith for heresy and removed him from his professorship at the Free Church College of Aberdeen, Lindsay testified in Smith's favor. At issue were Smith's entries for the *Encyclopaedia Britannica*, ninth edition, in which his historical and textual scholarship on the Bible raised doubts about God's authorship. (*DNB*; King, "Scottish Women's Suffrage Movement," 130; J. W. Rogerson, *The Bible and Criticism in Victorian Britain: Profiles of F. D. Maurice and William Robertson Smith* [Sheffield, England, 1995].)

9. Duncan McLaren (1800–1886) had allied himself with Richard Cobden and John Bright long before he won election to Parliament as the member for Edinburgh in 1865, and he helped to build the Liberal party in Scotland. In

1881, he retired from Parliament, where he was a firm supporter of woman suffrage. (*DNB*; Joseph O. Baylen and Norbert J. Gossman, eds., *Biographical Dictionary of Modern British Radicals*, vol. 2, *1830–1870* [Sussex, England, 1984], 326–29.)

10. Katharine Lucas Thomasson (c. 1841–1932), the daughter of Margaret Bright Lucas, married the wealthy, Quaker cotton manufacturer, John Pennington Thomasson in 1867, merging two families notable in the Anti-Corn Law agitation. Settled at Bolton, Kate Thomasson became active in the Manchester National Society for Women's Suffrage. When her husband won election to Parliament, where he served from 1880 to 1885, she took advantage of their time in London to host Liberal politicians as well as woman suffragists. During their time in London, both ECS and SBA were objects of her hospitality, at events SBA described as "splendid" and "elegant." (*Times* [London], 21 March 1932; *DNB*, s.v. "Thomasson, Thomas"; *Who's Who of British Members of Parliament*, vol. 1, s.v. "Thomasson, John Pennington"; Mills, *John Bright and the Quakers*, 1:293n; SBA diary, 6, 12, 18, 25, 29 June, 5, 6, 19 July 1883, *Film*, 22:814ff.)

11. ECS mixes the names of two places in the city, the Castle and Holyrood Palace. She probably meant the latter, a royal residence, at the eastern end of the city on the site of a medieval abbey. The Salisbury Crags rose several hundred feet over the city's southeastern corner.

12. Lydia Ernestine Becker (1827–1890), a hard-working founder of Britain's suffrage movement, former correspondent of the *Revolution*, and editor of the *Women's Suffrage Journal* since 1870, spoke at the Scottish National Demonstration. She was secretary of the society in Manchester and wielded considerable power through the Central Committee of the National Society for Women's Suffrage. By 1882, her willingness to abandon suffrage for married women, if that compromise won parliamentary support, put her at odds with many former allies, especially among members of the Bright circle. (*DNB*; Blackburn, *Women's Suffrage in the British Isles*, passim; Holton, *Suffrage Days*, 39–41. See also *Papers* 2.)

93 ~ PRISCILLA BRIGHT McLAREN TO ECS

Newington House Edinburgh [*Scotland*] Nov 14ᵗʰ 1882

My dear Mʳˢ C. Stanton

When I went to Glasgow I put yr valued note with some others in a "safe place" and I cannot tell now where that safe place is—but it will turn up some day—and I am obliged to send this to my sisters' to forward

I am thinking much of you & know you can have no time for letter reading on the eve of yr dear daughter's wedding—[1] I do feel for you and yet rejoice when I remember what you told me of your son in law— that he is worthy to be yr daughter's husband & yr son. I should have liked to have been in Town & have been present at the ceremony— accept <u>our</u> best wishes for all concerned in the event—

I must now thank you very warmly & affectionately for the copy of yr History of Womans Suffrage, bound in calf— I prize it exceedingly, and valuable as the books were before, I prize them more since we have had the honour & pleasure of having had you as our guest— Oh, how sorry I am you did not know my Husband when he could have conversed with you—he never said anything that was not worth hearing— he was so wise so calm in all his judgments. I have seen no account of the Manchester meeting[2]—but I feel how much you must have given the same help to it which ours rec^d from you— I sent thro' Kate Thomasson a laughable cartoon of us all for you to see— I think they have done you the best of anyone, they have given you some force of character.

I must not add—I have been out walking and lost myself in the mist so have not much time to catch the post— It was very good of you to send me a card from Manchester—a letter from my sister makes me quite envy her the privilege she had in travelling with you— again thanking you more than I can well express—and wishing every blessing may attend the pair so soon to be united[3]— I am with my Husbands kindest regards & mine yours very affectionately

❧ *Priscilla McLaren*

❧ ALS on stationery imprinted with address, Scrapbook 2, Papers of ECS, NPV.

1. Harriot and Harry Blatch were married on 15 November 1882 in the Portland Street Chapel in London in a ceremony conducted by William H. Channing. ECS had envisaged a ceremony led by both Channing and her friend Moncure D. Conway, also then in London, but Channing would not consent because Conway had forsaken the idea of marriage as a sacrament. So intense was Channing's hostility that Conway thought it better to decline ECS's invitation to be a guest at the wedding, lest ill will spoil the event. The Blatches left London after their wedding for a honeymoon to Dartmoor. (DuBois, *Harriot Stanton Blatch*, 52–54; George W. Smalley to ECS, 27 October 1882, M. D. Conway to ECS, 2 and 13 November 1882, W. H. Channing to ECS, 3 November 1882, in *Film*, 22:690–92, 696–99, 722–24.)

2. ECS traveled from Edinburgh to Manchester with Margaret Lucas to attend the annual meeting of the Manchester National Society for Women's Suffrage on November 7. In her remarks, ECS encouraged British women not to stop agitating, for a Parliament that did not represent women voters could easily reverse recent gains. (*History*, 3:926–27; *Women's Suffrage Journal* 13 [1 Dec 1882]: 189–91, *Film*, 22:712–14.)

3. ECS penned a note on this letter and forwarded it to Harriot. "Save this little note from good Mrs McLaren for me. I shall probably be in Edinborugh by the time you return & cannot say when we shall meet again. All your orders executed. Theodore returns to Paris on Tuesday."

94 🌿 INTERVIEW WITH SBA IN FORT SCOTT, KANSAS

[*c. 15 November 1882*]

Miss Susan B. Anthony is visiting her brother J. M. Anthony,[1] of this city, for a few days. A *Monitor* reporter paid his respects to the distinguished champion of female suffrage last evening and was graciously received. Naturally the conversation turned on the late election in Nebraska,[2] and Miss Anthony remarked:

"Well, we were snowed under about as badly as you Republicans were down here in Kansas,[3] but then I don't believe when the official returns come in that it will be so bad a defeat as it appears at present. You see there were so many important issues before the people that our question has been largely lost sight of. One thing I am satisfied of, that this question can never be settled by a popular vote. It is a hopeless case so far as that goes. I have worked hard in Nebraska, have spoken in forty counties and on all occasions our meetings were largely attended and enthusiastic, but I did not expect to carry the state."

"Where do you go from here?"

"I shall go to Leavenworth for a few days, and then directly to Washington. I want to be there at the opening of the session."

🌿 Unidentified and undated clipping, reprinted from *Fort Scott Monitor*, SBA scrapbook 9, Rare Books, DLC.

1. Jacob Merritt Anthony (1834–1900), the youngest of SBA's siblings and known always as Merritt, had lived in Fort Scott, Kansas, since 1869.

(Anthony, *Anthony Genealogy*, 173, 189; Andreas, *History of Kansas*, 2:1076; *Woman's Journal*, 23 June 1900.)

2. Nebraska's voters rejected the amendment in all but eleven counties by a statewide vote of 25,756 to 50,693. Like the referendum in Colorado in 1877, Nebraska's election was flawed by ballots with incorrect wording, inconsistent rules about whether separate ballot boxes were required, local decisions to count blank ballots as votes against the amendment, and some distribution of phony ballots printed by the leading antisuffrage editors. The loss sharpened positions that divided the National and American associations. SBA told co-workers at a post-election rally in Omaha that never again would the National attempt to canvass a state and win over voters; "the best way to succeed was to obtain a sixteenth amendment for suffrage through Congress." Lucy Stone and Henry Blackwell found the exercise in Nebraska equally fruitless, especially in states with large numbers of foreign-born voters like Nebraska; "Americans voted for the Amendment," Blackwell claimed, and foreigners did not. But firm in his conviction that the federal government had no role in voting rights, he hoped to turn all attention to the partial suffrage that legislatures could grant directly. (McPherson, *Hand-Book of Politics for 1884*, 102; Coulter, "History of Suffrage in Nebraska," 102–6; *Film*, 22:715; *Woman's Journal*, 4 November, 9 December 1882; H. B. Blackwell to Alice S. Blackwell, 24 September 1882, in Wheeler, *Loving Warriors*, 282–83.)

3. Democrats won the governorship in Kansas in 1882, defeating John P. St. John's bid for a third term. Republicans retained control over the legislature.

95 ≋ ECS TO ELIZABETH PEASE NICHOL[1]

10 Duchess street   Portland Place [*London*] Nov 16th [*1882*][2]

Dear Elizabeth Nichols,

I have thought many times of the few short hours I had at your pleasant home & of those valuable letters we had not time even to glance over.

I write to say that I will redeem my promise to visit you before I return to America if you will appoint the time. My daughter was married yesterday, all passed off well. She has gone on her wedding trip to be absent three weeks   she will then return & go to housekeeping.

Now if you will tell me when you will be at home & at what time my visit would suit you I will arrange my plans so as to suit you either in December or January. I have many things to talk over with you face to face, that I will not attempt to write. I cannot tell you dear friend how many pleasant & painful memories, the thought of all that has passed during the forty two years since we met, rushed on me when I first clasped your hand on the platform at Glasgow. Only think of forty two years, how long it seems, and what sorrows many of our mutual friends have passed ↑through↓ & what joys have gladdened the life of others. But all this we will talk over. With much love affectionately yours

➤ *Elizabeth Cady Stanton*

➤ ALS, *72M-101 (623), Letters to William Lloyd Garrison and Others, MH-H.

1. Elizabeth Pease Nichol (1807–1897) met ECS in 1840 at the World Anti-Slavery Convention and then again at the mass demonstration in Glasgow in 1882. Elizabeth Pease had married John Pringle Nichol, a noted astronomer at the University of Glasgow, in 1853 and settled in Scotland. After her husband's death in 1859, she moved to Edinburgh. A lifelong reformer, she joined the campaign against the Contagious Diseases Acts in the 1870s and was sympathetic to the movement for woman suffrage. Nichol retained her correspondence with leading American and British abolitionists; the sons of William Lloyd Garrison removed the collection in 1889 and later gave it to the Boston Public Library and Harvard University. (*Oxford DNB*; Baylen and Gossman, *Modern British Radicals* 2:369–71; Clare Midgley, *Women against Slavery: The British Campaigns, 1780–1870* [London, 1992]; SBA diary, 20 July–6 August 1883, *Film*, 22:814ff; Anna M. Stoddart, *Elizabeth Pease Nichol* [London, 1899], 296–97. See also *Papers* 1.)

2. ECS wrote "Mrs Nichols Nov 16th" on the last page of this letter. Both ECS and SBA stayed at this address, at a boarding house, with a woman named Mrs. Ellen Phillips. Nothing more is known about these arrangements.

96 ➤ KATHARINE LUCAS THOMASSON TO ECS

London. November 16, 18[82].

Dear Mrs Stanton:

I have seen Mr Bright[1] to-day and his daughter Mrs Clark,[2] and I write to say that Mr Bright will be at his rooms any morning between 10 and 12 o'clock, and will be glad to see you. He lives up two flights of stairs at 132 Piccadilly. Uncle will be in town as long as Parliament is sitting.

I hope you will call, and be very cautious in alluding to the Suffrage question. Who knows but that with caution you might assist him to see more clearly in the matter?[3] Affectionately yours,

⋙ *Katharine L. Thomasson.*

⋙ Typed transcript, ECS Papers, NjR.

1. John Bright (1811–1889) celebrated twenty-five years in Parliament in 1883. One of England's leading middle-class reformers, he helped to build the Liberal party and had insisted that household suffrage be the basis for extending the franchise in the Reform Act of 1867. At that time, he supported John Stuart Mill's effort to include women in the act, but Bright changed his mind thereafter and consistently voted against woman suffrage. (*DNB*; J. Bright to Theodore Stanton, 21 October 1882, in Stanton, *Woman Question in Europe*, 22–24n.)

2. Helen Priestman Bright Clark (1840–1927), John Bright's daughter by his first wife, married William Stephens Clark in 1866 and settled with him at Street, where he ran the C. & J. Clark Company. She followed her Priestman and Bright aunts in supporting woman suffrage. (Mills, *John Bright and the Quakers*, 1:474–78, 2:60–63; Percy Lovell, *Quaker Inheritance, 1871–1961: A Portrait of Roger Clark of Street, Based on His Own Writings and Correspondence* [London, 1970], 1–5, 260–61; Holton, "From Anti-Slavery to Suffrage Militancy: The Bright Circle"; *Times* [London], 17 January 1927.)

3. Different accounts of this interview are found in ECS's diary, 20 November 1882, in *Stanton*, 2:197, and in *Eighty Years*, 357. In the former, a half-hour visit steered clear of woman suffrage, "as I fear I could do nothing with a man who, after hearing Mill's able presentation of the subject," voted against it in Parliament. In the latter, "[f]ree trade and woman suffrage formed the basis of our conversation" during a one hour visit.

97 ⋙ SBA TO HARRIET HANSON ROBINSON

Room—151—Riggs House   Washington D.C. Dec. 7, 1882

My Dear Mrs Robinson

Yours of Dec. 5 is just here this A.M— Well! Well! haven't you walked into the very heart of the Hub— Hold your N.W.S.A. of Mass. meetings in the N.E. Womens club rooms at—5 Park street!![1] Well, well!!— I am glad you are working your way so delightfully into the central forces of Boston—& Miss May[2] to speak for you!— What does it mean?— I thought she was a firm adherent to Lucy!! Your plan with your book is capital—you will have to push yours and ↑we↓ ours—if there any sales made of them— I planted one or more sets of ours in every town I spoke in Nebraska—but I could ↑do for↓ nothing else— neither Mrs Gougar's Herald or your book—one can't press but one thing with an audience—so I of course took our History—

I hope you will stir up your women to each write a letter to each Mass. Member & Senator in Congress—urging upon him to push the passage of our 16th am't bill— I wish we had a million signed petition to present—[3] The Republicans seem very chary of our question so far as I have seen them here   It looks as if they were going to get down on all fours to the Whiskey elements of their party—to try & coax back the German Lager beer voters—[4] If they do—they'll fail in that not only— but alienate from the Prohibitionists forever—& so kill themselves absolutely— I saw Gen'l Butler—he will doubtless make some sort of woman suffrage recommendation in his message to your Legislature—[5] I think you ought to write him & urge him to urge municipal suffrage— if he thinks the Legislature has power to extend it—and to re-assert his belief in the 14th amendment & to urge a 16th am't—since the 14th is denied— I tell you he means business on our question quite as much as any Republican I know— I do hope he will make a splendid paragraph in his message for woman suffrage—such as shall shame every Republican Governors message in the nation—

You will soon get copy of Call for Wash. Con. from Mrs Sewall—it is to be Jan. 23, 24, 25, and by that time—our 16th am't bill will be reached on the Senate Callendar—and I hope before it, our House Com. will have reported favorably—[6] Both Senators Lapham & Blair have told me they should make a speech on the am't when it comes up—& all agree that it is best to push it to a vote this session

How Lucy does print every criticism of our national women in Nebraska—[7] Well let her have all the rope she pleases to take—she will surely hang herself sooner than she will any one else— I am glad you & Mrs Shattuck just go ahead quietly—your bills & circulars are good—

Mrs Stanton writes that she is settled in London for the winter—& hopes I will go over right away after our Wash. Con. is through—but I shall want to stay & watch progress of 16th amendment up to March 4th

Well Good Bye— I hope you will keep well & in good cheer to the end— I get awfully dissatisfied with myself every little while—feeling as if were doing next to nothing—unless actually out speaking every night—that is my natural work—

Love to Mrs Shattuck & yourself & your young daughter & her husband—[8] Sincerely yours

≈ *Susan B. Anthony*

≈ ALS, Robinson-Shattuck Papers, MCR-S.

1. The New England Women's Club, founded in 1868, shared honors with New York's Sorosis as the mother and model of women's clubs nationwide. More active in social reform than many clubs it inspired, it played an important role in gaining women a voice in the governance of public education in Massachusetts, first by running candidates for office, and later by supporting school suffrage for women. (Karen J. Blair, *The Clubwoman as Feminist: True Womanhood Redefined, 1868–1914* [New York, 1980], 15–38.)

2. Abigail Williams May (1829–1888) was a distinguished philanthropist and reformer in Boston—a founder of the New England Women's Club, a member of the Boston School Committee and the State Board of Education, and a vice president of both the New England and the Massachusetts suffrage associations aligned with Lucy Stone. (*NAW*; *ANB*.)

3. For the petition sent to Congress by the National Woman Suffrage Association of Massachusetts, see *Congressional Record*, 47th Cong., 2d sess., 11 January 1883, pp. 1107–8, 1125.

4. After their loss of a majority in the House of Representatives in the election of November 1882, Republican leaders were rethinking their alliances. To fight off competition from the Prohibition party, state leaders had proposed various weak temperance measures before the election, but this attempt to prevent the defection of prohibitionists alienated brewers and German-American voters, who resisted legislation that encroached on personal rights. (Mark Wahlgren Summers, *Rum, Romanism, and Rebellion: The Making of a President, 1884* [Chapel Hill, N.C., 2000], 77–90.)

5. In his inaugural address as governor of Massachusetts on 4 January 1883, Benjamin Butler repeated his belief that the Constitution already enfranchised women, although he acknowledged that the judiciary did not share his view. He also proposed that women be allowed the opportunity to vote on whether or not they should be granted municipal suffrage by the state legislature. ("Inaugural Address of His Excellency Benjamin F. Butler," *Acts and Resolves Passed by the General Court of Massachusetts in the Year 1883, Together with the Constitution, the Messages of the Governor, List of the Civil Government, Changes of Names of Persons* [Boston, 1883], 643–44.)

6. The short, second session of the Forty-seventh Congress opened on December 4. Through December, SBA was confident that the Senate Select Committee would introduce the joint resolution in mid-January. The committee failed to make that deadline. On January 19, SBA reported that the com-

mittee called off its meeting the previous week for lack of a quorum and would try again the next day to get a quorum and a majority vote. Her decision to sail for Europe in mid-February, rather than wait until the end of the session, may indicate that she knew by late January that the senators would not bring the joint resolution to the floor of the Senate in this session. (SBA to Benjamin F. Butler, 14 December 1883; SBA to Franklin B. Sanborn, 2 January 1883; SBA to Elizabeth B. Harbert, 19 January 1883; all in *Film*, 22:760–66, 23:4–5, 29–30.)

7. Presumably SBA refers to the *Woman's Journal*, 2 December 1882. There the editors reprinted an article from the *Omaha Republican* about a post-election meeting on November 8 at which Phoebe Couzins lost her temper in a tirade against several prominent local opponents of woman suffrage. According to the *Republican*, "on every hand were heard expressions of condemnation of Miss Couzins, the tenor of the criticisms being that she had lost her temper, that she had made an unjustifiable assault, had injured her cause, and had made a fool of herself." The *Woman's Journal* also carried an article by Elizabeth Harbert that retold the story but opined, "we do not feel that the fact that one of our speakers displayed some temper for a moment, is a reason why the several States of this Union should continue to disfranchise United States citizens on account of sex." Lucy Stone's own article in the issue credited the National's speakers with good work, though she omitted to name Phoebe Couzins among them.

8. Despite SBA's syntax, the younger daughter, Elizabeth Osborne Robinson (1852–1926), was still a single woman. She married George S. Abbott in 1885. SBA refers to Sidney Doane Shattuck (1855–1930), who married Hattie Robinson in 1878. The Shattucks lived in Malden with Harriet Robinson. (Bushman, *"Good Poor Man's Wife"*, passim.)

98 ↠ SBA TO LILLIE DEVEREUX BLAKE

Room 151—Riggs House   Washington D.C. Dec. 9, 1882

My Dear Mrs Blake

Yours of the 5th inst. is before me—[1] I doubt the wisdom of again pushing a bill similar to the Andrews bill[2] in Legislature— It strikes me just as does that of Presidential Suffrage[3]—or any bill about which there can be a difference of opinion as to its constitutionality— It seems to me far wiser to present & push only fair & fully established methods & measures— Then having so many different plans presented must detract from all it seems to me— I very much wish you & all of the different state workers of the National would concentrate on the one measure of a 16th amendment— Our Senate bill will be reached in the regular course of the Calendar by the middle of January—or soon after—and we ought to have the report ↑of the vote↓ of every Legislature that sits this winter to rush before the Senate with by that time— Of course I want you not to fail to press the vote in our N.Y. Legislature the very first thing— The first word I get from every member is "You got badly beaten in Nebraska"!!— Then I have to explain how 25,756 of the very picked men of Nebraska was a real <u>majority</u> vote of the brains & morals of the state—

Then they say—you could get the Nebraska Legislature to ratify a 16th am't now that the <u>people</u> have voted down woman suffrage— So you see our only possible hope of converting these Senators & M.C. to the possibility that any Legislature would ratify an amendment—is to show to them their votes on the resolution recommending its passage by Congress—to get such a resolution through the N.Y. Legislature should be the first effort of our friends at Albany— Mr Lapham & Mr Blair are both ready to make speeches on the wisdom of 16th am't method— But when it is reached on the callendar <u>one</u> objection can carry it over a day—& then it can come up for action only by a vote of the Senate—but that you see will be a good deal of a <u>test vote</u>— ~~Senat~~ ↑Gen'l↓ Butler says by all means push it to a vote in both houses—it will help you greatly even if you get no more than one third or one half of each house— It will show just how far your work has progressed—& so says Senator Blair—

Now, my dear Mrs Blake can't you, wont you help to get all our women in all the states concentrate upon the passage of this Resolution through their Legislatures?— What an immense political weight it would have here with Congress!— What I want all of you to see is the importance of getting the decision of our question lifted out of the hands of the rank & file of voters—into those of the representatives of the several states— Sincerely yours—

❧ *Susan B. Anthony*

❧ ALS, Lillie Devereux Blake Papers, MoSHi. In *Film* as enclosure in 19 December 1882.

1. SBA forgot to mail this letter but found it again on December 19. Blake received it as an enclosure in a letter written on the later date.

2. This bill for suffrage in New York State was named for its first sponsor,

Alexander Edward Andrews (1834–1908), a graduate of Hobart College and a Republican attorney from Binghamton, New York, who won election to the state assembly in 1878 and 1880. In March 1880, Andrews proposed an act to prohibit disfranchisement that read, "No person shall be debarred from voting at any election, or at any town meeting, school meeting or other choice of government functionaries whatsoever, by reason of sex." The bill reached a third reading that year. Legislators and the state suffrage association were following the legal advice of Hamilton Willcox, a long-time suffragist and lawyer in New York. Willcox argued that it was unconstitutional to treat as disfranchised any persons whose suffrage was not explicitly granted in the state constitution, and he amassed evidence that the legislature frequently corrected such mistakes by simple legislation. Suffrage for women should be granted by the same means. To increase the number of legislators favorable to the bill, Willcox created a new Woman Suffrage party, and leaders of the state association, including Blake, joined forces with him. Another Andrews bill was reported by the judiciary committee in March 1881, brought to a vote in the assembly on 11 May 1881, and supported by a majority in a vote of fifty-nine to fifty-five, short of the sixty-five votes needed for passage. During a third attempt in 1882, the attorney general submitted his opinion to the assembly that the bill was unconstitutional. According to the *New York Times*, this changed the minds of some of the bill's supporters, despite Willcox's rapid response to the attorney general, and on 16 May 1882, the assembly voted fifty-four to fifty-nine against the measure. SBA need not have worried about the state association's next step: the executive committee unanimously agreed on 27 May 1882 "that it would be almost suicidal" to pursue the bill any further. (*Biographical Review. This Volume Contains Biographical Sketches of the Leading Citizens of Broome County, New York* [Boston, 1894], 388–89; *Binghamton Press*, 13, 14, 17 February 1908; with the assistance of the Broome County Historical Society, Binghamton, N.Y.; *NCBB*, December 1880; *New York Times* 4, 12 May 1881, 4, 12, 17 May 1882; *History*, 3:426, 431, 434–35, 959–61; Minute Book 1, New York [City & State] Woman Suffrage Papers, NNC.)

3. By presidential suffrage, its advocates meant the right to vote for members of the Electoral College in each state. Article II, section 1, of the Constitution of the United States authorized legislatures "to determine the manner of appointing Electors in each state equal to the size of the state's congressional representation." Advocates argued that this language made the right to vote a matter of state election laws, beyond the reach of a state's constitutional definition of eligible voters, and thus it could be granted by legislative enactment rather than amendment. Henry Blackwell was the most conspicuous and persistent advocate of presidential suffrage into the twentieth century, but he was not alone. After Blackwell made his case at the annual meeting of the American association in 1880, a number of local activists, like Helen Gougar in Indiana, returned home to seek local, legal opinion and ask for presidential suffrage in their legislatures. (*History*, 2:860n; Kriebel, *Where the Saints Have Trod*, 84.)

·◁▬▬▬◦▦◦▬▬▬▷·

99 ❧ SBA TO JANE CANNON SWISSHELM[1]

Rochester N.Y. Jan. 2, 1883

My Dear Mrs Swisshelm

Here's a Happy New Year to you—and here's the call for our 15th Convention at Washington—[2] Wont you give us a letter? Do you see Ex. Senator Conklins argument before the Supreme Court—bringing to light the <u>secret</u> discussions on the 14th amendment—to prove that the framers <u>intended</u> its guarantees to protect others beyond <u>colored men</u>—[3] Oh shades of legal honesty—after denying them to foreign men in Rhode Island—& Women native & foreign of the entire nation—to now claim them for <u>R.R.</u> <u>Corporations</u>!!![4] I wish you would go after Senators Edmunds & Conklin with your <u>sharp pen</u>—& cut them up as they deserve—the argument was Dec. 20th—

Have you received Vol. II. of our History of Woman Suffrage? If not I want you to have it— Mrs Stanton is ↑in↓ Europe—so Vol. III. waits her return— I hope you are well—& enjoying life—& that your daughter is happy in her new life—[5]

Address me to care of Riggs House—Washington—D.C.—where I start for tomorrow   Sincerely yours

❧ *Susan B. Anthony*

❧ ALS, on NWSA letterhead for 1881–1882, William Bell Mitchell & Family Papers, MnHi. Envelope addressed to Swissvale and forwarded to Hyde Park, Illinois.

1. Jane Grey Cannon Swisshelm (1815–1884) published antislavery papers before the war and a Radical Republican paper in Washington, D.C., at the war's end. After losing a federal job, she divided her time between Pittsburgh and Chicago, published articles in the *Woman's Journal*, *Chicago Tribune*, and *Pittsburg Commercial-Gazette*, among others, and made occasional appearances in the suffrage movement in the early 1870s. Always argumentative and independent, Swisshelm grew more conservative and cranky as the decade progressed, and by 1878 she turned her acerbic pen against suffrage activists. (*NAW*; *ANB*; Louise R. Noun, *Strong-Minded Women: The Emergence of the Woman-Suffrage Movement in Iowa* [Ames, Iowa, 1969], 205–6, 215–19; *Woman's Journal*, 20 January 1872, 16 May 1874; *New York Tribune*,

8 June 1876, 14 February, 17 April, 13 June 1878; *Chicago Tribune*, 15 October 1874, *Film*, 18:118–20. See also *Papers* 1 & 3.)

2. Enclosure missing.

3. Roscoe Conkling, retired from the Senate, and George Edmunds, still a senator, were retained as attorneys by the Southern Pacific Railroad to appeal a case to the Supreme Court about taxing railroad property in California. To dramatize his belief that corporations were protected by the language in the Fourteenth Amendment barring states from depriving "any person" of property "without due process of law," Conkling presented himself as an expert on the amendment's intended results. Using the still secret journal of the Joint Committee on Reconstruction as a prop, he heaped scorn on the notion that the amendment was "one single expression" concerned "with the protection of the freedmen of the South." Section one was designed to "employ not the narrowest, but the broadest, words in denoting the subjects on which the several amendments were to act." The moment was significant in the history of corporate uses of the amendment and its due process clause, and the Court soon affirmed Conkling's reasoning. (William F. Swindler, "Roscoe Conkling and the Fourteenth Amemdment," *Supreme Court Historical Society Yearbook 1983* [Washington, D.C., 1983], 46–52; *California Railroad Tax Case. In the Supreme Court of the United States. County of San Mateo, Plaintiff in Error, vs. The Southern Pacific Railroad Company, Defendant in Error. Oral Arguments on behalf of Defendant by Roscoe Conkling, Geo. F. Edmunds, S. W. Sanderson* [Washington, D.C., 1883].)

4. SBA contrasts Conkling's flexible and broad interpretation of the amendment with the literal, narrow readings put forward in cases concerned with voting rights. In 1870, George Edmunds for the Senate Committee on the Judiciary had rejected the claim of a petition from Rhode Island that the state's stiffer voting requirements for naturalized citizens than for the native born violated the Fourteenth and Fifteenth amendments. The amendments, he reported, had very limited reach: their authors, indeed, rejected any application other than "race, color, and previous condition of servitude." In cases involving women's voting rights, the same history of intent was told. Ward Hunt's opinion in SBA's own trial for illegal voting was a case in point: "The 13th, 14th and 15th Amendments," he wrote, "were designed mainly for the protection of the newly emancipated negroes." (*Congressional Record*, 41st Cong., 2d sess., 19, 20, 26 May 1870, pp. 3605–6, 3649, 3828; McPherson, *Hand-Book of Politics for 1874*, 215–16; United States v. Susan B. Anthony, 11 Blatchford 200 [1873].)

5. Mary Henrietta Swisshelm (1852–?) married Ernest L. Allen in December 1881 in Chicago. She gave birth to a daughter either late in 1882 or early 1883. (Sylvia D. Hoffert, *Jane Grey Swisshelm: An Unconventional Life, 1815–1884* [Chapel Hill, N.C., 2004], 174–86.)

100 ❧ ECS TO ELIZABETH PEASE NICHOL

Basingstoke Hants [*England*]   Jan 10th [*1883*][1]

Dear Mrs Nichol,

Yours of the 3rd should have been answered sooner had I felt able to say precisely what I would do. Not having felt very well I have been unable to ~~say~~ decide whether I could with safety make a journey to Edinboro. I was obliged to leave London being threatened with congestion, on account of the fogs. In fact I have had a cough ever since I landed in England, & my physician warns me to be careful until somewhat acclimated.[2] Hence I think I better remain here, until the long days bring more genial breezes & warmer sunshine. My daughters home is on a hill, where we have a fine view & seldom see a fog even of the faintest hue. I never saw anything to equal the black fogs in London for days we burned gas in the streets & houses.

I shall not leave England without spending a few days with you to look over your interesting correspondence.[3] I have just been reading the report of your annual meeting, of the woman suffrage association, in which I was much interested.[4] Kind regards to Mrs M'Laren. Is it not remarkable that we must stand to day rehearsing the same old arguments for women that have been made for different classes of men over & over again? How long will it take us to recognize the fact that all human beings have the same love of liberty & justice, & whatever is good for white men is equally good for black men & women. I see by the American papers that a grand dinner was given to Frederick Douglass in Washington, thus is a former slave honored in the Capitol of the nation[5]   Well the next generation of women will reap the blessings we are now sowing, so let us work on in faith & hope to the end. Have you looked over our History of woman suffrage yet? With the best wishes of the season, sincerely yours

❧ *Elizabeth Cady Stanton*

❧ ALS, *72M-101 (623), Letters to William Lloyd Garrison and Others, MH-H.

1. An unknown hand added the year 1884 to this date and later corrected it to read 1883.

2. ECS brought to England letters of introduction from her brother-in-law Edward Bayard to two homeopathic physicians practicing in London, a Dr. Wilson, probably David Wilson (c. 1811–?), and Edward William Berridge (1843?–1920?). Both men served with Bayard in 1880 on a committee intending to publish works by the founder of homeopathy, Samuel Hahnemann. ECS described Wilson as "a good talker and very original." He did offer the advice "to get out of the London fogs as quickly as possible." Determined to meet both men, ECS proceeded to Berridge's office. Berridge earned an honorary degree from the Homeopathic Medical College of Pennsylvania in 1869, and from 1878 to 1881, he was a publisher of *The Organon*, an Anglo-American medical journal. ECS thought highly enough of him to recommend him to the Priestmans, at 30 October 1883, below. Confusion between E. W. and a spiritualist C. M. Berridge has led researchers to assign widely divergent dates of birth and death to Edward. (*History*, 3:934; Census of Britain, 1881; Thomas Lindsley Bradford, *The Life and Letters of Dr. Samuel Hahnemann* [Phildelphia, 1895], 501–3; Ithell Colquhoun, *Sword of Wisdom: MacGregor Mathers and "the Golden Dawn"* [London, 1975], 148–49; Leslie A. Shepard, ed., *Encyclopedia of Occultism and Parapsychology*, 3d ed. [Detroit, Mich., 1991].)

3. ECS's promises to return to Edinburgh were frequently mentioned (see, for example, 30 January and 6 February 1883 below), but it appears that she did not make the trip. At the end of June, she again had a plan, this time to accompany SBA in July, and again she changed it. (*History*, 3:925–26; ECS to Theodore W. Stanton, 27 June 1883, *Film*, 23:235–36.)

4. The annual meeting of the Edinburgh National Society for Women's Suffrage took place on 28 December 1882 and was reported in *Englishwoman's Review* 14 (15 January 1883): 34–36.

5. On the twentieth anniversary of the Emancipation Proclamation, African-American leaders honored Frederick Douglass at a banquet in Washington on 1 January 1883. (Douglass, *Papers*, 5:52.)

101 🔊 SBA TO BENJAMIN F. BUTLER

Riggs House   Washington D.C. Jan 23/83

Dear Mr Butler

What does it mean that your letter does not come?[1] It is now 11 Oclock ~~Wednesday~~ ↑Tuesday↓ night— Don't fail to have it here ~~this~~

tomorrow morning—at Lincoln that P.M— I am distressed lest it is lost— Sincerely—

S. B. Anthony

If you can possibly come into our Con. tomorrow or next day—let me know—& I want you to be both seen & heard on our platform— S. B. A

ᐳ ALS, on NWSA letterhead for 1881–1882, Benjamin F. Butler Papers, DLC.

1. The Washington convention of the National association opened on Monday, January 22.

102 ᐳ Benjamin F. Butler to SBA

Washington, D.C., Jan. 23, 1883.

My Dear Miss Anthony: I received your kind note asking me to attend the national convention of the friends of woman suffrage at Washington, for which courtesy I am obliged. My engagements, which have taken me out of the commonwealth, cover all, and more than all, of my time, and I find I am to hurry back, leaving some of them undisposed of.[1] It will therefore be impossible for me to attend the convention.

As I have already declared my conviction that the fourteenth amendment fully covers the right of all persons to vote, and as I assume that the women of the country are persons, and very important persons, to its happiness and prosperity, I never have been able to see any reason why women do not come within its provisions.[2]

I think that such will be the decision of the court, perhaps quite as early as you may be able to get through congress and the legislatures of the several states another amendment. But both lines of action may well be followed, as they do not conflict with each other. This course was taken in the case of the fifteenth amendment, which was supposed to be necessary to cover the case of the negro, although many of the friends of the colored man looked coldly upon that amendment, because it seemed to be an admission that the fourteenth amendment was not sufficient. Therefore I can without inconsistency, I think, bid you "God speed" in your agitation for the sixteenth amendment.

It will have the effect to enlighten the public mind as to the scope of the fourteenth amendment. I am, very truly, your friend and servant,

℥ *Benj. F. Butler.*

℥ Washington *National Republican*, 25 January 1883.

1. Benjamin Butler was sworn in as governor of Massachusetts on 4 January 1883. At the evening session of the Washington convention on January 24, SBA read this letter aloud to the audience.

2. Butler stated this position as a member of the House Committee on the Judiciary, in a report signed with William Loughridge of Iowa: House Committee on the Judiciary, *Victoria C. Woodhull. Views of the Minority*, 41st Cong., 3d sess., 1 February 1871, H. Rept. 22, Pt. 2, Serial 1464.

103 ℥ ECS TO ANNA M. PRIESTMAN[1]

Basingstoke Hants [*England*] Jan 30 [*1883*]

Dear Miss Priestman,

Your kind letter of the 23rd was received, & I am sorry to say that my daughter could not just now accept your invitation to speak in a series of meetings. She is encèinte & suffering the usual disturbances of that condition, but I hope much of her in the future, as wifehood, & motherhood rightly considered are a means of developement. Basingstoke is a very benighted conservative town of about 8000 inhabitants, & might with benefit be "stirred up" a little by some of your speakers. They have never heard the gospel of woman's equality here, in fact we find ourselves quite alone in all our radical ideas, on many points.

We are going up to London on the 5th to attend Lady Harberton's dress convention.[2] I am quite well again & am getting somewhat acclimated   After making some visits in & about London, we are going to Edinborugh for a week, & when we return to Basingstoke my plan is, if all goes well to slip down to Bristol for a few days, to see you & Mrs Clarke[3] but we will arrange that to suit your convenience. With kind regards for yourself & sister sincerely yours

℥ *Elizabeth Cady Stanton.*

My address in London will be 10. Duchess street, Portland Place

❧ ALS, Millfield Papers, Archive, C. & J. Clark Ltd., Street, England. Not in *Film*.

1. Anna Maria Priestman (1828–1914), who grew up in a family of Quaker reformers, was a younger sister of John Bright's first wife, Elizabeth, and with their sister Mary Priestman (1830–1914), helped to raise Bright's daughter, Helen Priestman Bright. Anna Priestman was active in the Bristol (later West of England) National Society for Women's Suffrage from 1868, helped to found the National Union of Women Workers in the 1870s, and organized Bristol's Women's Liberal Association in 1881. Mary Priestman shared in her sister's activities, but she identified most closely with Josephine Butler's Ladies' National Association for Repeal. The sisters lived at Durdham Park, Bristol, where ECS visited them in May 1883 to speak to their Women's Liberal Association, and SBA made a social visit in November (below at November 10). (*Oxford DNB*, s.v. "Priestman, Anna Maria" and "Tanner, Margaret Priestman"; Mills, *John Bright and the Quakers*, 1:384–85, 392–97; S. J. Tanner, *How the Women's Suffrage Movement Began in Bristol Fifty Years Ago* [Bristol, England, 1918]; Holton, *Suffrage Days*; Census of Britain, 1881; *The Shield*, January 1915; *Film*, 23:156; *Stanton*, 2:206–7.)

2. Florence Wallace Legge Pomeroy, Viscountess Harberton (1843?–1911), founded the Rational Dress Society in 1881 to promote dress reform and her own reform costumes. The society held a meeting on February 6 at the Steinway Hall. Lady Harberton also presided over at least two of the mass demonstrations for woman suffrage that were held in the major British cities between 1880 and 1882, and she served as a member of the Central Committee of the National Society for Women's Suffrage in 1885. Late in 1886, she declined ECS's invitation to work on the *Woman's Bible*, saying that her own religious views were "far from orthodox," and her name would only prejudice people against the work. She went on to say she doubted that the project would "help the woman question." (*Oxford DNB*; David Rubinstein, "The Buckman Papers: S. S. Buckman, Lady Harberton and Rational Dress," *Notes and Queries* 244 [January–February 1977]: 41–45; *Times* [London], 2 May, 8 July 1911; *History*, 3:867–69, 878–79, 890n; F. Harberton to ECS, 24 December 1886, *Film*, 25:124; *Englishwoman's Review* 14 [15 February 1883]: 84–85.)

3. That is, Helen Bright Clark.

·⟮⟯══⟯══⟯·

104 ❧ SBA TO LILLIE DEVEREUX BLAKE

The Riggs House   Washington D.C. Feb. 6/83

Dear Mrs Blake

Yours of a few days since is before me— I am glad you pushed things so well at Albany—& hope our Savans will heed our many prayers!!¹

I saw Mr White of Ky. this A.M— he feels very sanguine he'll get the majority favorable report introduced in the House before the 21ˢᵗ inst²—so that Rachel & I can carry the joyful word with us across the big blue sea!³

I have had a talk with Carlysle⁴ of Ky who hopes to speaker of the next House—& he says of course <u>you</u> shall have <u>your</u> <u>select</u> Com. again next Congress— In the Senate there is no danger of not getting it—and Mr White will insist on it in the House— I am satisfied that letters from a score of women to the leading friends in both House about it—will be better—or at least <u>will</u> do the work of securing the re-appointment of our Com's— At any rate—there is no money to pay any ones ↑expenses to come↓ here— You must write Miss Sheldon what you want done— she is to be the acting Cor. Sec'y—while Miss Foster is gone—

I do hope our 16ᵗʰ am't resolution will get through our Legislature—

I shall go up to Philadelphia Saturday at latest—shall stop at Miss Thomsons—114—North 11ᵗʰ street— We are to sail Feb. 21ˢᵗ—two weeks from tomorrow— I hardly expect to go over to New York—or home to Rochester— Sincerely yours—

❧ *Susan B. Anthony*

❧ ALS, Lillie Devereux Blake Papers, MoSHi.

1. After the failure of the Andrews bill in 1882, New York's state association changed its strategy for the legislative session of 1883, seeking a constitutional amendment to remove "male" from the state's qualifications to vote and a bill for municipal suffrage. In response to the attorney general's opinion against the constitutionality of the Andrews bill, the association also mobilized to defeat the attorney general in his bid for reelection in November 1883. (*History*, 3:436–37; Blake and Wallace, *Champion of Women*, 156; *New York*

Times, 3 April 1883; *Woman's Journal*, 28 April 1883, 3 January 1885; New York *Evening Post*, Supplement, 7 February 1885.)

2. Not until 1 March 1883, two days before the end of the Forty-seventh Congress, did the Select Committee on Woman Suffrage refer House Resolution No. 255 back to the House with a favorable report and place the measure on the calendar. Although John White said he reported "by unanimous consent," committee member William Springer, Democrat of Illinois, claimed he had not seen the report. (*Congressional Record*, 47th Cong., 2d sess., 3551; 47th Cong., 2d sess., Joint Resolution, H.R. 255; House, Select Committee on Woman Suffrage, *Woman Suffrage. Report*, 47th Cong., 2d sess., H. Rept. 1997, Serial 2160.)

3. SBA's plans for a trip to Europe now included traveling with Rachel Foster on the Continent in addition to visiting with ECS in England.

4. John Griffin Carlisle (1835–1910), Democrat from Kentucky, entered the House of Representatives in 1877 and served until 1890, when he won election to the Senate. As SBA predicted, the House of Representatives of the Forty-eighth Congress, in which Democrats gained a substantial majority over Republicans, elected Carlisle Speaker of the House. (*BDAC.*)

105 ⤳ ECS TO ELIZABETH SMITH MILLER

London, February 6, [*1883*]

Dear Julius:

Hattie and I are here for a spree of two weeks and intend to go to Edinburgh before returning home. Yesterday we called on Lady Harberton who is the head of the dress reform movement.[1] She had on the bifurcated garments, but so well arranged that no one could have discovered the fact.[2] The effect was much better than our bloomers—Oh, those tempestuous days!—and she says they give quite as much freedom as our more conspicuous experiment did. Lady Harberton feels as we did, and still do—but alas! the pain of the doing because of opposition and ridicule—that there is no hope of much advancement for women while they are so hampered in body by mere clothes.

During our visit, Frances Power Cobbe came in, and the conversation turned from the rags of women to the bodies of animals. (You know she is the moving spirit of the anti-vivisection society.)[3] She had a beautiful dog with her and put him through all his tricks for us. As after each feat he had to get his reward, the thin bread and butter on the tea-table was soon exhausted. We laughed afterwards at the simplicity and unconsciousness, like a dear child in love with her pet, with which Miss Cobbe robbed us of our viands. I do not think she knew what she was doing, for she never said a "by your leave" to Lady Harberton. The sugar bowl was reduced to such a state of emptiness that poor old Johnson had to content himself with one lump of sugar. But Hattie whispered as she passed me the bowl: "Forget your sweet tooth, and be thankful that canines don't like tea."[4]

I had just read Miss Cobbe's "The Peak in Darien."[5] You would find the chapter on medicine very rich. Only think what doses the human stomach has endured in all ages. I found many things to disagree with, and [t]old her I thought the chapter on the Agnostics very unfair. She replied [t]hat she was too radical to please the orthodox, and too orthodox to please [t]he radical, and thus stood alone.

She told us an amusing story of her taking the chair at a suffrage [m]eeting. One of the London papers had said that morning that women lost their bloom by entering public life, so she began her remarks by "you see [b]efore you a woman who has lost all her bloom." Of course it brought down [t]he house, for she is immense, weighing nearly three hundred pounds, and [w]ith the ruddiest roundest face I ever saw. She looks as jolly as Santa [C]laus. We are to have tea with her—and the dog—to-morrow, and then I [w]ill tell you more about her.

I have made some pleasant friends among the Positivists,[6] and [h]ave attended a great gathering of the Salvation Army in Exeter Hall.[7] So I go from one extreme to the other,—eyes and ears open to all that is going on.

⇒ *Elizabeth Cady Stanton.*

⇒ Typed transcript, ECS Papers, NjR. Letters in square brackets obscured by binding.

1. Lady Harberton lived on Cromwell Road in London.

2. The divided skirt was Lady Harberton's signature design. ECS described it as "so skillfully adjusted in generous plaits and folds, that while the wearer enjoys the utmost freedom, the casual observer is quite ignorant of the innovation." At least one manufacturer, a cooperative of seamstresses and owners, produced the dress as part of its line of "hygienic" clothing. (*History*, 3:924; *Englishwoman's Review* 14 [15 June 1883]: 284–85.)

3. Officially the Society for Protection of Animals Liable to Vivisection,

this was known as the Victoria Street Society. In 1876, under pressure from the society, Parliament passed a bill to license but not prohibit scientific and medical experiments on live animals. See Richard D. French, *Antivivisection and Medical Science in Victorian Society* (Princeton, N.J., 1975).

4. Another account of Cobbe's dog appears in ECS's diary, 6 February 1883, *Stanton*, 2:203–4.

5. *The Peak in Darien, with Some Other Inquiries Touching Concerns of the Soul and the Body* (1882), a collection of essays. ECS refers to the essays "Sacrificial Medicine" and "Magnanimous Atheism."

6. ECS's diary reports meeting unnamed Positivists at the home of Fanny Hertz on 26 November 1882, in *Stanton*, 2:198. The entry goes on to say that she found them "narrow in their ideas as to the sphere of woman." See also *History*, 3:930–31, and *Eighty Years*, 360.

7. On 28 November 1882. Descriptions of the meeting are found in her diary, in *Stanton*, 2:199, and *History*, 3:932–33. The Salvation Army organized in 1878 and expanded at its most rapid pace between that date and 1883. On this occasion, new officers were commissioned to carry on the army's work in the United States, Sweden, the Cape of Good Hope, and New Zealand. (Glenn K. Horridge, *The Salvation Army, Origins and Early Days: 1865–1900* [Godalming, England, 1993]; Robert Sandall, *The History of the Salvation Army* [London, 1946], 2:223.)

106 ⇛ FRANCES P. COBBE TO ECS

[*London,*] Feb. 13 [*1883*]

Dear Mrs Stanton

The umbrella is all safe. I wondered to whom it might belong of our visitors—[1] I wish I could take, or send it to you but I am dreadfully pressed at this moment & have no available messenger at the office. If I were to send it to you by Parcel's C^o it would be almost infallibly broken—[2] Till further orders it shall therefore remain in charge of Mrs Rhodes[3] at the office   She will keep it carefully & deliver it to anybody you may send for it—

I am so pleased, dear Mrs Stanton, at your approval of my office— Certainly that kind of work can only be carried on with order—, & for my own part I look on the "admired disorder" of ↑some↓ literary folk with as much dislike as you do—as verging on that most detestable thing Bohemianism— Of course you & I know how a single day's hard work may leave one's writing table a mass of papers which must not be touched by profane hands   It is <u>permanent</u> & perennial disorderliness which is so intolerable & <u>helpless</u>—

You are yourself an instance of the healthfulness of work for women— The thing which ruins women in this country & I fancy even more often in America,—is their senseless disregard of the claims of the body— I recollect a dear Yankee friend of mine who travelled with me a long journey, remarking to me one day half petulantly "Your wants are so <u>imperious</u>! If you are hungry you <u>must</u> eat! If you are sleepy— you <u>must</u> sleep!"— My reply was "My dear Friend I believe it is to the fact that in this respect my habits are more those of a man than of a woman that I owe my vigour"—

I think you will be interested in the enclosed letter[4] which I have just received from the great female Reformer of India of whose movement at Bombay the Times gave an account three or four months ago— She is giving her life to elevate her country women & is said to be marvellously eloquent— I think we ought all to write & encourage her with our sympathy ↑& admiration↓   Will you not do so as a Representative of America?

Please return the letter   I hope dear Mrs Stanton you & M^rs & Miss Blatch[5] will some afternoon come & look in on me here at tea time— I am going down to Clifton for a week but shall then be fixed at home Ever

❧   *F P Cobbe*

❧ ALS, on stationery imprinted with address, ECS Papers, DLC.

1. Cobbe wrote from her home at 26 Hereford Square in South Kensington about a visit ECS made to her office on Victoria Street. ECS remarked on the orderliness of the office again in *Eighty Years*, 362.

2. The London Parcels Delivery Company carried small packages around the city.

3. This was probably Georgine M. Rhodes. Cobbe described her as "a good German scholar" with a sound knowledge of the antivivisection movement. In 1892, Rhodes compiled the book *The Nine Circles of the Hell of the Innocent: Described from the Reports of the Presiding Spirits*, published at Cobbe's expense. Errors in the book's account of medical experiments— errors caused, Cobbe said, by Rhodes not following directions—caused a major confrontation between antivivisectionists and medical doctors over the accuracy of reformers' propaganda. (Frances Power Cobbe, *Life of Frances Power Cobbe* [Boston, 1894], 2:624–27; French, *Antivivisection and Medical*

Science, 249–50; Sally Mitchell, *Frances Power Cobbe: Victorian Feminist, Journalist, Reformer* [Charlottesville, Va., 2004], 338–40.)

4. Enclosure missing.

5. Alice Blatch (c. 1853–?), Harry Blatch's next younger sister, lived with her father in Basingstoke. As Harriot Blatch told the story, she and ECS made a project of Alice, to find her an occupation. After meeting with Emily Lord in London, Alice took up kindergarten teaching, later won election to the Basingstoke school board, and, after moving to London in the 1890s, served as a poor law guardian in Islington. In 1901, she married George Edwards, a much younger civil servant at Scotland Yard. (Census of Britain, 1881; Blatch and Lutz, *Challenging Years*, 68–70; DuBois, *Harriot Stanton Blatch*, 56, 173, 292n.)

107 ❧ INTERVIEW WITH SBA IN PHILADELPHIA

EDITORIAL NOTE: Much attention was paid to SBA's departure for Europe, a day later than scheduled. National newspapers carried the news of her trip and reported the tributes paid her by friends in Washington, Rochester, and Philadelphia. While she prepared for the trip, Philadelphians had arranged a formal dinner, a reception at the New Century Club, an address to students at the Girls Normal School, and a party hosted by the Citizens' Suffrage Association and Robert Purvis. The last of these included celebration of her sixty-third birthday. On February 22, a reporter greeted her on the dock, where friends and family members had gathered to wish her a safe voyage. (*Film*, 23:110–20.)

[*22 February 1883*]

In conversation with a *News* reporter Miss Anthony said she was not going to Europe on account of her health, by any means, for she felt perfectly well and had never known a day's sickness in her life—which was saying a good deal for one who was 63 years old last Thursday. The chief object of her trip was for recreation and also to meet several friends in England, notably Mrs. Elizabeth Cady Stanton and others. To use her own expression, "I don't see why I can't have a little fun the same as any one else." Miss Anthony proposes to visit London, Rome, Paris and Geneva, returning to London in May to attend the annual meeting of the British National Woman's Suffrage Association;[1] thence to Switzerland in the summer and probably returning to this country with Mrs. Stanton in September to write the third volume of "The History of Woman Suffrage." When asked how she was pleased with the election of several ladies as school directors on Tuesday she replied: "I was delighted; though, of course, I should have been better pleased if all had been successful. Nature didn't make any mistake when she made woman mother, and woman alone, is fit to be the teacher of the child."[2]

"Is this your first visit to Europe, Miss Anthony?" asked the reporter.

"Yes, I am about to cross the ocean for the first time, but I do not apprehend any ill-effects from it. As I told you, I am in perfect health and intend to occupy my time in the saloon writing and preparing for my future work, for I do not intend to be idle. Although I am going for recreation I shall combine some work with it, and shall probably deliver several addresses and lectures in different European cities before returning to America."

How She Will Be Received.

Miss Anthony expects to be received on her landing in England by a delegation of some of the most prominent members of the Woman's Rights Society, who are to meet in Liverpool for that purpose.

Miss Rachel Foster will not return with Miss Anthony, but contemplates a three years sojourn in Europe. The postal address of both ladies will be at the American Exchange in Europe, No. 449 Strand, London.[3]

At 10 o'clock the bell rang, farewells were exchanged and in a few minutes the steamer left her dock, and with head down stream proceeded on her voyage.[4]

❧ Philadelphia *Evening News*, 22 February 1883, SBA scrapbook 10, Rare Books, DLC.

1. This was the Central Committee of the National Society for Women's Suffrage, a constituent body with societies in most of the large cities of Great Britain. It was born out of a division in 1871, when Lydia Becker and Jacob Bright separated from the original suffrage committee led by John Stuart Mill. (*History*, 3:841–42, 851–52, 866; Blackburn, *Women's Suffrage in the British Isles*, 63–68, 119–21; Strachey, *The Cause*, 268–72; Caine, "John Stuart Mill and the English Women's Movement"; Holton, *Suffrage Days*, 37–39, 54.)

2. By amendment to the state constitution in 1873, women in Pennsylvania

became eligible to hold elective office as school directors, the title for members of the boards that oversaw each school district. The first contests occurred in 1874. In 1883, women appeared on the ballot in seven of Philadelphia's thirty-one districts. Two women won their contests. (*History*, 3:465–68; James Pyle Wickersham, *A History of Education in Pennsylvania, Private and Public, Elementary and Higher* [1886; reprint, New York, 1969], 304, 313–16, 343–44; *Philadelphia Inquirer*, 19, 20, 22 February 1883.)

    3. The American Exchange and Reading Room provided services to American travelers in London, including access to American newspapers, an address for mail, currency exchange, and banking.

    4. In fact, the *British Prince* came to a halt thirty miles down the Delaware River, unable to clear the sandbars. The ship finally left the river in the afternoon of February 23. (SBA diary, 1883, *Film*, 22:814ff.)

108 ❧ ARTICLE BY ECS

10 Duchess Street, Portland Place, London, March 15 [*1883*].

Your readers will no doubt be pleased to know that their distinguished countrywoman, Susan B. Anthony, arrived safely in England on the 6th of March, having had a smooth, pleasant voyage on the British Prince. (Rather out of character for our demure friend to choose the "Prince" when the "Queen," belonging to the same line, is an equally good steamer.) Meeting Miss Anthony at one of the great London stations, my first question was, "Were you ill on the voyage?" "Not at all," was her prompt reply. "I have been perfectly well every moment of the time. I have enjoyed the voyage, and had a delightful rest. The first ten days in my life I had nothing to do."[1]

But her rest ended on landing. After exploring the wonders of Liverpool, she hurried to this great metropolis of the old world, and commenced at once a career of sight-seeing and lion-hunting sufficient to exhaust any ordinary mortal in one week. The House of Commons, the theaters, meetings for every reform under the sun, dinners, receptions, drives in the parks, all passed in quick succession. Every nook of the Westminster buildings she explored, from the old orange woman at the entrance to the ladies' gallery on the third story.[2] She was rather surprised to find the daughters of the nobility and wives of the members of Parliament seated in that dark, lofty perch, behind a fine wire grating, looking from the opposite side of the house like hens in a coop. The only way the members of the government can be seen from this outpost is by pressing one's nose close to the wires and looking down in as straight a line as the eyes can be fixed without closing. In the House of Lords we fared better. There we had comfortable seats, where we heard Lord Granville[3] make a great speech on the Portuguese question, and with our opera glasses had a good view of all the Lords and the Chancellor.[4]

In the corridor of the House of Commons we met Miss Caroline A. Biggs[5] and Miss Lydia Becker, plying the various members with woman suffrage petitions. There seems to be no rest for these unhappy men who make the laws, neither in the old world nor the new. The same thing going on here as in our Capitol at Washington, only our statesmen are much better looking, speak with more grace and ease, and the women have more comfortable seats to see and hear them.

Everybody in London raves over Irving and Miss Terry in "Much Ado About Nothing,"[6] so we persuaded Miss Anthony to go and see them. At breakfast next morning she was asked how she enjoyed the entertainment. "It was so stupid I could hardly keep my eyes open," was her prompt reply. "Irving mouths the English language so that I could not understand a word he said, and what I did understand was not worth hearing, and he moves about in such a stiff way that one might imagine him just recovering from an attack of rheumatism. The only redeeming points to me were the beautiful scenery and the love-making, which was cooler, more distant, and more piquant than usual."[7]

The looks and exclamations of surprise that went round the table at such criticisms on this popular play and the idols of the hour were as varied as amusing. A brilliant reception at Mrs. Peter B. Taylor's,[8] where Miss Anthony had the honor of meeting many members of Parliament and other distinguished ladies and gentlemen, pleased her much better. Mrs. Taylor, a most charming woman, is the leader of the suffrage movement in this country. With sensible people and important questions for discussion, Miss Anthony is quite at her ease, and she never looked better than on this occasion, in an elegant black satin dress and point lace cape, presented her by loving friends on the eve of her departure from America.[9] Her toilet was completed with the beautiful suffrage badge given her by the friends in Philadelphia.[10] While my daughter was pinning the badge on her left shoulder an English lady remarked: "Won't that look very odd?" Not at all. Your Queen wears badges of distinction on state occasions, and why should not one of our queens. This morning Miss Anthony, in company with four other ladies,[11] left London for Rome, where they hope to celebrate Palm and Easter Sundays. She proposes quite an extensive tour in Italy, Switzerland, France, and Germany, to return here for a few months, and home in October, ready to besiege Congress at the opening of the next session for a sixteenth amendment to the National Constitution that shall secure to the women of the republic all the civil and political rights that are in justice theirs as citizens of a free government.

⤝ *Elizabeth Cady Stanton.*

⤝ Chicago *Inter-Ocean*, n.d., SBA scrapbook 10, Rare Books, DLC.

1. "Mrs Stanton with her flowing white curls & beaming face awaited us at Depot," SBA recorded in her diary on March 8, when she reached London. (SBA diary, 1883, *Film*, 22:814ff.)

2. London's fruit sellers were well known to readers of English literature, and the phrase "orange girl" or woman could be applied to someone selling any fruit. ECS made frequent mention of the ladies' gallery in Parliament and described it again in *History*, 3:931, and *Eighty Years*, 361.

3. Granville George Leveson-Gower, Earl Granville (1815–1891), was foreign secretary from 1880 to 1885. He responded to a question about negotiations underway with Portugal to recognize that country's claim to land along the River Congo. This was one small element of the competition in the 1880s among European powers for control of trade in Africa. (*Times* [London], 10 March 1883; Kenneth Bourne, *The Foreign Policy of Victorian England, 1830–1902* [Oxford, England, 1970], 140–41; Paul Knaplund, *Gladstone's Foreign Policy* [1935; reprint, Hamden, Conn., 1970], 92–93.)

4. Roundell Palmer, First Earl of Selborne (1812–1895), served as Lord Chancellor in the ministry of William Gladstone from 1880 to 1885. In that post, he presided over meetings of the House of Lords. (*Oxford DNB.*)

5. Caroline Ashurst Biggs (1840–1889), in company with Lydia Becker, called on SBA as soon as she reached London and entertained her on March 12. Biggs was a member of the Central Committee of the National Society for Women's Suffrage; editor, from 1870 until her death, of the *Englishwoman's Review*; foreign corresponding secretary of the National Woman Suffrage Association; and author of the chapter on Great Britain for the *History of Woman Suffrage*. Brought into suffrage activism by Clementia Taylor, Biggs was a secretary to the earliest London committee, until John Stuart Mill engineered her removal in 1871. A day of sightseeing in London with Biggs caused SBA to remark, "English women seem to know nothing of getting tired

out." (*Oxford DNB*; *Women's Suffrage Journal* 20 [1 October 1889]: 125; Mill, *Collected Works*, 17:1698, 1823–24, 1825, 1836, 1842–43, 1849, 1851, 1860; SBA diary, 9, 12, 13 March, 8, 9, 11, 25 October 1883; *History*, 3:833–94.)

The petitions supported a resolution that would put Parliament on record, in advance of debate on the Third Reform Bill, as favoring the extension of suffrage to women "who possess qualifications which entitle men to vote, and who in all matters of local government have the right of voting." Although the resolution's language about qualifications was similar to earlier motions dating back to 1867, the passage in 1882 of a Married Women's Property Act changed the terms of debate about its meaning. Married women, who met the property qualifications to vote, might now be deemed eligible, unless they still lacked the status of single and widowed women. (*History*, 3:872–73; Blackburn, *Women's Suffrage in the British Isles*, Chart I; Strachey, *The Cause*, 276–77; Mary Lyndon Shanley, *Feminism, Marriage, and the Law in Victorian England, 1850–1895* [Princeton, N.J., 1989], 102–30.)

6. Henry Irving (1838–1905) and Ellen Terry (1847–1928), two of England's most distinguished actors, performed many Shakespearean plays together on the London stage.

7. In her diary, SBA said of the play, "Good but not at all equal to Boothe," referring to the American Shakespearean actor Edwin Thomas Booth. (13 March 1883.)

8. On March 14. Clementia Doughty Taylor (1810–1908), one of Britain's earliest advocates of woman suffrage, hosted many receptions for radical politicians and reformers at Aubrey House, her home with Peter Alfred Taylor (1819–1891), a radical member of Parliament from 1862 to 1884. A founder of the Ladies' London Emancipation Society during the American Civil War, Mentia Taylor signed the suffrage petition to Parliament in 1866 and served as treasurer of the London National Society for Women Suffrage at its founding in 1867. She was also a member of the executive committee of the Married Women's Property Committee from 1876 to 1882. (Sally Mitchell, ed., *Victorian Britain, An Encyclopedia* [New York, 1988], and *Oxford DNB*, s.v. "Taylor, Clementia Doughty"; *Times* [London], 14 April 1908; Baylen and Gossman, *Modern British Radicals*, 2:497–99; *Who's Who of British Members of Parliament*, vol. 1; SBA diary, 14 March, 30 May, 12 June 1883.)

9. Cheney Brothers of Manchester, Connecticut, gave SBA a dress length of black silk to make a new dress for her trip. The point lace was a gift from suffragists in the District of Columbia. ("Women's Work," *Indianapolis Times*, n.d., SBA scrapbook 10, Rare Books, DLC; SBA diary, 17 February 1883.)

10. The Citizens' Suffrage Association presented SBA with this piece of jewelry at the National's annual meeting in May 1881. A gold bar pin inscribed "S. B. A." held a Greek cross on which "N.W.S.A" and "1848" had been inscribed. A message on the back of the cross read: "Presented to SBA by the Citizens' Suffrage Association of Philadelphia as a token of gratitude for her life-long devotion to the interests of women, May 1881." (*Boston Daily Globe*, 27 May 1881, *Film*, 21:993.)

11. SBA's party consisted of Alice Blatch, Rachel Foster, Hattie Daniels, and Fanny Keartland, making a party of "four spinsters and a widow," as ECS quipped. "They all wear spectacles and eyeglasses, so their sight-seeing may involve many optical illusions." Harriet, or Hattie, Daniels (c. 1840–?) grew up in Canandaigua, where she kept house for a widowed sister and a nephew. She accompanied ECS to the station to greet SBA, "as sort of escort" SBA observed in her diary. Daniels left the party on March 19 in Rome when she met up with a friend. (Federal Census, 1880; Lewis Cass Aldrich, comp., *History of Ontario County, New York, with Illustrations and Family Sketches of Some of the Prominent Men and Families* [Syracuse, N.Y., 1893], 243; SBA diary, 8, 19 March 1883.) Fanny Keartland (c. 1837–?), a widow who lived in London, may have been a friend of Alice Blatch. In addition to making the trip to Italy, she joined Alice at Basingstoke in June when SBA returned from the Continent. She also visited Edinburgh during SBA's stay there late in July, at which point SBA referred to her as "of Clifton." (Census of Britain, 1881; ECS to Mary S. Anthony, 16 March 1883, *Film*, 23:133, and SBA diary, 3, 5 June, 27 July, 2 August 1883, and address pages.)

109 ⇝ SBA TO DANIEL R. ANTHONY

Amalfi, Italy, April 1 [*1883*][1]

I dropped you a postal two weeks ago from Milan.[2] Since that we have spent a week in the "Eternal City," visited St. Peter's and sundry other cathedrals, less in size but equal in style in different ways. On Easter Sunday we saw the devotees most fervently kiss St. Peter's big toe.[3] One day we devoted to the palaces of the Caesars—all brought out by the most patient and careful excavations—one entire palace built on top of another. The old pavements, forty feet below the later ones, still preserve their Mosaic faces; the frescoes on the walls of the oldest and deepest one are still bright. I think the survival of the colors strikes me as quite as marvelous as any one thing.[4]

Our hotel at Rome was filled almost exclusively with Americans. Its name is Pension Chapman, 75 Nazionale; and if any of your Kansans are going to Rome it will be *the place* to find things somewhat homelike. We spent a week there, and return there again to-morrow. The last week we spent at Naples. Mr. and Mrs. Albert Chain,[5] of Denver, and two young ladies,[6] with our two English ladies, made up our party. We climbed Vesuvius;[7] the ascent is now made easy by an almost perpendicular railroad from the point where we leave the carriages to within two hundred yards of the old crater. But that distance was quite enough for my three-score-and-three. Not only is the ascent very steep, but the loose, deep lava causes one to slide back almost as far as one steps each time. But one feels richly paid when the puffing and exploding and the ascending of the red-hot lava meets the eyes and the ears.

The mountains, the Bay of Naples, the sail to Capri, and the blue grotto are fully equal to my expectation;[8] yes, and so are the ruins of Pompei and Herculaneum, to which we gave a day. I am getting but a bird's eye glimpse of things. But, the squalid looking people on the streets, their hopeless fate, makes one's stay at any of these Italian resorts most depressing. Troops of beggars beset you all along the streets and roads; with tradesmen there is no honesty, and the one thing every traveler is warned against being cheated—paying double and treble what a thing is worth. The rule is, that you are not safe to offer more than *one third* the price asked and even in doing that you may pay more than a thing is worth. For instance a man asked for a long comb shell twenty francs, he came down to seven, then six, then five and finally said, "What will you give?" I, never dreaming he would accept it, said "two francs" and he threw the comb in the carriage. Yesterday—Saturday—we took the cars from Naples to Salerno,[9] twenty-four miles, and a drive to the palace Amalfi twelve and a half miles. For the entire distance the road is cut in the rocks that jut into the sea, immense walls are built up to hold the road, and the ravines are crossed with splendid stone bridges. It was built in 1852, or finished then. The road is very crooked, winding in and out and around the mountain curves; each leading point crowned with the ruins of an old fort, built eight centuries ago, to protect the coast against the pirates of the Mediterranean. Every mountain side that has a seven by nine patch of soil in a place is terraced and grape vines and lemon trees—the latter yellow with fruit—now cover them. On many of them I counted twenty and thirty terraces, each with a solid stone wall to hold the soil in its place. It is wonderful to see what an amount of labor it costs to get even the little the natives seem to care for. Our hotel here is an old monastery, and on one side of its court is the cathedral, with its grotesque paintings. One gets awfully sickened with the ghastly spectacle of the *dead* Christ. It is amazing how little they make of the *living* Christ.

Rome, April 5.[10]

On Monday morning we drove back over that magnificent road, and took the train to Naples. In the afternoon we drove to Lake Averness, and went into the Grotto of the Sibyls, the entrance to Dante's Inferno,[11] and were carried on the backs of stalwart Italians through the knee-deep waters into various rooms, which clearly show themselves to have been parts of olden baths, into which by some convulsion of nature, the waters of the lake have found their way.

It was a dark, long, cavernous passage, and with the men's fluttering candles making the darkness but the more visible, we could but feel that there was reason for the old superstition. In going and returning to this lake we passed through a long tunnel, made, it is said, in the eighth century. It is now well lighted with gas and paved.

The narrowness of the streets of Naples—and they are without the pretense of a sidewalk—leave the men, women, children, horses and carriages, donkeys and their loads, the cows and little goats, each night and morning driven along, from house to house and halted at each door, while the pint cup full, more or less, is milked from them to supply the people, all these go marching along, jostling each other at every step.

But we are back in Rome now, where, in the newer parts of the city, the streets are wider, and bordered with narrow sidewalks, though in the older parts of the city they are the same as in Naples. This forenoon we spent in the picture galleries of the Vatican. I cannot describe them; one is simply dazed with the wealth of marble—not only the statuary, but the stairs, pillars and massive buildings. We stop here until the 9th, and then go to Florence, and reach Berlin about the 25th, where we are to be the guests of our American minister to Germany. I have already received letters of invitation and welcome from Mrs. Sargent.[12]

It is good for our younger civilization to see and study that of the olden days, and to see what still exists in this old world to-day—the hopelessness of lifting the masses of the people swarming these streets into freedom and freedom's industry, honesty and integrity. How any American, any lover of our free institutions, based on equality of rights for all, can settle down and live here is more than I can comprehend. It will be only by overturning and overturning the powers that be—that education and equal chances will come to the rank and file of the people. The hope of the world is indeed in our republic. So let us work to make it a *genuine democracy*, where every citizen—woman as well as man—shall be crowned with the one national symbol of equality—the ballot.

Last evening Miss Foster and I went to an Art Association's concert at which Ristori gave two recitations—one from Dante's Inferno and the other from Joan of Arc.[13] She is matchless in her power of expression, though I couldn't understand a word she said. She is most graceful, motherly and dignified in her appearance. The music, both singing and violin, was soft and sweet beyond anything I ever heard, and I wished sister Annie[14] could be there to enjoy it.

～ S. B. A.

～ *Leavenworth Times*, 29 April 1883.

1. SBA and her party reached Amalfi on this day.

2. She stopped in Milan on March 16 and 17.

3. For more on the visit to Rome, from March 18 to 26, see SBA to Mary S. Anthony, 23 March 1883, *Film*, 23:136. Easter fell on March 25. Noting in her diary this custom of kissing the toe of the bronze, fifth-century statue of St. Peter, SBA thought "the poor devotees" exhibited "all the religious awe of ignorance and superstition." (SBA diary, 1883, *Film*, 22:814ff.)

4. Excavations began at this site of several imperial palaces on Palatine Hill, including that of Augustus Caesar, in 1726 and continued well into the nineteenth century. SBA toured the ruins on March 21.

5. James Albert Chain (c. 1847–1892) and Helen Henderson Chain (1852–1892) joined the party in Rome for the trip to Naples. See also SBA to M. S. Anthony, 27 March 1883, *Film*, 23:138. The Chains left Denver for Europe in January 1883. Helen Chain was a well-known artist, and her husband was a partner in Chain and Hardy, booksellers and stationers. Frequent travelers, the Chains died when their steamer was destroyed by a typhoon on the China Sea. (*Rocky Mountain News*, 7 January 1883, and *Denver Republican*, 20 October 1892, courtesy of Kay Wisnia, Denver Public Library; Federal Census, 1880; city directory, 1876; Phil Kovinick and Marian Yoshiki-Kovinick, *An Encyclopedia of Women Artists of the American West* [Austin, Tex., 1998].)

6. Also added to the party were Genevieve Walton and Hattie Hoover. Genevieve Maria Julia Walton (1857–1932) grew up in Ypsilanti, Michigan. While attending St. Mary's Academy in Indiana, she studied art and began to paint. She and her parents lived briefly in Denver, which may explain why she traveled with the Chains. The Waltons returned to Michigan later in 1883. Walton changed careers in 1891, when she enrolled in a library course. She became librarian of the Ypsilanti Normal School the next year and held that post until her death. (Laurel Grotzinger, "Women Who Spoke for Themselves," *College & Research Libraries* 39 [May 1978]: 186–88; biographical

file, Archives, Eastern Michigan University, courtesy of Rosina Tammany; Saint Mary's College Archives; SBA to G. Walton, 2 January 1896, *Film*, 34:736–37.) Hattie Hoover appears in the census of 1880 as a girl of nineteen, born in Indiana and living with her widowed mother in Three Rivers, Michigan. She later married Charles F. Harding, an attorney in Chicago; in 1892, SBA recorded Hattie's married name and address in her diary. (Federal Census, 1880; back cover, SBA diary 1892, *Film*, 29:655ff; Chicago city directories, 1892 and 1893.)

7. On March 29. The Vesuvius Wire Rope Railway opened in 1880.

8. She sailed to Capri on March 30 and visited the Blue Grotto, a large water cave known to the Romans and rediscovered in the nineteenth century.

9. D. R. Anthony misread his sister's handwriting and reported their destination to be Palermo. At Amalfi, SBA stayed at the Albergo dei Cappuccini near the Cathedral of St. Andrea.

10. SBA returned to Rome on April 3 in the evening. See also SBA to M. S. Anthony, 5 April 1883, *Film*, 23:142.

11. On April 2. SBA was mistaken in her literary allusion: it was the Roman poet Virgil (70–19 B.C.), not the Italian poet Dante (1265–1321), who described, in the sixth book of the *Aeneid*, the Cave of the Sibyl next to Lake Avernus as the point at which Aeneas entered the underworld.

12. Aaron Sargent served as minister to Berlin from 1882 to 1884. In New York on 29 April 1882, SBA had accompanied the family, including the two daughters, to their ship. Elizabeth studied medicine in Zurich during this time, while Ella stayed in Berlin with her parents. (SBA to Elizabeth B. Harbert, 1 May 1882, *Film*, 22:471–72; and SBA diary, 21–23, 29 April, 1–3, 5–7 May 1883.)

13. At the International Association of Artists, Vicolo d'Alibert, they heard Adelaide Ristori (1822–1906), an Italian actress noted for her tragic roles.

14. Anna E. Osborne Anthony (1845–1930) married Daniel Read Anthony in 1864. (Anthony, *Anthony Genealogy*, 185; *U.S. Biographical Dictionary: Kansas Volume*, 56–63; biographical files, KHi. See also *Papers* 1–3.)

110 ⪼ SBA TO DANIEL R. ANTHONY

[Heidelberg, Germany, 11 May 1883][1]

As I have clambered among the ruins of the Heidelberg castle to-day I have thought of all my loved ones left in the new World, and wished for each in turn to come across old Ocean and look upon the remains of ancient civilization,—of art and architecture, of bigotry and barbarism.

I am enjoying my "flying" ever and ever so much. We have remained a week in only three places, in most cases not over two days, but I would not again make such a rush—it is too tiresome and confusing, seeing so many things so close on the heels of each other. But I am getting a good relish for a more deliberate tour at some later day. All of life should not be in running one's work at home, whether that is woman's suffrage, newspaper or government affairs. I have thought often that I would write you a decent letter of some of my sight-seeings, but I get too awfully tired every day to possibly think of touching a pen, much less thinking a thought.

We spent last week delightfully in the most hospitable home of our United States minister at Berlin. After being among people perpetually, not a word of whose language I could understand, it was doubly grateful to me to get into the midst not only of my countrymen but of my dearest friends, and I enjoyed their society so much that I almost forgot there were any wonders of art or architecture in Berlin.[2] But we did make an excursion to Potsdam[3]—a jolly company of us, Mr. and Mrs. Sargent and their gifted daughter, Ella, also the professor of Greek in your Kansas State University at Lawrence, Miss Kate Stephens.[4] I remembered the fact of her appointment four or five years ago, but had never seen her. She is "every inch a woman," dignified, easy, graceful, not a bit pedantic, and yet intelligent on every question, imparting information readily, speaking German like a native Dutchman, and interpreting the rapid utterances of the ever-present guide, for the edification of those of us to whom their jabber was worse than "Greek." Our minister has conquered the language in his one year's residence, both understanding and speaking it quite readily,—a great feat, I should say, and accomplished only by the most indefatigable study and practice.

At Potsdam we were shown the very rooms[5] in which Frederick the Great lived and moved and had his being, plotted and planned to conquer his neighbors; the very library, books, piano, music rack, the manuscript written by his own hand. On the door hangs a painting of Frederick playing his flute. In the little church, plain and unattractive, save for the myriads of flags, tattered and torn, taken in their many wars, hanging around the galleries, are two great stone caskets on either side of a dark vault, in which repose the bodies of Frederick the Great and his father, Frederick William, peaceful in death, however warlike in life.

We also visited the new palace[6] where the present Emperor William spends the summer months. The grounds are spacious and beautiful, the palace grand in proportions and magnificent in arrangement. I cannot describe the various rooms, but we saw the parlor, the dining room, the bedrooms, the very plain, narrow bed-stead the emperor sleeps upon, the great workshop, in which are tables, maps, all sorts of materials for study and planning how to hold and gain empires. In this room he receives Bismark, von Moltke and others of his private council. I even peered into the kitchen, and saw there the pitchers, plates, coffee-pots, stew-pans, etc., all duly placed on shelves and tables. It was my first sight of a real mortal living look of things! so I enjoyed this palace hugely. We saw the crown princess' bedroom,[7] also that of the Grand Duchess of Baden—there are rooms enough in these palaces for an army of people. But you must come and see them for yourself; no descriptions can make one realize how these concentrations of elegancies are heaped together for one family at the expense of the comforts and elevation of all the people outside. One is so constantly impressed with the fact that all of these magnificent displays of wealth in churches, palaces and castles, citadels, fortifications and glittering military displays of monarchical governments are only so many evidences of the poverty, ignorance and degradation of the masses, that all pleasure in seeing them is sullied with sadness, and I turn to our own land of "freedom and equality to all men" with hope for the highest development of race. It is only under such broad institutions as ours that true greatness of character can be attained; and when we shall have rounded out our government by the practical applications of its great principles of equality of rights to its whole people—not half, as now—our nation will have started on its career of grandeur that shall "make it the bright and shining example to all the world outside."

We stop at Strausburg[8] to see and hear the great clock on Sunday, then to Paris on Monday, and after a few days there, back to London for June.

∽ *Susan B. Anthony.*

∽ *Leavenworth Times*, 3 June 1883, not in *Film*. Reprinted in unidentified newspaper, in *Film* at date. Variant in *Anthony*, 2:560, also in *Film*.

1. An editorial introduction described this as a private letter to D. R. Anthony, dated at Heidelberg on May 11. According to her diary, SBA wrote

this letter on May 12. The party left Rome on April 9, stopped for a day in Pisa, and reached Florence on April 10 in the evening. The party began to break up: SBA and Rachel Foster left Florence on April 16 for Venice and Milan. After a visit to Zurich to see Elizabeth Sargent and stops in Munich, Nuremberg, and Dresden, Rachel and SBA arrived in Berlin on April 28. They reached Heidelberg on this date. Heidelberg Castle was a magnificent Renaissance ruin overlooking the Rhine. See also SBA to Mary S. Anthony, 23 April and 8 May 1883, and SBA to Elizabeth B. Harbert, 12 May 1883, *Film*, 23:147, 149, 152–54.

2. SBA made no mention at the time of an apocryphal adventure in Berlin reported later by ECS. After SBA mailed numerous letters written on the stationery of the National Woman Suffrage Association, a German official returned them all to the American legation. The German post office refused to handle envelopes imprinted with messages like "taxation without representation is tyranny." (*History*, 3:944.)

3. On May 3.

4. Kate Stephens (1853–1938) moved to Lawrence, Kansas, with her parents in 1868 and graduated from the University of Kansas in 1875. She became assistant professor of Greek when she received her master's degree in 1878 and was made full professor the next year. The university dismissed her from the faculty in 1885, and she worked primarily as an editor and author for the rest of her life. (*NAW*.)

5. The Old Palace, one of several in which Frederick II, king of Prussia (1712–1786), or Frederick the Great, lived at Potsdam, preserved his private rooms, as SBA describes. The Garrison Church contained his remains alongside those of his father, Frederick William I (1688–1740). The flags were French, some of them taken in the Franco-Prussian War in 1870 and 1871.

6. The New Palace, completed by Frederick the Great in 1769, was a residence of William I, emperor of Germany (1797–1888). Otto Eduard Leopold von Bismarck (1815–1898), first chancellor of the German Empire, was the architect of William's consolidation of Germany under Prussian control and his invasion of France. Helmuth Karl Bernhard von Moltke (1800–1891), chief of the Prussian general staff, reorganized the military and its tactics.

7. Victoria Adelaide Mary Louisa (1840–1901), a daughter of England's queen, married the crown prince in 1858. She and her family had a summer residence in the palace. The Grand Duchess of Baden was her sister-in-law, formerly Luise, princess of Prussia (1838–1923).

8. On May 13. Tourists gathered at the cathedral in Strasburg to watch this complex astronomical clock, with its many mechanisms that marked the fractions of each hour.

·⟨══════⟩·

111 ⤙ FROM THE DIARY OF SBA

[*14–25 May 1883*]

MONDAY, MAY 14, 1883. Left Strassburg—6.30—for Parris—arrived 5.30 P.M.— Theodore Stanton & wife Marguerite—met us at Depot—& accompanied us to the Palais Royal Hotel—opposite the Louve—[1] Rachel met here her friends Mr & Mrs Mills & daughter Ella—from Cincinatti—[2] We had a delightful ride the scenery some of it—lovely— it was through the <u>lost to France</u>-kingdoms of Alsace & Loraine—it seemed sad to me all day—& as if they must be given back to France—[3] Wars seem to have been the Chronic condition of poor France—

1. Hôtel de la Place du Palais Royal, rue de Rivoli.
2. This family is unidentified. They appear in SBA's diary only on the days in Paris reproduced here.
3. By the treaty ending the Franco-Prussian War in 1871, Germany gained control of the French border regions Alsace and Lorraine.

TUESDAY, MAY 15, 1883. In Paris—Hotel—Palais Royal—Rue Rivoli— Breakfast at 8.30— A letter from Madam d'Barrau—& a call—inviting me to be her guest during my stay in Paris—also invited & self to dine at 51-rue-de-Varenne at 7. this eve—which we accepted & had a very splendid dinner & nice visit— during the P.M. we called at American Bureau[1]—& at the Normandy Hotel[2] & saw J. Scott Anthony & bride—[3] Miss Ward's friend—Mrs Sharpstein not in—[4]

1. The American Exchange in Paris was affiliated with the London office and provided similar services.
2. On the rue de l'Echelle.
3. Scott J. Anthony (1830–1903), a distant cousin of SBA, was a business-man in Denver, Colorado. He is best known as the major in charge of Colorado's Fort Lyon at the time of the Sand Creek Massacre in 1864; though not held personally responsible for the murder of Indian women and children, he did not use his superior rank to stop or condemn the outrages. After the death of his first wife in 1878, Anthony married Frances Brown (c. 1840–?), a teacher in Denver. (*Portrait and Biographical Record of Denver and Vicinity, Colorado* [Chicago, 1898], 340–45; Federal Census, 1880; *Leavenworth Times*, 6 October 1903, Kansas Scrapbook Biography A, KHi; David Svaldi, *Sand Creek and*

the Rhetoric of Extermination: A Case Study in Indian-White Relations [Lanham, Md., 1989], passim.)

4. Possibly SBA refers to a friend of Eliza Titus Ward (c. 1838–1907), an activist in Washington who served on the finance committee at the National's recent convention. Known for "notable administrative ability and financial sagacity," Ward later became the auditor of the National-American Woman Suffrage Association. (Unidentified clipping, 27 July 1890, in SBA scrapbook 16, Rare Books, DLC; *Washington Post*, 15 November 1907; Federal Census, 1880.)

WEDNESDAY, MAY 16, 1883. In Paris—at Palais Royal Rue Rivoli— in A.M. to see [*line left blank*] in P.M. ↑at 4.↓ to Salon—to see the paintings & statuary of living artistes—with Miss Ella Mills—[1] at 4.30 to call (with Theodore) on Madam d Raismes—[2] at 6 dined at Restaurant with the Mills'— at 8 R[achel] & I went to the Opera—magnificent house scenery—equipage & all—but with my three lacks—in music— language & sight—I could not appreciate the artistic merit of the performance—& I feared, too, it was the "added ounce" for dear Rachel— got letter from Sister Mary—good news[3]

1. The Salon in the Palais de l'industrie held an annual exhibition of contemporary paintings and sculpture in May and June.

2. While in Paris, SA met the three key figures in the republican movement for women's rights in France: Maria Deraismes (1828–1894), Hubertine Auclert, and Léon Richer. By 1883, they worked separately, having reached different conclusions about how to expand women's civil and political rights without jeopardizing the Third Republic. Deraismes, a writer and brilliant orator, founded the movement in the 1860s and worked alongside Richer for more than a decade. They both had opposed the demand for woman suffrage, fearing that republican secularism could not survive if women brought their strong religious values to the polls. At the time SBA met with her, Deraismes presided over the Société pour l'amelioration du sort de la femme and edited the paper *Le Républicain de Seine-et-Oise*. In the fall of 1882, she began to express moderate support for woman suffrage, upsetting Richer and earning praise from Auclert. Deraismes was equally well known for her anticlericalism, and she contributed an essay on the interconnection between the liberation of women and the secular state to the chapter on France in Theodore Stanton, *Woman Question in Europe*. (*DBF*; Laurence Klejman and Florence Rochefort, *L'Égalité en Marche: Le féminisme sous la Troisème République* [Paris, 1989], 34–39, 57–85; Patrick Kay Bidelman, "Maria Deraismes, Léon Richer, and the Founding of the French Feminist Movement, 1868–1878," *Third Republic/ Troisième République* 3–4 [1977]: 20–73; Patrick Kay Bidelman, "The Politics of French Feminism: Léon Richer and the Ligue Française pour le Droit des

Femmes, 1882–1891," *Historical Reflections/Réflexions Historiques* 3 [Summer 1976]: 93–120.)

3. SBA wrote this entry on the page in her diary for Friday, May 18; caught her mistake; corrected the printed date; and wrote "move back" at the top of the page. She then entered May 17 and 18 on the two preceding pages, making the appropriate corrections to the printed dates.

THURSDAY, MAY 17, 1883. Paris— Rachel left—9.40—for London—[1] Miss Ella Mills went Depot with me to see R. off— Sad to see go & I left behind— She has been a most genial & loving companion through the whole trip— Miss Mills took me to the Madeline Cathedral—Greek architecture[2]—then to Am Exchange—then met her Father & he took me to the Louve— after that Lunch at the Palais Royal—then a long call from J. Scott Anthony & bride (Miss Brown) of Denver— then at 5 P.M. Cab to 51 ↑rue-de-↓Varenne Madam d Barrau's—to stay with her a few days—her home is delightful & she a most intelligent woman—thoroughly posted on all great questions—had a delightful evening— Theodore Stanton & wife have home here too—

1. Since the start of their journey, Rachel Foster had prepared to be presented at Court in London, wearing a dress made for her in Berlin that SBA described as a "cream-white satin, low neck, *no sleeves at all*, and a four-yard train!" (SBA to Jane S. Spofford, 20 May 1883, *Film*, 23:158.)

2. The Église de la Madeleine, built to resemble a Greek temple, is surrounded by large columns.

FRIDAY, MAY 18, 1883. In Paris—at Madam d'Barraus— Charming morning—the Robins & other birds singing—sun shining—air lovely— room south east corner—& bright & lovely— It does seem good again to be in a home with those who can talk English—though only Madam d'B—Theodore & Marguerite can do so here— Madam Berry[1] cannot speak or understand English—she is a very fine appearing woman— young to be ↑grand↓ mother of an This is my first real Continental breakfast—roll & butter & coffee bro't to my room at 8 A.M.— I enjoyed it much— Marguerite took me to Miliners for bonnet in A.M. failed— Theodore to see the University—Sorbonne—Notre Dam &c— Madam d Barrau at evening took me to anti C.D.A. meeting[2] where were passed Resolutions to Mr Stansfeld[3]

1. The announcement of Theodore and Marguerite Stanton's marriage was made by her parents, "Monsieur et Madame A. Berry." Harriot Stanton

Blatch, however, suggested that Marguerite's father died before her marriage. (*Film*, 21:976; Blatch and Lutz, *Challenging Years*, 55–58.)

2. Although France's regulation of prostitution, or police des moeurs, set the example for Britain's Contagious Diseases Acts, agitation to abolish regulation traveled in the opposite direction. Josephine Butler made several trips to Paris to encourage reform. The French movement never equaled the British model, but it met with some success just before SBA's arrival. Between 1880 and 1882, abolitionists in Paris forced the municipal government to restrain enforcers of the law, and they drew public attention to the false security against disease and the threat to women's liberty embodied in regulation. (John Chapman, "Prostitution in Paris," *Westminster Review*, no. 236 [April 1883]: 236–49; Stanton, *Woman Question in Europe*, 263–67; Karen Offen, *European Feminisms, 1700–1950: A Political History* [Stanford, Calif., 2000], 124–25, 154–56.)

3. James Stansfeld (1820–1898), a Liberal member of Parliament, woman suffragist, and opponent of the Contagious Diseases Acts, succeeded on 20 April 1883 in putting through a motion in Parliament to suspend the compulsory medical examination of women under the acts. (*DNB*; Baylen and Gossman, *Modern British Radicals*, 2:479–82; Paul McHugh, *Prostitution and Victorian Social Reform* [London, 1980], 220–27.)

SATURDAY, MAY 19, 1883. In Paris—at Madam Caroline d'Barrau's— Actually—was caught napping at quarter to 8 A.M. when the maid bro't roll & coffee— So I for my <u>first</u>—positively ate my breakfast in bed— what my dear Mother would pronounce—"most lazily"—

Got Postal from Rachel, writen yesterday A.M. she is well & getting on for Queenly seeing!!— Theo. got letter from Lydia E. Becker of London—that she is in Paris— T[heodore] M[arguerite] & self called on Miss Becker at 1.30— Madam d'Barrau invites her to dinner— walked through the Palais Royal arcade & stores with Madam d'B.— rode home— Miss Becker came at 7. & staid till 11.—interesting talk on the different gov'ts—she thoroughly believes in ↑a↓ Royal family for the people to look up to—Madam d'B. & I in royalty [*in margin*] of intelligence & worth

SUNDAY, MAY 20, 1883. In Paris— At Madam d'B's— Cloudy but pleasant—roll, sweetest of butter & coffe—in bed, again, 7.30— a letter from Hattie Stanton enclosing one from Laura Curtis Bullard[1] & card of Mr A. D. Worthington[2] Hartford Ct—for ↑the facts of↓ my life to be sent to him for Frances E. Willard to write sketch for a book he is getting up of Eminent American Women— After breakfast 12—noon—

Madam d'B—Miss Becker & self drove to a far part of city & called on M'lle Hubertine Auclert[3]—a bright young woman—editor of "La Citoyenne"—demanding suffrage for French women—then to see Leon Richer[4]—who deplores Miss Auclert's advance suffrage claim—then drove through the Champs Elysse

1. Laura J. Curtis Bullard (c. 1834–1912) of Brooklyn, New York, was living in England with her husband, Enoch Bullard, who retired early from the Curtis family's business in patent medicines. An ally of ECS and SBA in the equal rights association and at the Woman's Bureau, she succeeded ECS as editor of the *Revolution* when SBA sold the paper in 1870. Bullard was at work on a life of ECS for the book *Our Famous Women*. (Federal Census, 1870, 1880; *New York Times*, 20 January 1912; SBA diary, 30 May, 12, 15, 18 June 1883, *Film*, 22:814ff; Laura Curtis Bullard, "Elizabeth Cady Stanton," in *Our Famous Women* [Hartford, Conn., 1884], 602–623. See also *Papers* 2 & 3.)

2. Alfred D. Worthington (c. 1846–?) of A. D. Worthington & Company in Hartford, Connecticut, a publisher of subscription books, was assembling the chapters for *Our Famous Women*. He had selected Frances Willard to write about SBA. As SBA explained in her diary on May 29, Willard asked her in March to send details of her life, SBA did not stop her tour to do so, Willard became "indignant" and told Worthington to find another author, and ECS agreed to write the chapter with the proviso that SBA help her do it. SBA proceeded to Basingstoke as soon as she reached England in order to work on the chapter. (City directories, 1882 to 1884; Federal Census, 1880; SBA diary, 29–30 May, 16 June 1883; ECS, "Susan B. Anthony," *Film*, 23:1096–1117.)

3. Marie-Anne-Hubertine Auclert (1848–1914) broke with Maria Deraismes and Léon Richer in 1876 on the importance of the vote, and at the time of their Congrès internationale in 1878, she publically criticized them for their exclusion of political rights from the agenda. Since 1881, she had published *La Citoyenne*, a monthly paper, and just months before SBA's arrival, she founded a new group, Le Suffrage des femmes, with the stated intention of matching British and American suffrage organizations. (*DBF*; Hubertine Auclert, *La Citoyenne: Articles de 1881 à 1891*, ed. Édith Taïeb [Paris, 1982]; Klejman and Rochefort, *L'Égalité en Marche*, 57–85; Bidelman, "Politics of French Feminism," 93–120.)

4. Léon Richer (1824–1911), one of the founders of the movement in the 1860s, focused attention on changing the laws that disadvantaged wives and mothers and excluded women from education and work. He edited *Le Droit des femmes*. Votes for women, he feared, would empower a new religious bloc. When SBA called on him, he too had a new organization, La Ligue française pour le droit des femmes, established in 1882 and headed by Victor Hugo. With a long list of prominent names backing him, Richer sought close collaboration with politicians and the legislature to win changes in law. (Bidelman, "Maria Deraismes, Léon Richer, and the French Feminist Movement," 20–73;

Bidelman, "Politics of French Feminism," 93–120; Klejman and Rochefort, *L'Égalité en Marche*, 45–54, 57–85.)

MONDAY, MAY 21, 1883. [*in margin*] Wrote letters to Mrs. Sewall & Mrs Spofford this day—

In Paris—51-rue-de-Varenne— Marguerite went with me to get bonnet changed—but they would do nothing without extra charge—so had to pay for new Satin strings & also keep their lace ones &c—very mean!!! In P.M. Theo. took me to the Chamber of Deputies—to see how Frenchmen look in legislative assembly—very like Americans— we then walked A'm. Exchange—called on Mr Hines friend Dr Wilkie—a dentist—then walked to Normandy Hotel—found Mrs Sharpstein out again—then back home at 5— just tired out— So refused to go to Mr Gillig's[1] reception at the Binda Hotel[2]—& went to bed at 9 Oclock—

1. This was probably Henry F. Gillig, an American at the Paris office of the American Exchange. He published *Hints to the American Traveler Abroad* (1880), *The American Exchange Indicator Map of Paris* (1883?), and a series entitled *The "American Exchange" Travelers' Social Telegraph Code*. His brother Charles Alvin Gillig, at the London office, also published books for travelers.

2. The Hôtel Binda was on rue de l'Echelle.

TUESDAY, MAY 22, 1883. In Paris— At Madam d'Barraus Lovely A.M. read Felix Adler's article on "A secular view of moral training["]—very true & inspiring—[1] walked in the park of The Invalides—Soldiers Hospital in A.M.—[2] in P.M. Madam d'B. & self called on Mr & Mrs Wilbour—(C. B.)[3]—& I staid from 3 to 6. good chat—Mr W. very cordial & social—

1. Felix Adler, "A Secular View of Moral Training," *North American Review* 136 (May 1883): 446–54.

2. Completed in 1676, the Hôtel des Invalides housed disabled and needy soldiers. An esplanade leads from its facade to the Seine.

3. Charlotte Beebe Wilbour (1833–1914) and Charles Edwin Wilbour (1833–1896) moved to Paris from New York City in 1874, when Charles, a lawyer, came under scrutiny for his associations with the Tweed Ring. There he pursued his interest in Egyptology, amassing a great collection of books and artifacts, while living part of each year with his wife and four children aboard a boat on the Nile. Charlotte Wilbour had been a leading organizer of women in New York before their move: she was secretary of the Women's Loyal National League, an officer in the New York and National suffrage associations, a founder of the woman's club Sorosis, and planner of the first Woman's

Congress in 1873. The Wilbours lived on Boulevard Haussmann. (*NCAB*, 13:370; *ACAB*, s.v. "Wilbour, Charles Edwin"; *New York Times*, 26 December 1914; file on C. B. Wilbour, Sorosis Collection, MNS-S. See also *Papers* 1–3.)

WEDNESDAY, MAY 23, 1883. In Paris— After Lunch Theodore & M. went me to St Cloud by boat—& back on top of tram Car—[1] In evening Madam d Barrau took me to Mlle Auclert's suffrage meeting—seemed very good[2]

1. West of Paris on the Seine, Saint-Cloud was the site of ruins of a palace burned in 1870 during the Franco-Prussian War and of an extensive and elegant park.

2. According to an article reprinted in *La Citoyenne*, 4 June 1883, Auclert introduced SBA to the audience at this, the first in a series of weekday meetings about suffrage. See also SBA to Rachel G. Foster, 24 May 1883, and SBA to Elizabeth B. Harbert, 27 May 1883, *Film*, 23:159–62; and *Women's Suffrage Journal* 14 (2 July 1883): 114.

THURSDAY, MAY 24, 1883. In Paris— Walked to the Invalides—to see the Tomb of Napoleon—but it was not open till 12—[1] After breakfast Theodore & Marguerite went with me— It was—is very imposing— In evening all went to an out of door Caffe Concert—in Champs Elysse

1. Napoléon's remains were moved in 1840 into the Dôme des Invalides, once a royal chapel completed in 1708.

FRIDAY, MAY 25, 1883. In Paris— In P.M. Theodore went with me to call on Grace Greenwood—[1] also called on Mr & Mrs Chain & Miss Walton—but found them out—

1. Grace Greenwood was the penname of Sara Jane Clarke Lippincott (1823–1904), an accomplished American journalist and author of children's books, who had attempted to register and vote in Washington, D.C. A frequent traveler abroad, on this trip Greenwood went from Paris to London to work on a children's biography of Queen Victoria and oversee her daughter's singing debut. (*NAW*; *ANB*; *History*, 2:587, 3:813; *Papers*, 2:649–50; SBA diary, 15, 26 June 1883; *New York Times*, 22 July, 6 August, 4 November 1883.)

⤝ The Empire State Diary 1883, n.p., SBA Papers, DLC. Letters in square brackets expand initials.

112   SBA TO MARY S. ANTHONY

[*Paris*] May 26/83—

Saturday P.M.—no more letters since I wrote you— I shall go to London Tuesday next—the 29th Maud's birth day—18 years old!!—[1] If, when I get to London, I find you really have given up coming over this summer—I shall take a look at Scotland & Ireland & make for home in a very few weeks—unless somebody has power to make me see it for the best for me to stop longer—which I do not believe they can— I want to see the end of clearing out those boxes of papers & things this autumn— I am seeing very little of Paris—can't get about without Rachel to start me out—

  S. B. A—

  ANS on a postal card, SBA Papers, NRU. Postmarked at Paris; addressed to Rochester, N.Y. Not in *Film*.

1. Maude Anthony (1865–1950), later Koehler, was the eldest child of D. R. and Anna Anthony. She was a student at the Gannett Institute in Boston, and SBA hoped she would continue her education at the University of Kansas. "I am sure she would," SBA wrote to another niece, "if her father & mother felt as earnest to have her do so as does her aunt Susan." (Anthony, *Anthony Family*, 185, 187; *Los Angeles Times*, 24 January 1950; SBA to Lucy E. Anthony, 27 August 1883, and SBA to Kate Stephens, 8 June 1884, *Film*, 23:276–88, 784–88.)

113   FROM THE DIARY OF SBA

[*26–28 May 1883*]

SATURDAY, MAY 26, 1883. In Paris—51-rue-de-Varenne   Cloudy—did not go out— Mlle Loizillon called—[1] She has appointment from French Gov't on Educational matters—has recently returned from America—three months & reports that she found the people there opposed to Co-education—after ages of 12 & 1[3?]!!

1. Marie Célestine Loizillon (1820–?), a former teacher, held numerous posts as an inspector for France's ministry of public instruction. Her tour of the United States in 1882 resulted in her report, *L'Éducation des enfants aux États-Unis, rapport présenté à M. le ministre de l'Instruction publique, après une mission officielle, par Mlle Loizillon* (1883). (Isabelle Havelange, Françoise Huguet, and Bernadette Lebedeff, *Les inspecteurs généraux de l'instruction publique: dictionnaire biographique, 1802–1914* [Paris, 1986].)

SUNDAY, MAY 27, 1883. In Paris— In P.M. took street & Marguerite, Theodore & Madam d'Barrau went with me to La Chaise Cemetery & there saw the Communists by the thousands going to the spot & hanging wreaths on the wall where hundreds of their friends were shot down in 1871— It was a sad sight—all were most orderly—[1]

1. At Père Lachaise Cemetery, on 27 May 1871, one of the last battles in the destruction of the Paris Commune took place. Since the general amnesty of communards in 1880, ceremonies were conducted each year to remember those executed by the troops of the Versailles government.

MONDAY, MAY 28, 1883. [*above date*] rode ove[r?] to S̲t̲ L̲azare C̲harity̲ with Madam de Barrau this A.M.[1]

In Paris— At 12—noon—I went with Theodore Stanton to the College of France—to witness the last honors to the scholar & liberal Laboulaye[2]—recorded my name on the register—where the Savans, Senators—Deputies—the very brain of France—wrote theirs this A.M.— Saw his little parlor—& sadly saw the Catholic Priests perform their sorceries over his coffin in the Church— after return—Margurite rode with me for an hour or two—

1. Caroline de Barrau was director of the Oeuvre des libéreés de Saint-Lazare, a charity helping prostitutes find new work when they were released from the women's prison. (Stanton, *Woman Question in Europe*, 272.)

2. Edouard René Lefebvre de Laboulaye (1811–1883) died on May 23. He was administrator of the Collège de France, where SBA attended the services. A writer and politician, he was a great admirer of the United States, and he was also known for his interest in the rights of women. (Larousse, *Grand dictionnaire universel, Deuxième supplément*, 1490–91; Stanton, *Woman Question in Europe*, 242.)

⟜ The Empire State Diary 1883, n.p., SBA Papers, DLC. Square brackets surround uncertain reading.

·◁━━━━▶·

114 ↝ SPEECH BY ECS: "ON THE SOCIAL, EDUCATIONAL, RELIGIOUS AND POLITICAL POSITION OF WOMAN IN AMERICA"

EDITORIAL NOTE: When the executive committee of the Central Committee of the National Society for Women's Suffrage met on 3 May 1883, the members agreed to organize "a conversazione to welcome" ECS and SBA. The event grew into a large afternoon meeting on 25 June 1883 in the new Prince's Hall, Piccadilly, where Jacob Bright presided. SBA learned of the plan when Margaret Lucas greeted her in London on May 29 with a request that she and ECS consent to lecture. On June 7, the executive committee adopted this new "scheme of having addresses by these ladies on the position of Women in America." Neither ECS nor SBA had yet accepted the invitation on June 12, when committee members at a party beseeched SBA to say yes. SBA still feared for the meeting's success as late as June 23, when Ursula Bright wrote to say, "I think it will be all right." In the event, SBA spoke first, treating the subject of women's industrial, political, and legal progress in the United States. Rachel Foster prepared a synopsis of her speech for publication in the *Englishwoman's Review*. "Mrs. Stanton gave them the rankest radical sentiments," SBA wrote home, "but all so cushioned they didn't hurt." Jane Cobden asked ECS to submit her text to the editor John Morley for publication, presumably in his journal *Nineteenth Century*, but no published text of this speech has been found.

ECS wrote out her speech in advance, and then offered her daughter Harriot Blatch the opportunity to edit the manuscript—or so the evidence on the manuscript pages seems to indicate. Harriot penciled in suggestions above her mother's lines; most of her changes were then incorporated into the text by removing ECS's word or phrase and substituting new words written in Harriot's hand. On the eleventh page of the manuscript, the evidence of collaboration between mother and daughter is strong: Harriot changed words on the page, but the results were so messy that she struck out the entire page. ECS then turned over the sheet and wrote out a new page eleven incorporating the changes. When Harriot, working with a thicker pen, struck out text, ECS's original wording is still legible. The effect of her erasure of ECS's words varied: some rejected words were obliterated, some survive only as a syllable, but occasionally the original word is legible beneath Harriot's handwriting. Nonetheless, it is not possible to remove Harriot's intervention and leave a coherent text. There are, for example, entire pages in her hand. The text published here is that of the edited manuscript, reflecting the work of ECS and Harriot Blatch. In the notes and textual notes, the layers of their work are represented, with Harriot's work set off in braces to distinguish it from ECS's own emendations. (Ms. Minutes, Central Committee of the National Society for Women's Suffrage, Women's Library, London; SBA diary, 29 May, 12 June 1883, SBA to Mary S. Anthony, 22 and 26 June 1883, U. M. Bright to SBA, 23 June 1883, SBA's speech, and J. Cobden to ECS, 2 September 1883, *Film*, 22:814ff, 23:176, 177, 181–86, 234, 295–96.)

[25 June 1883]

¶1   Forty three years ago a world's antislavery convention was held here in London, in Freemasons Hall.[1] Delegates came from all parts of England, Ireland, Scotland, France, and America, and among them were six women from the United States,[2] one of whom was Lucretia Mott, a distinguished Quaker preacher, of years, experience, and rare abilities. The entire first day of the convention was taken up in the discussion as to whether the women could be admitted as delegates.

¶2   The clergy said no, it would be in violation of the spirit and letter of the Bible. Politicians said no, it would cause the meeting to be ridiculed in the morning papers. Sentimentalists said no, it would destroy the delicacy and refinement of woman. But all alike sang her praises loud and long, and then in solemn chorus voted her out of the convention by an overwhelming majority. But there were a goodly number of men who stood firmly by the principle of human equality. The most eloquent orators, such as George Thompson, Daniel O'Connell, Wendell Phillips, Henry B. Stanton, Dr Bowring,[3] bravely advocated the admission of the women. That long hot day in June was one of such refined torture as I had never before experienced. I remember even now how my pulse quickened, and my heart throbbed, listening to the noble utterances of those loyal to woman and the burning indignation that filled my soul, as our opponents strengthened with the creeds, and codes, and customs, of a barbarous age, assumed to speak as the representatives of God himself, in remanding all women to that sphere of safety, where never to be seen nor heard, is considered the acme of purity and virtue.[4] However my misery was somewhat mitigated by the placid comments, and smiles of derision that passed round the distinguished circle of women who were permitted to occupy seats in juxtaposition with the members of the convention. Facing such a galaxy of talent and philanthropy, as Elizabeth Fry, Amelia Opie, Mary Howitt, Elizabeth Pease, Mrs Hugo Reid, Lady Byron[5] and Lucretia Mott, no amount of masculine dogmatism could have convinced me of the heaven ordained inferiority and subjection of woman.

¶3 William Lloyd Garrison our great antislavery apostle, being delayed at sea, did not arrive until the third day. On hearing that the women were not admitted as delegates, he promptly said, then I shall not present my credentials, nor enter the convention. "I have opposed, said he, the slavery of the black race, not because they were black, but because they were human beings, and on the same ground I oppose all invidious distinctions between man and woman. If the difference in sex makes woman weaker, more helpless and incapable than man, then by every consideration of justice and chivalry should our laws, religion and social customs shield her with special safeguards. Governments, it is said, were formed to protect the weak against the strong, not to make the strong, stronger and the weak more helpless." Garrison in the gallery was the grandest feature in that convention, the central figure in the picture that will some day be historic. He came three thousand miles to take part in a great gathering, on a question to which he had devoted his life, but a principle of justice was crucified in the rejection of six women, so he chose to sit with the spirit of liberty outside, rather than shine as the bright peculiar star of that assembly of inconsistencies. It was from this, that the woman suffrage movement in England and America started. It was here that the fact was made to stand out in bold relief, that there were others beside Africans, in slavery. Accordingly on returning to America Lucretia Mott and I called the first woman[6] suffrage convention, and sent forth that daring declaration of rights, demanding for every grievance the redress which the next forty years of agitation proved feasible.

¶4 So audacious did this appeal for absolute equality with man seem to the nation that our declaration was received with derisive laughter from the Atlantic to the Pacific, from the Lakes to the Gulf.

¶5   A few years later Mrs John Stuart Mill dignified one of our conventions with highest encomiums in your Westminster Review.[7] Later, the Hon John Stuart Mill introduced a bill for household suffrage, with thousands of petitions in its favor into Parliament.[8] In the meantime enthusiastic conventions were held in the United States from year to year, and eloquent voices heralded the new gospel of justice, liberty, and equality for woman. Garrison, Phillips, Channing,[9] Higginson, Theodore Parker, Ralph Waldo Emerson swelled the grand chorus in the new world, quickly echoed back by the Mills, the Brights, the M[c]Larens, by your poet laureate in his Princess,[10] by George Eliot in her novels, Harriet Martineau[11] in her essays, and the Rev Charles Kingsley in his protests against the degradation of woman in the canon law. At last complete political equality for woman was accorded in two of our territories, then England passed her household suffrage bill, enfranchising in a measure thousands of women;[12] then we opened our colleges and professions, and gave to women school suffrage in twelve states of the union.[13] England then secured to married women their rights of property,[14] and extended municipal suffrage to the women of Scotland, until now we may truly say, that the glad sunlight, on the wild mountain tops of Wyoming, is already gilding the venerable dome of St Paul. And it is fitting this should be so: that England and America should march side by side, in these successive steps of progress on this, the most far-reaching, and momentous question that the nations of the earth have ever been summoned to consider. We are the same people as you, we speak the same language, when we left our mother country we took with us your system of Jurisprudence, and constitutional law, your literature, your theological ideas, your virtues and your vices. What has been the effect of our civilization on woman is the subject I am invited to consider. As Miss Anthony will speak to you on the political status of our countrywomen,[15] I will confine myself to[16] the social, educational and religious phase of the question.

¶6   Before introducing you to the women of America, let me relate an anecdote. Some twenty years ago, William H. Seward,[17] then Secretary of State, made a grand reception for the Burlingame delegation of Chinese. Charlotte Cushman, Lucretia Mott and other distinguished women were there, and through an interpreter were put into communication with the representatives of the great eastern empire. To all serious questions in regard to the government commerce and religion of China, the only reply was immoderate laughter. The ladies supposing that the interpreter was misrepresenting them, appealed to Mr. Seward, who inquired "why they laughed," they replied, "to hear women in all earnestness ask such profound questions."[18] "Why", said one, "your women walk about and talk as if they owned the country, and had a perfect right to go everywhere, and express their opinions on every subject." Arrayed in gorgeous silks, they hid themselves most of the evening behind their elaborately ornamented fans, so shocked were they to see ladies and gentlemen walking arm in arm, and chatting together. When some sang duets and waltzed, the Chinese would peep out first one side of their fans and then the other, convulsed with shame and laughter. Of all they saw in the United States, what surprized them most, was the independence and self assertion of[19] the women.

¶7   Now in giving you some facts in regard to your American sisters, let me ask you to sit down on your fans, and, unlike the Chinese embassy scan us frankly and openly, and so perhaps find us though different not degenerate.

¶8   I presume there never was a nation of men so chivalrous to women as in the United States, partly due to our republican institutions: to the leaven of equality acting on all classes, and partly to the necessary dependence of men and women on each other in a new and isolated civilization. Remember we were three thousand miles beyond the influence of Popes, and Kings, and old time social customs, without steamers or telegraphic communication for near a century! Time enough mid the grandeur and solitudes of nature for the young nation to measure its infinite capacity and learn the sacredness of individual rights.[20] With man woman shared the dangers of the May Flower on a stormy sea, the dreary landing on Plymouth rock, the rigors of a New England winter, and the privations of a seven years war. With him she bravely threw off the British yoke, felt every pulsation of his heart for freedom, and inspired the glowing eloquence that maintained our liberty through the century. It was mid such surroundings that the vision of enfranchised womanhood revealed itself in each passing generation, inspiring with lofty sentiments of liberty the lips of Abigail Adams, Mercy Otis, Hannah Lee,[21] Lydia Maria Child, Margaret Fuller and Angelina Grimké. Many influences have made American women more independent, self-asserting, versatile than those of other nations. Owing to the great difference in climate, our women are nervously more highly wrought, physically more delicate and slender, more excitable perhaps in manner, the voice pitched on a higher key.[22] The distinguished trainer of operatic singers at Vienna, gave it as the result of her experience that American women had the most musical voices in the world, and added "let any other nationality pitch the voice in conversation on so high a key, and the effect would be unbearable." A Paris paper some months since complained that the best talent of Europe wore itself out for American gold, and that in return none but third rate talent was ever sent from our shores. The peevish journalist did not know or failed to mention that at that very moment the first lady at the Paris Comic Opera was a citizen of the United States, and the prima donna in Italian Opera, a native of America, her name Albani being taken from her birthplace, Albany.[23] I cannot give two better instances of the peculiar characteristics, the natural products of our institutions, than in the writer Louise Alcott,[24] and the orator Anna Dickinson, alike born of intelligent parents, they were brought up in straightened circumstances, with no special advantages of education, yet one with her beautiful stories has made a world wide reputation and a fortune, and the other as an orator attained at one time an enviable position on the platform, speaking on the great political questions of the hour.

¶9   The sentiment of chivalry in our men served to modify our property laws, giving us in New York State as early as '48, the married woman's property bill,[25] the same just passed in England, through the influence of the Hon Jacob Bright,[26] sustained by the perseverance, and untiring labors of his estimable wife. Later was secured to married women the right to their children and earnings, and more reasonable laws of divorce. I notice from recent discussions in Parliament on the "deceased wife's sister's bill," that the laws of America were used to point a moral, and the slender bonds by which we are supposed to be held in the marriage relation cited as a warning against any liberal legislation in this country.[27] In speaking of the marriage and divorce laws in America it should be borne in mind that they differ in every state in the union. In all together we have eighteen different causes for divorce.[28] In my native state of New York there is but one cause for divorce, (adultery), it is the same in South Carolina. But as those living in these states can, by a residence of one year in Connecticut or Indiana, avail themselves of the broader laws, it is not fair, in making up statistics, to attribute all the divorces granted, to the permanent inhabitants. When it is said that a thousand marriages are dissolved in Connecticut in a single year, we must remember that the greater part were asked by non-residents. Before commenting on our liberal divorce laws in parliament it would be well for English statesmen to weigh the causes and effects. That our laws are not the result of a low state of morals, but of a steadily increasing high one, of the most exalted feelings as to the sacredness of a true marriage relation, as the debates in the several state legislatures, and the characters of those advocating the measures fully attest.[29] Our divorce laws are not the result of the fickleness of men, but of the growing independence of the women. It is in a majority of the cases that wives ask for the dissolution of the union. There is no country in the world where the relations of husbands and wives are mutually more respectful and tender and where children enjoy greater freedom, or where there is more real home happiness than in the United States. And this is because the principle of self government is slowly but surely making its way in every department of life, because individual rights, individual conscience and judgement are governing alike in the state, the church, and the home.

¶10 In the western states in the early days there was a scarcity of women, and often in pioneer life none at all; hence there was for them and children a wild worshipful feeling among men. Mr Billings,[30] long President of the Great Northern Pacific Railroad, who spent many years of his early life in California told me, that by chance an old bonnet found its way into the mining camp, which the men kept carefully hung up, and at night when the day's work was done, they would join hands and dance joyfully about it, singing "home sweet home."

¶11 At a theatre in San Francisco, a baby crying uproariously one night, the men called out stop the orchestra let us hear the baby.

Simple anecdotes but they illustrate a principle, and reveal the secret of woman's power in the roughest civilizations. Such influences have essentially modified the habits of our social life, making the men more ready to extend courtesies to all women. Foreigners who have been accustomed to see women wait on, and serve men, would draw very unjust conclusions from the differences in our manners towards each other. Professor Christlieb,[31] a distinguished German Clergyman, who attended the evangelical alliance in New York a few years since, expressed severe condemnation of the marriage relation as it existed in our country. After his return to Germany, an American gentleman called on him one day, and was most cordially received, but while he praised much that he saw in America, he sadly deplored the insubordination of the women. He said that on more than one occasion he had heard an American woman say to her husband, "Dear will you bring me my shawl," and her husband had brought it, and worse than this, he had seen a husband returning home at night, enter the parlor where his wife was sitting, in the very best chair perchance, and the wife not only did not go and get his slippers, and dressing gown but she even remained seated and left him to find a chair as he could. The Rev Knox Little,[32] a High-Church clergyman of England, spent a few weeks in the United States during the fall of 1880, and he felt himself called on to preach a sermon to women. The large church of St Clements Philadelphia was crowded. By the utter perversion of some of the plainest passages of scripture, and principles of our religion he proved woman's divinely ordained inferiority, and subordination to man. His ideas were so utterly opposed to the public sentiment of the country, that our secular papers ridiculed him beyond measure, and even our most orthodox religious journals repudiated his scriptural expositions. Unfortunately for the Rev Knox Little, who came to America to teach the "Bible position of women," women had themselves been reading that book in the original. Many of them had been trained in our theological schools. Many were preaching in their own pulpits, regularly ordained, over congregations acting as pastors, administering the ordinances. According to woman's exposition of texts of scripture, man[33] and woman were a simultaneous creation made alike in the image of God, and holding alike a title deed to this green earth. The masculine and feminine elements, two great powers in nature, exactly equal and balancing each other, like positive and negative electricity, like the centripetal and centrifugal forces, were necessarily a simultaneous creation, as there could have been no perpetuation of life otherwise.[34]

¶12 Among American institutions the contrast between adopted and originated principles is no where more clearly shown than in our method of education. In early days we looked to Europe for models in all things. We saw your colleges and universities firmly founded on old traditions, and imitating your system excluded one half the citizens of our republic from the higher branches of education. But in establishing our public schools, so absolutely necessary to the safety of a democracy, we had to seek a path of our own, not finding on this side of the Atlantic any such system. Here we were original, and to day many European educators turn to us, for ideas on training the masses. Led in no small measure by our political ideals, and forced by the necessities of a new country, we based our primary and high schools on co-education. American women have ever had such advocates for their intellectual developement, as our grand old Concord philosopher, Ralph Waldo Emerson, who complained that in most of our homes, "the gravest discourse has a savor of hams and powder tubs," adding that still worse is it "when this sensualism intrudes into the education of young women, and withers the hope and affection of human nature, by teaching that marriage signifies nothing but a housewife's thrift, and that woman's life has no other aim."[35] It was our ideal of individual freedom, that accorded to American women training far superior to other nations in the 18th century, and the logic of the necessities of a people, limited in means, and scattered over a vast country that gave us co-education. From this system we have no where departed, except where European ideas have undermined the wisdom of our Pilgrim Fathers in some of the large cities of the Atlantic sea-board. But go a hundred miles inland, and there is co-education again, and as you journey farther and farther into the heart of the country, into the great west, where indeed throbs the life blood of the nation, you find co-education based less upon expediency, more upon justice, until at last you see all the university doors, the departments of law, medicine, and theology, open to woman. Out there in that region of the rough, but true hearted humanities, there is a firm belief that mankind is mankind the world over and that however high superficial custom builds, there are some of the noble essentials of life that she cannot circumscribe. These rough hewn sons and daughters of nature, hold gentlest faith that the attractions, in their simplicity, of men and women to each other are good, are divine, and only in danger of degenerating into morbid sentimentalities when shallow unwisdom assumes command. It is their honest conviction, that in all relations man and woman were made for each other, that has given co-education to the prairie world of America. But where boys and girls are separated, there are always two schools exactly similar, no difference being made in the proficiency of the teaching, nor in the requirement of the pupils. Then our schools are absolutely free, even the use of necessary text books, is given gratis. Every girl in America, from the learning of her letters, gains a thorough preparatory training for college and university without paying one penny. You ask then, of what are American women complaining? We reply, that the private schools and seminaries, where our most wealthy classes send their daughters, are miserably superficial, and that many of our colleges, universities and schools of law, medicine, and theology in the east, refuse admittance to young women. But the public schools, primary, and high, and normal, all educate girls and boys, men and women together.

¶13   All over the world, where the Kinder Garten system is known, the infant idea, be it boy or girl is taught how to shoot in one and the same room.[36] American logic tends to believe that with equal safety the maturer ideas might in union, seek for Greek roots and Naperian logarithms.[37] The dead languages, and higher mathematics are not more demoralizing than the a, b, c. It is to our public schools, that every believer in co-education can point with pride, and assurance. In them, is reproof given to shallow argument against training men, and women together for the earnest duties of life.

¶14   And yet there are still University trustees, in America who argue that co-education would not be morally safe, that the admission of girls would lower the College standard of study, that the concentrated efforts of boys, would overtax the girl, mind and body. Such arguments are put forward in spite of the fact, that the moral effect of men and women upon each other in the institutions of co-education, is apparent to the most casual observer: in spite of the fact that a good proportion of the prizes are won by girls, in our public schools, and honors accorded in Universities to women: in spite of the fact that women pursuing severe courses of study, show by statistics higher average of health than those in society.[38] In the great intercollegiate contest in '76 when some of our best colleges were represented, a girl took the Greek prize.[39] The daughters of our women identified with the suffrage movement were the first to enter our colleges when opened.[40] But in spite of all facts conservatives will remain incorrigible. If the morals of men and women suffer by contact, they are surely safer pursuing their studies under the same roof, than performing a giddy waltz in a crowded ballroom. Invariable answer to all arguments "men and women boys and girls are better apart." But gentlemen, where have you seen this rule tried? Can you instance a single tribe, however free from all influence of art and civilization, in which nature gives to certain parents none but girls and to another none but boys, and in the first instance takes care to remove the father by death, and in the second the mother, in order to achieve what to you, seems a necessity, the separation of the sexes. You answer "in colleges and universities it would be detrimental morally and intellectually." But gentlemen, it is no longer a question belonging to conditioned time, but to past and present. Have you not heard the favorable verdicts of half a dozen Presidents of western colleges, where co-education is an accomplished fact, backed by the logic of having existed in America over a quarter of a century? Have you not heard the opinion of our late minister at Berlin President White[41] of Cornell University in New York state?[42] In speaking of the admission of women President White said, that it had the same effect in college life that the introduction of palace cars had on the travel on railroads. His were not hasty conclusions, but based on years of experience, in the institution at whose head he stands. But all argument is in vain with gentlemen, who deal in no tense of the indicative mood but a conditioned future.

¶15 Vassar college in New York, wholly for girls, disproves many conservative theories in regard to the higher education of women. It is almost a score of years since it graduated its first class.[43] Within its walls thousands of women have received thorough and complete university training. Here Prof. Maria Mitchell,[44] the distinguished astronomer, has instructed students in mathematical astronomy, giving them the benefit of instruments, which stand third only in the United states. The calculations of one of her classes, Prof. Mitchell used when she went to observe the total eclipse at Denver. The draw backs at Vassar are that it is exclusively for women and that its buildings which accommodate five hundred are so planned that the students live under a single roof. Smith College and Wellesley in Massachusetts are a later venture, unfortunate in being also for women only, and fortunate in being heavily endowed, and having adopted the plan of allowing its students to board in separate families.[45] Both these institutions prove that concentrated study is not detrimental to health.[46] Of Wellesley the President and Faculty are women, all graduates from Ann Arbor university. If on the hardest rock you let water fall, drop by drop, at last an impression is made. With all due patience, we have applied this knowledge to the wearing away of the conservatism of *our* Cambridge. The achievement is called Harvard Annex, and its working is something in this wise. "We cannot let you in, my daughters, say the Faculty, at the front door, but if you go round by that dark side passage, and tap very gently at that big high gate there, (don't ring the bell it will create a disturbance in the lecture room in front) the gate will be opened, you must not ask by whom, and you slip quietly into our classic scullery. If enough of you come to make it worth while we will send a professor, whom you will surely pay well for his magnanimity in answering all your questions. By and by you shall be examined, but we can't give you a degree, but you shall have a back door certificate."[47] Now, my friends, that is not what in America we call generous, but small favors are thankfully received. But we can record better things of the grand State Universities of Michigan, and New York;[48] there women are received exactly on an equal footing with man. They work side by side, compete for the same honors, and when won deliver before the audience assembled to witness the commencement exercises, their prize theses. On all sides the prospect for women is brightening in America. Even the Johns Hopkins University in Baltimore, Maryland where those who have already won their B.A. or M.A. degrees are assisted in carrying on their studies to the highest point, has accorded a fellowship in mathematics to a graduate of Vassar.[49]

¶16 The ancients did not praise a ship when decked with gay pinions

at her launching, but when she had out-ridden the storm, and returned to safe harbor with weather beaten sides, and ribboned sails;
so I, in speaking of the grand progress in so many directions, that we
have made in America, am asking you to do honor to no doubtful
ventures, but to superb achievements, which have battled victori-
ously with adverse winds, and returned to us freighted with promise
to sail the ocean yet other generations, in safety and success.

¶17 A stranger would note too the higher respect paid our women in
the halls of legislation. In our national capitol, when women visit the
House of Congress to listen to debates, they have large spacious
galleries, the very choicest seats, where they can see and hear; we are
not cooped up in a little dark corner behind a screen.⁵⁰ When
questions touching our interests are before the House, we are granted
personal appeals before the committees, where we can present our
claims in person.

¶18 Our movement for suffrage in America has arrived at the exact
point where we always thought triumph would be assured.⁵¹ At one
time only the most liberal men in politics, and religion were favorable, the press, the church, the bar, the bench, the world of fashion
were all against us; now our leading journals treat the question with
respect; popular reviews and magazines entertain it quite hospitably
in their pages, scientists even write voluminously on the difference
of sex. Judges and lawyers have come to discuss it as one of constitutional law, and the clergy are giving us new interpretations of
scripture in harmony with the spirit of the age. And now just as all
these classes are advancing in one direction, lo! our liberals come to
a dead stand. They say they are in favor of woman suffrage per se,
but they are afraid of the practical working of the principle. Women
they declare are naturally so conservative, so entirely under the
controul of their priests and bishops, that they would destroy the
secular nature of our government. We hear this objection alike in
America, England, and France. Well suppose by way of argument
we admit that women in general are narrow, bigoted, and timid; that
their influence would be steadily against every step in progress; that
if they had the opportunity to exercise direct political influence,
they would invariably reinforce the conservative party. The question naturally arises if this would be their direct influence, is not
their indirect influence precisely the same to day? Whether for good

or for ill, the influence of woman is ever insidiously doing its work, either beckoning man upward, to the diviner heights she has climbed herself, or holding him down in the valley of humiliation where she is bound. Their narrow ideas are sedulously educated into their children, and we see them reappearing in every legislative assembly, in every ecclesiastical council, generation after generation; the time and patience of our most advanced thinkers are wasted in combating the short sighted policy in political economy, the bigotry and prejudices of an old worn out theology, in the men believing what their mothers taught them. Could we but appreciate what an insurmountable obstacle to a high civilization is the religious faith of the women of a nation, we should see that light on this question is of the first consideration. I remember reading some years ago an able pamphlet on Catholicism written by your present Prime Minister,[52] in which deploring the spread of that faith, he said "as might be expected its most ready victims are women being influenced by their emotions rather than reason." A recent writer in The New York Times speaking of Egyptian civilization, said the great block in the way of advance there, is the condition of the women and all progress for them is hopeless because they are taught by their religion that their condition is in harmony with the will of God.[53] And this idea is responsible everywhere for the apathy and indifference of women under the most adverse circumstances. If we could substitute logic for emotion, reason for blind faith in the traditions of our Fathers, we might propose a significant question to ourselves. Seeing that the condition of women differs essentially in every country, which one is according to the divine will? As toilers in the rice swamps and cotton plantations of the southern states of the American republic, or as teachers and Professors in the best schools and colleges of the North, as beasts of burden in Germany and France, as petted slaves, wearing veils and masks in Turkish harems, or in Girton college,[54] contending for Greek and Mathematical prizes, or in Windsor palace, Queen of an Empire, head of the army and navy of the mightiest nation on the globe? Seeing these vast differences we cannot logically ascribe anyone of them to a direct fiat from Heaven but to human laws and customs, which we ourselves have the absolute right to modify, and improve, and change altogether. It is only through the utter perversion of the religious element in their nature that women are made the patient, hopeless slaves they are.

¶19 The loss to themselves of the highest developement of which they are capable is sad, but when this loss involves a lower type of manhood, a lower tone of civilization it is sadder still. The primal work to day in every country is the freedom and education of its women. Seeing that her powerful indirect influence is generally acknowledged, there is only one road to safety and that is to give woman all the advantages and opportunities for improvement that lie within her reach, and thus broaden her sympathies, clear her vision, enlarge her charity and strengthen her judgement, that the race may be lifted up a few degrees. Galton in his great work on Heredity says, "with the tangled problems of our present intense civilization the brain of man is overweighted and as in the nature of things even more complex questions will come up in the near future, something must be done to lift our statesmen a few degrees higher, to make them strong enough to meet successfully what lies before them."[55] And where shall we look for this new power but in a higher type of womanhood.

¶20 You are asking here in England for various bills for the protection of girls and women. The best bill that could be passed to this end is parliamentary suffrage. Whatever can be done to dignify woman in the eyes of man is a protection. If the same respect the masses are educated to feel for cathedrals, altars, symbols, and sacraments, was extended to the mothers of the race, as it should be, all these dis-tracting problems in which her interests are involved would be speedily settled, but alas! there is nothing so cheap as womanhood in the commerce of the world to day. You can scarce take up a paper that does not herald some outrages on woman, from the dignified matron on her way to church to the girl of fourteen, gathering wild flowers on her way to school. You cannot go so low down in the scale of being as to find men who would enter our churches, insult our priests, or desecrate our altars because they have been educated into a holy reverence for these. But is not woman as the mother of the race, more exalted than symbols, sacraments, altars and vast cathedral domes? Yet where shall we look for lessons of honor and respect to her. Do our sons in our law schools rise from their studies, where they read the invidious statutes, and opinions in regard to women, with a higher respect for their mothers? by no means! Every line of the old common law of England touching the interests of my sex is an insult to the intelligent womanhood of the 19th century. Do our sons in their theological seminaries rise from the commentaries of Scott[56] and Clarke on the passages of scripture touching woman with a higher respect for their mothers and sisters? By no means; they come oftimes fresh from their studies, perhaps with the dew of prayer upon their lips, to preach anew the subjection of one half the race to the other.

¶21 In the long debate just passed in parliament, on the deceased wife sister's bill, I looked in vain for one lofty sentiment of trust and confidence in woman.[57] I hold men in high places responsible for the actions of the lower orders. It is the sentiments expressed by legislators, that mould the morals of the highway. And yet that fine cobweb of faith that men and women have in each other is what holds society together; blighted and blasted as it has been again and again, it remains ever the same.

¶22 Strengthened, purified, exalted in equal conditions it is this faith that will at last make us one and immortal. It is this faith that is the foundation of the new form of religion we are now entering, the religion of humanity, in which instead of the unknown Gods, men and women will worship each other, striving together to make this life a blessing, and our earth a Paradise.

❧ AMs, ECS Papers, DLC.

1. This convention, called by the British and Foreign Anti-Slavery Society, met from 12 to 23 June 1840. Henry B. Stanton, a delegate, took his new bride, ECS, to London for the event. ECS first wrote a history of the convention and its impact in a speech for the Eighth National Woman's Rights Convention in 1858, *Papers*, 1:361–69, then reworked that account for *History*, 1:53–62.

2. Three antislavery societies selected women to be delegates to the convention, and seven of those chosen made the trip to London. Lucretia Mott represented the American Anti-Slavery Society. Her close friends from Philadelphia Mary Grew (1813–1896), Sarah Pugh, Abby Kimber (1804–1871), and Elizabeth Johns Neall (1819–1907), later Gay, represented the Pennsylvania society. From Boston, the Massachusetts society sent Emily Annette Winslow (1822–1904), later Taylor, and Ann Terry Greene Phillips (1813–1886). (Garrison and Garrison, *Life*, 2:353. See also *Papers* 1.)

3. Not previously identified are two members of Parliament, Irish national-

ist Daniel O'Connell (1775–1847) and English diplomat John Bowring (1792–1872), who both supported the admission of women as delegates to the convention and wrote public letters on the subject. (Mott, *Slavery and "the Woman Question,"* 29–30, 33, 34; W. L. Garrison to Oliver Johnson, 3 July 1840, and to Samuel J. May, 6 September 1840, in Garrison, *Letters,* 2:666, 696–99.)

4. Page five of the manuscript was removed, and the conclusion of its text was struck from the top of page six. Harriot Blatch then renumbered the page "5 & 6."

5. Although not delegates to the convention, these abolitionists befriended the American women in London. Those not yet identified are Amelia Alderson Opie (1769–1853), a Quaker poet; Mary Botham Howitt (1799–1888), another English Quaker and writer; and Anna Isabella Milbanke, Lady Byron (1792–1860), philanthropist and reformer. Marion Kirkland Reid (1815–1902), known as Mrs. Hugo Reid, published an early argument for rights, *A Plea for Woman,* in Edinburgh in 1843. ECS is the sole source for repeated, modern claims that Reid attended the convention, and it was on this occasion in 1883 that ECS first included Reid in her list. Reid remained in ECS's later lists in *History,* 3:838n, and *Eighty Years,* 80. But the evidence is strong that ECS had confused Mrs. Hugo Reid and Elizabeth Jesser Reid (1789–1866), a close friend of Harriet Martineau and a pioneer in women's education, who did attend the convention. For the lists of British women ECS published prior to this speech, without including either Reid, see *Papers,* 1:366, and *History,* 1:61. (Jane Rendall, entry on Marion Kirkland Reid, for *Biograpical Dictionary of Scottish Women,* eds. Elizabeth Ewen, Sue Innes, and Sian Reynolds [forthcoming from Edinburgh University Press], courtesy of the author; Mott, *Slavery and "the Woman Question,"* 54; Garrison, *Letters,* 2:663n; with the assistance of Clare Midgley, Jane Rendall, and Bonnie Anderson.)

6. After Harriot Blatch emended page eleven, beginning here, the page was struck out, and ECS copied the emended text on the verso. On ECS's collaboration with Lucretia Mott to call the woman's rights convention at Seneca Falls in 1848, see *Papers,* 1:67–68, 74–75.

7. Harriet Hardy Taylor Mill (1807–1858), the wife of John Stuart Mill, wrote "The Enfranchisement of Women," *Westminster Review* 55 (July 1851): 149–61, after reading about the First National Woman's Rights Convention at Worcester, Massachusetts, in 1850.

8. Mill presented the petitions in 1866, and when Parliament debated the Reform Bill of 1867, he proposed to remove the word "male" from the qualifications to vote. "Household suffrage" for women effectively limited the vote to widows and spinsters, who, unlike married women, could own property, but Mill avoided language that would draw attention to the distinction. (*History,* 3:839–42; Blackburn, *Women's Suffrage in the British Isles,* 53–63; Holton, *Suffrage Days,* 20).

9. That is, William H. Channing.

10. Alfred, Lord Tennyson (1809–1892), the English poet, published *The Princess* in 1847.

11. Harriet Martineau (1802–1876), a British writer and abolitionist.

12. ECS refers to municipal suffrage based on being a householder, not to parliamentary suffrage. In 1869, Jacob Bright succeeded in amending the Municipal Franchise Act to delete the word "male" and make explicit the right to vote of women who met the property qualifications. (*History*, 3:844–47; Blackburn, *Women's Suffrage in the British Isles*, 91–95.)

13. School suffrage gave women the opportunity to vote on issues regarding public education, though states differed in listing which issues those were. Some form of school suffrage existed in Colorado, Dakota Territory, Kansas, Kentucky, Massachusetts, Michigan, Minnesota, Nebraska, New Hampshire, New York, Oregon, and Vermont.

14. The revisions made to this sentence are contradictory. Here Harriot Blatch wrote "over," and on the sheet's verso wrote, "Years before she had extended municipal suffrage to the women of England & all her colonies". She also struck out words from ECS's original sentence and then wrote "stet" over some unmarked part of it. The editors have used ECS's original text.

By the Married Women's Property Act of 1882, English women gained greater control over and protection of their separate property, but Parliament rejected language that would grant them the status of single women. The difference in status came back to haunt the suffrage movement. (Lee Holcombe, *Wives and Property: Reform of the Married Women's Property Law in Nineteenth-Century England* [Toronto, 1983], 195–205, 247–52; Shanley, *Feminism, Marriage and the Law*, 102–30.)

15. SBA had already spoken.

16. Page seventeen, from here through "women were there, and through an," is entirely in the hand of Harriot Blatch.

17. ECS describes a party in Auburn, New York, given by Secretary of State William Henry Seward (1801–1872), in the weeks after he signed the Burlingame Treaty between the United States and China in 1868. He entertained the envoys from the Chinese foreign office, Zhi Kang (1819–?) and Sun Jiaku (1823–?). Charlotte Saunders Cushman (1816–1876), an American actress, was staying with Seward. According to ECS's account in the *Revolution*, Lucretia Mott, Martha Wright, and SBA were also present. (*Papers*, 2:160–62; *Rev.*, 20 August 1868, *Film*, 1:257–58; Frederick Wells Williams, *Anson Burlingame and the First Chinese Mission to Foreign Powers* [1912; reprint, New York, 1972], 100–101; Joseph Leach, *Bright Particular Star: The Life and Times of Charlotte Cushman* [New Haven, Conn., 1970], 338–39.)

18. Harriot Blatch added a new page nineteen in order to extend this anecdote through "opinions on every subject." The text returns then to ECS's original page nineteen, renumbered "19-a."

19. Here, at the end of page "19-a," Harriot Blatch inscribed a new page twenty through "a nation of men so chivalrous".

20. ECS marked her page "over" and wrote the next two sentences on the verso of her sheet.

21. Members of families active in the American Revolution, these were Abigail Smith Adams (1744–1818) of Massachusetts, whose letters to her husband, John Adams, were published early in the nineteenth century; Mercy Otis Warren (1728–1814) of Massachusetts, a poet and political satirist; and Hannah Lee Corbin (1728–1782) of Virginia, who told her brother in the Continental Congress that widows needed voting rights. See also *History*, 1:32–33.

22. Harriot Blatch took up the pen here in the middle of ECS's page twenty-three. She inscribed the next two manuscript pages, ending with "her birthplace, Albany." ECS took up the pen again at the bottom of her page twenty-five.

23. Dame Emma Albani (1847–1930) was a star in the opera houses of Europe. Born and educated in Montreal, she moved to Albany, New York, in 1864, and there her talent as a singer was noted. Funds were raised for musical education abroad, and, as ECS comments, she adopted her stage name to honor her benefactors. (*ApCAB*, s.v. "Albani, Marie Emma Lajeunesse"; W. Stewart Wallace, *The Macmillan Dictionary of Canadian Biography*, 3d ed. [London, 1963], s.v. "Gye, Marie Louise Emma Cécile Lajeunesse.") On the verso of page twenty-three, there is, in Blatch's hand and struck out, a draft of the passage that begins here in ECS's hand. It reads "Can I give two better instances of ~~our independence~~ these characteristics, two women more peculiarly products of our institutions than the writer Louise Alcott, and the orator Anne Elizabeth Dickinson".

24. Louisa May Alcott (1832–1888) achieved her greatest success with the publication of *Little Women* in 1868 and 1869, and she published her last novel in 1886.

25. New York's Married Women's Property Act of 1848 protected the real and personal property that women brought into marriage and any gifts they received during marriage. By the Act of 1860, wives gained control of their separate earnings and mothers became joint guardians of their children, with powers equal to those of fathers. However, in 1862, the legislature reversed the custody provision of the Act of 1860. Although women tried to modify New York's laws of divorce, they failed to do so. (Norma Basch, *In the Eyes of the Law: Women, Marriage, and Property in Nineteenth-Century New York* [Ithaca, N.Y., 1982], 136–99, 233–37. See also *Papers* 1.)

26. Jacob Bright (1821–1899), a younger brother of John, sat in Parliament from 1867 to 1874 and again from 1876 to 1895. When John Stuart Mill lost his seat in Parliament, Bright became the leader of woman suffragists until 1876. (*Who's Who of British Members of Parliament*, vol. 2; Banks, *Biographical Dictionary of British Feminists, 1800–1930*.) Ursula Mellor Bright (1835–1915) shared her husband's political interests. She joined the Manchester suffrage society, worked against the Contagious Diseases Acts, and led the Married Women's Property Committee from 1868 until its end in 1882. In the

debates leading up to the Reform Act of 1884, Jacob and Ursula Bright stood with advocates of votes for married as well as single women. (*Oxford DNB*; Holton, "From Anti-Slavery to Suffrage Militancy: The Bright Circle"; Holton, *Suffrage Days*, passim.)

27. Based on a reading of Leviticus 18:18, British law forbade the marriage of a widower and his wife's sister. The Marriage with a Deceased Wife's Sister Bill, under discussion in 1883, would legalize such marriages. ECS refers to a debate in the House of Lords on June 11 about the divorce rate in the United States. (*Hansard Parliamentary Debates*, 3d ser., vol. 280 [1883], cols. 147–48, 155; Margaret Morganroth Gullette, "The Puzzling Case of the Deceased Wife's Sister: Nineteenth-Century England Deals with a Second-Chance Plot," *Representations* 31 [Summer 1990]: 142–66.)

28. The numbers of divorces in the United States after the Civil War, exceeding those in any European country, attracted the attention of social conservatives and social scientists. Statisticians began to assemble data on the phenomenon in each state, and conservatives organized to limit access to divorce by writing stricter law. What began in 1881 as the New England Divorce Reform League became in 1885 the National Divorce Reform League. ECS draws attention to the extremes of American law. Well into the twentieth century, New York granted divorce only for adultery. Only South Carolina had stricter laws: it made no provision for divorce. ECS refers to a short-lived experiment, lasting from 1872 to 1878, when divorce on the grounds of adultery was permissible. At the other extreme were Indiana and Connecticut, where the laws recognized many possible reasons for granting divorce and enabled plaintiffs to establish state residency with relative ease. Statistics on divorces granted to migrants into those states were not kept in this period, but ECS's view of their importance was shared by most observers. Her statement that two-thirds of petitions for divorce were filed by women was widely accepted. (Roderick Phillips, *Putting Asunder: A History of Divorce in Western Society* [Cambridge, England, 1988], 403–5, 439–61; Nathan Allen, "Divorces in New England," *North American Review* 130 [June 1880]: 547–65; ECS, "The Need of Liberal Divorce Laws," *North American Review* 139 [September 1884]: 234–45, *Film*, 23:951–62.)

29. ECS indicated here to turn over the sheet. She wrote the next two sentences on the verso.

30. Frederick Billings (1823–1890), president of the Northern Pacific Railroad from 1879 to 1881, made his first fortune as a lawyer and landowner in California, where he arrived in 1848. (*ANB*.)

31. Theodor Christlieb (1833–1889), a professor at the University of Bonn in Germany, visited the United States in 1873 to attend the General Conference of the Evangelical Alliance. Matilda Gage recounted this story about his views on marriage in her chapter, "Woman, Church, and State," in *History*, 1:787–88. (*Allgemeine Deutsche Biographie*.)

32. William John Knox-Little (1839–1918), a popular Anglican preacher and High Churchman, found a congregation that welcomed his advocacy of Catholic

sacraments and social conservatism, when he preached at St. Clement's Church in Philadelphia. Among those who answered him was the journalist Anne E. McDowell. (*DNB*; *History*, 1:782, 3:471–72.)

33. Here, at the end of her page thirty-seven, ECS indicated to turn over the page. She rejected two drafts of the next page, one on the verso of her page thirty-eight and another on the verso of her page thirty-seven. She settled upon the text beginning here and continuing to the end of the paragraph, omitting references to Genesis.

34. Though ECS here placed a mark for an insertion, she struck out the verso of the page.

35. Ralph Waldo Emerson, "Love," in *Essays: First Series*, vol. 2, *Collected Works of Ralph Waldo Emerson*, ed. Joseph Slater (Cambridge, Mass., 1979), 107.

36. The kindergarten, based on the notion that young children could learn through directed play, was relatively new when ECS spoke, developed by Friedrich Froebel in Germany in the 1830s and introduced by his students into Great Britain and the United States in the late 1850s. In both countries by the 1880s, kingergarten movements, with strong leadership from women, had developed to promote Froebel's ideas, establish independent schools, and train teachers. See Joachim Liebschner, *Foundations of Progressive Education: The History of the National Froebel Society* (Cambridge, England, 1991), and Michael Steven Shapiro, *Child's Garden: The Kindergarten Movement from Froebel to Dewey* (University Park, Pa., 1983).

37. ECS means to say Napierian logarithms, named for the Scottish mathematician, John Napier.

38. ECS marked her text here with an X and "over," and the next two sentences appear on the verso.

39. Julia Josephine Thomas (1848–1930), later Irvine, won the Greek prize while a student at Cornell University, and her success was noted at the National Woman Suffrage Association's meeting in 1876. Her mother, Mary M. Thomas, was a noted suffragist in Indiana. Julia Thomas married Charles J. Irvine in 1875. After his death, she became professor of Greek and later president of Wellesley College. (*NCAB*, 12:221; *WWW1*; *History*, 3:6.)

40. A news item published in 1879 identified Julia Thomas; Florence and Emma Perkins, daughters of Sarah Perkins; and Harriot Stanton. ("Woman's Kingdom," Chicago *Inter-Ocean*, 27 September 1879.)

41. Andrew Dickson White (1832–1918), first president of Cornell University, was appointed ambassador to Germany by President Hayes in 1879. White urged Cornell's trustees to accept coeducation, and he oversaw the university's admission of women. (*ANB*.)

42. ECS marked her page to be turned over, where she added the next sentence.

43. Chartered in 1861, Vassar College accepted its first class in September 1865 and graduated four women in 1867.

44. Maria Mitchell (1818–1889), the astronomer, joined the faculty at Vassar in 1865. Mitchell engaged her students, among whom was Harriot Stanton, in her preparations for the solar eclipse of 1878, and she invited Harriot to accompany her to Denver for the observation. "The home verdict was in the negative," Harriot recalled, "and wholly based on the matter of expense. It makes my heart stand still and my head whirl whenever I think of the utter lack of imagination in my guardians in allowing such an opportunity to slip away from a young student." (*NAW*; *ANB*; Blatch and Lutz, *Challenging Years*, 39.)

45. Smith College and Wellesley College, both opened in 1875, housed students in small quarters designed to replicate a domestic setting. Distinguished by a faculty of women, Wellesley hired many alumnae of the University of Michigan, most notably Alice Freeman, later Palmer, professor of history in 1879 and president of the college in 1881. (Helen Lefkowitz Horowitz, *Alma Mater: Design and Experience in the Women's Colleges from Their Nineteeth-Century Beginnings to the 1930s*, 2d ed. [Amherst, Mass., 1993], 75–90.)

46. Marked with an X to insert the sentence that follows.

47. As ECS indicates, Harvard University moved at a glacial pace toward the education of women. By private arrangement, women could pay Harvard professors to prepare them for examinations, and the university would issue certificates. The legislature incorporated the Society for the Collegiate Instruction of Women in 1882, making the arrangement more formal but leaving the terms in place. Certificates from the Annex, as it was known, were first awarded in 1883. (Kim Townsend, *Manhood at Harvard: William James and Others* [New York, 1996], 202–6, 216–20.)

48. The University of Michigan became a coeducational school in 1870. By a state university in New York ECS probably means Cornell University, New York's land grant school, which began to admit women in the same year.

49. The Johns Hopkins University opened in Baltimore in 1876 as a research university for men. When Christine Ladd (1847–1930), later Ladd-Franklin, class of 1869 at Vassar, applied for admission to study mathematics in 1878, a faculty member recognized her name as the author of numerous publications in the field and insisted on her admission. She won a fellowship in 1879 to continue her studies and completed the requirements for a doctorate in 1882. The university refused to award her degree. (*NAW*; *ANB*.)

50. Here marked "over," where she wrote the sentence following.

51. ECS published this and the next paragraph as "The Liberals in Religion Afraid of Us," Boston *Index*, 21 August 1884, *Film*, 23:853.

52. W. E. Gladstone, *The Vatican Decrees in Their Bearing on Civil Allegiance: A Political Expostulation* (1874). William Ewart Gladstone (1809–1898) was prime minister of Great Britain from 1868 to 1874, 1880 to 1885, 1886, and finally 1892 to 1894.

53. When ECS published this paragraph in her article "The Liberals in Religion Afraid of Us," she cited not the *New York Times*, but the London *Times*, for this observation about Egypt.

54. Girton College, founded in 1869, aimed to provide women a way into Cambridge University on an equal footing with men. Since 1881 Cambridge admitted Girton students to its examinations, but the university did not award them degrees until 1921. (M. C. Bradbrook, *"That Infidel Place": A Short History of Girton College, 1869–1969* [London, 1969].)

55. ECS's source for this specific quotation is unidentified. For similar sentiments from Francis Galton, see note above at 1 September 1882.

56. Thomas Scott (1747–1821), an English clergyman known as "the Commentator," published *The Holy Bible, with Explanatory Notes, Practical Observations, and Copious Marginal References* between 1788 and 1792. Adam Clarke published his commentaries between 1810 and 1826. (Allibone.)

57. ECS added an X and "over" to insert the next two sentences.

TEXTUAL NOTES

Braces {} are used in these notes to set off the words and emendations written by Harriot Stanton Blatch and distinguish them from the changes made by her mother. Where it is possible to recover ECS's original wording, the strike out is shown within the braces.

¶1	*ll.* 3–4	among them {~~illegible~~ ↑were↓} six women from the United States, one of {~~them~~ ↑whom was↓}
¶2	*l.* 1 beg.	The clergy {~~in the convention~~} said no,
	ll. 2–3	it would cause the {~~convention~~ ↑meeting↓} to be ridiculed in the morning papers. Sentamentalists said no it would
	l. 8	eloquent orators {~~in the convention~~}, such as
	ll. 9–10	Henry B. Stanton, Dr Bowering, bravely
	ll. 12–13	quickened, & my ↑heart↓ throbbed,
	ll. 14–15	opponents {~~illegible~~ ↑strengthened with↓} the creeds, & codes,
[*conclusion from page removed*]		{~~I had been born any other living thing than a woman.~~}
	ll. 21–22	juxtaposition {~~illegible~~ ↑with↓} the members of the convention. {~~With~~ ↑Facing↓}
¶3	*l.* 1 beg.	William Loyd Garrison our great
	l. 2	until the third day {~~of the convention~~}.
	ll. 10–11	sheild her with special safeguards {~~honor, & protection~~}.
	l. 19	peculiar star of {~~the convention~~ ↑that assembly of inconsistencies↓}.
	l. 22	that there {~~was another class in slavery~~ ↑were others↓} beside Africans, {~~illegible some consideration~~ ↑in slavery↓}. Accordingly
	ll. 25–26	the redress ~~that~~ ↑which↓ the next forty years

[*original page 11, ¶3 and 4, and their emendations, all struck out*] suffrage convention & sent forth that {first} daring declaration of rights, demanding {the redress of ↑for↓} every grievance {illegible ↑the redress which the next↓} forty years of agitation {has} proved feasible.

So audacious did {the demands ↑this appeal↓} for {an} absolute equality {of rights} with man {everywhere, illegible on the ↑seem to the↓ ears of the} nation, that our declaration was received with derisive laughter, from the Atlantic to the Pacific, from the Lakes to the Gulf. A few years later Mrs

¶5   *ll.* 2–4   encomiums in your {widely known Quarterly the} Westminster Review. Later, the Hon John Stuart Mill {illegible ↑introduced↓} a bill for household suffrage, & ↑with↓ thousands of petitions ↑in its favor↓ into Parliament.

ll. 10–14   the Brights the McLarens {↑by↓} your poet laureate in his Princess, {↑by↓} George Eliot in her novels, Harriet Martineau in her {philosophy ↑essays↓} & ↑the Rev↓ Charles Kingsley in his protests against the ↑degradation of woman in the↓ canon law. At last complete ↑political↓ equality for woman

ll. 23–24   side by side, in the↑se↓ successive steps of progress on this, ↑the↓ most far-reaching

ll. 25–26   the same people {↑as you↓}, we speak

ll. 28–29   your social virtues & your vices{↑.↓; until now we are said to surpass you in political corruption commercial dishonesty, & in religious & social freedom: we certainly do in our inventive genius, our industrial arts & our implements of husbandry.} What has been

ll. 29–30   the effect of {this ↑our↓} civilization on woman

¶6   *ll.* 7–8   To all {the} serious questions in regard to the government commerce & religion of {their country their ↑China, the↓} only reply

ll. 17–19   When they ↑some↓ sang duetts & waltzed {together} the Chinese would peep out first one side ↑of their fans↓ & then the other, confused ↑convulsed↓ with shame &

¶8   *l.* 2   women as {are those} in the United States

ll. 5–6   civilization. ↑Remember we were↓ three thousand miles beyond

l. 15   maintained {illegible ↑our liberty↓} through the century.

l. 18   sentiments of liberty such the lips of Abigail Adams

ll. 19–25   Childs, Margaret Fuller & Angelina Grimké {whose yearnings at last took form & shape in conventions, speeches & resolutions}. {Such ↑Many↓} influences have made American women the most ↑more↓ independent, self-asserting,

versatile than those of {any} other nation. Owing to the
great difference in climate, {too} our women are {↑nervously↓}
more highly wrought, physically more delicate & slender,
more excitable {↑perhaps↓} in manner, the voice pitched on
a higher key. {Said} The distinguished

ll. 38–39   born of intelligent parents, ↑they↓ were brought

¶9   *l.* 1 beg   {This ~~illegible~~ ↑The sentiment↓} of chivalry {↑in our men↓
~~early modified~~ ↑served to modify↓} our property laws,
giving us {↑in New York State↓} as early as '48,

ll. 4–7   Jacob Bright, {~~illegible~~ ↑sustained↓} by the perseverance
& untiring labors of his estimable wife. {~~This illegible~~
~~cause has~~ ↑Later was↓} secured to married women the
right to their children & earnings, & more reasonable
laws of divorce. {~~emancipating refined virtuous women~~
~~from all gross associations with unworthy men.~~}

ll. 9–11   by which we are {↑supposed to be↓} held in the marriage
relation {~~illegible~~ ↑cited↓} as a warning against any liberal
legislation {~~on that question~~} in this country.

ll. 12–13   mind that the they differ in

ll. 13–14   In all ~~the states~~ together we have have eighteen different
causes for divorce {~~in some more in others less~~}.

ll. 17–21   Indiana, {~~obtain their release from unhappy unions, it~~
~~would not be~~ ↑avail themselves of the broader laws it is
not↓} fair, in making up statistics {~~for these states,~~} to
attribute all the divorces granted, to {~~their illegible~~ ↑the
permanent inhabitants↓.} When it is said that a thousand
{~~divorces are granted~~ ↑marriages are dissolved↓} in Connecticut in a single year {~~it is probable~~ ↑we must remember↓}

l. 24   effects. {~~Our~~ ↑That our↓} laws are not the result

l. 32   husbands & wives are ↑mutually↓ more respect~~able~~↑ful↓

ll. 34–37   And {~~it~~ ↑this↑} is because the principle of self government
is slowly but surely making its way in every department
of life, {↑because↓} individual rights, individual conscience
↑& judgement↓ are governing alike

l. 38   & the home. [*entire, emended passage struck out by Harriot
Blatch*] Our divorce laws are not the result of the fickleness
of men, but ↑the↓ growing independence of {~~the~~} women.
It is in a vast majority of the cases that wives ask for the
dissolution of the union, & not

¶10   *l.* 1 beg.   {~~Again in~~ ↑In↓}

ll. 2–3   & {↑often↓} in pioneer life {~~breaking up the lands, &~~
~~mining~~} none at all{↑;↓} hence there was {↑for them &
children↓} a wild worshipful feeling {~~for~~ ↑among↓ ~~women~~
~~& children~~}.

l. 7   the days work was done

¶11   *l.* 6   courtesies to all women {~~which the women accept as their just rights~~}.

     ll. 9–10   a distinguished German ~~Professor~~ ↑Clergyman↓,

     l. 31   orthodox religious {~~papers~~ ↑journals↓} repudiated

     ll. 34–35   Many of them {↑had been↓} trained in our theological schools {~~for the last half century~~}, many {↑were↓} preaching

     ll. 37–38   According to woman's exposition {↑of texts↓} of scripture {~~texts~~}, man

[*on verso of page 37 and struck out*] & woman were a simultaneous creation. Without going into any Bible expositions, I would simply call the attention of the women present to the 1st chapter of Genesis 27th & 28th verses So God created man in his <u>own</u> image, male & female created he <u>them</u> & gave <u>them</u> dominion over everything on the earth; but there is not a word said of giving man dominion over woman   If language has any meaning here is a plain declaration of the existence of the feminine element in the Godhead

     ll. 40–42   two great {~~forces~~ ↑powers↓} in nature, exactly equal & balancing each other, like {~~the~~} positive & negative electricity, {~~the north & south magnetism~~ ↑like↓}

     ll. 42–43   forces ↑were↓ necessaryly a simultaneous creation,

[*on verso of page 38 and struck out*] Without going into any Bible exposition, I would simply call the attention of the women present to the 1 chapter of Genesis 27th & 28th verses.

     As this is much more dignified than to have been merely an afterthought, the origin of sin, cursed of heaven, doomed to lasting subjection no doubt you will gladly accept the higher idea

     The Bible not opposed to woman suffrage

¶12   *ll.* 1–2   contrast between adopted & originated principles

     l. 4   We ~~found~~ ↑saw↓ your colleges & universities

     ll. 7–8   public schools, ↑so absolutely necessary to the safety of a democracy↓ we had to seek

     l. 11   Lead in no small measure

     ll. 27–28   sea-board, ~~b~~↑B↓ut go a hundred miles inland &

     ll. 32–33   medicine, & theology, ~~all~~ open to woman.

¶13   *ll.* 2–3   shoot in one & the same ~~*illegible*~~ ↑room↓.

¶14   *ll.* 19–20   "men & women ↑boys & girls↓ are better apart."

     l. 26   sexes. ~~They~~ ↑You↓ answer "in colleges &

     l. 33   [*marked further with arrows to indicate final order*] White of ~~the~~ ↑in↓ New York state ↑Cornell↓ University

¶15   *l.* 1 beg.   Vassar college ↑in New York,↓

	l. 5	Here ↑Prof.↓ Maria Mitchell,
	ll. 10–11	its buildings ↑which accommodate five hundred↓ are so planned
	ll. 12–14	Smith College ↑& Wellesley↓ in Massacheusetts is a later venture, unfortunate in being also for women ↑only↓, &
	ll. 27–28	slip quietly into ~~the~~ ↑our classic↓ scullery.
	ll. 29–30	professor, whom ↑you↓ will surely pay well for his magnanimity ~~to~~ ↑in↓ answer↑ing↓
	ll. 34–35	of Michigan, & New York, there women are
	ll. 38–39	prospect for women is brighening
	l. 40	University in Baltimore ↑Md↓
¶16	*ll.* 1–2	gay pinions at her lauching,
	l. 3	with {~~illegible~~ ↑weather beaten↓} sides, &
¶17	*ll.* 4–5	can see & hear. we are not cooped
¶18	*l.* 1 beg.	Our movement ↑for suffrage↓ in America
	l. 8	discuss {~~it~~ ↑our movement↓} as one of [*ECS then marked the passage to be returned to her original text*]
	l. 11	classes are {~~moving~~ ↑advancing↓} in one direction
	ll. 13–14	Women {~~say~~ they ↑declare↓} are naturally
	ll. 19–20	against every step in progress, that if
	l. 26	holding him down in ↑the↓ valley of
	l. 29	generation after generation, the time &
	ll. 36–37	pamphlet on Catholiscism, written
	ll. 38–39	its most ready victims ~~were~~ ↑are↓ women
	l. 47	reason {~~instead of~~ ↑for↓} blind faith
	ll. 50–51	~~Women toiling~~ ↑As toilers↓ in the rice swamps & cotten plantations
	ll. 56–57	navy of the mightest nation
	l. 60	& improve, & change ↑altogether↓ ~~altogether.~~
¶19	*l.* 5	Seeing that {~~this~~ ↑her↓} powerful
	ll. 11–12	problems of our present ↑intense↓ civilization
	ll. 13–14	complex questions ~~must~~ ↑will↓ come up in the near future, something must be ↑done to↓ lift ~~up~~ our statesmen a few degrees ↑higher↓
	l. 16	~~You are asking for various bills~~ And where shall we look
¶20	*l.* 1	asking here in England for various bill
	ll. 4–5	If the ↑same↓ respect the masses are educated
	l. 15	reverence for these. ~~But where shall we look for any lessons of respect~~

[*original page 75 struck out and turned over to become 76½*] but where shall we look for such worshipful regard for woman for that honor & respect worthy the age in which we live, & yet as mother of the race is she not more than symbols, sacraments, altars & vast cathedral domes

l. 26   By no means. they come oftimes fresh

¶22   *l.* 1 beg.   Strengthened purified exalted in equal conditions it is this faith that ↑will at last↓ makes us one & immortal.

115   ❧   URSULA MELLOR BRIGHT TO ECS

London, July 2, 18[*83*].

Dear Mrs. Cady Stanton:

I am sure you will not refuse to support Miss Craigen's amend[men]t on Thursday.[1] I cannot go to the meeting, and if I did, my husband [doe]s not like me to speak in public at all. He is afraid of me losing my [do]mestic character and being dragged into a round of public work which he [say?]s would kill me! I dare say he is quite right; but it is a little try[in]g at times when a thing like this has got to be done and one does not [kno]w whom to ask to do it. Believe me, Truly yours,

❧   *Ursula M. Bright.*

❧ Typed transcript, ECS Papers, NjR. Letters in square brackets obscured by binding.

1. Bright referred to the great demonstration called by the National Society for Women's Suffrage at St. James's Hall on July 5, the day before Parliament's scheduled vote on the suffrage resolution. Jessie Craigen's amendment would confront the problem of married women's status by changing the resolution to favor parliamentary suffrage for "women, whether married or single, who possess the qualifications which entitle men to vote." When Craigen stepped forward to introduce the amendment, she was interrupted by loud and repeated calls for the chair to rule her out of order. Instead, the chair took a confusing vote on whether to debate Craigen's amendment and announced that the meeting "ruled that the amendment was not to be entertained." ECS spoke at a different point in the meeting, making no reference to the dispute. (*Women's Suffrage Journal* 14 [19 July 1883]: 122–26, *Film*, 23:247–51; Holton, *Suffrage Days*, 62.)

116 ∽ FROM THE DIARY OF SBA

[*4–8 July 1883*]

WEDNESDAY, JULY 4, 1883. In London— Went round with Rachel to see about copying—trunks &c, &c

Mrs Mellens[1] Reception for Mrs Stanton & self—at 9.PM— A large company—& our American girls & women made a good showing of what freedom & equal chances will do for women   It was 2 Oclock when we got home—

1. Ellen Seymour Clarke Mellen (1836?–?) was an American widow, living in Pembroke Gardens, Kensington, with some of her seven children. For descriptions of this elegant event, see *History*, 3:946, and SBA to Mary S. Anthony, 13 July 1883, *Film*, 23:257. ECS and SBA saw Ellen Mellen on numerous occasions. In 1856, Mellen had married her sister's widower, William Proctor Mellen, a lawyer in Cincinnati, friend of Salmon P. Chase, and special treasury agent during the war. They moved to Flushing, New York, in 1866, but after the marriage of Mary Mellen, Ellen's stepdaughter, to the builder of the Denver & Rio Grande Railroad, William Jackson Palmer, the Mellens moved to Colorado Springs in 1872. Ellen Mellen and children stayed there after the death of William P. Mellen in 1873 until at least 1880. By 1890, according to notes in SBA's diary, Ellen Mellen lived on Washington Square in New York City. (ECS diary, 30 April 1883, *Stanton*, 2:205–6; SBA diary, 14, 25 June, 4, 5 July, 15 October 1883, and end pages 1890, *Film*, 22:814ff, 27:679ff; *History*, 3:927, 945–46; *Eighty Years*, 370; Federal Census, Colorado, 1880; Mitchell Sprague, *Newport in the Rockies: The Life and Good Times of Colorado Springs* [Denver, Colo., 1961], 315–16.)

THURSDAY, JULY 5, 1883. St James Hall—W.S. Demonstration—[1] A splendid audience— Mrs Millinett Garrett Fawcett[2] made a most excellent address—ditto Miss Scatchard[3] of Leeds—

Spent A.M. on Rachel's report of my Princess Hall speech—breakfast at Mrs Mellen's—then to W.S. Office[4]—Waterloo House[5] &c— &c—& home— at 5.30 went to Mrs Thomasson's to an elegant 6.30— dinner—all women—Mrs Lucas, Mrs M'Laren—Miss Tod—Miss Becker—[*blank*] Mrs Stanton, Harriot, Rachel & self—& thence to St James Hall—

1. At this "Great Meeting," ECS and SBA occupied the stage with other distinguished guests and members of Parliament.

2. Millicent Garrett Fawcett (1847–1929), wife of a member of Parliament, was, like her husband, a political economist and politician. Theodore Stanton chose her to write the essay on England's suffrage movement for his book, *Woman Question in Europe.* Her speech on this occasion was published as "Women and Representative Government," *Nineteenth Century* 14 (August 1883): 285–91. She held the view that if Parliament would admit spinsters and widows to the franchise, suffragists should accept that partial victory. (*DNB*; Stanton, *Woman Question in Europe*, 1–29.)

3. Alice Cliff Scatcherd (1842–1906) of Leeds, an effective speaker and organizer, made particular contributions to the British movement by her attention over many decades to working women. When SBA met her in Leeds in October, she remarked in her diary how much she liked Scatcherd, adding, she "is less bound by old customs than any woman I have met here." In 1888, Scatcherd visited the United States as a delegate to the International Council of Women. (Holton, *Suffrage Days*, passim; E. Sylvia Pankhurst, *The Suffragette Movement: An Intimate Account of Persons and Ideals* [1931; reprint, London, 1977], 118; Patricia Hollis, *Ladies Elect: Women in English Local Government, 1865–1914* [Oxford, England, 1987], 35–36, 155; *History*, 3:866n, 868n, 875, 923, 929, 941; SBA diary, 18–19 October 1883.)

4. At 29 Parliament Street, Southwest.

5. On Cockspur Street, Pall Mall East, it housed shops for haberdashers, silk mercers, and drapers.

FRIDAY, JULY 6, 1883. Mr Hugh Mason's[1] bill to come up in Parliament today—

Went W.S. office in A.M. Found not on returning from Mrs M'Laren & Mrs Thomasson saying the former would call for me at 8.15—had a seat for me—which she did & we waited in hall of Parliament building until 9. P.M. when we were let into the <u>coop</u>— Mr Mason introduced his bill & made a very <u>weak</u> speech—& so were all of them pro & con except Mr Jacob Bright's[2]—which had the ring of earnestness & principle— the vote was taken at 1. A.M. and I rode to Duchess street with Mr Walter M'Laren & wife—Eva Muller—[3] the vote stood 130 against & 114 for—

1. Hugh Mason (1817–1886), a Liberal member of Parliament from 1880 to 1885, became the parliamentary leader of woman suffrage the year of his election. When he presented the resolution (not a bill, as SBA states), Mason assured the members that he only "intended to cover women ratepayers who are spinsters and widows. I have not the slightest sympathy with those who advocate the conferring of this vote upon married women." (*Oxford DNB*;

Who's Who of British Members of Parliament, vol. 1; *Hansard Parliamentary Debates*, 3d ser., vol. 281, [1883], cols. 664–71.)

2. *Hansard Parliamentary Debates*, 3d ser., vol. 281, [1883], cols. 703–8. Bright distinguished his hope for "electoral equality" from the position taken by Mason, but he devoted most of his time to making the case for women's right to and need for suffrage.

3. Walter Stowe Bright McLaren (1853–1912), a son of Duncan and Priscilla McLaren and a businessman, won election to Parliament in 1886. He married Eva Maria Müller (1852?–1912) in April 1883. Before her marriage, Eva served as a Poor Law Guardian and formed the Society for Promoting the Return of Women as Poor Law Guardians. After marriage, she became active in the Manchester suffrage society. (*Oxford DNB*, s.v. "McLaren, Eva Maria"; Hollis, *Ladies Elect*, passim; *Who's Who of British Members of Parliament*, vol. 2; Bertha Mason, *Walter S. B. McLaren: An Appreciation* [London, n.d.], Women's Library, London.)

SATURDAY, JULY 7, 1883. In London— Went to Central Com. meeting at Office at 11—[1] much dissatisfaction with measure of Mr [Mason?]

Somerville Club[2]—Rachel spoke 15 minutes beautifully on need of <u>union</u> among women— she will surely make a good ↑speaker↓— I gave a little ballot argument— Mrs M'Laren spoke a little— The club has nice rooms & we had cup of coffee— Rachel left for Antwerp on 8 train—to meet her mother & sister— I feel as if my last hope had left me— She has taken entire charge of all money & business matters for me—up to moment of parting—

1. This was a conference of delegates, convened to discuss the parliamentary defeat. The published account of the meeting makes no mention of differences over married women's suffrage. (*Women's Suffrage Journal* 14 [1 August 1883]: 150.)

2. Founded in 1878 to provide a place for women to discuss social and political questions, the Somerville Club was regarded as London's first women's club. It moved its rooms in the summer of 1883 from 21 Mortimer Street to 405 Oxford Street. (*Englishwoman's Review* 12 [15 January 1881]: 29–30, 12 [15 April 1881]: 188, 14 [15 June 1883]: 281–82; Eva Anstructher, "Ladies' Clubs," *Nineteenth Century* 45 [April 1899]: 600.)

SUNDAY, JULY 8, 1883. In London & <u>Rachel</u> not with me & lonely enough

Went to Notting Hill with corrected proof of speech—& thence at 1.30 to Mrs Lucas' to dinner—Mrs M'Laren there—in P.M. Mrs Lillian Ashworth Hallett[1]—a niece called—and Mrs Moss & Miss Smith of Hyde—near Manchester—Factory women—& Mrs M'Cormic[2]—the getter up of the meetings— all are very anxious & feel that some one of the women must have coached Mr Mason to declare Married women not intended to be included in the Bill—&c—

1. Lilias Sophia Ashworth Hallett (c. 1844–?) was a daughter of another of the Bright sisters, Sophia Bright Ashworth, and like her cousins, she became active in the suffrage movement at an early age. After her marriage to Thomas George Palmer Hallett in 1877, she grew more conservative, and her loyalty to Lydia Becker and advocacy of suffrage only for single women put her at odds with numerous members of her family. (Census of Britain, 1881; Mills, *John Bright and the Quakers*, 1:177, 296n, 297, 398, 465; Lovell, *Quaker Inheritance, 1871–1961*, 41; Holton, *Suffrage Days*, 40, 65, 66, 167.)

2. The names of these three women appear often in reports of meetings in Manchester and the nearby milltown of Hyde. For instance, they were all on the platform of a suffrage meeting in Hyde in March 1880. All of them attended the conference of delegates at the Central Committee's offices on July 7. Mrs. McCormick, who was organizing agent for the Manchester National Society for Women's Suffrage as early as 1879, added to her local work by traveling to other cities in advance of large demonstrations to assist with logistics. (*Women's Suffrage Journal* 11 [1 April 1880]: 74, and 14 [1 August 1883]: 150; Blackburn, *Women's Suffrage in the British Isles*, 154; *Annual Report of the Central Committee of the National Society for Women's Suffrage Presented to the General Meeting, July 19th, 1883*, 12, Organizational Records, Women's Library, London.)

❧ The Empire State Diary 1883, n.p., SBA Papers, DLC. Square brackets surround uncertain reading.

117 ❧ ECS to Harriet Cady Eaton[1]

Basingstoke Hants [*England*] July 10th [*1883*]

Dear sister

I have just read your nice long letter, it did indeed bring the house, the town, the people, all vividly before me. I could almost make a drawing of the old Holland house.[2] I had a perfect vision of the dining room, the dish washing, & you at the writing desk, in black & white silk, & pretty morning cap with a jaunty bow on one side, the old family Bible on top of the desk, & the outlook on the grass, & the

Murray brick wall. You speak of my future domestic life. I shall return
with Susan the last of September or the 1st of October, according to the
state of Hatties health. We must finish the third volumn of our history.
Susan will either stay with me in Johnstown & Maggie spend the winter
with us, or I will stay with her in Rochester. As soon as that is finished
I shall return here to finish my days with Hattie & Theodore, unless in
the meantime I find that Paradise Nellie[3] speaks of in America. With
her for a companion I think most any spot would quite satisfy my heart.
Problems for extended discussion are multiplying on my mind daily &
I never felt more of the spirit of investigation, nor enjoyed more fullness in life than now. I want Nelly to read that last chapter in the first
vol. of my History on "Woman & the Church." I have just been reading
it aloud to Hattie to day, preparatory to writing another sermon, as I
am to fill Moncure D Conways[4] pulpit on the 22nd of July. If you or
Nelly have any new ideas on time & eternity send them over without
delay, as I can make good use of all my friends possess as well as what
I hold in my own right. I have a most charming friend "a spinster" of
thirty five[5] who is writing a fine essay on the grand sphere for single
women. She read it to me when I was in London. She believes in single
women having their own homes & occupation. Hattie & I spent several
days at her house. Her income is 600 pounds a year, she has a fine
house horses carriage & does just as she pleases. She has the right to
vote in all municipal elections & has been twice elected a member of
the School Board. All join in congratulations to Alexander Brown.[6] I
do hope he will get a good wife for Hatties sake as well as his own.
When you write to Hattie & Cady[7] give our love to them. I was indeed
glad to see Nellies pen tracks once more she must take this as an answer
to her as well as to you. Hattie & I are both well & our days pass
happily along without the least friction. Harry is as good as gold, his
devotion to Hattie is most soul satisfying to me, & of course to her [*in
margin of first page*] ever your loving sister

∽ *Elizabeth Cady Stanton.*

∽ ALS, Alice Paul Papers, MCR-S.

1. Harriet Eliza Cady Eaton (1810–1894) was an older sister of ECS who
married their cousin Daniel Cady Eaton. A widow since 1855, she often spent
summers in Johnstown, New York. (Allen, *Descendants of Nicholas Cady*, 174–
75; Gravestones, Johnstown, N.Y.; genealogical files, notes from Presbyterian
Church Records, NJost.)

2. ECS names features of the Johnstown neighborhood near the Cady house at Market and Main streets.

3. Ellen Dwight Eaton (1832–?), known as Nellie, was a niece of Harriet Cady Eaton and a child of ECS's cousin Amos Beebe Eaton. Nellie and ECS met in 1860 and became fast friends. ECS once described her as an invalid. (Allen, *Descendants of Nicholas Cady*, 175; Sophie Selden Rogers, Elizabeth Selden Lane, and Edwin van Deusen Selden, *Selden Ancestry. A Family History, Giving the Ancestors and Descendants of George Shattuck Selden and His Wife Elizabeth Wright Clark* [Oil City, Pa., 1931], 167; ECS to Ann G. Phillips, before 9 January 1866, *Film*, 11:265–70. See also *Papers 1.*)

4. Moncure Daniel Conway (1832–1907) was an American reformer and Unitarian minister, living in London since 1863. In London, ECS and SBA often visited him and his wife, Ellen. Conway heard ECS and SBA speak at the meeting of June 25, and he approached ECS with the request that she preach in his freethinking South Place Chapel on July 22. She chose to answer the question, "What has Christianity done for Woman?" In 1901, she published the text of what she thought was this sermon under the title "Woman's Position in the Christian Church." (*ANB*; *History*, 3:928; *Stanton*, 2:208–9; *Film*, 23:263–67.)

5. Frances Henrietta Müller (1846?–1906) was born in Valparaiso, Chile, the daughter of a German-born businessman who became a British subject. Henrietta, as she was known, entered Girton College in 1873, and upon graduation, she stood for election to the London School Board in 1879 and drew the most votes of any candidate. Winning two more elections, she served on the board until 1885. In 1884, to protest Parliament's failure to include women in the Reform Bill, she refused to pay her taxes, publicized her action, and invited women to observe the seizure of her property. Using the nom de plume Helena B. Temple, Müller edited the *Women's Penny Paper* from 1888 to 1890, renamed it the *Woman's Herald*, and continued publishing until 1892. Müller entertained both ECS and SBA in 1882 and 1883. (*Oxford DNB*; Cambridge University, Girton College, *Girton College Register, 1869–1946* [Cambridge, England, 1948], 5–6; Hollis, *Ladies Elect*, 100; *History*, 3:950–51; *Woman's Journal*, 12 July, 9 August 1884; *Woman's Herald* 4 [28 November 1891]: 915–16; *Times* [London], 6 January 1906.)

6. Alexander Brown (1858–1949), Harriet Eaton's grandson, was the only child of Harriet Eaton Brown (1835–1893) and her husband, George Stewart Brown, of Baltimore, Maryland. A graduate of Princeton College in 1878, he spent two years abroad before joining his father's banking house, Alexander Brown & Sons. The cause for congratulations is not known; he did not marry until 1887. (*ACAB*; *New York Times*, 14 May 1949; Allen, *Descendants of Nicholas Cady*, 174–75; Frank R. Kent, *The Story of Alexander Brown & Sons* [Baltimore, Md., 1950], 171–80.)

7. This Daniel Cady Eaton (1837–1912), one of several in the family, was the

son of Harriet Eaton and an art historian. He was Professor of History and Criticism of Art at Yale University from 1869 to 1876, and after two years in Europe, he resided in New York City until returning to Yale in 1902. (Allen, *Descendants of Nicholas Cady*, 175; *WWW1*; D. Cady Eaton Papers, CtY.)

118 ⇜ FROM THE DIARY OF SBA

[*11–16 July 1883*]

WEDNESDAY, JULY 11, 1883. At Miss Muller's—London— Both of remained in the house all day—and talked ove the whole social question—she thinks she will forever eschew marriage—for her public work—has an intimate man friend[1]—who is not content to allow her to do so—but she feels that she is strong enough to resist—indeed that it is no self-denial—but that her mission to help the world is a higher one & apart from marriage

    1. At 28 October 1883 below, SBA identified him as Charles Martin.

THURSDAY, JULY 12, 1883. Miss Müller sent me over to Duchess in her carriage—drew from American Exchange £50.— the last of my Letter of Credit—$1000— to pay for an India shawl— Lunched at Duchess—did sundry errands—rain came on—took cab back to Miss Muller's at 5—wrote letter to Rachel—& got one from her—her mother & Julia arrived at Antwerp this A.M. 7 Oclock— Miss M. did not get home from School Board till 9 P.M.—so we dined at that hour— She was awfully tired—her work is very constant & hard—

FRIDAY, JULY 13, 1883. [*above date line*] This is the 66th anniversary of dear Fathers & mother's wedding day—July 13, 1817!!

    Left Miss Mullers at 11. drove to Civil Service store—& gave order for a longer & wider trunk to be made—[1] called Farmer & Rogers—117 Regent st—& paid $250. for India shawl—a tremendous sum to put into one wrap—but it is for rest of my life time & for nieces after me—then to ~~Duchess to Lunch—after it~~ Mrs Jacob Bright's to call— She is right in her demand—but almost alone in courage to speak it—"Married women too"! Then to Duchess to Lunch— Found note from Mrs M'Laren for me to go to Barne Elms—her Son Charles'—& Laura—

home to dinner[2]—so telegraphed Mrs Rose[3] I go to her tomorrow—& wrote letters to Sister Mary[4] & Mrs Stanton till 5.30—then Mrs M & Mrs Lucas took me in Carriage to dinner—splendid peaches—

1. Officially named the Civil Service Supply Association, the Civil Service Stores on Victoria Street began as a membership cooperative for bulk purchases of groceries. (*London Encyclopaedia*.)

2. ECS described her own visit to Barn Elms, an ancient estate along the Thames, with a manor house rebuilt in 1694 and extensive waterworks and gardens, in *History*, 3:929–30, and *Eighty Years*, 358–59.

3. SBA first called upon Ernestine Rose in March and "found her very sad & suffering." She hoped to persuade Rose to return with her to the United States. (SBA diary, 9, 10, 13, 14 March, 13 June 1883, *Film*, 22:814ff.)

4. *Film*, 23:257.

SATURDAY, JULY 14, 1883. Left London 11.50 A.M. Arrived Tunbridge Wells—at the Spa—Santarium—2.30— Found Mrs Ernestine L. Rose looking bright as ever and full of rheumatic pains in body & mind as ever— She was 73— the 13th of last January—so was born January 13, 1810—while I was born February 15, 1820—ten years difference in our ages—

SUNDAY, JULY 15, 1883. At Tunbridge Wells—Spa—with Mrs E. L. Rose— Rode over the hills & through the lanes & garden farms from 11.30 to 1 PM— Cool & lovely day—very little like a home July Sunday— It is very sad to see so great and grand an intellect—at close of so grand a life work so incapable of making the best of the inevitable— accepting it cheerfully— I do hope I shall not live to feel that no one cares for me—or can help me to conditions of enjoyment— I am made fearfully sad with dear Mrs R's mental sufferings—apart from her bodily pains—

MONDAY, JULY 16, 1883. At Tunbridge Wells Spa— Spent entire day listening to & talking with & reading to dear Mrs Rose— read the Speech of glorious Wendell Phillips before Old Harvard alumni— Phibeta cappa—of two years ago—the one he handed me last January & said "here is probably my last speech"![1] & I said "Oh—no—you must not say so!!["] I have used all my persuasive powers to get Mrs Rose to go back to America with me—but to no avail—

1. Wendell Phillips, *The Scholar in a Republic: Address at the Centennial Anniversary of the Phi Beta Kappa of Harvard College, June 30, 1881* (1881). On the fiftieth anniversary of his graduation from Harvard, Phillips chastised

those with education who became enemies of popular rights. The true duty of the scholar was to lead in the agitation of such great subjects as temperance, universal suffrage, the rights of women, and labor's right to organize. As Phillips predicted to SBA, this was his last major address.

⚬ The Empire State Diary 1883, n.p., SBA Papers, DLC.

119 ⇝ ECS to SBA

Basingstoke, England, July 17, 1883.

Dear Susan:

If you are in London, do go and see what the new movement proposes.[1] I have written to the promoters exactly what I think about the narrow de[m]and for spinsters and widows, and advised them to base themselves on a [p]rinciple and not on the fraction of one.[2] You may take what position your conscience dictates; I shall follow my own. If my influence can help broaden the English platform, it shall go in that direction. It has gone in that direction ever since I came into the country and shall till I leave it. In haste,

⚬ *Elizabeth Cady Stanton.*

⚬ Typed transcript, ECS Papers, NjR. Letters in square brackets obscured by binding.

1. ECS may refer to a specific meeting in advance of the Central Committee's annual meeting on June 19.

2. ECS's diary entry for July 8 reports this correspondence. "I have written a letter to Mrs. M'Laren and Mrs. Lucas, which I ask them to read to the Brights and Thomassons, on the wisdom of broadening their platform. I impress on them the fact that to get the suffrage for spinsters is all very well, but their work is also to elevate the position of women at all points, and that in calling attention to every form of injustice and laying bare every inequality, they take the shortest way to educate women into rebellion and self-assertion, and men into consideration of women's rights and wrongs. That the married women in this movement in England consent to the assumption that they are, through marriage, practically represented and protected, supported and sheltered from all the adverse winds of life, is the strongest evidence of their own need for emancipation. Any other course is as illusory as was working for the black man's emancipation and enfranchisement at the close of our Civil War." (*Stanton*, 2:208–9.)

120 ⤜ PRISCILLA BRIGHT McLAREN TO ECS

Bath, [*England*] July 17, 1883.

My dearest Mrs. Stanton:

I do not think it is possible for you, with your wide unpre[ju]diced views, thoroughly to comprehend our position here. Though I see the [ri?]ght and justice of all you say, I assure you it would set our cause back [at] least twenty years were we to act upon your advice. I abhor the idea [of] degrading marriage as much as my sister Ursula Bright by any positive [pr]ohibition of a right because of marriage.[1] But we should be running our [he]ads against a wall were we to go in all at once for all the rights you [ad]vocate. Besides, the women of our country are not prepared for some of the [th]ings you advise us to put upon our flag. We have to prove our fitness [fo]r some of them by increased education. I am convinced that, with what [ed]ucation they have had, the women are as fit as men to hold the offices many [me]n hold. But <u>our world</u> does not think so. The way women have acted on [sc]hool-boards, &c., has opened the eyes of many men who now admit that they [de]serve still further advance; and in consequence, many have been brought [ro]und to our suffrage views. The real practical reformer must be willing to [cl]imb step by step. In a young country, you may go ahead; but here, we must [tr]ead cautiously, not timidly, but wisely. You must forgive me, dear, noble, [cl]ear-minded friend, if I cannot knock down at once all our Old World [fe]nces. We must creep under them, or climb over them, as best we can, and, [by] letting the privileged proprietors of all the sister domains see that we [wa]lk surely and spoil nothing, make them gradually willing to open all the [ga]tes, to other domains, of which they have so long held the key.

How good of Susan B. Anthony to go and see Mrs. Rose. It brightens [my?] heart to think of that poor woman having a light thrown across her [da]rkened path,—a path over which she herself will admit no ray of heavenly [li]ght.

⤜ *Priscilla M'Laren.*

⚜ Typed transcript, ECS Papers, NjR. Letters in square brackets obscured by binding.

1. Ursula Bright sent a letter to the Central Committee's annual meeting on July 19 with these views about demanding suffrage for married women. (*Women's Suffrage Journal* 14 [1 August 1883]: 154–55.)

121 ⚜ FROM THE DIARY OF SBA

[17–18 July 1883]

TUESDAY, JULY 17, 1883. Left Tunbridge Wells at 3.30 P.M. dear Mrs R. riding to Depot with me— Nothing I could propose seemed possible or attractive to her— she mourns her loss of her adoring husband[1]—he was never exhausting in doing for her— after dinner I called on Mr & Mrs Justice[2]—he is Executor for Mrs R.—& says ↑as does Mrs R. that↓ she has money enough to carry her along comfortably—that is is such a comfort—but they know not what to propose to her—so we agreed that she must make her own home as she could—since no one is able to suggest acceptably—

1. William Ela Rose (c. 1813–1882), an English jeweler and silversmith, moved to the United States with his wife in 1836 and returned with her to England in 1874. He died suddenly of a heart attack in January 1882. (Yuri Suhl, *Ernestine L. Rose and the Battle for Human Rights* [New York, 1959], passim.)

2. Philip Syng Justice (1819–1901) and Helen Mary Cobb Justice (c. 1819–1893), formerly of Philadelphia, settled in London after the Civil War. From a business in hardware, Philip Justice had moved to importing and then manufacturing steel rails and wheels for American railroads. In England, he still oversaw his American business. SBA and Ernestine Rose had called on the couple in Philadelphia in 1854. (John W. Jordan, *Colonial Families of Philadelphia* [New York, 1911], 1:826–27, 866; *Friends' Intelligencer* 50 [1893]: 392, 58 [1901]: 295; SBA diary, 12 April 1854, *Film*, 7:879ff.)

WEDNESDAY, JULY 18, 1883. In London—at Duchess st— Mrs Stanton writes she ↑has &↓ shall counsel English women to take the broad ground for Married women too— My point is simply that I do not feel it in good taste for either of us to advise <u>public</u> opposition—to the bill before Parliament—

Mrs Blanchard[1] with me—ordered onyx & gold chain—£10. and the two cameos set £10—$100—in all—of Mr Frank Flower[2]—George Blogg & Co.—4— Albemarle st— in P.M. called at W.S. Office—saw Miss Becker—who set forth the impracticability of pushing more than the one point of <u>sex</u> disability now—

1. Mrs. Blanchard may have boarded at 10 Duchess Place.

2. SBA tipped into her diary the business card of Frank Flower and this prominent firm of international jewel brokers and dealers in precious stones, noting on the verso, "Where I purchased my watch chain." SBA had ordered two cameos carved of herself while she was in Rome, one for Jane Spofford, one for Mary Anthony. (SBA diary, 22 March, 5, 7, 9 April 1883, *Film*, 22:814ff.)

❧ The Empire State Diary 1883, n.p., SBA Papers, DLC.

122 ❧ SBA TO RACHEL G. FOSTER

London, July 19 [*1883*].

My Dear Rachel:

. . . I am to attend a suffrage meeting at the Westminster Palace Hotel Hall this afternoon,[1] and tomorrow at 10:25 A.M. I start for Edinburgh with Mrs. Moore.[2] I am bound to suck all the honey possible out of everybody and everything as they come to me or I go to them. It is such unwisdom, such unhappiness, not to look for and think and talk of the best in all things and all people; so you see at threescore and three I am still trying always to keep the bright and right side up. I am expecting a great ferment at the meeting today, for those who agree with Mrs. Jacob Bright have asked Mrs. Stanton to confer with them about what they shall do now. She advises them to demand suffrage for all women, married and single; but I contend that it is not in good taste for either of us to counsel public opposition to the bill before Parliament. . . .

I wrote you about Miss ———.[3] She is settled in the conviction that she will never marry any man—not even the one with whom she has had so close a friendship for the past ten years. She feels that to do the work for the world which she has mapped out she must eschew marriage, accepting platonic friendship but no more. I tell her she is giving her nature a severe trial by allowing herself this one particular friend, that if he does not in the end succeed in getting her to marry him, it will be the first escape I ever heard of. She is a charming, earnest, conscientious woman, and I feel deeply interested in her experiment.

☞ *Anthony*, 2:567–68. Ellipses in original.

1. The Central Committee of the National Society for Women's Suffrage held its annual meeting at the Westminster Palace Hotel on this date. (*Women's Suffrage Journal* 14 [19 July 1883]: 117, [1 August 1883]: 135, 150–55.)

2. Rebecca Fisher Moore (1820–1905) wrote the column of English correspondence for the *Revolution* from 1868 to 1870, while she worked with Lydia Becker in the suffrage movement in Manchester. In March, when SBA arrived in London, Moore paid her a call. From a family of Irish abolitionists and Quakers, she married Robert Ross Rowan Moore before 1847, but he left her and she raised their son alone while teaching school. Moore was an early activist in the Garrisonian female antislavery societies, and Elizabeth Pease Nichol was an old friend to whom she made frequent visits. On this trip, she and SBA stayed with Nichol until August 6. (Midgley, *Women Against Slavery*, passim; Douglas Cameron Riach, "Ireland and the Campaign against American Slavery, 1830–1860," [Ph.D., University of Edinburgh, 1976], 131–33, 313; Blackburn, *Women's Suffrage in the British Isles*, 59; SBA diary, 13, 14 March, 3 July, 20 July–6 August, 20 August, 8, 12 October 1883, *Film*, 22:814ff; Stoddart, *Elizabeth Pease Nichol*, 264–67, 277–79, 286–88, 292; *Woman's Journal*, 3 June 1905.)

3. Henrietta Müller.

123 ☞ FROM THE DIARY OF SBA

[*19–20 July 1883*]

THURSDAY, JULY 19, 1883. In London— ~~Mrs Blanchard, in A.M. went with me~~— ↑In A.M.↓ wrote letters to May Wright Sewall—Rachel—& sister Mary & Mrs Stanton and in P.M. went to the West minster Palace Hotel W.S. meeting (annual)— the whole shaping & moulding of the National Society is left to one person—L. E. Becker—all other members & speakers seem to presume nothing of control— a letter was read from Mrs Jacob Bright who stands so alone in objecting to such ↑one woman↓ control—[1] at close of meeting Mrs Lucas, Miss Tod & self went home with Mrs Thomassons to tea & dinner—had nice time—

then back to Duchess & packed till 1 A.M.—and then couldn't sleep for the cup of coffee indulged in at dinner—

1. Neither Jacob nor Ursula Bright attended the meeting. The other members of Parliament all warned against dividing the movement on the question of married women and counseled the two sides to be tolerant of each other. Ursula Bright's letter was noted but not published in the official report. (*Women's Suffrage Journal* 14 [1 August 1883]: 135, 150–55.)

FRIDAY, JULY 20, 1883. Leave London—Kings Cross Station—at 10.25 A.M. for Edinburgh—Scotland—Huntley Lodge—Mrs Eliz Pease Nichol's— Mrs Lucas met me at Depot with box of strawberries & lovely cherries— Took a 3$^{\underline{d}}$ Class ticket & with Mrs Rebecca Moore— had a pleasant journey—arriving at Edinboro at 8.30—and receiving a most cordial welcome from dear Mrs Nichol—the most lovely—queenly face—like dear Martha C. Wright more than any one I ever met— She is one of the few left of the 1840 World's Con. Was put in the same room occupied by glorious Wm L. Garrison in /67 & 77—when here[1]

1. See also SBA to Mary S. Anthony, 22 July 1883, *Film*, 23:261.

⪥ The Empire State Diary 1883, n.p., SBA Papers, DLC.

124 ⪥ SBA TO H. LOUISE MOSHER

Imperial Hotel—Belfast—[1] Ireland—Sept. 3^{d} 1883—

My Dear Niece Louise

I was very, very glad to get your good letter of Aug. 16th telling me of your present enjoment of both health of mind & body—and your aspirations for useful occupation of both—also—[2] It was very pleasant that all of your dear Mother's children[3] could be thus merrily together for those few days in the "Jarsays"—and I am glad that Wendell had found such a loving & lovely home as that of the Jones[4] to introduce you to—and I hope both of you will ever prove grateful for and worthy of their kind attentions. Which it is a great comfort to me to feel sure you will ↑both↓ strive to do.

You do not speak of missing your four years constant companion in all your studies, pleasures &c—in Rochester—but I know, nevertheless, that both you & Lucy E. must feel sort of lost in being apart from each other!⁵

I met a lady the other day in Edinburgh who showed me the way in ↑which↓ she kept her Journal when making tours through pleasant places—that book was of a tour through the English Lakes—and the book was such as your School Drawing books—had ↑printed↓ on the cover—"Sketch Book"—and on each right hand page she had sketched the house & surrounding of the place she stopped over night—or the Lake & Mountains she had visited—and the corner of it she had nicely printed the name of the place—the date—& the events of the day— So she had preserved not only a word painting of what she had seen & enjoyed—but a pencil sketch of the scenes that had most pleased— And I at once thought of my Niece Louise—& said I will tell her about this beautiful way for to keep her journal of the places she visits this summer—this came to me—or you came to me thus—because I have heard you say, if you had any special love for any one school study that was your drawing!! Now my dear—begin with making a sketch of the lovely house & home your are in at Germantown— and then there is a quaint old house—the home of a very dear friend of mine—Miss Sarah Pugh—on Church Lane—I think it is—not far from the Indian name Depot—"Station"—they always say here—& nothing advertises ones Americanism more surely than saying "Depot"—instead of "Rail Road Station"!! Dear Miss Pugh is now over eighty years of age—and if you should call on her—she would enjoying hearing you read my letter— She was the most dear and intimate friend of Lucretia Mott—whom you remember of seeing at the Unitarian Church—at time of our Woman Suffrage Convention in Rochester in 1878—⁶ Miss Pugh was with Mrs Mott then— If you do call on her—give to her Aunt Susan's best love— and tell her I have often heard her name spoken by dear Mrs Nichol of Edinburgh—and there heard ↑read↓ some of her old, 1840, letters to Mrs Nichol relative to the World's Anti Slavery Convention, held in London, that year—

Then there is Mrs Hannah Whiteall Smith, in Germantown a dear friend of mine—and a most lovely woman—and she has a lovely daughter, too—⁷ Miss Frances Willard visits her—and also the Mrs J. Ellen Foster⁸—who you remember with her little boy, spent a night with us at Madison street last sumber— Mrs Smith is a great Temperance woman— & Bible Reader— Go & hear one of her readings if you can— Perhaps the Jones know her—if so—get them to introduce you & tell her you are my niece— I hope you have been to the Unitarian Church in Germantown— I do not know their minister now—but did their last one the Rev. Samuel Longfellow[9]—and a most beautiful man he was, too.—

Monday P.M. Sept. 3[d]— I have just come in from a five hours sight seeing in company with Miss Tod—a bright nice Irish lady—and this evening at 6 she & I are to take tea at Mrs O'Brien's[10]—and tomorrow P.M. we are to be driven round the city by Mrs Crawford[11]—next day I go to a little Irish Village with Miss Tod—where she is to give the good people a lecture on Temperance[12]—& the next day we visit the Giants Causeway—the next drive round the Coast of Antrim— So you see, I am fairly started in for Irish Sight seeing—and at every step of the way I think first of dear Aunt Mary and wish she were with me—and then Louise & Lucy & Maud[13]—and wish their trio were seeing it all ↑with me↓— We have visited the largest factory for making envelopes— Christmas cards & all sorts of <u>fancy</u> things in the Stationery—also the <u>Linen</u> Warehouse—the lovely h'k'ff's—hand embroidery & finest lawn— make one's mouth water—$25 & $50— apiece—then the lovely damask towels & table-cloths— I'd just love to invest all round—but then the heavy <u>duty</u> on all the goods on arriving at New York would make the prices almost double what they are here—so I simply look & admire!! But I hope the day will come when you & Wendell & all the rest can enjoy all & more than Aunt Susan has the past six months— So with dearest love to Wendell & yourself as ever I am Your Affectionate Aunt

≟ *Susan B. Anthony*

≟ ALS, SBA Papers, NRU.

1. After three weeks in Edinburgh visiting Elizabeth Nichol, SBA toured Scotland and northern England and landed in Belfast on the morning of September 2 to start a month of touring Ireland.

2. On 27 August, SBA complained to another niece that though she had written twice to Louise, Louise had not written to her; "It seems very unlike her old ways." (SBA to Lucy E. Anthony, 27 August 1883, *Film*, 23:276–88.)

3. When Hannah Lapham Anthony Mosher (1821–1877) died, she left her daughter, Louise, and three older sons: Arthur Anthony (1851–1932), who lived in St. Louis with his wife and two children; Frank Merritt (1857–1951), who probably lived in Rochester; and Wendell Phillips (1858–1946), who recently moved to Philadelphia. (*Insurance Times*, February 1891, in SBA scrapbook 17, Rare Books, DLC; Anthony, *Anthony Genealogy*, 183–85;

Chamberlain and Clarenbach, *Descendants of Hugh Mosher*, 312, 549–50; Aldridge, *Laphams in America*, 156, 222–23. See also *Papers* 3.)

4. These good friends of Wendell Mosher and hosts of Louise, who also became friends of SBA, lived in Germantown but are otherwise unidentified.

5. Louise had recently graduated from the Rochester Free Academy, along with her cousin Lucy, a daughter of Merritt Anthony.

6. On this, the Third Decade Celebration, held in Rochester on 19 July 1878, thirty years after the convention at Seneca Falls, see *Papers*, 3:386–99, and *Film*, 20:313–56.

7. Both of Hannah Smith's daughters, Mary (1864–1945) and Alys (1867–1951) were probably at home at this time. When SBA visited the Smiths in 1882, Mary was away at college. (Strachey, *Remarkable Relations*.)

8. Judith Ellen Horton Avery Foster (1840–1910), a lawyer from Iowa and a suffragist, headed the Woman's Christian Temperance Union's Office of Legislation and Petitions, but she opposed moves by Frances Willard to commit the union to supporting the Prohibition party. Their differences increased, until Foster pulled out of the union in 1888 to form the Non-Partisan Woman's Christian Temperance Union. Foster was the mother of two sons, William Horton, born in 1863, and Emory Miller, born in 1870. (*NAW*; *ANB*.)

9. Samuel Longfellow (1819–1892) served as minister of the Unitarian church in Germantown from 1878 to 1882. (*ANB*.)

10. According to her diary, SBA and Isabella Tod went on this date to the home of George O'Brien, 39 Botanic Avenue, for "a very pleasant evening" with his daughter Mary and four sons. On the next day, Mary O'Brien took SBA on tours of her father's laundry and a children's hospital for the poor. (SBA diary, 1883, *Film*, 22:814ff.)

11. Mrs. Crawford was also a guest at Isabella Tod's reception for SBA on September 7. (SBA diary, 1883.)

12. Isabella Tod spoke on total abstinence to a large audience on September 5 at Garvagh, north of Belfast. SBA found it notable that Tod did not encourage discussion of the more moderate strategy of licensing grog shops. (SBA diary, 1883.)

13. That is, Maude Anthony, another of SBA's nieces.

125 ⫸ FROM THE DIARY OF SBA

[*27–29 October 1883*]

SATURDAY, OCTOBER 27, 1883. In London   wrote letters & packed till
5 P.M— then went to Miss Mullers to spend Sunday— She took me to
the Savoy Theatre—to see Iolanthe—[1]

1. *Iolanthe, or The Peer and the Peri*, the seventh operetta by W. S. Gilbert
and Arthur S. Sullivan, opened in London on 25 November 1882 and ran for
four hundred performances.

SUNDAY, OCTOBER 28, 1883. In London   at Miss J. Henrietta Müller's—
58 Cadogan Place—W—
   Went with her & her friend Charles Martin—to Windsor & had a
row on the Thames for four hours or more—[1]
   In evening I went in Hansom to Hall of Science—to hear Mrs Annie
Besant[2]—on What Christianity has taken from Solar Worship— She is
a strong woman intellectually—

1. Müller once explained, "I used to get my rest and recreation by going
down to the river from Saturday to Monday. I kept a boat of my own for seven
years and at one time I could row twenty miles; I couldn't do so now."
(*Woman's Herald* 4 [28 November 1891]: 917.)
2. The Hall of Science was the headquarters of the National Secular Society. Annie Wood Besant (1847–1933) was a leading secularist and close friend
of Charles Bradlaugh. Together they were prosecuted in 1877 for publishing
a book on birth control. At this stage of a long and varied career as a reformer,
Besant was interested in science. She studied science at London University
from 1878 to 1880, and although she never earned a degree, she lectured on
many scientific topics in the interest of promoting freethought. (*Oxford DNB*;
Joyce M. Bellamy and John Saville, *Dictionary of Labour Biography* [London,
1977], 4:21–31.)

MONDAY, OCTOBER 29, 1883. Returned to No. 10 Duchess—couldn't
quite consent to be guest of Miss M. until I left London as she desired—
   Miss Muller called at evening & took me to Claremont Hall—
Pentonville[1] to see & hear Charles Bradlaugh[2]—on the Miracle of the
Resurrection—a close reasoner—
   Attended in P.M. society ↑for↓ medical women for India—[3]

1. Pentonville, in north London, was an eighteenth-century suburb, slipping by 1883 toward a slum. Claremont Chapel, on Pentonville Road, was built as a Congregational church in 1819. (*London Encyclopaedia*.)

2. Charles Bradlaugh (1833–1891) was a leading freethinker and an editor of the *National Reformer* with Annie Besant. Although elected to Parliament in 1880, 1881, and 1882, he was repeatedly denied his seat because he would not swear the required oath on the Bible, and Parliament would not pass an act to allow affirmation. The most recent vote to exclude him occurred in July 1883. (*DNB*; Joseph O. Baylen and Norbert J. Gossman, *Biographical Dictionary of Modern British Radicals*, vol. 3, *1870–1914* [Sussex, England, 1988], 111–18; *Who's Who of British Members of Parliament*, vol. 3.)

3. On the interest of British women in the medical education of Indian women, see Antoinette Burton, *Burdens of History: British Feminists, Indian Women, and Imperial Culture, 1865–1915* (Chapel Hill, N.C., 1994), especially pp. 112–14.

✍ The Empire State Diary 1883, n.p., SBA Papers, DLC.

126 ✎ ECS TO ANNA M. PRIESTMAN, MARY PRIESTMAN, AND MARGARET PRIESTMAN TANNER[1]

Basingstoke Hants [*England*] Oct 30th [*1883*]

Dear "Widows & Spinsters"

In writing letters all day I have exhausted my paper, & yet in saying farewell to my English friends I must not forget you, if you will excuse a hasty line on this ragged scrap of paper. I shall long remember the pleasant talks & drives we had in Bristol, and those merry chats with peals of laughter over the photos. I send you some much better taken in London. I had a lovely little grand daughter born on the 30th of September.[2] Mother & baby both doing well Nov 5th I go to London to spend a week with Miss Müller, then Miss Anthony & I will visit friends in Manchester & Liverpool & sail for America in the Servia on the 17th of Nov. Remember me to Mrs Clark & tell her I was delighted to hear of her & Miss Cobden[3] at Leeds.[4] I would like to know if that fine little boy of Mrs Clarke's[5] has recovered from the disease in his scalp. I urged them to consult Dr Berridge a skillful Homeopath in London. I have met so many noble women in England, that every corner of my heart will be filled with love for you all, & I shall leave you with deep regret. I want you all to know the daughter I leave behind me, & help her to earnest work, in all the great reforms for the developement of humanity. Remember me to the dear little woman with whom we dined, who has had so much sorrow. I should know her if I met her anywhere but cannot recall the name. I hope she may find comfort & happiness in her children, that they may be all a fond mothers heart could wish.

I think Miss Anthony met Mrs Turner at Leeds.[6] I am sorry she has not seen you in your pleasant home   I shall always be happy to hear of you & of Mrs Clarke's family. Farewell dear friends. So long as we can write to each other, recall our words & lineaments we are not wholly separated, though an ocean may roll between us. very cordially yours

➤ *Elizabeth Cady Stanton*

➤ ALS, Millfield Papers, Archive, C & J Clark Ltd., Street, England. Not in *Film.*

1. Margaret Priestman Wheeler Tanner (1817–1905) was another of the Priestman sisters, aunt to Helen Clark, and a particular friend of John Bright. She was twice widowed, in 1848 and 1869, and though often with her sisters in Bristol, she lived in Sidcot, Somerset. Like Mary Priestman, she worked closely with Josephine Butler in the Ladies' National Association and held the post of treasurer from 1871 to 1881. The Mid-Somerset Liberal Association named her a delegate to the Conference on Parliamentary Reform in October 1883. (*Oxford DNB*; "Dictionary of Quaker Biography," typescript, UkLQ; Mills, *John Bright and the Quakers*, 1:384–85, 392–96; Blackburn, *Women's Suffrage in the British Isles*, 159n.)

2. This was Nora Stanton Blatch, named for the lead character in Henrik Ibsen's play *A Doll's House*. Henrietta Frances Lord's English translation from the Norwegian was published in London in 1882 under the title *Nora: A Play.*

3. Emma Jane Catherine Cobden (1851–1947), known as Jane and later as Jane Cobden Unwin, after her marriage in 1892, was one of Richard Cobden's four daughters and an activist in the Liberal party and the suffrage movement. She entertained both ECS and SBA during their stays in England. The Midhurst Liberal Association chose her as a delegate to the Conference on Parliamentary Reform. (*Oxford DNB*; *Times* [London], 9 July 1947; Blackburn, *Women's Suffrage in the British Isles*, 159n; SBA diary, 24 June 1883, and J. Cobden to ECS, 2 September 1883, *Film*, 22:814ff, 23:295–96.)

4. The Liberal party's Conference on Parliamentary Reform, chaired by John Bright, opened at Leeds on 17 October 1883 to discuss the upcoming

Reform Bill and the party's aim of extending parliamentary suffrage to house-holders who lived outside parliamentary boroughs. Among the two thousand delegates were nine women chosen by their local Liberal associations. When their allies proposed to amend the main resolution to say that "any measure for the extension of the suffrage should confer the franchise upon women," Helen Bright Clark and Jane Cobden, daughters of two of the party's founders, addressed the delegates. The Manchester *Guardian* reported that "so judicious were the advocates of this proposal in the arguments they employed that it was adopted almost unanimously." Though the event fueled optimism about women's chances to be included in the Reform Bill of 1884, opponents in the Liberal party later denied that a majority of delegates backed the amendment. (Manchester *Guardian*, 18 October 1883; *Women's Suffrage Journal* 14 [1 November 1883]: 191–92, 194–95; *History*, 3:874–75, 936–37; Blackburn, *Women's Suffrage in the British Isles*, 159; Holton, *Suffrage Days*, 63–64; *Pall Mall Gazette*, 14, 15, 17, 19 January 1884; David Rubinstein, *A Different World for Women: The Life of Millicent Garrett Fawcett* [Columbus, Ohio, 1991], 60–61.) ECS erred in writing later that SBA was there for the vote. She reached Leeds at night on October 17, and on the next day, met with delegates at Alice Scatcherd's house and heard John Bright speak. (*History*, 3:936–37; SBA diary, 17–18 October 1883, *Women's Suffrage Journal* 14 [1 November 1883]: 199, and SBA to Mary S. Anthony, 27 October 1883, *Film*, 23:320, 322.)

5. Helen Clark was the mother of two sons, John Bright Clark (1867–1933) and Roger Clark (1871–1961).

6. ECS means Margaret Tanner. Tanner and SBA were guests at the same house near Leeds during the Liberal conference. (SBA diary, 17–19 October 1883.)

127 ≈ From the Diary of SBA

[*30 October 1883*]

TUESDAY, OCTOBER 30, 1883. In London 10— Duchess— Spent the noon part of day with dear Mrs Rose 32— Petersburgh Place— Lunched with her—returned at 4— found Cousins F. & C.[1] at 10— they went to spend evening with a friend— Miss Muller called & took me to St James Hall to see & hear Michael Davitt[2]—on The Nationalization of Land—he is an earnest sincere man & made most impressive speech Helen Taylor[3] move vote of thanks to Davitt most beautifully—

1. Charles Dickinson (1858–1935), the youngest child of SBA's aunt Ann Eliza Dickinson of Chicago, arrived in England with his sister Fannie after her

graduation from the Woman's Medical College of Chicago earlier in 1883. Their visit lasted fourteen months, during which Fannie studied ophthalmology with prominent surgeons in London and Darmstadt. When they returned to Chicago, Charles worked in the family's seed business with his brothers. (Smith, *Descendants of Nathaniel Dickinson*, 234; Sperry, *Group of Distinguished Physicians of Chicago*, 150–51; *The Book of Chicagoans: A Biographical Dictionary of Leading Living Men and Women of the City of Chicago, 1917* [Chicago, 1917]; *Who's Who in Chicago* [Chicago, 1926]; *Chicago Tribune*, 3 September 1935.)

2. Michael Davitt (1846–1906), Irish revolutionary and labor leader, spent the first half of 1883 in jail in Dublin for sedition and the second half of the year lecturing on the nationalization of land. Through discussion of the "land question," liberal reformers and agricultural workers criticized the vast and idle landed estates sustaining the aristocracy and raised the possibility of reallocating land for small farms that would ease unemployment and urban crowding. SBA met with him in Dublin in September. (*DNB*; Eugenio F. Biagini, *Liberty, Retrenchment and Reform: Popular Liberalism in the Age of Gladstone, 1860–1880* [Cambridge, England, 1992], 55–59, 184–91; SBA diary, 12 September 1883, *Film*, 22:814ff.)

3. Helen Taylor (1831–1907), the stepdaughter of John Stuart Mill and an early advocate of woman suffrage, won election to the London School Board for the Southwark section of London in 1876 and was returned at elections in 1879 and 1882. Famously difficult to work with, she alienated Liberals but earned the respect of the Irish. From support for the Irish Ladies' Land League, she moved to the advocacy of nationalizing land and taxing its value in England. Sympathy with socialism led her in 1881 to the Democratic Federation, later known as the Social Democratic Federation. (*DNB*; Hollis, *Ladies Elect*, 90–110.)

❧ The Empire State Diary 1883, n.p., SBA Papers, DLC.

128 ❧ LYDIA E. BECKER TO ECS

Manchester, [*England*] October 31, 1883.

My dear Mrs. Stanton:

At our committee to-day there was an earnest appeal passed, [t]hat you should be present at the annual meeting.[1] We are just preparing [o]ur great placard in which I have ventured to enclose your name. If you were [a]dvertised, people would be dreadfully disappointed not to see you. Hoping [f]or a favorable reply, I am, Yours truly,

≈ *Lydia E. Becker.*

≈ Typed transcript, ECS Papers, NjR. Original on letterhead of Manchester National Society for Women's Suffrage. Letters in square brackets obscured by binding.

1. This was the annual general meeting of the Manchester National Society for Women's Suffrage, scheduled for 14 November 1883.

129 ≈ FROM THE DIARY OF SBA

[*31 October–6 November 1883*]

WEDNESDAY, OCTOBER 31, 1883. Left London at 10.15 for Surbiton[1]— to visit cousins Charles & Fanny Dickinson—took a row on the Thames— & had very pleasant time—

called at <u>Lost</u> things office—21 Whitehall Place—but found no umbrella looking like mine left in Cab last Saturday night—

1. Surbiton, near Kingston and the Thames and now a part of Greater London, lies on the main rail line from London to Southampton.

THURSDAY, NOVEMBER 1, 1883. Left Surbiton at 10.30   Arrived Basingstoke at 11.30—found all well at The Mount—a wee baby—of 9 lbs now—at 5 almost six weeks   weighed 7 lbs at first—

FRIDAY, NOVEMBER 2, 1883. At Basingstoke— Went to Winchester in afternoon to see Mrs Mary A. Friend[1]—the aunt of our Postman at Rochester   got letter from Mrs Helen Bright Clark—Street—inviting me to visit her—[2]

Called on Mrs J. E. Butler—at Winchester—but found her out at Church—or somewhere

1. Mary A. Friend (c. 1816–?), a widow, worked as the senior servant in Chernocke House, a residence for boys attending Winchester College. The city of Winchester lies southwest of Basingstoke toward Southampton. (Census of Britain, 1881.)

2. The Clarks lived in Street, a town in Somerset County, near Glastonbury.

SATURDAY, NOVEMBER 3, 1883. At Basingstoke   Mrs Caird[1] took Lunch with Hattie—and at 4.49 Mrs Stanton & I left for London— Went to Miss Mullers & took dinner—& then went to 10— Duchess street

1. Alice Mona Alison Henryson Caird (1854–1932), known as Mona Caird, published her first novel, *Whom Nature Leadeth*, in this year. She continued to write, producing six more novels and many essays. Her essay "Marriage," published in the *Westminster Review*, August 1888, set off an uproar with its account of a failed institution that obstructed woman's search for self-development. She had herself married in 1877 to James Alexander Henryson Caird, a gentleman farmer in Scotland. Her only child was born in 1884. (*Oxford DNB*; Ann Heilmann, "Mona Caird (1854–1932): Wild Woman, New Woman, and Early Radical Feminist Critic of Marriage and Motherhood," *Women's History Review* 5, no. 1 [1996]: 67–95.)

SUNDAY, NOVEMBER 4, 1883. At 10— Duchess— Rained all day— Wrote 20—& more letters—& in evening went to Portland Hall & heard Helen Taylor give a masterly lecture on Nationalization of Land—[1] Mrs Stanton & Mrs Mellen with me [*no entry was made for November 5*]

1. ECS summarized Taylor's lecture in her diary at this date, *Stanton*, 2:212. "It was an able address in favor of the soil being as free to all as the air. . . . [A]s by acts of parliament the land had been legislated into the hands of the few, so it might be legislated by acts of parliament into the hands of the many."

TUESDAY, NOVEMBER 6, 1883. In London In P.M. to call at Mrs Rose's

❧ The Empire State Diary 1883, n.p., SBA Papers, DLC.

130 ❧ ECS TO WILLIAM H. BLATCH, JR.

London, November 7, 1883.

How did Hatty get a cold in her head? Some carelessness of course. Scold her well for me. We must begin to treat sick people as criminals and administer reproof rather than sympathy.

It is a great satisfaction to me, dear Harry, in parting to think that we have lived together for nearly a year in uninterrupted harmony. From the day you and Hattie became engaged, I took you to my heart as part of her. I flatter myself you have not found in me the much dreaded typical mother-in-law. Affectionately,

⇌ *Elizabeth Cady Stanton.*

⇌ Typed transcript, ECS Papers, NjR.

131 ⇀ FROM THE DIARY OF SBA

[*7–17 November 1883*]

WEDNESDAY, NOVEMBER 7, 1883. In London—10 Duchess   Helen Mellen[1] to call & go to stores with me—

1. Helen S. Mellen (c. 1858–?) was one of Ellen's daughters.

THURSDAY, NOVEMBER 8, 1883. In London   Lunch at Miss Müllers with Mrs Milosent Garrett Fawcett—   Dinner at dear Mrs Lucas— Cousins C. & F. there also Dr Mary Hall—[1] all went to hear Mr Fawcett M.P.—[2] Mrs Lucas & I stood all the evening—splendid speech—

1. According to ECS, this was Dr. Mary J. Hall, "the only woman practicing homeopathy in England." (*History*, 3:940.)
2. Henry Fawcett (1833–1884) was a Liberal member of Parliament, Postmaster General in Gladstone's government, and professor of political economy at Cambridge. A disciple of John Stuart Mill in political economics, Fawcett also followed Mill's lead as a supporter of woman suffrage, voting to include female householders in the Reform Act of 1867. Millicent Fawcett sent a long extract from his speech on this occasion to the National Woman Suffrage Association meeting in March 1884. (*DNB*; *Who's Who of British Members of Parliament*, vol. 1; *Times* [London], 9 November 1883; *Report of the Sixteenth Annual Washington Convention, 1884*, pp. 25–26, in *Film*, 23:573ff.)

FRIDAY, NOVEMBER 9, 1883. I London   Reception at Miss Muller's from 3 to 6— made my last & most painful call on dear Mrs Rose—her last words were upbraiding because I hadn't been to her more often!!— large numbers at Miss Mullers—   Staid to dinner then home to 10 Duchess & worked or packed trunks & boxes till after midnight

SATURDAY, NOVEMBER 10, 1883. Left London at 9. A.M. Dear Mrs Phillips went station with me—   Reached Clifton—Mary Estlin's[1] about noon—had warm welcome—took lunch & she went with me to the

Misses Pristman—large reception— Helen Bright Clark there— Staid
to dinner & spent evening most delightfully

[*added later*] Jane Mott[2]—elder sister of Lydia—died this A.M at 5
Oclock—short illness pneumonia—

1. Mary Anne Estlin (1820–1902), a leader in the Bristol and Clifton Ladies'
Anti-Slavery Society, was well known to American reformers as an ally of
William Lloyd Garrison and advocate of immediate abolition. By correspon-
dence and a visit to the United States in 1868, she maintained a wide circle of
American friendships. Since emancipation, she redirected her reform work,
aiding the campaign against the Contagious Diseases Acts, petitioning for
woman suffrage, and supporting the National Union of Women Workers.
(*Oxford DNB*; Midgley, *Women Against Slavery*, 134–35, 168–69, 172–73, 181;
Holton, *Suffrage Days*, 31, 35, 43.)

2. Jane Mott (1796–1883) was an older sister of Lydia Mott (1807–1875).
SBA had cared for them both through serious illnesses and returned in 1875 to
help nurse Lydia as she died. The Motts' house in Albany was for many
decades the headquarters for social reformers in the antislavery, woman's
rights, and woman suffrage movements. (Thomas C. Cornell, *Adam and Anne
Mott: Their Ancestors and Descendants* [Poughkeepsie, N.Y., 1890], 134, 219;
History, 1:744–45n; *Woman's Journal*, 28 August 1875; *Papers*, 1:517, 3:203n.)

SUNDAY, NOVEMBER 11, 1883. In Clifton—at Mary A. Estlin's   went
Friends Meeting with the Priestmans— Took tea with them Mrs Clark
still there— Had much good talk with Mis Estlin at her house—she too
feeble to go out with me much   her Aunt Mitchell called on me—her
uncle ill

MONDAY, NOVEMBER 12, 1883. Left Clifton at 10—& reached Penketh
near Warrington—Mrs Margaret E. Parkers[1] about 6 P.M— Weather
cold—her daughter the housekeeper

1. Margaret Eleanor Walker Parker (1828?–1896), a temperance leader,
former president of the British Women's Temperance Association, and a
woman suffragist, met SBA on several occasions when she visited the United
States in 1876. She lived both in Dundee, Scotland, and Penketh, in Lancashire.
Her only daughter, Mary (c. 1859–?), continued to live with her mother in
Britain and, in the 1890s, in California. (*Oxford DNB*; *SEAP*; Frances E.
Willard, *Woman and Temperance: Or, The Work and Workers of the Woman's
Christian Temperance Union*, 5th ed. [Chicago, 1886], 114–18; Eliza Daniel
Stewart, *The Crusader in Great Britain, Or, The History of the Origin and
Organization of the British Women's Temperance Association* [Springfield,
Ohio, 1893], 226–28; Census of Britain, 1881; *Papers*, 3:261–62.)

TUESDAY, NOVEMBER 13, 1883. Very cold— after Lunch—Left Mrs Parkers for Alderly Edge[1]—via Crewe—arrived at 6—found Mrs Stanton at station & Mr Jacob Bright there for her— was warm welcome from him & his noble wife—& son & daughter[2] [*added later*] Jane Mott— Albany N.Y. buried this day—

1. The Jacob Brights lived near Manchester, at Alderley Edge in Cheshire.
2. Probably these were the youngest of the three children of Jacob and Ursula Bright, Esther, about fifteen years old, and John Gratton, about twelve. Esther later became a close friend of Annie Besant and a proponent of Theosophy. (Census of Britain, 1881; Esther Bright, *The Ancient One: To the Young Folks at Home* [London, 1927], 26, 31, 59.)

WEDNESDAY, NOVEMBER 14, 1883. At Mr Jacob Bright's— Mrs Stanton had sever cold—so she remained in bed— I went up to Manchester to W.S. meeting— Mrs McLaren & Mrs Lucas there— A stiff cold affair[1]

1. The Manchester National Society for Women's Suffrage met in the Town Hall. SBA spoke briefly about the cordial reception she had received in Great Britain and the progress made in the United States. Most of the time was given over to reports, appointments, and resolutions of thanks to members of Parliament. Priscilla McLaren proposed a resolution thanking Alice Scatcherd for her efforts "to secure the adoption of a resolution at the recent Leeds conference in favour of the franchise being conferred on women." (*Women's Suffrage Journal* 14 [1 December 1883]: 214–16, *Film*, 23:339–41.)

THURSDAY, NOVEMBER 15, 1883. Mrs Bright gave an elegant reception at her lovely home from 4 to 7— large numbers came—

FRIDAY, NOVEMBER 16, 1883. Left Alderly Edge—Mrs Bright—Lucas— Mrs McLaren—Mrs S. & I at 11— Reached Liverpool at 1.30 & attended reception at Dr E. Whittles[1]—65—Catharine st—Parliament Terrace—from 3 to 6— Mrs Scatchard came was glad to see her— Tried to get started early this A.M. to see Miss Becker—but failed— Cousins Fannie & Charlie came

1. Ewing Whittle (c. 1814–?), a physician in Liverpool and an author on political and medical subjects, assisted with the campaign to repeal the Contagious Diseases Acts and supported woman suffrage. He and and his wife were named to the committee of correspondence formed at his reception. (Census of Britain, 1881; *Report of the Sixteenth Annual Washington Convention, 1884*, p. 114, in *Film*, 23:573ff; McHugh, *Prostitution and Victorian Social Reform*, 226.)

This reception gained later significance as the founding of the International Council of Women. Margaret Parker made the motion, seconded by Priscilla McLaren, that the gathering "appoint a committee of correspondence, preparatory to forming an International Woman Suffrage Association." Members were named in England, Scotland, Ireland, France, and the United States. This much is known from notes made by Parker. An edited and poorly dated letter from ECS to her daughter suggested further decisions were made: that Jacob Bright would preside over the association, vice presidents would include men as well as women, one member from each country would make up an executive committee, and each country would have a secretary. Although nothing in their papers from 1882 and 1883 documents prior discussion of this plan, later accounts ascribed the idea to ECS, who "pressed its consideration on the leading reformers" in France and England, and talked it over with SBA. As soon as ECS and SBA reported their actions at home, the National Woman Suffrage Association invited overseas members of the committee of correspondence to attend or write to the National's convention in January 1884. Nearly all of them responded with words of encouragement, and Scotland was represented at the meeting by Jessie Wellstood of Edinburgh. (Holton, *Suffrage Days*, 64–65; *Eighty Years*, 375; *History*, 3:952; May Wright Sewall, comp., *Genesis of the International Council of Women and the Story of Its Growth, 1888–1893* [N.p., n.d.], 1–3; *Report of the Sixteenth Annual Washington Convention, 1884*, 25–26, 53–55, 96–116; ECS to H. S. Blatch, 16 November 1883; *Report of the International Council of Women, 1888*, p. 9; the last four in *Film*, 23:342–43, 347–48, 573ff, 26:154ff.)

SATURDAY, NOVEMBER 17, 1883. Sailed from Liverpool—on the Steam Ship Servia at 10— A.M.—the dear Bright sisters & Mrs & Miss Parker & Mrs Scatcherd & Mrs Phillips & Miss Whittle[1] bid us good bye on the tug—Charlie & Fannie went to the ship with us—

the sea was rough and I surrendered to the fiend sea-sickness

1. Two daughters of Ewing Whittle lived at home with their parents, Margaret (c. 1852–?) and Laura (c. 1858–?). At the demonstration in London on 5 July 1883, Laura Whittle was identifed as a delegate from Liverpool; both daughters attended the conference of delegates on July 7. (Census of Britain, 1881; *Film*, 23:247–51; *Women's Suffrage Journal* 14 [1 August 1883]: 150.)

⪼ The Empire State Diary 1883, n.p., SBA Papers, DLC.

132 ⇝ WILLIAM F. CHANNING TO ECS

Providence R.I.   Sunday, Nov. 18—1883.

My dear Mrs. Stanton:

I have just read in the Woman's Journal that you & Miss Anthony sailed yesterday in the Servia! Mrs. Channing, Grace[1] & myself expect to be in New York next week <u>at</u> <u>the</u> <u>time</u> <u>of</u> <u>your</u> <u>arrival</u>! I can not tell you how glad I shall be to see you, & how sincerely I welcome you home! We have corresponded indirectly through Hattie,—and about Hattie I have no end of questions. You will let me have a little of your time, even in the first days of your return! We shall be in New York three or four days on our way to Florida for the winter. So we shall try to find you while we can.

We send kindest greetings to Miss Anthony as well as (all of us) to yourself.

Does it add to your happiness to know that others feel richer with you on the same continent again?[2] Affectionately,
yr friend,

⇝ *Wm F. Channing.*

⇝ ALS, Scrapbook 2, Papers of ECS, NPV.

1. Grace Ellery Channing (1862–1937), later Stetson, was the second of three children of William F. and Mary Jane Channing. She was suffering from tuberculosis, and the family sought a better climate than Providence, moving first to Florida and soon to Pasadena, California. (*WWW1*; Freedman, *William Douglas O'Connor*, 312, 316.)

2. Sending this letter along to Harriot Blatch, ECS wrote on it: "Many sweet letters of welcome have come to me already. I am rich in loving friends & I count them a great blessing. Words cannot tell how happy I feel in my country my family my friends. Yes life is worth living & to day I feel as if I would take a lease for another seventy years were it possible".

133 ⬦ REMARKS BY SBA TO THE FIFTIETH
ANNIVERSARY OF THE AMERICAN ANTI-
SLAVERY SOCIETY

EDITORIAL NOTE: SBA rode the night train from Rochester to reach
Philadelphia early in the morning of 4 December 1883 for the fiftieth
anniversary celebration of the American Anti-Slavery Society at Horticultural Hall. She found, she noted in her diary, "a wonderful
audience of aged people—mainly." Scheduled to lecture that evening
in Easton, Pennsylvania, she stayed only for the morning session.
(SBA diary, *Film*, 22:814ff.)

[4 December 1883]

The Chairman.[1]—Susan B. Anthony; no introduction is needed.

Susan B. Anthony.—Mr. President and Friends; I feel that I have nothing to add to all the good words that have been uttered here this morning,
but simply to say to you, that I have just landed from the Old World, after
a play-time of almost a year. I heard of this meeting yesterday afternoon,
by telegraph, and took the train to come here; but I can not stay here, and
I feel sorry, and I want you all to feel sorry for me.

I want to say that my soul has been dipped into the deepest sympathy with the early workers in this cause. I was not one of the early
members. I was only thirteen years old when this Society was organized, which we have assembled to celebrate to-day. It is a great while
that the work has been going forward. When my father moved to the
city of Rochester, N.Y., I there came to know the Abolitionists. The
first I met were Amy and Isaac Post,[2] and Mary and William Hallowell.
I was there among the many friends and the landmarks and pioneers of
this movement in the city of Rochester. Dr. Furness[3] tells of being born
again. I think if anybody was ever born again, spiritually, that it was
myself, under the teachings of Stephen and Abby Foster,[4] who first
took me to an anti-slavery meeting. From that day forward (it was in
1850) to the abolition of slavery, I worked, with what little capacity I
had, in coöperating with the Anti-Slavery Society, and, as I wrote to
Wendell Phillips, upon his seventieth birthday,[5] next to the approval

of my conscience and my God, was the approval of William Lloyd Garrison, Wendell Phillips, and Lucretia Mott.

I feel that I am one of the children of that great anti-slavery movement; and I wish to say to the young people who are here to-day, for what little there is of me, what little work I have done for the public weal, I am indebted largely to the education received in working for and with the American Anti-Slavery Society. A young man once went to Dr. Furness and asked him where were the best elocutionary schools, where he could get the best education to make a good speaker of himself. Dr. Furness said: "Engage yourself as a lecturer for the Anti-Slavery Society."

Now you would not expect me to sit down without saying what every one of you is thinking; that, though this American nation has put away the foul blot of slavery; though this government placed the ballot—the symbol of equality and right—in the hands of the colored men of this nation, great and grand as that work has been, still you would not expect that I should stand here, or sit here, and be silent in regard to a still-existing injustice, in the face of the great and fundamental principle of equality and rights to all. All *men*, native and foreign, of all complexions and nationalities, of all grades of education and of wealth, or of ignorance or poverty, every *man* outside of States prison or lunatic asylum, wears upon his head the crown of citizenship—the symbol of equality; but the women of this republic, one-half of the entire people, are yet left outside. And I want to say this to the young people here to-day: Do not think the work is all done when the monstrous wrong of slavery is blotted out; but strive to make the American people see and feel the monstrous injustice that is being done to one-half of the people of this republic in withholding from them their inalienable right to a voice in the government and in the making of the laws they are bound to obey. I think I should not have slept to-night if I had not said so much to you.

A Gentleman.—I notice there are no names of women appended to the Declaration of Sentiments at the Convention;[6] although I understand that some were there and took an active interest in the proceedings. Will some one explain this?

Miss Anthony.—Lucretia Mott was there and suggested an amendment to that Declaration; but when they came to write their names, not a man or woman of them ever thought it would be possible for a woman to sign such a document. Woman had not been discovered fifty years ago. I am making the discovery to-day; and that is what I want all of you to think over at home. Woman everywhere, in church, in State, in schools, and colleges, everywhere, is yet to be recognized, and her opinion counted as equal to that of man.

The Chairman.—With the permission of Miss Anthony, I would say in regard to the women who were present at that Convention, and who contributed very much to its interest, that many suggestions were made by them. The amendment to the Declaration, by Mrs. Lucretia Mott, I distinctly recollect. When the sentence was read in which we declare that "we may be personally defeated, but our principles never can be"; she rose in her place, and asked that the words, "can be," should be omitted, which was agreed to, and then the sentence read, "we may be personally defeated, but our principles never."[7]

⤝ American Anti-Slavery Society, *Commemoration of the Fiftieth Anniversary of the Organization of the American Anti-Slavery Society, in Philadelphia* (Philadelphia, 1884), 32–35.

1. Robert Purvis presided. He was one of four surviving signers of the Declaration of Sentiments, the pledge in 1833 "to overthrow the most execrable system of Slavery that has ever been witnessed upon earth . . . and to secure to the colored population of the United States all the rights and privileges which belong to them as men and as Americans."

2. Isaac Post (1798–1872), the late husband of Amy Kirby Post, was at the center of Garrisonian abolitionism in western New York. (*ACAB.*)

3. William Henry Furness (1802–1896) was pastor emeritus of Philadelphia's First Unitarian Society. In remarks just before SBA spoke, Furness recounted his late conversion to abolitionism: "I should think it was six years afterwards, that after wrestling with the truth, it then became too strong for me, and I committed myself to the cause. It was a good experience. I felt then as if I had experienced religion for the first time." (*ANB.*)

4. The late Stephen Symonds Foster (1809–1881) and his wife, Abigail Kelley Foster (1811–1887), were both outstanding lecturers and organizers against slavery. SBA met them at the Western New York Anti-Slavery Society meeting at Rochester in January 1851, and she joined Abby Foster on a tour that winter. (*ANB*; *Papers*, 1:182–84.)

5. Phillips acknowledged this letter after his birthday in November 1881. (*Film*, 22:157–58.)

6. The Declaration and the names of its signers were read at the start of the meeting.

7. At the anniversary celebration of the American Anti-Slavery Society in 1863, Mary Grew asked the same question about the absence of women's

names and prompted a review of attitudes in 1833 and women's role at the society's start. Lucretia Mott remembered her contribution differently: "when our friends felt that they were planting themselves on the truths of Divine Revelation, and on the Declaration of Independence, as an Everlasting Rock, it seemed to me, as I heard it read, that the climax would be better to transpose the sentence, and place the Declaration of Independence first, and the truths of Divine Revelation last, as the Everlasting Rock; and I proposed it." (*Proceedings of the American Anti-Slavery Society, at Its Third Decade* [New York, 1864], 40–43.)

134 ⭢ SBA TO ELIZABETH BOYNTON HARBERT

Washington, D.C.[1] Dec. 9th, 1883

My Dear Friend

Your good welcome of Dec. 4th followed me on to this great central station of the republic— It is very, very good to feel that all of you are glad to have me back on my native heath again— I surely am delighted to be here—though the work that looms up on all sides looks apalling— actually weighs me down

Dec. 11th Again I will try to talk to you! Yesterday the vacancies of the Senate Committees were filled—& our W.S. Com. stands thus— Lapham, (Chairman) Anthony, Palmer, Blair, Fair, Jones of Florida and Brown—[2] No one knows how Palmer of Michigan—stands—but I hope you will urge every one of the friends to write letters to each member & urge him to urge a speedy & favorable report— Personal reminders from women constituents is now our best mode of attack it seems to me—

We have about decided to hold our Wash. Con. the first week of Lent—the 4th 5th 6th of March—instead of in the fashionable season as hitherto— So many Senators & M.C's wives have said they would attend &c. &c but that their other duties forbid—but so soon as Lent opened—they were free!! hence we propose to test them!!— But to answering your several questions & points

1st As to the Conference between the leaders of the Temperance & Woman Suffrage movements— I should be very glad to meet the Temperance leaders—but I do not see what could come of it practically—

They as Temp. women—can ask the ballot only as a <u>weapon</u> with which to fight their battle—as a <u>means</u> to an end—while we ask it wholly & solely on the ground of <u>Right,</u> of <u>U.S. Citizenship</u>—whether its possession shall prove a means to one end or another! whether it gives us prohibition or license of the Liquor traffic!— <u>They</u> would need to have their petitions & memorials state that they made the claim for the <u>one specific reason</u>—with which only a fraction of our Woman Suffrage women could unite! Then to have the conference—the Temp. women must unite with us— Does Miss Willard, Mrs Foster[3]—or any one of their leaders wish to confer or unite with us?— My impression is that none of them could join us only as an individual—in no sense for ~~their~~ ↑her↓ great W.C.T.U.—

Then, if you mean a conference with the Prohibition <u>men</u>—I see no strength to us in that— <u>We</u> ↑women↓ can do nothing for <u>them</u>—until we <u>get</u> <u>the</u> <u>ballot</u>—and <u>they</u> can do nothing for <u>us</u> until they <u>get</u> <u>into</u> the <u>majority</u>!!— And for us of ↑the N.↓W.S.A—to ally ourselves with the Prohibition Party, would be to <u>divide</u> our ranks—just as it would if we were to ally ourselves with either of the great National Parties— Indeed I see no possible good to come to us by anything but a thoroughly independent position of all parties & sects—rejoicing over every word & work of each that shows favor to our great principle—and leaving our individual members to work with & for whichever party & person she sees it her duty to do— I am delighted at the progress the N.W.C.T.U. is making suffrage-ward—but any attempt to ally <u>our</u> <u>out</u> & out suffrage society to them—would frighten ↑many timid women↓ & set back the tide for a time at least— My feeling, therefore, is to let them work out their Suffrage Salvation by themselves & in their own way— Dear Mrs Wallace[4] can safely be trusted to lead her W.C.T.U. army on as rapidly as is safe & sure— But I think she would make a blunder by an effort to join her forces to ours— I hope she will urge her children to petition Congress for a 16th am't—& pour in a constant stream of petitions from all the states—

Yes—I like the <u>one</u> "Woman's Tribune"[5] I have seen—but I hope Mrs Colby will not involve herself pecuniarily— I fear Mrs Gougar has plunged into a bottomless sea with her paper— We surely need a great & grand National Woman's paper—but it can only be when all the states will combine & concentrate upon <u>one</u> <u>paper</u>—instead of each state & each woman starting a separate little sheet for itself & herself!!

If all the state & local societies & women would make use of the columns of their local papers already in circulation—as you do in the Inter Ocean—Mrs Sewall in Indianapolis Times—&c. &c—and then all unite to support a <u>national organ</u> of the movement—there would be some hope!

I trust you will be able to be at our Washington Con. this Winter—and between this time & that—I hope you will rouse the women every where to write their Senators & M.C's—telling them of their wish for them to ↑en↓act the Suffrage demand—

The history will lie at rest until congressional & Washington work is over—but I hope we shall get out our 3ᵈ Vol. in time for the 84 Fall Trade!!

Mrs Stanton is at Geneva—but expects to be here after new years—she is very well & so am I—

Mrs Stebbins has <u>150</u> names to a call for a Michigan State Con. & wants me to go out & help them re-organize—& so I would gladly do—if I only could be in two places & do twenty things at a time—[6]

Hoping to hear from you again & with love to Mr H,[7] yourself & the wee ones I am as ever sincerely yours

⇜ *Susan B. Anthony*

P.S.—Please send me your paper— If I had a dollar bill, it should go into this letter—but I want to know what you are saying— I wish every state had a <u>practical</u> Mrs Duniway—her work is bringing forth splendid fruit in that great North West![8]

⇜ ALS, on letterhead of Riggs House, Box 2, Elizabeth Harbert Collection, CSmH.

1. SBA reached Washington on December 7 and settled into a room at the Riggs House. She began to call on members of Congress the next day.

2. At the start of the Forty-eighth Congress, three new committee members were added to the Select Committee on Woman Suffrage. Elbridge Lapham (chairman), Henry Anthony, Henry Blair, and James Fair, from the old committee, were joined by Thomas Witherell Palmer (1830–1913), newly elected Republican of Michigan; Joseph Emerson Brown (1821–1894), Democrat from Georgia, who served in the Senate from 1880 to 1891; and Charles William Jones (1834–1897), Democrat of Florida, who entered the Senate in 1875. Then on 5 February 1884, Jones asked to resign from the committee, Lapham asked to be relieved of the chairmanship, and Francis Marion Cockrell of Missouri was named as the new member and new chairman. (*Congressional*

Record, 48th Cong., 1st sess., 10 December 1883, 5 February 1884, pp. 50, 876, 879; *BDAC*.)

3. That is, Judith Foster.

4. Zerelda Gray Sanders Wallace (1817–1901), a leader of the Indiana Woman's Christian Temperance Union and a cofounder of the Indianapolis Equal Suffrage Society, was an early promoter of woman suffrage within the Woman's Christian Temperance Union. (*NAW*. See also *Papers 3*.)

5. Clara Colby edited the *Woman's Tribune* for the Nebraska Woman Suffrage Association. The first issue appeared in August 1883. The association withdrew its support in 1884, but Colby kept the paper going until 1909. (E. Claire Jerry, "Clara Bewick Colby and the *Woman's Tribune*, 1883–1909: The Free Lance Editor as Movement Leader," in Martha M. Solomon, ed., *A Voice of Their Own: The Woman Suffrage Press, 1840–1910* [Tuscaloosa, Ala., 1991], 110–28.)

6. After voters defeated Michigan's woman suffrage amendment in 1874, no statewide suffrage association remained active, but several strong, local societies were planning to reorganize. Their founding convention of the Michigan Equal Suffrage Association met in Flint on 21 May 1884, but SBA declined to attend because she was at work on the *History of Woman Suffrage*. (*Report of the Sixteenth Annual Washington Convention, 1884*, pp. 85–87, and SBA to Mary B. Clay, 24 April 1884, *Film*, 23:573ff, 725–32; *History*, 4:755; *Woman's Journal*, 27 January, 10 March, 27 October 1883, 7 June 1884. See also *Papers 3*.)

7. William Soesbe Harbert (1842–1919) graduated from law school at the University of Michigan after serving in the Civil War. He practiced law in Chicago. (*NCAB*, 18:232; University of Michigan, *Catalogue of Graduates, Non-Graduates, Officers, and Members of the Faculties, 1837–1921* [Ann Arbor, Mich., 1923], 470.)

8. Oregon's legislature of 1882 voted in favor of the woman suffrage amendment by larger majorities than its predecessor of 1880. On October 3, the senate passed the measure by a vote of twenty-one to seven, and on the next day, the house passed it forty-seven to nine. This set the stage for a statewide referendum in June 1884. (*New Northwest*, 5, 12 October 1882.) In Washington Territory, on 23 November 1883, women gained the right to vote by an act of the legislature entitled "An Act to amend Section 3050, Chapter 238, of the Code of Washington." By this act, the word "male" no longer appeared as a qualification for electors, but two years later, the federal supreme court of the territory ruled that because the title failed to express the purpose of the legislation, the law was void, and women could no longer vote. In 1884, large numbers of women took advantage of their vote in local and federal elections, and they began also to serve on juries, where to be an elector qualified one to serve. (T. A. Larson, "The Woman Suffrage Movement in Washington," *Pacific Northwest Quarterly* 67 [April 1976]: 49–54; Stella E. Pearce, "Suffrage in the Pacific Northwest: Old Oregon and Washington," *Washington Histori-*

cal Quarterly 3 [1912]: 111–12; Rosencrantz v. Territory of Washington, 2 Wash. Terr. 267 [1884]; Harland v. Territory of Washington, 3 Wash. Terr. 131 [1887].)

135 ⚡ ECS to Elizabeth Boynton Harbert

Geneva [*N.Y.*,] Dec 9th [*1883*]

Dear Friend,

Your letter was forwarded here. I am visiting the daughter of Gerrit Smith[1] the great apostle of antislavery. I have seen nothing more charming in the old world than this beautiful home on the banks of Seneca Lake in western New York. It is a grand old mansion with a piazza twelve feet wide on three sides. Here you can imagine me pacing up & down many times a day, thinking of all I have seen in the old world, & the work that remains for us to do in the new. I shall return to New York in a few weeks to spend the winter. I am happy to be here again. After a year under the leaden sky of England our ~~beautiful~~ ↑grand↓ harbor just at sunrise, in our clear atmosphere seemed more beautiful than ever, & the trip up the Hudson & Mohawk valley impressed me as never before.

Miss Anthony & I have been received most cordially in public meetings, & in the hospitable homes of our English, Scotch & Irish friends. The women engaged in the suffrage movement are all of a high order, & most earnest & energetic in the work. The wives, sisters, daughters of the Bright & Cobden[2] famil~~y~~↑ies↓ maintain the lustre of those names in their devotion to this reform. If we can judge of the civilization of a nation by its women, England must rank high above all countries.

The many charming acquaintances I have made there, inspire me with new hope for my sex, & the memory of them will enrich the sunset of my life. There are however divisions in their suffrage ranks, as in ours here, a difference in principle, & as to the manner of carrying on the work. Mrs Jacob Bright thinks the demand for "spinsters & widows" is too narrow in its scope, hence she & her coadjutors ask the suffrage for all women on the same qualifications on which men are allowed to vote. To exclude married women from the privilege is to offer a bounty on celibacy, & reflect on the dignity of the married state. Mr & Mrs Bright take the same ground John Stuart Mill did when he championed this measure in parliament.[3] The meetings of the English women however do not compare in dignity & speaking with ours in this country. Theirs are but for a few hours with ten minute speeches, all from one standpoint, everything in which they differ carefully excluded, hence no discussion, or interruption of the programme which with the resolutions & speakers is printed. As the resolutions cover the narrowest possible ground, the speeches generally has no more to do with the resolution than the clergyman's text with his sermon. Our conventions on the other hand continue for one two & three days, with carefully prepared speeches, & interesting debates of many principles involved in the enfranchisement of woman. We print our resolutions after they have been thoroughly discussed & adopted, and these resolutions from year to year take higher bolder ground, drawn for the express purpose of educating the women into broader ideas, & not for the unthinking unanimous endorsement of the convention. Hence our conventions are schools for the consideration of the first principles of government, where our women are educated in every phase of the question they advocate. I heard no speech from a woman in England equal to that in logic & power to that of Matilda Joslyn Gage on United states citizenship none so beautiful as that of Phoebe Couzzins, "a woman without a country," nor any so piquant & amusing as Helen Goughar, answering the objections to woman's voting. Then the English women all speak with their bonnets on, which destroys the artistic effect of the person & the platform & all sense of freedom. I suppose they do this in obedience to Paul's directions that when women appear in public they ↑should↓ have their heads covered.[4] What would the London public say if Mary Anderson[5] should always appear on the stage, with some outlandish bonnet tied under her chin? Bonnets have not yet arrived at that perfection that a woman with a well shaped head does not look better without one. I met one lady the wife of a Professor at the military academy in Sandhurst,[6] who has rebelled against Paul, & walked into the established every Sunday for two years bonnet in hand, & created a vast amount of agitation on this violation of a well established conventionalism If women may bare their heads in the theatre & opera why not in the church & the convention. I have just been reading Mrs Deveraux Blake's answer to the Rev Mr Dix.[7] I think she has met him at every point triumphantly. Miss Anthony & I return with renewed strength & vigor to push our grand reform. I hope to see you at the Washington convention. We crossed the atlantic with one of your friends, Mrs ↑Buchanan↓ Sullivan,[8] just returning from Ireland. We had many pleasant conversations on the responsibilities of American women, in helping to make our republican institutions ↑in fact↓ all that our National constitution & Declaration of Independence set forth in principle. With kind words of greeting for all my western friends through the Woman's Kingdom sincerely yours

        ⇝ *Elizabeth Cady Stanton*

⇝ ALS, Box 7, Elizabeth Harbert Collection, CSmH. Also published in "Woman's Kingdom," Chicago *Inter-Ocean*, 22 December 1883.

 1. Gerrit Smith (1797–1874), philanthropist, abolitionist, and radical reformer, was ECS's first cousin and the father of Elizabeth Smith Miller.
 2. Richard Cobden (1804–1865), father of Jane Cobden, was the moving force behind the Anti-Corn Law League and a close political ally of John Bright.
 3. ECS refers to Mill's and the Brights' shared support of married women's suffrage.
 4. 1 Cor. 11:4–8
 5. Mary Anderson (1859–1940) was an American actress who made her London debut in 1883.
 6. Telling this story in the *History of Woman Suffrage*, ECS identified this as "Mrs. Seville, whose husband was a professor at Sandhurst College." Records at the Royal Military College indicate that Captain A. R. Savile was an instructor (later professor) in tactics, and according to the Census of Britain, 1881, Captain Albany R. Savile was married to Sybilla Savile, then age thirty-seven and the mother of five children. (*History*, 3:951; with the generous assistance of Dr. A. R. Morton, Archivist, Sandhurst Collection.)
 7. Morgan Dix (1827–1908), rector of Trinity Church in New York City, delivered a course of Lenten lectures on the "Calling of a Christian Woman" in February and March 1883. Of the second in the series, the *New York Times* said it was "one of the roundest beratings that the woman's rights movement has received, from the pulpit at least, since the movement sprang into being." Lillie Blake had crossed paths with this opponent many times since 1873, when her campaign for the admission of female students to Columbia University first met stiff resistance from trustee and chairman of the committee on higher education for women, Morgan Dix. She decided to answer Dix's assault on woman's rights in her own series of lectures that garnered as much publicity as his, including reports in English newspapers. By year's end, both

series of lectures had been published. (*ANB*; Blake and Wallace, *Champion of Women*, 151–54; *New York Times*, 17, 24, 26 February, 3, 5, 10, 12, 17 March 1883; Lillie Devereux Blake, *Woman's Place To-Day. Four Lectures, in Reply to the Lenten Lectures on "Woman" by the Rev. Morgan Dix, D.D., Rector of Trinity Church, New York* [New York, 1883]; Morgan Dix, *Lectures on the Calling of a Christian Woman, and Her Training to Fulfil It. Delivered during the Season of Lent, A.D 1883* [New York, 1883].)

8. Margaret Frances Buchanan Sullivan (1847–1903) was an Irish-born journalist from Chicago, who wrote *Ireland of To-day; the Causes and Aims of Irish Agitation* (1881). (*WWW1*; D. J. O'Donoghue, *The Poets of Ireland: A Biographical and Bibliographical Dictionary of Irish Writers of English Verse* [1912; reprint, Detroit, Mich., 1968]; SBA diary, 18 November 1883, *Film*, 22:814ff.)

136 ⤳ SBA TO MARY B. CLAY

[*Washington, D.C., 17 December 1883*][1]

has already put in a 16th am't bill[2]—and we hope your Kentucky <u>Speaker</u>[3] will give us a splendid Committee in the House— Wont you write him & urge him to select <u>woman</u> ↑suffrage↓ Democrats to put on ~~the~~ ↑our↓ Committee— You see the <u>Chairman</u> & <u>four</u> <u>others</u> of our House Com must be Democrats—hence to have a majority favorable we must have one or two of them woman suffrage!!

We have found that our new member from Rochester, N.Y. is a woman suffragist[4]—also Mr Moulton of Illinois—[5] So I hope Mr Carlyle will put those two men on our Com—

Stir up your Sister & all the other southern women you can to write to their Senators & members urging them to push our 16th am't proposition to a discussion & a vote in both Houses of Congress this session—

I had fully intended to have visited Michigan this Autumn & helped them to re-organize their state society—but my <u>late</u> return home prevented me—so now I do not expect to go out West before April or May—between the close of this Session & the opening of the next I hope to help the state work on all round—

I am rejoiced to hear that Lucy Stone is getting so broad & catholic in spirit as not to require you to eschew your allegiance to the National

W.S.A— as a qualification for the Presidency to her society![6] It augurs well for our cause—the <u>common cause</u>—I mean—and I shall be delighted when all our women grow in mental & spiritual stature so as to fully cooperate for the end we all so much desire—that is lay aside personal animosities—& think only of helping on our work—

I hope if you succeed in organizing a society in Ann Arbor—you'll influence it, either to stand independent of <u>both</u> National organizations—or else to <u>vote itself auxilliary to both</u>!!— I have always in the past—urged all state & local societies to hold themselves independent & free to cooperate with any & all other societies—but those who separated from the National sixteen years ago have not pursued the same line of action—but on the other hand have perseveringly ↑worked to↓ secured <u>formal</u> ↑votes making them↓ auxilliary ~~votes~~ to the American—which makes all such state & local societies <u>seem</u> to <u>invidiously</u> <u>discriminate</u> <u>against</u> the <u>National</u> & in <u>favor</u> of <u>the</u> <u>American</u>—which <u>seeming</u> is unjust to the vast majority of the women who make the membership of the state & local societies!! for the vast majority are like you & your noble Sister—equally cordial with everybody ↑& every society↓ which earnestly works for our good cause.

I throw this suggestion out to you—because I know you will wish to avoid even the <u>seeming</u> of invidious influence or expression against us of the National— I am glad you accepted the presidency under the testimony you have— I wish each & all would be thus faithful & true to themselves & to others as you showed yourself— Divisions & ostracisms would then be no more!!

I wish we had the money to make an <u>organ</u> of the National possible— but we have not— to make it do the work needed, it must be a <u>Missionary</u> <u>sheet</u>—not a <u>paying</u> newspaper!!— What we have to say editorially ought to go to every teacher in our schools every preacher in our pulpits—& every editor in our nation!! It is such a paper that I long for—one that we can send where there is no dollar asking for its coming!!— Mrs Gougar is a very earnest, plucky little woman— I admire her courage & persistency—& hope her paper will pay its way—& I think she'll make it do so—because she constantly lectures & solicits subscribers—& that is the only way to make a W.S. paper pay— The Woman's Journal has had thousands & thousands of dollars contributed by the friends to carry it these fourteen years— Their first installment was $10,000— and how many thousands since that was gone—I do not know— It probably pays running expenses now after all these years—but nobody will get rich out of it!!— A reform paper is always a heavy load on somebody—

Dear Mrs Duniway—has kept her New Northwest afloat the past thirteen years, by just Travelling over Oregon & Washington Territory—& holding meetings in every school district every year—over and over! over & over!!— And Wash. Ter. Legislature's work is due more to Mrs. D's persistent canvassing for her paper—than to any or all other influences—and because of her constant lecturing & drumming up of subscribers for her paper—the rank & file of the people of Oregon are better educated on our question than in any other State—and my hope of winning a majority vote at their next June election is proportionally larger than it was for Nebraska!!

I wish I could help Mrs Duniway financially— But I have seen none of the said Legacy yet—and fear I shall not in time to be of any use for that State.

With many thanks for your good letter & for your good work all round & with love to those dear boys[7] & to your dear Sister Mrs B.[8] and to your Mother & other two sisters—I am very sincerely yours

⪦ *Susan B. Anthony*

⪦ ALS incomplete, Cassius M. Clay Papers, Manuscripts Department, KyLoF. Envelope addressed to Ann Arbor, Michigan, and postmarked at Washington, 17 December 1883.

1. Dated by postmark on envelope.

2. The start of this sentence, on a missing sheet of the letter, named one or both of the joint resolutions for a woman suffrage amendment already introduced in the Senate and the House. On 6 December 1883, Elbridge G. Lapham introduced Senate Resolution 19. It was referred to the select committee. On December 10, John White introduced House Resolution 25. It was referred to the Committee on the Judiciary. In both instances, the amendment read, "The right of citizens of the United States to vote shall not be denied or abridged by the United States or by any State on account of sex." (*Congressional Record*, 48th Cong., 1st sess., 48, 78; 48th Cong., 1st sess., Joint Resolution, S.R. 19, and Joint Resolution, H.R. 25.)

3. That is, John G. Carlisle. The House Select Committee on Woman Suffrage expired with the end of the Forty-seventh Congress.

4. Halbert Stevens Greenleaf (1827–1906), a manufacturer of locks in Rochester, New York, won election as a Democrat to the Forty-eighth Congress in November 1882 and came to Washington in time for the start of the first session in December 1883. After SBA called on his wife, Jean Brooks Greenleaf,

on December 13, she wrote in her diary, "found her earnest suffragist also the M.C." Greenleaf voted with the Republicans on December 20 in favor of a committee for woman suffrage. He returned to business at the end of one term but served again from 1891 to 1893. (*BDAC*; SBA diary, 1883, *Film*, 22:814ff.)

5. Samuel Wheeler Moulton (1821–1905), Democrat of Illinois, served in the House of Representatives from 1865 to 1867 and again from 1881 to 1885. He was among the Democrats who supported the committee on woman suffrage in 1882, and he voted for it again on December 20. According to SBA's diary on December 15, Ruth C. Denison brought her the news about this second woman suffragist discovered in Congress. (*BDAC*; SBA diary, 1883.)

6. Mary Clay became president of the American Woman Suffrage Association in October 1883.

7. Clay was the mother of three boys, Clay Herrick (1867–1935), Francis Warfield Herrick Clay (1869–1919), and Green Clay (1872–?). Clay Herrick lived with his father in Ohio and retained his father's name. The younger boys stayed with their mother and took her surname. Frank and Green Clay both enrolled in the University of Michigan but took degrees from other schools. (University of Michigan, *Catalogue of Graduates*; *Ohio Authors and Books*, s.v. "Herrick, Clay"; Federal Census, East Cleveland, Ohio, 1880; Clay family genealogical notes on-line, in project files.)

8. SBA singles out Sallie Clay Bennett.

137 ❧ FROM THE DIARY OF SBA

[*19–24 December 1883*]

WEDNESDAY, DECEMBER 19, 1883. In Wash— Mrs Spofford & self went the H.R. to see & hear report from Com. on rules— All the Select Com's, except our W.S.—had majority of the Com's sanction— Mr Kiefer was ordered to present ours & ask the opinion of the House— which of course killed it with the Democrats—since the Dem's on the Com. had refused to report it!— The decision went over until tomorrow—[1]

1. The House Committee on Rules refused to express an opinion about the merits of establishing a new select committee, but it directed J. Warren Keifer to introduce a resolution on the subject for the consideration of the House. Opponents quickly raised objections to this unusual procedure, and the debate was postponed until the next day. (*Congressional Record*, 48th Cong., 1st sess., 196.)

THURSDAY, DECEMBER 20, 1883. In Washington— Mary F. Davis[1] of Orange N. Jersey called—just as Mrs Spofford, Miss Sheldon & I were starting for the H.R. to see the vote on our Select W.S. Com—which after ↑a↓ weak speech by Reagan[2] of Texas—& good replies by Belford[3] of Colorado & Kiefer[4] of Ohio—was lost by 124 to 85— only 4 of the nays were Republicans—while 13 of the ayes were Democrats—[5]
Mrs Nason's son Willie[6] returned from school for Holidays

1. Mary Fenn Robinson Love Davis (1824–1886), an early ally of SBA in New York State and well-known woman's rights activist, was a spiritualist and woman suffragist, active in the New Jersey state association. (*NAW; ANB*. See also *Papers* 1.)

2. John Henninger Reagan (1818–1905), Democrat from Texas and former Confederate cabinet member, served in the House from 1875 to 1887, when he resigned to enter the Senate. He objected that because only states had the power to regulate suffrage, a committee on woman suffrage could not introduce any bill that would be constitutional. Later in the debate, he added that he had "too much respect for [women] to see them taken out of their true sphere of action and placed where the God of nature and the common judgment of mankind never intended they should be." (*BDAC; Congressional Record*, 48th Cong., 1st sess., 217, 219.)

3. James Burns Belford (1837–1910), Republican from Colorado, served partial terms in the House in 1876 and 1877 and then served from 1879 to 1885. After a sarcastic remark about Reagan's sudden interest in the Constitution in the wake of his rebel past, Belford pointed out that Congress surely had the authority to propose a constitutional amendment on woman suffrage. Moreover, women had a constitutional right to petition Congress, and the committee's primary purpose was to receive their pleas. (*BDAC; Congressional Record*, 48th Cong., 1st sess., 217.)

4. Keifer reinforced Belford's points and added that Congress had the authority to legislate on suffrage for the territories and the District of Columbia. He also reminded members that women had already made considerable progress toward suffrage, even in parts of the country controlled by Democrats. (*Congressional Record*, 48th Cong., 1st sess., 217–19.)

5. SBA's numbers were off slightly. In a roll call vote, fourteen Democrats voted with the Republicans in favor of a committee, while six Republicans helped to defeat the measure. (*Congressional Record*, 48th Cong., 1st sess., 219.)

6. William Nason (c. 1868–?), the son of Mary Snow Nason, lived with his widowed mother at the Riggs House before going away to school. (Federal Census, 1880.)

FRIDAY, DECEMBER 21, 1883. In Washington   Sent off ten of Cong. Records to our W.S. Women Editors— Mrs Davis not able to call as promised— Drove to Georgetown with Mrs Spofford & called on Mrs Wilson—

SATURDAY, DECEMBER 22, 1883. In Wash— At Riggs Wrote all day— letters to stir up friends to work toward 16th am't by this Congress— Miss Victor of Ohio—spent an hour or more trying to get me to take hold of a war claim of hers—for loss of School House in Louisiana— Couldnt see it— Mrs C. H. Dall[1] called—had long time to find me— said she had called twice before—!!

Didn't go out for a walk—even— Mrs Lockwood & the Mrs Russell[2] the new warden of the women's jail called in the evening—

1. Caroline Wells Healey Dall (1822–1912), writer, reformer, and woman's rights activist, moved from Boston to Washington, D.C., to live with her son, a scientist at the Smithsonian Institution. (*NAW*; *ANB*. See also *Papers* 1–3.)

2. This was Elizabeth Russell, whose name appeared as Elizabeth A., Elizabeth B., and Elizabeth J. In the report of a temperance meeting in February 1884, presided over by Belva Lockwood, Elizabeth B. was described as of Chicago. The city directory lists her as resident at Lockwood's house on F Street, N.W. Her appointment as matron of the jail was announced on this date. Activists in the District of Columbia, including Lockwood, secured two changes in the systems for the detention of women in 1883: establishment of a ladies' room at the court house with a matron assigned to it and appointment of a deputy warden or matron at the District jail. Although Russell's appointment was confirmed and her salary fixed, she did not begin her new job until 16 March 1884, due to a dispute over controlling the fund that paid her. (*Report of the Sixteenth Annual Washington Convention, 1884*, p. 13, *Film*, 23:573ff; *History*, 4:571; *Washington Post*, 22 December 1883, 21 February, 16 March 1884; city directory, 1884.)

SUNDAY, DECEMBER 23, 1883. In Washington— 100th anniversary of Gen'l Washington's surrender of his Military Commission—to Congress—[1]

Mrs Dall called & I went with her to tea at Mrs Johnsons—12th street—[2] Snowing & the snow six inches deep—

1. George Washington (1732–1799), later first president of the United States, surrendered his commission as commander of the army to Congress at Annapolis, Maryland, on 23 December 1783. Because the centennial fell on a Sunday, President Arthur's proclamation suggested religious services might make appropriate mention on that date and directed that at noon on Monday, December 24, national salutes be fired from all the nation's forts. (*New York Times*, 22 December 1883.)

2. Probably this was Nancy Maria Donaldson Johnson (1794–1890), a friend of Caroline Dall and the widow of the scientist Walter Rogers Johnson. She lived at 506 Twelfth Street, Northwest. (City directory; research by Helen Deese.)

MONDAY, DECEMBER 24, 1883. At Washington

  The Empire State Diary 1883, n.p., SBA Papers, DLC.

138   SBA TO ELIZABETH BOYNTON HARBERT

The Riggs House   Washington, D.C.—Dec. 25/83

My Dear Mrs Harbert

A Merry Christmas to you—& your "Woman's Kingdom"— I cannot do without the weekly Inter Ocean to see every week what you say and propose about women and their enfrancisement— So I enclose to you the $1—Greenback—please tell them to address it to me here— Riggs House Washington—D.C.—

Do please say to your W.K. readers[1] that the House of Representatives' vote that we should not have a Select Woman Suffrage Committee—simply remanded our question the most able & influential Committee of Congress—The Judiciary—which will, undoubtedly, not only give us a candid hearing—but also bring in a ~~favorable~~ report in favor of the submission of our 16th amendment proposition to the Legislatures of the several States—and then bring the question to a discussion and division in the House— Thus you see we are now likely to get a much weightier report—than could have been one from the best select Committee!!— At any rate—"Don't give up the Ship"—shall be our motto— The Judiciary Com. consists of Messrs—Tucker—Va— Hammond—Ga— Culberson—Tex.— Moulton—Ill— Broadhead Mo— Dorsheimer—N.Y.— Collins—Mass— Seney—Ohio— Reed—Me— E. D. Taylor—Ohio— M'Coid—Iowa— Browne—Ind— Poland—Vt—[2] Sincerely yours

  Susan B. Anthony

Moulon, Reed, Taylor & M'Coid—voted ⬆4—⬇ yes— on our proposed Select Com.

Cameo cut by Pio Siotto of Rome and set in gold by the London jeweler George Blogg & Co., inscribed on verso to Mary S. Anthony. Siotto worked both from a photograph of Susan B. Anthony, taken in March 1883 by G. Borelli in Rome, and from life, at sittings in his studio. Anthony, who gave a second cameo to Jane Spofford, pronounced the work "quite good I think."
(Photograph courtesy of Rare Books and Special Collections,
University of Rochester Library.)

Margaret Bright Lucas (1818–1890) and Elizabeth Cady Stanton. Lucas, a sister of the English politicians and reformers John and Jacob Bright, presided over the British Women's Temperance Association and joined the women of her extended family in the suffrage movement. Photograph by Cyrus Voss Bark at his studio in Clifton, England, taken in May 1883 when Stanton spoke to the Bristol Women's Liberal Association. Later, recalling their "peals of laughter over the photos" taken in Bristol, Stanton sent better pictures to her friends in that city.
(Theodore Stanton Papers, Special Collections and University Archives, Rutgers University Libraries.)

Henry Brewster Stanton (1805–1887). In 1881, Elizabeth Cady Stanton wrote that her husband "looks about fifty, scarcely any gray hairs in his head." When Stanton died on 14 January 1887, his editor at the New York Sun observed that "his mind retained its sharpness and vigor. . . . [N]o one who knew Mr. Stanton thought of him as an old man." Marks on this undated tintype, one of two poses taken by an unidentified photographer, indicate that family members once kept it in an oval frame.
(Courtesy of Coline Jenkins/Elizabeth Cady Stanton Trust.)

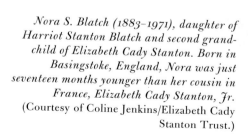

Nora S. Blatch (1883–1971), daughter of Harriot Stanton Blatch and second grand-child of Elizabeth Cady Stanton. Born in Basingstoke, England, Nora was just seventeen months younger than her cousin in France, Elizabeth Cady Stanton, Jr.
(Courtesy of Coline Jenkins/Elizabeth Cady Stanton Trust.)

Priscilla Bright McLaren (1815–1906).
The sister, wife, mother, and aunt of
members of Parliament, McLaren, with
other members of the Bright family,
exercised wide influence in Britain's
suffrage movement. She befriended
Elizabeth Cady Stanton and Susan B.
Anthony during their stays in Great
Britain. By an unknown engraver.
(From E. C. Stanton, S. B. Anthony, and
M. J. Gage, *History of Woman Suffrage.*)

Rachel G. Foster (1858–1919). Foster, who
accompanied Susan B. Anthony on a
European tour in 1883, initiated the
practice among younger activists of
addressing her as "Aunt Susan." In her
position as corresponding secretary of the
National Woman Suffrage Association, to
which she was elected in 1881, Foster
assumed many of Anthony's executive
responsibilities. Engraving by John
Chester Buttre from a photograph by
J. Ganz of Brussels.
(From E. C. Stanton, S. B. Anthony, and
M. J. Gage, *History of Woman Suffrage.*)

"THE LADIES' BATTLE."

(*The Women's Suffrage Demonstration in the St. Andrew's Halls, 3rd November, 1882.*)

Drawn by Alexander Stuart Boyd, or TWYM, for the humorous journal Quiz, "The
Ladies' Battle" depicts Elizabeth Cady Stanton addressing the Scottish National
Demonstration of Women in Glasgow on 3 November 1882. Priscilla McLaren
called it a "laughable cartoon of us all," but assured Stanton "they have done
you the best of anyone, they have given you some force of character."
(Quiz, 10 November 1882, by courtesy of the Mitchell Library,
Culture and Leisure Services, Glasgow City Council.)

John Daugherty White (1849–1920). Photographs taken at
Matthew Brady's studio in Washington.
(Brady-Handy Photograph Collection, Library of Congress,
Prints and Photographs Division, LD-DIG-cwpbh-04710.)

White, in the House of Representatives from Kentucky, and Hoar and Palmer, in the Senate
from Massachusetts and Michigan, served woman suffragists as energetic advocates of a
constitutional amendment. In a speech, delivered in 1885 and distributed by the National
Woman Suffrage Association, Palmer opined, "The right of women to personal representation
through the ballot seems to me unassailable, wherever the right of man is conceded and
exercised. I can conceive of no possible abstract justification for the
exclusion of the one and the inclusion of the other."

George Frisbie Hoar (1826–1904). Photographed by Abraham Bogardus of New York City before 1887, when Bogardus sold his business.
(Courtesy of Concord Free Public Library.)

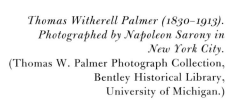

Thomas Witherell Palmer (1830–1913). Photographed by Napoleon Sarony in New York City.
(Thomas W. Palmer Photograph Collection, Bentley Historical Library, University of Michigan.)

Joseph Emerson Brown (1821–1894).
Photographed by Charles Parker in
Washington, D.C., and dated 1889.
(Courtesy of Hargrett Rare
Book & Manuscript Library,
University of Georgia Libraries.)

Francis Marion Cockrell (1834–1915).
Photograph taken at Matthew Brady's
studio in Washington.
(Brady-Handy Photograph Collection,
Library of Congress, Prints and Photo-
graphs Division, LC-DIG-cwpbh-03817.)

Senators Brown of Georgia and Cockrell of Missouri were assigned to the Select Committee on Woman Suffrage despite their venomous opposition to the cause. In the first of their minority reports from that committee, dated 1884, they compiled their arguments. "Society acts unwisely when it imposes upon [woman] the duties that by common consent have always been assigned to the sterner and stronger sex." Politics "draws [woman] out from the dignified and cultivated refinement of her womanly position, and brings her into a closer contact with the rougher elements of society." Moreover, suffrage "is a local question, which properly belongs to the different States of the Union, each acting for itself."

Harriet Hanson Robinson (1825–1911).
Robinson invited the National Woman
Suffrage Association into Massachusetts,
to compete directly with the rival Ameri-
can association based in Boston. Her
successful organizing in the state eroded
Lucy Stone's control over New England's
suffragists. Tintype, taken when Robinson
was forty-seven.
(Schlesinger Library, Radcliffe Institute,
Harvard University.)

Elizabeth Avery Meriwether (1824–1917).
Meriwether, a writer who glorified
the Old South, was one of the first southern
Democrats drawn to the National Woman
Suffrage Association. Her convictions about
states' rights collided with the association's
commitment to national citizenship.
Photo taken at age fifty-eight.
(From Minor Meriwether, *Lineage of the*
Meriwethers and the Minors, courtesy of Earl Gregg
Swem Library, College of William and Mary.)

Clara Bewick Colby (1846–1916). From her home in Beatrice, Nebraska, Colby built a state-based newspaper, the Woman's Tribune, *into a national publication affiliated with the National Woman Suffrage Association. Photographed by Aaron Veeder of Albany, New York. Veeder and his wife, Adelaide, offered pictures of leading reformers at a discount to be sold for the benefit of temperance and woman suffrage societies. The frontispiece portraits of Elizabeth Cady Stanton and Susan B. Anthony also came from the Veeder studio.* (Image WHi-26612, Wisconsin Historical Society.)

May Wright Thompson Sewall (1844–1920). An educator from Indianapolis, Sewall chaired the executive committee of the National Woman Suffrage Association for a number of years. Engraving by John Chester Buttre from a photograph by D. R. Clark of Indianapolis. (From E. C. Stanton, S. B. Anthony, and M. J. Gage, *History of Woman Suffrage*.)

51.

the United States. And ~~this~~ is
because the principle of self government
is slowly but surely making its
way in every department of life,
~~because~~
individual rights, individual
conscience, judgement are growing alike
in the state, the church, & the
home. ~~Our divine laws are not~~
~~the result of the fickleness of men,~~
~~but growing independence of the~~
~~person. It is in a vast majority~~
~~of the cases that gives ask for~~
~~the distribution of the union, and~~

On this page from the speech Elizabeth Cady Stanton delivered in London on 25 June 1883,
Stanton's fine-tipped pen is overwhelmed by her daughter's blunt instrument.
Harriot Stanton Blatch edited the entire speech, though her mother
did not accept every change she proposed.
(Elizabeth Cady Stanton Papers, Manuscripts Division, Library of Congress.)

Frederick Douglass (1818–1895) and Helen Pitts Douglass (1838–1903). Photographed at
Niagara Falls in the summer of 1884, perhaps in a studio against a
backdrop of bridges and churning water.
(National Park Service, Frederick Douglass National Historic Site.)

Tucker, Culberson, Broadhead, Dorsheimer, Seney,—5—voted <u>no</u> Hammond, Collins, Browne, Poland—4—were absent—

❧ ALS, A-68 Mary Earhart Dillon Collection, Series III, Box 2, MCR-S. Printed in "Woman's Kingdom," *Inter-Ocean*, 29 December 1883, in *Film*.

1. Prior to writing this letter for Harbert to include in her newspaper column, SBA wrote her a longer, private letter on December 23, setting forth the same analysis of prospects for a favorable report from the House Judiciary Committee. (*Film*, 23:428–37.)

2. The Democratic members of the House Committee on the Judiciary were John Randolph Tucker (1823–1897), who served in the House of Representatives from 1875 to 1887; Nathaniel Job Hammond (1833–1899), who served from 1879 to 1887; David Browning Culberson (1830–1900), who served from 1875 to 1897; James Overton Broadhead (1819–1898), who served from 1883 to 1885; William Dorsheimer (1832–1888), who served from 1883 to 1885; Patrick Andrew Collins (1844–1905), who served from 1883 to 1885; George Ebbert Seney (1832–1905), who served from 1883 to 1891; and Samuel W. Moulton, already identified. The Republican members were Thomas B. Reed, already identified; Ezra Booth Taylor (1823–1912), who served from 1880 to 1893; Moses Ayers McCoid (1840–1904), who served from 1879 to 1885; Thomas McLelland Browne (1829–1891), who served from 1877 to 1891; and Luke Potter Poland (1815–1887), who served from 1883 to 1885. (*BDAC*.)

139 ❧ FROM THE DIARY OF SBA

[*25–26 December 1883*]

TUESDAY, DECEMBER 25, 1883. At The Riggs House   Stormy day— snow & slush the order—

Letter from Mr & Mrs Minor—[1]

Christmas Cards from niece Louise Mosher—Mrs Jones—with whom L. Boards   Miss Van Lew[2] of Richmond now in the Treasury Department and one from S. D. L. (City) & who S. D. L. is I cannot imagine— and a lovely Boquet of flowers from Mrs Lord—a Card case from Mrs Spofford—also a Card case from niece Louise!

1. Francis Minor (1820–1892), an attorney in St. Louis, collaborated with his wife, Virginia, in defining the legal argument about women's constitutional right to vote and preparing a test case that reached the Supreme Court. (Alumni records, Archives, NjP; *St. Louis Republic*, 21 February 1892; *Woman's Journal*, 5 March 1892. See also *Papers* 2 & 3.)

2. Elizabeth L. Van Lew (1818–1900) was a federal spy in Richmond, Virginia, during the Civil War, and in recognition of her service and loss of livelihood, President Grant named her the city's postmistress in 1869. President Hayes removed her, and her later attempts to regain the office failed. In 1886, she was named an honorary vice president of the National association. (*NAW*; *ANB*.)

WEDNESDAY, DECEMBER 26, 1883. In Washington— Saw that Mrs J. E. Foster was at Temple Cafa—& rushed down to see her—[1] she is just from Iowa & full of hope that suffrage will carry there this time—[2]

Went thence to Mrs Lockwoods—& we together worked over Call for Wash. Con— We had both Mrs Sewall's & Mrs Stantons before us—passed three hours— I mailed a copy of <u>our</u> call to Mrs S. with hers—& one of ours to Mrs Sewall with hers—& begged both to push ahead somehow—[3]

At Eve. Mrs Senator Logan[4] of Ill. & friend called on Mrs Spofford & me—very pleasant—

1. At other times, SBA knew how to spell Temple Café, located on Ninth Street, Northwest, apparently within the Temperance Temple at 432 Ninth. It served both as a hotel, sometimes used by delegates to the National's meetings, and as a residence for working women. (City directory, 1883, listing of "Halls" and residence of Celia B. Ashby; SBA to Lillie D. Blake, 16 January 1883, *Film*, 23:25–27.)

2. Iowa's Nineteenth General Assembly, in 1882, passed a joint resolution to strike male from the qualifications for voters by a vote of sixty-one to thirty-one in the house and twenty-seven to eighteen in the senate. The measure was to come before the next session in 1884 for its second passage. Adopted by the senate, it lost in the house. (*Report of the Sixteenth Annual Washington Convention, 1884*, pp. 37–40, *Film*, 23:573ff; *History*, 3:623–24, 4:633.)

3. For this call to the National association's sixteenth annual Washington convention, 4 to 6 March 1884, see *Film*, 23:506.

4. Mary Simmerson Cunningham Logan (1838–1923), the wife of Senator John A. Logan and a leader in Washington society, was involved in the newly formed Woman's Relief Corps, the auxiliary to the Grand Army of the Republic. (*NAW*.)

↜ The Empire State Diary 1883, n.p., SBA Papers, DLC.

·⟨⫻⟩·

140 ⪼ SBA TO THE EDITOR, *CINCINNATI COMMERCIAL GAZETTE*[1]

The Riggs House, Washington, D.C., December 29, 1883.

To the Editor of the *Commercial Gazette*:

Where did you get the wood-cuts of Mrs. Stanton and Miss Anthony printed in your paper of December 23, 1883? If you still have them, will you be so kind as to destroy them? They are too horrible to have our names written under them. Mrs. Stanton is a very fine-looking woman, and the press, if they send out pictures pretending to represent her, ought at least to get a photograph from her that she considers tolerably fair.

As for myself, it can not be said I am a beauty; therefore am I more sensitive at being made to look more ugly than truth absolutely demands.

The cuts are not, evidently, meant for caricatures, since the sketches indicate the desire to be even complimentary. I wish the editors would send to us for a good photograph when they wish to make a wood-cut of us.[2]

To-day brings me the Philadelphia *Call* with a picture of me that looks as if it were printed from the very same wood-cut! I wish the press would at least try again, start anew, and see if they can not make us look more like civilized human beings. Very respectfully yours,

⪻ *Susan B. Anthony.*

⪻ *Cincinnati Commercial Gazette*, 2 January 1884. Not in *Film* in this version; a partial reprint in *Film* at before 5 January 1884.

1. Murat Halstead (1829–1908) was editor-in-chief of this paper, recently created by the merger of the *Cincinnati Commercial* and *Cincinnati Gazette*. On 23 December 1883, the paper published woodcuts of ECS and SBA to accompany biographical sketches that praised their significance as reformers and complimented their appearance. Of SBA, the author wrote, "There is nothing of the unseemly or unkempt radical air about Miss Anthony's personal appearance. She looks like a Quakeress, dresses in somber fashion, and makes it a point to make herself felt wherever she goes." The paper described ECS as possessing "the most lovable face of all the best known feminine agitators who have made their mark in the United States."

2. When the *Commercial Gazette* published SBA's response, the editor appended a droll reply, attributing the admittedly unflattering woodcuts to the artist's lack of talent and promising to request SBA's photograph next time. After noting that to destroy the woodcuts would not prevent use of the images by other publications, he did promise to "stamp on ours to express her contempt for them by proxy."

141 ↭   LUKE P. POLAND TO SBA

Washington, D.C., Jany 19, 1884.

Dear Miss Anthony

Had I been present I would have voted for the formation of a Committee on Woman Suffrage; and should the question come up again, should so vote.—[1]

At the same time I ought to say, that I have ↑not↓ yet become convinced that the extension of the right of suffrage to women is necessary for the protection of all their rights and interests, or that it is advisable. But it is a question that is largely agitated in the country, and ↑there exists↓ a great contrariety of opinion on the subject. I would therefore do any proper thing to give its advocates the fullest and fairest opportunity to express their views and to make them prevail if their reasoning and arguments, are sufficient to that end.—

I believe in full discussion on all subjects, and if any of my own opinions cannot stand that ordeal let them go under. Yours very truly

↭   *L P. Poland*

↭ ALS, on letterhead of House of Representatives, HM 10597, Ida Harper Collection, CSmH.

1. Poland no doubt replies to a query from SBA like one addressed to "Sir" and dated 18 January 1884, that asks "Will you kindly tell me if you would have voted for the resolution for a Select Committee on Woman Suffrage, had you been in the House when the vote was taken Dec. 20? Or rather—would you vote for a Committee if another motion were brought before the House?" (*Film*, 23:470–71.)

142 ⚜ SBA TO ECS

[*Washington, D.C.*] Jan. 27, 1884

My Dear Mrs Stanton

I do hope you wont put your foot into the <u>Douglass</u> question, of <u>the intermarriage of</u> the <u>races</u>! It <u>has</u> <u>no</u> <u>place</u> <u>on</u> <u>our</u> <u>platform</u>, any more than the question of <u>no</u> marrige at all—or of polygamy! And so far ↑as↓ I can prevent it—it shall not be brought there.[1]

The papers all stated that the <u>woman</u> <u>was</u> <u>a</u> <u>suffragist</u>! Her name is not on our books—and so far, I have seen no one who knows her—↑But↓ Mrs Dr. Winslows[2] interview says she helped edit the Alpha some time since—

If a <u>white</u> <u>male</u> <u>head</u> of a Department had married one of the women clerks under him, it would ↑not↓ have <u>elevated him</u> in the opinion of the sensible people—nor would it have lifted the woman above the suspicion of marrying for a <u>home</u>!—and surely this case—is no better— He & she have, against the wish & judgement of <u>their</u> <u>own</u> <u>families</u>, taken the step—and I do not propose to be any party to the indiscretion—and I beg <u>you</u> not to congratulate him by letter![3] He has by this act compromised every movement ↑in which↓ he shall be brought to the front!— We don't push Dr. Mary Walker,[4] Victoria Woodhull,[5] or any other person who shocks public sentiment on <u>any</u> <u>other</u> or <u>side</u> <u>question</u>—because ↑our↓ <u>demand</u> <u>is</u> <u>not</u> <u>identity</u> of dress—or one or more wives or no legal wife at all—but simply <u>perfect equality of</u> <u>Rights</u>—<u>civil</u> and <u>political</u>—for <u>all women</u>— Were there a proposition to punish the woman in this affair—and leave the man to go scott free— then <u>we</u>—as suffragists—would have a protest to make against the invidious discrimination—

The question of the amalgamation of the different races is a scientific one—affects women & men alike! & I do not propose to have ↑the suggestion,↓ the discussion or ↑the↓ settlement of it upon our woman suffrage platform— Had you or I, as leading representatives of our movement—in our own persons ↑done any thing that↓ made our presence on the platform, <u>raise</u> <u>the</u> question of race intermarriage—then the rank & file of our suffrage constituency <u>might</u> <u>rightfully</u> ask us to resign our posts—they surely would never elect us again to be their representatives—and it now ↑is the same↓—in the Case of Douglass—while he has just shocked the ~~the~~ general feeling—the general sense of propriety— (he may be right—& the general feeling wrong) it doesn't matter to my point)—[6] Our intent at this grandest Convention ever held, will be to make every one who sees or hears or reads—<u>believe</u> in the grand principle of Equality of rights & chances for Women—and if they see on our program—and on our platform—the name ↑of↓ Douglass—every one's thought will be turned <u>to</u> the question of amalgamation of the races—and hence turned away from the <u>one</u> <u>question</u> of <u>woman</u>—and <u>her disfranchised</u>!!

Neither Douglass, nor you, nor I, have the <u>right</u> to complicate nor compromise <u>our</u> <u>question</u>—by first shocking the public sense in any other direction—and if we take the bits in our teeth in another line—we mustn't expect our compeers to follow us there! If we do thus expect— we shall surely find ourselves mistaken!

It has been all that Mrs Spofford, Mrs Dennison, Dr Susan Edson, Mrs Joy, Mrs OConnor[7]—and all the D.C. women could stand to see & hear him on our platform here—for years—not because he is colored— but because of <u>his</u> <u>falseness</u> to <u>them</u>—when they went to the courts—to stand by <u>unfortunate</u> <u>girls</u>—during his U.S. Marshalship—he told them it was no place for them to go—actually insulted them! You know they have told this to you & me—over & over—and yet we have persisted in inviting him— I did it—even—last year—but he refused to come to the platform— and <u>now</u>—I shall <u>not</u> invite him—and if you do—you will outrage the best feelings of the best friends here—[8] I have ↑not↓ been able to brush the <u>silly old man</u> performance ↑out↓ of my thought—after all he said of Purvis' outraging the feelings of his family—for him to go & do the same thing to his!![9]

Tuesday Jan. 29th

Now—understand—I <u>will</u> <u>not</u> <u>in</u> <u>any</u> <u>way</u> <u>be</u> <u>committed</u> to <u>this</u> <u>mad</u> <u>passion</u> <u>business</u>!— And you very well know that if you plunge in as your letter of to-day proposes—that <u>your endorsement</u> will be <u>charged</u> <u>upon me</u> & <u>all</u> <u>the</u> <u>woman</u> <u>suffrage</u> <u>women</u> <u>of the</u> <u>entire</u> <u>nation</u>! And I feel & say that you have <u>no right</u>—while your are Pres. of the N.W.S.A. to thus <u>publicly</u> <u>commit</u> yourself to and thereby bring ~~down~~[10] the thought of the public to the question of a <u>negro marrying a white woman</u>! and shocking & repelling the vast numbers of people who are just beginning to look kindly toward us— <u>I</u> would cut my right hand off before I would thus set back the growing feeling of friendliness toward our cause! If you publish such a letter—I do hope you wont—in justice to truth you should do it as a private person—& disclaim in any sense speaking as Pres. of the National W.S.A. or as representing the rank & file of its members—for I am sure such endorsement ~~illegible doesnt~~! ↑does not↓!

All the forepart of this remonstrance & appeal—I wrote on Sunday eve'g—& then said to myself—If I send this—it may <u>make</u> her do the very thing I want her not to! So I tucked it away—and this A.M. brought your feeble attempt at irony—on the black man stooping to take a white woman!— If you were going to get a <u>parallel</u> case—it should have some <u>Old</u> <u>White</u> <u>fellow</u> in <u>his</u> <u>dotage</u> stooping to mary one of his employees—not a grand noble enterprising woman—being denied her right to earn an honest living!—

I don't believe you ever thought of the fact that by your doing what you propose—you would be committing the whole woman suffrage movement to this <u>incident</u>— There is no <u>principle involved</u> in this marriage of Douglass—had there been he would have sought a white woman who was <u>his</u> <u>peer</u> in <u>intellect</u>, <u>position</u> & <u>wealth</u>!— He has just gotten under the magnetic influence of the woman—let his sentiments & passions get the better of his judgement—& married the woman that would, ↑no doubt,↓ have more gladly brought under her spell a <u>white man</u> of <u>equal</u> <u>conditions</u>!

Now, for heavens sake—for <u>woman's freedom</u> <u>sake</u>—dont through↑w↓ round this blind & reckless infatuation the halo of pure & lofty sense of <u>duty</u>—to break down ↑the↓ lines of race!!— There is nothing higher ↑in it↓ than in the ten thousand other foolish, impulsive marriages!

But enough—only for <u>my</u> <u>sake</u>—if no other—don't proclaim yourself as endorsing this act! Your sympathy has run away with you! Lovingly & Fearfully yours,

❧ Susan B. Anthony

P.S.—An Interviewer probed me—I said—["]I have but one question— that of equality between the sexes—that of the <u>races</u> had no place on our platform—" Only to think how Douglass threw the principle of

Equality of Political Rights to women—overboard—in /69—& all along—saying himself first & you afterwards![11] If there were no other reason—you should now let him carry his own burden—if he has voluntarily picked one up— S. B. A

N.B. I want you to let Maggie[12] see this—& then I want her to tell me if she thinks you'd better run before you're sent to help Douglass reconcile the world to his marriage!!

❧ ALS, SBA Papers, NRU.

1. This letter went through at least three different stages of emendation after SBA wrote it: changes in the text are indicated in ink, blue pencil, and black lead pencil. Some of the changes are clearly in the hand of Ida Harper. The text printed here reflects, to the extent possible to discern, SBA's original composition and the changes she made using the same ink. Where it is impossible to distinguish the author and the sequence of changes, the difficulty is described in notes to the text.

On 24 January 1884, Frederick Douglass married Helen Pitts (1838–1903), a clerk in his government office, the Recorder of Deeds for the District of Columbia. A northern New Yorker by birth, Pitts graduated from Mount Holyoke College in 1859, taught freedmen in Virginia during the Civil War, took part in suffrage societies in Washington, and worked at one time as an assistant editor of the *Alpha*, the newspaper of the Moral Education Society. Neither Douglass nor Pitts informed family members in advance of the evening ceremony at the home of the Reverend Francis J. Grimké, but a reporter found out, and the story made national news on January 25. Helen Pitts was a white woman, and that fact made Douglass's decision to remarry especially controversial. By January 26, newspapers in Washington and New York reported how various prominent African Americans reacted to the news. The story continued to grow, eliciting virulent racism from many whites and accusations of betrayal from many blacks. (Douglass, *Papers*, 5:145–47n; Mount Holyoke College, Alumnae Association, *One Hundred Year Biographical Directory of Mount Holyoke College, 1837–1937* [South Hadley, Mass., 1937], 95; McFeely, *Frederick Douglass*, 318–23.)

2. Caroline Brown Winslow (1822–1896) came from England to Utica, New York, as a child and studied medicine in New York and Ohio. After moving to Washington during the war, she founded a homeopathic dispensary and hospital in the city and became active in the Universal Franchise Association. She went on to attempt to vote in the District of Columbia in 1871 and held office in the National Woman Suffrage Association. An early opponent of licensing prostitution, Winslow helped to organize the Moral Education Society and for many years published its journal, the *Alpha*. There she became acquainted with Helen Pitts. One interview with Winslow appeared in the

Washington Post, 26 January 1884. (*Cleave's Biographical Cyclopaedia of Homeopathic Physicians and Surgeons* [Philadelphia, 1873]; *American Women*; Moldow, *Women Doctors in Gilded-Age Washington*, passim.)

3. When she began this letter on the twenty-seventh, SBA had seen something written by ECS on the subject of Douglass's marriage. That text has not been found. She received another communication from ECS before she resumed the letter on January 29. That second letter at least resembled what ECS wrote to Douglass on January 27 and sent to him in May: the passage that SBA labels as ECS's pitiful irony is found in the letter to Douglass, published below as an enclosure to ECS's letter of 27 May 1884.

4. Mary Edwards Walker (1832–1919), a physician and dress reformer, attended most of the Washington suffrage conventions, interrupting the proceedings and, in the opinion of ECS, distracting the press from the political purposes of the events. (*NAW*. See also *Papers* 2 & 3.)

5. Victoria Claflin Woodhull (1838–1927) set new directions for the National association in 1871 with her plea to Congress for a declaratory act that would recognize women's existing right to vote under the Fourteenth and Fifteenth amendments. However, to credit her for that leadership cost the association supporters who recognized only Woodhull's defense of free love and charges of adultery against Henry Ward Beecher. By this date, Woodhull, living in England, had married for a third time and taken her husband's name of Martin. (*NAW*; *ANB*.)

6. Possibly none of the three parentheses was written by SBA.

7. Of these activists in Washington, Jane Spofford and Ellen O'Connor are already identified. Ruth Carr Denison (c. 1829–?) had been active in the suffrage movement in the District of Columbia since at least 1871, when she joined the large group of women attempting to register and vote. Skilled as a lobbyist, she served on the National's congressional committee in 1876 and 1877 and became auditor in the 1880s. (Federal Census, 1870; city directories, 1870 to 1881; *History*, 3:813, 956, 4:27, 567–68n. See also *Papers* 2 & 3.) Susan Ann Edson (1823–1897) graduated from the Cleveland Homeopathic Medical College in 1854 and served in army hospitals during the Civil War. Settling in Washington, she worked with Caroline Winslow to establish homeopathic medical facilities in the city; helped to organize the local suffrage movement, beginning with the Universal Franchise Association in 1867; and built her own medical practice, that included the family of James Garfield. She attended Garfield after he was shot in 1881, and Congress paid her for the service. In 1886, she became a trustee of the newly incorporated National Woman Suffrage Association, and she presided over the District of Columbia Woman Suffrage Association for many years. (Jarvis Bonesteel Edson, *Edsons in England and America and Genealogy of the Edsons* [New York, 1903], 583; *History*, 3:809n, 813, 4:295, 567n; Moldow, *Women Doctors in Gilded-Age Washington*, 12, 17, 107; *Woman's Journal*, 11 December 1897.) Little is known about Jerusha G. Joy (c. 1830–?), a native of Massachusetts, whose husband worked at the

Government Printing Office in Washington. In 1880, she attended both the annual meeting of the National association in Indianapolis and its mass meeting in Chicago as a delegate from the District of Columbia, and thereafter she often served on committees for Washington conventions. She was also treasurer in 1883 of the Washington Society for Moral Education. That group noted her removal from Washington in April 1884 without indicating her new residence. (Federal Census, 1880; city directories, 1880 to 1884; *History*, 3:175n; *Alpha*, May 1884; *Film*, 23:23.)

8. According to the Washington *National Republican*, 6 March 1884, *Film*, 23:651–53, Frederick and Helen Douglass "were conspicuous figures on a front seat" at the convention's public session in the afternoon of March 5.

9. In this comparison with Robert Purvis, SBA might see two distinct offenses—interracial marriage and remarriage by widowers. She was devastated when her brother-in-law Aaron McLean sought female companionship after the death of his wife, Guelma Anthony. (*Papers*, 3:76n; SBA diary, 30, 31 March, 1, 6 April 1874, *Film*, 17:491ff.)

10. Although left in the text as SBA's strikeout, this change could have been made later.

11. SBA refers to Douglass's stance not only in 1869 but as early as 1866, when he assumed responsibility for rallying woman suffragists to the cause of manhood suffrage. In speeches to dozens of woman suffrage meetings, he argued that all women were well represented by men. For examples, see his speeches of 20 November 1866, 14 May, 19 November, 11 December 1868, in Douglass, *Papers*, 4:146–48, 172–86, and his letter to Josephine Griffing, 27 September 1868, in Philip S. Foner, *The Life and Writings of Frederick Douglass* (New York, 1955), 4:212–13.

12. That is, Margaret Stanton Lawrence.

143 ≫ JANE COBDEN TO SBA

10 Oxford and Cambridge Mansions, London, N.W., Feb. 5, 1884.

My Dear Miss Anthony:

Many thanks for your letter of January 9th. With you I wish sincerely I could be at the Annual Convention of the National Woman Suffrage Association of America, to be held in Washington on the 4th, 5th and 6th of March.

I hope the question on your side of the Atlantic is making the way it is on this. If so, we shall simultaneously and shortly see the enfranchisement of women in both countries. Here the agitation for adding this act of justice to our statute-book is gaining in strength daily; the Liberals have called for it throughout the country, through their representatives at the Leeds Liberal Conference in October last, and Liberal Associations, one after the other, are passing resolutions in favor of this reform. We have, therefore, the Liberals of England with us, and so we may feel sure of a speedy victory.

I feel all the more certain of the righteousness of the work, in which I am so much engaged, because I know from words spoken and written by my father as far back as 1845, that, had he been living at the present day, I should have had his sympathy. He was nothing if not consistent, and so he said in a speech delivered in London in 1845, on Free Trade: "There are many ladies, I am happy to say, present. Now, it is a very anomalous and singular fact that they cannot vote themselves, and yet they have a power of conferring votes upon other people. I wish they had the franchise, for they would often make a much better use of it than their husbands."[1] The reference to the power of conferring votes relates to the creation of forty-shilling freeholds. By this quotation you will see that my father was in favor of Woman Suffrage.

I wish you all success in the struggle you are carrying on so bravely in America, and I know your hearty sympathy is with us here. Yours most sincerely,

⇜ *Jane Cobden.*

⇜ *National Woman Suffrage Association. Report of the Sixteenth Annual Washington Convention, March 4th, 5th, 6th and 7th, 1884* (Rochester, 1884), 98.

1. "Free Trade," 15 January 1845, in *Speeches on Questions of Public Policy by Richard Cobden, M.P.*, eds. John Bright and James E. Thorold Rogers (London, 1870), 1:245. In an effort to strengthen the political power of towns over counties, Cobden encouraged advocates of free trade to buy small plots of land in order to take advantage of an ancient law that entitled owners of forty-shilling freeholds to vote in the counties. In this speech, he particularly urged fathers and mothers to convey freehold qualifications to their sons in time for the next election.

·⊏━━━━━━━⊐·

144 | ⤳ ECS to Mary England[1]

No 8. West 40th street [*New York*] Feb 8th [*1884*]

My dear Friend,

Your pleasant note I received last evening. I fear I shall not be able to accept your invitation for Sunday, as only three days remain before I leave for my new home.[2] I have many last things to do, many last calls to make, & I am not feeling very vigorous in body, & many things to depress me in spirit. I long for rest in my old home, with its many sweet associations. I shall go & hear Adler[3] on Sunday, if I can see that I can make time, as I would like to know his estimate of Wendell Phillips. Vanderbelts gallery[4] is well worth seeing you must try to go next time. We "old ladies" were all too lazy to do them (the pictures) up thoroughly, but we enjoyed what we had the strength to look at. Mr Villard's house[5] is also well worth seeing. But I find a very little sight seeing & visiting tires me out. Letters from Hattie to day say that she is rapidly gaining strength & begins to feel like her old self. I have been sitting up until twelve at night reading Mr Isaacs,[6] the closing pages are exquisite in their philosophy. Perhaps this habit of sitting up late may account for my sleepiness by day. If you see our magnificent knight Gitteaux again present him my compliments. You must write us an occasional epistle to cheer our solitude in Johnstown. To get letters is one of my greatest pleasures. With kind regards for Mr England sincerely yours

⤳ *Elizabeth Cady Stanton*

⤳ ALS, Knollenberg Collection, Manuscripts and Archives, CtY.

1. Mary England (c. 1832–?) was Mrs. Paddock when she married the widower Isaac W. England (1832–1885) in 1872 and filled a household near Ridgewood, New Jersey, with seven children, by ECS's count, or five children, according to his obituary. Isaac England worked as a printer before becoming a journalist and editor. He knew the Stantons through Henry Stanton's work at the New York *Sun*, where England was one of the paper's owners and manager of its business department. ECS wrote a vivid description in *Eighty Years* of her friendship with Mary England, centered on their

numerous children. In 1876, SBA described one visit of the England and Paddock children to Tenafly lasting seven days and bringing progress on the *History of Woman Suffrage* to a halt. (New York *Sun*, 26 April 1885; *New York Tribune*, 26 April 1885; *Eighty Years*, 322–23; Federal Census, 1880; George A. Stevens, *New York Typographical Union No. 6: Study of a Modern Trade Union and Its Predecessors* [Albany, N.Y., 1913], 661–65; *Papers*, 3:256, 259.)

2. She refers to Johnstown, New York, where ECS and Henry Stanton settled for the next year.

3. Wendell Phillips died on 3 February 1884, and Felix Adler celebrated his life before a large audience at Chickering Hall in New York City on February 10. (*New York Times*, 11 February 1884.)

4. William Henry Vanderbilt (1821–1885), president of the New York Central Railroad, opened his private collection of art in his house at Fifth Avenue and Fifty-first Street to visitors and provided a guide, the *Collection of W. H. Vanderbilt, 640 Fifth Avenue, New York*, published in 1884.

5. Henry Villard (1835–1900), journalist and president of the Northern Pacific Railroad, built his house on Madison Avenue between Fiftieth and Fifty-first streets. Designed by the architectural firm of McKim, Mead & White, Villard's was but one of six row houses built around a courtyard in Italian Renaissance style. Villard and his wife, Fanny Garrison Villard, moved into their unfinished house in December 1883, just as Villard's finances collapsed, and they gave up the house in the spring of 1884. ECS knew the Villards through her connections to the Garrison family and also through her brother-in-law Samuel Wilkeson, secretary of the Northern Pacific. (*ANB*; William C. Shopsin and Mosette Glaser Broderick, *The Villard Houses: Life Story of a Landmark* [New York, 1980].)

6. *Mr. Isaacs. A Tale of Modern India* (1882) was the first and very successful novel of Frances Marion Crawford (1854–1909), a nephew of Julia Ward Howe and student of Sanskrit at Harvard. An Islamic jewel merchant who anglicized his name for business purposes, Isaacs undergoes a transformation in his views of women as he moves from polygamous marriage to a sublime love for an Englishwoman, and at last to a concept of spiritual union. (*DAB*.)

145 ⇝   MILLICENT GARRETT FAWCETT TO SBA

51 The Lawn, S. Lambeth Road, London, February 14, 1884.

Dear Friends in Convention Assembled:

I think we may fairly ask those who have not yet come to any conclusion on the subject of Women's Suffrage, whether on the whole they believe representative government to be preferable to despotic government; and, if so, why the reasons which lead them to this opinion lose their cogency when those who are asking for representation happen to be women?

It is appropriate that England and America, the strongholds of representative government, should be leading the way in this question of the representation of women. The demand of women for the Suffrage is but a branch of the great movement towards democracy which received its first impulse from America in 1774, and is still going on, gathering force and volume year by year in the Old World as well as in the New.

≈ Millicent Garrett Fawcett

≈ *National Woman Suffrage Association. Report of the Sixteenth Annual Washington Convention, March 4th, 5th, 6th and 7th, 1884* (Rochester, 1884), 25.

146 ≈ LYDIA E. BECKER TO SBA

29 Parliament Street, London, S.W., Feb. 15, 1884.

Dear Miss Anthony:

I am glad you are safely returned, and have resumed your work. I gladly send a line of hope and encouragement for your meeting. Your visit to our country will have shown you how much women have gained in England of electoral rights, and I trust your great Nation will not long be content to lag behind. You will have observed that the government of Canada has again brought forward their electoral bill, which gives the franchise to women.[1] It will probably soon become law, and this will give fresh impetus to the cause in the mother country, and in her colonies as well as in the States. The men of Oregon will hardly refuse to their women rights, which the British government proposes to concede in the Dominion.

You will learn the progress of our cause through the *Journal*, and I will only ask you to convey to your Convention the sympathy and good wishes of their sisters on this side the water. Yours truly,

≈ Lydia E. Becker.

⤚ *National Woman Suffrage Association. Report of the Sixteenth Annual Washington Convention, March 4th, 5th, 6th and 7th, 1884* (Rochester, 1884), 100.

1. Conservative Prime Minister John A. Macdonald proposed suffrage for property-holding single and widowed women as one element of a federal franchise bill introduced in the Canadian Parliament in 1883 and 1884. The bill passed in 1885 only after members voted to remove the woman suffrage clause. (Catherine L. Cleverdon, *The Woman Suffrage Movement in Canada*, 2d ed. [Toronto, 1974], 105–9; Carol Lee Bacchi, *Liberation Deferred? The Ideas of the English-Canadian Suffragists, 1877–1918* [Toronto, 1983], 134–36.)

147 ⤙ SBA TO WILLIAM LLOYD GARRISON, JR.

Riggs House—Washington—Feb. 17th 1884

My Dear Friend W[m] L. G. Jr.

Enclosed is the Call for our 16th annual Convention under the shadow of the Capitol of this "land of the free & home of the brave!"[1] Will you not be present with us on this occasion and help us shout the shameful fact that ↑in the face of this boast—↓ one ↑half↓ of the people are still <u>political slaves</u>!! I very much ↑wish↓ you could stand on our platform here & speak your strong word for perfect equality ↑of↓ rights for women—civil & political—! That is all we ask— After such practical equality is establised by law—if women fall behind in the race of life—it will be their own fault—not the laws' nor men's fault!!

But if you cannot be with us—Do, please, not fail to send us a letter that shall make sure of your presence <u>in</u> "<u>letter</u> & <u>spirit</u>"—if not in person—[2] I am sure ↑you↓ will not fail to give us your good word—but oh, I do so wish you & Ellen could be here with us—and I think you would be, spite of all the hindrances—if you could fully appreciate the weight of your influence on our platform! but I shall ↑be↓ profoundly grateful for your letter—to read before our Con—& have published in the papers of the city—and also to go into our pamphlet report—& ↑there↓ form a part of our <u>Standing</u> Woman Suffrage document for the coming year!—[3]

I cannot tell you & Ellen—& Frank—& Wendell too—how much I enjoyed my visit at Roxbury—and what a lovely picture it has left on

↑the↓ tablet of memories many & varied stowed away for all time—to be ever & anon called up & bring anew the pleasure!![4]

Gen'l Butler sent me telegram Thursday P.M—saying—"Eddy case heard— Judge Allen decides in favor of woman"—[5] But I suppose this does not estop the case going up to the full bench in March— Still it is one good opinion ~~of~~ to start with—and I hope it foreshadows equally good results from the full bench!

But I shall feel that you will keep an eye on the progress of the case— Mr Ransom has not written me—but undoubtedly he knows of the favorable opinion of Judge Allen—

I essayed to write Lucy Stone—& ask her if ~~she~~ ↑we↓ should put her name on our program as one of our speakers—and what should be the title of her speech!—[6] And then I was afraid I might set her back— instead of helping her to come—and so decided to keep silent! But if you see her—I wish you would, incidentally, ↑—not from me—↓ ask her if she is going to the Wash. Con—& get the point on which she proposes to speak—& ask her if you shall not write me to put her name & subject in the program— If she comes I want to give her the best place at an evening session! And you can see that to do that I must know that she will be here before our program is printed!!

With ever so much love to Ellen & yourself & ↑the↓ dear children[7] & brother Frank—I am Very Sincerely & Affectionately

❧ Susan B. Anthony

❧ ALS, on NWSA letterhead for 1884, Garrison Papers, MNS-S.

1. Enclosure missing.

2. See W. L. Garrison, Jr. to SBA, 24 February 1884, *Report of the Sixteenth Annual Washington Convention, 1884*, pp. 126–27, *Film*, 23:573ff.

3. This intention to publish a pamphlet reporting on the convention, congressional action, and work in each of the states in the years 1883 and 1884 was formalized at an executive session of the National association on March 4. May Sewall agreed to edit the report, but when she found the task too big, ECS and SBA put aside their work on the *History* for a month to do it themselves. ECS later promised that she and SBA would prepare annual reports "to bind together handsomely as future volumns of the history." (*Report of the Sixteenth Annual Washington Convention, 1884*, p. 5, ECS to SBA, 17 March 1884, SBA to Mary B. Clay, 24 April 1884, ECS to Elizabeth M. Harbert, 21 May 1884, *Film*, 23:573ff, 701, 725–32, 755–58.)

4. SBA attended the funeral of Wendell Phillips at Boston's Hollis Street Church on February 6, and she stayed with William and Ellen Garrison in

Roxbury until February 11. There she encountered sons of William Lloyd Garrison whom she had not seen for many years: Francis Jackson Garrison (1848–1916) worked at the Riverside Press in Cambridge, and Wendell Phillips Garrison (1840–1907) was an editor of the *Nation* in New York. (Garrison, *Letters*, 6:12, 14, 18.)

5. Jerome Bacon's complaint against the heirs of the Eddy estate was heard by one judge of the Supreme Judicial Court for the Commonwealth. On 11 February 1884, Benjamin Butler filed a demurrer to the complaint and argued the case before Justice Charles Allen (1827–1913). Allen, in sustaining the demurrer, was of opinion that Eddy's will created no trust but gave property outright to Stone and SBA for them to do with as they chose. As SBA assumed, the case was next heard by the full court. (*DAB*; Bacon et al. v. Ransom et al., Bill of Complaint, Supreme Judicial Court for the Commonwealth of Massachusetts, Docket No. 324 in Equity, Archives, Supreme Judicial Court, Boston; *Boston Daily Globe*, 17 February 1884.)

6. While she stayed with the Garrisons, SBA received many guests, and among them, according to the *Boston Daily Traveller*, 11 February 1884, were Lucy Stone, Henry Blackwell, and Alice Stone Blackwell. (SBA scrapbook 10, Rare Books, DLC.)

7. There were five children of Ellen and William Garrison: Agnes (1866–1950), Charles (1868–1951), Frank Wright (1871–1961), William Lloyd Garrison III (1874–1964), and Eleanor (1880–1974). (Wright genealogical files, Garrison Papers, MNS-S.)

148 ❧ Hubertine Auclert to SBA

"La Citoyenne," 12 Rue Cail, Paris, Feb. 17, 1884.[1]

Dear and Distinguished Friend:

I rejoice at the victory which you have just gained in Washington Territory. America will soon be, through your efforts, a true land of freedom for all humanity. Your success gives us renewed courage here in France. We keep up the good fight, but, if we except a few moral gains, we are still far from the goal. In our impatience to throw off man's despotic yoke, we stretch our hands to you, O sisters almost enfranchised. We call upon you to come to our aid, as your countrymen, a century ago, besought France to help them escape the subjection of England. Will you not come to our help as Lafayette[2] and his legion flew to yours? You are fitted to act as liberators. As veterans of the cause, you should take the initiative in calling together at Paris, capital of the world, a Universal Congress in favor of Woman Suffrage. Such a congress could not but have a great influence on public opinion, and would powerfully aid the movement for woman's emancipation throughout the whole world.

I submit this suggestion to the consideration of the Convention, and I beg of you to accept for the American Suffragists, and for yourself, distinguished friend, my warmest expressions of sincere admiration.[3]

⮜ *Hubertine Auclert.*

⮜ *National Woman Suffrage Association. Report of the Sixteenth Annual Washington Convention, March 4th, 5th, 6th and 7th, 1884* (Rochester, 1884), 116.

1. This translation was likely made by Theodore Stanton, who transmitted this letter and the one below from Léon Richer dated February 19 to the National's Washington convention.

2. Marie-Joseph-Paul-Yves-Roch-Gilbert du Motier de Lafayette (1757–1834) withdrew from French military service to enter the Continental army in the American Revolution.

3. Auclert retained a copy of her letter, now in Auclert Papers, Box 5, Bouglé Collection, Bibliothèque Historique de la Ville de Paris, and in *Film*, 45:381–82. It reads:

Miss Antony   chère et illustre amie

J'applaudis à la victoire que vous venez de remporter dans le territoire de Washington; bientôt grâce à vos efforts, l'Amérique sera véritablement une terre libre pour toute l'humanité

En France, nous nous inspirons de votre actions; nous luttons, mais malgré certains résultats moraux obtenus, nous sommes encore bien loin du but à atteindre

Dans notre impatience de secouer le joug despotique de l'homme, nous tendons nos bras d'esclaves vers vous ô soeurs presque affranchies. Nous vous appelons à notre aide, comme il y a un siècle vos compatriotes ont appelé la France à leur aide pour délivrer l'amérique du joug anglais. Viendrez-vous à notre secours comme Lafayette et sa légion ont volé au votre?

Le rôle de libératrices vous convient. En votre qualité de vétéranes de la cause vous pourriez prendre l'initiative d'organiser à Paris capitale du monde un congrès universel en faveur du suffrage des femmes.

Ce congrès de nature à influer sur l'opinion publique, aurait un immense retentissement très favorable à l'emancipation des femmes du monde entier

Je soummets ce projet à l'appréciation de vos comités et je vous prie d'agréer pour les américaines suffragistes et pour vous illustre mademoiselle l'expression de ma plus sympathique admiration

·(⊂⸺⸺≫≪⸺⸺⊃)·

149 ⤳ LÉON RICHER TO SBA

"Le Droit des Femmes," 4 Rue des Deux Gares, Paris, Feb. [*19*],
1884.[1]

Madam: You do me the honor of asking me to send a few words to the grand meeting which is to be held at Washington in March. I am very much touched by this mark of esteem on your part, and I seize this opportunity to express to you publicly my deep sympathy for your noble efforts in favor of the political rights of women.

Because I have devoted myself above all to securing the legal rights of French women, some people imagine that I draw back before their political equality. Far from it. I made this demand twenty years ago. But France postpones; France is timid. I turn to the most pressing reforms, and devote my chief efforts to measures which can be soonest obtained.

I admire your free America. I salute with respect those brave women who, like Mrs. Elizabeth Cady Stanton and yourself, consecrate their whole lives to the grand cause of equality, justice and progress, to which I, too, am devoted.

Continue the good work in the future as in the past. Be sure that the success of your valiant labor will, sooner or later, be felt in the Old World. The rights secured in the United States and England will serve as examples to lagging nations. You are the advance-guard, and I salute you with respect.

Please convey my compliments to the delegates to your great meeting, and accept for yourself my sincerest expressions of regard.[2]

⤳ *Leon Richer.*

⤳ *National Woman Suffrage Association. Report of the Sixteenth Annual Washington Convention, March 4th, 5th, 6th and 7th, 1884* (Rochester, 1884), 116.

1. Although the source text dates this letter February 9, Richer dated it February 19. On the origin of this translation, see note at 17 February 1884 above.

2. The text of this letter that Léon Richer published in *Le Droit des femmes*, 7 avril 1884, reads:

Vous me faites l'honneur de me demander quelques lignes pour le grand meeting qui doit s'ouvrir à Washington en mars prochain.

Je sens tout le prix de cette marque d'estime de votre part et j'y réponds avec d'autant plus d'empressement, qu'elle me fournit l'occasion de témoigner publiquement de toute ma sympathie pour vos généreux efforts en faveur du droit politique des femmes.

Parce que je m'attache surtout, dans mon pays, à la conquête de l'égalité civile, certaines personnes s'imaginent que je recule devant l'égalité politique.

Moi, reculer devant l'égalité politique! Il y a vingt ans que je l'affirme! Mais la France retarde; la France a peur. Je cours au plus pressé, et je m'attache plus étroitement aux réformes immédiatement applicables.

J'admire votre libre Amérique; je salue les femmes courageuses qui, comme Mme Cady Stanton et vous, consacrent leur vie entière à la grande cause d'égalité, de justice et de progrès dont j'ai fait mon oeuvre, moi aussi.

Travaillez, Mesdames, sans relâche, comme vous l'avez fait jusqu'ici. Dites-vous que les succès de votre vaillante propagande auront, tôt ou tard, leur contre-coup sur le vieux continent.

En affranchissant les femmes de votre grand pays, vous préparez l'affranchissement des femmes du monde entier. Les droits conquis en Amérique et en Angleterre serviront d'exemples aux nations retardataires. Vous êtes l'avant-garde; je vous salue avec respect.

Veuillez être l'interprète, dans le meeting, de mes sentiments de dévouement profond, et recevoir pour vous, Mademoiselle, l'assurance de ma considération très distinguée.

150 ⪼ Margaret Walker Parker to SBA

The Home Lea, Penketh, near Warrington, Feb. 20, 1884.

My Dear Miss Anthony:

Most gladly do I send greetings to you and the noble women assembled in Convention in Washington. I shall be with you in spirit during all your sittings. I only wish that in bodily presence I could say, "all hail!" and enjoy seeing you face to face. To be engaged in so holy a cause as the demand for full justice for women is to be on the winning side—for God is ever with the right.

In looking back over the years, we see how much has been gained in both Great Britain and America. Thanks to the noble workers who have trod with bleeding feet the path that now is full of promise to the women of to-day. We are looking to the bill for the extension of the franchise, hoping it will include equal Suffrage for women rate-payers.[1] Your visit, and that of Mrs. E. C. Stanton, has been a fresh inspiration to us. I trust that ere long we shall have an International Woman Suffrage Association, that the women of all lands may join hands and pledge each other to labor till every vestige of disability be removed and the crown of perfect equality be placed on the brow of the mothers of the race. Yours for human equality,

  Margaret E. Parker.

  National Woman Suffrage Association. Report of the Sixteenth Annual Washington Convention, March 4th, 5th, 6th and 7th, 1884 (Rochester, 1884), 113–14.

1. William Gladstone introduced the Third Reform Bill at the end of February 1884. Woman suffragists intended to offer an amendment to the measure when it came up for discussion late in the spring. Based on the payment of rates, or taxes, the bill promised nearly universal adult, male suffrage.

151   ECS TO SBA

Johnstown, [N.Y.] February 23, 1884

[D]ear Susan:

I am very sorry to admit it, but really I am in no condition for a [c]onvention. I have been so troubled with short breath that I could go [n]owhere in New York. My heart is the threatening trouble. I have not written [t]o you about it, because I did not want it known or talked about.[1] I am really [s]orry, my beloved, that I cannot be in Washington to share your anxieties; [b]ut I fear I should only add to them. If I should climb up those stairs in [L]incoln Hall, it would take me five minutes to recover my breath. Don't tell [a]nybody all this; just say I have a cold.

I shall have my speech copied to-day and will send it on Monday.[2] If

[t]here is a niche where you have nothing better to place, read it. I have [t]hought of two or three ideas for resolutions. I will prepare and send them, [n]ot necessarily for adoption but as suggestions. Lovingly,

≈ *Elizabeth Cady Stanton.*

≈ Typed transcript, ECS Papers, NjR. Letters in square brackets obscured by binding.

1. Once she reached Johnstown, ECS did not reverse direction to attend the National association's Washington convention. The official reason, by the time the delegates gathered on March 3, was that "the sickness of her sister" kept ECS away, or, as SBA told it, ECS was in Johnstown "where a dear sister was lying very ill, expecting death every hour." This explanation appeared first in a letter to SBA, written on March 1, when ECS mailed her letter to the convention. "I never wanted to be at a convention so much in my life," she wrote, "but I cannot with my dear sister perhaps dying. . . . A letter to-day says she is worse." This letter of February 23 and the one of March 1 both exist only as transcripts edited by the Stanton children; there is no known way to check the reliability of this rapid shift from heart problems to a cold to a dying sister. All of ECS's sisters survived for many more years. (ECS to SBA, [1 March] 1884, and Washington *National Republican*, 5 March 1884, *Film*, 23:572, 649–50; Washington *National Republican*, 4 March 1884.)

2. ECS sent a speech entitled "Self-Government the Best Means of Self-Development." No one read it for her at either the convention or the subsequent congressional hearings. It was included in the second half of the pamphlet report on the Washington convention and is described there as her "argument prepared for the committees." Many copies of the pamphlet report lack this second section, subtitled *Congressional Action in the First Session of the 48th Congress, 1883, 1884*, including the copy in *Film*. A copy of ECS's speech from the pamphlet, found clipped and pasted into a scrapbook, does appear in *Film*, though its original source was unknown. (*Film*, 23:681–84; *History*, 4:40–42.)

152 ≈ ECS TO THE NATIONAL WOMAN SUFFRAGE ASSOCIATION

Johnstown, Fulton Co., N.Y., March 1 [*1884*].

My Dear Friends in convention assembled: I deeply regret that I cannot be present at this, the fourteenth, annual convention in Washington, but family illness prevents.

After an absence of two years in the old world, I had hoped at this time to see again the usual familiar faces I have so often greeted on this platform, and to welcome with renewed pleasure the earnest young women, coming from year to year, to fill the vacant places that time is gradually making in our ranks.

Though absent in person, I shall be with you in spirit; happy in the success of the convention, proud in the wisdom and moderation that will, no doubt, as usual guide the proceedings of the platform. Our American journals in times past were wont to point us for example to the superior manner in which the suffrage agitation was carried on in England, but after spending a year there, and attending many of their suffrage meetings, I return quite well satisfied with the dignity of our conventions, the appearance of our women, the eloquence of our speakers, and the enthusiasm of our audiences.

There is only one great advantage they have over us, and that is in the large number of honorable gentlemen interested in the movement, who always take part in their meetings. This, no doubt, is due to the fact that these women have municipal and school suffrage; belong with men to the liberal leagues; hold some municipal offices, thus having a direct influence in local politics. Hence, their public men take note of this growing power.

Our politicians, on the contrary, think that woman suffrage in this country is still too far off to make it necessary for the present generation of Congressmen to take note of the interests of women.

I think some of our friends should interview the prominent Presidential candidates, learn how they stand on the franchise question, and also ascertain if there is any possibility that either of the leading parties will place a woman suffrage plank in its platform. If not, I trust this convention, in numbers and influence, may be to our enemies like the hand-writing on the wall of old, warning them that they have been weighed in the balance and found wanting.

While greeting those of our friends who are with you in health and vigor, my thoughts dwell, too, on those who are absent to return to us no more forever.

I would remind you of that noble coworker, Elizabeth B. Schenck,[1] of California, the first to demand equal rights for women on the Pacific slope. In her rare common sense, dignity, and wisdom she was a worthy representative of the grand movement she helped to inaugurate.

We have been suddenly called in the past year to part with one of the youngest members of our association, Jennie Channing O'Connor.[2] Earnest, talented, conscientious, we cannot too highly estimate the loss of one so full of promise, so deeply interested in the enfranchisement of woman.

Where shall we find again such an able, eloquent advocate of the rights of woman in our day and generation as we had in Wendell Phillips? In looking over the glowing testimonials to him as philosopher, philanthropist, scholar, and gentleman, I have been amazed to find how many liberal writers even have qualified their praise with regrets over his recent utterances on the reforms of the day.[3] As that form of slavery to which he devoted his early life ended, and the great victory passed into history, the most faint-hearted moralist can now with safety say, "Well done, good and faithful servant";[4] but for the struggle with other forms of oppression still respectable and popular, they have no words of encouragement for the living or praise for the dead.

The same hatred of injustice that made Wendell Phillips advocate emancipation for the African race moved him also to speak out boldly for the rights of women and the laboring masses, for prohibition and a better system of finance. What shortsighted writers have pointed out as his weakness was indeed his strength. He was conscientious throughout; ever as true to the great principles of freedom and justice as the needle to the pole. As he once said, "he was not born to be an abolitionist merely, but to speak the truth on all the wrongs of society that he saw and felt." And he did it bravely and boldly to the end, followed by the regrets of timid friends and the deprecations of time-serving enemies. Great soul! Peerless in moral courage, self-denial and steadfastness of purpose! Though possessed of abundant wealth, while refined and artistic in his tastes, he lived economically in the humblest surroundings. In his renunciation of the elegancies and luxuries of life, of all its temptations and ambitions, he lived alone in the world, while faithfully fulfilling his duties in it.

Socrates before the court in Athens, or Luther before the Diet of Worms[5] do not present grander scenes in human history than Wendell Phillips before the Harvard Phi Beta Kappa Society in June, 1881. In such a conservative assemblage of presidents, professors, scholars, authors, and editors, what other man would have dared to hurl such thunderbolts of indignation at the national crimes and outrages of his times?

The great Athenian and the German reformer had but their own cases to plead, to touch but a few points of Christianity and morals, but Wendell Phillips swept the whole gamut of human suffering and crime in such words of glowing eloquence as no human lips have ever surpassed. He stood there calm and earnest, though almost alone in his convictions in that vast audience; but the profound silence and fixed attention proved that while they rejected his opinions they reverenced the moral courage of the man. It was on that occasion he said: "If in this critical battle for universal suffrage—our fathers' noblest legacy to us, and the greatest trust God leaves in our hands—there be any weapon which once taken from the armory will make victory certain, it will be as it has been in art, literature, and society, summoning woman into the political arena.

"The literary class, until within a half a dozen years, has taken note of this great uprising only to fling every obstacle in its way. The first glimpse we get of Saxon blood in history is that line of Tacitus in his Germany which reads: 'In all grave matters they consult their women.'[6] Years hence, when robust Saxon sense has flung away Jewish superstition and Eastern prejudice, and put under its foot fastidious scholarship and squeamish fashion, some second Tacitus, from the valley of the Mississippi, will answer to him of the Seven Hills, 'In all grave questions we consult our women.'"[7]

While we hold Wendell Phillips in grateful remembrance for the great services he has rendered our cause for nearly forty years, let us not forget to mention the noble woman, whose sympathy in his life work has been a constant inspiration.

In closing I might suggest that a resolution, expressive of the tenderness and respect we who know her best feel for her in this hour of deep affliction, be sent to Ann Green Phillips from this convention. Sincerely yours,

🔊 *Elizabeth Cady Stanton.*

🔊 "Woman's Kingdom," Chicago *Inter-Ocean*, 22 March 1884, ECS Papers, DLC. Corrected by ECS.

1. Elizabeth T. Schenck (?–1884) became a subscriber to the *Revolution* in 1868, the National association's vice president for California in 1869, and a founder of the California Woman Suffrage Association in 1870. ECS and SBA

were her guests on their trip to San Francisco in 1871. Schenck also wrote the California chapter for the *History of Woman Suffrage*. (Roger Levenson, *Women in Printing: Northern California, 1857–1890* [Santa Barbara, Calif., 1994], 50, 61,. 96, 100; *History*, 3:750–54, 761, 4:61; city directory, 1871. See also *Papers* 2.)

2. Jean O'Connor (1858–1883) of Washington, daughter of Ellen Tarr O'Connor and niece of William F. Channing, died on May 5 at the Channing house in Providence, Rhode Island. She had attended the Washington convention in 1882, where she met ECS and SBA. (Freedman, *William Douglas O'Connor*, 80, 311–17.)

3. Many obituaries of Phillips, including those written by abolitionist allies, lamented a lack of discrimination evident in his postwar support for woman's rights, socialism, nihilism, paper currency, and labor's right to organize. SBA assembled a collection of the obituaries, preserved in SBA scrapbook 10, Rare Books, DLC.

4. Matt. 25:21.

5. Socrates (c. 470–399 B.C.), the Greek philosopher, was tried and condemned for religious unorthodoxy, as Martin Luther was in the sixteenth century.

6. Apparently a loose translation of the Roman historian Cornelius Tacitus (c. 56–c. 120), *De origine et situ Germanorum*, chap. 8, sec. 2: "inesse quin etiam sanctum aliquid et providum putant, nec aut consilia earum aspernantur aut responsa neglegunt."

7. "The Scholar in a Republic," Phillips, *Speeches, Lectures, and Letters, Second Series*, 354.

153 ᔰ **TESTIMONY OF SBA BEFORE THE SENATE COMMITTEE ON WOMAN SUFFRAGE**

EDITORIAL NOTE: The Senate Select Committee on Woman Suffrage granted a hearing to members of the National Woman Suffrage Association on the morning of 7 March 1884, while the Washington convention was still in session. With all committee members in attendance, Francis Cockrell of Missouri presided, but he turned over to SBA the management of speakers. She introduced each one: Harriette Shattuck, May Sewall, Helen Gougar, Abigail Duniway, Caroline Rogers, Mary Howell, Lillie Blake, Clemence Lozier, Elizabeth Harbert, and Sarah Wall. Before concluding the hearing, SBA made her own remarks to the committee. On March 8, she managed a similar hearing with different speakers before the House Committee on the Judiciary. (*Film*, 23:685–88.)

[7 March 1884]

Miss Anthony. I wish I could state the avocations and professions of the various women who have spoken in our convention during the last three days. I do not wish to speak disparagingly in regard to the men in Congress, but I doubt if a man on the floor of either house could have made a better speech than some of those which have been made by women during this convention. Twenty-six States and Territories are represented with live women, traveling all the way from Kansas, Arkansas, Oregon, and Washington Territory.[1] It does seem to me that after all these years of coming up to this Capitol an impression should be made upon the minds of legislators that we are never to be silenced until we gain the demand. We have never had in the whole thirty years of our agitation so many States represented in any convention as we have had this year.

This fact shows the growth of public sentiment. Mrs. Duniway is here, all the way from Oregon, and you say, when Mrs. Duniway is doing so well up there, and is so hopeful of carrying the State of Oregon, why do not you all rest satisfied with that plan of gaining the suffrage? My answer is that I do not wish to see the women of the thirty-eight States of this Union compelled to leave their homes and canvass each State, school district by school district. It is asking too much of a moneyless class of people, disfranchised by the constitution of every State in the Union. The joint earnings of the marriage copartnership in all the States belong legally to the husband. If the wife goes outside the home to work, the law in most of the States permits her to own and control the money thus earned. We have not a single State in the Union where the wife's earnings inside the marriage copartnership are owned by her. Therefore, to ask the vast majority of women who are thus situated, without an independent dollar of their own, to make a canvas of the States is asking too much.

Mrs. Gougar. Why did they not ask the negro to do that?

Miss. Anthony. Of course the negro was not asked to go begging the white man from school district to school district to get his ballot. If it was known that we could be driven to the ballot-box like a flock of sheep, and all vote for one party, there would be a bid made for us; but that is not done, because we cannot promise you any such thing; because we stand before you and honestly tell you that the women of this nation are educated equally with the men, and that they, too, have political opinions. There is not a woman on our platform, there is scarcely a woman in this city of Washington, whether the wife of a Senator or a Congressman—I do not believe you can find a score of women in the whole nation—who have not opinions on the pending Presidential election. We all have opinions; we all have parties. Some of us like one party and one candidate and some another.

Therefore we cannot promise you that women will vote as a unit when they are enfranchised. Suppose the Democrats shall put a woman-suffrage plank in their platform in their Presidential convention, and nominate an open and avowed friend of woman suffrage to stand upon that platform; we cannot pledge you that all the women of this nation will work for the success of that party, nor can I pledge you that they will all vote for the Republican party if it should be the one to take the lead in their enfranchisement. Our women won't toe a mark anywhere; they will think and act for themselves, and when they are enfranchised they will divide upon all political questions, as do intelligent, educated men.

I have tried the experiment of canvassing four States prior to Oregon, and in each State with the best canvass that it was possible for us to make we obtained a vote of one-third. One man out of every three men voted for the enfranchisement of the women of their households, while two voted against it. But we are proud to say that our splendid minority is always composed of the very best men of the State, and I think Senator Palmer will agree with me that the forty thousand men of Michigan who voted for the enfranchisement of the women of his State were really the picked men in intelligence, in culture, in morals, in standing, and in every direction.[2]

It is too much to say that the majority of the voters in any State are superior, educated, and capable, or that they investigate every question thoroughly and cast the ballot thereon intelligently. We all know that the majority of the voters of any State are not of that stamp. The vast masses of the people, the laboring classes, have all they can do in their struggle to get food and shelter for their families. They have very little time or opportunity to study great questions of constitutional law.

Because of this impossibility for women to canvass the States over and over to educate the rank and file of the voters we come to you to ask you to make it possible for the legislatures of the thirty-eight States to settle the question, where we shall have a few representative men assembled before whom we can make our appeals and arguments.

This method of settling the question by the legislatures is just as much in the line of States' rights as is that of the popular vote. The one question before you is, will you insist that a majority of the individual voters of every State must be converted before its women shall have the right to vote, or will you allow the matter to be settled by the representative men in the legislatures of the several States? You need not fear that we shall get suffrage too quickly if Congress shall submit the proposition, for even then we shall have a hard time in going from legislature to legislature to secure the two-thirds vote of three-fourths of the States necessary to ratify the amendment. It may take twenty years after Congress has taken the initiative step to make action by the State legislatures possible.

I pray you, gentlemen, that you will make your report to the Senate speedily. I know you are ready to make a favorable one. Some of our speakers may not have known this as well as I. I ask you to make a report and to bring it to a discussion and a vote on the floor of the Senate.

You ask me if we want you to press this question to a vote, provided there is not a majority to carry it. I say yes, because we want the reflex influence of the discussion and of the opinions of Senators to go back into the States to help us to educate the people of the States.

Senator Lapham. It would require a two-thirds vote in both the House and the Senate to submit the amendment to the State legislatures for ratification.

Miss Anthony. I know that it requires a two-thirds vote of both Houses. But still, I repeat, even if you cannot get the two-thirds vote, we ask you to report the bill and bring it to a discussion and a vote at the earliest day possible. We feel that this question should be brought before Congress at every session. We ask this little attention from Congressmen whose salaries are paid from the taxes, women do their share for the support of this great Government. We think we are entitled to two or three days of each session of Congress in both the Senate and House. Therefore I ask of you to help us to a discussion in the Senate this session. There is no reason why the Senate, composed of seventy-six of the most intelligent and liberty-loving men of the nation, shall not pass the resolution by a two-thirds vote. I really believe it will do so if the friends on this committee and on the floor of the Senate will champion the measure as earnestly as if it were to benefit themselves instead of their mothers and sisters.

Gentlemen, I thank you for this hearing granted, and I hope the telegraph wires will soon tell us that your report is presented, and that a discussion is inaugurated on the floor of the Senate.[3]

❧ Senate, Committee on Woman Suffrage, *Report to Accompany S.R. 19*, 28 March 1884, 48th Cong., 1st sess., S. Rept. 399, Pt. 1, Serial 2175, pp. 13–14.

1. A list of delegates can be found in *Report of the Sixteenth Annual Washington Convention, 1884*, pp. 74–75, *Film*, 23:573ff.)

2. At the November election of 1874, voters in Michigan defeated the proposed amendment for woman suffrage, 40,077 to 135,957. (*Tribune Almanac, 1875*, 86–87. See also *Papers 3*.)

3. The committee's majority—Anthony, Blair, Lapham, and Palmer—presented their report in favor of the amendment on March 28. Brown and Cockrell filed minority views against the amendment on April 23. The committee attached to its report the stenographic record of this hearing on 7 March 1884 and of the hearing before the Senate Committee on the Judiciary on 23 January 1880. No debate on the amendment occurred during this session. (Senate, Committee on Woman Suffrage, *Report to Accompany S.R. 19* and *Views of the Minority*, 48th Cong., 1st sess., S. Rept. 399, Pts. 1 and 2, Serial 2175.)

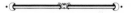

154 ❧ Lucy Stone to SBA

Boston, Mar. 18 1884

Dear Susan

Mr. Ransom came in yesterday to tell me, that we have no chance now, till the November term, of having our claim to Mrs. Eddy's legacy settled.[1] It is very trying. But I had told Mrs. Duniway I would raise $1000. for her. The case seems so hopeful there, that it is worth this effort—[2]

Mrs. Duniway spoke to a very large audience in Tremont Temple last Sunday afternoon, and to great acceptance.[3]

I was very glad to see that you had a really fine convention in

Washington and so successful every way. We have been badly beaten here.[4] yours truly

         Lucy Stone

ALS, on letterhead of *Woman's Journal*, Blackwell Papers, DLC.

   1. Chandler Ransom referred to the hearing before the full bench of the court.

   2. Stone made good on her promise by other means: the American Woman Suffrage Association provided one thousand dollars to Duniway in advance of the June referendum in Oregon. (*Woman's Journal*, 21 June, 5 July 1884.)

   3. After the Washington convention, Abigail Duniway spoke in a number of eastern cities before heading home to Oregon. (*Woman's Journal*, 22 March 1884.)

   4. After debates on March 12 and 13, the Massachusetts General Court defeated a bill for women to be granted municipal suffrage by the unusually large negative vote of one hundred and fifty-five to sixty-one. Activists presented massive petitions in favor of the measure, while antisuffragists organized against it. (*History*, 4:721–22; *Woman's Journal*, 15 March 1884.)

155   ECS TO SBA

                   Johnstown, [*N.Y.*] March 20, 1884.

Dear Susan:

   My English friends have all utterly failed to grasp our idea. We merely proposed to take the initiative steps by way of correspondence to form a few years hence an international association. It is not a thing to be done in a hurry. But those English women are all too timid to do anything until Miss Becker says so.[1]

   I am ready when you are to begin to work on the History. If you could spend April here and lay out work for me for the summer, so that I could take it leisurely, I could accomplish something. Affectionately,

         Elizabeth Cady Stanton.

Typed transcript, ECS Papers, NjR.

   1. The National association was a step ahead of ECS on plans for international work. At the recent meeting in Washington, delegates resolved "That, as there is a general awakening to the rights of women in all European countries, the time has arrived to take the initiative steps for a grand international

woman suffrage convention to be held either in England or America." (Washington *National Republican*, 6 March 1884, *Film*, 23:651–53.) On the dispute within the British movement over these plans, see Holton, *Suffrage Days*, 64–65, and Holton, "'To Educate Women into Rebellion': Elizabeth Cady Stanton and the Creation of a Transatlantic Network of Radical Suffragists," *American Historical Review* 99 (October 1994): 1125. None of ECS's British correspondence on this matter survives.

156 ⤳ SBA TO BENJAMIN F. BUTLER

Rochester May 2, 1884

Gen'l B. F. Butler   My Dear Friend

I received your note saying you thought the <u>Eddy Will Case</u> would be reached in the June Term of Court— I am trusting implicitly that you will leave no stone unturned, on our side, to be ready, and to push the case to a decision! Every postponement will add to the expenses— and thus lessen the amount to go to the Woman Suffrage Cause—and I want you to study & work to save as much as possible to come to us—

What or who can block the way to a decision in the June Term?— Hoping that nothing and nobody can or will do so—I am very sincerely

⤳ *Susan B. Anthony*

⤳ ALS, on NWSA letterhead, Benjamin F. Butler Papers, DLC. Docketed "Rochester N.Y. May 2, 1884 Anthony Susan B. Relative to the Eddy Will Case" and answered "May 25/84."

157 ⤳ SBA TO HARRIET HANSON ROBINSON

Johnstown N.Y. May 12/84

My Dear Mrs Robinson

Here I am—<u>settled</u> in Mrs Stanton's old time home-town—a block & a half away from her place—in a lovely sunny—parlor chamber—of a widow lady—with one daughter[1] & a niece—"we four & no more"[2]— are to be the family— My room fronts East with two good old fashioned windows—& extends back the full width of the house—with one west window—into which—now—the sun is streaming in most lovely through a lovely white lilac bush—or tree— So you ↑can↓ think of me, all this blessed Summer & mayhap away into autumn—basking in both the morning & evening sunlight!! It is the nicest bit of good luck for me— the Hotel man & everybody said it was no us to look—that every house was ful that would take a boarder!— This is the <u>glove</u> <u>making</u> <u>world</u> so every woman & girl that must eke out her income or make one stitches ↑on↓ gloves—the two girls here make ~~their~~ button-holes—& nothing else!!

Well my dear—Can you imagine what I want you to do? I imagine you can!—so round out and boil down your Mass. Chap. at your earliest convenience and send it on to us— I wish you would get what is not in print—copied with a type writer—so we ~~could~~ ↑can↓ read it easily— It is awful hard on our three-score & nine & four eyes to battle with such quantities of obscure chirography!

How come you on?— I don't hear a lisp of Boston!— I want—must have the Woman's Journal— Will you mail it to me regularly—or shall I subscribe for it?— I heard of another <u>nice</u> <u>piece</u> of <u>fairness</u> in newspaperdom when at Rochester—a friend of mine—Mrs Jenny Marsh Parker[3]—a literary woman—who is now writing up the History of Rochester—which celebrates its 50th anniversary in June—and who has made honorable mention of its citizen S. B. A. in her book—& also put S. B. A's picture in it—among the honored men of the city— Well—this lady ↑told me that↓ a year ago—through the appeal of some one to Lucy Stone—to send her the W.J. and ask her to write an article for it now & then, as return compliment—wrote an item—including the testimonial of Rochester's best men & women to S. B. A. on her departure for Europe—giving the names of the signers—the President ↑& Professors↓ of our University—the ministers—Doctors—lawyers, Judges—&c—the Mayor—the School Superintendent of the city &c— And <u>little</u> <u>Lucy</u> wrote her back that she couldn't publish it—that she had already made sufficient mention of Miss Anthony's departure!!!— Isn't that <u>growing</u> <u>friendly</u>?— Lovingly yours

~   *Susan B. Anthony*

[*in margin of first page*] Love to Harriette & Mr Shattuck &c—

~ ALS, on NWSA letterhead, Robinson-Shattuck Papers, MCR-S.

1. Jane Akin Henry (1816–1902) was the widow of George Henry, a printer and once the publisher of the *Fulton County Republican*. He died in 1883. Emma Gertrude Henry (1850–1923) was the only one of seven or eight children still living at home, though many of her siblings settled in Johnstown. Gertrude, as she was known, stayed with her mother until at least 1900, but sometime between that year and 1913 she married David Fox. On the glove-making industry that employed many men and women in Johnstown and nearby Gloversville, see Barbara McMartin, *The Glove Cities: How a People and Their Craft Built Two Cities* (Caroga Lake, N.Y., 1999). (Federal Census, 1870, 1880; Washington Frothingham, *History of Fulton County* [Syracuse, N.Y., 1892], 241–42, 271, 283; city directories, 1875, 1879, 1883, 1900; "Cemetery Recording 1979, City of Johnstown, Fulton County, N.Y., Johnstown Cemetery, Book Number 1," typescript, Gloversville Free Library; with research assistance of Alyce Lanphere, Gloversville, N.Y.)

2. From a well-known selfish prayer, "Bless me and my wife, son John and his wife, we four and no more." In some versions it ends "us four and no more."

3. Jane Marsh Parker (1836–1913), a prolific writer of journalism, juvenile literature, and local history under the name Jenny Marsh Parker, published *Rochester. A Story Historical* in 1884. In it she reprinted the testimonial SBA describes below, sent to Philadelphia for SBA's birthday in 1883 by eighty prominent men and women of Rochester. They described themselves as "old friends and neighbors, adherents to her cause—and those who are not." (*ANB*; *Film*, 23:117; Rochester *Democrat and Chronicle*, 20 February 1883.)

158 ❧ BENJAMIN F. BUTLER TO SBA

Boston, Mass., May 25, 1884.

My dear Miss Anthony:—

I cannot make the Courts go any faster than they will. I hope the Courts will take up the Eddy Will case in June. I shall do nothing to hinder its being brought up and aid it in every I can. Yours truly,

❧ *Benj. F. Butler.*

❧ TL, letterbook copy, Benjamin F. Butler Papers, DLC.

159 ⤳ ECS TO FREDERICK DOUGLASS, WITH ENCLOSURE

Johnstown Fulton Co   New York May 27th [*1884*]

My dear Douglass

I enclose you a little peice of American history. When the hue & cry began at your marriage, I resolved to "pitch in" & defend your action in public as I did everywhere in private   I wrote two articles sent one to a friend in the New York press & one to Washington, intended as an open letter to you ridiculing this ridiculous prejudice of color. Both parties kept them declaring I should not mix in that controversy on the eve of the Woman suff convention. I did feel strongly about the matter, for just at that time there was another fuss about burying a colored man in a "white" cemetery,[1] & then came Mrs Miller & her little boat on the Mississippi,[2] & I did feel as if I would like to fire ten pounds of dynamite at the heels of all these contemptible prejudices as to sex & color. But they were too small for an outlay of dynamite so I took ridicule. I send you enclosed that you may know my sympathies were with you as they always have been   But the colored people in their late conventions have behaved as badly as those who call themselves white. Well Douglass I have suffered all my life just as you have, you have endured one curse I another   I do not believe you have passed through a shade of feeling I do not understand. To be the equals yea the superiors of those who have the impudence to prescribe our spheres is enough to exasperate a saint. I know that with your intense pride & self respect you have suffered more perhaps than any other American slave that ever trod this planet. I know I have more than any other women I ever met   I have always been in chronic condition of rebellion. If I had not naturally a sunny temperment & good health, I should have been the princess of feminine devils.

In the English literature class one day in school reading something invidious to my sex, I burst into angry tears, threw the book aside & rushed out the room. The teacher rushed after me & asked me what was the matter. I told her she ought to be ashamed to give us such degrading things to read. Why said she that is considered one of the most beautiful passages Irving has written.[3] I think it was his vine & oak effusion. Well my friend if it is any comfort for you to know that there is another soul that though absent, is walking the vine press with you, know that every squib about your marriage brought the blood to my face & quikened my pulses, just as the vulgar squibs do about my sex. I have never been able to find words to express my indignation, when I think of woman's position. I have so little patience left when I meet these jackasses in the opposition, that I sit so silent & apparently indifferent that they do not even have the satisfaction to know that I care what they say. Well, well my best wishes for you & your wife sincerely yours

⮜ *Elizabeth Cady Stanton*

⮜ ALS, on NWSA letterhead, Frederick Douglass Papers, DLC.

ENCLOSURE

New York, 8 West 40th street   Jan 27th 1884

Frederick Douglass   Esteemed Friend,

Allow me to congratulate you, on your recent marriage, & express my sincere wish, that all the happiness possible in a true union may be yours.

In view of all you have suffered & all you have achieved, the sunset of your life should be one of peace & enjoyment, but the days of your persecution seen not yet to be ended.

I hear much hostile criticism on your condescention in marrying a <u>white</u> <u>woman</u>. After all the terrible battles, & political upheavals we have had in expurgating our constitutions of that odious adjective "white" it is really remarkable that you of all men should have stooped to do it honor   "The white" feature of this contract is bad enough, but "the woman" is still worse.

To think that you a full fledged citizen of this republic, one of the male aristocracy, a sovreign in your own right, who can make & unmake Presidents, Senators, & Congressmen, amend constitutions, capable as a scholar & statesmen of occupying the loftiest position in the gift of the American people, to think that you should unite your future destiny with "a woman."

In choosing a domestic companion from this anomalous order of being, did you forget that according to some authorities, a woman is not even "a person," much less "a citizen," ranked with idiots, lunatics, & criminals in our state constitutions, an outlaw, a pariah, not fit according to the present Solicitor of the Treasury[4] to pilot a little steamboat, up the muddy Mississippi? No wonder your large circle of admiring friends protest against such self-sacrifice on your part.

In defence of the right to pilot ships, or marry whom we please we might quote some of the basic principles of our government, we might suggest that in some things individual rights, & tastes should control.

If a woman wishes to perfect herself in the science of navigation it might be said that unbounded liberty to do so is her inalienable right. If a good man from ~~Virginia~~ ↑Maryland↓ sees fit to marry a disfranchised woman from New York, there being no legal impediments to the union, full liberty of choice in such relations should be conceded

But alas! if we settle all these questions on the principle of right & justice, what is to become of our time honored customs, prejudices & sentimentalisms? On what could the Kenneth Rayners, & the members of the press expend their eloquence?

If we press Mrs Miller & her steamboat, Mr Douglass & his wife into the compass of a syllogism, & prove logically that "United States citizens" have a right to choose their own wives & employments, half the writing & speaking in ~~the world on color & sex~~ ↑this country as to class privileges↓ might be ended. I hail the day when in the discussion of human rights exact & equal justice will be ~~secured to~~ ↑demanded for↓ all without distinction of race or sex. With my kind regards to your wife, & my best wishes for your happiness, very sincerely yours

             ~ *Elizabeth Cady Stanton.*

~ ALS, Frederick Douglass Papers, DLC.

1. At the time ECS wrote her original letter to Douglass in January, newspapers carried the story of the Hackensack Cemetery Company in New Jersey refusing to bury Sam Bass, an African-American sexton of the First Baptist Church of Hackensack. (*New York Times*, 26, 29 January 1884.)

2. Mary Millicent Garretson Miller (1846–1894) applied late in 1883 for a license to be master of a steamboat on inland rivers, including the Mississippi. With years of experience on the rivers alongside her husband, Miller passed the examination administered by local inspectors of the Steamboat-Inspection Service in New Orleans. The supervising inspector sought the advice of his

superior at the Treasury Department about licensing a woman. The inspector-general approved the license, but the solicitor of the Treasury stepped in to reverse his decision. When ECS wrote to Douglass in January, the solicitor's action had just been announced. Early in February, Treasury Secretary Charles J. Folger overruled the solicitor and told local inspectors to determine Miller's eligibility. Miller obtained her license on February 16. (Eugenia K. Potter, ed., *Kentucky Women: Two Centuries of Indomitable Spirit and Vision* [N.p., 1997], 118–19; *New York Times*, 7 December 1883, 26 January, 3, 19 February 1884.)

   3. Washington Irving (1783–1859), the American writer. ECS recalls his words in "The Wife" about the help women offer their husbands in times of trouble. "As the vine which has long twined its graceful foliage about the oak, and been lifted by it into sunshine, will, when the hardy plant is rifted by the thunderbolt, cling round it with its caressing tendrils and bind up its shattered boughs; so is it beautifully ordered by providence, that woman, who is the mere dependent and ornament of man in his happier hours, should be his stay and solace when smitten with sudden calamity, winding herself into the rugged recesses of his nature; tenderly supporting the drooping head, and binding up the broken heart." (*The Collected Works of Washington Irving*, vol. 8: *The Sketch Book of Geoffrey Crayon, Gent.*, ed. Haskell Springer [Boston, 1978], 22.)

   4. Kenneth Rayner (1808–1884) was appointed solicitor of the Treasury by President Hayes in 1877 and served until his death on 6 March 1884. (*ANB.*)

160   FREDERICK DOUGLASS TO ECS

Washington D.C. May 30, 1884

My dear Mrs Stanton:

   I am very glad to find, as I do find by your kind good letter, that I have made no mistake in respect of your feeling concerning my marriage. I have known you and your love of Liberty so long and well, that without one word from you on the subject, I had recorded your word and vote against the clamor raised against my marriage to a white woman. To those who find fault with me on this account I have no apology to make. My wife and I have simply obeyed the convictions of our own minds and hearts in a matter wherein we alone were concerned and about which no body has any right to interfere. I could never have been at peace with my own soul or held up my head among

men had I allowed the fear of popular clamor to deter me from following my convictions as to this marriage. I should have gone to my grave
a self accused and a self convicted moral coward. Much as I respect the
good opinion of my fellow men, I do not wish it at expense of my own
self-respect. Circumstances have during the last forty years thrown me
much more into white society than in that of colored people. While
true to the rights of the colored race my nearest personal friends owing
to association and common sympathy and aims have been white people—
and as men choose wives from friends and associates, it is not strange
that I have so chosen ~~mine~~ my wife and that she has chosen me. You,
Dear Mrs Stanton, could have found a straight smooth and pleasant
road through the world had you allowed the world to decide for you
your sphere in life—that is had you allowed ↑it↓ to link your moral and
intellectual individuality into nonentity. But you have nobly asserted
your own and the rights of your sex—and the world will know here
after that you have lived and worked beneficently in the world.

 You have made both Mrs Douglass and myself very glad and happy
by your letter and we both give you our warmest thanks for it. Helen is
a braver woman than I am a man and bears the assaults of popular
prejudice more serenely than I do. No sigh or complaint escapes her.
She is steady firm and strong and meets the gaze of the world with a
tranquil heart and unruffled brow. I am amazed by her heroic bearing
and am greatly strengthened by it. She has sometimes said she would
not regret though the storm of opposition were ten times greater.

 I would like to write you a long letter, but I must be off to the
Chicago Convention[1] and must leave this to be folded and directed by
Helen. How good it is to have a wife who can read and write, and who
can as Margaret Fuller says cover one in all his range. Always truly
yours

❧ *Fred^k Douglass.*

❧ ALS, ECS Papers, DLC.

 1. The Republican National Convention met in Chicago from June 3 to 6,
and Douglass was in attendance.

161 ❧ SBA TO EDWARD M. DAVIS

Johnstown N.Y. June 12, 1884

My Dear Friend

Mrs Stanton is trying to grind out something for the Penn. Chapter—for our W.S. History—Vol. III—and in all the papers & points
collected by our dear & absent Rachel Foster—we cannot find so much
as the ↑date of the↓ organization of the Citizen Suffrage Society, or the
Radical club—or the original Penn or Phila. Society[1]—and Mrs Stanton
bids me write Edward M. instanter—and tell him if she writes anything
worthy of all the work done—he must give her all the facts in the case—
and more—she says—he must get some person to write up the whole of
the different societies works! I have written dear Mary Grew to write
out their society's record to the present— But you will have to tell the
story from the beginning down—

Did you send petitions into the constitutional Convention in 1873?—[2]
Was there any special work done over the state influence the Con. Con.
We have a copy of J. B. Broomall's[3] speech in the Con. Con—& Bishop
Simpson's[4] before it— Now who else spoke before that Con. Con—&
what was done?

You will see that it will be impossible for us to Phila—Cit. Suf. & all
justice—unless you yourselves will help us to do so— Here—I cannot
get at any Phila. paper—my ~~olny~~ only possible book of reference is ~~the~~
↑a file of the↓ Woman's Journal—which, as you know is a blank as to
your work & all of ours!! So I pray you—see to it—that the work of
writing out the main points of your work—you needn't mind the rhetoric—only give the facts & dates & what you can of the spirit of things—

tell when the different Societies were formed—why so many—&c—
&c— Sincerely yours

❧ *Susan B. Anthony*

[*above date on first page*] Johnstown—<u>Fulton</u>—not <u>Clinton</u>—Co.

[*in hand of ECS on envelope*] We have not room for much but we want
that little strong. If you want justice done "Cit & Rad" bestir yourself.

We have no dates of birth or death either   Flora[5] has just returned from Auburn, Eliza has taken down 50 pounds by dieting   I am about to follow her example

⤜ ALS, Holden Collection, Manuscripts Division, Department of Rare Books and Special Collections, NjP. Envelope addressed to Philadelphia.

1. Edward M. Davis was instrumental in organizing both of these groups, whose members worked with the National association: the Citizens' Suffrage Association and the Radical Club. They offered alternatives to the Pennsylvania Woman Suffrage Association, headed by Mary Grew from 1869 to 1892 and affiliated with the American association. In answer to SBA's requests, Mary Byrnes sent a short history of the Citizens' Suffrage Association, and John K. Wildman wrote a report on the state association. (*History*, 3:457–63. See also *Papers* 2 & 3.)

2. During the yearlong constitutional convention in Pennsylvania, beginning in November 1872, all the state's suffrage associations urged the delegates, through petitions and hearings, to enfranchise women. On this effort, see *History*, 3:460–61, 463, 465; Ira V. Brown, *Mary Grew: Abolitionist and Feminist (1813–1896)* (Selinsgrove, Pa., 1991), 148–52; and *Journal of the Convention to Amend the Constitution of Pennsylvania: Convened at Harrisburg, November 12, 1872; Adjourned November 27, to Meet at Philadelphia, January 7, 1873*, 2 vols. (Harrisburg, Pa., 1873).

3. John Martin Broomall (1816–1894) led the advocates of woman suffrage in the constitutional convention. His speech to the convention was not included in the *History of Woman Suffrage*. (*BDAC*; *Papers*, 1:568–70; *History*, 3:464.)

4. Matthew Simpson (1811–1884), bishop of the Methodist Episcopal church, had a long history of engagement in political and social questions. For his recent support of suffrage, see M. Simpson to SBA, 2 April 1884, *Film*, 23:717. Simpson died six days after this letter was written. (*ANB*.)

5. That is, Flora McMartin Wright, who visited Cady relatives in Johnstown and Wright relatives in Auburn. She brought word of her sister-in-law Eliza Wright Osborne (1830–1911), a daughter of Martha and David Wright, who lived in Auburn, New York, with her husband and four children. She was active in the New York State Woman Suffrage Association. (Wright genealogical files, Garrison Papers, MNS-S; Garrison, *Letters*, 6:214n; *Woman's Journal*, 12 August 1911.)

162 ❧ WILLIAM F. CHANNING TO ECS

Providence, R.I., July 4, 1884.

My dear Mrs Stanton:

I want to call your attention to Ouida's new novel, "Princess Napraxine," just published.[1] It is the strongest and boldest of her anatomisations of marriage and sexual life. It is morbid anatomy but none the less of scientific value, and psychological interest. It is her first novel since she joined the Catholic Church, and on that account has a special interest. If you need any light(?) literature as stimulus to your mind in its leisure moments during your present work, you will find nothing more stirring.[2] Indeed, it will prove a very intense stimulus and perhaps over-freight your mind for its present voyage. Faithfully yours,

❧ *Wm. F. Channing.*

❧ Typed transcript, ECS Papers, NjR.

1. Ouida was the penname of Marie Louise de la Ramée (1839–1908) a prolific English novelist living in Italy. In *Princess Napraxine*, published in 1884, Ouida created a love triangle, through which she explored opposing ideals of womanhood, pitting angelic femininity against enchanting assertiveness. Marriage made a martyr of the innocent, self-sacrificing peasant, and it entrapped the bold, manipulative title character. Channing's reference to Ouida's conversion to Catholicism echoed reports in the British and American press in December 1883. Ouida had denied them. (*New York Times*, 9 December 1883, 10 February, 5 July 1884; Talia Schaffer, *The Forgotten Female Aesthetes: Literary Culture in Late-Victorian England* [Charlottesville, Va., 2000], 138–49.)

2. Channing probably refers to ECS's work not on the *History* but on her article "The Need of Liberal Divorce Laws," *North American Review* 139 (September 1884): 234–45, *Film*, 23:951–62.

163 ☙ APPEAL BY ECS AND SBA

Johnstown [*N.Y.*], July 30, 1884.

STAND BY THE REPUBLICAN PARTY.

To the Members of the National Woman Suffrage Association:

The choice of a President once in four years by 60,000,000 of people is an event of such magnitude as to impress all thoughtful minds with a realizing sense of the personal responsibility that rests on every citizen of a Republic. Although the individual sovereignty of woman is not fully recognized, yet as she is heir to all the general blessings that flow out of free institutions, she is equally interested with man in this supreme event in the Nation's life. Hence, in the present turmoil of dividing parties it is well for her to consider where to give the weight of her influence, and the stimulus of her enthusiasm.[1]

For this reason we would make some suggestions to our co-workers why they should remain steadfastly with the political party that for the last quarter of a century has most faithfully represented the fundamental principles of Republican government. During the many years we have memorialized Congress for a 16th amendment to the National constitution, "to prohibit the several States from disfranchising United States citizens on account of sex," Republicans, both in the Senate and the House, have presented our petitions and advocated our demands. They have given our Association respectful hearings before their committees, and made favorable reports, recommending the submission of a 16th amendment to the Legislatures of the several States. Distinguished Republican lawyers[2] in the United States Courts, have maintained woman's right to vote and practice law under the guarantees of the 14th Amendment. All these constitutional arguments and congressional reports, sent broadcast by thousands over the country, have done an immense educational work among the people.

In 1882, for the first time in the history of our Government, Congress appointed special committees in both Houses to look after the interests of woman, thus at last raising her political status to the dignity of the Indian. For this special consideration we were mainly indebted to Republicans, as only three Democrats in the Senate and eleven in the House, honored us and themselves by voting for the measure.[3] In 1884, when the House refused to renew "the committee on the political rights of women," by one hundred and twenty Democratic votes, there were only four Republicans recorded with them.[4]

At the opening of the next session, with our bills and reports waiting their turn on the calendars of both Houses, it is to Republicans we must look for a discussion and division on our question; and did they constitute a two-thirds majority, we should confidently hope for the passage of the resolution to submit a 16th amendment. But we have nothing to expect from any of the other parties now struggling into existence.

As to the Greenback[5] and Anti-Monopoly[6] parties, with their quasi-recognition of woman's political equality in their platforms, and the rank and file of seceding Democrats and workingmen who will constitute his supporters, the Hon. Benjamin F. Butler would be powerless to help us. True, he has long been a valiant champion of our cause, and presented in Congress, in 1871, an exhaustive report on woman's right to vote under the 14th Amendment[7]—an argument that lifted our question from that time into one of constitutional law. But with all his varied powers and great executive ability, what could General Butler do as President for us, with a Congress that would never entertain our demands.

Some of our coadjutors feel that we should give our moral support to the Prohibition Party, because it has a woman suffrage plank in its platform, and a Presidential nominee, Gov. St. John, who is an openly avowed advocate of our demands.[8] But, unfortunately, the wording of their plank shows their exact estimate of the minor importance of our question. While they demand an amendment to the National Constitution to prohibit the Liquor traffic, they remand woman for the adjudication of her rights to their infinitesimal party in the several States; that is, a National law against a beverage which a fraction of the population may choose to make and sell; while the fundamental personal and property rights of one-half the people are left to the arbitrary dictation of a third party in the several States.

The comparative magnitude of the question of woman's enfranchisement seems never to have entered into the calculation of Prohibitionists. To make woman suffrage a tail to their kite, is to defy the laws of gravitation. Prohibition could not secure woman suffrage, but woman suffrage is the only power by which prohibition could be made possible.

There are various propositions being discussed by the people for National legislation, viz: A bankrupt law; a divorce law; a prohibition law; the election of the President by a popular vote; the recognition of God in the constitution; but woman's right to self government is of infinitely more importance than all these put together. We would remind those demanding the last, that the best recognition the men of this Nation can make of God in the constitution, is to secure exact justice to their mothers. "If you love not woman whom you have seen how can you love God whom you have not seen."[9] The 16th amendment belongs to woman, both in the order of precedence and importance. Our demands for National protection have been before Congress for twenty years and our petitions by hundreds of thousands are piled up in the archives of the Capitol at Washington. Advocates of other measures may ask for 17th, 18th or 19th amendments, but we claim the 16th, and our case stands first on the calendar.

The recent defection of some of our most prominent friends from the Republican party,[10] who have spoken bravely and eloquently for many years on our platform, must not mislead the unwary, as their action has been in no way influenced by their interest in the woman suffrage question. In fact their remarkable somersault, as far as we can see, is not to illustrate any vital principle, but merely to gratify a personal pique. It is not that they hate Cleveland[11] less, but Blaine more, that such men as George William Curtis, James Freeman Clarke, and Thomas Wentworth Higginson[12] have come down from their high moral platform to swamp their votes with the Democratic party. The result of this last secession, were its proportions equal to its virtuous pretentions, would be to throw the administration of our government into the hands of the Democratic party, not into those of Mr. Cleveland, who though he were possessed of all the cardinal virtues claimed, and in addition thereto, the crowning excellence of adhesion to the great principle of political freedom for woman, he could do nothing for any reform with a Congress and a constituency nine tenths of whom are blind and bitter opponents of all liberal measures.

Suppose, on the other hand, the Republican nominee, James G. Blaine, were wanting in all the public and private virtues, with a

Congress and a constituency three-fourths of whom are our friends, he could do nothing to hinder the passage of an amendment. But he is friendly. His name stands recorded with the "ayes" on all questions affecting the interests of woman brought before Congress for many years.[13] Thus in Mr. Blaine we have a nominee in harmony with the Republican majority in Congress. Hence our hope of securing the initiative step to make suffrage for woman the supreme law of the land lies in the triumphant success of the Republican party.

For these reasons, as we have no votes to offer, we should give our earnest conscientious support to the Republican party whose chosen leader is one of the ablest statesmen our country can boast, and who if elected will, with the noble women of his family circle, honor the White House, and the highest office in the gift of the American people.

ᴀ *Elizabeth Cady Stanton, President.*

ᴀ *Susan B. Anthony, Vice President.*

ᴀ Circular, SBA scrapbook 10, Rare Books, DLC.

1. Delegates to the National association's Washington convention in March 1884 agreed after some debate only to oppose any presidential candidate who opposed woman suffrage, and editors of the *Woman's Journal* advised women to remain nonpartisan in the race. Nonetheless, partisanship among suffragists was high, and the *Journal*'s columns filled with partisan statements from readers, including this appeal by ECS and SBA. The *Journal*'s editors challenged the legitimacy of the appeal as an expression of views within the National Woman Suffrage Association, noting first that ECS and SBA wrote only "over their own names," and, in a later riposte, scolding that they "made a mistake in signing their appeal as officers of the National Woman Suffrage Association without authority." In the meantime, members of the National association from Polk County, Iowa, to Boston registered their disagreement with the stand taken by ECS and SBA. In September, ECS reiterated her support of the Republican ticket. (*Woman's Journal*, 9, 23, 30 August 1884; *Amsterdam Daily Democrat*, 1 August 1884; *Our Herald*, September 1884; *Film*, 23:876.)

2. An asterisk here in the text led to this footnote: "Matthew H. Carpenter, in the case of Myra Bradwell, of Illinois; Henry R. Selden in that of Susan B. Anthony, of New York; and Francis Minor, in that of Virginia L. Minor, of Missouri."

Matthew Hale Carpenter (1824–1881), Republican senator from Wisconsin, argued before the Supreme Court in *Myra Bradwell v. State of Illinois* (1873) that the Fourteenth Amendment protected Bradwell's rights against discriminatory state law. (*BDAC*.) Henry Rogers Selden (1805–1885), a founder of the Republican party in New York, defended SBA in her federal criminal trial for illegal voting, *United States v. Susan B. Anthony* (1873). (David McAdam et al., eds., *History of the Bench and Bar of New York*, [New York, 1897], 1:472–73; Peck, *History of Rochester and Monroe County, N.Y.*, 1:450–52.) Francis Minor acted as counsel in his wife's suit for woman suffrage, *Virginia Minor v. Reese Happersett*, decided by the Supreme Court in 1875.

3. *Congressional Record*, 47th Cong., 1st sess., 9 January 1882, p. 268, and 25 February 1883, p. 1448. In the Senate, the Democrats who voted in support of the committee were Charles W. Jones, David Davis (1815–1886) of Illinois, and Matt Whitaker Ransom (1826–1904) of North Carolina. In the House of Representatives, thirteen Democrats (not eleven) voted for the committee. Five were New Yorkers: Lewis Beach (1835–1886), Archibald Meserole Bliss (1838–1923), Roswell Pettibone Flower (1835–1899), Waldo Hutchins (1822–1891), and Michael Nicholas Nolan (1833–1905). They were joined by Samuel Moulton of Illinois, Augustus Albert Hardenbergh (1830–1889) and Henry Schenck Harris (1850–1902) of New Jersey, George Leroy Converse (1827–1897) and George Washington Geddes (1824–1892) of Ohio, George Robison Black (1835–1886) and Alexander Hamilton Stephens (1812–1883) of Georgia, and Jesse Johnson Finley (1812–1904) of Florida. (*BDAC.*)

4. *Congressional Record*, 48th Cong., 1st sess., 20 December 1883, p. 219. In fact, six Republicans in the House of Representatives helped to defeat the committee. They were Edward Breitung (1831–1887) of Michigan, Richard William Guenther (1845–1913) of Wisconsin, David Bremner Henderson (1840–1906) of Iowa, Sereno Elisha Payne (1843–1914) of New York, William Drew Washburn (1831–1912) of Minnesota, and Archibald Jerard Weaver (1844–1887) of Nebraska. (*BDAC.*)

5. Benjamin Butler received nominations for president in 1884 from the Greenback National party and the National Anti-Monopoly Convention, but he failed in a bid to be the Democratic candidate. The Greenback party, meeting in Indianapolis on May 28, agreed in their platform that, "[f]or the purpose of testing the sense of the people upon the subject, we are in favor of submitting to a vote of the people an amendment to the Constitution in favor of suffrage regardless of sex, and also on the subject of the liquor traffic." (*National Party Platforms*, 70; Edward T. James, "Ben Butler Runs for President: Labor, Greenbackers, and Anti-Monopolists in the Election of 1884," *Essex Institute Historical Collections* 113 [April 1977]: 65–88.)

6. The Anti-Monopolists met in Chicago on May 14. The fourth plank of their platform might be construed as a reference to woman suffrage: "That in the enactment and vigorous execution of just laws, equality of rights, equality of burdens, equality of privileges, and equality of powers in all citizens will be secured." But delegates rejected a woman suffrage plank by a vote of eighty to twenty-nine. (*National Party Platforms*, 64; *Woman's Journal*, 24 May 1884.)

7. House Committee on the Judiciary, *Victoria C. Woodhull. Views of the Minority*, 41st Cong., 3d sess., 1 February 1871, H. Rept. 22, Pt. 2, Serial 1464.

8. The Prohibition party met in Pittsburgh, Pennsylvania, on July 23 and nominated John P. St. John. The sixth plank of their platform directed that "the Congress shall submit to the States an Amendment to the Constituion forever prohibiting the importation, exportation, manufacture and sale of alcoholic drinks." On the question of woman suffrage, the ninth plank endorsed the principle and "relegate[d] the practical outworking of this reform to the discretion of the Prohibition party in the several States according to the condition of public sentiment in those States." (*National Party Platforms*, 71–72.)

9. Adaptation of 1 John 4:20.

10. The Independent Republicans, or Mugwumps, waged a crusade against political corruption, and they rejected the Republican presidential nominee, James G. Blaine, as a corrupt man. At a meeting in New York City on July 22, they announced their support for the Democratic candidate. Prominent among the Mugwumps were well-known supporters of woman suffrage in Boston and New York, most of whom were allies of the American Woman Suffrage Association. (Geoffrey Blodgett, *The Gentle Reformers: Massachusetts Democrats in the Cleveland Era* [Cambridge, Mass., 1966], 1–47; Summers, *Rum, Romanism, and Rebellion*.)

11. Grover Cleveland (1837–1908), former mayor of Buffalo, New York, and current governor of New York State, won the Democratic nomination for president of the United States on July 12. When ECS and SBA published this letter, word about Cleveland's sexual indiscretions and illegitimate child was just spreading beyond his hometown of Buffalo. It is not evident whether they chose not to comment on the stories or lacked information about them. Those stories and debates about the relative importance of public and private virtue soon changed the political discussion, especially in the *Woman's Journal*, where T. W. Higginson, on the one side, and Lucy Stone, on the other side, debated the significance of Cleveland's moral failings to his public life.

12. Prominent among the Mugwumps, T. W. Higginson and James Freeman Clarke (1810–1888), a Unitarian minister and reformer in Boston, represented the Massachusetts base of the movement. (*DAB.*) George William Curtis (1824–1892), editor of *Harper's Weekly*, helped mobilize independents in New York. (*ANB.*) Higginson and Curtis spoke at the meeting on July 22. (*New York Times*, 23 July 1883.)

13. Notable among Blaine's votes for women were those he cast in support of Belva Lockwood's efforts to gain admission to the bar of the Supreme Court of the United States. See *Papers 3*.

·◦⊶———※⊷———◦·

164 ❧ ECS and SBA to Benjamin F. Butler

Johnstown Fulton Co   New York Aug 12th [*1884*]

Hon. Benjamin F. Butler, Dear Sir,

Miss Anthony & I are much embarrassed in our public work, by the delay in the settlement of Mrs Eddy's will.

For several years we have been writing "The History of Woman Suffrage" two volumns are already published but we are blocked on the third for lack of funds, & our publishers are not willing to advance the money

Hence we write to ask you to loan us $5000. if you feel sure that the case will be settled in our favor in November. No one can know as well as you do, the certainty in this matter.[1]

As we ask you to take no risk of loss, having the case in your own hands, & as it will be an incalculable advantage to us to finish the work we hope you will oblige us, by promptly advancing the money

As your name has honorable mention in our work & its pages show our high appreciation of your services, for your minority report of 1871 is published in full, you have some interest in helping us to complete our undertaking, & thus add to your immortality. With our best wishes for your success in the Presidential campaign, we remain Yours sincerely

❧ *Elizabeth Cady Stanton*
❧ *Susan B. Anthony*

❧ ECS ALS, on NWSA letterhead, Benjamin F. Butler Papers, DLC. Docket notes "<u>In re</u>. the 'Eddy Will Case.'"

1. On an earlier offer from Wendell Phillips and Chandler Ransom to advance money from the Eddy estate, see above at 23 September 1882.

·⊂————⊃x⊂————⊃·

165 ∾ SBA TO BENJAMIN F. BUTLER

Johnstown N.Y. August 19, 1884

My Dear Friend

Your Pronunciamento on the political parties and their platforms is before me—[1] And once read—I hasten to thank you for your good & true words for working women and their need of the ballot for their protection!

It is the best word yet uttered by any man from a political stand point— And if my <u>wishing</u> would accomplish it—the rank & file of the producing classes of the men of this nation would vote solid for you— so that you would welcome the officers of our National Woman Suffrage association to the White House in Jan. 1886—as its rightful occupant and dispenser of hospitality— And if they would thus vote—I know your Inaugural address would not fail to repeat ↑the demand for↓ the <u>right</u> <u>of</u> <u>women</u>—to an equal voice in the government!

As I read & as I feel now—I can see ↑resting down upon you↓ the approving smile of the glorious & sainted Wendell Phillips! And to feel worthy of his approval is above the fleeting flattery of any & all living mortals— So I congratulate you again upon your truthful & [fa]r-seeing utterances for the laboring [cl]asses—the women included—and remain Yours Sincerely & Gratefully

∾ *Susan B. Anthony*

∾ ALS, on NWSA letterhead, Benjamin F. Butler Papers, DLC. Square brackets surround letters obscured by docket. Inscribed by secretary "<u>In re.</u> the National Woman Suffrage question".

1. Butler's address to his constituents was published in major newspapers on this date. It called upon Anti-Monopolists, Greenbackers, and labor to form a People's party that would split the electoral vote in each state and hold the balance of power in the election. In his platform, Butler described woman suffrage as a necessity for the laboring woman; without it, she "becomes virtually a slave!" He posed the question, "Why has not some Republican statesman given a few hours in these later years when Southern troubles have passed away, or been overlooked, to the question whether the women of the nation, if not protected by other legislation, should not be allowed the ballot

with which to protect themselves, as that party gave it for like purposes to the negro?" (*New York Times*, 19 August 1884; James, "Ben Butler Runs for President," 78–80.)

166 ⇝ WILLIAM F. CHANNING TO ECS

Providence R.I. Oct. 12, 1884—

Dear Mrs. Stanton,

I have yours, <u>probably</u> of Oct. 10, endorsing the "North American" note to you, of the 9th—[1]

I am very glad of the offer. It shows that you have not lost caste by your previous article. Do not let them trap you into writing a <u>truculent</u> article on the present subject. Write suavely that you may influence the countless multitude whose <u>feelings</u> are more bound up in Christianity than their reason. Of course write uncompromisingly. The Christian <u>Church</u> has been bad enough in its treatment of women, & in nothing worse, perhaps, than in its wicked Mariolatry, I mean its ascetic doctrine of virginity, & its <u>convents</u>. But the spirit of Christianity, (kicking out Paul,) has been benign, & has helped through the centuries to develope the idea of the feminine forces & virtues, as higher than brute force. Christ mingled the woman with the man. ~~His ideal~~ The ideal of his character has helped to exalt woman Spencer[2] says ↑somewhere,↓ (so Dr. Bartol[3] ↑once↓ told me) "Christ was a maid ere he was shapen as a man." <u>Old testament</u> Christianity has always trampled on woman, just as it did on the slave. You can instance the Old testament polygamy as one of the outrages on woman, & so set yourself right on that point.[4]

I have not time or brains to suggest any mischief to you. You are usually fertile enough in <u>coups des plumes</u>. I resign Christianity to your tender mercies. If any thing comes to me, I will send it to you. I have written Mr. Cabot[5] asking him to write you. Yr friend truly—

⇝ *Wm. F. Channing*

⇝ ALS, ECS Papers, DLC.

1. Though the editor's letter and ECS's note to Channing are missing, they no doubt concerned the invitation to write "Has Christianity Benefited Woman?" *North American Review* 140 (May 1885): 389–99, *Film*, 24:294–304. The

journal also invited Bishop John Lancaster Spalding to respond to ECS in the same issue.

2. Herbert Spencer (1820–1903), an English philosopher and prolific writer, applied the principles of evolution to societies.

3. Cyrus Augustus Bartol (1813–1900), a Unitarian leader of Boston, was a founder of the Free Religious Association. (*DAB*.)

4. Possibly Channing refers to ECS's statement on polygamy in "The Need of Liberal Divorce Laws." Countering Noah Davis's claim that monogamy was "an Hebraic Christianized idea," she wrote: "The Hebraic part of that idea was pure polygamy; the Christianized part was the unchanged polygamy of the early Christian church, except where and until it came in contact with the monogamic Greek and Roman civilizations . . . . Neither Christ nor his disciples ever attempted to change polygamous into monogamic marriage." (*North American Review* 139 [September 1884]: 239, *Film*, 23:956.)

5. That is, Frederick Cabot.

167 ✎ ECS to Benjamin F. Butler

Johnstown [*N.Y.*] Oct 16th [*1884*]

Dear Mr Butler

I sincerely desire while you are in my native town, that you will honor us with your presence.[1] Mr Stanton as you know is one of the editors of The Sun,[2] & has been wielding his pen in your praise during the campaign. I have been singing your praises ever since your grand minority report on woman suffrage in Congress.

My son who is the bearer of this will escort you to our house if you will honor us with a call,[3] which would give Mr Stanton & myself great pleasure   very sincerely yours

✎ *Elizabeth Cady Stanton*

✎ ALS, Benjamin F. Butler Papers, DLC. Inscribed by secretary "Invitation to visit and lunch."

1. Butler's campaign train reached Johnstown in the afternoon of this date, several hours before he was scheduled to speak. He accepted ECS's invitation, and a crowd gathered at the Cady house to hear ECS welcome him. Possibly Henry Stanton wrote the report in the New York *Sun*, 17 October 1884: "A surging mass of citizens pressed against the house and battled for a glimpse through the windows." When Butler spoke later that day, "[t]he houses were emptied, and the streets swarmed with people. . . . [S]quads of

workmen from the glove factories, carrying their dinner pails, hastened to the edges of the multitude from all sides."

2. The New York *Sun* supported Butler's candidacy for president.

3. Filed with this letter in Butler's papers are the calling cards of ECS and D. Cady Stanton.

168 ⇒ SBA to ECS

Rochester N.Y. Oct. 23/84

My Dear Mrs Stanton

I reached home Tuesday night—after a two weeks stay in New York—where I went to get a glimpse of Mrs Moore[1]—which I did on three several occasions at the home of our dear Mattie Griffith Brown[2]—142—East 19th street— last Saturday ~~night~~ ↑evening↓ I was present at Miss Boothe's reception—and Sunday P.M. took tea with her!—and she & I talked over your duty to live in New York—and to be at home to receive friends on certain afternoons & evenings—and thus help on—and Mrs Phelps[3] talked of you thus—too—and said she stood ready to invite guests to meet you—& that you should be at no expense— I am sure of one thing—and that is that Johnstown is as good, or bad, as a burial-place— You are there lost to the work of pulling down the strong holds of prejudice against Woman—either publicly or privately!! I cant bear to think of your mewing up there for the Winter—it is an awful mistake for you—

Am glad to hear that Harriot is feeling well & going to visit at Berlin & Paris— I had a lovely letter—to-day—from dear Mrs Nichol—of Edinburg— I sent her—by Mrs Wellstood[4]—yours & my lithographs and also my photo—by Kent[5]—and she is delighted with them—and by Mrs Moore—I sent her Theodore's Women of Europe—got it at the Putnams—for publishers price $2.82— Mr P.[6] told me they would lose money on it— I talked with him about taking our History— Said if I were now asking him—he should probably take it—but he would not entertain the idea of taking hold of Vol. III— Fowler & Wells will do it on same terms as the other two volumes— I haven't decided whether to let them do it thus—or to take it in hand myself—or in name of "National Woman Suffrage Association Publishing Company"— If that could be <u>shortened</u>—I'd like it— I think to take it thus—and have all the friends <u>know</u> that <u>all the profits went into</u> the National Treasury—there to help bring out other publications—it might be a stimulus to them to buy—whereas now—they don't become enthusiastic to buy to help along the Fowler & Wells firm— You see it would make a great difference with us too—in making our appeals to the friends—if we could tell them every dollar of the profits went into the Society's Treasury— Don't you think we had better thus place the History—and leave it so that the National Association may have it as a source of income??— It wouldn't be likely to make it <u>rich</u>! but it would read well!!

I have just opened the W.J. with Princeton Review article[7]—will send it to you—but you must not forget to return it—as I want to keep the file— What a fool T. W. H. does make of himself— I heard Lawyer Merrick[8] of Washington—the Star Route Lawyer & Mr <u>Dorsheimer</u>— last night—and such trumpings up—to inveigh against Blaine & the Repub. Party—it was sickening!![9] I heard Belva in New York—[10] The Academy of Music <u>stage</u> had her alone on it—& some 300 people in it!! rather slim—and she ran over short comings of all parties—and <u>kept too little</u> on her own specific ground—of <u>woman</u> & <u>her disfranchised</u>— her speech was too much like a re-hash of the men's speeches!! She wore her hair ala Martha Washington[11]—save it was no longer a handsome iron gray—<u>but</u> a <u>dead, dyed brown</u>!! So human are poor mortal strongminded women!!

I begin lecturing Nov. 7th Have promised to attend R. Island Annual meeting Dec 3 & 4—[12] Good Bye with Love as ever yours[13]

ᴥ *Susan B. Anthony*

ᴥ ALS, on NWSA letterhead, ECS Papers, DLC.

1. Rebecca Moore and Lydia Becker were among the suffragists who sailed to North America for meetings of the British Association for the Advancement of Science, held in Montreal from August 27 to September 3. Becker visited SBA in Rochester before she sailed home from Quebec in September. Moore and other women not named by SBA sailed from New York City on October 18. E. M. Davis helped to pay for a reception for the visitors in New York. (Blackburn, *Women's Suffrage in the British Isles*, 167; SBA to Lillie Blake, 20 August 1884, 11 September 1884, *Film*, 23:845–48, 871–75.)

2. Martha, or Mattie, Griffith Browne (c. 1833–1906) served on the executive committee of the Women's Loyal National League, held office in the

American Equal Rights Association, and was a vice president of the National Woman Suffrage Association in its first year. After her marriage to Albert Gallatin Browne in 1867, she lived in Boston until her husband's editorial work for New York newspapers brought them back to the city. (Garrison, *Letters*, 5:117n; *Woman's Journal*, 9 June 1906; *NCAB*, 19:316.)

3. Elizabeth B. Phelps (c. 1805–?), now a wealthy widow, helped SBA to publish the *Revolution* and in 1869 opened the Woman's Bureau at 49 East Twenty-third Street to house artists' studios, offices for women's organizations, and overnight accommodations for women visiting the city. Although she lived on Fourth Avenue for several years, she returned to the house on Twenty-third in 1884. (Federal Census, 1870; *Quaker Genealogy*, 3:250, 254; city directories, 1874 to 1884. See also *Papers* 2 & 3.)

4. Jessie Morrison Wellstood (c. 1823–1898) of Edinburgh made frequent trips to the United States, where her husband, Stephen Wellstood, began his business in the manufacture of stoves. SBA met her in 1876, when she visited the Centennial Exhibition in Philadelphia to attend the Women's International Temperance Convention, and again in 1883 in Scotland, when the Wellstoods entertained her on several occasions. At the Washington convention of 1884, Wellstood, the only international delegate in attendance, reported for the Edinburgh National Society for Women's Suffrage. (*History*, 3:144n, 868n, 926, 955, 4:18–19; *Report of the Sixteenth Annual Washington Convention, 1884*, pp. 53–55, *Film*, 23:573ff; SBA diary, 21, 24–25, 27, 31 July 1883, *Film*, 22:814ff; on-line photograph of grave in Quaker Burial Ground, Edinburgh.)

5. John H. Kent (c. 1829–?) was a portrait photographer in Rochester who took numerous pictures of SBA. (Federal Census, 1880; city directories, 1882, 1883; *Rochester History* 52 [Winter 1990]: 22–23.)

6. George Haven Putnam (1844–1930) was president from 1872 to 1930 of the publishing firm G. P. Putnam & Son at 27 West Twenty-third Street. (*ANB*.)

7. In two issues, 4 and 11 October 1884, the *Woman's Journal* reprinted Francis King Carey, "Women of the Twentieth Century, First Article," from the *Princeton Review*, September 1884. Carey traced the sexual division of labor to the relatively recent triumph in England of the common law, with its absurd faith in the oneness of husband and wife. Both issues of the *Journal* included columns by T. W. Higginson about Grover Cleveland's probity and social purity. After the election, Higginson resigned his position at the *Journal* and refused reelection to office in the American association. (Lucy Stone to Mrs. Hussey, 28 November 1884, and to T. W. Higginson, 18 December 1884, in Wheeler, *Loving Warriors*, 287–89; *Woman's Journal*, 27 December 1884.)

8. Richard Thomas Merrick (1826–1885), a distinguished lawyer of Washington, D.C., and a Democrat, prosecuted the Star Route Cases in 1882 and

1883, cases that revealed widespread corruption in financing special southern and western mail routes. Although Merrick used his experience to illustrate the need for a Democrat in the White House, neither political party escaped the investigation entirely. (*ACAB.*)

9. Democratic Congressman William Dorsheimer joined Richard Merrick in a series of large Democratic rallies in northern New York, at which the atmosphere in Washington was deemed "hostile to purity and economy" and James G. Blaine was described as incapable of reform. (*BDAC*; *New York Times*, 22 October 1884.)

10. Belva Lockwood entered the presidential race on September 3, when she accepted the nomination of a new Equal Rights party based in California. Earlier in the campaign season she had disagreed publicly with the advice of SBA and ECS to stand by the Republican party and urged suffragists, instead, to back John P. St. John and the Prohibition party. SBA remained aloof from Lockwood's campaign. To Elizabeth Harbert, she wrote on October 6 that she would leave it to journalists to react. "They are making good natured items thus far," she observed. The campaign, she believed, "has no solid foundation." Evidence has not been found to support the frequent claims that SBA acted or spoke in public against Lockwood's candidacy. (*New York Times*, 20 October 1884; *Our Herald*, September 1884; *Woman's Journal*, 23 August 1884; *Film*, 23:966–71; Jill Norgren, "Lockwood in '84," *Wilson Quarterly* 26 [Autumn 2002]: 12–21.)

11. Martha Dandridge Custis Washington (1731–1802), wife of George Washington.

12. After lecturing in Brockport, New York, on November 7, SBA continued west into Ohio, where she spoke in Cleveland, Painesville, and Toledo, among other places, and continued to Indianapolis, where she visited May Sewall around November 22. (*Film*, 23:994–95, 997–1004.)

13. Sending this letter to her children, ECS wrote on it, "Perhaps you & Hattie may enjoy Susan's letter & Marguerite too as she knows her now."

169 ❧ SBA TO THOMAS W. PALMER

Johnstown N.Y. Dec. 1, 1884

My Dear Friend   Senator Palmer

It just occurs to me that the President of the Senate[1] will have to appoint a member on our W.S. Com. to fill the vacancy of Senator Anthony[2]—and I want to beg of you to use your influence to get a good & strong man placed there—say

Hoar of Mass.—[3]
Cameron— "   Wis—
Logan—   Ill—
Platt —   Ct—

—you may know others equally strong who are friendly—[4]

And—I want to say to you—that I hope you will watch the approach of our 16th am't bill—on the Calendar—and have all of your Committee—& our friends on the floor of the Senate—standing ready to make sure of action upon it—and their best speeches in its favor—as well as their good votes—

My feeling now is that the wisest step for the Republicans in Congress is to make every possible effort to secure the <u>passage</u> of our 16th am't resolution—and thus put the decision of woman's political emancipation into the hands of the state legislatures—and thus place the question where we may hope to get the proposition ratified before our next Presidential election!! Who doubts that if the women of the nation could have voted—that we should have been saved the humiliation of seeing Grover Cleveland installed in the White House!![5]— Now do help all the Republicans to see this necessity for woman's help— Hoping for the best—I am very sincerely yours

                          Susan B. Anthony

❝ ALS, on NWSA letterhead, Women's History Collection, Division of Political History, National Museum of American History, DSI.

1. George Edmunds was president pro tem of the Senate.

2. Senator Henry Anthony died in Providence, Rhode Island, on 2 September 1884.

3. In addition to George Hoar and John Logan, SBA lists Angus Cameron (1826–1897), Republican of Wisconsin, and Orville Hitchcock Platt (1827–1905), Republican of Connecticut. Cameron served in the Senate from 1875 to 1885. As a member of the Senate Committee on Privileges and Elections in 1878, he supported Aaron Sargent's constitutional amendment for woman suffrage. Platt entered the Senate in 1879 and served until his death. (*BDAC*; *Papers*, 3:346, 367–68n, 410, 429.)

4. Next to SBA's list, Palmer wrote "Sheffield" for William Paine Sheffield (1820–1907), who was appointed in November to take Henry Anthony's seat. Sheffield served only until 20 January 1885, when an elected successor took his place. He was appointed to the Committee on Woman Suffrage on December 4. (*BDAC*; *Congressional Record*, 48th Cong., 2d sess., 51.)

5. Grover Cleveland won the presidential election by the very slim plurality

of twenty-three thousand votes but a more decisive majority of thirty-seven votes in the Electoral College.

170   SPEECH BY SBA TO THE RHODE ISLAND WOMAN SUFFRAGE ASSOCIATION

EDITORIAL NOTE: SBA spoke several times at the two-day annual meeting of the Rhode Island Woman Suffrage Association, where she joined Lucy Stone, Henry Blackwell, Frederick Douglass, and William Lloyd Garrison, Jr., at the invitation of Elizabeth Chace and Frederic Hinckley. Early in the meeting, SBA delivered a variant of her well-known lecture "Bread and Ballot." Later, she urged suffragists to work for those votes in the power of the legislature to grant and, as she advised in other states, seek municipal suffrage. On the final evening, when the meeting had moved from the State House to Blackstone Hall, SBA followed Henry Blackwell to make this speech about the importance of Congress. If reconciliation was the intent of gathering the divided leadership into one place, differences of opinion could not be erased. Garrison chastised those who would ally the cause with the "demagogue" Benjamin Butler or any other corrupt politician, and another speaker so insulted Belva Lockwood for her support of Mormons that Douglass felt obliged to rise in her defense. (*Film*, 23:1012–24.)

[4 December 1884]

Miss Susan B. Anthony was received with hearty applause. She paid a grateful tribute to the memory of Paulina Wright Davis, and to the memory of Senator Anthony, one of their best and noblest friends. The year had been sad with the record of distinguished dead, who had been firm and prominent in their support of woman suffrage. Among these she mentioned Bishop Simpson, Senator Anthony, who, on the 12th day of December 1866, made a motion to strike the word "male" from a bill regulating the suffrage in the District of Columbia, and made that capital speech in its behalf,[1] Sarah Pugh, the friend and companion of Lucretia Mott,[2] and other famous names. Miss Anthony discussed at some length the question of extending the suffrage. Miss Anthony urged that her hearers should aid her in endeavoring to obtain the consent of Congress to submit to the State Legislatures an amendment providing that no citizen shall be disfranchised on account of sex. She spoke in strong terms of gratitude of the report of a majority of a committee of the Senate last spring, in favor of submitting a woman suffrage amendment to the States. Senator Anthony appended his consent to that report in the following clause:

> The constitution is wisely conservative in the provision for its own amendment. It is eminently proper that, whenever a large number of the people have indicated a desire for an amendment, the judgment of the amending power should be consulted. In view of the extensive agitation of the question of woman suffrage, and the numerous and respectable petitions that have been presented to Congress in its support, I unite with the committee in recommending that the proposed amendment be submitted to the States.[3]

"Well may Rhode Island be proud," said Miss Anthony, "of the hand that penned that clause. I wrote to Senator Anthony that it was worth a whole volume of rhetoric, because it acknowledged that the agitation was sufficiently respectable in numbers and character to justify the submission of the proposed amendment to the States. In a communication, under date of March 4, 1884, Senator Anthony wrote to me as follows:

> The enfranchisement of woman is one of those great reforms which will come with the progress of civilization, and when it comes those who witness it will wonder that it has been so long delayed. The main argument against it is that the women themselves do not desire it. Many men do not desire it, as is evidenced by their omission to exercise it, but they are not therefore deprived of it. I do not understand that you propose compulsory suffrage, although I am not sure that that would not be for the public advantage, as applied to both sexes. A woman has a right to vote in a corporation of which she is a stockholder, and that she does not generally exercise that right is not an argument against the right itself. The progress that is making in the direction of your efforts is satisfactory and encouraging."

Miss Anthony went on to state that of 124 members who voted against the proposed amendment in the House, all were Democrats except four; of the eighty-five who voted "yes," all were Republicans except thirteen.[4] Miss Anthony earnestly urged the Congressional agitation as the method most likely to secure success. Miss Anthony was applauded at the close.

∽ *Providence Daily Journal*, 5 December 1884.

1. Henry Blackwell had just spoken about Henry Anthony and his speech in the Senate during debate on the District of Columbia franchise bill in December 1866. Anthony did not make the motion to include women in the bill's provisions, as here indicated, but he was one of the rare Republicans who spoke and voted in its favor. His speech was reproduced in *History*, 2:106–8. See also *Papers*, 2:8–10.

2. Sarah Pugh died in Germantown, Pennsylvania, on 1 August 1884.

3. Henry Anthony joined the majority in its favorable report on the amendment, but rather than signing the report he wrote, "My view of the subject is embodied in my qualified assent to the report heretofore made," and repeated what he wrote in 1882, here quoted by SBA. (Senate, Committee on Woman Suffrage, *Report to Accompany S.R. 19*, 28 March 1884, 48th Cong., 1st sess., S. Rept. 399, Pt. 1, Serial 2175.)

4. On SBA's calculations about the House vote on a committee for woman suffrage (not an amendment), see notes above at 20 December 1883 and 30 July 1884.

171 ∽   SBA TO THOMAS W. PALMER

Rochester N.Y. Dec. 12/84

My Dear Friend   Senator Palmer

Yours of the 8th is here— That the 12,000 women voters of Washington Territory out of the 42,000—that is one third—could not carry the election of the Republican candidate for Congress—should not be counted against the women altogether—[1] I know that Mrs Duniway made a thorough canvass of the Territory in behalf of the Republican Party— You may possibly find that the Democratic candidate is in <u>favor</u> of Woman Suffrage—and the Republican opposed— if so—that might account for the women's voting for the Democrat—provided they did so vote—which I do not know— But—whichever way they voted—we must have <u>more</u> <u>Woman</u> <u>Suffrage</u>—

And now I see that Dacota is asking to come into the Union—[2] If the bill to admit her has the little word "<u>male</u>"—in its suffrage clause—will you see to it that a motion is at once made to strike it out?— Or that such a motion is made at the proper time— For we surely must not allow another exclusively <u>male</u> state to come into the Union—

Hoping that you will set <u>our</u> Select Committee about this work of protest against any further exclusion of women—I am very sincerely yours

~ *Susan B. Anthony*

~ ALS, on NWSA letterhead, Women's History Collection, Division of Political History, National Museum of American History, DSI.

1. In the November election for Washington's territorial delegate to Congress, voters chose the Democrat Charles Stewart Voorhees (1853–1909) over Republican James M. Armstrong (1844–?), a man closely tied to the Northern Pacific Railroad. Voorhees won by only one hundred and forty-six votes, but to blame the women was farfetched. Voorhees trounced Armstrong in Kings County where Republican voters shared his hostility to the Northern Pacific. (*BDAC*; H. K. Hines, *An Illustrated History of the State of Washington* [Chicago, 1893], 380–81; Robert E. Ficken, *Washington Territory* [Pullman, Wash., 2002], 199–200.)

2. On 9 December 1884, the Senate debated a bill (S. 1682) introduced in the previous session to enable the southern portion of Dakota Territory to form a state government. (*Congressional Record*, 48th Cong., 2d sess., 103, 106–11.)

172 ~ SBA TO ELIZABETH BOYNTON HARBERT

The Riggs House   Washington D.C. Dec. 21, 1884—

My Dear Elizabeth B. H.

I have heard it whispered that there was talk of <u>your</u> taking "<u>Our Herald</u>"— to Chicago— I can see that if Mrs Gougar & Mrs Colby would both give their papers over to you as managing editor—<u>at Chicago</u>—and each of them devote herself to lecturing—organizing & soliciting subscriptions—that the ↑one↓ paper might be made a success—financially—and <u>many</u> times more of a success morally & intellectually—

I do wish all the women who want a paper—on this side the Rocky Mountains—would concentrate upon <u>one</u> paper—either in Chicago or New York— I do not care very much which— Mrs Blake would be a good supervisor in New York—& Mrs Harbert in Chicago— This settled upon—then our National auxilliaries & officers in all the states would be urged by us to work for building up the paper— The W.C.T.U. have thus concentrated now—and their ⁺one↓ paper is vastly more than the <u>two</u> used to be!¹

Now my dear—do you see the way to any adjustment in this direction— It is an impossibility for <u>each</u> state to sustain a <u>local paper</u>—but quite possible for all the States to sustain <u>National</u> paper—that should publish the work of each state & all local work & workers— I feel very deeply about the matter—and some plan ought to be devised by which our best <u>speaking talent</u> in each state shall not be fastened to the <u>editorial</u> & <u>publishing chair</u>!— If all the states—say our Vice Presidents—will join in pledges to get subscribers for one paper—it would be safe— Can't you present a plan—<u>practicable</u>—that we may discuss & perchance adopt—at our executive sessions here!!

Our 16ᵗʰ am't bill is sure to be reached very soon in January— Will you not your-self write—and stir up ever so many others to do the same—to each of your Ill. Senators—begging him to stand ready to both speak & vote for it— Every one the 76 Senators ought to be pelted with scores of letters from scores of the best women of their state— Do help to stir up as many as possible to thus write— Will you be able to be with us this Winter?—

Oh—another question— Shall we not make one more tremendous effort to roll up a mammoth petition—to be presented at the 1ˢᵗ Session of the 49ᵗʰ Congress—that is to say at the next session—1885 & 1886— If the Lucy Stone—& the W.C.T.U. women would join with us—it seems to me we might make a larger petition than ever before? How can we bring a <u>heavy</u> pressure to bear upon the 49ᵗʰ Congress? Lovingly yours

❧ *Susan B. Anthony*

❧ ALS, on NWSA letterhead, Box 2, Elizabeth Harbert Collection, CSmH.

1. Beginning in January 1883, the National Woman's Christian Temper-

ance Union published the *Union Signal* weekly from Chicago. It brought together the *Signal*, begun in 1875 as a national but very weak paper, and *Our Union*, the paper of the Illinois union.

173 ⮜ SBA TO ECS

The Riggs House   Washington D.C.   Dec. 21/84

My Dear Mrs Stanton

Here is the result of my appeal in your behalf[1]—so you may as well set your self about compiling the <u>laws</u> <u>for</u> <u>women</u>—in the several states & countries— I judge he means—legal—educational & industrial—at any rate the department will give you broad scope—

Senato Palmer—is preparing his speech on our 16th am't bill during these recess days—he specially wants the statistics of <u>women</u> who support themselves— can you give him any facts—if so send them to T. W. Palmer   Detroit—Mich—

Senator Miller[2] of our state says he shall make a speech for us—& Senator Lapham is all ready to do— Did I tell you Gen'l Butler says the Will case will come on by the middle of January—and if it does—& goes in my favor—I will pay your board here—for a month—so that you can meet the Senators—especially the <u>southern Senators</u>— I hear they complain that they are never approached by us—

I shall stop to see you a day or so—but my work is <u>here</u>—until our bill is reached—discussed & voted upon in the Senate— So get ready to do your work here too— I do wish our best women had cash to work with—

⮜ *S. B. A*

⮜ ALS, A-68 Mary Earhart Dillon Collection, Series III, Box 2, MCR-S. Written on verso of D. O. Kellogg to SBA, 19 December 1884, and in *Film* at that date. Was enclosed in ECS to E. M. B. Harbert, 23 December 1884.

1. SBA wrote this letter on the verso of one from Day Otis Kellogg (1837–1904), written from Vineland, New Jersey, on 19 December on letterhead of the *Encyclopaedia Britannica—American Reprint*. Kellogg thanked ECS for unspecified aid in completing an entry on popular suffrage and acknowledged SBA's suggestion that ECS contribute directly to his publication. "I contemplate . . . taking up the general subject of women and their legal position when

we reach that letter of the alphabet," he wrote, "& shall be most happy to assign that to Mrs Stanton if she is then willing to take it." The entry "Women, Their Education and Enfranchisement in the United States" was written by Ellen M. Henrotin in Kellogg's edition of 1897. Kellogg left his post as an Episcopal minister in Providence, Rhode Island, to become professor of English literature and history at the new Kansas State University in 1870. Returning east in 1874, he settled in Philadelphia, where he took an interest in organizing the city's charities and assumed his late father's job as editor of the encyclopedia. (Day Otis Kellogg, ed., *New American Supplement to the Latest Edition of the Encyclopaedia Britannica* [New York, 1897], 5:3180–82; Kate Stephens, "In Memory of Dr. Day Otis Kellogg: Sometime Professor of English Literature and History," *Graduate Magazine of the University of Kansas* 3 [March 1905]: 212–16; Clifford S. Griffin, *The University of Kansas: A History* [Lawrence, Kan., 1974], 54–55, 63, 68; *New York Times*, 28, 29 January 1904; with assistance of the University Archives, University of Kansas.)

2. Warner Miller (1838–1918), elected to the House of Representatives as a Republican from New York in 1879, resigned when he won election to the Senate in 1881 to complete the term of Thomas C. Platt. He lost his bid for reelection in 1887. (*BDAC*.)

174 ⤙ ECS TO SBA

[*Johnstown, N.Y., after 21? December*][1] 1884.

[D]ear Susan:

My trunk is all packed and all my arrangements made, and, what is [m]ore, I am longing for the fray. I am actually glad in the prospect of a [c]onvention and meeting with all our co-adjutors once more. A year shut up [i]n a community of snails has developed in me an amount of enthusiasm that [i]s a surprize to myself. They say people always revive just before they [g]o out altogether; so if immediately after this performance I have symptoms of softening of the brain, you need not be surprized. Sincerely,

⤙ *Elizabeth Cady Stanton.*

⤙ Typed transcript, ECS Papers, NjR. In *Film* at December? 1884.

1. Dated only "1884" by the transcribers of the lost manuscript, this letter may have answered SBA's of December 21. See also ECS to Elizabeth M. Harbert, 23 December 1884, *Film*, 23:1069–72, about ECS's plans to go to Washington.

175 ≫ MATILDA HINDMAN TO SBA

20 Stockton Ave. Allegheny City Pa   Dec. 25ᵗʰ 1884.

Dear Miss Anthony,

I am again at home, and wishing to hear from you. I write hoping you will receive this. On my way from Boston I stopped over in Philadelphia two days.[1] Miss Adaline Thomson, your true friend, most kindly entertained me, and aided me in meeting the friends of suffrage. How many noble, true-hearted women we meet in this work. I had the pleasure of meeting Mr. Robert Purvis in his own home, he and other friends seem willing to do all they can to help us with the paper.

Miss Grew also gave me much encouragement. The State Asso. will ↑raise↓ money and devote it to the same. Now dear Miss Anthony I must tell you what I have done. Mrs. Livermore, Mrs. Lucy Stone, Mr. Wᵐ I. Bowditch[2] and Hon John M. Broomall ↑also Miss Eastman↓[3] have all consented to become contributors, Mrs. Livermore's first article will be in this week's issue, I therefore have put your name and Mrs. Stanton's in also, as contributors. You can realize that the 200,000 readers of this paper should have the best thoughts of the leading thinkers in this movement, and as the columns will be open to all our friends we wish to place all on an equal footing in presenting the cause. You understand, and I do hope you and Mrs. Stanton will not think I have done wrong, for I feel certain you will both favor us with your views ↑through the paper↓.

I hope to be able to attend the Washington Convention and talk over plans of work, for henceforth my work will be confined to my own state, and with proper plans we may be able to do much this year.[4]

I wish I could go to New Orleans but I fear I cannot.[5] May I hear from you soon. Send me anything you wish to have published and I will make room for it. Direct to 20 Stockton Ave., Allegheny City, Pa. With much love I remain Your friend

≫ *Matilda Hindman*

The daily circulation of the paper is 21,000, the weekly, 32,000. These are different classes and as the weekly goes into the families of the leading citizens in Western Pennsylvania and eastern Ohio you can readily see what a work can be done, for there are probably not less than four times that number of readers [*sideways at margin*] over

Will you not try and persuade Mrs. Stanton to write, I have written to her so often I do not like to write again. If she absolutely ↑refuses↓ of course I will take her name off the list. M. H.[6]

❧ ALS, Box 2, Elizabeth Harbert Collection, CSmH.

1. Matilda Hindman, who had seen SBA at the Rhode Island Woman Suffrage Association's annual meeting earlier this month, describes plans for a column, "Woman's Realm," that she would edit in the *Pittsburgh Commercial Gazette*. Her visits in Philadelphia to Robert Purvis of the Citizens' Suffrage Association and Mary Grew of the American Woman Suffrage Association suggest a calculated effort to bridge the divided movement. The same theme is evident below in her list of contributors to the column. All the writers named, except Mary Livermore and ECS, had also attended the meeting in Rhode Island.

2. William Ingersoll Bowditch (1819–1909), of Brookline, Massachusetts, was a real estate lawyer, abolitionist, early investor in the *Woman's Journal*, author of pamphlets on woman's rights, and current president of the Massachusetts Woman Suffrage Association. (Garrison, *Letters*, 6:379; Prospectus of *Woman's Journal*, 14 October 1869, NAWSA Papers, DLC.)

3. Mary F. Eastman (c. 1834–1908), of Tewksbury, Massachusetts, was a teacher before discovering her talent as a lecturer. She was closely identified with the American Woman Suffrage Association. (Federal Census, 1880; Julia Ward Howe, ed., *Sketches of Representative Women of New England* [Boston, 1904], 484–89; *Woman's Journal*, 21 November 1908.)

4. Hindman and Edward Davis represented Pennsylvania at the National's meeting in January 1885, where Hindman was named to the nominating committee and selected to deliver an evening lecture. (Washington *National Republican*, 21, 22 January 1885, *Film*, 24:3–7.)

5. The National Woman Suffrage Association had announced plans for a meeting in New Orleans on 6 and 7 January 1885, at the World's Industrial and Cotton Centennial Exposition. The event was later canceled. (*Film*, 23:1043.)

6. When SBA sent this letter on to Elizabeth Harbert, she wrote upon it the message, "Dear Mrs Harbert— This is to add to your Press report— I do hope you can send us your report—if you cannot come & bring & give it!!"

176 ⤳ ECS TO LAURA CURTIS BULLARD

Johnstown [*N. Y.*] Dec 28th [*1884*]

Dear Laura,

Have you yet reached your native shore? I long to hear how & where you are, & what you are thinking of the great questions, of time & eternity.

I hear of Theodore[1] occasionally through my children, & the last I heard from you was ~~the~~ of the day you dined with them in Paris.

Do write & tell me of your wanderings, your voyage, your hopes & fears. I am amusing myself shocking people with all manner of heresies, political, religious, social. When I can discover your retreat I will send you some of my pronunciamentoes, though not with the faintest hope of shocking you, unless you have indeed had "a change of life" for which I have some reason to hope as you had the advantage of the salvation army excitement while abroad[2] & now of Moody[3] in our own country. Did you return in time to enjoy the sweets of our presidential campaign. Burchards[4] alliteration, & Beechers[5] indictment of the chastity of our fathers, husbands, brothers, & sons? Well we ↑have↓ learned one thing that chastity is a virtue, intended preeminently for women, for which the sons of men in high places have no use. Even the immaculate T. W. H. in the Woman's Journal said it was not a necessary qualification for a political official.[6] Lucy published the sentiment without comment, & the people said Amen, & elected their President who did not possess that jewel, & discarded Blaine because of divers lapses from political virtues. I suppose as we cannot vote, & hence have no political virtues, that social purity is more important for us, as we must have something to stand on. With love for yourself & mother[7] good night [*in margin of first page*] sincerely yours

⤳ *Elizabeth Cady Stanton.*

⤳ ALS, ECS Papers, DLC.

1. That is, Theodore Tilton.
2. Despite its rapid growth and talk of its merger with the Anglican church, the Salvation Army remained a controversial religious organization that met

popular and official opposition in Britain. By one count, there were six hundred army members imprisoned in 1884 for behavior judged to disturb the peace. (Horridge, *Salvation Army, Origins and Early Days*, 109.)

3. Dwight Lyman Moody (1837–1899), an American evangelist, led revivals in England while ECS was abroad and returned to the United States in July 1884. Through the fall, he conducted revivals across the northern tier of New York State. (James F. Findlay, Jr., *Dwight L. Moody: American Evangelist, 1837–1899* [Chicago, 1969], 355–56; *New York Times*, 13 September, 11, 20 November 1884.)

4. Samuel Dickinson Burchard (1812–1891), the pastor of the Murray Hill Presbyterian Church in New York, uttered the fateful description of Democrats as the party of "rum, Romanism, and rebellion," when he welcomed James Blaine to a rally of ministers in New York on 29 October 1884. Democrats made haste to use the phrase to discredit Blaine with voters. (*DAB*.)

5. Henry Ward Beecher (1813–1887), the minister of Brooklyn's Plymouth Church, abandoned the Republican party in 1884 to campaign for Grover Cleveland. To audiences in Brooklyn and Jersey City, Beecher declared, "If all the men in the State who have broken the seventh commandment would vote for Cleveland, we would elect him." His explicit defense of men's sexual sins amused those who still believed that Beecher had seduced his parishioner Elizabeth Tilton. (*ANB*; Paxton Hibben, *Henry Ward Beecher: An American Portrait* [New York, 1927], 341–48; *New York Tribune*, 28, 29 October 1884; *New York Times*, 28 October 1884. See also *Papers* 1–3.)

6. T. W. Higginson drew this distinction clearly in an editorial headed "Public and Private Virtues," in the *Woman's Journal*, 30 August 1884. In selecting a president, public virtue should be the primary consideration, he wrote; honesty and a willingness to destroy the spoils system were the only pertinent standards for a candidate. That Grover Cleveland had "once fallen before what may be, under some circumstances, one of the strongest of human temptations, does not necessarily so disqualify a man," because chastity was a secondary standard for a president. ECS was unfair to Lucy Stone to say she did not counter Higginson. In the same issue of the *Woman's Journal*, Stone rejected his distinction between public and private virtue and opined that the safety of home and family was no less important than public integrity.

7. Lucy W. Curtis (c. 1809–?).

177 ⇒ LUCY STONE TO SBA

Boston, Jan. 2 1885.

Dear Miss Anthony

I owe you an apology for delay in reply to yours of the 24th ult. But I have been over busy.

Of course, I have had no opportunity since its receipt to consult the officers of the association. But as the American association has always urged a 16th amendment there is no doubt they would unite in an Extra Effort to push for it. But I am sure they would want their part in it to be counted to their credit—

The Woman's Journal will encourage the united plan. It will make its own statement and take charge of ↑the↓ part that will especially come to the American association, and be ready to cooperate according to its judgment and in a spirit of good will with the whole movement[1]

Wishing you a happy new year and as many of them as you may desire Yours for our common cause

⇒ *Lucy Stone*

⇒ ALS, on letterhead of Massachusetts Woman Suffrage Association for 1884, year corrected, Blackwell Papers, DLC.

1. On 26 February 1885, John D. Long presented to the House of Representatives a memorial of the American Woman Suffrage Association in support of a constitutional amendment. (*Congressional Record*, 48th Cong., 2d sess., 2224.)

178 ～ ECS TO THE EDITOR, "WOMAN'S REALM"

[*Early January 1885*]¹

To the Editor of Woman's Realm.

BILL FOR EXTENDING PARLIAMENTARY FRANCHISE TO WOMEN.²

Be it enacted by the Queen's most Excellent Majesty, by and with the advice and consent of the Lords Spiritual and Temporal, and Commons, in this present Parliament assembled, and by the authority of the same, as follows:

1. This Act may be cited as the Representation of the People (Extension to Women) Act, 1884.

2. For all purposes of and incidental to the voting for members to serve in Parliament women shall have the same rights as men, and all enactments relating to or concerned in such elections shall be construed accordingly.

Provided that nothing in this Act contained shall enable women under coverture to be registered or to vote at such election.

(Prepared and brought in by Mr. Woodall, Mr. Illingworth, Mr. Coleridge, Mr. Stansfeld, Mr. Yorke and Baron Henry de Worms.)³

The above is the bill now before Parliament demanding in one section "that women shall have the same rights as men," and in the closing sentence making marriage a "disability" for women, though not for men. How can women have the same rights as men if in marriage, where the vast majority are, their civil and social rights are ignored, because their political equality is not recognized? How those grand women, who are the hope of England, who lead in this movement, can be so blind to this false position as to the ethics of this question, I am at a loss to understand. The principle recognized in this bill is that monstrous idea at the foundation of all law for women, the old common law of England, which makes the wife the abject slave of her husband.

The basic idea of this bill is the slavery of woman in marriage, which statesmen and bishops fully believe, and which the women who consent to this bill now fully indorse. "Wife beating" is one of the crying sins in England, and the lower orders carry out practically the theories of their leaders. Perhaps they do not understand the origin and significance of the word "coverture," but they have learned the essence and spirit of it, from the centuries of degradation and misery that statesmen and churchmen in their codes and creeds have inflicted on women. It is a very short-sighted policy to claim Parliamentary suffrage for "spinsters" at such a sacrifice of principle. It is no answer to this to say that in England suffrage is based on property, because by recent legislation married women can hold their property independently of their husbands. Hence they may be the house-holders and taxpayers practically though in that position described by the hateful phrase "under coverture."

Some of the women in the suffrage movement there see all this, and have made an active opposition to such half-measures, but the majority are blinded and cajoled by the special pleading of their friends in the House of Commons. Yet it is both pitiful and amusing to see that with all their care to keep the "spinsters" uppermost in the minds of their legislators, that whenever the bill comes up for debate the discussion always turns on the effect the enfranchisement of married women will have on the family. There's the rub. "Men hate," as John Stuart Mill says, "to have a recognized equal at their own fireside."[4]

  Elizabeth Cady Stanton.

  "Woman's Realm," *Pittsburgh Commercial Gazette*, n.d., SBA scrapbook 11, Rare Books, DLC. In *Film* at December? 1884?

1. The date of this article from an undated clipping falls between Christmas Day 1884, when Matilda Hindman wrote that ECS had not yet answered her letters, and the start of the National association's Washington convention on 20 January 1885. Just below this article, in the same column, Hindman noted that SBA was in Washington preparing for that convention.

2. On 12 June 1884, members of Parliament rejected suffragists' attempt to amend the Third Reform Bill to give parliamentary suffrage to women. Chang-ing their strategy, suffragists in the House of Commons introduced a separate bill on November 10 to confer parliamentary suffrage on "duly-qualified women." This bill gained the support of Jacob Bright, but on November 17, when it was scheduled for a second reading, William Woodall, who had replaced Hugh Mason as parliamentary leader, withdrew the bill. On November 19, he returned

with the bill quoted in full by ECS, known as the "Parliamentary Franchise (Extension to Women) (No. 2) Bill," but he had lost the support of Bright. Woodall (1832–1901), a Liberal, sat for Stoke-on-Trent from 1880 to 1885. (*History*, 3:877–90; Blackburn, *Women's Suffrage in the British Isles*, Chart I and 161–65; Holton, *Suffrage Days*, 67–68; *Hansard Parliamentary Debates*, 3d ser., vol. 293 [1884], col. 1439, 1855, and vol. 294 [1884], col. 23; *Who's Who of British Members of Parliament*, vol. 2.)

3. The bill's other backers were Conservatives Henry De Worms (1840–1903), John Reginald Yorke (1836–1912), and Coleridge John Kennard (1828–1890), and Liberal Alfred Illingworth (1827–1907). (*Who's Who of British Members of Parliament*, vols. 1–2.)

4. ECS rewrites a sentence in John Stuart Mill, "The Subjection of Women," in Mill, *Collected Works*, 21:299.

179 ✒ LUCY STONE TO SBA

Boston, Jan 20 1885

Dear Susan

Yours came yesterday & I directed the complete sets of our tracts to be sent you.[1]

Will you send me please the papers that contain the best accts of the Washington convention that I may make up a report? A good debate in the Senate will be invaluable. I hope you may have as pleasant weather as we are having.

Mr. Ransom told me yesterday that our case will come up on Friday next probably, but that we shall not hear any decision before Apr or May— But <u>then</u> he fully expects it will be on our side— What a blessing it will be to have so much with which to work! Yours truly

✒ *Lucy Stone*

✒ ALS, on letterhead of *Woman's Journal*, Blackwell Papers, DLC.

1. Among the tracts was a new one by Daniel P. Livermore, *Woman Suffrage Defended by Irrefutable Arguments, and All Objections to Woman's Enfranchisement Carefully Examined and Completely Answered* (1885), written to answer Boston's antisuffragists. According to the Washington *National Republican*, 22 January 1885, the two hundred page book was available at the door as delegates entered the National association's convention. (*Film*, 24:6–7.)

·(⟵————⟩⟩⟨————⟩)·

180 ⭒ MEETING OF THE NATIONAL WOMAN SUFFRAGE ASSOCIATION

EDITORIAL NOTE: The National Woman Suffrage Association met in Washington for three days, beginning on 20 January 1885, with executive sessions each morning at the Riggs House and public sessions in the afternoon and evening at the Universalist Church of Our Father. ECS presided. Resolutions read to the audience in the evening of January 20 urged Congress to pass the suffrage amendment, remembered supporters who died in 1884, and praised the Woman's Christian Temperance Union for its support of the amendment. Set apart from the others was a lengthy resolution about women and the churches. On January 21, after delegates adopted the first resolutions without debate, ECS spoke about the religious one, indicating that discussion on it would take place the next day. Despite her efforts, discussion began immediately. (Washington *Evening Star*, 21 January 1885, *Film*, 24:11.)

[21 January 1885]

Then followed the reading of the resolution concerning which so much has been said. It was as follows:

> *Whereas*, The dogmas incorporated in the religious creeds derived from Judaism, teaching that woman was an afterthought in creation, her sex a misfortune, marriage a condition of subordination, and maternity a curse, are contrary to the law of God as revealed in nature and the precepts of Christ; and,
>
> *Whereas*, These dogmas are an insidious poison sapping the vitality of our civilization, blighting woman and laying their palsying hand upon humanity; therefore,
>
> *Resolved*, That we denounce these dogmas wherever they are enunciated; and we will withdraw our personal support from any organization or person so holding and teaching. And,
>
> *Resolved*, That we call upon the Christian ministry, as

leaders of thought, to teach and enforce the fundamental idea of creation that man was made in the image of God, male and female, and given equal dominion over the earth, but none over each other. And further, we invite their co-operation in securing the recognition of the cardinal point of our creed, that in true religion there is neither male nor female, neither bond nor free, but all are one.[1]

The following report of the discussion was almost entirely furnished by the stenographer.[2] After the reading of the resolution Mrs. Stanton said:

As this is a very radical resolution we will have it come up for consideration to-morrow. It claims what has never been claimed before—the full and complete equality of woman everywhere, in church as well as state. Woman has no recognition in the church, and we now claim our proper place there. She has been licensed to preach in the Methodist church;[3] and some of the Baptist, Unitarian and Universalist churches have recognized the equality of woman. But the majority do not recognize women in any way, although for the first three centuries after the proclamation of Christianity, woman had a place in the church. They were deaconesses, and elders, and were ordained, and administered the Sacrament. Yet, through the Catholic church, these rites were done away in Christendom, and they have never been restored. Now we intend to demand equal rights in the church. Inasmuch as we compose the principal membership of the church; make all the gowns; work the altar-cloths, and do other work, we propose to have some recognition[4] there as equals. And that is the idea of this new Gospel—full and perfect equality of the feminine element. Surely, if worth recognition anywhere, it is in the religions of our country.

A lady in the audience (Mrs. McPherson, of Iowa):[5] I would like a word. That resolution is a little hard on Judaism. I don't deny but that it is the custom to ignore women as there stated, but I do hold that the Bible does not teach it. It says that Christ is the equality of the law. Christ's teachings are opposed to that selfishness that keeps women out.

Miss Anthony: I feel like making an amendment. It does not matter where the dogma came from. It would seem much better to cut out that part of the resolution which says "derived from Judaism," and simply say, "the dogma that teaches this inequality."

Dr. McMurdy,[6] of Washington, (the man that got up the famous ministers' dinner in New York that brought out Parson Burchard): I don't think that any cause is subserved by stating anything which is not true. Anything which is untrue when stated, creates prejudice and drives off people. Nothing this Association can do will affect my action; I have the right to my own opinion upon this subject. The more comprehensive and broader your views, the sooner you will achieve your victory. No political party can restrict or confine its action to the few. There is a positive statement in that platform. It is not true that the Jewish religion teaches what the resolution says. Women were teachers under the old dispensation. It is not true that the old churches ever departed from this custom. The Roman Catholic church has its women set apart and ordained, and given the title of "reverend." And some of those most noble ladies deserve that title. And they are ordained in the Episcopal church. Bishop Potter[7] has ordained Deaconesses. Their object is to do just what was done in the early ages of the church. Can these ladies show that they are not doing that? I speak not as a sectarian when I say the Catholic church will come up to its duty. I have the most profound respect for the lady (Mrs. Stanton), and if she has evidence that women have administered the Lord's Supper, it will be something entirely new to me. I know of no such thing in the church; but I do know that women baptized, and do so to-day. This baptism may be irregular in some cases, but is considered good. I trust no extravagant position will be taken—none that will merely provoke contention in the wrong direction. You have a great work to do, and I hope you will have the wisdom to confine yourself to it. The best men in the anti-slavery movement kept to one idea.

Mr. John B. Wolf:[8] While I agree with Miss Anthony in regard to striking out certain words in regard to this dogma being found in the Talmud, the Koran, or the Bible, nevertheless it is true that that dogma has its foundation somewhere, and when you have accomplished your purpose, you will uproot both cause and sequence together. While I agree with the greater part of what the gentleman who preceded me said, I would like to ask him if it is true that the church, Catholic, Episcopal, Methodist, or any other, recognizes the right of woman to be ordained a bishop and lay her holy hand on others. Until women attain full equality in the highest places, and can perform the highest functions, based upon their right to do so, the work will never be accomplished. Whence this dogma, if not in the religions of the past and present? Whence the greatest opposition to this movement? Whence the opposition to that great guerrilla movement, the woman's temperance movement which is bringing it into harmony with the suffrage movement? When the temperance movement was started, it found its chief opposition in the pulpit. I have myself been barred out of a church, and left it for a neighboring grog shop where I organized a total abstinence society at the bar. This suffrage movement has to encounter a sort of pulpit infallibility.

A lady from New York (who refused to give her name): I hope before this resolution is adopted you will remember how many Christian women among the temperance workers are your friends. I would ask the leaders here if the Methodist church has not stood foremost for women? I challenge any one to show a greater number in any Christian body who have voted for woman suffrage than among the ministry of the Methodist church. I know the relative proportion of voices among the Methodist clergy that are raised for woman's rights and temperance. I do not believe the dogmas referred to in that resolution can be found in the Bible. If faults have crept in we must not blame the Bible.

Miss Anthony: I was on the old Garrison platform, and found long ago that this matter of settling any question of human rights by people's interpretation of the Bible is never satisfactory. I hope we shall not go back to that war. Colonel Higginson once said it was like two persons going into the woods and never meeting. No two can ever interpret alike, and discussion upon it is time wasted. We all know what we want, and that is the recognition of woman's perfect equality—in the home, the church, and the state. We all know that such recognition has never been granted her in the centuries of the past. But for us to begin a discussion here as to who established these dogmas would be anything but profitable. Let those who wish, go back into the history of the past, but I beg it shall not be done on our platform.

Mrs. Shattuck, of Mass.: I agree with Miss Anthony. We do not want to antagonize the force that is working for us. The church is conservative; we are radical; but the church is coming up to our help. Let us not introduce anything extraneous to the question. I believe the church is on our side. Only last Sunday I heard the Rev. Heber Newton[9] state his belief in the political equality of women with men. And others are coming forward in the same way. Do not let us antagonize our friends.

Mrs. Clara B. Colby, of Nebraska: I think there is a misunderstanding about this resolution. Allow me to read it again. I agree with the lady from New York that the Bible is not in fault, but this resolution is aimed not against religion or the Bible, but against dogmas and man's interpretation. (Reads and comments.) Who can deny that these dogmas have been held and taught? And who can deny that they are an insidious poison? Out of these have grown the two standards of morality which are the curse of society, and this dogma of woman's divinely appointed inferiority has, as the resolution states, sapped the vitality of our civilization, blighted woman and laid its palsying hand upon humanity. As a Christian woman and a member of an orthodox church, I stand on this resolution; on the Divine plan of creation as set forth in the first chapter of Genesis, where we are told that man was created male and female, and set over the world to have equal dominion;[10] and on the gospel of the new dispensation, in which there is neither male nor female, bond nor free, but all are one. This resolution avows our loyalty to what we believe to be the true teachings of the Bible, and the co-operation of the Christian ministry is invited in striving to secure the application of the Golden Rule to women.[11]

Mr. E. M. Davis, of Philadelphia: I am glad the resolution has been offered; it will lead to enlightenment. I am surprised to find my friend, Susan B. Anthony, is afraid of discussion. Are you afraid of discussion against rum? If we are to restrict ourselves to suffrage, pure and simple, we have no right to denounce drunkenness. Some one says the Jews favor woman suffrage, and the Catholics, and Episcopalians, and Methodists; but we are not talking of individual members, many of whom do favor it. When the question comes up before them as a church they repudiate it! Show me a religious body in the land that has expressed itself in favor of the equality of women with men! You can't find one—not even among the Quakers. I am glad the resolution came up. I want to hear from its author, Mrs. Stanton—for she, I am sure, was the inspiration of it. I want to say that the great stumbling-block to every reform has always been the clergy, and is to-day. We are told that we must not attack them. But when they fling their fists in our faces, we strike back. That is a part of our duty.

Mrs. Stanton: I am not the author of the resolution as it stands.[12] I wrote one that went to the committee, where it was changed. However, I agree with it substantially. I want to say in reply to one of the gentlemen who have spoken here, that women *did* administer sacraments for three centuries after Christ. I have not the proof with me, but can bring it this evening. There is abundant proof that women did have all these rights in the churches, and that one by one, they were taken away from them. I have studied this question. You may go over the world, and you will find that every form of religion that has breathed upon this earth, has degraded woman. There is not one that has not always made us subject to man. Men may rejoice in them because they make man the head of the woman. I have been traveling over the old world the last few years and have found new food for thought. What power is it that makes the Hindoo woman burn herself on the funeral pyre of her husband? Her religion. What holds the Turkish women in the harem? Their religion. Man, of himself, could not do this; but when he says: "Thus saith the Lord," of course he can do it. By what power do the Mormons perpetuate their abominable system of polygamy? They do it through their religion. So long as ministers stand up and tell us that as Christ is the head of the Church, so is man the head of the woman, how are we to break the chains that have held women down through the ages? You Christian women can look at the Turkish, the Mormon, and the Hindoo women, and wonder how they can be held in such bondage. Look to-day at the work women are doing for the churches! *The church rests on the shoulders of women.* Have we ever yet heard a man preach a sermon from Genesis i:27–28, which declares the full equality of the feminine and masculine element in the Godhead? I never heard such a thing in my life. They invariably shy over that first chapter. They always get up in their pulpits and read that second chapter.[13] Now I ask you if our religion teaches us the dignity of woman? It teaches us that abominable idea of the sixth century— Augustine's idea[14]—that motherhood is a curse; that woman is the author of sin, and is most corrupt. Can we ever cultivate any proper sense of self-respect as long as women take such sentiments from the mouths of the priesthood? Now what we demand is an expurgated edition of the Bible. Men have written it—translated it—revised it, and put in and taken out whatever suited their own ideas. Now what we want is to call a council of women for an expurgated edition of the Bible that shall place us in our true position as equals on this Christian earth. I am not willing that our sons and daughters shall read the Bible as it stands to-day and become poisoned with these ideas of woman's inferiority. I went into many a Catholic church in Europe, where no woman is allowed to sing in the choir. I asked the reason why. I knew; but I wanted to see what they would say. They said it was only because women were not allowed to enter the altar. Women were the authors of sin; we have been the sex that has been denounced from the fifth to the eighteenth century. History shows one continual persecution of woman. It was this that brought about the dark ages. In England I went into the church of good old Dean Stanley.[15] One of the two daughters who showed me around, said: "Do you notice that cover on the altar? Sister and I worked that." I said: "Were you allowed to enter the altar to put it on?" She said: "O, no." I asked her why, and she didn't know. "Shall I tell you?" I said. "It is because the Christian religion has taught that woman was the author of sin, and is therefore a dangerous element, always dragging man down from his high heavenly position—from his spiritual life."

I have been gathering together three or four volumes of the canon laws. They are infamous—so infamous that a council of the Christian church was swamped by them. In republican America, and in the light of the nineteenth century, we must demand that our religion must teach a higher idea in regard to woman. People seem to think we have reached the very end of theology; but let me say that the future is to be as much purer than the past, than our immediate past has been better than the Dark Ages. We want to help roll off the soul of woman the terrible superstitions that have so long repressed her. We want to teach woman self-respect. Self-respect has been educated out of them, or else we could not find them sitting under the preaching of such men as Morgan Dix and Knox-Little. Some one in the Pan-Presbyterian Council in Philadelphia[16] had the audacity to introduce a resolution favoring a little more liberty for women; but that body of Pan-Presbyterians laughed the idea to scorn. When I read that, I was thrilled to the soul with indignation. I cannot tell you the indignation I feel to see teachers and preachers, who pretend to preach divine truth, so degrade woman by preaching the nonsense they do.

Now I hope this resolution will pass. I tell you it is the religious bondage of woman that is to-day the great blockade to her progress. It must be removed.

Mrs. Perkins,[17] of Ohio: I am perfectly willing that man should be the head of the woman as Christ is of the Church, viz: to give his life for her.

Laura De Force Gordon:[18] I hope this resolution will be taken up and discussed to-morrow in the same kindly spirit in which it was written. Let us understand that there is a difference between religion and theology. Understanding that, I think the most timid and ungrown in soul will not be much terrorized. The difference is as broad as that between the teachings of Christ and the theology of Paul.

> EDITORIAL NOTE: According to the *Evening Star*, there was, at this point, great confusion in the hall, and ECS cut short the discussion by adjourning the session. At the executive session on January 22, delegates, in anticipation of further discussion that afternoon, amended the resolution "by omitting the objectionable part referring to Judaism." No record of a formal discussion on the third day has been found; the *National Republican* commented that those people expecting "some interesting developments . . . were doomed to disappointment." The paper also reported that ECS announced that the executive session "had decided that the religious resolution should be debated by the women alone, and had therefore laid it over for a year." In the evening, Laura Gordon spoke at length on canon and feudal law and the separation of church and state. She "took the position that woman does not owe her favorable position to the teachings of the church and that her enfranchisement would not tend to restore the supremacy of ecclesiasticism." She showed "that in proportion as Church and State were united was humanity, especially woman, degraded." At the conclusion of Gordon's speech, ECS rose to close the meeting. (Washington *Evening Star*, 22 January 1885; Washington *National Republican*, 23 January 1885; and *Woman's Tribune*, March 1885; all in *Film*, 24:8, 11, 14–22.)

[22 January 1885]

Mrs. Stanton closing the convention said:

I want to say that there is a great deal of significance in the discussion we have listened to to-night. It is important that women should have brought before their consideration all that pertains to government. Men have learned the importance of disconnecting church and state and it is very necessary that women should see the danger of betraying the state into the hands of ecclesiasticism. Under the Roman law women had more liberty than woman has ever had since. The canon law laid its withering hand on woman, and our statutes were derived from the canon law.

Men come oftimes fresh from these studies, with the dew of inspiration on their lips to preach the inferiority of woman. Do you suppose that their teachings inspire our sons to a higher respect for their mothers? No lessons of respect for womanhood are taught anywhere. Men have been educated with holy reverence for the rites and offices of the church, but when have they been taught a holy reverence for woman? And yet are we not as the mothers of the race more exalted than symbols and sacraments? I want an expurgated edition of the Bible. Men have revised it again and again and they have not yet revised it so as to make the mother of the race equal with the father. Next time a council is called we must take our part in the revision. We must try to see that everywhere at last woman is the acknowledged equal of man. We may differ about what steps we should take, but this I do know that if we are to save our republican form of government, we must realize in fact the grand principles we have laid down in its formation. A gentleman told me recently—and I often hear such remarks, that he despaired about the future of our nation. There has never been a moment when I doubted the ultimate triumph of our Republic. Men despair and say our republican form of government is a failure. No, my friends it is not. We have gone steadily onward ever since the landing of the Pilgrim Fathers, step by step towards the realization of our grand idea. From my visit to foreign lands, I have come back feeling more than ever proud of my country, and proud of the principles on which it is based. Oh, do not let the sons of the Pilgrims say that the idea of the Republic is a failure. Let us go on until we shall establish a government of justice and equality for all its citizens.

❧ *Woman's Tribune*, March 1885.

1. Gal. 3:28.

2. That is, Frances Ellen Burr (1831–1923), the sister of the publishers of the Democratic *Hartford Times* and an activist in the state and national suffrage associations since 1869. She was also the secretary of the newly organized Hartford Equal Rights Club. (Charles Burr Todd, *A General History of the Burr Family*, 4th ed. [New York, 1902], 305; *New York Times*, 10 February 1923; *History*, 3:334–38. See also *Papers* 2 & 3.)

3. Licensed preachers could lead a church, but only the more thoroughly educated minister who received ordination could offer the sacraments. Officially, the General Conference of the Methodist Episcopal Church in 1884 rejected a proposal to license and ordain women, but in practice, at least one woman received a license in 1869 and still preached. (*New York Times*, 17, 18 May 1884; *Woman's Journal*, 31 May 1884; "Bessie Bramble," Pittsburgh

Dispatch, 25 January 1885, SBA scrapbook 11, Rare Books, DLC; *ANB*, s.v. "Van Cott, Maggie Newton"; Kenneth E. Rowe, "The Ordination of Women, Round One: Anna Oliver and the General Conference of 1880," *Methodist History* 12 [April 1974]: 60–72.)

4. This word was left incomplete in the source text.

5. Mary E. McPherson (c. 1832–?) worked as a clerk in the Internal Revenue office in Washington. A widow and mother, she was born in Ohio, married a man from North Carolina, and gave birth to her daughter in Iowa about 1870. The National association sometimes counted her as a delegate from the District of Columbia and at other times credited Iowa for her presence at the Washington conventions. (Federal Census, 1880; city directories, 1881, 1883 to 1886, 1888 to 1890; *Register of Federal Officers*, 1883, 1885; *Our Herald*, n.d., and *Report of the Sixteenth Annual Washington Convention, 1884*, pp. 74, 148, *Film*, 23:49–51, 573ff.)

6. Robert McMurdy (1819–1892) is described parenthetically with reference to the dinner for clergymen supporting James Blaine's presidential candidacy at which Burchard uttered the infamous phrase "Rum, Romanism, and Rebellion." He was an Episcopal clergyman and educator and a leading advocate of international arbitration, with a long career as a Republican party operative. (*TwCBDNA*; "The Reverend Robert McMurdy, Doctor of Divinity and Doctor of Laws," *The Annual of Washington and Jefferson College for 1887* [Washington, Pa., 1888], 116–42; R. McMurdy to Benjamin B. French, 6 October 1864, Abraham Lincoln Papers, DLC; R. McMurdy to John A. Logan, 23 August, 2 September, 5 November 1884, and Alfred H. Love to R. McMurdy, 9 October 1884, John A. Logan Family Papers, DLC; with assistance of Anna Mae Moore, Washington and Jefferson College.)

7. Henry Codman Potter (1835–1908) was the rector of Grace Church in New York City and assistant bishop of New York in the Episcopal church. Since at least 1871 he had urged the church to recognize the promise of engaging women in the ministry as deaconesses. In the early Christian church, deaconesses attended to charitable work, and in the nineteenth century, bishops in several denominations sought to revive the office. Not until 1887 did Potter restore the ordination of deaconesses, but before that date, he, like other bishops, instituted less formal (and less controversial) ways of designating them as special servants of the church. (*ANB*; Mary P. Truesdell, "The Office of Deaconess," in *The Diaconate Now*, ed. Richard T. Nolan [Washington, D.C., 1968], 159–61.)

8. John B. Wolfe, or Wolff, a member of Section 12 of the International Workingmen's Association in New York, often attended suffrage meetings in Washington and New York. He was also active in the Universal Peace Union and the American Labor Reform League. (Samuel Bernstein, *The First International in America* [New York, 1962], 90; Timothy Messer-Kruse, *The Yankee International: Marxism and the American Reform Tradition, 1848–1876* [Chapel Hill, N.C., 1998], 248. See also *Papers 3*.)

9. Richard Heber Newton (1840–1914), an Episcopal clergyman, was rector

of All Souls' Church in New York City and a defender of critical studies of the Bible. (*ANB*.)

10. Gen. 1:26–28.

11. Matt. 7:12. The "Golden Rule" reads "Therefore all things whatsoever ye would that men should do to you, do ye even so to them: for this is the law and the prophets."

12. A note in an unknown hand, preserved in a scrapbook at the Huntington Library, explains that the convention considered texts drafted by ECS but modified by Clara Colby. In the diary of ECS prepared by her children, she is made to say that her own "short" resolution was thought "rather too pronounced," and the committee on resolutions replaced it with the text brought to the meeting, "which places all the blame on Judaism. This form raised a row among some Jews in the convention, and precipitated a discussion on the whole question." Below, at before 25 March 1885, ECS reclaims authorship. (*Film*, 24:23; *Stanton*, 2:223.)

13. Gen. 2:21–23. In this account Eve is created from the rib of Adam rather than simultaneously with Adam.

14. Saint Augustine of Hippo (354–430), an influential theologian in the early Christian church, argued that man fell from grace into sin through woman, and that women, the personification of Original Sin ever after, were in all their relations temptresses. God's punishment for disobedience, he taught, was to make sexuality shameful and childbirth both a burden and a curse. For a modern exposition of Augustine similar to ECS's, see Karen Armstrong, *The Gospel According to Woman: Christianity's Creation of the Sex War in the West* (Garden City, N.Y., 1987).

15. Arthur Penrhyn Stanley (1815–1881) was dean of Westminster Abbey from 1864 until his death. Elsewhere ECS notes that while visiting the Jacob Brights in November 1883, she visited Stanley's birthplace nearby at Alderley Rectory. (*DNB*; *Eighty Years*, 375.)

16. This was the Pan-Presbyterian Council of 1880. When the council's program appeared in the press without a single mention of women, ECS wrote an indignant open letter to the group. After the meeting concluded, she praised a proposal to ordain deaconesses in order to engage women in the urban church where social services were needed. (*Film*, 21:413–21, 512.)

17. Sarah Maria Clinton Perkins (1824–1905), an ordained minister in the Universalist church and an experienced lecturer on woman suffrage, moved to Cleveland in 1880, after the death of her husband. She held positions of leadership in Ohio's suffrage association, and at this meeting of the National association, she served on the committee on resolutions. She was best known for her work in the temperance movement. (*SEAP*; *American Women*; *Woman's Journal*, 16 December 1905; *Papers*, 3:100–102.)

18. Laura De Force Gordon (1838–1907) was an early organizer of the suffrage movement on the West Coast and an executive committee member of the National association in the 1870s. In 1879, she and Clara Foltz won a decision from the California Supreme Court that required Hastings College of Law to

admit women. A year later, Gordon opened a law office in San Francisco. She was admitted to practice before the Supreme Court of the United States while on this trip to Washington in 1885. At this meeting, Gordon was named to the committee on resolutions. (*NAW; ANB.* See also *Papers* 2 & 3.)

181 ⤳   INTERVIEW WITH ECS IN WASHINGTON,
DISTRICT OF COLUMBIA

EDITORIAL NOTE: In response to the National association's discussion of religion, Howard University's president, W. W. Patton, preached a sermon on "Women and Skepticism" at Washington's First Congregational Church on Sunday, January 25. With ECS, SBA, and Jane Spofford listening from the pews, Patton, in the *Washington Post*'s summary, "laid down the proposition that the enlargement of woman's sphere tended to immorality; that women are governed by their emotions and are incapable as advisers in the world of action." Under the headline "A Hornet's Nest about the Ears of the Woman Suffragists," the *Post*'s article continued with this interview of ECS and a summary of the sermon delivered on Sunday evening by Olympia Brown on the same topic.

[*25 January 1885*]

Among the reverend gentleman's auditors were Mrs. Stanton, Miss Anthony, and Mrs. Spofford, who listened attentively to his remarks. At the close of his discourse, Mrs. Stanton and Miss Anthony advanced and Miss Anthony, extending her hand, said: "Dr. Patton, your mother, if you ever had one, ought to take you across her knee and give you what you deserve—a good spanking."

Without waiting for a reply Mrs. Stanton added: "O, no, Doctor; allow me to congratulate you on your discourse. I have been trying for years to make the women understand that the very worst enemies they have are in the pulpit and you have illustrated the truth of my assertion."

These somewhat ironical congratulations were not replied to.

A *Post* reporter who noticed this incident asked Mrs. Stanton her opinion of the discourse. "It was illogical, and in some respects brutal," she replied.[1] "He made woman responsible for the excesses of the French revolution. He served up, so to speak, Madame Roland,[2] a noble woman, in my opinion. He discoursed on the immorality of

George Eliot,[3] and spoke depreciatingly of Frances Wright and Mrs. Wollstonecraft.[4] Harriet Martineau was also treated slightingly. Perhaps the most outrageous statement made by him was to the effect that the leader of the woman suffrage movement and a fair representative of the cause is Victoria Woodhull.[5] Why should he not have been honest and named as the pioneer in the movement that glorious woman, Lucretia Mott? Instead of selecting some of the representative good women of the day he went out of his way to name women against whom, perhaps, serious charges would lie."

≈ *Washington Post*, 26 January 1885, SBA scrapbook 11, Rare Books, DLC.

1. Through many weeks of controversy, Patton refused to provide the text of his sermon for publication, but he offered his own summaries to dispute those made by his critics. Defending himself in a letter to the *Woman's Journal*, he described the sermon as "a defence and glorification of woman in her high moral and religious nature, and in her devotion to the gospel which has so elevated her." (Washington *National Republican*, 26 January 1885, *Film*, 24:39; Washington *Evening Star*, 26, 30 January 1885; *Alpha* 10 [1 February 1885]: 9–10 and [1 March 1885]: 9; *Woman's Journal*, 7 February 1885.)

2. According to the summary of the sermon in the *National Republican*, 26 January 1885, Patton described the French revolutionary Jeanne-Marie Philipon Roland (1754–1793) as a woman "whom too much liberty had ruined and who died without religion."

3. Patton named George Eliot and Harriet Martineau in a list of nineteenth-century figures who displayed "perverted womanhood."

4. The *National Republican* noted Patton's naming of Frances Wright (1795–1852) without providing his characterization of her. A freethinker and critic of women's subordination in marriage, Wright provided a model for the antebellum movement for woman's rights. Mary Wollstonecraft (1759–1797), author of *A Vindication of the Rights of Women*, published in London in 1792, "liv[ed] an immoral life," according to Patton.

5. The *National Republican* reported what ECS says here: that Patton named Victoria Woodhull as "the representative of the movement in this country," a movement that "gave evidence of atheism and immorality." The *Republican*'s reporter asked the further question, what had been Woodhull's role in the movement? ECS replied: "She came here thirteen years ago with a splendid argument for suffrage and was introduced to a committee of congress by Gen. Butler, . . . We did not know anything about her free love doctrines, if indeed she had any then, and welcomed her as a fortunate and able advocate. She only attended one convention, at which I was not present. That was her sole connection with the movement."

182 ❧ SBA TO NELSON W. ALDRICH[1]

Washington, D.C., Feb. 1st 1885.

My Dear Sir

The Committee on Woman Suffrage promise to bring up our 16th amendment bill early this week—[2] May I not rely on you to vote for its submission—also to speak in its favor—and do all you can to secure its passage by the Senate?

Please accept the package of pamphlets accompanying this—and oblige Yours Respectfully

❧ Susan B. Anthony

❧ ALS, on NWSA letterhead for 1885, Nelson W. Aldrich Papers, DLC.

1. Nelson Wilmarth Aldrich (1841–1915), Republican of Rhode Island, resigned from the House of Representatives in 1881 to enter the Senate, where he served until 1911. (*BDAC.*)

2. When it was announced on 20 January 1885 that Senate Resolution No. 19 was the next item on the calendar, Francis Cockrell asked that it be passed over. Then, on 4 February, Thomas Palmer announced that he would call up the resolution on 6 February "for the purpose of offering a few remarks upon it." (*Congressional Record*, 48th Cong., 2d sess., 850, 1246.)

183 ❧ SBA TO ELIZABETH BUFFUM CHACE

[*Washington, D.C.*] Feb. 10th, 1885.

I give you the copy of your senators' replies to me. I wrote each of the 76 senators on Sunday, Feb. 1st,[1] asking him if I might *count* him among the senators who would vote for our 16th Amendment bill. Senator Chace[2] writes: "I am obliged for thy good words to me in thy letter of the 1st instant. I have little hope of being able to *fill* Senator Anthony's seat, or to answer the expectations of his friends and mine who have placed me there. I notice thee asks me to speak. One of the traditions of the Senate is that a new member is expected to keep quiet for a season; a constraint hardly necessary for me, for I shrink from much speaking, and never do it except when impelled by a sense of absolute duty."

Senator Aldrich wrote: "Dear Madam, I beg to acknowledge receipt of your letter of the 1st inst. with enclosures."

Now my dear, our bill is *promised to come up* in the senate without fail, and I want you, and as many of your women as you can stir up, to write letters to both your senators. I have no doubt but Mr. Chace will vote *Yes*, though he doesn't absolutely say he will do so, but I am not so sure of Aldrich: his reply evades the subject matter of my letter to him altogether. Without letting him know of my sending you this copy of his reply, do just have him literally pelted with appeals to vote for our bill. It would be a shame for one of R. Island's senators to vote no, or not vote at all.

❧ Lillie B. C. Wyman and Arthur C. Wyman, *Elizabeth Buffum Chace, 1806–1899* (Boston, 1914), 2:213–14.

1. In addition to her letter to Nelson Aldrich above, her letters on the same date to George Edmunds, John Logan, and Philetus Sawyer are in *Film*, 24:63–69.

2. Jonathan Chace (1829–1917), Republican of Rhode Island, was elected to the seat of the late Henry B. Anthony and entered the Senate on 20 January 1885. He also assumed Anthony's place on the Committee on Woman Suffrage. He served in the House of Representatives from 1881 to 1885. (*BDAC*; *Congressional Record*, 48th Cong., 2d sess., 3 February 1885, p. 1218.)

184 ❧ ECS TO MARGUERITE BERRY STANTON

Johnstown [*N.Y.*] March 8th [*1885*]

My dear Marguerite

It is a long time since I directed an epistle to you, but I always intend all I write Theo for you & the baby also   I have been from home six weeks this winter attending conventions & legislative hearings, visiting &c.[1] When in New York I went to the theatre with Bob & Kit, had a large reception given to me at a stylish new Hotel on Park avenue five hundred invitations given out. The parlors & halls were crowded.

I thought I should suffocate, & the worst of all was that I was called on for a speech   After talking & shaking hands, standing & trying to be brilliant two hours you may imagine that my speech was not up to the high water mark. You will say all this is quite dissipation enough for one now in her 70th year. But everybody says my trip abroad renewed my youth, & that I returned brighter than ever, so you need not look forward to 70^{ty} with any misgivings, if you will continue to eat well, sleep well, exercise all your powers of mind & body, & try to be cheerful & happy under all circumstances, which I think you & Theodore are both inclined to do. Dear little Lizette how I do long to see both of the babies & hear them talk![2] I have laughed many times thinking what a good plan you hit on to keep Lizette still when you had a dinner party. I can see her with her little fat hands, red in the face [walking?] the kitchen furniture, puffing & tugging to the point of exhaustion. How fortunate that she did not walk ↑upon you all↓ in her fatigue costume. Mr Stanton Neil[3] & I compose the family at Johnstown. Maggie is coming the first of April. Our plans for the summer are not yet decided upon. Bob has grown very large, & wise, he is a great fellow. He ↑&↓ Kit live in great style both in their house & offices.[4] Kit has just joined the Union Club[5] of which Mr Evarts[6] is President. They have a magnificent building one block from Aunt B's on Fifth Avenue. Cady Eaton[7] had a fall a few weeks ago & broke two of his ribs & has been confined to his bed ever since. All the rest of the family circle are in their usual health   I enjoy Theodore's letters very much. I feel very sorry for poor Louise Michel.[8] Why dont you women send in petitions for her release. Roll up an immense petition, ask for a hearing in the Chamber of Deputies, & get some of your orators either men or women to plead her case. It is a shame to have her incarcerated if guilty of no crime. You must do something to rouse your women to see that justice is done to all your citizens. We never know how much we can do until we try. Now that Theodore has come to be such a good writer I want him to cultivate his speaking talents. Bob told me he used to be one of the best speakers in Cornell   I hear good news from H^e, baby rosy & happy & all goes well with them. Hattie has been highly complimented for her speeches at several parlor meetings in London. Good night with love & kisses

⪻ *Mother*

[*in margins of first page*] Neal & Mr Stanton join in love & good wishes for your happiness. My love to Marie when you write

❧ ALS, ECS Papers, DLC. Square brackets surround uncertain reading.

1. When she left Washington for New York, ECS joined the state suffrage association's effort to pass a new bill to prohibit disfranchisement, introduced in the assembly by James Husted in January 1885. After a short stay with Tryphena Bayard in New York City, ECS established a base near Albany on a ten-day visit with Caroline Rogers in Lansingburgh. From there, she traveled to Albany to lecture in the senate chamber on February 5, spoke in Troy at the Unitarian Church on February 8, and entertained local suffragists at a large party given by her hostess. On February 11, she returned to New York City to attend the annual meeting of the state association and a reception given in her honor at the Murray Hill Hotel on February 12. Back in Albany on February 18, she spoke again to the legislature, before returning to Johnstown on February 20. (*Woman's Journal*, 5 January 1885; *History*, 4:853–54; Blake and Wallace, *Champion of Women*, 159–62, 223; *Film*, 24:43, 73–76, 94–101, 121–36, 45:383–84; *Troy Daily Telegram*, 2 February 1885; *Stanton*, 2:224–25.)

2. That is, Lizette Stanton and Nora Blatch.

3. D. Cady Stanton, or Neil, alternated his residence between Logan, Iowa, and New York. Here as elsewhere in the historical record, ECS is silent about Neil's personal life. He had married Frederika F. Anthony in Chicago on 17 April 1884, but according to her complaint for divorce in 1886, they separated in September 1884, when Neil sent her back to Chicago from Iowa. Florence Lanyon Stanton was born on 10 January 1885. Again according to the complaint, Neil neither visited the baby nor paid anything toward the support of mother and child. Frederika Stanton was granted a divorce on 27 December 1886, and Neil was ordered to support his child. (Marriage license no. 80957, Illinois Regional Archives Depository, Chicago; Frederika F. Stanton vs. D. Cady Stanton, Circuit Court of Cook County, December Term, 1886, Cook County Circuit Court Archives, Chicago.)

4. According to the city directory issued in May 1885, Henry Stanton, Jr., and Robert Stanton had moved their law firm, Stanton and Cass, into the Mutual Life Building at Nassau, Cedar, and Liberty streets, and moved in together on West Thirty-sixth Street.

5. The oldest social club in New York City, the Union Club occupied a building at Fifth Avenue and Twenty-first Street. ECS places it near the home of Tryphena and Edward Bayard.

6. William Maxwell Evarts (1818–1901), a former secretary of state and a distinguished lawyer who represented Henry Ward Beecher in the Beecher-Tilton case, was elected to the Senate from New York in January 1885. (*ANB*.)

7. It is unclear whether this was Daniel Cady Eaton (1837–1912), ECS's

nephew, the art historian already identified, or Daniel Cady Eaton (1834–1895), her cousin, a professor of botany. (*ANB*.)

8. Louise Michel (1830–1905), a French anarchist and communard, returned to France from exile in New Caledonia in 1880 and was jailed in 1883 for anarchist agitation. Michel refused several efforts to pardon her in the winter of 1885. (Edith Thomas, *Louise Michel*, trans. Penelope Williams [Montreal, 1980], 240–46.)

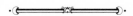

185 ✿   SBA TO HARRIET HANSON ROBINSON

New Orleans La—[1]   March 14, 1885

Dear Mrs R.

I received the package of your History—weight 72—lbs—cost $5.35—your letter to Mrs Sewall—came same day—& so I opened & read it—

We have a <u>table</u> on which our Histories—pamphlet reports—newspapers & tracts are piled—for the passers by to behold— and I now expect Mrs Colby—who is here—will take her seat at the table—sell books & take subscribers for her Woman's Tribune—& give away the leaflets—

I have visited (& spoken) to the Girl's High School[2]—the only Boys Grammar School that has a woman principal[3]—the McDonnoh School no 11.[4]—& the Straight University—Colored[5]—and yesterday I attended a lecture on <u>physiology</u>—to the City Teachers—in the Medical college room—by Prof. Shalley[6]—and at close of his lecture—he introduced me—& I spoke to the nearly 300 women teachers of the city of New Orleans—& Monday A.M. I am to go to the Webster School for Girls[7]—there is plenty of missionary work waiting some one here— Mrs Sewall & I address a fine audience last Monday the 9th by invitation of the Women's Club[8]—& arrangements are in progress for me to lecture in their largest & best hall—before I leave the city—[9] Everybody is most cordial—and the time now is for us to canvass the south with our gospel of equal rights for woman   Very Sincerely yours

✿   *Susan B. Anthony*

P.S—I received the $50— from your Treasurer[10]—that was a great deal more than I dreamed of your sending or giving me—but it will all go to help on our good work— S. B. A

N.B.—<u>Dont</u> send on any more tracts by express—the cost is too enormous—

⚞ ALS, on NWSA letterhead, Robinson-Shattuck Papers, MCR-S.

1. SBA, accompanied by Adeline Thomson, arrived in New Orleans on March 4 to attend the World's Industrial and Cotton Centennial Exposition. It was her first trip into the South. Within the exposition's Woman's Department, the local Woman's Christian Temperance Union provided a table where members of the National Woman Suffrage Association could introduce themselves to visitors. (*Film*, 23:1119, 24:111–15, 152–53, 160–65; Samuel C. Shepherd, Jr., "A Glimmer of Hope: The World's Industrial and Cotton Centennial Exposition, New Orleans, 1884–1885," *Louisiana History* 26 [1985]: 271–90; *Woman's Journal*, 25 March 1885.)

2. SBA, May Sewall, and Adeline Thomson visited the Girls' Central High School, Academic, No. 2, at 144 Clio Street, on March 6. See *Film*, 24:158–59.

3. Miss M. R. Chevallie was listed in city directories as the principal of the boys' Bienville School at the corner of Bienville and North Robertson streets. SBA, however, referred to her in another letter as Rosalie Chevallie. Miss Rosalie Chevalier and M. R. Chevallie resided at the same address in 1885, but the former was listed not as a principal but as a teacher. "Mrs. Chevalier" sat on the platform at SBA's lecture to teachers on March 19. (City directories, 1884, 1885; SBA to Elizabeth B. Harbert, 18 March 1885, and New Orleans *Times-Democrat*, 20 March 1885, *Film*, 24:198–203, 207.)

4. The McDonogh School, No. 11, was a girls' school at the corner of Prieur and Palmyra streets.

5. Straight University was founded by the American Missionary Association in 1868 to offer education from elementary school through college to African Americans. After its first campus was destroyed by arson in 1877, the school was rebuilt on Canal Street at the corner of Tonti.

6. Stanford Emerson Chaillé (1830–1911), professor of physiology and pathological anatomy in the medical faculty at the University of Louisiana, later Tulane University, offered a free course of lectures on physiology and anatomy to teachers. (*ANB*; *History*, 3:797–98.)

7. The Webster School was at the corner of Dryades and Erato streets.

8. At Continental Guards' Hall opposite Lafayette Square, Sewall and SBA "attracted the largest audience ever seen in New Orleans at an entertainment of this character," according to the New Orleans *Daily Picayune*, 10 March 1885, *Film*, 24:169.

9. At Tulane Hall on Dryades Street at the invitation of the city's teachers on March 19. See *Film*, 24:206–7.

10. This was Sara A. Francis Underwood (1838–1911), an author and editor, who contributed to the *Revolution* in 1868 and 1869, published *Heroines of Freethought* in 1876, and edited the Boston *Index* with her husband, Benjamin Underwood. (*WWW1*; *DAB* and Gordon Stein, ed., *The Encyclopedia of Unbelief* [Buffalo, N.Y., 1985], s.v. "Underwood, Benjamin Franklin"; Sara A. Francis Underwood, "Memories of Elizabeth Cady Stanton," *Free Thought Magazine* 21 [January 1903]: 20–22; *Papers*, 2:200–201.)

186 ⚙ SBA TO HARRIET HANSON ROBINSON

Bloomfield, Iowa,[1] April 16 1885

My Dear Mrs R.

I wonder if I have ever acknowledged your note with report of Court decision—it went all the way round to Washington New Orleans & Rochester & thence to some of my lecturing points— it was my <u>first</u> positive knowledge of the fact—[2] Many thanks to you— Well I am now booked to be at Mr Ransom's Savings Bank on Monday A.M. the 27th inst—my last lecture is the 21st & I go thence to Leavenworth for <u>one night</u> only—and then take train for Boston direct—not stopping over a train at home— I shall go direct to the Parker House—shall try & get there on Sunday evening—but not be able to do so—[3]

Had I known I was to have been summoned to receive the bequest—so soon—I should have ordered lecture engagements stopped off earlier— I had planned to spend the next three weeks after the 22d visitng my brothers & Kansas—

Of all—we will chat when we meet in Boston Sincerely yours

⚙ *Susan B. Anthony*

⚙ ALS, on letterhead of Trimble House, Bloomfield, Iowa, Robinson-Shattuck Papers, MCR-S.

1. SBA lectured in the Midwest for nearly a month after she left New Orleans. Some of her engagements in Illinois and Iowa are documented in *Film*, 24:208–10, 225, 233–36, 239.

2. Word reached SBA while she was on the road that the Massachusetts Supreme Judicial Court dismissed the Bacons' bill in equity with costs, sending the matter back to the Suffolk County Probate Court. Lawyers argued the case before the Supreme Judicial Court on 18 March 1885, and the court recorded its decision on the next day, concluding that Eliza Eddy's will imposed no trust upon the property left to Lucy Stone and SBA but rather granted money to them absolutely. In letters now missing, SBA received orders to report to Boston on April 27. On that day, Chandler Ransom filed another inventory of the estate, showing a balance of $48,230 in deeds, bonds, mortgages, and stocks to be divided equally between Stone and SBA. (Albert F. Bacon et al., executors, & others v. Chandler R. Ransom, executor, & others, 139 Massachusetts Reports 117 [1885]; Third and Final Inventory, Suffolk County Probate Court, Docket

No. 66836, Archives, Supreme Judicial Court, Boston; SBA to Benjamin F. Butler, 29 March 1885, *Film*, 24:214–15.)

3. On Monday, April 27, SBA wrote Robinson to say she stayed instead at the Adams House and would go to William Lloyd Garrison's house for the night of the twenty-seventh, meet again with Chandler Ransom on the twenty-eighth, and leave town that afternoon. These plans complicated relations with Lucy Stone, who later complained that she invited SBA "to come and spend the day with us" at Dorchester and received in reply "a hateful note, that made me feel the last plank between us had been broken." (*Film*, 24:245–46; L. Stone to Antoinette B. Blackwell, 10 January 1886, in Lasser and Merrill, *Friends and Sisters*, 250.)

187 *⇝* ECS TO F. ELLEN BURR AND THE HARTFORD EQUAL RIGHTS CLUB, WITH DISCUSSION

EDITORIAL NOTE: Ellen Burr brought the National Woman Suffrage Association's debate about religion back home to the new Hartford Equal Rights Club. Members discussed the resolution at a meeting just weeks after the club formed. Burr, the club's secretary, sent minutes of that meeting to ECS, and on 10 April 1885, she read ECS's response to the members, who resumed their discussion. The minutes were again sent to ECS, and the exchange of ideas continued at this meeting on April 24. The Equal Rights Club encouraged debate and disagreement among its members, and then distributed its minutes widely. As Burr explained in the *History of Woman Suffrage*, the club's "proceedings are reported pretty fully and published in the *Hartford Times*, which has a wide circulation, thus gaining an audience of many thousands and making its proceedings much more important than they would otherwise be." (*Film*, 24:226–28; *History*, 3:338.)

[24 April 1885]

The secretary read the following letter she had received from Elizabeth Cady Stanton:

Many thanks for your paper containing the report of your club of April 10th. I read it carefully, and would reply to each point. One said, "Many good suffragists do not coincide with Mrs. Stanton."[1] It is not my opinions, but the facts of history to which I invite the attention of women. Miss Hall[2] questions "whether it would be wise to dig into the past." That is just what all our religions do; the farther back they can trace authority for these dogmas and miracles, the firmer the basis, they think, on which they stand. The Bible is the record of the dim past. It is into the shadows and speculations of the customs and faith of the world's ancient peoples that we are continually going for precedents. If Miss Hall would settle all questions by common sense, reason, and what we see ourselves of the facts around us, she and I would exactly agree. But if she wishes to dig back 1,800 years to find out what Paul and Timothy, James and John said, then I wish to tell her what St. Chrysostom, Augustine, John Calvin, Luther, John Wesley[3] and the rest said. If she can quote favorable words and action of certain clergymen of her acquaintance in regard to woman's equality, I can quote innumerable utterances and published volumes to show what many more have said against the extension of any further rights for women, beside the uniform hostile action of the vast majority of all church organizations. My one interest in the religions is what they have taught concerning women. I have no quarrel with any of the creeds or catechisms, the bulls or the bibles, on any point of the thirty-nine articles,[4] except where they touch the creation and destiny of woman, and there I will accept none of them, for they all alike degrade the sex, and make us slaves and subjects, Pariahs and outcasts. The church at the present, is in spirit what it was in the past, modified by advancing civilization, as are all other institutions. It never did teach the dignity and equality of woman, and it does not to-day. I send each of the ladies who led your discussion an article in the "Index," showing an item of its recent action.[5]

Women are in some sects theoretically allowed a voice in the business matters of the church, but they are discouraged in many ways from ever using it. In how many churches do you ever see a woman made a trustee, a deacon, an elder, or a pastor? And if a woman were nominated for one of these offices, the majority of her sex would vote against her, so demoralized are women by church teaching in regard to their own rights, duties and interests. It is the long, bony fingers of the canon law stretching through the centuries that hold the church women outside our suffrage movement to-day. The clergy hold and contend for the benefit of themselves and the churches, all that enthusiasm and religious fervor that should be expended in their own education. The most important fact in the universe always was, is, and ever will be, the status of woman, the mother of the race. Around this fact centers all human progress. And yet our church women to-day think that all the doxys,[6] the sacraments, the altars and spires of their temples of worship of more account than themselves. The sprinkling of a baby; an organ; a choir; psalms without metre, or with; the doctrine of free will as against foreordination; salvation by faith, or by works; the plenary inspiration of the scriptures,—all these things great and small, have divided protestants into numberless sects, but not one has yet divided on the great fact of woman's nature, creation, and true position in the scale of being. She is still an afterthought, a helpmeet, a weaker vessel, second in the order of being. And she herself thinks it of more consequence that she should be dipped or sprinkled, join the church, take the communion, and attend the weekly prayer meeting, than that she should be recognized as the Heavenly Mother, the feminine element eternal in the godhead, as essential as the masculine in all creation, in the beginning, now and ever, as there could have been no perpetuation of being, but in the simultaneous creation of these great forces. The first step towards a pure religion is the infusion with the doctrines and discipline of the church an equal share of the feminine element; equal dignity, honor and glory for woman. There is no question in the social, religious, or political horizon that can compare in importance with this, and equality everywhere should be the primal demand of women professing Christianity, as equality was the burden of all the teachings of Jesus. And in the early church, women did preach and teach and administer the sacraments, and were robbed of these rights by licentious ecclesiastics, denounced as an impious sex, cursed of God, forever in collusion with the devil, and unfit for companions of holy men. Yours truly,

ELIZABETH CADY STANTON.

We select a few points here and there from the discussion that followed.

Mrs. Kimball:[7] I think great allowance should be made for our religious prejudices—prejudices we are unconscious of. I think it is due more to St. Paul's utterance, "Let your women keep silent in the church,"[8] than to "the long bony fingers of the canon law" that women are to-day held in subjection by the church.

The Secretary: St. Paul is older than the canon law, and it is difficult to tell to which to date the prejudice back. The ministers are now ahead of their creeds, as a general thing.

Mrs. Barnes:[9] The Methodists and Baptists are more liberal than other sects in giving liberty to women. I have known of their being told to sit down when attempting to speak in a Congregational church.

Mrs. Kimball: I think the Congregational church would not object to a woman reciting a hymn, but would object to her getting up and delivering a speech or a sermon.

The Chairman: St. Paul's remark was made with reference to a certain state of things in those days, when education was considered to militate against the virtue of women; the wife of Socrates, even, was not educated.[10] Women who made themselves public at all were supposed to be lewd.

The Secretary: I would like to read a little extract I have just run across from a speech by Mrs. Stanton at the last New York suffrage convention:[11] "The worst objectors to woman suffrage are fashionable women. At Newport I saw ladies dancing with low-neck, short-sleeved dresses; and at the breakfast table next day, they said they were shocked to read that there had been a woman suffrage meeting in Newport. They were shocked to think of a woman talking from the platform. I told them it was a matter of taste: that I would rather do it than put on a low-necked dress and dance in the arms of a man. 'But the names of the women who spoke are in the paper,' objected one of the ladies. 'Well,' I said, 'so are the names of the ladies who danced; and those whose names were not printed, were not at all pleased.'"

Mrs. Kimball: I know that fashionable ladies think it highly proper to dress in the most *décolleté* style and perform in theatricals on the stage, and these same ladies would indignantly resent a proposition to speak in a modest dress in a woman suffrage meeting.

The Chairman: These are good points for women to reflect upon, and I am sorry that the ladies are not all here, but it is the annual spring house-cleaning time and they have probably to oversee that business.

The Secretary: The political house needs cleaning more than the domestic one; they can afford to overlook a little dirt in the latter occasionally for the sake of the former.

❧ *Hartford Daily Times*, 25 April 1885, in Minute Book 1, Hartford Equal Rights Club Record, 1885–1919; Archives, History, and Genealogy Unit; Ct.

1. This was Emily Parmely Peltier Collins (1814–1909), chairman of the club, who moved to Hartford in 1879 from Louisiana, years after she organized what was thought to be the first woman's rights society in the nation at South Collins, New York, in 1848. Collins was, by this date, twice widowed. She first married Charles Peltier in Michigan, and the son of that marriage, Pierre D. Peltier, a physician, provided her home in Hartford. In 1841, she married a lawyer, Simri Collins, who died in Louisiana in 1876. A second son, Emmett Burke Collins, died in 1872. (*History*, 1:88–94; *American Women*; Isabella B. Hooker to Virginia L. Minor, 1 April 1879, *Film*, 20:789–93; *New York Times*, 30 April 1909; *Woman's Journal*, 29 May 1909.)

2. Mary Hall (1843–1927), who practiced law in Hartford, took a leading part in all of the discussions about ECS's ideas, and she made this statement about the past at the meeting of April 10. After Hall studied with John Hooker, husband of Isabella Hooker, and passed the examination for admission to the bar, the state supreme court held that state law permitted women to practice as attorneys. Hall was active in the equal rights club and the state suffrage association. (*American Women*; *New York Times*, 16 November 1927; information from Connecticut Women's Hall of Fame; In re Hall 50 Connecticut Reports 131 [1882].)

3. To counter Mary Hall's reliance on four authors of the New Testament's Gospels, ECS turns to later religious authors. Saint Augustine, Martin Luther, and John Wesley are already identified. Saint John Chrysostom (c. 347–407) was an influential leader and writer in the early Christian church, and John Calvin (1509–1564) was a French theologian and early Protestant.

4. The summary of basic beliefs in the Church of England.

5. Enclosure missing.

6. Though usually doxies when plural, a doxy was a religious opinion. The same word also means wench.

7. Emily O. Richardson Kimball (c. 1831–1902) was a painter and the wife of John Calvin Kimball, pastor of Unity Church of Hartford from 1878 to 1888. The couple left Hartford when John Kimball became a college lecturer on evolution. (Federal Census, 1880; *WWW1*, s.v. "Kimball, John C."; on-line biographical record of class of 1854, Amherst College, Mass.)

8. 1 Cor. 14:34.

9. Mrs. Barnes is unidentified.

10. As reported in Xenophon, *Symposium*, 2.10, Socrates said that he did not educate his famously difficult wife, Xanthippe, for the reason that by learning to endure her, he trained himself to get along with any human being.

11. At the annual meeting of the New York State Woman Suffrage Association on 12 February 1885. Two reports, neither identical to the one read here, are in *Film*, 24:94, 98.

188   ECS TO SARA FRANCIS UNDERWOOD

Tenafly N.J.   May 9th [*1885*]

Dear Mrs Underwood,

Many thanks for the tract, scraps, & your letter.[1] I wish to be in regular communication ↑with you↓ on all phases of the religious question. There are so few women who seem to feel the slightest interest in being emancipated from their religious terrors, & so few that are emancipated that have the least pity for others that when I find one like yourself, I want the help & inspiration of such communion.

Whenever you get a new thought on any of these religious points do share it with me

To rouse woman to a sense of her degradation under the canon law & church discipline, is the work that interests me most, & to which I propose to devote the sunset of my life. I am very busy just now moving back to Tenafly New Jersey, my old place of residence. as soon as I get through the confusion I intend to take a thoughful look at Bishop Spalding[2]   The old New York Observer had nearly two columns of criticism[3] & most of the religious papers have had something to say. All this I trust will rouse some women to thought. It matters little what they say of me, so that attention is called to the facts of history. Your kind expressions are very grateful for while I do not heed the criticism of opponents, I prize the approval of friends. With kind regards for yourself & husband sincerely yours

        ✍ *Elizabeth Cady Stanton.*

✍ ALS, Papers of ECS, NPV.

1. Sara Underwood no doubt wrote about ECS's article in the *North American Review* 140 (May 1885): 389–99, "Has Christianity Benefited Woman?" *Film*, 24:294–304. Taking on the popular claim that women owed her present, elevated position to Christianity, ECS countered that "All religions thus far have taught the headship and superiority of man, the inferiority and subordination of woman." While "material civilization" and secular leaders accepted progress toward woman's liberty, sectarian leaders encouraged "the perversion of her religious sentiments" within the church and opposed secular

change outside. In passing, she noted the need for "another revision of the Protestant Bible [that] shall strike from its pages all invidious distinctions based on sex."

2. John Lancaster Spalding (1840–1916), bishop of the Roman Catholic diocese of Peoria since 1877, rebutted ECS's article in the same issue of the *North American Review*, pp. 399–410, and denounced her. She had displayed her "ignorance of Christian teaching," voiced views "at once ignorant and coarse," and taken a "false and therefore offensive tone." "[A]dvocates of woman's rights," he continued, "speak like people who have grievances, and to have a grievance is to be a bore." (*ANB*.)

3. The unsigned editorial in the Presbyterian *New York Observer*, 30 April 1885, deemed the Bible and "the views of the Female Suffrage Society" to be antithetical. After admitting to a general dislike of "any thing which Mrs. Stanton or Susan Anthony may say or do," the editor dismissed ECS's views on Christianity out of hand, and proclaimed, "No, Mrs. Stanton, Protestants will not tinker the Bible to please you." Spalding's affirmation that Christianity "always and everywhere uplifted, purified and emancipated woman" won the editor's approval.

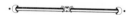

189 ☞ SBA TO CAROLINE THOMAS MERRICK[1]

17 Madison street   Rochester N.Y. May 15, 1885

My Dear Mrs Merrick

Just before leaving home for the Ohio State Woman Suffrage Convention[2] at Painesvill—last Monday the 11th—I received & read with great delight the paper with the report of Ex. Gov. Hoyt's speech on Wyoming[3]—& said what an immense ↑help↓ this fine report in the N.O. papers will be—& now, Friday, your letter mailed the 9th awaited my return—and to know that the cause ↑is↓ indebted to <u>you</u> for that enterprise of reporting & getting to the office in good time—& thus telling the Governors good word to so many people—and that in addition to all that you bethought you to have speeches of Mr Phillips & Mrs Mill scattered through the audience—[4] I am more delighted than I can tell—to think of & to do all that, was equal ↑to↓ the <u>best</u> of the <u>pioneer</u> <u>workers</u>—and <u>our</u> <u>success</u> lies in the amount ↑of↓ such quick thought & action to <u>improve</u> every possible occasion in that way— Your promptness delights my heart more than any cash contribution could—because such <u>practical</u> <u>work</u> is better than gold to our cause—

You rightly read J. W. H.—[5] It is most amazing to me that any woman should not be anxious to bring out & to the front every woman who can speak or act— She seems to feel that she herself is the <u>only</u> woman possessed of brain & culture to open her lips—whereas the fact is there are hundreds of the young women of to-day who possess both of those necessary qualities to a vastly greater degree than her lady-ship!! And I am bound you southern splendid women shall see & hear & know <u>others</u> of our northern women—& those, too, who feel them-selves made of the same sort of stuff as other mortals— I think we shall be able to plan & carry out a series of meetings & conventions in all the larger cities of of the Gulf States the coming winter with Mrs Stanton & myself & some others as speakers—and then we shall want you & Mrs Saxon & Mrs Chapin[6] & every possible southern <u>born</u> woman to come in and go with us—& speak in our meetings & help us <u>organize</u> every state—so that we shall have a good working centre in every one— I know you will hail such a canvass & will give all the "aid & comfort" to <u>such</u> <u>an</u> "<u>invasion</u>" that you possibly can—

I thought of you & how you would enjoy seeing & hearing & speaking—at the Ohio meeting—it was a splendid gathering—

I have written to Mrs Spofford—Riggs House—Washington to send to you a "<u>pair</u>" of pictures—those of Stanton & Anthony—and I mail you my photograph—from which the Litho—was taken—

I am delighted that you will gather & put together all you can of woman in La & the South—for ꜛour History—Vol. III—꜌[7] and when you see your Confreres—Mrs Saxon & Dr Keating[8] give my love to them— Mrs Saxon <u>did</u> send me a brief paper—but it is at Mrs Stanton's—with all the rest— if it will be a help to you—I will send it when I get to Mrs Stantons—

Do give my love to the teachers, to Mrs Field[9]—Mrs Nicholson,[10] & all the good women I met—and Mrs [Hornby?][11] the <u>Captain</u> of the W.C.T.U. Boothe—and with profound respect for the Judge & for "Ned"—and best of love for yourself

ᴁ *Susan B. Anthony*

ᴁ ALS, on NWSA letterhead, Merrick Family Papers, Historic New Orleans Collection. Square brackets surround uncertain reading.

1. Caroline Elizabeth Thomas Merrick (1825–1908), one of the women who

appeared before Louisiana's constitutional convention of 1879 to seek the removal of women's legal disabilities, continued to work with Elizabeth Saxon for woman suffrage and served as the state vice president for the National association. She also became president of the Louisiana Woman's Christian Temperance Union. On the final days of SBA's stay in New Orleans, she was a guest of the Merrick family. (Glenn R. Conrad, ed., *A Dictionary of Louisiana Biography* [New Orleans, 1988]; *NAW*.) Her husband, Edwin Thomas Merrick (1808–1897), was a prominent lawyer and former chief justice of the state supreme court. Edwin Thomas Merrick, Jr., (1859–1935) lived with his parents and practiced law with his father. (Conrad, *Dictionary of Louisiana Biography*; *ANB*; Federal Census, 1880; SBA to Elizabeth B. Harbert, 18 March 1885, *Film*, 24:198–203.)

2. On May 12 and 13. See *Film*, 24:274–75.

3. This unidentified and undated clipping is in SBA scrapbook 11, Rare Books, DLC. John Hoyt spoke on the subject of woman suffrage in Wyoming at noon at the territory's headquarters in the Government Building at the exposition.

4. The speech given by Wendell Phillips to the National Woman's Rights Convention of 1851 and Harriet Taylor Mill's article "Enfranchisement of Women," published in 1851 about the convention of 1850, were tracts one and three of the Woman's Rights Tracts first published in 1853 and kept in print for half a century thereafter.

5. The appointment of Julia Ward Howe (1819–1910) of Boston to be chairman of the Woman's Department at the Louisiana exposition stirred controversy even before she arrived in New Orleans in December 1884. Southern women interpreted her selection as an insult to their own capabilities. To the southern organizers, the presence of the author of the "Battle Hymn of the Republic" aptly symbolized the exposition's goal of reconciliation between North and South. Howe's hard work to fund the department softened some critics during her stay, but her abrasive manner left others complaining until her departure in May 1885. (*NAW*; *ANB*; Shepherd, "Glimmer of Hope"; Deborah Pickman Clifford, *Mine Eyes Have Seen the Glory: A Biography of Julia Ward Howe* [Boston, 1979], 236–43.)

6. Sarah Flournoy Moore Chapin (1830?–1896), known as Sallie F. Chapin, was president of the Woman's Christian Temperance Union in South Carolina and superintendent of the national union's department of southern work. She worked closely with Caroline Merrick. (*NAW*; *ANB*.)

7. Caroline Merrick's chapter on Louisiana is in *History*, 3:789–801.

8. Harriette Charlotte Harned Veazie Keatinge (1837–1909), a niece of Clemence Lozier, practiced medicine in New Orleans. She moved south during the war with her second husband, Edward Keatinge, an engraver of Confederate currency, and she stayed in South Carolina for several years with her children after he returned to New York. At what was probably the time of

her husband's death, Keatinge enrolled in the New York Medical College for Women. After graduation, she settled in New Orleans. There in 1878 and 1879, she joined Janet Norton, Caroline Merrick, and others in their quest for suffrage, and from 1881 onward, she was active in the National association. Later in the 1880s, Keatinge moved back to New York to take over Clemence Lozier's medical practice. (*NCAB*, 18:129–30; Federal Census, Columbia, South Carolina, 1870, and New Orleans, 1880; *Woman's Journal*, 16 June 1888; *New York Times*, 12 November 1909.)

9. Martha Reinhard Smallwood Field (1855–1898), known to her readers as Catharine Cole, grew up in New Orleans and returned to the city as a widow with a young daughter to support. She joined the staff of the *Daily Picayune* in 1881 and became the best-known southern woman in journalism. Field was a champion of the city's poorly paid schoolteachers. (Conrad, *Dictionary of Louisiana Biography*; Joy J. Jackson, *New Orleans in the Gilded Age: Politics and Urban Progress, 1880–1896* [Baton Rouge, La., 1968], 198–99.)

10. Eliza Jane Poitevent Holbrook Nicholson (1849–1896) moved from literary editor to publisher and editor of the *Daily Picayune* when her first husband died in 1876. While bringing financial success to the paper, she expanded its audience by offering features that attracted families to the daily, including society pages, advice columns, and literature. In 1884 she served as president of the Women's National Press Association. (*NAW*; *ANB*.)

11. SBA first drew a line in lieu of a name here and returned later to write a nearly illegible name over her line.

190 ⤳ SPEECH BY SBA TO THE PENNSYLVANIA YEARLY MEETING OF PROGRESSIVE FRIENDS

EDITORIAL NOTE: The Longwood Yearly Meeting, or Pennsylvania Yearly Meeting of Progressive Friends, in Chester County, met annually from 1853 to 1940. Welcoming "all who recognize the Equal Brotherhood of the Human Family," the meetings attracted reformers from far beyond the county's borders and outside the circle of dissident Friends. Stenographer George W. Black reported SBA's speech. (Christopher Densmore, "Be Ye Therefore Perfect: Anti-Slavery and the Origins of the Yearly Meeting of Progressive Friends in Chester County, Pennsylvania," *Quaker History* 93 [Fall 2004]: 28–46; Albert F. Wahl, "Longwood Meeting: Public Forum for the American Democratic Faith," *Pennsylvania History* 42 [January 1975]: 43–69.)

[6 June 1885]

The Chairman:[1]—Friends, the subject for consideration this morning is Woman Suffrage, and if any person has a right to be heard on that certainly that person is Susan B. Anthony.

Miss Anthony said:—Mr. Chairman and Friends, I have been just reminded this morning, that for thirty-three years these annual meetings have been held at Longwood. For thirty-three years the gospel of equality of rights has been preached to this people. Every one who was a child at least thirty years ago, has had line upon line, precept upon precept, not only upon the question of the abolition of slavery, on the question of temperance, prison reform and every other possible reform, but also upon the question of the equality of the rights of women. Certainly, for me to come at this late day, after all these years, to speak to you, is like the old story of carrying coals to New Castle. I do not feel any special inspiration to go over now the fundamental principles of this great movement for the emancipation of women from political slavery in this country. The ground has been gone over and over for the last forty years of our Government. I remember twenty years ago, nearly, at the time of the Constitutional Convention in my own state of New York, I met George Wm. Curtis just before he made his most admirable argument before our Constitutional Convention[2] in behalf of our question in the new Constitution which was there to be framed, and he said to me, "This whole question of the equality of human rights, is in a circle, and in a circle not larger than a peck measure, and all we have to do, is to go round and round that circle." Well, this is not only true of the whole movement, but so far as I am concerned, that measure is smaller than a peck measure. I have stood before the people all these years, and I am before you to-day, as the representative of this one idea. You could not even draw me out yesterday upon the question of what religion was.[3] I don't know what religion is. I only know what work is, and that is all I can speak on, this side of Jordan.[4] I can then on this morning talk simply of work. There is not, probably a human being in this house, that is not thoroughly educated upon the main question. Not one, I venture to say, if there is one here, I will not talk to him. It is to you who are educated, you who have stood with us for these last thirty or forty years that I wish to speak. I don't think that the day has entirely gone by for agitation, but I do believe the day for action on the part of the people has fully arrived. Now, there are various methods by which the practical result of all our talk can be obtained—the first and most active method thought of is that of each individual legislature submitting the question to be voted upon by the rank and file of the electors in each state, as to whether that adjective "male" shall be stricken out from the state Constitution. We have thought of no other method, through all the years, and that has been the method which the politicians have thought to be the only practical way. And there have been five states in this Union, whose legislatures have submitted to the people the proposition to strike from the state Constitution the word "male";—Kansas, Michigan, Colorado, Nebraska, and Oregon;[5] and in each of the states except Oregon, I have taken an active part in the canvass and have travelled from one part of the state, to another, speaking each day in each one of the counties for three months or six weeks prior to the election. I have seen thus a great deal of the temper of the people, and I stand here to-day to say that I believe that method utterly hopeless, for after all the good work we have done, what has come of it?

In Oregon, the state last named, Mrs. Duniway, the editor of "The New Northwest," one of our most admirable workers, a woman of rare intellectual ability, has worked for the last fifteen years with might and main canvassing the state each year over and over for votes, and soliciting subscriptions for her newspaper and making speeches. There is probably no state in the Union, that for the last fifteen years has had as much thoroughly good educational work done in it and for it, as the state of Oregon, and yet when the question was submitted to the popular vote, less than one third, a little more than one man out of four, went to the ballot box and voted "yes," while almost three men out of every four went there and voted "no." In each of the other states mentioned not only the local workers took part in the campaigns preceding the elections, but scores of us went out and worked day and night for this question with about as discouraging a result. In Nebraska we spent fully $10,000, and many of us travelled all over the state, to endeavor to persuade these men to go up to the ballot box and vote in favor of striking out the word male, but the result was, after spending all that money and labor, I say the result was precisely the same as it was in Oregon, as it has been in all the other states. In Michigan in 1874 there was a splendid canvass made and she was supposed to be the most liberal of states, and yet only forty thousand men voted in favor and nearly one hundred thousand voted "no." Well then, we have arrayed against us the ignorance of every state, for the ignorant woman if she could have voted on this question, would have voted as the ignorant man did. The main objection to making the popular vote the final appeal is, that the ballot box is not the place for the adjudication of such a great question of Constitutional law, as is the question of the right of each citizen to a voice in the Government. Now, I will illustrate the character of the voters. Colorado was a new state, the Centennial state. There was a most thorough canvass made, and I was in that campaign, and at the close or rather during the campaign, I remember at one place I met the Governor of the state and he said to me "The question is going to carry the state, the four hundred negroes of Denver will vote solidly for it,"[6] and I said "Governor Routt, I know nothing of the individual negro man of Denver, but I do know the school that the negroes of the nation have been educated in, and slavery never educated master or victim into the great principles of equality of rights to all people, I don't believe it"; and when the election came, just ten out of the whole four hundred voted in favor of giving the women a vote. Then in the Legislature and in the Constitutional Convention of that new state, there were Mexicans. The Chairman of the Committee on the Suffrage question was a Mexican,[7] and he voted against all his interests in our direction, but when the vote was taken scarcely one of them voted in favor of the enfranchisement of women. To give you an idea of the intelligence and progression of civilization and the arts, particularly in agriculture, as I travelled over those magnificent valleys, I frequently saw Mexicans harvesting their wheat. They cut it by hand in some way and then having laid it down in circles on the ground with the head of the wheat on the outer side of the circle, they drove little goats around to thresh it,[8] and yet each one of these men, though not one of them could speak or understand a word of English, was entitled to go to the ballot box to put in his vote to decide as to whether the women of his race in that state, as well as of the intelligent native American, should have the right of franchise. There were intelligent men among the miners there, Germans, Irishmen and Native born, who were believers in Woman Suffrage, but when the election day came, the majority of the miners in that state voted "no." Then there is another class. Every man who belongs to what is known as the "Christfield Ring"[9] is opposed to allowing his mother, or his sister, his wife or his daughter to have any voice at the ballot box. This whole class voted solidly against us, and will espouse the opposite party in every case where this question is submitted. Then there is still another class of people, very excellent people who read their Bible, and some others very good people, who are afraid that St. Paul's feelings will be hurt if women are allowed to vote. Now when you put all these classes together and submit the question to them whether there shall be equality of rights you will find the overwhelming majority will vote "no." I therefore appeal to you as friends who desire to see the day when women shall be allowed to vote on equal terms with men, that you apply to your State Legislature to secure the suffrage by some other method than that of the popular vote. I have not been in a lawyer's office where I could examine your Constitution but I believe your State Legislature has the power to enact a law that shall forbid disfranchisement on account of sex. In New York, we have been trying to get a law passed by our State Legislature, which shall forbid the continuance of the practice of disfranchising women, and in the last Legislature we came within a very few votes of carrying the bill through one branch.[10] You can perceive that if that method be legal and constitutional, which the large majority of the lawyers of our state say it is, it will be a much more hopeful way of gaining the suffrage than through the action of the less intelligent rank and file of the people. At any rate that is the method that has been adopted in my state and we have an immense number of precedents there wherein the legislature has enacted laws to extend the suffrage to classes not provided for under the original suffrage clause of the constitution. For instance in 1821 when the constitution was revised:—The next to the last time the legislature met we had in that state a property qualification of two hundred and fifty dollars, and that legislature passed a law that men who were not worth that amount should be allowed to vote, upon the ratification of the proposed amendments to the constitution.[11] Now if the legislature of New York when the constitution says that all male citizens worth two hundred and fifty dollars of real estate shall be entitled to the right to vote, had the power and the right to pass a law giving to all men who did not possess the two hundred and fifty dollars the right to vote on that most important question of the revision of the fundamental law of the state, it has an equal right to pass a law saying that women, one-half of the people of the state who are simply disfranchised by not being mentioned, shall also have the right to vote. It is on that basis that we are pressing this method in New York and since the defeat in Oregon we have been at work on this plan and felt very sanguine that the legislature would pass the bill, but it was defeated notwithstanding the splendid arguments urged in favor of it by some of the ablest lawyers who were retained to plead the cause before the committee. Now I appeal to you to study up your constitution, go to friendly lawyers and see if you in Pennsylvania cannot make your legislature pass such a law as will forbid the further disfranchisement of women on account of sex. That is the way in which I recommend you to go to work and if you find that the state constitution is so framed that the legislature cannot extend the suffrage in the state, there is still a little bit of suffrage that every state legislature has a right to grant and that is municipal suffrage. Secure the right to vote in the cities as they have in England.

In this country the city or the village is the creation of the state legislature and the state legislature has the right to dictate conditions to this creation of its own, and therefore has the right to pass a law that shall allow all women to exercise their right to vote at all municipal elections. If you had had in Pennsylvania what we call municipal suffrage and what your legislature has a perfect right to grant the women of the state, then at your last election, if it was at Kennett Square[12] every woman would have been allowed to go to the ballot box and vote as to who should be your town-officer etc., and also upon the supervisors, upon every officer and justice of the peace, every officer who has to do with executing the municipal arrangements of your village. That would push the whiskey question with you, and every woman should have the right to say whether the sale of whiskey shall or shall not be licensed. It would put the women of the state in such a position that they could elect only such men as would execute the laws. Therefore there are two kinds of work that you can do. I won't ask for school suffrage that is too small a thing to work for, but I do ask first if you possibly can do it, that the legislature shall enact a law that shall secure all the women of the state their right to vote on equal terms with men. And second, that you demand municipal suffrage. I was out in Ohio, and the United States Judge[13] said to me "Miss Anthony, the legislature of Ohio has not the right to pass a law to protect women in their right to vote in municipal elections." I asked him the question "Who gives the charter to the municipality?" "The Legislature." "Has the legislature the power to control the things it creates?" "Of course it has." I want to go a step farther. I appeal to the friends of the cause not simply to come here once a year, or once a week, or however often you may assemble in this beautiful place, to listen to talk on this question, but put your hand to the work. Go to your state legislature, raise money, not seventy-five dollars simply to pay for publishing the report of the talk of this meeting, but raise five hundred or one thousand dollars and go to your next state legislature, and have a good committee to stay there through the winter and to work this bill through the legislature, just as men go there and work when they wish to pass a bill beneficial to any class of people, miners, manufacturers or farmers. Send your delegation to the state capitol to stand in the lobby and press the work that has to be done. If we ever get our bill passed, then in addition to that work I want you to come with us to Washington, where our National Association has been acting for the last eighteen years by means of conventions and petitions, for we began to petition congress at the close of the war to make no further legislation on this question except such as shall be equal for man and for woman. We demanded in the fourteenth amendment the recognition of women, and defeated there, we demanded that the word "sex" should be added to the fifteenth amendment. We were again repulsed and from that day down to the present time the National Woman Suffrage Association has been present in Washington during the session of every Congress, in conventions, by petitions, and by hearings before Congressional Committees. We have appealed until it would seem that the Congress of the United States if for no other reason than that of the unjust judge would be ready to say "yes," to get rid of us.[14] The last Congress had special committees appointed to consider the question of our petition (the last Congress before this) and at the close of the last session of that Congress, both the Senate and House committees, presented favorable reports but too late for action.[15] During the last Congress, the committee in the Senate was new, and that committee made a favorable report and gave us a hearing of two hours.[16] The House by a vote of one hundred and twenty-four to eighty-four refused to give us a special committee to consider the question, so it was referred to its judiciary committee, said to be the ablest committee ever appointed on questions of Constitutional law. At the head of that committee was Mr. Tucker, of Virginia, and they also gave us a long hearing.[17] The majority brought in an unfavorable report, but the minority headed by Mr. Reed, of Maine, brought in a most able and conclusive minority report in our favor.[18] Now here is where the question stood at the opening of the last session of the last Congress, and during the whole winter I remained in Washington, hoping we should at least secure a discussion and vote in the Senate. At last what we did gain was a speech from the Hon. Thomas Palmer of Michigan,[19] a new Senator, an able man and a champion of whom the cause may well be proud, and I am very sorry that I have not a number of copies of his speech here to scatter among you. He was our champion, and doubtless in the coming Congress will be made the Chairman of our Committee.

Now here is where we stand to-day, and we are to start with the Forty-Ninth Congress exactly as if we had never been there before. We ask that you send your petitions through your representative, and then it will be the business of Congress to put these petitions again into the hands of the proper committees, and then we shall go again, we hope, to our National Convention, and appeal for the submission of this proposition to the State Legislatures, and keep on petitioning and appealing until the work is done.

Pennsylvania Yearly Meeting of Progressive Friends, *Proceedings of the Pennsylvania Yearly Meeting of Progressive Friends, Held at Longwood, Chester County, Penna., 1885* (Kennett Square, Pa., 1885), 55–63.

1. Frederic Hinckley presided.

2. George W. Curtis was elected a delegate-at-large to the New York State constitutional convention of 1867. The speech he delivered on 19 July 1867 when he introduced an amendment to remove the word "male" from the qualifications for voting, was entitled *Equal Rights for All*, when ECS arranged for its publication. Many editions followed, to make the speech one of the most popular tracts of the woman suffrage movement. (*Papers*, 1:85; *History*, 2:288–303.)

3. Religion was the topic for discussion on Friday morning. Rising in support of the view that true religion makes the present world a better place, Richard B. Westbrook said, "I have been trying to get Miss Anthony to tell us something of her views of religion, for I knew she would be sure to tell us that it is a part of religion to enfranchise woman, and I believe every word of that." (*Proceedings of the Pennsylvania Yearly Meeting of Progressive Friends, Held at Longwood, Chester County, Penna., 1885* [Kennett Square, Pa., 1885], p. 36, *Film*, 24:312ff.)

4. The River Jordan separates this world from the promised land and thus marks the transition from life to death.

5. Voters in Oregon defeated the woman suffrage amendment on 2 June 1884, 11,223 to 28,176. SBA did not take part in the canvass leading up to this vote because Duniway preferred to limit the campaign to local women. (*New Northwest*, 5 June 1884; McPherson, *Hand-Book of Politics for 1884*, 103.)

6. John Long Routt (1826–1907), the first state governor of Colorado, won election in 1876 and served until 1879. SBA first reported her conversation with Routt in 1877, just after Colorado voters defeated a constitutional amendment for woman suffrage. (*BDGov*; *Papers*, 3:327–31.)

7. This was Agapito Vigil (c. 1840–?), the delegate from Huerfano and Las Animas counties in southern Colorado and a farmer. He signed the minority report at the territory's constitutional convention of 1876 in support of woman suffrage. During the year of the Colorado amendment campaign in 1877, he was named to the executive committee of the state suffrage association. (*History*, 3:717–18, 720n; Federal Census, 1880.)

8. SBA may indeed have seen these agricultural practices, but her description matches quite precisely what Lucy Stone wrote in the *Boston Daily Globe*, 28 September 1877, in one of a series of letters about her travels in Colorado.

9. Possibly SBA said "Whiskey Ring."

10. James Husted's bill to prohibit disfranchisement was reported favorably from the New York Assembly's Committee on Grievances on March 9 and considered in committee of the whole on March 19. Members defeated an attempt to offer a constitutional amendment in its stead by a vote of twenty-five to eighty-five. When the bill came to a vote on April 7, an insufficient majority, fifty-seven to fifty-six, voted in its favor. (Blake and Wallace, *Champion of Women*, 159–62, 223; *History*, 4:853–54; *Woman's Journal*, 3 January 1885; *Albany Argus*, 15 January, 7 February, 10, 20 March, 8 April 1885.)

11. Hamilton Willcox published *Cases of the Legislature's Power Over Suffrage* in a second, revised edition in March 1885. On the legislative decision in New York in 1821 to set aside the property requirements to vote in order to allow all adult males to vote for delegates to the constitutional convention, see Charles Z. Lincoln, *The Constitutional History of New York* (1906; reprint, Buffalo, N.Y., 1994), 2:298–300.

12. A Chester County town near the meetinghouse.

13. The judge is not identified. No discussion of municipal suffrage at the annual meeting of the Ohio Woman Suffrage Association in May 1885 was reported. In November 1884, municipal suffrage was a topic when SBA spoke in Toledo as the guest of the city's woman suffrage association. See *Film*, 23:997–1000, 24:274–75.

14. In Luke 18:1–8, the unjust judge avenged the widow "lest by her continual coming she weary me."

15. SBA's history of congressional action begins with reports on the federal amendment issued during the Forty-seventh Congress: Senate, Committee on Woman Suffrage, *Report to Accompany S.R. 60*, 5 June 1882, 47th Cong., 1st sess., S. Rept. 686, Serial 2007; and House, Select Committee on Woman

Suffrage, *Report to Accompany H.R. 255*, 1 March 1883, 47th Cong., 2d sess., H. Rept. 1997, Serial 2160.

16. Senate, Committee on Woman Suffrage, *Report to Accompany S.R. 19*, 28 March 1884, 48th Cong., 1st sess., S. Rept. 399, Pt. 1, Serial 2175. The report includes a stenographer's record of the hearing before the committee.

17. On 8 March 1884. The testimony was published at congressional expense as *Arguments before the Judiciary Committee of the House of Representatives by a Committee of the Sixteenth Annual Washington Convention of the National Woman-Suffrage Association in Favor of a Sixteenth Amendment to the Constitution of the United States, That Shall Protect the Right of Women Citizens to Vote in the Several States of the Union* (Washington, D.C., 1884), *Film*, 23:685-88.

18. House, Committee on the Judiciary, *Report to Accompany H.R. 25*, 24 April 1884, 48th Cong., 1st sess., H. Rept. 1330, Serial 2257. Views of the minority are included within this report.

19. Thomas Palmer spoke as promised on 6 February 1885 in support of Senate Resolution No. 19, and the measure was then returned to the calendar. He supplied the National Woman Suffrage Association with three thousand copies of his speech, sending out most of them under his own frank. (*Congressional Record*, 48th Cong., 2d sess., 1322-25; *Universal Suffrage. Speech of Hon. Thomas W. Palmer, of Michigan, in the Senate of the United States, Friday, February 6, 1885* [Washington, D.C., 1885]; SBA to Elizabeth B. Harbert, 15 February 1885, *Film*, 24:106-9.)

191   SBA TO AMELIA JENKS BLOOMER

Rochester N.Y. June 23, 1885

My Dear Mrs Bloomer

I have changed printers—so that the entire of Vol. III.is to be re-set and—re-stereotyped—[1] I am at home looking after the starting of the first chapters—the book is being done in Rochester!—and I find a letter of October 4, 1884—from you relative the corrections Miss Hindman wished made saying that you still ↑had↓ the Iowa Chapter proof— uncalled for by me— I am glad you have it in hand—and shall be very glad if you will make such changes—such additions and subtractions as you see fit & send it to me— I was on the point of sending you a proof I had—entirely forgetting that you had one—

The ↑book↓ is now going to see "<u>finis</u>" written—by October or

November, at latest— We have all set about it with this resolve to push
it to completion— So close up your corrections & changes & send on
Iowa as soon as may be—direct it here— I think you had better strike
out the Woodhull mentionings— We have given her all the importance
she deserves in the 14th amendment chapter of Vol. II—and it seems to
me unwise for the state chapters to give her the prominence of a
mention, even.[2]

But use your own judgement & send it on at your earliest convenience—& oblige yours sincerely

              ✍   *Susan B. Anthony*

✍ ALS, on NWSA letterhead, Amelia Bloomer Papers, Seneca Falls Historical Society.

1. Using money from Eliza Eddy's bequest, SBA became the publisher of
the third volume of the *History of Woman Suffrage*. The title page bore her
name and home address, and she alone held the copyright. All the pages
previously set into type by Fowler & Wells were set again. Publishing was a
costly enterprise. "I am compelled to spend ↑money↓ heaveily on this huge
book," she wrote Elizabeth Harbert, "and I groan inwardly at the way it goes
every breath . . . I am spending the money & shutting my teeth—hoping to get
to the point of turning some of the books into cash." Though the Charles
Mann Printing Company of Rochester was identified simply as the book's
printer, Charles Mann worked closely with SBA on every aspect of production. She said he was "a splendid rhetorician—& close critic—& often very
much improves even Mrs Stanton's best sentences." (SBA to E. B. Harbert, 26
October 1885, *Film*, 24:585–94.)

2. Chapter twenty-three, "The New Departure under the Fourteenth Amendment," notes the presence of Victoria Woodhull at meetings of the National
association in 1871 and 1872, includes several speeches by other women that
make favorable reference to her claim that women had the right to vote under
the Fourteenth and Fifteenth amendments, and reproduces both her memorial to Congress at the end of 1870 and her speech to the House Committee on
the Judiciary on 11 January 1871.

192 ❧ SBA TO LILLIE DEVEREUX BLAKE

Rochester N.Y. July 10/85

My Dear Mrs Blake

Your Wide-Awake letter is just here—[1] My ball & chain will hold me fast this summer and into the autumn— I do most sincerely hope you have struck a lead this time— There has never been any <u>lack of law</u> to enable us to <u>vote</u>—only men willing to interpret & execute it—and women ready to test its powers—

But—go ahead— I wish you could rouse a few thousand women to try to vote this fall—and I wish I could join you in the stirring up business— But I have vowed the vow not to be or do aught else—until Vol. III. is off my head, heart & hands— Mrs Stanton—remember is no longer a New Yorker—but relapsed again into a Jerseyman!!

Oh—if there could be united, concerted work all along the line—but each woman seems to catch a glimpse of something & start off in its pursuit— If ever I get my neck out of this history yoke—I shall hope to be of some use in the world again—

Give my best love to Dr Cushing—[2] I well remember my visit at her home eight years this autumn— Good for you— Go ahead—

I am awfully ashamed I let the time slip & <u>no</u> letter to darling Bessie[3]—but tell her a <u>set</u> of W.S. History—is to my wedding present— I do hope she is & will continue to be the happier for her marriage— Lovingly yours

❧ *Susan B. Anthony*

[*sideways on first page*] Of course I shall want you to come & see my in my den—if I am at home—& come any way—my sister will give you of our humble way of living— S. B. A.

❧ ALS, on NWSA letterhead, Lillie Devereux Blake Papers, MoSHi.

1. Blake probably wrote to SBA about joining her on a tour of New York State. The state association and the Woman Suffrage party were encouraging women to register and vote in as many towns and cities as possible, testing the state election code. Hamilton Willcox had concluded that the code itself said

nothing about barring women from the polls; only nonbinding instructions to registrars and inspectors of elections mentioned the exclusion of women. In a later letter, SBA promised to register in Rochester but urged Blake to put off a campaign until the month before the election, lest women be scared away from the polls by a well-organized opposition. (SBA to L. D. Blake, 28 July 1885, *Film*, 24:406–9; *Woman's Journal*, 7 February, 1, 15 August 1885; Hamilton Willcox, *Women Are Voters! New York Suffrage Law. Full Text of the Parts of the New York Constitution and Laws Concerning the Right of Suffrage* [New York, 1885].)

2. Sarah Lamb Cushing (c. 1818–?) settled in Lockport, New York, at the end of the Civil War to practice medicine. Educated at the Albany Female Academy, she earned her medical degree at Starling Medical College in Columbus, Ohio, and cared for soldiers during the war. Cushing arranged for SBA to speak in Lockport on 5 September 1877 and hosted a luncheon where SBA met some of the city's prominent men. She was active in the New York State Woman Suffrage Association for many years. (SBA diary, 1877, *Film*, 19:12ff; Federal Census, 1880; *History*, 3:429, 4:847n; William Pool, ed., *Landmarks of Niagara County, New York* [Syracuse, N.Y., 1897], pt. 3, p. 15.)

3. Lillie Blake's daughter Bessie married John Beverly Robinson, an architect, on 1 July 1885. (*New York Times*, 2 July 1885.)

193 ✑ FRANKLIN G. ADAMS TO SBA

[*Topeka, Kan.,*] July 17 [*188*]5

My Dear Miss Anthony:

I inclose you a letter which I received from Miss Nellie C. Nichols,[1] granddaughter of Mrs. C. I. H. Nichols nearly three months ago, and which now, on re-reading I think you should read, because it answers an inquiry which your kind heart led you to make of me concerning the pecuniary circumstances of Mrs. N's. children in California. You feared they might not have been able to make her comfortable in her declining days. You and the cause so dear to her heart were in her thoughts at the very last. You will be gratified to know this. Please to return the letter when you have done with it. Yours truly

✑ F. G. Adams.

✑ ALS letterpress copy, Records of the Kansas State Historical Society, Letterpress Books, Department of Archives, KHi.

1. After the death of Clarina Nichols on 11 January 1885, SBA asked F. G. Adams if he knew "aught of the financial condition of her sons." Perhaps, SBA opined, the money raised in Kansas for an engraving of Nichols should have gone to support Nichols instead. Adams conveyed SBA's concern to Helen Clarina Nichols (c. 1868–?), known as Nellie, the younger daughter of George B. Nichols, with whom Clarina Nichols lived in Pomo, California, until her death. In this letter to SBA, Adams enclosed Nellie's reply of 23 April 1885 (in *Film* as enclosure with SBA to F. G. Adams, 28 July 1885). Nellie assured Adams that the family was "able to provide every comfort and gratify her every wish." She also reported that the name of SBA was the last word Nichols spoke, and she expressed her own hope that SBA "may long be spared to carry on the good work so many have left in her hands." SBA later attended Nellie's wedding in San Rafael, California, on 4 October 1896. (Family notes, Clarina I. H. Nichols Papers, MCR-S; Federal Census, 1880; SBA to F. G. Adams, 11 February 1885 and 28 July 1885, and SBA diary, 1896, *Film*, 24:78–81, 400–405, 34:877.)

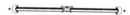

194 ≫ ARTICLE BY ECS

[23 July 1885]

HAS CHRISTIANITY BENEFITED WOMAN?

Commenting in the July number of the *North American Review*, Mrs. Harriet R. Shattuck says, "If the human race has been benefited by Christianity, and if woman is a part of the human race, then the only logical conclusion is that woman has been benefited by Christianity."[1] The difficulty with Mrs. Shattuck's syllogism is that her major premise is yet to be substantiated.

When we consider the very small portion of the human race that have ever heard of the Christian religion, and the still smaller portion that accept and believe it, it is nonsense to talk of its benefits to the whole human family.

"The Buddhist religion is the one most extensively accepted in the world, having, in round numbers, about 340,000,000 adherents. There are not more Roman Catholics in the world than people of all other religious classes. The total number of Roman Catholics is about 200,000,000 against about 80,000,000 of the Greek Church, 100,000,000

Protestants, and 6,500,000 of other Oriental churches than the Greek. Of the 1,400,000,000 people in the world, about 1,000,000,000 are not Christians, but, with the exception of the 6,000,000 Jews, are what are called heathens."[2] This shows that we cannot speak of the benefits of the Christian religion to the races of mankind. And even in professedly Christian countries, the benefits of its principles are limited to a few favored classes.

Look at the mighty multitude in the slums of the cities in England and America, as ignorant, impoverished, and brutalized as humanity is anywhere on the face of the earth. Look at the weary, wizened children as well as men and women in our factories and workshops. Look at the hard battles awakened labor is everywhere fighting for itself to-day against Christian institutions and monopolies. The equality of the human family is the glittering generality taught alike in what we choose to call the Christian religion and republican government; but the idea is nowhere as yet believed or acted upon, and in neither case has the slightest practical application to the masses.

Every form of religion and government has thus far been based on the principle of caste and class, and the greatest blessings of advancing civilization have been monopolized by the few at the expense of the many; and women have invariably belonged to the ostracized classes. But, while many are awake to their degradation in the State, and are demanding new laws and amendments to the constitutions, their religious emotions so entirely obscure their judgment that they are wholly oblivious to their degradation in the Church that sedulously teaches their inferiority and subjection.

Imagine a black man in the old days of slavery, working in the rice swamps in the broiling sun, commenting thus in the *North American Review*: "If the human race has been benefited by a republican form of government, and if the black man is a part of the human race, then the only logical conclusion is that the black man has been benefited by a republican form of government."

True, for two centuries he was worked within an inch of his life, scantily fed and clothed, his back scarred with the lash, he was kept in hopeless ignorance of all his natural rights; and now, on the slightest provocation, he is imprisoned, tortured, and worked by the civil authorities in most of the Southern States. If the master has been benefited by republican government, he certainly has not: the black skin still draws down on him unrelenting persecution.

The blessings and benefits of each step in progress do not come to all classes. It takes centuries for the simplest principles of justice to be so applied as to mitigate the miseries of the masses. All religions and governments being alike the outgrowth of human experience, differing in different latitudes, no one of them can be said to have brought any special benefit to the human race as a whole, and much less to all classes under any one of them.[3] The recent revelations now shaking London society to its foundation do not show that womanhood in that city has received any special benefit from Christianity. Nothing more horrible has ever blackened the pages of history than the reports we read of the annual sacrifice in London of 20,000 girls to men who make the laws of the kingdom and hold high places in all the professions. Think of English law making a girl of thirteen responsible for her own protection! There is no greater mistake than to suppose that blessings contributed[4] by human powers, like the rain and sunshine, come alike with refreshing influence to all.

The grand principles that Confucius, Buddha, Mohammed,[5] Jesus, and Theodore Parker proclaimed have all had their influence, inspiring here and there the lives of the few refined and receptive, through a happy combination of circumstances, and these few indirectly moulding the lives of others. Thus, the little leaven working through the centuries has ever and anon shown us the goodness of which human nature is capable. In this way, no true word spoken, no noble deed done, has been without some influence through the ages; but, in each slowly passing generation, the few have invariably robbed the many of their rightful heritage.

A religion that teaches the inferiority and subjection of the mother of the race; that ostracizes her in the practical affairs of the Church, giving her no voice in its discipline or rulers; that makes man the head of the family, while the wife is the weaker vessel owing obedience,—such a religion cannot be said to benefit woman.

The law of life and growth is liberty, justice, equality; and whatever spirit robs woman of her natural rights,—to think, to know, to be all of which she is capable,—and relegates the whole sex to certain limits of man's choosing, cannot be the spirit of a true religion.

The Christian religion has done this eighteen hundred years, if we are to accept the facts of life, the teachings of the Bible, the action of the Church, and the popular sentiment of Christian communities.

⤳ *Elizabeth Cady Stanton.*

⤳ Boston *Index*, 23 July 1885.

1. H. R. Shattuck to Editor, *North American Review* 141 (July 1885): 95–96. Although Shattuck did not mention ECS by name, she aimed her criticism at ECS's article in the May issue of the *Review*, "Has Christianity Benefited Woman?" Shattuck continued: "And the church, instead of causing the middle ages and woman's humiliation, was really the only beam of light in the midst of the darkness. Indeed, one might as well try to prove that civilization has not benefited woman."

2. ECS's source on the world's religions is not known. Similar proportions, though not exact numbers, appeared in James Freeman Clarke, *Ten Great Religions: An Essay in Comparative Theology*, originally published in 1871 and reissued frequently thereafter.

3. ECS asked the Underwoods on July 11 to add this and the next three sentences to her article, giving Benjamin Underwood authority "to work this in at some point." On that date, the New York *Sun* carried a detailed summary of William T. Stead's investigative reports for the *Pall Mall Gazette*, on the "Maiden Tribute of the Modern Babylon," about the forced prostitution of large numbers of girls in London. Stead caused an uproar in London among those offended by the lurid details he included and those shocked by conditions he exposed. Public reaction pushed Parliament to raise the age of consent from thirteen to sixteen years of age and make the procurement of prostitutes illegal. (ECS to S. F. Underwood, 11 July 1885, *Film*, 24:377–82; *Pall Mall Gazette*, 4–10 July 1885; Strachey, *The Cause*, 218–21.)

4. In her letter of July 11, this word appears to be a misspelling of "controlled" rather than "contributed," as Underwood read it.

5. Founders of three of the world's great religions, these are Confucius, or K'ung Ch'iu, (551–479 B.C.), Chinese philosopher; Buddha, or Siddhartha Gautama, (c. 563–c. 483 B.C.); and Muhammad (c. 570–632), founder of Islam.

195 ➤ SBA TO AMELIA JENKS BLOOMER

Utica—N.Y.[1] Aug. 1, 1885

Dear Mrs Bloomer

Unless you prefer to do more—you needn't feel obliged to but make corrections of facts and dates— I have one of the <u>first</u> page proofs ↑of Iowa,↓—but still I would prefer—if we do the final fixing—to work from that—because it has had the Des Moine eyes over it[2]—also Mrs M'Kinney's—[3] So I cannot but feel it must be not very far from accurate—and now if you fix it up so you can put upon it your <u>imprimateur</u>—I shall feel doubly sure— But mark the <u>order</u> of possibility is <u>small</u> <u>space</u>— I am flying back to Mrs Stanton with our remaining <u>National</u> <u>work</u> chapters—to get her to cut them <u>down</u>, <u>down</u> because I find we cannot get the <u>half</u> in this Vol. III—unless we do condense everything down to its <u>barest</u> fact statements— I would greatly prefer that Iowa should be <u>shorter</u>—than a page longer—and I am glad you will not leave that awful foot note there—the work done by each of us tells the best story of each of us—

You are not alone in fearing Mrs Stanton's reviewing of your chapter—all are the same— Still I can assure ↑you↓ that every chapter she has been over has been greatly improved— I have just,—in compliance with absolute order of the author,—allowed <u>one</u> state chapter to go to press with↑out↓ first being carefully gone over by Mrs Stanton—and I shall not allow another to go thus—and the author of it—I think— would have acknowledged the improvement if it had had the tautalogy & repetitions eliminated by Mrs Stanton—& it would have saved 10 or 15 pages of space for the rest of the chapters— So trust Mrs Stanton— I beg of you—& just make the paper tell the truth—& I will try & keep all of that—

➤ S. B. A

N.B. Remember the entire chapter is to be set <u>anew</u>—so you can cut & trim and shape as you please—only send us a clear, concise, copy— I shall be mightily glad if you send it so trimmed down—that Mrs Stanton cannot find an extra adjective to cut out— Almost every one does just as we have done all along—that is writes loosely & hurriedly—as if they had a <u>10 acre</u> lot to spread over—or a Dacota 10,000 acre wheat-field—even— Lovingly S. B A

❧ ALS, on NWSA letterhead, Amelia Bloomer papers, Seneca Falls Historical Society.

1. SBA was in transit: she left Rochester on July 29 to visit Matilda Gage, and on this day, she left Fayetteville for Tenafly. (SBA to Harriet H. Robinson, 1 August 1885, *Film*, 24:418–22.)

2. On 19 July 1885, SBA explained to Bloomer why other women in Iowa had a hand in the chapter on their state. "<u>I</u> did <u>not</u> ask any one to <u>write Iowa</u>—but I did—after hearing that there was a feeling that Des Moines might not get its full meed of praise—send a copy of the proof to Mrs Coggeswell—& ask her to call together the leading friends & read to them ~~your~~ what we had." SBA went on to explain that the group, organized by Mary Jane Coggeshall (not Coggeswell), made almost no changes except to correct the spelling of names. Bloomer continued to question the arrangement in later letters. (*Film*, 24:386–90.)

3. Jane C. Amy McKinney (1832–1905) lived in Decorah, Iowa, where SBA helped her organize the Winnesheik County Woman Suffrage Association in 1875. Working for suffrage societies and the Woman's Christian Temperance Union, McKinney acquired skill as a legislative lobbyist. As the National association's vice president for Iowa, she had shown her interest in the state's history with her detailed report to the Washington convention in 1884. Educated in Cleveland and at Oberlin College, McKinney taught school both before and after her marriage. When her daughter enrolled in the Chicago Kindergarten Training School in 1888, McKinney also enrolled as a student and at the end of her course, stayed in the city to direct a number of kindergartens. She also became president of the Cook County Equal Suffrage Association. (*American Women*; *Woman's Journal*, 6 January 1906; Oberlin College, *General Catalogue of Oberlin College, 1833–1908* [Oberlin, Ohio, 1909], 20; *History*, 3:623; *Film*, 18:503.)

196 ❧ SBA TO LILLIE DEVEREUX BLAKE

Tenafly, N.J. Sept. 6, 1885

My Dear Mrs Blake

The plot thicken with me—so that I see no prospect of my being able to be absent from here the necessary time to enable me to legally register & vote in my city of Rochester— I believe it is <u>30 days</u> previous to election day—that I must be in the city—and that will be out of the question—without putting an end to ↑the↓ finishing of Vol. III. before New Years—and that I cannot think of jeoparding— So it must be you younger women who <u>make</u> the <u>test</u> of N.Y's State constitution— I have written my sister to tell Mrs Smith[1]—the dear brave woman that she is—and that she—my sister <u>must</u> <u>lead</u> ~~on~~ the women of our city in the work of registering & voting—

We take in hand the <u>Middle States</u>—tomorrow—are finishing up the <u>New England States to day</u>— Our one severe task is <u>cutting</u> <u>out</u> <u>every</u> superfluous word & sentence— We are now come to the necessity of condensing the 38 states into 400 pages of Vol. III—and it is a fearfully difficult job—to retain the <u>points</u> and condense the <u>verbose</u> chapters— many of them—sent to us—

How do you come on?— I do hope—just as we go to press—to be able to say that <u>New</u> <u>York</u> State women have voted by the thousands!! Sincerely yours

≫   *Susan B. Anthony*

≫ ALS, on NWSA letterhead, Lillie Devereux Blake Papers, MoSHi.

1. Lewia C. Hannibal Smith (1811–?), better known as Mrs. L. C. Smith, was a widow from Clarkson, New York, who moved to Rochester in the 1850s and became a notable local activist. After attempting to register as a voter in 1872, she was made president of the Women Taxpayers' Association of Monroe County, founded during the criminal prosecution of the women who did vote. She also served on the National association's executive committee in 1877. In 1885, Smith organized a women's political club in the city. At Smith's ninety-fourth birthday party, SBA credited her with work for suffrage since 1865 and called her "the champion worker in the way of begging money in this city." (Federal Census, 1880; *History*, 3:413; Nancy A. Hewitt, *Women's Activism and Social Change: Rochester, New York, 1882–1872* [Ithaca, N.Y., 1984], 208, 210–11, 214; L. C. Smith to National Woman Suffrage Association, 28 June 1876, L. C. Smith to ECS, 27 May 1880, and Rochester *Democrat and Chronicle*, 15 June 1905, all in *Film*, 5:58, 18:866–69, 44:561.)

197 ~ SBA TO ELIZABETH BOYNTON HARBERT

Tenafly N.J. Sept. 12, 1885

My Dear Elizabeth

Yours of the 8th is just here—a most welcome comer too—

Mrs Stantons birth-day is Nov. 12th—which comes this year, on the second <u>Thursday</u> of the month— Mrs. Colby wished me to tell her what way Mrs S's 3 score & Ten years could be celebrated—and I didn't know what to say, any more than I now do—to you—[1]

But it must be in some <u>very simple</u> & <u>very</u> <u>inexpensive</u> way—because the women who most honor Mrs S. & our cause—have neither the leisure nor the cash for any other sort of celebration— I asked Mrs Sewall early last June to fix upon a plan— If it were nothing other than a letter or Post-Card of greeting—that would do— A dinner—with one or two representative women from the different states—would be nice— or a <u>purse</u>—the product of a thousand or ten thousand of the <u>mites</u> of women—would be nice—or for the friends in every locality—to hold a meeting—a reception—or some sort of gathering—to discuss the worth of the words & deeds of Mrs S.—and each meeting to send a Telegram to her— If there were any one <u>in</u> <u>New York City</u> to lead off—something might be done there—but I fear there are none there— Mrs Blake and Dr Lozier—are the only real workers—and their time & cash are both limited— thus you see I am utterly at sea—as to any plan to recommend to you— I forward your letter to Mrs Sewall—with the hope that her youthful brain may see something—

Yes—I hope you will say in your Sept. Era—that Vol. III. is more than half done—400 pages are actually stereotyped— I am getting out a circular letter—also a sheet of testimonials of Vol. I—but I fear they will be too late for this months paper— But you may say—that the book is to be ready for the holidays—and that all who send the cash before Feb. 1, 1886—I will sell the entire set—three volumes—for $12— in cloth binding & for $15— in Leather—and that Vol. III. will contain a good <u>Index</u> of the entire three volumes— I shall of course pay you for the advertisement you have kept standing—as well as the new one—

Mrs Duniway writes me that she will hold herself ready—when the right time comes—for a grand combination of all the local papers into one solid, splendid one at Chicago—to merge her N. Northwest—and to do her level best at canvassing for subscribers to it— And of cours Mrs Colby would say & do the same—for it is a mere question of time, how long any <u>one</u> woman—can carry a paper—<u>alone</u>— We must have a <u>cordial cooperation</u>—financially and editorially—no <u>one person</u> must feel to absolutely control everything about it— if <u>one person only</u> does control it—then the interest in & cash for it—centres down that which the one person has the power to attract!! No <u>one</u> woman in these new days—when there are thousands—when there used to be a hundred— who <u>cared</u> what a paper was—can speak for all— there must be a willingness to concede—on the part of each—a little something to the others—who are equally true & earnest with ↑the↓ <u>each</u>—

But I know you see!! 25 & 30 years ago—Each woman went on her own hook—without thought of any other one's caring what she said or did!! While now—each <u>one</u> who speaks or writes or acts—there is a large constituency of thinking, intelligent, earnest women who feel themselves honored or disgraced—as the <u>one's</u> words or actions—may be judged good or bad!!—Strong or weak—discreet or reckless—hence <u>mutual</u> understandings & agreements—as to public utterances and actions are vastly important to-day—as never before— I wish I could be with you & Mrs G.[2] and that Mrs Colby & Mrs Duniway & Mrs Sewall—& the <u>leading</u> <u>minds</u>—could a score of them at least—be with us—to talk of ways & means & methods! Yours &c

～ *Susan B. Anthony*

～ ALS, on NWSA letterhead, Box 2, Elizabeth Harbert Collection, CSmH.

1. Harbert settled on her own plan for ECS's birthday within a few days: she decided that the entire November issue of her monthly journal, the *New Era*, would be a tribute to ECS. Harbert recapitulated ECS's life under such headings as "Mother," "Patriot," "Reformer," and "Friend." Margaret Stanton Lawrence and Amelia Bloomer contributed articles; old friends like Frederick Douglass, Theodore Tilton, Giles and Catharine Stebbins, and John and Isabella Hooker sent greetings; Harbert culled a number of articles about ECS's life and work from the pages of *History of Woman Suffrage*; and SBA paid for an engraving of ECS to be bound into every copy. Harbert published the *New Era* for only one year, after she purchased *Our Herald* from Helen Gougar and renamed it. In what proved to be the paper's last issue in December

1885, Harbert announced that she would discontinue publishing "for a year at least." (*New Era* 1 [November 1885]: 321–48; SBA to E. M. Harbert, 17, 24, 28 September, 11, 14 October 1885, *Film*, 24:478–79, 488–91, 495–99, 536–39, 543–48.)

   2. That is, Helen Gougar.

198 ∽ ECS to Benjamin F. Underwood[1]

Tenafly N.J. Oct 19, [1885]

Dear Mr Underwood,

   The scrap you sent me was so badly expressed "Mrs Stanton" nine times repeated that I put the gist of it in better language so that you can say what I send yourself without quoting anybody[2]

   My sickness to which you refer[3] (Sub rosa) was occasioned by the warnings from you & Judge Hurlbut[4] to stay at home from that Albany complication   Fortunately, I had a crick in my knee two or three days at that time, to save me from misrepresentation. But I was punished for my special pleading by innumerable letters of inquiry as to my health. As I pride myself on being always well, it is humiliating to me to be considered otherwise. I have often thought of you & Mrs Underwood & The Index, but I have had no time to write as I ↑am↓ very busy proof reading & preparing material with the printers close on my heels. To read a thousand pages of proof four times after selecting from bushels of papers & manuscripts the facts we want makes the work of the last ten years a hard one for my old eyes & hands, & specially hard now as I have passed from the political to the religious phase of this question, for I now see more clearly than ever that the arch enemy to woman's freedom skulks behind the altar. With best regards for Mrs Underwood & yourself, sincerely

∽   Elizabeth Cady Stanton

I send you a letter from my Theodore from which you might make the extract I marked.[5] I take great pride in this son, because he is a pure noble young man, who never had since birth the slightest tendency to evil. All his tastes are refined. And he is deeply interested in my life work & sympathizes with me as fully as my daughters. All that he writes for various papers is high toned. I never heard him use a profane or obscene word in his life. Contrasting him with my four other sons (though as good as the usual run of young men) he seems to me as near perfection as a young man can be. I am glad to see his articles occasionally in the Index   I enjoy The Index from week to week & the moment we can say finis ⊤to Vol III⊥, I shall write some articles that are clamouring in my brain for utterance for both the Index & North American Review

⤳ ALS, on NWSA letterhead, Papers of ECS, NPV.

1. Benjamin Franklin Underwood (1839–1914) edited the Boston *Index* from 1880 to 1886, when he and his wife, Sara Underwood, moved to Chicago to edit the *Open Court*. He was a prominent freethinker, lecturer, and author. (*DAB*; Stein, *Encyclopedia of Unbelief*.)

2. Under "Current Topics," in the *Index*, 29 October 1885, Underwood announced plans to celebrate ECS's birthday in different localities and described her work on the *History*, closing with this unattributed report: "This valuable work, Mrs. Stanton recently remarked to a friend, would be her bequest to the coming generation of women, and the best monument she desired to her own steadfastness of purpose and unflinching loyalty to her sex."

3. Underwood asked her about news that she was too ill to attend the annual meeting of the New York State Freethinkers Association in Albany, September 11 to 13, as reported in the *Truth Seeker*, 19 September 1885. When Courtland Palmer invited her to speak at the meeting, ECS accepted but also wrote Underwood for advice: "would I compromise myself in anyway by being on their platform?" Freethinkers remained divided over how to counter the censorship exercised by Anthony Comstock, as he zealously enforced postal regulations against mailing obscene material and used them against radicalism and blasphemy. Liberals disagreed about whether to seek repeal of the postal regulations or take a stand against obscenity. Underwood had tried for many years to craft language that protected social reform and religious critics without offering the same protection to obscenity, and ECS trusted him to explain where the New York State freethinkers stood. (*Truth Seeker*, 19 September 1885, extract in *Film*, 24:476; ECS to B. F. Underwood, 11 April 1885, and C. Palmer to ECS, 27 August 1885, *Film*, 24:229–32, 443–45; Sidney Warren, *American Freethought, 1860–1914* [New York, 1943], 195–200; Stow Persons, *Free Religion: An American Faith* [New Haven, Conn., 1947], 118, 121, 124–25.)

4. Elisha Powell Hurlbut (1807–?) was active in the National Liberal League and the New York State Freethinkers Association, generally taking the more conservative line that would distinguish obscenity from sexuality and freethought and allow regulation of the former. ECS had known him since the 1840s, when he served on the New York Supreme Court with her father, Daniel Cady.

Hurlbut authored *Essays on Human Rights, and Their Political Guaranties* (1845), an influential attack on the common law and its disasterous impact on woman's rights, from which ECS and her collaborators drew language for the Declaration of Sentiments in 1848. (Henry H. Hurlbut, *The Hurlbut Genealogy, or Record of the Descendants of Thomas Hurlbut, of Saybrook and Wethersfield, Conn.* [Albany, N.Y., 1888], 232, 350–51. See also *Papers* 1.)

5. Enclosure missing. A short piece by Theodore Stanton that described all the work of the sculptor Frédéric-Auguste Bartholdi to be found in the United States appeared in the *Index*, 29 October 1885. The *Index* first published Stanton's work in the issue of 26 February 1885, and by fall of the year, his articles on French culture, religious liberalism, and women in Europe appeared nearly every month.

199 ⤋   SBA TO LILLIE DEVEREUX BLAKE

Tenafly N.J. Oct. 27/85

Dear Mrs Blake

Your note is here— I must say yes—to your invitation to be at the reunion at Dear Dr Loziers the evening of Nov. 12.?— What shall it be— a <u>dress</u> occasion?— I shan't know how to behave— I am all rusted out—know nothing know nothing but <u>history</u> plodding!!

Tell me your exact plan of proceedure! as I understand—you do not want Mrs Stanton there! Is that so?—

I am delighted that some women succeeded in registering—and I do hope some of them will get their votes into the ballot box—and then— I hope some street corner groceryman will complain of them—so they will have to go through the courts—[1] Still to get the votes in—& counted—<u>and</u> <u>no</u> <u>suit</u>—would be a tacit assent to their legality—

Why do not you & Mrs Lozier sue the Inspectors? Mrs Stanton says her son Robert would delight to study up the case—and take it through for nothing!! Sincerely yours

⤋   *Susan B. Anthony*

⤋ ALS, on NWSA letterhead, Lillie Devereux Blake Papers, MoSHi.

1. Women's attempts to register to vote were extensive. On 21 October 1885, the *New York Times* reported that fifty women in Brooklyn and others in New York City made the effort, and a few of them succeeded. Blake did not succeed. After the election in November, she reported additional attempts to

register or to vote in Buffalo, Albany, Ithaca, Ogdensburg, Utica, Poughkeepsie, Rochester, Freeville, Canastota, Randolph, and West Winfield. (*Woman's Journal*, 10, 17 October, 7 November 1885; *New York Times*, 21 October, 4, 6 November 1885.)

200 ✌ ECS to Lillie Devereux Blake

Tenafly N.J. Oct 30 [*1885*].

My dear Mrs Blake,

If you care to do anything in honor of my seventieth birthday I will tell you what I should like. In our good Dr Loziers parlors sacred to so many of our suffrage gatherings I should like to meet about two or three dozen of our most earnest <u>women</u> (not one man) for a pleasant talk among ourselves as to our work past present & to come. On the occasion I will read an essay on "the pleasures of old age" that I am now preparing for a paper at the request of the editor[1]   I do not like receptions or dinners or anything that involves trouble & expense, but a quiet social time with women alone is always agreeable to me. When my mind is interested I am bright & happy but all ordinary visiting tires me out speadily. The young women now earnestly working in this great movement are of more interest to me than all the world beside & to them I should be glad to devote the closing hours of my three score years & ten. We will all take our dinners at our own homes & meet say at eight o'clock for a pleasant informal chat. The thought of public performances of any kind puts me in a tremor. Let us have a very few of our most earnet & faithful coadjutors. Jennie June[2] is not with us in spirit   She never appreciated the dignity of our movement & I would not desire to be illustrated in the new fangled way in our newspapers. A seventieth birthday is something too serious for mirthful illustration. Now you have my idea, how does it strike you. Add twenty years to your life if you can in imagination, & think how sober you will begin to feel. Sincerely

✌ *Elizabeth Cady Stanton*

✌ ALS, Women's Rights-U.S.-Biography, MNS-S.

1. Gertrude Garrison was a writer and literary editor for the American

Press Association, a supplier of ready copy for at least fifty newspapers in the United States, from its New York City offices. Her career began in Indianapolis, where she learned to set type and became an associate editor of the. *Saturday Herald*, leaving when the editor sold the paper at the end of 1879, and joining him at the *Saturday Review*, also published in Indianapolis. She wrote poetry, and her friends from Indiana included Emily Thornton Charles and James Whitcomb Riley. Riley may have introduced her to another midwestern poet-journalist Ella Wheeler Wilcox, a close friend. While still in Indiana, Garrison also became interested in the suffrage movement. She represented the state at the National association's annual meeting in St. Louis in 1879, and in 1881, she worked on the campaign for a state suffrage amendment. She left Indianapolis in 1882. During her tenure at the American Press Association, until the spring of 1887, she published many of her own short stories as well as *General Grant, Sketches of His Life* (1885). Garrison accepted an invitation to ECS's birthday celebration, and ECS recorded that she consulted with Garrison on her plans for the *Woman's Bible* at about the same time. According to city directories, she was a widow in the 1880s. (*History*, 3:142n, 541n, 555–56; Charles Johanningsmeier, *Fiction and the American Literary Marketplace: The Role of Newspaper Syndicates, 1860–1900* [Cambridge, England, 1997], 42–48; Riley Mss., Lilly Library, InU; Gertrude Garrison Papers, MCR-S; G. Garrison to Ella W. Wilcox, 12 January 1884, Ella Wheeler Wilcox Papers, MCR-S; New York City directories, 1886, 1887; SBA to G. Garrison, 7 November 1885, *Film*, 24:640–42; *Eighty Years*, 392; with assistance from Charles Johanningsmeier and Andrea C. Hawkes.)

2. Jane Cunningham Croly (1829–1901), known as Jennie June, was a journalist, writing at this time for *Demorest's Monthly Magazine*, and a leader in the development of women's clubs, most notably founding Sorosis in New York City in 1868. (*NAW*; *ANB*.)

201 ⪢ ECS TO ELIZABETH BOYNTON HARBERT

[Tenafly, 2? November 1885][1]

Many thanks dear friend for your efforts to hand me down to immortality. It is really quite pleasant to celebrate these birthdays as we find out what people will say of us when we are dead. I have just written a fitting word of you & Mr Harbert in the Illinois chapter,[2] & I want him to know that it was not called out by his tribute to me,[3] but by his own individual merits. Susan will testify that I wrote mine several days ago. If I were not kept humble by continual cuffing by the opposition I am really afraid this number of The Era, would fill me with conceit. Then you would have the blame of destroying all my cardinal virtues. Maggies report of our tantrums[4] is really quite humiliating for such dignified saints as [*in margins of second page*] Susan & I are supposed to be. Maggie has gone to England to visit her sister so we shall have no one now to report our follies [*in margin of first page*] With kind regards for Mr Harbert & yourself

≫ *E. C. S.*

≫ ALS, on NWSA letterhead, Box 7, Elizabeth Harbert Collection, CSmH.

1. On November 2, SBA reported to Elizabeth Harbert that the birthday issue of the *New Era* arrived at ECS's house in Tenafly at eleven o'clock that morning. (*Film*, 24:625–28.)

2. *History*, 3:592–93.

3. *New Era* 1 (November 1885): 344–45.

4. *New Era* 1 (November 1885): 322–24. See appendix to this volume.

202 ≫ SBA TO MARY L. BOOTH AND ANNE W. WRIGHT[1]

Tenafly N.J. Nov. 7, 1885

My Dear Miss Boothe & Mrs Wright

A few of the <u>elect sisters</u> are to meet at the house of Dr Lozier—103— West 48th on the evening of November, 12, next Thursday—to make note of our beloved Mrs Stanton's 70th birth day—and I would love to have you two noble friends present—and if you know of Abby Sage Richardson[2]—in the city—would you invite her— Only a few of the best & most earnest friends are to be invited—it is to be wholly informal—that is not a dress affair at all— Lovingly yours

≫ *Susan B. Anthony*

P.S—Of course Mrs Stanton's "<u>lean friend</u>" of thirty years standing— will be present— S. B. A

P.S—If Mary Mapes Dodge[3] is with you—& would be please to see & hear Mrs Stanton invite her please— Mrs Stanton will give a short address—on "<u>The Pleasures of age</u>"!!

⌇ ALS, on NWSA letterhead, Papers of SBA, NPV.

1. Anne W. Wright (c. 1825–?) was Mary L. Booth's companion. A friend from childhood, Wright was the widow of a sea captain, with whom she had gone to sea. Of her life with Booth, a friend said Wright "lifted every care from Mary, and all Mary's friends were hers." (*ANB*, s.v. "Booth, Mary Louise"; Federal Census, 1880; Harriet Prescott Spofford, *A Little Book of Friends* [Boston, 1917], 124–25.)

2. Abby Sage McFarland Richardson (1837–1900) had been at the center of a scandal about marriage, divorce, and murder in 1869 and 1870, when her ex-husband mortally wounded her fiancée, Albert Deane Richardson; she married Richardson as he lay dying; and McFarland was found not guilty of murder. Since that time, she had turned to the study of literature, writing numerous books, lecturing on literary subjects, and writing for the stage. (*WWW1*; Madeleine B. Stern, "Trial by Gotham 1870: The Career of Abby Sage Richardson," *New York History* 28 [July 1947]: 271–87. See also *Papers* 2.)

3. Mary Elizabeth Mapes Dodge (1831?–1905), whose children's book *Hans Brinker; or, The Silver Skates* (1865) was a popular success, edited the children's magazine *St. Nicholas* in New York. (*NAW*; *ANB*.)

203 ～ ECS TO AMELIA JENKS BLOOMER

Tenafly N.J. Nov 10 [*1885*]

My dear Mrs Bloomer

You are certainly unfair in your last epistle to Susan, in complaining that you have not the full meed of praise you deserve in the History   In the first place your picture cost $100. Many have paid that themselves to go in, you go in free gratis. Now see in how many places you are mentioned

	See Vol. I. page	465
		457
		485
	footnote	487[1]
		488
	twice on	489
	The N.Y. Tribune	490
		491

We told you in the Iowa chapter to say what you wished said of yourself

& that I would put my initials to it. what more could I do? I wish you could know what our labor has been for the last ten years, & all the carping we have had on all sides. No body is pleased with their pictures, with the space accorded them. They seem to think the history was written specially to relate every incident of their lives   You say it is easy to get dates; that is the one thing people fail to give up. As to the points you speak of   Of course Susan & I both know we met for the first time May 1851 & yet our attention has never been drawn to the mistake in my reminiscences.[2] Writing I probably thought of the interview & not of the dates. Just as this mistake was made without the intention of defrauding any body so others are made   We should have no reason for giving Miss Clarke's laurels to Antoinette Blackwell.[3] We have asked every one who found mistakes to let us know that ~~they~~ ↑we↓ may have them corrected in the next edition. We have found it very difficult to collect facts & dates from anybody   But you will have a taste of what we go through yourself, when the Iowa chapter is finally launched in Vol III   You have done your best to be exact & fair but you will see how Tray Blanche & sweetheart[4] will all bark and howl. If you could see the letters we get, the growling we hear, about everything you would wonder that we had not thrown up the whole thing in disgust long ago. I liked the New Era very much. I do not think the minor things of which you speak are of the slightest consequence, but it is late and night yours

⇝ E. C. S.

[*in margin of first page*] Who cares two pins as to which fox cut his [*in margins of second page*] tail off first, so long as we were all ashamed of having cut them off at all[5]

⇝ ALS, Amelia Bloomer Papers, Seneca Falls Historical Society.

1. Bloomer's name appears on page 486, not page 487; otherwise ECS's list is accurate.

2. ECS's prose creates an impression that the two friends met in 1848, though a long quotation from Theodore Tilton dates the friendship to 1850. In fact, they met in 1851. Bloomer knew the correct date because SBA was her guest in Seneca Falls at the time. See *History*, 1:456–57, and *Papers*, 1:182–84.

3. Bloomer spotted an error in accounts of women's early temperance work in *History*, 1:472–513, where Emily Clark and Antoinette Brown (later Blackwell) are mentioned repeatedly. Emily Clark was a founding member and officer of the Women's New York State Temperance Society and, with SBA, an agent of

the society in 1852 and 1853. She is identified only through that work: she was single, and the press described her as of LeRoy, Genesee County. (*Papers*, 1:196–98, 197n, 204n, 217, 218n, 229.) Antoinette Louisa Brown Blackwell (1825–1921) was the first American woman to be ordained a minister. Before her marriage in 1856, when she lived in Henrietta, New York, she too worked in the women's temperance movement. (*NAW*; *ANB*. See also *Papers* 1–3.) Bloomer may have disputed the account on page 489 about a delegation consisting of Clark, Brown, and Bloomer who were sent to the legislature in 1853 with temperance petitions. Dexter Bloomer's memoir of his wife took pains to explain that the delegation in fact consisted of Clark, Bloomer, and H. Attilia Albro. (Dexter C. Bloomer, *Life and Writings of Amelia Bloomer* [1895; reprint, New York, 1975], 95–96.)

    4. William Shakespeare, *King Lear*, act 3, sc. 6, lines 20–21.

    5. ECS included a short account of dress reform in the 1850s within her chapter of reminiscences, and she compiled a list in the appendix of the women who wore the Bloomer costume with shortened skirts. Amelia Bloomer's name appeared in the appendix but not in the chapter, where ECS credited Elizabeth Smith Miller with designing and first donning the costume. See *History*, 1:469–71, 844.

204 ~ ANTOINETTE BROWN BLACKWELL TO ECS

Elizabeth N.J Nov. 10, 1885.

Dear Mrs. Stanton

    Many happy returns of the day! Increasing happiness and honors with revolving years! You must live to be at least 95 or you will fall sadly short of your best privileges as a strong minded woman able to control a healthy body. But of course you will do that. Strike for a hundred.

    Haven't you gone forward somehow in date? My next birthday, six months hence, will be the sixty first. Surely you did not use to be so far away. I thought you, Susan, Lucy, Prof Mitchell, Mrs Howe and several others all came within one year. But 70! So much the better. It is just the prime of life, is it not?

    It is grand that all of our lifetime workers refuse to grow old. They make splendid illustrations of the good results which come from the steady use of brains—especially of "pluck" and Will. Illustration is the grand revolutionizer after all. "Seeing is believing."[1]

Well, accept my best wishes and very sincere congratulations Your friend

⥲ *Antoinette Brown Blackwell.*

⥲ ALS, Blackwell Papers, MCR-S.

1. An English proverb.

205 ⥲ "THE PLEASURES OF AGE": SPEECH BY ECS

EDITORIAL NOTE: Fifty women gathered at Clemence Lozier's home on West Forty-eighth Street to celebrate ECS's seventieth birthday with speeches, refreshments, and music on 12 November 1885. Lillie Blake introduced the guest of honor, who spoke, by one account, for twenty minutes on "The Pleasures of Age." All available texts of this speech date from many years after the event. According to SBA, the speech disappeared: "We thought it was forever lost," she noted on clippings sent to the Library of Congress in 1904, until she and Ida Harper stumbled upon the text late in 1903. However, ECS had found the speech earlier and submitted it to the *Boston Investigator* for publication in 1901. It is not clear from SBA's notes whether she found the 1901 printing or an earlier one; she sent an unspecified copy to Harriot Stanton Blatch and the *Investigator* version to the Library of Congress. Harriot Blatch advertised copies of the speech for six cents, published by her brother's European Publishing Company in New York, in time for celebrations of her mother's birthday in 1904. Three different imprints of a pamphlet survive, all lacking a date and clues about the publisher; one bears an inscription by Margaret Stanton Lawrence in 1928, while another is designed in a style consistent with items Blatch published in 1915. The Blatch text of the speech, alike in all the pamphlets, differs from the text published in 1901. Gone are the tributes to Lillie Blake and Clemence Lozier, along with other references particular to the birthday celebration. What follows is the text of 1901, but how closely it matches what ECS said in twenty minutes sixteen years earlier is not known. (*New York Tribune*, 13 November 1885; *Woman's Journal*, 15 October 1904; SBA's notes, scrapbook 2, ECS Papers, DLC; *The Pleasures of Age*, inscribed copy in Seneca Falls Historical Society, N.Y.; copy in scrapbook 2, Papers of ECS, NPV; copy from the estate of Mary Hillard Loines, Women's Rights Collection, MCR-S.)

[12 November 1885]

A friend asked me one day to write an article on "The Pleasures of Age" for her Journal, to which request I readily responded; being on the threshold of seventy, I felt myself peculiarly fitted to write an essay on that theme.

Before giving my views, however, I thought I would ask those of my friends whom I chanced to meet who had passed threescore and ten what they had to say on the question. Accordingly, seated at the breakfast table one morning, at a mansion up town, with several friends revolving round the seventies and eighties, I launched my question for their serious consideration.[1]

The octogenarian at the head of the feast, after a few moments thought, replied sadly, "There is no pleasure in old age."

> Whatever poet, orator or sage,
> May say of it, old age is still old age,
> It is the waning, not the crescent, moon,
> The dusk of evening, not the blaze of noon.[2]

As my friend's life had been one of great usefulness, enjoying good health and all the ordinary comforts of wealth and position, I was rather surprised at this reply. Another said perhaps one may find some pleasure in being deaf, as then you do not hear the nonsense of ordinary talk. Another said blindness, too, may have its advantages, as then your eyes are shut to many things you fain would never see. Another said there is comfort even in being crippled, as then, like the old woman in the song, who was always tired, one need do nothing but rest forever and ever.

Most discouraging negations from a group of educated people from which to extract an essay on the pleasures of old age. And many more I have asked in the ordinary walks of life without one triumphant response as to the joys of this grand period of our mortal life. Even the poets and philosophers speak with no certain sound.

So I turned to my calendar of October 8th, as it was prepared by a woman on the shady side of sixty, Elizabeth Smith Miller.[3] I hoped to find something encouraging there. I read the following:

> Under the eternal laws of the universe I came into being, and under them I have lived a life so full that its fulness is equivalent to length.

There has been much in my life that I am glad to have enjoyed, and much that generates a mood of contentment at the close. I never dream of wishing that anything were otherwise than as it is; I am frankly satisfied to have done with this life. I have had a noble share of it, and I desire no more. I neither wish to live longer here, nor to find life again elsewhere.—Harriet Martineau.[4]

As Miss Martineau lived to be over seventy, and had labored assiduously with her pen for all the reforms of her day, her willingness to rest through eternity is not surprising.

To my young disciples looking forward with apprehension to the time when the joys of youth have passed, to that period so deplored by all, I bring a message of hope, of triumph, of victory. By making the best possible use of the passing days, you have the opportunity to make your old age all that you desire.

If we analyze the pleasures of youth, middle life and old age, we find all alike depend on the capacity of the individual for enjoyment. In other words, on organization, education, development. One child will amuse herself all day without toys or scenes of diversion, seemingly thinking of the nature of everything about her, using her little brain, in its feeble beginnings, peering into the soul of the universe, watching the motion of the trees outside, or the play of the sunbeams on the nursery walls, always healthy and happy, as a well-organized child should be. Another is restless, peevish, with all the change of attention that love and affection can give, with all the books and toys that Yankee invention has taxed itself to produce. The former, in the girl of sweet seventeen, is like a beam of sunshine wherever she goes, reflecting, like the prism, the glorious colors of the light. Her reports of balls, parties, skating-rinks, the school, the teacher, the home, the parents, are all gilded with her own glad outlook on life. She is linked with everything that is good and true and beautiful in Nature, in harmony with herself and her surroundings. Never on the outlook for personal attention, she is never neglected; not on the watch for the meed of praise, she is rarely disappointed. Her thoughts are not centred in herself, hence she has no envy, hatred or malice. She is still seemingly thinking of the mysteries of life and her relations to the outside world. The peevish, restless child is the discontented girl, more and more unhappy as the years roll round. She is in the same world with our sunbeam, but reflects in *her* atmosphere only the pale, white light. She has all the outward appliances of happiness, wealth, position, beauty, talent, but there is no music in her soul; to her unskillful touch discords only answer back.

Middle age, too, repeats alike the virtues and the follies of our youth. Our girls are now wives of senators in Washington.[5] One in a simple, comfortable establishment, outside the whirl of fashion, performs the social duties incumbent on her position with becoming etiquette, giving her best hours and faculties to a higher world of thought. She reads Comte, Buckle, Darwin,[6] Spencer, John Stuart Mill, American jurisprudence, Constitutional law, the Congressional Record, keeping pace with the debates on all great questions of government. She is interested in the reforms of the day, possibly attends the woman's rights conventions, and, through her influence, her husband may be the champion in the Senate of all bills for just and progressive legislation. Good men visit her to have their moral purposes strengthened to new endeavor, to be encouraged in patriotic sentiments and labors for the real good of the nation. Her ambition for her husband and children is that they may lead pure, grand lives, and by every word and action to leave the world better than they found it; to make themselves links in the chain of influences by which humanity may be lifted to a higher plane of action. With Mazzini,[7] the great Italian apostle of liberty, she labors: first, for justice and equality to all; second, for the love of country; third, for the best interests of the family; fourth, for her own highest good and development. With her the universe is not built on the Ego, but the Ego is the outgrowth of the universe.

It is easy to predict what the old age of such a royal soul must be. She knows no vacant, restless solitude. Her library is full of old acquaintances, whose noble deeds and words are as familiar as those of living friends. When tired of reading she can recite by the hour inspiring sentiments in prose and verse, and, if she has cultivated a taste for music, and can play on some instrument, then, in diviner language than any words can reach, she will touch the deepest, tenderest chords in the human soul; and thus with boundless resources to entertain herself, she will always be a charming companion alike to old and young.

And how fares our other matron in her gilded palace home, so spacious, richly furnished, adorned with pictures and statuary, brilliant with the gala-day receptions of leading belles and statesmen, lords and ladies from foreign lands, amid scenes surpassing far the luxury and elegance of the Caesars in the palmiest days of Rome? As the wife of a senator she has attained the highest position in our Republic. Rich in diamonds, velvets and laces, she is the observed of all observers, in beauty and grace she is the one peculiar star envied by all her class; but, alas, the peevish child, the restless girl, is but reproduced in the fashionable, worldly-minded woman. Her notes are still, as ever, notes of discord in the great psalm of life. With her the true order of human duties are reversed from that of our ideal woman. Now it is: 1st. Herself; 2nd. Family; 3d. Country; 4th. God, or the eternal principles of justice and truth. Beauty, wealth, position gone, evanescent possessions at the best, what has this matron left in poverty and solitude to gild the sunset of her life, or to make her company attractive?

Old age to such as these must be as varied as their experiences in bygone years. The life of those obedient to law, linked with the birds, the flowers, the majestic trees and mountains, and the eternal stars revolving with one common purpose around the great central source of light and truth, knows no old age; it is continued progress step by step in harmonious development.

The great Humboldt,[8] resting from his prolonged researches into the facts of science, sitting on the mountain side, in converse with his friends on Nature's mysteries, was wont to say: "I find all things governed by law." The same message the lovers of science bring back to us from the jeweled arches in the caves of the earth, from the eternal snows on mountain peaks, from ocean depths and realms above the clouds, they tell us, too, "all things are governed by law." And this law is as immutable in the moral as in the material world, in its control over man, as over all inferior forms of animal life. The first point in education, says Herbert Spencer, "is to learn the laws that govern our own organization and our relations to the outside world," and make our lives harmonious with them.[9] We shall find that the keynote in our human relations is love and the grand chorus is equality.

The pleasures of age depend on what constitutes the threads of our lives and how they are woven together. The silk worm hatched from a sound egg, well fed, in a genial atmosphere will weave his allotted skein of silk, his own winding-sheet, and rest from his labors; but in the resurrection he comes forth a pure white butterfly. There has been no friction in his quiet life, no failure in its purpose. So all that is woven into our lives will step by step reveal itself in a purer, higher development. Those who have obeyed the physical laws will have sound bodies and they will not be racked with pain and disease; they will work, eat, sleep and rise again to fulfill the round of human duties until the machinery runs down to work no more. If they have obeyed the moral laws, a blessed peace and joy pervade their lives, unbroken as the years roll on. The forces wasted by so many erring ones in vain regrets, by them are garnered up and used in noble deeds. If they have obeyed the laws of mind and enriched their lives with broad culture, with a knowledge of art, science and literature, and wisely used it all in philanthropic endeavors, they will have boundless resources in themselves for their own happiness and to make social life pleasant and profitable for others. They will be a pillar of light in this wilderness of life to the ignorant and the unfortunate, and a star of hope to the miserable and the despairing.

With good health, moral purpose and mental vigor, the pleasures of age are many and varied. If they differ from those we enjoyed in younger days, they are not less real and satisfying. In the place of active we enjoy passive exercise. Rolling in an easy phaeton is more to our taste than a gallop in the saddle. If our dancing days are over we still enjoy the harmony in music and motion, and the graceful posing of youth and beauty. While at ease in a comfortable rocking-chair we can imagine that the waltzing, the quadrille, the Virginia reel are all, as for the kings of old, gotten up for our special entertainment. Instead of going through the fatigue of skating, well wrapped in furs we can drive about in a sleigh and see the fun without the danger of cracking our skull, or of having our toes, ears and nose half frozen. If we can no longer run and hunt the fox we can take a pleasant stroll, at the twilight hour, over the autumn leaves and enjoy the rustle and crackling as much as ever, with all the added memories of early days that, like a picture gallery, we can review at our leisure.

The young have no youthful memories with which to gild their lives, none of the pleasures of retrospection. Neither has youth a monopoly of the illusions of hope, for that is eternal, to the end we have something still to hope. And here age has the advantage in basing its hopes on something rational and attainable. Instead of building castles in the air we clear off the mortgages from our earthly habitations. Instead of waiting for the winds of good fortune to waft us to elysian fields and heights sublime, we plant and gather our own harvests and climb step by step on ladders of our own making. After many experiences on life's tempestuous seas we learn to use the chart and compass, to take soundings, to measure distances, to shun the dangerous coasts, to prepare for winds and weather, to reef our sails, and when it is wise to stay in safe harbor. From experience we understand the situation, we have a knowledge of human nature, we learn how to control ourselves, to manage children with tenderness, servants with consideration, and our equals with proper respect. Years bring wisdom and charity, pity, rather than criticism, sympathy, rather than condemnation, for the most unfortunate.

I often hear women say, after their children are grown up and established in life, husband dead, perchance, that they have nothing to live for. I would point them to the broad fields of philanthropic work, to the wants and needs of humanity, calling for faithful service on every hand. It is unworthy any woman to say "my work is done" so long as she has energy and talent to fill the vacant places in this struggling, suffering sphere of action. I point such women to their own undeveloped faculties, to their duty to improve every talent they possess, to the study of the useful sciences, the fine arts, to practical work in the trades and professions, for brave souls, true women, are needed everywhere. "Yes," they say, "I might have done something years ago, but I am too old now to begin." Not so. Fifty, not fifteen, is the heyday of woman's life, then the forces hitherto finding an outlet in flirtations, courtship, conjugal and maternal love, are garnered in the brain to find expression in intellectual achievements, in spiritual friendships and beautiful thoughts, in music, poetry and art. It never is too late to try what we may do. In the words of Longfellow:

> Ah! Nothing is too late
> Till the tired heart shall cease to palpitate;
> Cato[10] learned Greek at eighty; Sophocles
> Wrote his grand Oedipus, and Simonides
> Bore off the prize of verse from his compeers
> When each had numbered more than fourscore years,
> And Theophrastes, at fourscore and ten,
> Had but begun his characters of men;
> Chaucer, at Woodstock with the nightingales,
> At sixty wrote the Canterbury Tales;

Goethe at Weimar, toiling to the last,
Completed Faust when eighty years were past.
These are indeed exceptions; but they show
How far the gulf-stream of our youth may flow
Into the Arctic regions of our lives,
Where little else than life itself survives![11]

The hurry and bustle of life over, if prosperity is ours, surely each of us may take up some absorbing congenial work to dignify the sunset of our lives, and if poverty is our lot, labor should be a necessity, rather than an idle life of dependence.

Professor Swing, of Chicago, thought people ought to read novels enough to keep up the colorings and warmth of youth through middle life and old age.[12]

Certainly let us read novels, mingle with the young, and enter into whatever we really enjoy. It was a custom with my father,[13] who was the oldest judge that ever sat on the bench in this country (84), always to take a novel in his valise when on one of his circuits, to read when waiting at the depot, or for his breakfast, or on the bench before the clerks and lawyers were ready to open the Court, and many are the tears he has shed over the miseries of imaginary characters. His sympathies were warm and tender to the end.

The old idea used to be that after fifty our special business was to prepare for death, that our reading should comprise the Bible, the lives of saints,[14] Zimmerman on "Solitude,"[15] Bickersteth on "Prayer,"[16] Harvey among the tombs,[17] Young's "Night Thoughts,"[18] and Baxter's "Saints' Rest,"[19] quite forgetting that the best possible preparation for death, is active work and generous services to our fellow-men. And what is death, that we should contemplate it with sorrow and gloom? Simply to fall asleep when our work here is finished, our limited powers exhausted, to awake with renewed energies and to more soul-satisfying pleasures, in a higher sphere of action. Why torment couches[20] with the medieval theologies of an angry God, a judgment seat, an all-powerful devil, and everlasting torments in hell—ideas that emanated from the diseased brains of dyspeptic celibates? These masculine theologies, all so foreign to the mother soul, should have no place in our thoughts. They should no longer be permitted to shadow our lives.

In the fuller development of the feminine element in humanity we shall have the impress of woman's thought and sentiment in government and religion, exalting justice and equality in the one, love and tenderness in the other, anger and vindictive punishment having no place in either. Harriet Martineau said that the "happiest day of her life was the day she gave up the charge of her soul."[21] I can say that the happiest period of my life has been since I emerged from the shadows and superstitions of the old theologies, relieved from all gloomy apprehensions of the future, satisfied that as my labors and capacities were limited to this sphere of action, I was responsible for nothing beyond my horizon, as I could neither understand nor change the conditions of the unknown world. Giving ourselves, then, no trouble about the future, let us make most of the present, and fill up our lives with earnest work here. The time has passed for the saints to withdraw from the world, to atone for their sins in fasting and prayer. Our good St. Clemence[22] here, on the shady side of her seventieth year, diligently laboring at her profession, healing the sick, bearing messages of hope to many a bedside of anguish, active in the great movement for woman's enfranchisement, opening her parlors month after month for our convocations, ready to test every new loop-hole of escape from bondage, now pleading with statesmen under the very dome of the Capitol at Washington, and now with the guardians of the ballot-box in the precincts of her district. Our St. Clemence, always active on the watch-tower of faith and hope, with her bright face and busy hands, is of more value to her day and generation than a regiment of saints who spend their time weeping and praying over the sins of the people. She is a worthy example for our younger co-workers to emulate, as she has carved her own way to fortune, and is pre-eminently a self-made woman. Moreover, our St. Clemence enjoys more real happiness than all Newport belles that have danced the summers away for the last twenty years. Who would dread an old age like hers? I am sure you all join with me in wishing many years of happiness and usefulness yet to our good St. Clemence.

Again, to speak of our representative in a younger generation. I would ask, is not Mrs. Lillie Devereux Blake[23] more dignified in traveling from town to town and city to city, trying to rouse women to some thought in regard to the laws and constitution of the Empire State, than she would be seated in her parlor with her feet on the grate, netting a tidy and bemoaning the fact that she is nearing the fifties and had nothing to do, or in spending her time in making calls and attending balls and receptions? There is just the same difference in dignity and importance between women engaged in some earnest life-purpose and those who do nothing that there is between men who labor in the trades and professions and those who spend their time in yachts, horse-races and general amusements. Yes, my youthful coadjutors into whose hands we are now passing the lamp of this great reform, that has lighted us through so many dark days of persecution, rest assured that your labors in this movement will prove a double blessing;—to yourselves in the higher development it will bring to you, and to the world in the nobler type of womanhood henceforth to share an equal place with man. In the words of Tennyson:

> Everywhere
> Two heads in council, two beside the hearth,
> Two in the tangled business of the world,
> Two plummets dropped as one to sound the abyss
> Of science and the secrets of the mind.[24]

It is the general opinion that with age must come decrepitude, that its inevitable accompaniments are wigs, spectacles, ear trumpets, false teeth, weak knees, asthma, neuralgia and rheumatism. This is by no means the case. I know several old gentlemen on the shady side of eighty who read without spectacles, whose hearing is as keen as a rabbit's, who can walk as briskly as most men of forty, and have as keen a zest as ever in all there is in life worth enjoying. One of our most celebrated dancing-masters in western New York, Mr. Cobleigh,[25] played on his violin and danced as lightly as a boy of sixteen long after he was seventy years old. I have no doubt if we kept up gymnastic exercises and a diligent rubbing every day, we should retain our suppleness of limb and motion to a good old age. "I suppose the time will never come when women, or men, either, will delight in crow's feet, wrinkles or gray hairs, but the time will come—aye, and now is—when they will view these blemishes as but a petty price to pay for the joy of added wisdom, for the deeper joy of closer contact with humanity, and for the deepest joy of worthy work well done."

But if our senses are not so keen as in youth, our spiritual eyes behold the unfolding of many glories we never saw before. We hear the music in the air, the harmonies of Nature unheeded in the early days, the interior life grows brighter as the years roll on, the horizon of thought broadens, new vistas open to unknown paths, we see visions and dream dreams of celestial harmony and happiness of the complete fulfillment of all our earth-born plans and purposes, begun in youth, in doubt and weakness, but finished at last in faith and victory.

> For age is opportunity, no less
> Than youth itself, though in another dress;
> And as the evening twilight fades away,
> The sky is filled with stars invisible by day.[26]

≈ *Boston Investigator*, 2 February 1901, in ECS Papers, DLC. In *Film* at 2 February 1901.

1. SBA annotated the copy of this speech she deposited in the Library of Congress. Here she noted in the margin "her sisters Mrs Eaton—Mrs Wilkeson—& Mrs McMartin!! all lovely women." (*Film*, 41:934–37.)

2. Henry Wadsworth Longfellow (1807–1882), "Morituri Salutamus," written for the fiftieth reunion of the Bowdoin College class of 1825.

3. An asterisk here marks a footnote: "Only daughter of Gerrit Smith, the philanthropist."

4. *Harriet Martineau's Autobiography*, ed. Maria Weston Chapman (Boston, 1877), 2:106–7.

5. SBA commented here, "I think Mrs Stanton must have had in mind Mrs Ellen C. Sargent wife of Senator A. A. Sargent of California."

6. In her list of nineteenth-century intellectual giants, those not yet identified are Auguste Comte (1798–1857), French philosopher; Henry Thomas Buckle (1821–1862), English historian; and Charles Robert Darwin (1809–1882), English naturalist.

7. In *The Duties of Man*, translated into English by Emilie Ashurst Venturi in 1862, Giuseppe Mazzini (1805–1872), champion of the unification of Italy under a Republican government, ranked the importance of man's duties as first to Humanity, then to Country, to Family, and finally to Self.

8. ECS's likely source was Robert Ingersoll's lecture "Humboldt," marking the centennial of the birth of Alexander von Humboldt (1769–1859), a German naturalist. Ingersoll included it in his collection *The Gods, and Other Lectures* (1874), a book ECS read in 1877. The phrase "The Universe is Governed by Law" was the lecture's subtitle and its last line, as Ingersoll paid tribute to a scientist who challenged superstition. (*The Works of Robert G. Ingersoll* [New York, 1929], 1:93–117; *Papers*, 3:279.)

9. In *Education: Intellectual, Moral, and Physical* (1861), Herbert Spencer placed science at the heart of all worthwhile education. ECS's words may not be Spencer's, but the idea is evident in Spencer's simplification of his argument: "all social phenomena are phenomena of life—are the most complex

manifestations of life—must conform to the laws of life—and can be understood only when the laws of life are understood." (Herbert Spencer, *Essays on Education and Kindred Subjects* [1911; reprint, New York, 1977], 28.)

10. From the classical world, Longfellow names the first century Roman poet Publius Valerius Cato, the Greek playwright Sophocles (c. 496–406 B.C.), the Greek poet Simonides of Ceos (c. 556–c. 468 B.C.), and the Greek philosopher Theophrastus (c. 372–c. 287 B.C.). He also singles out the English poet Geoffrey Chaucer (c. 1342–1400) and the German poet Johann Wolfgang von Goethe.

11. Longfellow, "Morituri Salutamus."

12. The Chicago preacher David Swing often lectured on literary subjects, urging his audience to read widely, keep up with new ideas, venture away from their specialities, and explore novels. Collections of his lectures available by 1885 included *Truths for To-Day, Spoken in the Past Winter* (1874), *Motives of Life* (1879), and *Club Essays* (1880).

13. Daniel Cady (1773–1859) served on the bench of New York's Supreme Court from 1847 through 1854.

14. Alban Butler, *The Lives of the Fathers, Martyrs, and Other Principal Saints* (1756–1759), better known as *Lives of the Saints*.

15. Johann Georg Zimmermann (1728–1795), a Swiss physician and writer, published *Über die Einsamkeit* in 1756. The many English translations of the work were variously titled *Solitude* or *Solitude Considered*. ECS listed this and the works by Baxter, Hervey, and Bickersteth in her lecture "Our Boys" as examples of "those heavenly minded books nobody ever reads." ("Our Boys," p. 46, *Film*, 45:75ff.)

16. Edward Bickersteth (1786–1850), an English evangelical clergyman, first published *A Treatise on Prayer: Designed to Shew Its Nature, Obligation, and Privilege* in 1818.

17. James Hervey (1714–1758), not Harvey, wrote very popular devotional literature in England, including *Meditations among the Tombs*, published in 1746.

18. Edward Young (1638–1765), an English poet, published the first in his series called *The Complaint; or, Night-Thoughts on Life, Death and Immortality* in 1742. The full series, through *Night the Ninth*, became available in 1750.

19. Richard Baxter, *The Saints Everlasting Rest: Or, a Treatise of the Blessed State of the Saints in Their Enjoyment of God in Glory* (1688).

20. The variants published by Harriot Blatch read "torment the dying." Possibly the typesetter misread ECS's writing of "ourselves."

21. This idea, though not the words, is found in *Harriet Martineau's Autobiography*, 1:493. When she no longer viewed Christianity "as a scheme of salvation," Martineau cherished "the blessed air of freedom from superstition," and acknowledged "that not for the universe would we again have the care of our souls upon our hands."

22. An asterisk here marks a footnote: "Dr. Lozier, among the earliest women to enter the medical profession."

23. A footnote at this point reads: "A Southern woman, born in North Carolina."

24. Alfred Lord Tennyson, "The Princess," pt. 2, lines 155–60.

25. Mr. Cobleigh taught dancing in Rochester. (*Rochester History* 8 [April 1946]: 3.)

26. The final lines of Longfellow's "Morituri Salutamus."

206 ~ ECS TO MARGARET STANTON LAWRENCE

Tenafly Nov 15, [*1885*]

Dear Maggie,

Well my birthday went off brilliantly in all respects. I had cablegrams, from distinguished people in France Germany England, beautiful letters; & letters & telegrams from all the associations in the Union[1] and presents, of books, silver, mosaics, pictures, & baskets of fruits & flowers. Aunty Had[2] sent me some handsome blankets & a new dress. Hattie Brown a check for $50. Frances Power Cobbe wrote me a beautiful letter[3] All our associations held parlor meetings the afternoon or evening of the day All the Massachusetts people even Lucy sent telegrams of congratulation.[4] They came by the dozens all day & to the evening meeting in New York Many of the Journals had puffs even The Tribune mentioned Mrs Henry B. Stanton's birthday reception[5] I read an address about thirty minutes long on "the pleasures of old age" which was pronounced very good. There again I had three magnificent baskets of flowers presented me. I had a grand dinner at Aunt B's[6] Flo & Edith were there en route for Florida. Friday Susan & I came back & took up our pens & went to work as usual. I had a letter from Mrs Bullard, she is at home again feeling very poorly. Women have been educated into the idea that at fifty they must undergo some remarkable change, pass through great perils, something like the sun in the equinoctial storm, which is all pure nonsense I hope you & Hattie will never get that absurd idea into your little heads & as you approach that period begin to shiver on the brink of Jordan imagining that your time has come to pass over. I never saw the slightest variation in my health either beginning nor ending the monthly period, & yet you will hear women with bated breath on all sides speak of these dangerous crises in a womans existence, pure stuff & nonsense. I mention this now not that you are nearing fifty, but as when you do I may not be here to warn you that you have nothing new to encounter. Just keep your heads & hands busy & your hearts warm with love of grand souls thoughts & labors & you will pass the line without knowing it. I do wish you ↑would↓ send me a word often if only a postal, as it is my greatest comfort to hear from you all on that side of the great waters. We are still having warm & delightful weather whole weeks of sunshine right along   Poor Mr Norris[7] is in a very bad way. He was boozy as usual & fell off the cars & broke his nose & was otherwise much injured. Mrs Norris sent me some splendid roses from her conservatory. Cousin Lizzie sent me a bushel basket full of preserves. She & Nannie[8] both wrote me very pretty letters. We have had but little need yet of anything but a little wood fire morning & evening. Three years ago to day we were busy making the final preparations for Hatties marriage at 10. Duchess street, & two years ago I was at Mrs Jacob Brights about to sail for America & now here I am again comfortably fixed in my own nest once more. Things move along very nicely with love for all

≪ *Mother*

≪ ALS, on NWSA letterhead, Scrapbook 2, Papers of ECS, NPV.

1. Margaret Stanton Lawrence sailed for England to visit her sister before her mother's birthday was celebrated. Lists of those who sent birthday greetings to ECS and some of their messages are in *Film*, 24:658–59, 661–62, 674.

2. That is, Harriet Cady Eaton. Her daughter, Harriet Eaton Brown, is also named in ECS's list.

3. See *Film*, 24:661.

4. At a Suffrage Sociable in Boston on November 11, "[i]t was voted, on motion of Mrs. Stone, that congratulations be sent to Mrs. Stanton on her seventieth birthday." (*Woman's Journal*, 14 November 1885.)

5. See *Film*, 24:672. Editors at the *Tribune* adopted the use of "Mrs. Henry B. Stanton" in all references to ECS in July 1869, and successors to Horace Greeley continued the practice. See *Papers*, 2:77n.

6. That is, at the home of Tryphena Cady Bayard, where they were joined by ECS's niece Flora McMartin Wright and Flora's daughter Edith Livingston Wright (1874–1960).

7. Possibly this was William Norris (c. 1840–?), a New York City dealer in wholesale woolen goods, who resided in Tenafly with his wife, Juliet G. Norris. (Federal Census, 1880; city directories, 1885, 1886.)

8. That is, Elizabeth Smith Miller and her only daughter, Anne Fitzhugh Miller (1856–1912). Nannie Miller, who lived with her parents in Geneva, New York, joined the suffrage movement in the 1890s as an organizer of political equality clubs in Ontario County and a regular participant in the state suffrage association. (*Geneva Daily Times*, 2 March 1912, and *Geneva Advertiser-Gazette*, 7 March 1912, courtesy of the Geneva Historical Society and Museum.)

207 ⇝ SBA TO GROVER CLEVELAND

Tenafly N.J. Nov. 16, 1885

To the President of the United States   My Dear Sir

May I not hope that in your forthcoming message to Congress you will urge the passage of a resolution submitting to the several Legislatures a proposition to so amend the National Constitution as to protect the women of all the states and Territories in the enjoyment of the right of suffrage on equal terms with men?[1] Very Respectfully Yours

⇝ *Susan B. Anthony*

⇝ ALS, on NWSA letterhead, Grover Cleveland Papers, DLC.

1. In his annual message, delivered on 8 December 1885, President Cleveland mentioned women only in the context of his attack on polygamy in Utah. (Israel, *State of the Union Messages*, 2:1514–55.)

208 ⇝ SBA TO LILLIE DEVEREUX BLAKE

Tenafly N.J. Nov. 18, 1885

My Dear Mrs Blake

Yours of yesterday is just here— <u>All right</u>—the only blunder you have made is ~~to have~~ in having borne & forborne so long with I. O. J. H. W.—[1] I heartily glad you have decided to get a "bill of separation," if not of "Absolute divorce"—for the N.Y. State Society—from all of <u>his</u> <u>Tom-foolery</u> of a <u>Woman Suffrage Party</u>. It is high time— Of course any one who can & will <u>tell absolute falsehoods for</u> a cause or himself—

will do the same against others!!— Your package hasn't yet come—but doubtless will at the P.M. mail—

Now I have had a bright thought—that is if you will go to Washington at the opening of Congress—and <u>work</u> <u>up</u> matters—[2]

1st In the Senate—secure good men on our select Committee   You know the last Congress put an enemy—& <u>small</u> one at that as chairman—[3] at least if they will put a democrat there—let it be a strong one— I think Senator Palmer will be a good chairman— So would Senator Hoar—he wouldn't take it before—but he might now—

2^d Work for the appointment of a Select Com. in the House—& if the vote is carried to raise one—then to secure good men on it—

3^d To canvass the House to get a vote to grant the use of it to National W.S.A. for a <u>hearing</u>—with all the M.C's & Senators—President & Cabinet—& Supreme Court invited to be present—and have Mrs Stanton prepare & make there <u>the speech</u> of her life— Surely R̶e̶p̶ the House of Representatives ought to open its portals to that woman before she dies— Perhaps we might add others to speak—but I think it would be more likely to carry—if asked for <u>one</u> <u>person</u> <u>specifically</u>—as it did for Parnell[4] in 1878— & more likely to be carried for Mrs Stanton than any other woman!!— Now isn't all this very bright—of course I will pay your board at the Riggs—& your travelling expenses—if you can go & work—say the first three weeks of Congress—or to the adjournment for the holidays— and by that time I shall hope to be through with this big history job—so that I can go to Washington at the re-convening of Congress and pick up & finish what you get started—

Now do you feel like plunging into this work pell mell?— And do you feel that you can do it & still push on—or at least not jeopard your New York work?— I looked over the whole country for <u>the woman</u>— last night before sleep would come—and could see none other but Mrs Blake who could be even hoped for, to do this work— Dear Phoebe Couzins is too ill—and I know of none other who understands how to do it—save yourself—it requires experience and tact—

I will write Mrs Spofford— Is there any other place you would prefer to board— Mrs S. sister Miss Snow is there now & between her & Mrs S. I think you could always be sure of an escort— Yours Sincerely & hopefully

⚞ *Susan B. Anthony*

P.S. You see the book cannot—will not be done until plump New Years—& for me to break out of its work now—is suicide to that job— So <u>some</u> one else must go to W. & do the work there— I have written Mr Reed of Maine—asking him if he would be our Leader in the House—& Senator Palmer for the Senate— I have also written Cleveland to recommend W.S. in his message to Congress— Do you write him also—every woman ought to do so!— S. B A

N.B. In jumping [fast?] so cannot re-read [now?]

N.B.—Do you know what the Gen'l Assembly did with the Rev. Isaac See's case?[5] if so please tell me— We have it only to the end of the Newark Presbytery's action—& thence it was appealed to the Gen'l Assembly!! If you have it send it to me instanter!!

❧ ALS, on NWSA letterhead, Lillie Devereux Blake Papers, MoSHi. Square brackets surround uncertain readings.

1. Blake's letter to SBA is missing, but she also announced her break with Hamilton Willcox in the *Woman's Journal*, 14 November 1885. There she wrote that direct action had failed, Willcox's educational efforts with the inspectors of elections had no effect, and women should resume their campaign with the legislature. Although she made a point of mentioning that "Mr. Willcox has been sustained by money and the support of many friends," she voiced only mild criticism and acknowledged her own part in promoting his ideas as "an excellent means of agitation." One week later, in the *Woman's Journal*, 21 November 1885, Blake sharpened her attack, reminding supporters "that the Woman Suffrage Party, of which Mr. Willcox is so active an officer, is not the same as the New York State Woman Suffrage Association," and that "sending money and letters to Mr. Willcox is not the same as sending money to the Association." Moreover, she added, most of the officers of the association were women. John Keappock Hamilton Willcox (1842–1898), whose activism dated back to the Universal Franchise Association in postwar Washington and continued when he returned to his native New York City to practice law and found the Woman Suffrage party, was a difficult ally, who increasingly took credit for much of what the National and New York suffrage associations accomplished. (SBA to L. D. Blake, 15 November 1885, *Film*, 24:683–86; Columbia University, *Alumni Register, 1754–1931* [New York, 1932]; *Woman's Journal*, 4 December 1898; Walter Dyson, *Howard University, The Capstone of Negro Education. A History, 1867–1940* [Washington, D.C., 1941], 163, 335; *History*, 3:959–61, 4:856; *Papers*, 2:140n, 3:399n.)

2. The Forty-ninth Congress was scheduled to open its first session on 7 December 1885.

3. Francis Marion Cockrell (1834–1915), a Democrat from Missouri, was a former Confederate army officer who won election to the Senate in 1875 and served until 1905. Named chairman of the Senate Committee on Woman Suffrage in 1884, he coauthored the committee's adverse reports with Joseph E. Brown in 1884 and 1886. (*BDAC.*)

4. Charles Stewart Parnell (1846–1891), Irish nationalist leader and member of Parliament, was granted permission to speak to the House of Representatives on 2 February 1880, while he visited the United States. (Robert Kee, *The Laurel and the Ivy: The Story of Charles Stewart Parnell and Irish Nationalism* [London, 1993], 217–20.)

5. Isaac McBride See (1829–1902) was charged by the Presbytery of Newark, New Jersey, with disobeying biblical injunctions against women preaching in church, after he allowed two members of the Woman's Christian Temperance Union to speak from his pulpit in 1876. In a show of support for See, Blake had attended the proceedings against him. The charges were sustained by the General Assembly of the Presbyterian church in 1878, as the editors were able to report in the *History.* (John Haven Raven, comp., *Biographical Record. Theological Seminary, New Brunswick, New Jersey, 1784–1934* [New Brunswick, N.J., 1934], 97, with assistance of Kenneth J. Ross, Presbyterian Historical Society, Philadelphia; Lois A. Boyd, "Shall Women Speak? Confrontation in the Church, 1876," *Journal of Presbyterian History* 56 [Winter 1978]: 281–94; *History,* 3:484–88; *Papers,* 3:285–86, 289n.)

209 ⚬ ECS TO ELLEN DANA CONWAY[1]

Tenafly N.J. [*after 13 December 1885*][2]

My dear Mrs Conway,

Your reception card reached me, & every week since Mrs Anthony & I have said as soon as this rush of the printers at our heels is over we will go over & see those dear friends whose acquaintance we so much enjoyed in the old world. And the prospect of doing so is brightening as we shall send our last chapter before Christmas & then in one month the hurry with proof will be over & we shall have time to enjoy the living present. Have we ever sent you the two first volumns ↑of the History of Woman Suffrage↓, if not we will do so at once. Let us know The third one will be out by April, then you will have a complete record of our struggle for forty years, as long as the children of Israel were in the wilderness.[3] When I tell you that these volumns are 1000 pages each you will appreciate how busy we have been since June in arranging material & correcting proof, & how weary we are with the continual labor. I have not been in the city but once, & that was to speak at a parlor meeting the evening of my seventieth birthday. The first call I make shall be on you, in the meantime if you & Mr Conway could find a spare day to spend here we should be very glad to see you. Our country home is heated with a furnace so you need have no fears of freezing. Tell Mildred my daughters are having a delightful time together in England sight seeing. A letter from Theodore this evening sends warm regards to you   He takes it for granted that we have met often already, & inquires as to what you are doing, saying, thinking, & how you like the change from England to America. I saw by the papers that Mr Conway had been fated in Boston, & preached for Adler last Sunday[4] & brought down the house, so he is busy, shocking the people [*in margin of first page*] just as they need to be. Now do write & tell us [*on new sheet*] What you are all about   Mildred & the boys as well as yourselves. Hattie asks in her letters as well as Theodore. The prospect is that Hattie will come over next summer. I long to see that blessed baby. What a revolution they are having in English politics quite equal to our own a year ago.[5] Really it is enough to kill Gladstone outright. Miss Müller lost her election,[6] so she intends to take a trip to Constantinople   not to straighten out Egyptian affairs I suppose, but for rest & recreation. Miss Becker's paper comes to us regularly so we keep posted on the suffrage movement there. Miss Anthony joins me in kind regards to one & all sincerely yours

❧ *Elizabeth Cady Stanton.*

P.S. What did Mildred do with her yellow cat?

❧ ALS, on NWSA letterhead, Moncure D. Conway Papers, Rare Book and Manuscript Library, NNC.

1. Ellen Davis Dana Conway (1833–1897), the wife of Moncure Conway since 1858, was the mother of three children: Eustace, born in 1859; Dana, born in 1865; and Mildred E., born in 1868. The two younger children were born in England. The Conways moved back to the United States late in 1885. (Moncure D. Conway, *Ellen Dana Conway: Born in Cincinnati, June 11, 1833. Died in New York, December 25, 1897* [New York, 1898]; Collection Register, Moncure Daniel Conway Family Collection, Dickinson College; *Woman's Who's Who 1914*, s.v. "Sawyer, Mildred Conway.")

2. Dated with reference to Moncure Conway's sermon "last Sunday," or 13 December 1885.

3. Num. 14:33.

4. Conway addressed the Society for Ethical Culture in Chickering Hall on "The Evolution of Religion." (*New York Times*, 12 December 1885.)

5. Gladstone resigned as Prime Minister in June 1885 and was replaced by a Conservative until new elections could be held in November. When ECS wrote this letter, the results were just in: Liberals still outnumbered Conservatives in Parliament, but the Home Rule party held the balance of power and, for the moment, aligned itself with Conservatives. Not until late January 1886 did this political configuration dissolve and Gladstone begin his third ministry. (Angus Hawkins, *British Party Politics, 1852–1886* [New York, 1998], 242–50.)

6. Henrietta Müller lost her bid for reelection to the London School Board in November 1885. (*Englishwoman's Review* 16 [14 November 1885] 494–99; *Women's Suffrage Journal* 16 [1 December 1885] 198; Hollis, *Ladies Elect*, 108–10.)

210 ❧ ECS TO ANTOINETTE BROWN BLACKWELL

Tenafly N.J. Dec 29 [*1885*].

Dear Mrs Blackwell,

We are not free quite yet, but shall be happy to visit you sometime in the near future, as well as to see you here

I enclose a time table,[1] that another attempt may be more successful. But you better plan when you have another day to spare to stay all night. I wish you could come & bring Lucy Stone that we might have one pleasant reunion before we pass to the next sphere of rest or action.[2]

I have none of your books, & should be very happy to place them in my library, & I am quite sure Susan would also.[3] She has gone to Philadelphia with Rachel Foster who returned on the Arizona yesterday.[4] Having lost her mother in Switzerland she is in great affliction. Nothing less would have taken Susan from work here. With kind regards for Mr Blackwell[5] & yourself yours sincerely

❧ *Elizabeth Cady Stanton*

❧ ALS, Blackwell Papers, MCR-S. Year added later in another hand.

1. Enclosure missing.

2. When Antoinette Blackwell delivered this suggestion, Lucy Stone replied that "meeting Mrs. Stanton is out of the question with me." According to Stone, ECS had described her in correspondence to a Mr. Shattuck as "'the biggest liar and hypocrite she had ever seen.'" The man to whom ECS allegedly wrote these words, possibly the husband of Harriette Shattuck, read the letter aloud to Stone in front of other people. "I cannot with any self respect," Stone continued, "meet her with a pretence of good fellowship." (L. Stone to A. B. Blackwell, 10 January 1886, in Lasser and Merrill, *Friends and Sisters*, 250–51.)

3. Antoinette Blackwell's books at this date were: *Studies in General Science* (1869), *The Island Neighbors: A Novel of American Life* (1871), *The Sexes Throughout Nature* (1875), *The Physical Basis of Immortality* (1876), and *The Comparative Longevity of the Sexes* (1884).

4. The senior Julia Foster died suddenly on board a train in Switzerland on November 12, and her daughters sailed from Liverpool with their mother's body on December 19. SBA met them in New York and accompanied them to Philadelphia. (*Film*, 24:675–77, 756–59.)

5. Samuel Charles Blackwell (1823–1901), a brother of Henry Blackwell and a businessman in New York and New Jersey, married Antoinette Brown in 1856.

211 ≈ SBA TO MARIETTA HOLLEY[1]

Riggs House, Washington, D.C., Jan. 31, 1886.

My Dear Miss Holley

First—let me thank you for "<u>Sweet</u> <u>Cicely</u>"— We have read it aloud here—Mrs Spofford & I & her sisters! and laughed until we cried over it!!— A very bright newspaper scribbler in Philadelphia ~~say~~—Miss Anna M'Dowell[2]—says she cannot stand it much longer—with <u>Josiah</u>— it is time to kill him off—and for Semantha to marry a <u>smarter</u> man!!— But your getting into all sorts of people's interior—and speaking exactly as they woud or do! is perfectly wonderful—and you did pile up the broken hip—& false teeth stories nicely!—

And now I want you to send us a letter—or better—come here yourself—and give a real earnest talk to Congress in person!! I believe you could speak if you would try—and move the hearts of these lawmakers—just as you do in your books—only a great deal more!!

Our Senate Committee—through H. W. Blair of New Hampshire—

will report favorably on Tuesday[3]—then will come the discussion & vote—by & by—

But if you cannot come in person—you will surely send a letter to be read in our meeting—and a little of what Kossuth[4] called the "material aid"—so essential to carry forward this most momentous revolution the world has ever seen—

With delightful memories of the evening you called on me at the Hotel at Adams[5]—and many, many thanks to you for all the good work you have done through you many books—I am—very sincerely yours

⤙ *Susan B. Anthony*

⤙ ALS, on NWSA letterhead, Marietta Holley Letters, NWattJHi.

1. Marietta Holley (1836–1926), author and humorist, published *Sweet Cicely, or Josiah Allen as a Politician* late in 1885. In this fourth of her books about Samantha and Josiah Allen and the woman question, Josiah's ambition to join the corrupt and unprincipled world of Washington politics leads his wife to make the trip herself in order to lobby President Arthur, James Blaine, and others for prohibition and woman suffrage. Framing its sharp satire of male politics are the stories of several female characters whose lives were damaged by their legal disabilities and their husbands' alcoholism. While writing the book, Holley sought SBA's help in identifying specific laws and illustrating their consequences. Holley incorporated SBA's popular story about a wife whose ill-fitting false teeth belonged to her husband (160–61). (*NAW*; *ANB*; SBA to M. Holley, 29 May 1884, *Film*, 23:772–77.)

2. Anne Elizabeth McDowell (1826–1901), a pioneer in journalism, published the *Woman's Advocate* in Philadelphia from 1855 to 1860. Thereafter she wrote for several of the city's daily papers. McDowell joined the festivities marking SBA's departure for Europe in 1883. (*NAW*; *Papers*, 2:507–11; *Film*, 23:113–17.)

3. Senate, Committee on Woman Suffrage, *Report to Accompany S.R. 5*, 2 February 1886, 49th Cong., 1st sess., S. Rept. 70, Serial 2355. Henry Blair was joined in the majority by Thomas Palmer, Jonathan Chace, and Thomas Bowen.

4. Louis Kossuth (1802–1894), the Hungarian leader, arrived in New York in December 1851 in search of American support for a Hungarian republic. "Material aid" was one category of the support he proposed in his speeches. The *New York Herald*, 13 December 1851, defined Kossuth's "material aid" as "men, arms, ships, and munitions of war," all of them "dependent on financial aid."

5. SBA lectured in Holley's hometown of Adams, New York, at the end of September 1880.

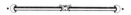

212 　 ECS TO THE NATIONAL WOMAN SUFFRAGE
ASSOCIATION

Tenafly, N.J., Feb. 15 [*1886*].[1]

To the National Woman Suffrage Association in Convention Assembled
Dear Friends: My convictions from year to year have been growing
stronger that before we can secure woman's emancipation from the
slavery and superstitions of the past we have an important work to do
in the church. Hence, I would suggest in "our plan of work" for the
coming year, that we now begin the same vigorous agitation in the
church that we have kept up in the state for the last forty years, as the
canon law, with all the subtle influences that grow out of it, is more
responsible for woman's slavery to-day than the civil code. With the
progressive legislation of the last half century we have an interest in
tracing the lessons taught women in the churches to their true origin,
and a right to demand of our theologians the same full and free discussion in the church that we have had in the state, as the time has fully
come for the woman to be heard in the ecclesiastical councils of the
nation. To this end I suggest that committees and delegates from all
our state and national associations visit the clergy in their several
localities and attend their various convocations of general assemblies
to press on their consideration the true position of woman as a factor in
a Christian civilization. Woman to-day, as ever, supplies the enthusiasm that sustains the church, and she has a right in turn to ask the
church to sustain her in this struggle for liberty, and not only as
individuals, but as influential organizations, to take some decided
action with reference to this momentous and far reaching movement.

It matters little that here and there some clergyman advocates our
cause, on our platform, so long as no sectarian organization has yet
recognized our demand as a principle of justice, and the debate is
rarely opened in their councils, being generally treated as a speculative, sentimental question unworthy serious consideration. Neither
would it suffice if they gave in their adhesion to the demand for political

equality, so long as by scriptural teachings they perpetuate our social and religious subordination.

The state has ever[2] granted us respectful hearings, before congressional committees and legislative assemblies, and it is now full time for the church to follow her example; lawyers and judges have listened to our arguments, while the civil code has been essentially modified, and some of the worst features of the old common law abolished.

Leading statesmen have taken part in the debates on the constitutional rights of women, and recognized our claims as citizens of a republic. Scientists in a rigid analysis of sex have proved by innumerable facts that the primal form of all life is feminine, exploding the fable that man was first in the creation.

And now the time has come for theologians to give expression to some well digested ideas on this question and substitute arguments for the sophistries too often used in our pulpits. In view of the intelligence, morality, and liberal education of the women of this period, all those texts of Scripture and parables referring to her as "the author of sin," as "an inferior," a "subject," a "weaker vessel," should no longer be read in our churches, as they humiliate and destroy the respect that is her due from the rising generation. All these old ideas should be relegated to the ancient mythologies as mere allegories, having no application whatever to the womanhood of this generation.

Everything points to a purer and more rational religion in the future, in which woman, as mother of the race, will be recognized as an equal in both the church and the state. Archdeacon Farrar, in an article in the January number of the *North American Review*,[3] says: "The three elements which are essential to the teaching of a strong living church are tolerance, freedom and progress." He gives in this article suggestions on various popular questions, in which he says it is the duty of the church to make its voice heard. To his list I add "justice, equality, and liberty for woman"—a more important question than any to which he refers, as it involves not only the sacred rights of one-half the race, but the most vital interests of all humanity. Our system of theology is based on woman's degradation, and as long as her religious sentiments, the strongest in her nature, are subsidized to false creeds and doctrines, with the promise of salvation, she will readily sacrifice freedom in this life to save her soul in the life hereafter. No opinions are so obstinately adhered to, no feelings so sedulously cherished as those based on religious superstitions.

It is not civil or political power that holds the Mormon woman in polygamy, the Turkish woman in the harem, the Hindoo woman on the funeral pyre of her husband, nor the American woman as a subordinate everywhere. The central falsehood from which all these different forms of slavery spring is the doctrine of original sin and woman as a medium for the machinations of Satan, its author. On this idea other demoralizing superstitions are based, all having a common origin in the ancient eastern mythologies.

To change the position of woman in dogmatic theology, where she is represented as the central figure in Paradise lost and regained, the medium alike for rebellion and redemption, is to revolutionize the system; hence all those who believe in progress within the church should hail the present movement for woman's emancipation, as that brings us to the next onward step in the new religion.

⮞ *Elizabeth Cady Stanton.*

⮞ Unidentified and undated clipping, SBA scrapbook 11, Rare Books, DLC. Not in *Film* from this source.

1. At the opening of the convention on January 17, SBA announced ECS's absence "on account of trouble with her throat, from which she had been suffering for some weeks." SBA also read two paragraphs from a personal letter: "I cannot tell you how sorry I am not to be with you, but the strongest sometimes are weak.

"Well, I have held on pretty well, seventy years; working steadily for woman suffrage for near half a century, and now my young coadjutors must fill my place;—much more easily done than you imagine." (*Woman's Tribune*, March 1886, *Film*, 24:900–908.)

2. Although the source text reads "never," common sense indicates, and other publications of the text support, reading the word as "ever."

3. Frederic William Farrar (1831–1903), archdeacon of Westminster and later dean of Canterbury, on a visit to the United States, wrote "The Work of the Church in America," *North American Review* 142 (January 1886): 25–35. The quotation is on page 32.

·⟨══════❧══════⟩·

213 ❧ EXECUTIVE SESSIONS AND EXECUTIVE
COMMITTEE OF THE NATIONAL WOMAN
SUFFRAGE ASSOCIATION

[17–20 February 1886]

The executive sessions were held in the parlors of the Riggs and were attended by a large number of members.

The first session opened at 10 A.M., Wednesday, Mrs. Sewall in the chair. The roll-call showed delegates present from nineteen states.

The following committees were appointed:

Resolutions—Miss Anthony, Mesdames Shattuck, Neymann,[1] Minor and Gougar.

Finance—Mrs. Spofford, Mrs. Denison, Misses Julia Foster, Mary Anthony and Caroline Sherman.[2]

Press—Miss Sheldon, Mrs. Field, Miss Ricker,[3] Mrs. Denison.

The Report of the Committee appointed last year on *Basis of Representation*, was then called for.[4] The committee were Mrs. Shattuck, Mrs. Colby and Mrs. Sewall. The report was as follows:

BASIS OF DELEGATE REPRESENTATION.

The Vice President for each State or Territory, shall, at least once a year, call together the members of this association resident in her State or Territory, for the purpose of electing delegates to the annual convention, and doing any other national work desirable. Each State and Territory shall be entitled to one delegate for every twenty-five members, or fraction thereof, and the delegates actually present shall be entitled to as many votes as the membership of their respective States or Territories commands. Or, delegations not full, may complete their number from members of the association present, who are residents of their respective States and Territories.

When any permanent auxiliary organization is formed from this membership, it may retain seventy-five *per cent* of its membership fees for its local work. Also, any State suffrage association may send two delegates, each of whom shall have one vote.

Regularly accredited delegates shall be entitled to vote at all meetings, but none others shall vote except by unanimous consent of the whole delegation.

After a full discussion the report was unanimously adopted.

A standing committee on *Plan of Work* was then appointed as follows: Mrs. Sewall, Ind.; Mrs. Ewing, Iowa;[5] Mrs. Colby, Neb.; Mrs. Robinson, Mass.; Madame Neymann, N.Y.; Mrs. Shattuck, Mass.; Mrs. Meriwether, Mo.; Mrs. Gougar, Ind.; Mrs. Southworth, Ohio.[6]

The report of the nominating committee, Miss Anthony, Mrs. Shattuck and Mrs. Colby was then received, each name of the officers at large was presented separately, and others were presented by States. Changes were suggested by persons present, and after full discussion and revision, the report was adopted. Mrs. Stanton was re-elected president, Miss Anthony vice-president, and Mrs. Spofford, treasurer. The full list of officers elected will appear later.

[18 February 1886]

SECOND SESSION.

Minutes of previous meetings were read and adopted.

Letters were received from Dr. Mary F. Thomas,[7] of Ind., Mrs. A. M. Swain[8] and Mrs. Lucinda B. Chandler,[9] of Ill.

It was then decided to have the report of committee on resolutions presented in executive instead of open session as heretofore.

The report was called for. The resolutions finally adopted were given in the March *Tribune*.[10] Over the report of this committee the liveliest and most interesting debates of the convention took place, and the public audiences were great losers by the decision to have the resolutions presented in executive session.

The first resolution related to the national method and clauses therein were supposed to contain an allusion to "State Rights," although not so intended by the committee. (I regret I have not this resolution as first presented. Ed.)[11] It was immediately taken up. Mrs. Meriwether, of St. Louis, avowed her adherence to the doctrine of State Rights. Mrs. Perkins, of Ohio, thought our duty was first to our conscience, then to our home, then to the State, then to the nation, then to the universe. Mrs. Bennett, Kentucky, took the ground we were already enfranchised. Mrs. Shattuck, Massachusetts, advocated the appeal to the nation for the protection of our rights in the States; we must stand by the national idea. Mrs. Meriwether said we do not owe allegiance to the United States because they have never protected our rights, but she was willing to take her freedom from the government. She moved to amend by striking out the words "owe our allegiance first to the nation." Madame Neymann, New York, agreed with Mrs. Shattuck that the whole was more important than its parts. Mrs. Minor, Missouri, said the matter was settled in the South; not a teacher could hold a position who did not take the oath of allegiance. Mrs. Gougar, Indiana, said that the National Association was working on the National Constitution. The supreme court has decided that women are citizens, but that citizen and voter are not synonymous terms. This resolution is well-timed. It sets forth the plan of the Association to appeal to the United States first, to the States afterwards. Miss Anthony said our primal citizenship was in the United States, our secondary citizenship in the States. Mrs. Colby, Nebraska, spoke of the necessity of women being enfranchised by the nation, otherwise a woman might be a voter in one State or Territory and not in another. Mr. Davis, Pennsylvania, was surprised that such a clause had been included in the resolution. It was strong enough without. A question may be a political truth, but not a moral truth. So the supremacy of the nation over the State may be established in politics, but not settled in the individual conscience. Mr. A. S. Willcox,[12] New York, thought it would be very impractical to go to Congress asking for something, at the same time telling Congress it was all wrong. Mrs. Southworth, Ohio, said State rights was an issue of the past, we obey national laws.

The re-reading of the resolution was called for.

Mrs. Shattuck said this provision tells why we go to Congress. Mrs. Meriwether moved to amend by striking out this clause about owing allegiance first to the United States, saying that to retain that clause would cut us off from all expectations from a democratic Congress.

Mrs. Colby moved to amend Mrs. Meriwether's amendment by striking out only the words "rather than to the particular States to which they belong." Mrs. Bennett, Kentucky, wanted this matter of State rights left alone. We are now a Union and citizens of the nation.

Mrs. Gougar moved to table Mrs. Colby's amendment which was carried by a vote of 24 to 4. Mrs. Gougar moved to table Mrs. Meriwether's amendment. Carried by 25 to 4.

Mr. Davis moved that the preamble be stricken out, on which Mrs. Gougar and Mrs. Shattuck both argued that that would make the resolution meaningless. Mrs. Colby moved as an amendment to Mr. Davis' motion that the resolution be referred back to the committee with a request for its revision so that it might receive the support of women of all sections. Mrs. Perkins said she did not like the wording and it would seem wise to recommit. Mrs. Shattuck, (chmn.,) said the committee would not make any change in it. Whereupon Miss Anthony, a member of the committee, said she had not been present at the meeting of the committee, and for one, she should want it changed. Several persons spoke in support of the motion to refer back. Mrs. Gougar moved to table Mrs. Colby's amendment. Mr. Davis asked Mrs. Gougar to withdraw her motion and give him an opportunity to secure a direct vote on the resolution. Mrs. Gougar being unwilling to do this, her motion was lost by a vote of 19 to 25. The vote was then taken on Mrs. Colby's amendment and the resolution was referred back to the committee by a vote of 26 to 4.

Other resolutions were then adopted. The proposition of Mrs. Ricker to purchase 3,000 leaflets prepared by the National W.S.A., of Massachusetts, and expounding the methods of the National Association for free distribution at the Convention, was carried.[13]

Mrs. Gougar spoke of the *Woman's Tribune* and wanted the Society to support it cordially and thus secure the dissemination of the reports of the National Association. Mr. Davis moved that a thousand copies of the Convention number of the *Woman's Tribune* be purchased by the Association and distributed by order of Miss Anthony and the treasurer. Carried.

The following resolution sent by Mrs. Stanton, was then read:

> *Whereas*, The greatest barrier to woman's emancipation is found in the superstitions of the church; and the literal renderings of scripture texts and allegories, by which those in authority are armed with the potent words "thus saith the Lord," to compel woman's subjection and belief in dogmas that cripple her development and freedom,

Therefore Resolved, That a thorough consideration of this question should now be urged in the American church, and for this purpose, delegates from State and national associations should be sent to all sectarian conventions; and committees appointed to visit the clergy in their own localities, to urge more enlightened teaching in their pulpits in regard to woman.

With the resolution Mrs. Stanton sent the letter which was published in the March *Tribune* and which should be read at this point to do Mrs. Stanton justice.[14] The letter was read by Miss Anthony. The discussion, which followed, although not given in full, is taken from the notes of the stenographer of the Convention, Miss Frances Ellen Burr, of Hartford, Connecticut, and the proceedings of the third session on this same resolution are included here to complete the record of one of the most interesting phases of the convention.

Mrs. Helen Gougar moved that the resolution be laid upon the table. She said: "A resolution something like this came into the last convention, and it has done more to cripple my work and that of other suffragists than anything that has happened in the whole history of the woman suffrage movement. When you look this country over you find the slums are opposed to us, while some of the best leaders and advocates of woman suffrage are among the Christian people. A bishop of the Roman Catholic church stood in my meeting in Peoria not long since. We cannot afford to antagonize the churches. Some of us are orthodox, and some of us are unorthodox, but this association is for suffrage and not for the discussion of religious dogmas. I am free to say that if I could live to say that if I could live to see Mrs. Stanton and Miss Anthony I could die in happiness that moment,[15] but I cannot stay within these borders if that resolution is adopted, from the fact that my hands would be tied. I hope it will not go into open convention for debate. The discussion between Mrs. Stanton and Bishop Spaulding in the *North American Review* has done more to injure our cause than any one thing in the last twenty-five years."[16]

Mrs. Perkins, of Ohio: I think we ought to pay due consideration and respect to our beloved president (Mrs. Stanton). I have no objection to sending missionaries to the churches asking them to pay attention to women suffrage; but I dont think the churches are our greatest enemies.

They might have been so in Mrs. Stanton's early days, but to-day, if she went over the United States, as I do, she would find the ministers our best helpers. If it were not for their co-operation I could not get a hearing before the people. And now that they are coming to meet us half way dont let us throw stones at them. I hope that resolution as worded will not go into the convention.

Mrs. Meriwether, of St. Louis: I think the resolution could be amended so as to offend no one. The ministers falsely construe the scriptures. For my part, I think we can overwhelm them with arguments for woman suffrage—with biblical arguments. We can hurl them like shot and shell. Herbert Spencer once wrote an article on the different biases that distort the human mind, and among the first he reckoned the theological bias.[17] In the early Christian days and in Christ's time, women were on an equality with men. But in those times there was no liberty, everyone was under the despotism of the Roman Caesars. But women were on an equality with men, and the religion that Christ taught, included women equally with men. He made none of the invidious distinctions that the churches make.

Mrs. Shattuck, of Massachusetts: We did not pass the resolution of last year so it could not harm anybody. But I protest against this fling against masculine interpretation of the Scriptures. Men can interpret the scriptures as well as women.

Mrs. Minor, of St. Louis: I object to the whole thing—resolution and letter both. We have had a long discussion here on state rights, and now we have got on to religion, and the Lord only knows what we shall get on to next. I believe in confining ourselves to woman suffrage.

Mrs. Colby, of Nebraska: Mrs. Chairman:[18] I was on that committee of resolutions last year and wrote the modified one which was presented and I am willing to stand by it. I have not found it hurts the work, save with a few who do not know what the resolution was, or what was said about it. The discussion was reported word for word in the *Woman's Tribune* and I think no one who read it would say that it was irreligious or lacked respect for the teachings of Christ. I believe we must say something in the line of Mrs. Stanton's idea. She makes no fling at the church. She wants us to treat the church as we have the state—viz. negotiate for more favorable action. We have this fact to deal with, that in no high orthodox body have women been accorded any privileges. I move that the resolution be referred back to the committee.

Mr. Edward M. Davis, of Philadelphia: I must say that I am overrunning with sympathy for the people outside of this house who dont know what is going on here. I dont think we have ever had a resolution offered here so important as this. We have never had a measure brought forward that would produce better results. I agree entirely with Mrs. Stanton on this thing, that the church is the great barrier to woman's progress. I am surprised that one who takes so active a part here as Mrs. Shattuck, should announce that last year's resolution was killed. She forgets the minutes she made, and she forgets the fact that the resolution is alive yet. Our friend Mrs. Gougar says this resolution would drive us to the slums, rather than to the clergy—

The Chairman: Mr. Davis is out of order.

Mr. Davis: We dont want to proclaim ourselves an irreligious, or a religious people. The question of religion does not touch us either way. We are neutral.

Madame Neymann: Because this resolution is so important, I concur with Mrs. Colby and ask that it be referred back to the committee. Because the clergy has been one-sided, we dont want to be one-sided. I know of no one for whom I have a greater admiration than for Mrs. Stanton. Her resolution antagonizes no one.

Mrs. Brooks,[19] of Nebraska: Let us do this work in such a way that it will not arouse the opposition of the most bigoted clergyman. All this discussion only shows that the old superstitions have got to be banished.

Mrs. Snow,[20] of Maine: Mrs. Stanton wishes to convert the clergy.

Mrs. Dunbar,[21] of Maryland: I dont want the resolution referred back to the committee. Out of respect to Mrs. Stanton and the manner in which she has been treated by the clergy—

The Chairman: Mrs. Dunbar is out of order. She is discussing the original resolution when it is an amendment that is under discussion.

(An amendment, and an amendment to an amendment, had been previously introduced.)

Mrs. Dunbar: I am speaking of referring this back to the committee. I dont want to lose the wording of the original resolution and therefore want it taken up here.

Mrs. Shattuck: I am teetotally opposed to the whole thing anyway. This resolution properly belongs to the committee of Plan of Work, and not to the committee on resolutions. It seems to me the Plan of

Work commmittee could suggest some way out of the trouble. I agree with a great many that the spirit of the church is all right and the letter all wrong, but dont let this resolution go back to the committee on resolutions. It would complicate matters.

Mrs. Gougar: I think it is quite enough to undertake to change the National Constitution without undertaking to change the Bible. I hope this will be sent to the committee on Plan of Work. I heartily agree with Mrs. Stanton in her idea of sending delegates to church councils and convocations, but I dont sanction this resolution which starts out: "The greatest barrier to woman's emancipation is found in the superstitions of the church." That is enough in itself to turn the entire church—Catholic and Protestant—against us.

Mrs. Nelson:[22] The resolution is directed against the superstitions of the church, and not against the church, but I think it would be taken as against the church.

Mrs. McPherson: Let it go to the Plan of Work committee. I am not in favor of telling the clergy what fools they are, and how ignorant and tyrannical. Let us not set ourselves up to criticise them.

Miss Anthony: As the resolution contains the essence of the letter, I would move that the whole thing go to the Plan of Work committee.

The Chairman: The question before us is a motion to refer the original resolution back to the committee on resolutions.

Motion lost by a vote of 18 to 22. Miss Anthony then moved that the letter and the resolution be placed in the hands of the committee on Plan of Work. Mr. Davis wanted to know if the object was to suppress it. He was assured it was not. Mrs. Neymann said she knew the committee and thought it perfectly safe to submit both letter and resolution to them. Meeting adjourned without action and on Friday morning the same subject was resumed. A motion to table Mrs. Stanton's resolution was lost. Miss Anthony then moved that both letter and resolution be placed in her hands as the representative of the president of the association to be read in open convention as her letter and resolution without any endorsement. "I dont want any one to say that we young folks go in here and strangled Mrs. Stanton's thought," said Miss Anthony.

Dr. McMurdy, of Washington: I dont intend to oppose nor favor the motion; but as a clergyman and a High Church Episcopalian, I cannot see any particular objection to Mrs. Stanton's letter. The scriptures must be interpreted naturally. Whenever Paul's remarks are brought up I explain these in the light of this nineteenth century as contrasted with the first. In this way I get the people on my side. When I try to antagonize them, it doesn't work.

Mrs. Pell:[23] I think we have been afraid of the clergy long enough. For eighteen years we have met universal opposition. Miss Anthony desires to read the letter and the resolution before open convention and I hope her motion will prevail.

It was finally voted that the letter be read *without* the resolution.

[19 February 1886]

THIRD SESSION.

After the reading of the minutes of the previous session the unfinished business of the Stanton resolution was disposed of. The first vote on reading Mrs. Stanton's letter in open convention showed 27 for to 21 against. On motion the vote was reconsidered and resulted 32 for to 24 against.

The resolution committee being ordered to resume their report the first resolution brought in was the one which had caused such discussion the previous day but which in its revised form was adopted without dissent. The following is the resolution as adopted:

> *Whereas,* women as well as men are citizens of the United States with an equal claim upon the national government for protection in the rights of citizenship; and
>
> *Whereas,* the right to the ballot should be protected in all the women of the nation alike, and thus secured from reversal by state legislatures or limitation by state lines: therefore
>
> *Resolved,* First, that we reaffirm our confidence in the national method of securing the ballot to women through an amendment to the federal constitution;
>
> 2d, That we call upon the forty-ninth Congress, in the name of justice, to submit at once to the states the resolution, now pending, which provides that once and forever "the right of citizens of the United States to vote shall not be denied or abridged by the United States or by any state on account of sex."

The resolutions passed without comment save the following:

> *Whereas*, a bill now pending before Congress proposes, under the pretense of suppressing polygamy, to disfranchise all the women of Utah, Gentile as well as Mormon: therefore,
>
> *Resolved*, That while approving the action of Congress in making disfranchisement a penalty for the crime of polygamy, we indignantly protest against the injustice of punishing Gentile and non-polygamous Mormon Women for crimes never committed, and that we call upon the national House of Representatives to strike out section 7 of this bill.[24]

The point of difference was on the clause approving the action of Congress making disfranchisement the penalty for polygamy.

It was voted to send a copy of this resolution also the one on national action to each member of Congress.

[20 February 1886]

MEETING OF THE N.W.S.A. EXECUTIVE COMMITTEE

On Saturday afternoon the officers of the Executive Committee met in council. The principal subject for consideration was the report of the Plan of Work committee. The points were as follows:

Vice-Presidents instructed to keep a list of all members of the Association in their respective states, and hold the membership ready for action.

The Vice-President and executive officers resident in each state appointed a committee to interview all ecclesiastical bodies sitting in the State with a view to securing their recognition of the equality of women.

To hold Conventions in the South as early as practicable.

To have headquarters in Washington in charge of the Cor. Secretary.

To establish a lecture bureau in Chicago.

To issue three leaflets: 1st a manual of information on the history of this movement; 2nd a programme of work for societies; 3d one on the objects and methods of this association.

To establish two distinct and auxiliary lines of work. *First*, a department of Domestic Science under charge of Emma P. Ewing, of Iowa. *Second*, an Industrial Department under charge of Lillie Devereux Blake, of New York.

The two last points were much debated. The first department was created in order to bring the proposed plans of Mrs. Ewing into relation to the Association with a view to securing local co-operation in the study of Domestic Science. The second was urged as a step towards bringing the ranks of wage-earning women to see the necessity of the ballot to secure favorable conditions, and to bring the influence of the Association to bear upon the needs of working-women.

It was voted that the president, first vice-president, the corresponding secretaries, the chairman of the executive committee and the vice-president resident in the District be a programme committee to provide for the annual convention with full power to invite speakers and make all arrangements concerning them.

It was voted not to pay the expenses of delegates to succeeding conventions.

The matter of having a committee of the Association incorporated for the purpose of receiving bequests and gifts for the uses of the Association was then considered and Miss Anthony and Mrs. Spofford were requested to secure a committee.

≈ *Woman's Tribune*, April 1886.

1. Clara Low Neymann (c. 1840–?), whose name often appeared as Clara B. Neymann, was a German-American freethinker and noted lecturer, active in the New York city and state suffrage societies. She joined the Nebraska campaign of 1882 as a German-speaker, and in 1912, she performed the same role in Wisconsin. She had recently returned from a long stay in Germany after the death of her husband. Neymann later served on the Woman's Bible Revising Committee. Her daughter Olga graduated from Cornell University, and by 1887 practiced as a dentist. (Federal Census, 1880; city directories, 1880 to 1891; *Woman's Who's Who 1914*, s.v. "Glucksmann, Olga Neyman"; *Woman's Journal*, 23 February 1884; *New York Times*, 10 January 1886; *History*, 6:702.)

2. Caroline A. Sherman (c. 1839–1907) worked in the War Department and in 1886, became one of two recording secretaries of the National association. She moved to Washington from New York during the Civil War and found a job in the Quartermaster General's office as a copyist. Rising to clerk, she stayed in her job into the 1890s, sometimes working alongside another suffragist, Ellen H. Sheldon. In 1871, Sherman was one of the women who attempted to

register and vote in Washington. (Federal Census, 1880; city directories, 1871 to 1894; *Register of Federal Officers*, 1865, 1867, 1871, 1873, 1875, 1877, 1879, 1881, 1883, 1885, 1887, 1889; *History*, 3:813n, 957; *Washington Post*, 7 December 1907.)

3. Marilla Marks Young Ricker (1840–1920) practiced law in Washington, D.C., where she often worked in concert with Belva Lockwood. She began to attend meetings of the National association in 1875 and held office in succeeding years. (*NAW*; *ANB*.)

4. At issue was article six of the National's constitution: "All Woman Suffrage societies throughout the country shall be welcomed as auxiliaries and their accredited officers or duly appointed representatives shall be recognized as members of the National Association." In 1882, the association agreed to consider a system of representation at its meetings (above at 25 January 1882), and a committee named in 1883 reported to the convention in 1884. At that time, Harriette Shattuck proposed that all suffrage societies be welcomed as auxiliaries and allowed five delegates. "Discussion ensued relating to limitation of number of delegates having power to vote in the Association," and the matter was referred back to committee for a report in 1885. Shattuck reported in 1885, but no newspaper recorded either her plan or responses to it. Other accounts of this discussion in 1886 explained that societies in distant states, whose members found it more difficult to attend annual meetings, sought to balance the representation of near and distant states. (*Report of the Sixteenth Annual Washington Convention, 1884*, p. 6, and Washington *National Republican*, 22 January 1885, 18 February 1886, *Film*, 23:573ff, 24:6–7, 897.)

5. Emma Pike Ewing (1838–?) was a professor in the School of Domestic Economy at Iowa Agricultural College. At this meeting, the National association agreed to collaborate with her on a department of domestic science, the details of which were not reported. Ewing had staked out a career and social mission: "to encourage and assist all classes of women in obtaining a *Thorough Knowledge* of Domestic Economy," especially by teaching "Cookery in its scientific aspects." After publishing *Cooking and Castle Building* in 1880 and launching a series of *Cookery Manuals* in 1882, she established the Chicago School of Cookery, moved to Iowa in 1884, left for Purdue University in 1887, and spent one year at an independent cooking school in Kansas City, Missouri. By 1891, she headed the summer cooking school of the Chautauqua Assembly in New York, while lecturing the rest of the year. In 1892, she founded the Housekeepers' National League to improve training and standards in household work, and in 1898, she opened the Model Home School of Household Economics in affiliation with Marietta College in Ohio. She was alive but ailing in 1900. (*American Women*; *WWW4*; University Archives, Iowa State University, courtesy of Tanya Zanish-Belcher; Special Collections, Purdue University, courtesy of Sammie L. Morris; Special Collections, Marietta College, courtesy of Rebecca Poe.)

6. Louisa Stark Southworth (1831–1905) of Cleveland, Ohio, the wife of a

businessman, known for her philanthropic and woman's rights work. She credited the American association with raising her interest in suffrage, when it held a convention in Cleveland in 1870. In 1880, she responded to ECS's call for messages to the Republican National Convention and in 1885, attended the National association's meeting in Washington for the first time. Within a few years, she took charge of a large project to enroll the names of women who wanted to vote and present the lists as needed to city, state, and federal politicians. To expand that work, she also served as Ohio superintendent of franchise for the Woman's Christian Temperance Union. Southworth wrote for the *Woman's Bible*, and, at the end of the century, she was active in the anti-imperialist movement. Both ECS and SBA were her guests in Cleveland on many occasions. (Mrs. W. A. Ingham, *Women of Cleveland and Their Work: Philanthropic, Educational, Literary, Medical, and Artistic* [Cleveland, Ohio, 1893], 338-42; *Anthony*, 2:623, 801, 840, 3:1337; *Woman's Tribune*, 28 December 1895; Cleveland Necrology File, Cleveland Public Library; *History*, 3:897n, 956, 4:137, 219, 250, 878-79, 939n, 5:146; Kathi Kern, *Mrs. Stanton's Bible* [Ithaca, N.Y., 2001], 146, 258n.)

7. Mary Frame Myers Thomas (1816-1888) practiced medicine in Richmond, Indiana, where she was active in the state's earliest woman's rights society and a founder of the Indiana Woman Suffrage Association. In 1880, she served as president of the American Woman Suffrage Association. (*NAW*.)

8. Adeline Morrison Swain (1820-1899) lived in Illinois at this date, but her work for woman suffrage dated back to her early days in Fort Dodge, Iowa, where she settled in 1858. There she hosted SBA on 23 April 1872, and the two met again on 17 March 1878, when SBA lectured in the town. In 1881, Swain was the Greenback party's candidate for state superintendent of public instruction. Still loyal to the party in 1884 and a delegate to its national convention, she disputed the advice of ECS and SBA to stand by the Republican party, insisting that the small third parties offered far more to women than the Republican party. (*American Women*; *History*, 3:144n, 617, 623, 4:1102; SBA diary, 1872 and 1878, *Film*, 15:888ff, 19:791ff; *Woman's Journal*, 6 September 1884; biographical files courtesy of the Iowa Women's Hall of Fame, Iowa Commission on the Status of Women.)

9. Lucinda Banister Chandler (1828-1911) was a proponent of enlightened motherhood, a uniform sexual standard, and women's control of their own bodies. Active in the National association since 1872, she urged women in 1886 to test again their existing right to vote and carry their cases to the Supreme Court. (*ANB*; *Woman's Tribune*, March 1886, *Film*, 24:900-908. See also *Papers* 3.)

10. For the final text of all the resolutions, see *Film*, 24:899.

11. The final text of this resolution appears below within this document. According to notes made by Harriette Shattuck after the convention, the original motion read: "Whereas: women, as well as men, are citizens of the United States owing their first allegiance to the U.S. rather than to the particular

state in which they reside &c." (Scrapbook 111, Robinson-Shattuck Papers, MCR-S.)

12. Probably this was Albert Oliver Willcox (1810–1897), a New York merchant, abolitionist, and lifelong supporter of woman suffrage. He was the father of Hamilton Willcox. (*ACAB*; *Woman's Journal*, 4 December 1897.)

13. Harriet R. Shattuck, *The "National" Method*, Leaflet No. 6, National Woman Suffrage Association of Massachusetts, n.d., in SBA scrapbook 11, Manuscripts Division, DLC.

14. Above at 15 February 1886.

15. On her copy of this article, Harriette Shattuck edited this clause to read, "I am free to say that if I could live to see Mrs. Stanton and Miss Anthony once". (Scrapbook 111, Robinson-Shattuck Papers, MCR-S.)

16. On this exchange, see notes above at 9 May 1885.

17. The titles to chapters eight through twelve of Herbert Spencer, *The Study of Sociology* (1873), matched this description. Spencer identified biases of education, patriotism, class, politics, and theology.

18. That is, May Sewall.

19. Harriet Sophia Brewer Brooks (1828–1888) was a former president of the Nebraska Woman Suffrage Association and edited the woman's department in the *Omaha Republican*, edited by her husband, Datus Chase Brooks. While living in Ann Arbor from 1857 to 1864, she joined the efforts to open the University of Michigan to women. When her husband moved to Chicago, she was active in local and regional suffrage societies and an officer of the National association. In 1876, D. C. Brooks took over as editor of the *Republican*, and Harriet emerged as a leader in her new home. (*Woman's Journal*, 21 July 1888; *Omaha Daily Herald*, 23 June 1888, SBA scrapbook 13, Rare Books, DLC; *History*, 2:545n, 3:105n, 176n, 516n, 682, 684.)

20. Although Sophronia Snow was not married, the reference is probably to her.

21. It is likely that this was Lavinia C. Dundore, not Dunbar, formerly of Baltimore, where she organized an equal rights association in 1867 and attempted to vote in 1870, and a resident of Washington since about 1880. By 1886, the city directory listed her as a widow. For a time after moving to the capital, Dundore worked as a pension and claims agent with Belva Lockwood, but she soon started her own business, Lavinia C. Dundore & Co. By 1891, this was an employment bureau. (*History*, 2:522, 542, 583, 3:73–74, 128, 151, 815, 816, 4:248; city directories, 1880 to 1892; *Papers*, 3:395, 398n, 580.)

22. Julia Bullard Nelson (1842–1914), a widow from Red Wing, Minnesota, and a long-time teacher of African-American students in the South, taught at this time in Jonesboro, Tennessee. She was a founding member in 1881 of the Minnesota Woman Suffrage Association and an early advocate within the Woman's Christian Temperance Union of suffrage. Nelson, who moved back to Minnesota in 1888, became a regular organizer and lecturer for the National

association in state campaigns. (Julia Wiech Lief, "A Woman of Purpose: Julia B. Nelson," *Minnesota History* 47 [Winter 1981]: 303–14.)

23. Mary Rodman Howland Pell (1810–1892) of Flushing, New York, became active in the state suffrage association in the early 1870s and served as a delegate to meetings of the National association beginning in 1878. In 1886, she was the National's honorary vice president for New York. Raised in the Society of Friends, she was disowned at the time of her marriage to Morris Shipley Pell in 1830 as he was not a Quaker. (*Quaker Genealogy*, 3:173, 252; *History*, 3:117n, 142n, 197n, 406, 436, 956; William M. Emery, *The Howland Heirs, Being the Story of a Family and a Fortune and the Inheritance of a Trust Established for Mrs. Hetty H. R. Green* [New Bedford, Mass., 1919], 395–98.)

24. Section seven of Senate 10, a bill passed by the Senate on 8 January 1886, read: "That it shall not be lawful for any female to vote at any election hereafter held in the Territory of Utah for any public purpose whatever, and any and every act of the governor and legislative assembly of the Territory of Utah providing for or allowing the registration or voting by females is hereby annulled." This was but one section of a complex bill, introduced by Senator George Edmunds in December 1885, that would make it easier to prosecute Mormons for polygamy and allow the federal government to seize property of the Church of Latter-Day Saints. When debate began on 5 January 1886, Senator George Hoar moved immediately to delete section seven, but the Senate defeated his effort the next day by a vote of thirty-eight to eleven. Three senators who favored woman suffrage and opposed section seven voted against the entire bill on January 8. The House of Representatives had not yet debated the bill. (*Congressional Record*, 47th Cong., 1st sess., 5, 6, 8 January 1886, pp. 405–8, 457, 565–66; 47th Cong., 1st sess., A Bill to Amend the Revised Statutes in Reference to Bigamy, 11 January 1886, S. 10; Sarah Barringer Gordon, *The Mormon Question: Polygamy and Constitutional Conflict in Nineteenth-Century America* [Chapel Hill, N.C., 2002], 147–81.)

214 ⫸ REMARKS BY SBA TO THE NATIONAL
WOMAN SUFFRAGE ASSOCIATION

[19 February 1886]

Miss Anthony rising to close the convention referred again to the fact that the Senate Committee had reported favorably on the bill for 16th amendment. At this point a resolution was passed thanking Senators Blair, Palmer, Boyd[1] and Chace for this report, to Representative

Reed for introducing the bill into the House,[2] and to Senator Hoar and all senators who opposed the passage of the Edmunds bill on account of its disfranchising the women of Utah.

Miss Anthony then referred to her long association with Mrs. Stanton, to the fact that Mrs. Stanton had stood at the front of the movement ever since she inaugurated it in company with Lucretia Mott; and after a beautiful tribute to her work Miss Anthony read the letter from Mrs. Stanton which was published in last issue and then said that the resolution referred to had been discussed in executive session and its suggestion of endeavoring to secure conference with evangelical bodies had been embodied in plan of work.

Reviewing the former status of the clergy Miss Anthony said that in many places where the early speakers went to hold meetings they had every minister in town warn his congregation against them. Special prayer meetings had been appointed for the night of their lectures. It was men who had been inspired to write the Bible and men alone had been allowed to study Greek and Hebrew and tell us what it meant. Until the Bible has been translated by women and preached by women, Miss Anthony said she would not believe it was against women. Whenever there was anything revealed that taught woman's subjection or, as in the case of the revelation of polygamy to Joseph Smith,[3] brought about her degradation, it was always revealed to some man: God never revealed one of these monstrosities to a woman.

Miss Anthony then explained the reason for going to Congress for 16th amendment. It was too big a job for us without party, without church, without congregation, without close organization to educate every individual.

With the remark that the advocates of woman suffrage were the only persons who rightly interpreted the constitution of the United States and the 14th and 15th amendments, Miss Anthony declared the convention adjourned.

⇒ *Woman's Tribune*, April 1886.

1. Either SBA or the reporter erred in naming this fourth senator. Thomas Mead Bowen (1835–1906) signed the majority report. A Republican from Colorado, he served one term, from 1883 to 1889. (*BDAC*.)

2. On 1 February 1886, Thomas Reed introduced House Resolution No. 109, a measure identical to Senate Resolution No. 5. The Committee on the

Judiciary, to which it was referred, granted a hearing to members of the National association on February 20. (*Congressional Record*, 49th Cong., 1st sess., 1034; 49th Cong., 1st sess., Joint Resolution, H. Res. 109.)

3. Joseph Smith (1804–1844), who claimed to receive *The Book of Mormon* from an angel, founded the Church of Jesus Christ of Latter-Day Saints in 1830.

215 ❧ SBA TO LILLIE DEVEREUX BLAKE

Riggs House, Washington, D.C., March 3, 1886.

My Dear Mrs Blake

I am amazed & distressed—that Mrs Gougar should repeat her action of two years ago[1]—and I have so written her—enclosing your note to me—and telling her that ~~she~~ ↑it↓ was not only unwise but cruel in speaking in Albany at this time—except at or on <u>your invitation</u>— just as you or any one of our number would have been to gone to Topeka—against <u>her</u> judgement—when she was pressing her bill before the Kansas Legislature—[2] <u>She</u> complained bitterly to me—of Bertha <u>Ellsworth</u> talking to the members then on the 3^d Party movement—& thereby killing her bill—or lessening its chances— I hope she will be able to see the point!!— I do hope your bill will go through—but the work for the year is clear whichever way this bill is acted upon— I several times told the audiences why you were not here—& that much as I regretted your absence here—I was glad you had a ~~weighter~~ weightier call at Albany— I rejoice in your good work—& feel that <u>no state</u> in the <u>Union</u> is so judiciously & thoroughly worked as New York— I do hope you will be successful—and that you will report progress to Mrs Colby— every month—give her the essence of your work—that is— I hope you & all of us will rally round Mrs C. and help her to make her paper live— I am very glad <u>her's</u> is the one to survive all the rest of the <u>Middle Western papers</u>; for she is clear sighted, strong & judicious— I am very hopeful of her paper— Lovingly yours

❧ *Susan B. Anthony*

❧ ALS, on NWSA letterhead for 1885, year corrected, Lillie Devereux Blake Papers, MoSHi.

1. Helen Gougar lectured for a temperance society in Albany on March 2 on "Prohibition in Kansas, versus High License in Any Place," a lecture she also delivered in New York City on February 28. At the time, the legislature was considering a municipal suffrage bill proposed by the state suffrage association. To complicate Blake's work for the bill, Gougar attacked prominent New Yorkers who sought to restrict liquor without resorting to prohibition and promised that with suffrage women would "level every brewery, distillery, and saloon in this land." (*New York Times*, 15 January, 11 February, 1 March 1886; *Albany Argus*, 3 March 1886; *History*, 4:854.) SBA may also refer to Gougar's presence in Albany in March 1884, when she and other delegates to the National's Washington convention attended the New York State Woman Suffrage Association's annual meeting on March 11 and 12. On that visit, Gougar addressed the assembly's judiciary committee on March 13, at an event arranged by Lillie Blake. Blake's account in the *History of Woman Suffrage* continues, "A few days later the same committee gave a special hearing to Mrs. Gougar, who made the journey from Indiana to present the case" (3:438).

2. SBA compares Gougar's behavior in Albany to her expectations while working with the Kansas Equal Suffrage Association to gain municipal suffrage. Gougar was on hand in Topeka when the association was founded in 1884, and she authored the municipal suffrage bill introduced in January 1885. In that year, the bill died without a vote, despite Gougar's lobbying. When the legislature took it up again in January 1886, opponents entangled the measure in so much controversy that the bill's advocates decided not to risk a vote. Gougar had complained to SBA about Bertha H. Ellsworth (1847–1907), the corresponding secretary, state organizer, and lobbyist of the equal suffrage association, but whether she complained in 1885 or 1886 is not clear. According to Ellsworth and Laura Johns, accusations in 1886 that suffragists backed a third party were not of their own doing but rumors circulated by opponents of the municipal suffrage bill. Before moving to Kansas, Ellsworth lived in Elgin, Illinois, where she worked at the watch factory and edited a paper called the *Lady Elgin*. A school teacher, a poet, and the wife of a farmer, Ellsworth began to work for suffrage in 1880 alongside Anna C. Wait in Lincoln, Kansas. The society in Lincoln sent her to Washington for the National association's meeting in 1884, and at the founding of the state association three months later, she was named an officer, organizer, and chair of the plan of work committee. Early in 1887, just before municipal suffrage was won, Ellsworth wrote a history of the campaign. She moved to Califonia in 1890, remarried a Mr. Manley, and died in Ventura County. (Federal Census, 1880; *Elgin Daily News*, n.d., and *Lincoln Beacon*, 10 April 1884, in SBA scrapbook 10, Rare Books, DLC; Michael Lewis Goldberg, *An Army of Women: Gender and Politics in Gilded Age Kansas* [Baltimore, Md., 1997], 86–94; Carolyn De Swarte Gifford and June O. Underwood, "Intertwined Ribbons:

The Equal Suffrage Association and the Woman's Christian Temperance Union, Kansas, 1886–1896," unpublished paper in editor's possession; *History*, 3:700–703, 708, 709n, 4:638–39; *Woman's Journal*, 7, 14 February, 28 November 1885, 6, 27 March 1886; *Report of the Sixteenth Annual Washington Convention, 1884*, pp. 49–51, *Film*, 23:573ff; *Lincoln County Sentinel*, 25 July 1907, courtesy of Tracee Hamilton.)

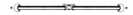

216 ⪼ ECS TO BENJAMIN F. UNDERWOOD

[*Tenafly, before March 11 1886*][1]

Dear Mr Underhill,

Don't you think where God & the Devil come in juxtaposition that the latter gentleman should be in Capital as well as the former[2] But for him what would become of our whole theological system   In fact he is the main spoke in the wheel   we could have had "no fall," "no redemption" "crucifixion" "ressurrection," without him. "Original sin," "salvation" through faith, the "judgement seat" "everlasting punishment"   all these delightful mythologies, would have been lost without him. I say by all means let us print him with a big D. I should like at least a dozen copies of the next number to send some to my native town, where there are people who still remember the old church.[3] sincerely yours

⪼ *Elizabeth Cady Stanton*

⪼ ALS, on NWSA letterhead, Papers of ECS, NPV.

1. Dated with reference to ECS's article "Religion for Women and Children," Boston *Index*, 11 March 1886, *Film*, 24:937–38.
2. She objected to the typesetting of her description of the needy poor as "hungering souls oppressed with fear of an angry God, an all-powerful devil, a judgment day, and everlasting punishment."
3. The article concluded with a description of the gloomy atmosphere surrounding the Presbyterian Church of her childhood in Johnstown, New York.

217 ⇝ SBA TO LILLIE DEVEREUX BLAKE

Rochester N.Y. March 16/86

Dear Mrs Blake

Was there ever any thing so provoking as that the <u>three</u> assembly-men from my own county—Monroe—should have voted against the suffrage bill! "<u>Turn the rascals out</u>"—must be the cry of their constuents!![1]

Now—my dear—while I shall be delighted to be present at the reception in honor of dear Dr Lozier—and to be in the Masonic Hall audiences—I tremble at the thought of trying to speak—[2] I am all out of practice— I could preside or throw in little tid-bits here & there—but to attempt to make a speech would scare me out of my senses!!— So fill in the time with speakers—& leave me only a 10 minutes talk at any of the sessions— Something may come to me—but it doesn't seem possible now that anything will!!—

The probability is—if an attempt is mad to bring up the bill again— the <u>enemy</u> will be <u>wide-awake</u> & read[y] to vote it down more strongly than before! and as the lack of only <u>two votes</u>—is a good showing to carry before the Constitutional Convention[3]—the question is, if you hadn't better let the case rest as it is!! But you have managed the matter so admirably at Albany that I hardly feel like venturing a suggestion even!!

I am home helping through the press the very last chapter of our huge [boo]k— I hope to see the end of ↑it↓ this week—

Well—the world jogs on slowly—<u>too slowly</u>—for me— Still it jogs!! With Love & Admiration

⇝ *Susan B. Anthony*

⇝ ALS, Lillie Devereux Blake Papers, MoSHi. Square brackets surround letters torn from corners.

1. Near midnight on 11 March 1886 after a lengthy debate, the state assembly voted on the municipal suffrage bill. It was a close vote, and supporters skirmished to reach the required number of votes. In a scene described as "active and exciting," the leadership prevailed on two members to change their votes to the affirmative, and the tally reached sixty-five ayes. But before

the results were announced, three members—Robert W. Evans of Oneida and Michael Brennan and Charles Smith of New York City—changed their votes to the negative to defeat the measure by a vote of sixty-three to fifty-two. Monroe County was represented in the assembly by Francis, or Frank, Gardner (c. 1837–1905), a farmer from the town of Mendon; Charles R. Pratt (1850–1914), a contractor from Rochester; and George W. Sime (1844–1924), a farmer from the town of Sweden. (*Albany Argus*, 12 March 1886; *Woman's Tribune*, April 1886; Edgar L. Murlin, *The Red Book, An Illustrated Legislative Manual of the State* [Albany, N.Y., 1895], 437; *Landmarks of Monroe County, N.Y.*, pt. 3, p. 27; Federal Census, 1880.)

2. At the annual meeting of the New York State Woman Suffrage Association on March 23 and 24. The association honored Clemence Lozier at a reception at the Park Avenue Hotel in the evening of March 23. (*Film*, 24:951–55.)

3. New York's constitution of 1846 called for a constitutional convention in 1866 "and in each twentieth year thereafter." The legislature had agreed to submit the question of calling the next convention to the voters in November 1886. Despite a huge majority voting in favor of a convention, the state's next constitutional convention met in 1894. (New York Const. of 1846, Art. XIII, sec. 2; Lincoln, *Constitutional History of New York*, 3:3–4.)

218 ⤳ ECS TO F. ELLEN BURR AND THE HARTFORD EQUAL RIGHTS CLUB

EDITORIAL NOTE: Ellen Burr read this letter to the club's meeting on 20 March 1886. Her published minutes reported that discussion followed "as to Mrs. Stanton's statement that 'nothing' had been gained during the past forty years. The unanimous voice of all present was that a good deal had been gained." Burr went on in her own voice to say, "Pioneers like Mrs. Stanton are getting tired of crumbs; they want the whole loaf. And it is not strange. The result seems small for the labors of half a century."

[*before 20 March 1886*]

I often think that the less people care for the real merits of our question the more tender they are about its reputation. Now I have such unbounded faith in its tenacity for life that I have not the slightest fear of killing it myself; nor that any other person will enjoy that distinction. I have no fears even of Mrs. Gougar. [Mrs. Gougar had opposed the introduction of Mrs. Stanton's resolutions into the convention in Washington, on the ground that similar resolutions of the year before had hindered her suffrage work.] As long as she retains her sweet face, pleasant manners and natural gifts for oratory, there is not the slightest danger that any of my heresies will block her way. Notwithstanding the resolutions on the church that brought out that spirited discussion in our Washington convention a year ago, she boasts of having had substantial church support throughout the year. How does she know but my gentle knocking at the door has aroused the clergy to thought and action, and perhaps been as beneficial as her "let alone" policy? Who can tell? Inasmuch as we cannot calculate influences we must utter the *highest* truth we see when we feel impelled to do so, knowing that in due time it will work its way. Our business is to protect each other in a free expression of opinion, no matter how widely we differ. A good many people have the idea that reforms are carried by clap-trap, and not by the slow process of education into great principles. Mrs. Gougar thinks she can wheedle the church and the clergy into our movement; but the priesthood have out-generaled woman too often for us to have any hopes of leading them blindfold. They know that woman is the very prop of the whole Christian theology—a theology that makes her the author of original sin and the fall of man. On this hangs the devil; a hell; an angry God; a sacrifice to perpetuate his wrath; a Saviour; a crucifixion; and a redemption; when the woman comes in again as the virgin mother. So you see the system begins and ends with woman as the chief factor. Now to change her position is to revolutionize theology; and it will take forces outside the church to do that. The clergy see clearly enough all that our movement involves, and they will be very slow to accord Justice, Liberty, and Equality to woman. They will gladly let women do all the church work they desire as subordinates; and they will continue to fan their enthusiasm in all organizations under their control; but they do not propose to overturn their Scriptures and theologies, their canon laws and ecclesiastical pronunciamentos for centuries, by recognizing the individual right of conscience and judgment for an inferior being; one created to be man's subject; a being cursed in thunder tones by her Creator in the beginning. All this will never do. That we must do for ourselves, and the sooner we begin the better.

I am discouraged as to making any impression on our statesmen until we first overturn the old religious ideas. I feel that our worst enemies are behind the altar; and that is the phase of the question in which I am now most interested.

Another thing: It is humiliating for a woman of my years to stand up before men twenty years younger, and ask them for the privilege of enjoying my rights as a citizen in a republic. I feel that I can never do it again. Think of eighteen years before Congressional committees; forty before the Legislature of New York, and nothing gained. We can make no impression on men who accept the theological view of woman as the author of sin, cursed of God, and all that nonsense. This *débris* of the centuries must be cleared away before our arguments for equality can have the least significance to any of them. They have but one idea of women, and that is that they were made to gratify their passions and bring children into the world. I should expect to get as much justice from a council of Indians in a wigwam as from any legislative assembly in this nation. Sincerely yours,

❧ *Elizabeth Cady Stanton.*

❧ *Hartford Daily Times*, 22 March 1886, in Minute Book 2, Hartford Equal Rights Club Records; Archives, History, and Genealogy Unit; Ct. Square brackets in original.

219 ❧ ECS to Benjamin F. Underwood

[*Tenafly, before 25 March 1886*][1]

Dear Mr Underwood

If you can squeeze my letter & resolution that I sent to the Washington convention into The Index even in fine print I wish you would as our suffrage papers do not publish it.[2] The resolutions both last year, & this were mine not Mrs Colby's, & have stirred up more agitation than all the rest of the convention work together.

If I can be there next year I will present & carry one stronger than ever   The shortest way to educate the women, is to make them religiously free   We have pecked away at the state half a century to no purpose   I have tried all along to show the women that our worst enemies were skulking behind the altars, & that our guns should be

turned on the church but it is difficult to make them see it. No prejudices so strong as those entrenched in superstition. Have you seen the
new Magazine called "The Forum" published in New York?[3] I shall
have an article in that on the Sunday question in the April number[4]
With kind regards for Mrs Underwood & yourself sincerely ever

       Elizabeth Cady Stanton

❧ ALS, Papers of ECS, NPV.

1. Dated with reference to publication in the Boston *Index*, 25 March 1886,
Film, 24:961, of the letter and resolution ECS sent to the Washington convention.

2. The resolution did not appear in the *Woman's Tribune* until the issue
dated April 1886. Without quoting the text, the *Woman's Journal*, 27 February 1886, inaccurately described the resolution as "the church resolution of
last year, drawn up by Mrs. Clara B. Colby, and presented by Mrs. Stanton,
which had been laid over for consideration until this year."

3. In March 1886, Lorettus Sutton Metcalf founded the *Forum*, a monthly
journal that paid particular attention to reform movements.

4. "Our Boys on Sunday," *Film*, 24:1011–18. The "Sunday question"—
whether public and cultural institutions should close for the Christian sabbath—frequently surfaced in public debate in the late nineteenth century. For
example, in the winter of 1885 and 1886, the American Secular Union circulated petitions demanding that the Metropolitan Museum of Art and the
American Museum of Natural History open their doors on Sunday, and the
state assembly approved a bill permitting this change. (Warren, *American
Freethought*, 170; *New York Times*, 18 November, 18, 27 December 1885, 17
January, 10 March, 2 April 1886.)

220 ❧ JOHN G. MACCONNELL[1] TO ECS

       Pittsburgh, [*Pa.*,] April 19, 1886.

Mrs. Elizabeth Cady Stanton:—Madam,—Pardon a stranger for writing and trespassing upon your time, but your most excellent and
instructive article published in "*The Forum*" of this month, entitled
"Our Boys on Sunday," and the manner in which it has borne good
fruit in this immediate neighborhood, is my sole excuse.

My friend Mr. Henry Phipps, Jr.,[2] of Allegheny City, read it at about
the same time I had the pleasure of reading it. On the following Monday

morning in comparing notes as to our Sunday reading, we came to the conclusion that your article had the most merit, was exceedingly instructive, and pointed out the true course to save, promote, and elevate "our boys." To such an extent did Mr. Phipps appreciate it, that on the 9th inst. he addressed a letter to the Superintendent of the Allegheny City Parks, presenting that city with the handsome sum of $25,000, to be used in the erection of plant-houses in the parks, stipulating, however, "that the houses should be kept open on Sundays during such hours and under such restrictions as they (the Park Committee) may deem necessary for the protection of the plants."

The Sabbatarians at once raised the hue-and-cry, that it should not be accepted, as it was the entering wedge to other ways of "desecrating" the Sabbath day. Presbyteries passed resolutions condemning that portion relating to the houses being kept open on Sunday, appointed Committees of clergy and laity to wait upon Mr. Phipps, seeking to have the objectionable part, from their stand-point, bigotry, stricken out. Mr. Phipps, to his great honor and credit, remained firm and steadfast in his determination in having the plant-houses remain open on Sunday as stipulated by him in his gift, and thus promoting the interests and happiness of that large portion of our community who are compelled to work hard for six days, and have therefore neither time nor opportunity of visiting such places of enjoyment and improvement, unless the first day of the week is given to them.

I take pleasure in enclosing herewith some cuttings from the newspapers of this city, so that you may see the feeling of our people on this subject, and the interest they are taking in it, as well as to show you that Mr. Phipps gives to you much credit.[3]

Hoping that your good pen may indite many more such articles on this question, and that they will not cease to bear fruit until the museums, public halls, public gardens, plant-houses, libraries, &c., &c., will be open seven days in the week, and "our boys," thus lifted out of and from temptation of the baser sort, and the churches, instead of being used for the purpose of reeling off prosy sermons, and old platitudes, will be used for the better purpose of giving short, bright, instructive addresses, on all subjects tending to elevate and promote the masses, by both men and women who have the courage to study and think for themselves, and in thus studying, thinking, writing, and talking, benefiting their neighbors, as well as humanity at large, is the wish of a father of three boys.

With respect and many thanks, I am, Madam, your obedient servant,

⤳ *John G. MacConnell.*

⤳ *Boston Investigator*, 12 May 1886. In *Film* at before 12 May 1886.

1. John Gilmore MacConnell (1840–1907) was a cigar manufacturer. ECS included his letter with hers to the editor in the *Boston Investigator*, 12 May 1886. (Federal Census, 1880; on-line records of family members in editor's files.)

2. Henry Phipps, Jr. (1839–1930) was a partner of Andrew Carnegie in the steel firm of Carnegie, Phipps & Company. His conservatory opened in Allegheny City's West Park in 1887. (*DAB*; *Memoirs of Allegheny County Pennsylvania: Personal and Genealogical, with Portraits* [Madison, Wis., 1904], 1:18.)

3. One of MacConnell's clippings, copied into ECS's letter to the *Investigator*, reported the actions of a presbytery in Allegheny whose members agreed to resist the gift from Phipps, if he insisted on disregarding "the conscientious convictions of so large a part of the community as compose the Christian element in our city."

221 ⤳ ECS TO SBA

Tenafly, [*before 27 April 1886*].[1]

Dear Susan,—You have not made me take your position.[2] I repudiate it from the bottom of my soul. It is conservative, autocratic, to the last degree. I accept no authority of either bibles or constitutions which tolerate the slavery of women. My rights were born with me and are the same over the whole globe. I may be denied their exercise in the mines of Siberia, in the empire of China and in the State of New York, through force, fraud, and sophistry; but they remain the same everywhere. Does my watch cease to be mine because some thief has taken forcible possession thereof? Of the three branches of government, the legislative, representing the people, is the primal source of power. I perceive that one of the lawyers you have consulted admits one of my points—that the legislature is above the courts; and yet the courts can declare null and void the acts of the legislature. But if the legislature can be above the courts and yet at times be in conflict with them, why on the same principle can it not be above the Constitution and yet in conflict with it? How do you amend the Constitution? The legislature, directly representing the people, decides that the Constitution needs amending, frames the amendment and submits it to the people, the majority saying yea or nay. Now where is the primary source of power? In the majority of the people. All this seems so plain to me that I wonder you halt so long over it. Think of you accepting the man-made constitution, the man-interpretation thereof, the man-amendment submitted by a convention of aristocrats, and the old secession reverence for a constitution. Why Garrison, who kicked and cuffed the old document for forty years, would turn in his grave to see printed in our *History of Woman Suffrage* your present ideas as to the authority and majesty of any of those constitutions, state or national. Ah, beware, Susan, lest as you become "respectable," you become conservative. One-half of the people have had no voice in the setting up of this constitution of New York, and I, for one, would not let a member of the legislature skulk behind the constitution so as to hold me at bay for years until that document were amended. On the contrary, I would say to him: "You represent me and it is your duty to see that justice is done. Set aside technicalities and accepted interpretations of special acts, and on broad principles recognize my citizenship." The legal rule of interpretation is in the spirit of the document. The legislature has the right to enfranchise the women of New York. Susan, you must rise to the dignity of Lord Mansfield[3] who, when law, popular sentiment, religion, custom, everything and everybody, believed in slavery, declared that no slave could breathe on English soil. You may, if you choose, write ten thousand footnotes giving in your adhesion to these man-made constitutions and appending your own name thereto, but wherever in your last revision of the proofs you have made me responsible for such todyism, I shall always bow my head with shame and sorrow.

≈ *Stanton*, 2:163–65. Dated 10 January 1880 in *Stanton*; in *Film* at April 1886.

1. Dated with reference to letter at 27 April 1886, below, that appears to follow this one in a series now largely missing. ECS's letter survives only in this heavily edited (and misdated) variant published by her children.

2. SBA disputed ECS's contention, in the preface to the *History of Woman Suffrage*, that the power of legislatures exceeded that of courts and constitutions. As finally published in *History*, 3:v, the passage reads: "We who have studied our republican institutions and understand the limits of the executive, judicial and legislative branches of the government, are aware that the legislature, directly representing the people, is the primary source of power, above all courts and constitutions." See also ECS speech to the Committee on Grievances of the New York Assembly, 18 February 1885, *Woman's Tribune*, 1 April 1885, *Film*, 24:123–24.

3. In 1772 chief justice of the Court of Kings Bench, William Murray, Earl of Mansfield (1705–1798), freed the slave James Somersett, who was brought to England from Virginia, ruling that in the absence of positive law creating slavery, slaves could not lawfully be kept in England.

222 ⇒ SBA TO MATILDA JOSLYN GAGE

Rochester N.Y. April 27/86

Dear Mrs Gage

When <u>Two</u> of the historical doctors disagree—who but the third should ~~be~~ decide!! Please scan the <u>law</u> & the <u>logic</u>—of Mrs Stanton's <u>assertion</u> that the legislature is <u>above</u> courts & constitutions—and hence have undoubted authority to enact laws in direct opposition to specific limitations or extensions of rights—in that instrument— I talked over & over my view of the matter, when at Tenafly—and last week—I wrote over eight pages—stating & re-stating the absurdity of her position—as asserted in this preface— She has itereated the same thing in a half dozen of the last chapters—against my constant protest— And now I do not want the, <u>to me</u>, absurd statement to stand forever in the preface— to me it is ridiculous—to say that we, ↑the people,↓ make a constitution—either for nation, state or association—and then retain the power & right to legislate in direct opposition to it!!— Can you ~~recast~~ not—if you see that the assertion is wrong—make it express the fact—and so state it that <u>she</u> can see it?— I do not want <u>my name</u> to <u>stand</u> to it as now stated!! ~~If~~ But if you & she see the matter alike—of course I shall surrender—

⇒ *S. B. A.*

⇒ ALS, on NWSA letterhead, SBA Papers, DLC.

223 ❧ ECS TO ANTOINETTE BROWN BLACKWELL

[*Tenafly,*] April 27, [*1886*]

Dear Antoinette,

I have been intending for some time, to thank you for the books which I am very happy to have. I have not yet given them the careful reading I intend to do as soon as I have a little leisure. I am in the midst of divers controversies with Bishops & Priests who combat my oft repeated assertion that "no form of religion as yet has taught the equality of woman." I have been trying for two years to key our women up to the discussion of the attitude of the church, & to demand equality there as well as in the state. And to do this for two reasons, 1st Because as long as the religion of the country teaches woman's subjection her status is necessarily degraded in the state. One half the difficulty in the labor problem to day is the religious idea taught, that these distinctions of class are "heaven ordained" "blessed are the poor in spirit" "the poor ye have always with you"

2nd There is no way in which we could get such wide spread agitation, on the whole question of woman's true position, as in opening a vigorous attack on the church. We have labored in the state nearly half a century, & in comparing our prolonged labors, with the result, the prospect is indeed discouraging. The political argument is exhausted it makes no impression, no one cares about it no one objects on any basis involving reason. But touch the religious phase & you have a hornets nest round your ears in a twinkling, because there our strongest enemies entrench themselves   Most of the women in our movement to day care more about their church   their religion, the salvation of their souls, than they do about enfranchisement. To concentrate their interest & enthusiasm on their own emancipation   their faith in the old theological superstitions must be unsettled. And to help do this work I ask your your aid & consideration   Our legislative assemblies are simply playing with us a cat does with a mouse. They agree among themselves to give us a good vote to keep us quiet, & they came so close to doing the thing outright in New York recently that two men in hot haste changed their votes at the last moment. We have had hearings before Congress for eighteen years steadily, good reports good votes, but no action. I am discouraged & disgusted, & feel like making an attack on some new quarter of the enemies domain. Our politicians are calm & complacent under our fire, but the clergy jump round the moment you aim a pop gun at them like parched peas on a hot shovel. I desire to hear from you on this phase of our question, through the Woman's Journal. I send you a tract of mine to read.[1] Do write something on these points pro or con & stir up some ↑new↓ thought on our question. With kind regards for Mr Blackwell & yourself sincerely

⇌ *Elizabeth Cady Stanton*

⇌ ALS, Blackwell Papers, MCR-S.

1. Enclosure missing.

224 ⇝ SBA TO HARRIET TAYLOR UPTON[1]

Leavenworth Kan. May 23, 1886

My Dear Mrs Upton

Your good father in sending me a copy of his report on our 16th amendment proposition,[2] requested me to forward you the enclosed item from one of the editors of your state.[3] Is it not a little remarkable that the modern knights of the quill almost invariably attribute the ridicule of our reform in the early days to the uncouth manners and unfashionable clothes of its advocates—when those who stand at the front to-day as the leaders of our movement are the same women who inaugurated it? Surely, Elizabeth Cady Stanton and Lucy Stone were not less attractive in manners forty years ago in the vigor and freshness of their young womanhood than now under the weight of their allotted three score years and ten? And surely no one will admit that any of the younger women who stand on our platform are superior in culture or earnestness—in the power of eloquence or logic to those pioneers of our crusade for equality of rights for women. Hence the change of attitude toward our cause ~~can~~ ↑must↓ come from the changed condition of the public mind as ↑to↓ the merits of our claims, rather ↑than↓ any improvement in the dress or address of its advocates!!

Your fathers report is excellent— I am having it sent to the leading editors and friends—and hope it will be extensively noticed by the press—

I hope you are enjoying these lovely May-days— I am taking a run west to visit my two brothers—one resides here in Leavenworth—and the at Fort Scott, Kansas— With kind regards yours sincerely

⪻ *Susan B. Anthony*

⪻ ALS, on NWSA letterhead, SBA Papers, NRU.

1. Harriet Taylor Upton (1853–1945) was the daughter of Congressman Ezra Taylor of Ohio. Since Harriet Upton did not yet believe in the need for woman suffrage, according to all accounts, her father may have hoped to open the communication that would later bring Upton into prominence in the National association. (*NAW*; *ANB*.)

2. House, Committee on the Judiciary, *Woman Suffrage. Report*, 49th Cong., 1st sess., H. Rept. 2289, Serial 2442. In the committee's report on May 6, the majority refused to restate their opposition, referred members to the report issued in the Forty-eighth Congress, and recommended that the joint resolution be tabled. Ezra Taylor's favorable minority report stated that women were "now entitled to immediate, sure, and absolute enfranchisement." The House agreed to place the resolution on its calendar.

3. Enclosure missing.

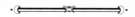

225 ⪼ SBA TO ELIZABETH BOYNTON HARBERT

Fort Scott—Kansas— June—3, 1886—

Dear Elizabeth B.

Can you help Mrs Briggs[1] to the full account of the great Chicago Sanitary Fair?— I cannot—

I was too lazy the two days I was in Chicago to let any one know I was there—but when on my return east next month—I hope to visit both you & my cousins out at Lake Geneva— they think your place must be on the opposite side of the lake from theirs—Boyles & Dickinson—are the names of the two families of my cousins![2]

I am off duty now—for a month—resting—while the Indexer[3] & the Binder finish up Vol. III.!! The Indexing of the three huge Volumes is a big job—and I hope it will be a good one too— Mrs Stanton's foreign married <u>son</u> Theodore & daughter Harriot are about landing now—on a visit to her—& her heart is full of joy—for they more fully enter into the spirit of our reform with their mother than any of the others of the seven!!—

Our friends in the U.S. Senate think it best to let our 16th am't resolution wait[4]—until after the House has acted on the <u>Washington</u> Territory Bill for admission—lest the full discussion and vote might wake up the enemy to combine against the admission of Washington into the Union!! because of its <u>women's</u> holding the ballot!!—[5] There may be force in the plan—but I see no other or at least no better way than ↑to↓ let our champions on whom we must depend for action—work in their own way & time— Lovingly

✒ Susan B. Anthony

N.B.—Please give me a list of the names & addresses of those to whom you have sold or given Vol's. I & II—also state whether they have cloth or leather bindings—that is if you wish me to send Vol. III. direct to each—and also tell me which paid you for the whole <u>three</u> volumes—& which only for one—or two— I shall return home in time to send out Vol. III—to each & all who already have Vols. I & II—Some 1,500—in all—

Or would you prefer all sent to you—and you take charge of furnishing a copy to each person?—please tell me exactly—

I hope the Fowler & Wells did not exact full pay of you for books on hand— I had always thought your books were charged to me—they ought to have been—but I could not find the bills for any sent to you—so I suppose they are right—when they say that you paid them—for them— S. B. A.

✒ ALS, on NWSA letterhead, Box 2, Elizabeth Harbert Collection, CSmH.

1. Probably she refers to Emily Pomona Edson Briggs (1830–1910), a well-known Washington journalist and hostess who wrote under the name "Olivia." Briggs also served as the first president of the Women's National Press Association, founded in 1882. The Chicago Sanitary Fair in October 1863 was a landmark in demonstrating women's talent for managing large events and raising money, in this instance for the Northwestern Sanitary Commission. (*NAW*; *ANB*.)

2. Lake Geneva, lying in three townships within Walworth County, Wisconsin, was reached in the nineteenth century by the Chicago & Northwestern Railroad. The Dickinson family owned large plots of land at the eastern

end of the lake in Buttons Bay, just south of the town of Lake Geneva. The Harberts owned a much smaller parcel of land on the lake's northern shore, near the town of Williams Bay. (North West Publishing Company, *Plat Book of Walworth County, Wisconsin: Drawn from Actual Surveys and County Records* [Philadelphia, 1891], 28–29.)

3. John L. Weinheimer of the *New York Tribune* had agreed to index the three volumes of the *History of Woman Suffrage* in time to include the index in the third volume. At different times at the *Tribune*, Weinheimer was given the titles editor, reporter, and librarian, but his lasting work was to compile and publish the yearly indexes to the newspaper. Until the mid-1880s, he lived in Brooklyn, but moved before 1888 to Kensico in Westchester County. (City directories, 1880 to 1889.)

4. The Senate passed over Resolution No. 5 twice in February 1886 and would again in July. On the last day of the session, Henry Blair announced that he would move for its consideration on the first day of the second session. (*Congressional Record*, 49th Cong., 1st sess., 23, 24 February, 8 July, 5 August 1886, pp. 1690, 1720, 6647, 8014.)

5. In April 1886, while the Senate considered the admission of Washington Territory to statehood, James Eustis, Democrat of Louisiana, moved to amend Senate 67 to bar women from voting on the adoption of a state constitution. He insisted that by its vote in January on woman suffrage in Utah, the Senate established the "wise and proper policy, that females in the Territories of the United States should be disfranchised and should not be entitled to the right of suffrage." His amendment was defeated by a vote of twenty-five to fourteen, and the Senate went on to pass the statehood bill. At this date, as the session neared its close, the House had not taken action on the bill. (*Congressional Record*, 49th Cong., 1st sess., 8, 9, 10 April 1886, pp. 3259–63, 3314–26, 3349–50; Keith A. Murray, "The Movement for Statehood in Washington," *Pacific Northwest Quarterly* 32 [July 1941]: 378–81.)

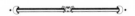

226 ❧ SBA TO JOHN W. WEINHEIMER

Rochester Aug. 13, 1886

Dear Mr Weinheimer

I send by same mail—proof, with copy—of Index—from G. to end of N—and shall be able to send you the remainder very soon now— The delay in the type-setting has been atrocious!!!

I have been over the ↑last of the↓ copy before the Compositor took it in hand—because I saw a few things I wanted to <u>classify</u>—for instance—

where I knew different persons had figured at other periods than the ones you had dated—I hunted them up & added—and when I came to <u>School</u> Suffrage—and found only <u>three</u> states under it—I hunted up & added thereto the ten or twelve other states & countries—and put, ↑all↓ under that head ↑of <u>Suffrage gained</u>↓—

I am reminded of the Story of the great discover—Columbus[1]— when his friends told him his discovery was no great feat—["]any body could have done the same"!—and he Columbus said "<u>can</u> any of you make this egg stand on the <u>small</u> end"?— they all tried & none could— he then hit it ↑and cracked it, and↓ at once the egg stood on the small end— So now—after—you have shown me the secret of <u>Index making</u> I quite feel that I could make one—and being cognizant of every person and every occurrence—nearly—and the date and place ↑they are↓ spoken of in the books—gives me help all along the line—

Under the heads of <u>Woman</u> & <u>Woman Suffrage</u>—I have cut out <u>immensely</u>—<u>everything</u> in the books being <u>about</u> <u>Woman</u>—it is but a repetition t̶o̶ ↑and would require↓ put↑ting↓ every incident in the books under <u>Woman</u>!!— I went carefully over the long list—& left only such things as were not—are not given under their proper letters— a few <u>were</u> <u>not</u> thus given—so I had to leave the heading <u>Woman</u>—

Under Suffrage ↑<u>attempted</u>↓—I would like to have put every attempt of every Legislature to pass a bill—but I cannot take the time— I shall get there every state that has voted upon it—

Hoping soon to send you the remainder—& that this will be returned very soon—Sincerely yours

⇜ *Susan B. Anthony*

P.S—Do you know you have not sent your bill to me? S. B. A—

⇜ ALS, on NWSA letterhead, Henry Simms, San Antonio, Texas. Not in *Film*.

1. Christopher Columbus (1451–1506), the explorer.

227 ⤳ ARTICLE BY ECS

[19 August 1886]

THE WOMAN'S BIBLE.

A number of English and American women are now in correspondence for the purpose of organizing a committee to revise the Scriptures, and to bring within the smallest compass all the texts that refer to the status of woman under the Jewish and Christian dispensations. To this end the committee will study the Old and New Testament both in the original and translations, and give short concise commentaries on chapters in their regular order.

The few who have inaugurated this movement are already in communication with women distinguished for their knowledge of Hebrew and Greek, and their general scholarly attainments.[1]

Women are told that they are indebted to the Bible for all the advantages and opportunities of life that they enjoy to-day, hence they reverence the very book, that above all others, contains the most degrading ideas of sex. This anomaly in human experience can only be accounted for on the assumption that women do not know what the Book really does say.

Man has written, translated and expounded for centuries his highest ideal of the great First Cause and his manner of dealing with the race, and assumed divine inspiration for his compilations. He has claimed a full knowledge of the eternal past and future, and bound his crude speculations together under the title of "The Holy Bible." With advancing civilization he has recast his creeds and dogmas, and from time to time thrown out texts, chapters, even whole books, and interpolated new theories at his discretion. Many revising committees of learned men, at different periods, have been organized for this work, but none have as yet seen fit to modify one letter of the law, to secure justice, liberty, or equality for woman. Through all history, sacred and profane, the one sorrowing, heavy-burdened figure, ever fleeing from the wrath to come, has been the mother of the race.

While Scribes and Pharisees have left her among thieves on the highway, no good Samaritan has as yet risen to shoulder her burdens, or to hold up her drooping head. No revising committee of learned men have as yet prepared an expurgated edition of the Bible, eliminating all passages invidious to woman, but on the contrary all the obscene records of her status in a barbarous age, are published and republished, bound up in the sacred volumes and scattered, the world over, spreading their baleful influence over every civilized nation.

All these the committee will collect, printing those passages too obscene for the general reader in Latin, giving chapter and verse for those who wish to prove that the text is correctly quoted.

Every civilized nation has now its representative class of educated women, and the time has fully come for them to revise the Scriptures that men claim to be of divine authority, and decide for themselves whether they will accept a "thus saith the Lord" that makes woman the author of sin; marriage, a condition of slavery; maternity, a curse; sex, a badge of degradation everywhere, even in the burnt offerings of the Jewish ritual.

Believing that the source and centre of woman's degradation is in the religious idea of her uncleanness and depravity, as set forth with innumerable reiterations in the Old Testament, and the contemptuous directions for the regulation of her life in the New, the committee feel it to be their conscientious duty to investigate the authenticity of the Scriptures.

If convinced that they emanate from the customs and opinions of a barbarous age, and have no significance in the civilization of the 19th century, they hope to free women from the bondage of the old theologies, by showing that The Woman's Bible rests simply on the authority of man, and that its teachings are unfit for this stage of evolution in which the sexes occupy an equal place in the world of thought.

⇒ *Elizabeth Cady Stanton.*

⇒ Boston *Index*, 19 August 1886.

1. See Antoinette B. Blackwell to ECS, 10 August 1886, *Film*, 24:1076–80.

228 ⤜ ECS TO HARRIET HANSON ROBINSON

[*Tenafly,*] August 27 [*1886*]

Mrs Robinson,

If you take The Index read my article on "The Woman's Bible" August 19, & tell me if you & Mrs Shattuck would join a Committee for "the revision of the scriptures" I think it would have a good effect on women themselves to assume the responsibility of such a work. I am writing to distinguished women in England as well as America & have thus far secured two English & four American. The details of the plan we shall decide on later. You will find an article on the subject from Miss Frances Lord[1] (English) in this weeks Index. Yours

⤜ *E C Stanton.*

⤜ ALS, Robinson-Shattuck Papers, MCR-S.

1. Henrietta Frances Lord (c. 1848–?) arrived in Tenafly from England early in August and began work with ECS on the *Woman's Bible.* In "The Woman's Bible," Boston *Index*, 26 August 1886, Lord wrote that the committee would discover whether the Bible contained "a mass of contradictions or a consistent code of right and wrong," and then ask if women "ought to obey it." She also disputed prevailing views of the Bible: its "plenary inspiration," or the view that every word was the word of God, and its "progressive morality," or the view that the book showed societies revising their morals. Neither was adequate for women. After studying at Girton College, Lord had joined her sister Emily in the kindergarten movement, served as a poor law guardian in London, and made a mark as the translator of Hendrik Ibsen's plays *The Doll's House* and *Ghosts.* Both ECS and SBA met her in London. Lord's passion for the Bible project was short-lived. From New Jersey, she traveled to Chicago to study Christian Science, or Mind Cure, with Emma Curtis Hopkins, and she stayed to edit a Christian Science journal for women. ECS had no patience with Lord's "mental bewilderment." After Lord's return to England in 1887, she published *Christian Science Healing: Its Principles and Practice.* (Cambridge University, Girton College, *Girton College Register, 1869–1946* [Cambridge, England, 1948], 8; Census of Britain, 1881; Allibone Supplement; Kern, *Mrs. Stanton's Bible*, passim; *Eighty Years*, 374, 377, 390–92; SBA diary, 27 June, 1, 3 July 1883, and ECS to Sara F. Underwood, 5 April, August?, 1 November 1887, *Film*, 22:814ff, 25:391–94, 658–63, 774–79.)

229 ~ ELIZABETH SMITH MILLER TO ECS

Geneva, N.Y., September 2, 1886.

Beloved Johnson:

Father believed the Bible was opposed to slavery, and did his best to oppose the contrary belief which the slaveholders supported.[1] Do you believe the Bible approves the doctrine of equal rights for man and woman? Whether it does, or does not, I, who do not believe in its inspiration, cannot expect my views to be accepted by those who most reverently regard it as the Word of God. When the doctrine of equal rights is established (and all must see the rapid progress being made in that direction) these Bible people will have the benefit—the beautiful result of <u>civilisation</u>. But I don't think it worth while to meddle with that book; and in order to show the world that it is not adapted to this day, why not let it alone and go on with the work which has already attained such grand proportions? Your loving,

~ *Julius.*

~ Typed transcript, ECS Papers, NjR.

1. For Miller's earlier refusal to work on the Bible, see E. S. Miller to ECS, 29 August 1886, *Film*, 24:1098. On her father's convictions about the Bible's alignment with social reform, see Ralph Volney Harlow, *Gerrit Smith: Philanthropist and Reformer* (New York, 1939), passim.

230 ~ ECS TO ELIZABETH BOYNTON HARBERT

Tenafly N.J. Sept 13 [*1886*]

Dear Mrs Harbert,

To begin with the last of your letter instead of the first, I have written many letters to leading women in the old world & the new to form a committee. Have as yet but <u>ten names</u>.[1] Plan of work, where, when, & how the committee can consult meet & compare notes is all yet to be arranged after we get a committee large enough for the importance of the undertaking. Miss Francis Lord an English lady has been staying with me six weeks & we have had this matter all the time under consideration & I will tell you what we have done. 1ˢᵗ We went through the whole Bible & marked all the passages referring to woman. Then we bought four cheap Bibles 25 cts apiece cut out these verses pasted them chapter by chapter at the top of a page in a black book, & wrote our commentaries thereon. In this way we have gone through the Penteteuch, carefully reading Clarkes commentaries[2] to see if he could throw any light on woman's position. We decided that many passages were too obscene to print in the English language & must appear in Latin with English commentaries. We shall reverse the order in most commentaries & put the texts in smaller print than the commentaries. We thought after securing a committee, we would divide the books among them. There are 65 books suppose we had a committee of 25, & each one would take three books or where two are near each other they would together take five, the work could be easily & quickly done. About one tenth of the Bible contains all that refers to woman, hence you see five books would not contain much. The committee should all be liberal read & comment as they would on the letter & spirit of any book of human origin, taking the orthodox view in regard to woman, that it does make woman man's inferior subject, subordinate slave. There is no use to shirk this idea it is plainly taught in the old testament & the new. But if our committee differ we can have different notes on the same text with the initials of the author. You see in Clarkes notes he often gives the opinion of several that differ from his own. We should try & make the commentaries sparkling as well as earnest, pathetic as well as pleasing learned as well as popular. If we could get twenty five intelligent well educated good common sense women we could make "The Woman's Bible" a great feature of the general upris-ing, in this 19ᵗʰ century If we accept the orthodox basis & write from that standpoint, declaring the human origin of the book because of this fact, our Rev gentlemen will begin at once to explain away all the odious features. Like the constitution much can be said on both sides and we can incorporate the various shades of thought Suppose for example you & Frances Williard should read over the Penteteuch after Francis Lord & I had completed our work, & should add a few sen-tences, making some criticisms on our seeming inconsistencies, that would only add to the interest & suppose Francis Lord & I should do the same to yours. Our differences would make our readers think, & teach them to respect the right of individual opinion conscience judgement   I do not see the beginning nor end, we must grow into the best way to accomplish this work. But let us get a committee & begin, the names of Hannah Whitehall Smith & Zerelda Wallace are desirable. I know them both & will write inviting them I wish you & Miss Williard would do the same   Will you & Miss Williard give [*in margins of page*] your names? With best regards

⬱ *Elizabeth Cady Stanton*

We have nine good names pledged, 3 English & 6 American. [*in margins of first page*] It would be well if we could have two or three good Hebrew & Greek scholars if we can find them among women. We can consult wise men individually as much as we please, but do not let us have them on our committee [*in margins of next to last page*] Miss Lord is going to California, she will spend a few days with May Wright Sewall. If you would like to see her invite her for a day or so as she will be in Chicago & would like to see some of you.

⬱ ALS, Box 7, Elizabeth Harbert Collection, CSmH.

1. The ten members (or nine, as ECS claims later in this letter) included herself, Harriot Blatch, Frances Lord, and Mary Livermore. In a letter written 10 October 1886, ECS named Olympia Brown, Ellen Burr, and Phebe Hanaford as others who accepted her invitation. (Mary A. Livermore to ECS, 1 September 1886, ECS to May W. Sewall, 10 October 1886, *Film*, 24:1101–5, 25:28–36.)

2. Adam Clarke, *The Holy Bible, with a Commentary and Critical Notes*, published between 1810 and 1826.

231 ⬱ APPEAL BY ECS TO THE GOVERNORS OF THE THIRTEEN COLONIAL STATES

Tenafly, N.J., Sept. 16 [*1886*].

Honorable Gentlemen—The programme is announced for the meeting preparatory to the celebration of that great event in our history, the adoption of a national constitution, which occurred fourteen years after we declared ourselves a nation.[1]

You are to have the honor of meeting in Carpenter's Hall, rich in so many memories of the early struggles of our forefathers, you are then to adjourn to Independence Hall, whose venerable bell rang forth the joyful news of a nation's birth and liberty to all its people.[2]

You have the promise of a barbecue in the park too, and a season of devotion in the same sacred temple, where the immortal Washington bowed his head in worship; and that all this may be realized with becoming decency and order, Col. G. E. Payton[3] will conduct you from point to point. It will be his duty to see that the effects of the barbecue are fully effaced before you enter the vestibule of the church.

But the point of time when the interest of the women of the thirteen original states and their descendants center round you, is immediately before the barbecue, while yet in solemn conclave in Independence Hall.

There, in your normal condition, your minds still unclouded by the viands heedless purveyors are sure to spread before you, if admitted to your presence, "We, the people"—that is, one-half the people—would propound to you the following questions:

What part, if any, are the women to have in the celebration of the New Centennial? Will the consideration of the great principles of the constitution throw any new light on their disfranchised condition? Will the distinguished governors who gather in Philadelphia to recall the noble deeds and words of their ancestors, return to their homes determined to secure liberty, justice, and equality for women?

In asking the co-operation of the younger states, and a representative regiment to make an imposing and appropriate military spectacle, you make no mention of women. Perhaps you include them in the word co-operation, and propose that they shall co-operate as they did in the centennial of 1876, viz: to do all in their power to make it a brilliant success, in raising money and serving in all subordinate positions, but to be ostracised as citizens at the great jubilee on the 4th of July.[4]

If, gentlemen, you desire a fine spectacular effect, no military display could be so imposing and appropriate as a long procession of disfranchised women, representing every state in the union, dressed in the national colors, with flags and banners bearing the inscriptions, "Taxation without representation is tyranny"; "No just government can be formed without the consent of the governed"; "Equal rights to all"; "The ballot is the columbiad of our political life, and every citizen who holds it is a full armed Monitor."

These mottoes might serve as so many reminders to thoughtful men, that there still remains, under this republican government, a class of citizens for whom these fundamental principles have as yet no significance.

It might be chivalrous, to say the least, for the governors of the several states now assembled to take some action in regard to the political rights of women.

The pages of our colonial history furnish abundant proof that in line with English precedent women did vote and hold office in several of the early colonies, and had an undoubted right to do so in all. In this view, we ask the present governors of the several states to recommend to their respective legislatures to pass bills restoring to women their ancient rights and privileges, taken from them in many cases by an arbitrary act of the legislature, without a constitutional amendment. It is plain to anyone capable of reasoning, that if a state legislature has the power to deprive a class of citizens of rights already exercised, it must have the power to confer rights also on new classes.

In the state of New Jersey, women voted as late as 1806, when by an arbitrary act of the legislature the right was denied them.[5] Being a citizen of this state, a property holder and tax-payer, I ask the governor of New Jersey[6] to recommend, in his next message, the passage of an act to restore to the women of this state the rights they once enjoyed under the constitution.

The effect of a governor's message in the legislature cannot be over-estimated. It is well known that on the recommendation of Governor Hubbard,[7] of Connecticut, the legislature passed a bill, securing to married women their property rights. Hence, in the celebration of the New Centennial, we ask the governors of the several states to recommend in their annual messages the enfranchisement of women, the only class of citizens still denied the right of self-government. Nothing that you could do, honorable gentlemen, would add greater dignity and honor to the coming celebration, than this act of justice to your mothers, wives, and daughters, who have an equal interest with yourselves in the success of the grand experiment of republican institutions.

ᷛ *Elizabeth Cady Stanton.*

ᷛ *Woman's Tribune*, October 1886.

1. On 17 September 1886, representatives from ten of the original thirteen

states met in Philadelphia to plan for the celebration of the centennial of the Constitution. Their schedule of speeches, marches, visits to historical sites, and barbecue in Fairmount Park closely matched what ECS describes herein. (Hampton L. Carson, ed., *History of the Celebration of the One Hundredth Anniversary of the Promulgation of the Constitution of the United States* [Philadelphia, 1889], 1:261–71; *New York Times*, 18 September 1886.)

2. Carpenters' Hall was the site of the first Continental Congress in 1774. The Declaration of Independence was adopted and the Constitution written in Independence Hall.

3. Jesse Enlows Peyton (1815–1897), known as the "Father of Centennials," was a promoter behind the Centennial of 1876 and the celebration of the Constitution in 1887. (*ACAB* Supplement; *New York Times*, 28 April 1897.)

4. ECS combines the story of the exploitation of the official Women's Centennial Executive Committee by the Centennial Commission with the separate story of the National Woman Suffrage Association, whose leaders were denied the chance to read their protest at ceremonies on the Fourth of July 1876. (Mary Frances Cordato, "Toward A New Century: Women and The Philadelphia Centennial Exhibition, 1876," *PMHB* 107 [January 1983]: 113–35; *History*, 3:1–40; *Papers*, 3:224–51.

5. New Jersey's constitution of 1776, in force until 1844, permitted adult inhabitants, including women, to vote, if they met the property qualifications. In 1807, however, the legislature enacted a law that limited the franchise to white male taxpaying citizens. (Judith Apter Klinghoffer and Lois Elkis, "'The Petticoat Electors': Women's Suffrage in New Jersey, 1776–1807," *Journal of the Early Republic* 12 [Summer 1992]: 159–93.)

6. Leon Abbett (1836–1894) was governor of New Jersey from 1884 to 1887.

7. Richard Dudley Hubbard (1818–1884) was governor of Connecticut from 1877 to 1879. His role in passage of a married women's property act is told in *History*, 3:324–27.

232 ⪼ MARY JANE TARR CHANNING TO ECS

Pasadena, California, September 26, 1886.

My dear Mrs Stanton:

I rather think it a good plan. It will frighten a great many women and men. Have you ever read Mrs Child's "<u>Progress of Religious Ideas</u>"?[1] I read it when it was first published and it emancipated me completely from Bible thraldom. I find it hard to keep in my mind the fact that so many otherwise enlightened people are bound by the words of the

Bible, however absurd, unjust or wicked they may be. My Grace, who is an omnivorous reader, says: "I would read it if it were interesting, but I do not think it is"; and I always find much of it uninteresting.

Did not Dr Channing get for you a curious book by an old divine showing the strongest Bible authority for polygamy? Do you know the Koran? And I have been told that the Eastern sacred books all have these same low ideas and estimates of woman. Yours most truly,

⹊ *M. J. Channing.*

⹊ Typed transcript, ECS Papers, NjR.

1. Lydia Maria Child, *The Progress of Religious Ideas, Through Successive Ages* (1855).

233 ⹊ ECS TO HARRIET HANSON ROBINSON

Tenafly Sept 30 [*1886*]

Dear Mrs Robinson,

It is quite evident from both yours & Mrs Shattucks letters[1] that you do not understand what we propose to do in "revising the Scriptures." <u>Our</u> <u>work</u> <u>has</u> <u>never</u> <u>been</u> <u>done</u> <u>before.</u> But one tenth of the Bible refers to women, we propose to put that in one volumn with our commentaries. It is not necessary that all the committee should be Hebrew or Greek scholars. We have a sufficient number who have accepted ~~already~~ to make a respectable committee, & have already quite a number at work. Miss Frances Lord & I have devoted ourselves all summer to the Penteteuch & that is ready to submit to the advisory committee. I had intended to do the whole work with my daughter's aid, but I thought it would be more dignified to have a committee of able women than any one individual. Many like your daughter & yourself have declined from distrust of their capacity to lend any effective aid,[2] & a want of appreciation of the importance of the work. To such there is nothing more to be said. Many others who are awake to the demoralizing influence of woman's position in all the sacred books, of all the religions, are enthusiastic in the compilation of the proposed book. I am going to England with my daughter the last of this month, to avail ourselves of the great library in the British Museum, to make a faithful study of woman's position under the various religions, & the claims put forward under all alike of divine inspiration. When our work is finished we shall have a grand convocation in London or New York of all the special committees who have done the work & of the advisory committee for final action on the commentaries. We have announced in Vol III that we shall hold an International suffrage convention in Washington in the winter 1888,[3] immediately after that while foreign ladies are here we shall have our Bible convention in New York, unless for some reason it may be best to have it in London, but N.Y. seems to me the place now. If you & Mrs Shattuck decline to give your names on the advisory committee, do not I pray you directly or indirectly depreciate the dignity of "a committee of women" to revise the scriptures. The Smith sisters work[4] was not at all what we propose. The assumption of a committee of women to revise the scriptures pertaining to the origin nature, & destiny of their own sex will have its influence in a new & broader agitation of our rights and when the work is accomplished there will be such a shaking of the dry bones of conservatives as we have not yet witnessed. Revolve the plan in your minds, look at it from all points of view before you decide that it is an inconsequential undertaking. With kind regards sincerely yours

≋ *Elizabeth Cady Stanton*

≋ ALS, Robinson-Shattuck Papers, MCR-S.

1. The authors' copies and transcripts made by the Stanton family of these two letters are in *Film*, 24:1113–17, 25:1–4.

2. Harriette Shattuck wrote on 8 September 1886 that she did "not feel competent to undertake the 'revision of the Scriptures.'" The transcript of her letter records ECS's comment to Harriot Blatch, "The revision is evidently needed for this poor little sister. She is the one you met at Concord who was converted by the Mormon argument to doubt the right of suffrage."

3. *History*, 3:952.

4. Harriet Robinson, on 29 September 1886, mentioned the biblical translation by Julia Smith as an existing source that treated women impartially. Julia Evalina Smith (1792–1886) and Abby Hadassah Smith (1797–1878) published Julia's translation of the Bible in 1876 as *The Holy Bible: Containing the Old and New Testaments; Translated Literally from the Original Tongues.* (*NAW; ANB.*)

234 ⇝ SBA TO ELIZABETH BOYNTON HARBERT

[Kan., before 19 October 1886][1]

Now—If I am not at Sandwich at the beginning of the Con[2]—Do you exhibit the History & the Woman's Tribune—and tell the audience that to every one who buys the History—Miss Anthony will present them the Tribune & membership of both National & State W.S. societies!! I want you to Let Harry & Lucy see that you are just as earnest to support the Tribune as you were the New Era— Everything of good work in the west depends on the sustaining of the <u>one</u> paper that is started & not starting any more

I fairly tremble at that of Mrs Colby's having to give up her paper as you had to yours & I had to mine— And I shall work all I can to prevent the sad fate coming to her—as I would have done to have saved myself—had I known how—and to save you had it not been that I was bound hand & foot—head & heart & purse to Vol. III—!! I can't tell you ↑how↓ relieved I feel that it is done— Lovingly—

⇝ *S. B. A*

P.S. Mrs Colby has gone home to get out her Oct. Tribune but expects to meet us at Witchita— She will go over to your State Con. at Sandwich—so we can easily fill a <u>third day</u> if the powers that be are willing to have us do so—

The friends in this state do not dream but that Lucy Stones meeting at Topeka next week belong to our National[3]—they write it up as the <u>National</u>—and announce Mrs Stanton, Miss Anthony Mrs Saxon & Mrs Colby—and two or three times I have seen all of our names and neither Lucy's nor Harry's!!! They dont succeed worth a cent in giving them selves a separate & select individuality—but instead in the public mind are all mixed up with the rest of us!!

⇝ ALS incomplete, Box 2, Elizabeth Harbert Collection, CSmH.

1. Dated by reference to an event at Wichita, scheduled for October 19. Clara Colby left Kansas for Nebraska before October 15, when she missed the meeting in Salina; thus, SBA could have written this earlier. See *Film*, 25:38.

In a renewed effort to gain municipal suffrage in Kansas, the National association, Kansas Equal Suffrage Association, and Kansas Woman's Christian Temperance Union organized a canvass of the state's congressional districts. Traveling with Colby and Elizabeth Saxon, SBA spoke at twelve of the meetings across the state from October 4, when she helped launch the tour at Leavenworth, to November 2, when she made her last appearance at Lawrence. (Gifford and Underwood, "Intertwined Ribbons"; *Film*, 25:18–19, 24–27, 37–38, 43–48, 52, 56–60, 63, 65.)

2. The Illinois Equal Suffrage Association held a three-day, seventeenth annual meeting in Sandwich, Illinois, beginning on 3 November 1886. SBA, Lucy Stone, and Henry Blackwell all spoke at an evening session on November 4, and on the next day, they joined discussions of a plan of work. (*Union Signal*, 2 December 1886, *Film*, 25:67; *Chicago Daily Tribune*, 5, 6 November 1886.)

3. The American Woman Suffrage Association opened its annual meeting in Topeka on October 26.

235 ❧ REMARKS BY SBA TO LUNCHEON IN WICHITA, KANSAS

EDITORIAL NOTE: When the congressional district convention in Wichita, Kansas, opened in the Methodist Episcopal Church on 19 October 1886, the first order of business was to organize a local society, whose members promptly resolved, "That the Wichita Equal Suffrage Association be a non-partisan organization, in accord with the attitude of the Kansas Equal Suffrage Association." National and local speakers weighed in on the same topic at a luncheon in the Manhattan Hotel during a midday recess on October 20 as guests of Dr. Nannie Stephens. After lunch, the public meetings resumed, with Mary Lease in the chair and SBA, Elizabeth Saxon, and Clara Colby taking turns as speakers. More than fifteen hundred people crowded Memorial Hall on the second evening, and the national speakers agreed to stay an extra day. (*Wichita Beacon*, 22 October 1886, *Film*, 25:46–47.)

[20 October 1886]

The midday was delightfully filled by a dinner at the Manhattan, given by Dr. Nannie Stephens[1] to the visitors and the committee on entertainment, Mrs. Saxon unfortunately not being able to be present on account of the severe cold from which she suffered during the entire trip, and which at times almost prostrated her. With the coffee toasts were in order. Mrs. Lease[2] proposed a toast to Miss Anthony which was replied to by Miss Anthony with a bright speech in which she claimed that the occasion offered the strongest proof that the condition of woman had changed for the better since the agitation of the question began. That a woman could be a physician, and a sufficiently success-ful one financially to be able to give a dinner like this was proof positive that woman's status had changed. Dr. Stephens proposed a toast to the new suffrage society replied to by Mrs. Colby. Mrs. Cuthbert,[3] of Belle Plaine, toasted the third party to which Mrs. Lease responded, claim-ing the third party as the one that favored women. Mrs. Johns[4] then proposed a toast to the Republican party and called on Miss Anthony to respond which she did enumerating the various votes in Congress and legislatures in which the favorable members were largely Republi-cans. The Kansas Republicans also had a plank in their platform of 1882. Miss Anthony claimed that as women had no votes to help a party and their friends were in all parties, a suffrage organization should hold itself non-partisan. In order to conform strictly to this idea, Mrs. Colby proposed a toast to the Democratic party so that no one could feel slighted. With the closing toast, that of Mrs. Johns to the fair hostess, the party adjourned to the place of meeting, but with a pleasant memory of the event and of the many bright and witty remarks made by the ladies in the toasts and responses.

❦ *Woman's Tribune*, November 1886.

1. Nannie A. Stephens (1854–?) graduated from the Woman's Medical College of Chicago in 1878 and attended medical lectures in Philadelphia, before opening her practice in Wichita, where her husband, Ralph Stephens, was proprietor of a livery and feed stable. (Andreas, *History of Kansas*, 1401; Federal Census, 1880.)

2. Mary Elizabeth Clyens Lease (1853–1933), later well known as a Populist orator, settled to Wichita in 1883, studied law, and founded a women's club for the discussion of public affairs. She also joined with the Union Labor party, a successor to the Greenback and Anti-Monopoly parties, and her introduction of SBA to the congressional district convention expressed her admiration for the Knights of Labor. Local suffragists elected her president of the Wichita Equal Suffrage Association. (*NAW; ANB; Film*, 25:43–48.)

3. Belle Plaine is about twenty miles from Wichita. A Mrs. Cuthbert living in that location has not been identified.

4. Laura Lucretia Mitchell Johns (1849–1935) moved to Kansas in 1883 and

became active in the Woman's Christian Temperance Union in Salina. There Bertha Ellsworth drew her into the Kansas Equal Suffrage Association. Johns organized the congressional district conventions underway in the fall of 1886. The state association elected her president in 1887, and she retained that position until 1895. (*American Women*; *Woman's Who's Who 1914*; Amy A. Mitchell, "Reminiscences of Laura Lucretia Johns," typescript, Alma Lutz Collection, NPV; Goldberg, *Army of Women*, 72–74, 88; Rebecca Edwards, *Angels in the Machinery: Gender in American Party Politics from the Civil War to the Progressive Era* [New York, 1997], 107–9.)

236 ❧ ANTOINETTE BROWN BLACKWELL TO ECS

Elizabeth [*N.J.*] Oct. 25 1886

Dear Mrs. Stanton:

So you are off without delay for England and work![1]

Well, success to your very live project. Push it, but <u>dont</u> hurry it; and when it is done let it be the very best that could be done by women.

I have read your various manifestoes which have a good ring and only write to speed your parting with a sincere word.

My long toil about the foundations of things goes on; and so all of us are busy. But dont <u>you</u> call this piece of work the "crown" of a long life The crown may be in the last act far ahead   Yours

❧ *A. B. Blackwell*

❧ ALS, ECS Papers, DLC.

1. ECS sailed on October 26. (*Stanton*, 2:233.)

237 ❧ SBA TO RICHARD W. GUENTHER

Ripon, Wis.[1] Nov. 12, 1886

Hon Richard Guenther   My Dear Sir

You will see by the enclosed bill[2]—that every Congressional District of your state is being invaded by the so called "<u>Strong Minded Women</u>"—

I do not know your views upon the queston of woman's enfranchisement[3]—but since it is to come before Congress during the next session—

I may hope that you will do us the favor and the honor to give us the weight of your influence by your presence and good word at our Convention at Oskosh the 13th 15th & 16th inst—

I hope you will be present at our opening session, tomorrow evening— at the Universalist Church of your city, but if that is not possible— please drop a note at the Post Office—telling me at which of the sessions you will be present— Monday & Tuesday evening meetings are to be held at the Opera House—and I very much hope you will allow me to announce that you ↑will↓ say a few words at one of them— Very respectfully yours

           ❧   *Susan B. Anthony*

❧ ALS, on NWSA letterhead, Richard W. Guenther Papers, Archives Division, WHi.

1. At Ripon on November 11 and 12, SBA and Clara Colby joined Olympia Brown for one in a series of eleven conventions in Wisconsin's congressional districts, beginning at Racine on November 8. They met next in Oshkosh. On this tour, see *Film*, 25:83–87, 101–2.

2. Enclosure missing.

3. Richard Guenther opposed the formation of a House committee on woman suffrage in the vote on 20 December 1883. (*Congressional Record*, 48th Cong., 1st sess., 219.)

238   ❧   ECS to Victoria Woodhull Martin

           Basingstoke [*England*] Nov. 12, [*1886*]

Dear Mrs Martin

Many thanks for the papers & your husband's admirable speech.[1] I was pleased to hear from your sister[2] that your domestic trials had ended so happily, & that you were in a safe harbor at last. Accept my congratulations I shall certainly call on you when I visit London. I do not know when that will be, as I am very busy. Vol III of History of Woman Suffrage is published you can get it at the same office where you found the others in Burner street[3] With sincere wishes for your happiness as ever your friend

           ❧   *Elizabeth Cady Stanton.*

P.S. Have you any catalogue of Lord Cook's gallery? What days is ↑it↓ open to visitors?

⪼ ALS, Victoria Woodhull Martin Papers, Special Collections, ICarbS.

1. On 31 October 1883, Victoria Woodhull married John Biddulph Martin (1841–1897), managing partner of one of England's oldest banks. The couple lived at 17 Hyde Park Gate in London. Educated at Harrow and Oxford, Martin had a range of intellectual interests from statistics to archaeology. Perhaps his wife sent a speech from his presidency in 1886 of the statistical and economic section of the British Association. (Lois Beachy Underhill, *The Woman Who Ran for President: The Many Lives of Victoria Woodhull* [New York, 1995], 277–91; *New York Times*, 22 March 1897.)

2. Tennessee Celeste Claflin (1845–1923) married Francis Cook (1817–1901), a London merchant, in October 1885. Cook had assembled a distinguished art collection in Doughty House, his London residence, to which he welcomed visitors. He was made a baronet in March 1886, and the couple were known as Lord and Lady Cook. (*DNB*; *NAW*.)

3. ECS probably means Berners Street, and if so, copies of the *History of Woman Suffrage* may have been available in the editorial offices of the *Englishwoman's Review* there.

239 ⪼ INTERVIEW WITH SBA IN OSHKOSH, WISCONSIN

[*13 November 1886*]

"Well, what do you want me to say?" The speaker was Susan B. Anthony and her remark was addressed to a *Northwestern* reporter who called upon her at the residence of Samuel Lawrence[1] on Washington street, where she is staying while in the city attending the woman's suffrage convention. "I'm sure I'll be glad to tell you anything I know," continued Miss Anthony.

"Well, what are you here for," asked the reporter.

"I am here to stir up the people on the question of woman's suffrage. My home is at Rochester, but I am helping the women of Wisconsin in the series of conventions which they are now holding. How do you interpret the amendment giving women the right to vote on all school matters, queried the scribe.[2] Do you think with Rev. Olympia Brown that the women according to that amendment can vote for governor?

Certainly I do, replied Miss Anthony. The only way the women can gain anything in this country is to assume their rights. In 1872 I was arrested and fined $100 for trying to exercise my rights of citizenship according to the 14th amendment, and the women in Wisconsin will have to stand up and demand their rights."

Do you really believe that women should have the right to vote?

"Of course I do. Don't you think your mother is as smart as you are?" she continued. The scribe replied that he thought there was only one woman in this town that was competent to vote, in answer to which assertion Miss Anthony declared that there are only two smart men in the city of Oshkosh.

"Who are they?" was asked.

"Oh! I don't know but I say as a rule there are only about two men in every municipality who are really men of learning. If you are going to take that matter into the question there are just as many smart women as there are men."

"How long do you think it will be ere we have woman suffrage in the United States?"

"When those who are now boys go to ballot box and give us the right, no sooner."

"Oh! I want to stir up the people of this city. I have written letters to Senator Sawyer[3] and Congressman Guenther to be present at the meetings, and I hope Congressman-elect Clark[4] will be there also. We want their influence and votes when the sixteenth amendment comes up in congress next winter. Now just rouse the people and make them come out to our meetings.

"I shall lecture Monday night on 'Woman wants Bread, not the Ballot.' I shall treat the subject from an industrial basis. We want an even chance with the men to earn our bread. The only way we can obtain it is through the ballot."

❧ Oshkosh *Daily Northwestern*, 13 November 1886. Not in *Film*.

1. Samuel B. Lawrence (1824–?), a lumberman who moved from Maine to Oshkosh in 1855, lived at 421 Washington Street. (Federal Census, 1880; *History of Northern Wisconsin, Containing an Account of Its Settlement, Growth, Development and Resources* [Chicago, 1881], 1153.)

2. At the election in November 1886, voters in Wisconsin approved a bill for school suffrage that the legislature passed in March 1885. Woman suffragists, including some legislators, held out hope that the statute's indefinite language

opened the door to municipal and some statewide suffrage. The statute referred to women's residence in election districts, rather than school districts,
and it granted voting "in any election pertaining to school matters." As one
activist explained to the *Woman's Journal*, a "liberal construction of the law"
would allow women to vote for the governor, "the election of such mayors as
appoint members of school boards, and the election of aldermen who perform
a like duty." (*Woman's Journal*, 27 November 1886, 5 November 1887; Brown
v. Phillips 71 Wisconsin Reports 239 [1888]; Theodora W. Youmans, "How
Wisconsin Women Won the Ballot," *Wisconsin Magazine of History* 5 [Sep-
tember 1921]: 3–32; Genevieve G. McBride, *On Wisconsin Women: Working
for Their Rights from Settlement to Suffrage* [Madison, Wis., 1993], 117–27.)

3. Philetus Sawyer (1816–1900), a Republican from Oshkosh, entered the
Senate in 1881, after a decade in the House of Representatives. He served in
the Senate until March 1893. (*BDAC.*)

4. Charles Benjamin Clark (1844–1891), a Republican from Neenah, Wisconsin, won election to the Fiftieth Congress, where he took his seat in March
1887. (*BDAC.*)

240 ❧ ECS TO SARA FRANCIS UNDERWOOD

Basingstoke Hants [*England*]   Nov 15th [*1886*]

Dear Mrs Underwood,

If you have any more of my last letter to The Index please send me
half a dozen slips.[1] I distributed most of mine in America before coming hither. Most of the English women to whom I have written are
terribly afraid of the project.[2] A letter yesterday from Julia Ward Howe
declining on account of <u>capacity</u>.[3] The humility of the educated women
is quite <u>praiseworthy</u>. "Blessed are the poor in spirit for they shall see
God"[4] Perhaps they hope to see God, by trying to make him believe,
that ~~their~~ ↑they are↓ encompassed in a garb of humility, in sack cloth &
ashes.[5] (They may deceive him but they do not themselves nor me).
Well when we get the volumn completed I hope they will have sufficient capacity to read & understand it. Well we have had considerable
agitation out of it already, one object secured. Whatever good ideas
suggest themselves to your mind please communicate & act on. What
do you think of publishing chapter by chapter in some paper. Put
yourself in communication with Clara Neyman. ~~Has~~ ↑Have↓ any Greek

or Hebrew scholars presented themselves as yet to your notice? When will you go to Chicago?[6] Frances Lord is still there looking into the <u>mind</u> <u>cure</u>.[7] Will The Index die a natural death or pass into other hands. Moncure D Conway ↑called↓ on me the night before I sailed, he said the project of a new paper in New York was given up, as they could not raise the necessary funds. Did you write to Susan B. Anthony Rochester N.Y. to send you the third volumn of the Woman Suffrage History to review. If you have not the other volumns ask for a complete sett on my account   With best regards for Mr Underwood [*in margin*] & yourself yours cordially

≽ *Elizabeth Cady Stanton*

≽ ALS, Papers of ECS, NPV.

1. "The Woman's Bible," *Film*, 25:49.

2. Letters from Clementia Taylor, 28 August 1886 and 12 November 1886; Ursula Bright, 28 September 1886; and Priscilla McLaren, 12 November 1886 are in *Film*, 24:1094–97, 1131, 25:74–76.

3. Julia Ward Howe to ECS, 23 October 1886, *Film*, 25:53–54.

4. ECS combines Matt. 5:3 and 5:8.

5. An indication of one's penitence, as in Dan. 9:3.

6. The Boston *Index* published its last issue on 30 December 1886 by a vote of the executive board of the Free Religious Association. Subscribers were offered the chance to receive either the *Open Court* or *Unity*, both published in Chicago. Benjamin and Sara Underwood edited the *Open Court* together from its first issue in February 1887, but they left the journal in November of that year. ECS agreed to be one of their contributors.

7. Mind cure, based on a belief that matter and body were creations of the mind, promised to heal sickness through directing the patient's thoughts. Chicago became an important center of training and publishing, as the movement grew in popularity, especially among women, from 1885 onward. (Beryl Satter, *Each Mind a Kingdom: American Women, Sexual Purity, and the New Thought Movement, 1875–1920* [Berkeley, Calif., 1999].)

241 ⋙ CAROLINE COULOMB DE BARRAU TO ECS

Paris, November 15, 18[86].

My dear Mrs Stanton:

At present, the French are disbelievers and agnostics or materialists; or they are Catholics and sound Protestants. Such as myself who still am not a sceptic, though neither Protestant nor Catholic, are now very few. I think I hardly know any. Quite different is the condition of religious ideas in England and among the Anglo-Saxon race generally; there the believers in the Bible are very numerous. Consequently, I do not think your Bible revision idea will excite much interest in France. It will be regarded as a curiosity and seem singular that anybody has anything to do with the Bible, that great minds like yours can give time to it.

The matter of women's intellectual culture is receiving a great set-back just now in France because of the contention of the hygienists who, falsely I think, hold that the number and extent of subjects which women should study ought to be limited, because, they declare, our brains cannot support many and higher studies.[1] Of course many and good arguments can be opposed to this view. But we find our men willing and glad to seize this occasion to assert the inferiority of woman. So there is a sad turning backwards, at this moment, of the movement in favour of equality. A large number of mothers say that they prefer their daughters to remain ignorant rather than have their health undermined by study! Sincerely yours,

⋙ Caroline de Barrau.

⋙ Typed transcript, ECS Papers, NjR.

1. On conflicts over the effects of French education for women, see Offen, *European Feminisms*, 176–81; and Karen Offen, "The Second Sex and the Baccalaureat in Republican France, 1880–1924," *French Historical Studies* 13 (Autumn 1983): 252–86.

242 ☙ SBA TO ELIZABETH BOYNTON HARBERT

Madison Wis— Dec 1/86[1]

Dear Mrs Harbert

Mrs Roby[2] writes me you are working up a meeting for Dec. 9th— Now I hope—if you are—that you will invite our dear Rev. Olympia Brown to speak at it— She is going to give her time to our good cause for a time—& I want all of us to help her to feel that she can do more good to the world by working for W.S. than by church preaching—[3] Mrs Colby can be with you—too— I am glad of that for <u>she</u> <u>grows</u> on me every day— Now I am going to take the 8. A.M. train Northwestern—for Chicago—on <u>Friday</u> <u>morning</u>—and shall get to the <u>Baltimore</u> & <u>Ohio</u> Depot—to take the very earliest train possible that P.M. or evening— So if I see you it must be by your catching me on my flight across the city <u>Friday</u> P.M.—[4] Write me to the Riggs House— I hope to land there Saturday night and see lots of Senators during Sunday the 5th— Lovingly yours

☞ S. B. A

Oh—yes—I wrote you & Mrs Roby—that the only night I could possibly give to you at Chicago this winter—was Jan. 13th and that can only be done by my making my last speech at the Topeka Con. on the night of the 11th and then taking the A.M. train of the 14th for Lansing, Mich— where I am engaged for that night—Jan. 14th—[5]

But I should vastly prefer <u>not</u> to stop off at Chicago it will so crowd me—& more I have no <u>new</u> <u>speech</u> & all my old words have been spoken over & over in Chicago— Still—if you so command—I will stop—& do my very best to be decent—but I enjoy a great deal better— <u>speaking</u> in <u>new</u> <u>places</u>—where I can feel <u>all</u> have not already heard all I know!! Sincerely—S. B. A

P.S. I want to know <u>positively</u>—whether you command me to stop—so I can get my R.R. tickets accordingly—

☞ ALS, Box 2, Elizabeth Harbert Collection, CSmH.

1. At Madison on December 1 and 2, SBA concluded her circuit of congressional district conventions in Wisconsin.

2. Ida Hall Roby (1857–?) managed the women's lecture bureau in Chicago, established pursuant to a resolution of the National association's executive committee (above at 17 February 1886). She moved to Chicago about 1881 and supported herself (and possibly a son) as a bookkeeper, living apart from her husband, Alfred H. Roby, a salesman. By 1887, she had opened a pharmacy on Thirty-first Street, two years before her graduation from the Illinois College of Pharmacy in 1889. While continuing her business, Roby presided over the Woman's Pharmaceutical Association of Illinois, founded in anticipation of professional visitors from across the country during the World's Columbian Exposition in 1893. She also oversaw the woman's pharmacy that was both exhibit and dispensary for visitors. In 1895, she employed George H. Roby, of the same home address, as a clerk in her store, and in 1899, when Ida Roby's name disappeared from the city directory, George was listed as the druggist at the same address. (*American Women*; Metta Lou Henderson, *American Women Pharmacists: Contributions to the Profession* [New York, 2002], 18–19; Federal Census, Cook County, 1880; city directories, 1880 to 1900; School of Pharmacy Student Records, Northwestern University Archives, with the assistance of Patrick M. Quinn; "The Woman's Pharmacy," *Pharmaceutical Era* 10 [1893]: 427–29; "Women in Pharmacy," *Druggists Circular* 51 [1907]: 151–53; Chicago *Inter-Ocean*, 11 December 1886.)

3. Brown's letter of resignation from her pastorate in Racine, Wisconsin, was dated 27 December 1886. (Coté, *Olympia Brown*, 125–26.)

4. The passenger station of the Chicago & Northwestern Railway lay north of the Chicago River, at the corner of Wells and Kinzie streets; that of the Baltimore & Ohio Railroad was on Monroe Street east of Michigan Avenue, in what was then known as Lake Park. (Assistance from the Chicago Historical Society's research center staff.)

5. SBA's schedule in early January included a two-day meeting of the Nebraska Woman Suffrage Association in Lincoln on the sixth and seventh, an appearance at the Cook County association on the thirteenth, and attendance at the Michigan Equal Suffrage Association in Lansing on the fourteenth. She was scheduled to attend the annual meeting of the Kansas Equal Suffrage Association in Topeka on January 11, but she telegraphed from Leavenworth to say she was ill. (*Film*, 25:146, 152–55; *Woman's Tribune*, February 1887.)

243 ≫ SPEECH BY SBA TO CONGRESSIONAL
DISTRICT MEETING, MADISON, WISCONSIN

EDITORIAL NOTE: On this, the second day of the congressional district meeting in the senate chamber of the state capitol, SBA spoke after Olympia Brown and Clara Colby.

[2 December 1886]

Susan B. Anthony then delivered an address upon "Moral Influence vs. Political Power." She said that in the present stage of society young women were told not to have anything to do with the young man who drinks or chews. She asked what the young girl of our age would do if she followed out that theory. The fact is, the girls have to take the young men just as they are or else go without them. In this respect the young men are masters of the situation. She thought the present marital relation was based upon the theory that the young man can manage the girl. However, soon after the marriage a divorce results, and the cause is that the young man can't manage the wife and the young woman can't endure the husband. All this, she declared, could be remedied by making the woman in every respect the equal of man. She desired a law that would make it impossible for a man in indorsing a note for a friend to jeopardize the home and comforts of his wife. She held that moral suasion, to be effective, should be backed up by the ballot. It was hard to overcome legal suasion by moral suasion in itself. A body of women with a petition for any purpose in a legislative body will be listened to, if they have the power of the ballot back of them, but without it moral suasion makes but little progress.

≈ *Milwaukee Sentinel*, 3 December 1886.

244 ⤳ SBA TO JANE SNOW SPOFFORD

[*Madison, Wis.? 3? December 1886*]

I intend now to make straight for Washington without a stop. I shall come both ragged and dirty. Think of two solid months of conventions, speaking every night! Don't worry about me. I was never better or more full of hope and good work. Though the apparel will be tattered and torn, the mind, the essence of me, is sound to the core. Please tell the little milliner to have a bonnet picked out for me, and get a dressmaker who will patch me together so I shall be presentable. Now for the Washington convention: Before settling upon the Universalist church, you would better pocket the insults and refusals of the Congregational church powers that be and send your most lovely and winning girls to ask for that.[1] If you can't get it or the Metropolitan or the Foundry or the New York Avenue or any large and popular church, why take the Universalist, and then tell the saints of the fashionable churches that we dwell there because they refused us admission to their holy sanctuaries. Don't let us go into the heterodox houses, much as I love them, except because we are driven away from the orthodox.

⪦ *Anthony*, 2:612.

1. The Universalist Church of our Father was located on Thirteenth Street at the corner of L Street, Northwest. Of Washington's two Congregational churches, SBA probably refers to the First Congregational Church at Tenth and G streets, Northwest. In her list of alternatives, by Metropolitan Church, SBA may refer to the Methodist Episcopal church of that name at the corner of 4½ and C streets, Northwest. The Methodist Episcopal Foundry Church was at G and Fourteenth streets, Northwest. The Presbyterian New York Avenue Church was between Thirteenth and Fourteenth streets, Northwest. (City directory, 1886.)

·⟨══════⟩⟨══════⟩·

245 ⇝ SBA TO ELIZABETH BOYNTON HARBERT

The Riggs House Washington D.C. Dec 10/86

My Very Dear Friend E. B. H.

Here is a minority report made in the Senate—last April—by Messrs Brown & Cockrell—to antidote the splendid one made on Feb 3ᵈ—1886—by Senator Blair—[1] I had never heard of it until Senator Blairs speech referred to it—[2] Can it be that a woman wrote those "Chimney Corner" letters—and if so—who can she be? Do find out if possible—Mr Blair serves it up splendidly—

We have purchased a lot of Senator Blairs speech of Dec. 8[3]—and I would like to send a package to some person who could & would see that they were wisely placed in the hands of Illinois Legislators!— How to get the most agitation out of these various reports is now <u>the question</u>!!

I have now been in Washington a week—<u>waiting</u> for Mrs Colby to send me a package of the Call for our Wash. Con.[4] and for Mrs Sewall to send me the result of her efforts to learn who would be the speakers at our Wash. Con. and what the titles to their speeches—but a line from either woman has yet come!! Can you come—& if so what will be your topic or title?

I am convinced that <u>our</u> <u>National</u> help to the states should be like that given to Kansas & Wisconsin—that is that we join—cooperate—with the state societies in holding Cong. Dis't Conventions—nothing short of that number in a state <u>stirs</u> <u>up</u> <u>thought</u>—much less action in a state— The National ought to aid each state in organizing a state society & also a Cong. Dis't society in each of its district—and at our Executive sessions next January we must decide upon such aid to the states—& also which of the states we shall thus

⇝ AL incomplete, on NWSA letterhead, Box 2, Elizabeth Harbert Collection, CSmH.

1. Enclosure missing. It was: Senate, Committee on Woman Suffrage, *Views of the Minority*, 29 April 1886, 49th Cong., 1st sess., S. Rept. 70, Pt. 2, Serial 2355. In this report, rather than voicing their own views, Joseph Brown and Francis Cockrell submitted excerpts from the antisuffrage tract, *Letters from a*

Chimney Corner: A Plea for Pure Homes and Sincere Relations between Men and Women (1886), written by "a highly cultivated lady, Mrs. —— of Chicago." The author, the senators wrote, "discussed the question with so much clearness and force that we make no apology to the Senate for substituting quotations from her book in place of anything we might produce." That author was Caroline Elizabeth Fairfield Corbin (1835–1918), a writer and once a supporter of woman suffrage. Her book began as letters to the Chicago *Inter-Ocean*, where Elizabeth Harbert had worked. Corbin later founded the Illinois Association Opposed to the Extension of Suffrage to Women. (*BDAC*; *Women Building Chicago*; Jane Jerome Camhi, *Women Against Women: American Anti-Suffragism, 1888–1920* [Brooklyn, N.Y., 1994], 238–39.)

2. *Congressional Record*, 49th Cong., 2d sess., 34–38. On 8 December 1886, Henry Blair asked the Senate to take up for consideration Senate Resolution No. 5, the proposed sixteenth amendment. After some sparring with Senator Cockrell, he spoke at length in support of the measure, but he agreed with Cockrell that a vote should be postponed until Senator Brown could be present.

3. *Woman Suffrage. Speech of Hon. Henry W. Blair, of New Hampshire, in the Senate of the United States, December 8, 1886* (Washington, D.C., 1886). Neither a congressional document nor a pamphlet of the National association, this appears to be a publication that Blair arranged himself.

4. The Washington convention of the National Woman Suffrage Association was scheduled to begin on 25 January 1887.

246 ⟫ SBA TO CAROLINE HEALEY DALL

Rochester N.Y. Dec 30/86

My Dear Mrs Dall

Your note came to me duly the next day after I got a glimpse of you at the Church while you were shaking hands with Mr Savage[1] and I was waiting for a chance to do the same—and when my chance had come— & I, freed from its seeking,—it was ↑looked for you to↓ find you gone— and as I rushed into Sunday school room & rear hall—you to the pavement you were out of sight everywhere!! and I intended to call on you the very day I got your card & note—& then failing—I intended to go Friday evening—but alas days & evenings are too short for me— whether in or out of Washington—

No I had not heard of the death of your good husband—[2] Do you know that I never even saw him—hence it is difficult to associate you with a husband— But a man who has been the father of a woman's children must seem a part of herself—

Hoping that the clouds may be lifted and that much good work awaits your days & years yet to come—I am as ever very sincerely yours

⚞ *Susan B. Anthony*

⚞ ALS, on NWSA letterhead, C. H. Dall Collection, MHi.

1. Minot Judson Savage (1841–1918), a popular Unitarian minister, usually preached at Boston's Church of the Unity, but he came to Washington in December 1886 to preach and lecture. (*ANB*; *Washington Post*, 13, 19 December 1886.)

2. Charles Henry Appleton Dall (1816–1886), a Unitarian minister, sailed for India in 1855, leaving Caroline in Boston with their children, William Healey Dall (1845–1927) and Sarah Keene Healey Dall Munro (1849–1926). Charles Dall died in India on July 16. (*ANB*; with the assistance of Helen R. Deese.)

247 ⚞ ECS to SBA

[*Basingstoke, England, 8 January 1887*][1]

Dear Miss Anthony:

Your budget of Congressional Records, Minority Reports, and Senator Blair's able speech on Senate Resolution No. 5, found me in the South of England, trying to cultivate patience;—that "passion of great souls";[2]—with the tardy action of our oppressors, in doing justice to women. But I fear all my efforts to attain the passive virtues will prove futile, for my feelings and reason alike dictate aggressive measures towards all institutions that hold woman in subjection.

The fact is, that trick in the New York Legislature last winter, when two members changed their votes, after our bill passed, in order to defeat the measure they had pledged themselves to sustain,[3] destroyed the last particle of my faith in the sincerity of our representatives. A similar trick was played on the women of England, in the House of Commons, when 104 members pledged to vote for the woman's amendment to the reform bill, at one crack of Mr. Gladstone's party whip, turned against it.[4] Our legislators are simply playing with us, as a cat does with a mouse, to sacrifice us at their pleasure. They have their prototype in King Pharaoh of old in his treatment of the children of Israel.[5]

What we need is a Moses with his magic wand to punish, with the seven plagues of Egypt, these Saxon rulers for their tergiversations. No doubt locusts, frogs, flies, hail, thick darkness, the Potomac and Thames rivers turned to blood, would have more effect, in the halls of legislation, than the most logical arguments. Moses knew that tender appeals would have no effect on Pharaoh, and he told Jehovah that as he was slow of tongue, and had not the gift of eloquence, some more active measures must be devised, to bring the king to terms.[6]

For half a century we have tried appeals, petitions, arguments with thrilling quotations from our greatest jurists and statesmen, and lo! in the year of our Lord 1887, the best answer we can wring from Senators Brown and Cockrell, in the shape of a minority report, is a "chimney corner letter" written by a woman; ignorant of the first principles of republican government; which they say, gives a better statement of the whole question, than they are capable of producing. Verily this is a new feature in congressional proceedings! Though a woman has not sufficient capacity to vote, yet she has superior capacity to her representatives in drawing up a Minority Report. No wonder Senator Cockrell feeling his inability to grasp so grave a question, "is anxious to have the matter disposed of."[7]

I was rather surprised that Senator Blair also said, "I desire at the opening of the session if possible that there be a vote, so that we may be relieved of the question, at least for this session, and perhaps for some congresses to come."[8] In spite of the Senator's good speech, that sentiment rather grates on my heart strings. If he had said I desire a vote, that women may be relieved from their crushing disabilities, that would have had a touch of magnanimity. If that is the kind of relief our champion desires well and good, as there is only one way to be relieved of this question and that is by passing Senate Resolution No. 5.

But if Senators Cockrell and Brown hope "to dispose of the question" by remanding us to "the chimney corner" we trust their constituents will send them to keep us company, that they may enliven our retirement, make us satisfied in the "sphere where the Creator intended we should be,"[9] by daily intoning for us their inspired minority report.

The one pleasant feature in this original document is the harmony between the views of these gentlemen and their Creator. The only drawback to our faith in their knowledge of what exists in the Divine mind, is in the fact, that they cannot tell us when, where and how they interviewed Jehovah. I have always found that when men had exhausted their own resources, they generally fell back on "the intentions of the Creator." Their[10] platitudes have ceased to have any influence with women who believe they have the same facilities for communication with the Divine mind as men have.

Again the right and liability to be called on to fight, if we vote, is continually emphasized by our opponents, as one of the greatest barriers in our way. But with all the modern appliances for warlike achievements, this difficulty is rapidly diminishing. With torpedoes, bomb shells, and all manner of explosives, with balloons and carrier doves for messengers, women could now easily cope with their oppressors, on the low plain[11] of force and strategy. In the recent evictions of Irish tenants, on Lord Clanricarde's estate, the women rendered active service in holding the enemy at bay, by pouring scalding hot lime water on the heads of their assailants.[12] If all the heroic deeds of women recorded in history, and our daily journals and the active virtues so forcibly illustrated ever and anon in domestic life, have not yet convinced our opponents that women are possessed of superior fighting qualities, the sex may feel called upon in the near future to give some farther illustration of their prowess. Of one thing they may be assured, that the next generation will not argue the question of woman's rights with the infinite patience we have for half a century, and to so little purpose.

To emancipate women from the fourfold bondage she has so long suffered in the state, the church, the home and the world of work, harder battles than we have yet fought are still before us. Let no motives of policy or rose-colored views of man's chivalry blind us to the fact that no political party or religious sect have as yet demanded complete equality for women. With best wishes for the success of the convention and warm greetings to our coadjutors on the platform, cordially as ever yours,

⚯ *Elizabeth Cady Stanton.*

⚯ *Woman's Tribune,* March 1887.

1. The date of composition was reported by the Washington *Evening Star*, 25 January 1887, on the day the letter was read to the convention of the National Woman Suffrage Association. (*Film*, 25:207.)

2. Possibly an allusion to James Russell Lowell, "Columbus": "Endurance is the crowning quality, / And patience all the passion of great hearts".

3. On this vote on municipal suffrage in March 1886, see above at 16 March 1886.

4. Before members of Parliament voted in June 1884 on an amendment to the Third Reform Bill, Prime Minister William Gladstone argued that the amendment would be the extra weight that sank the bill for parliamentary reform. Liberal members followed his direction and defeated the amendment by a vote of 271 to 135. Supporters of woman suffrage estimated that 104 friends of the cause voted against the amendment. (Blackburn, *Women's Suffrage in the British Isles*, 161–65.)

5. ECS draws on stories of the clash between Moses and the Pharaoh in Exodus, chapters 1–10.

6. Exod. 4:10.

7. On 8 December, when Senator Blair asked for consideration of the amendment, Cockrell assured his colleagues, "I am anxious to get the matter disposed of." (*Congressional Record*, 49th Cong., 2d sess., 34.)

8. Blair's unfortunate phrase came at the end of a plea for Senate action in which he also said: "The matter has been before the Senate during several Congresses, and there never has been any actual vote whatever upon the resolution, although it has been reported favorably from committees at least twice." (*Congressional Record*, 49th Cong., 2d sess., 34.)

9. The phrase appears in the opening sentence of the minority report that Brown and Cockrell wrote in 1884 and attached to their report in 1886. Throughout their report, they relied on "an abundance of evidence both in the works of nature and in the Divine revelation" that "in the Divine economy," man was the head of the family. (Senate, Committee on Woman Suffrage, *Views of the Minority*, 29 April 1886, 49th Cong., 1st sess., S. Rept. 70, Pt. 2, Serial 2355.)

10. The *Evening Star* read this word as "These".

11. In the *Evening Star*, the metaphor appeared as "in the low plane".

12. Late in August 1886 in Woodford, Ireland, tenants resisted eviction from the estate of Lord Clanricarde in a battle that lasted several days. The tenants used such weapons as boat hooks, stones, and swarms of bees against bailiffs and five hundred policemen. The London *Times* noted that women provided an abundant supply of "scalding meal, lime and tar" to shower on the heads of their besiegers. Hubert George De Burgh Canning, earl of Clanricarde (1832–1916), inherited his lands and title in 1874 and achieved infamy for the levels of violence seen on his estate. (*DNB*; *Times* [London], 30 August 1886; Laurence M. Geary, *The Plan of Campaign, 1886–1891* [Cork, Ireland, 1986], 18.)

248 ❧ ECS to Theodore W. Stanton

[Basingtoke, England, after 14 January 1887][1]

Your father was an eloquent speaker, a forcible writer, and an admirable conversationalist. Those who possess oratorical gifts are seldom able with their pen, and it is rare that a good writer is also a good speaker. Phillips was fine on the platform, so was Gerrit Smith, but neither could put his thoughts on paper without discovering a certain lameness. Garrison, on the other hand, could write better than he could speak. None of them were equal to your father in conversation. I never knew any one who could on the spur of the moment rise and express himself more appropriately on all subjects and on all occasions, whether he was called upon to deal with temperance, anti-slavery, education, agriculture, religion, politics, science, art, or music. Some times when I have been serenaded or expected to say a few words I have pushed him forward to express what I could not without preparation, and, at such moments, he was always happy in speaking from my standpoint as well as from his own. He was asked one evening to respond to a toast on music. Now, said I to myself, for once he will be at a loss for something to say. But after a few general remarks on national aptitudes for music, especially among southern nations, he went on and spoke charmingly of the beauty of the negro melodies and the solace music had been to our slaves in their weary bondage. It being in the days of our anti-slavery excitement, he always seized every opportunity that offered to call public attention to the "irrepressible conflict."

No man was better acquainted with the politics and politicians of the last century both in England and America than he was. Very conversant with history and literature, he had an inexhaustible[2] fund of anecdotes of the living and the dead, authors, statesmen, and artists. His memory was really wonderful, and he never forgot what he saw, read, or heard. In another respect he was also very remarkable: he was uniformly in good spirits. Although of a nervous temperament and capable of the highest enthusiasm, he never suffered corresponding depression, but was always ready for cheerful conversation. His industry was truly praiseworthy. He was continually busy reading, writing, or working outdoors.

When speaking before an audience, he was very quick to turn to account any unexpected occurrence. On one occasion he was delivering a temperance lecture on a platform covered by a thick oil-cloth that protruded two or three inches over the edge of the boards in front. In the midst of one of his most eloquent passages, he was comparing the inebriates' downward course to the falls of Niagara, and the struggle with drink to the hopeless efforts of a man in the Rapids. Just as he reached, in his description, the fatal plunge over the precipice, he advanced to the edge of the platform, the oil-cloth gave way under his feet and in an instant he went down headlong into the audience, carrying with him desk, glass, pitcher and water. Being light and agile, he was quickly on the platform again, and immediately remarked with great coolness: "I carried my illustration further than I had intended to. Yet even so it is that the drunkard falls, glass in hand, carrying destruction with him. But not so readily does he rise again from the terrible depths into which he has precipitated himself." The whole house cheered again and again, and even Gough[3] never struck a more powerful blow for temperance.

Your great delight, when a little fellow 4 or 5 years old, was to have him make speeches to you, he pretending that you were a judge and himself an advocate. He used to seat you on the piano and then, with vehement gestures and pirouettings, would argue the case. Not one word of the speech did you understand. But you remained spell-bound by the passion that was displayed, by the denouncing of witnesses and opposing counsel, by the laying down of the law to the judge—yourself—and by appeals to the jury—your older brothers, who were not less amused than you were by the whole performance. You never smiled nor took your eyes off of him for ten minutes on the stretch, when the court adjourned. One day in your father's absence I tried to amuse you in the same way, but I had scarcely uttered two sentences when the judge coolly clambered down from the bench and walked off, whether because moved by a masculine dislike of a feminine advocate, or the comparatively lifeless presentation of the case, I have never learned to this day. I never repeated the humiliating experiment.

Your father had a strong taste for agricultural pursuits. He enjoyed planting trees, grafting, raising fruit and vegetables, and never a day passed in summer that he did not go the round of the garden. He once made a wager with a friend that he could raise the largest melon, and won. He watched the growing fruit day after day, and when the big fellow was ready for the table invited his friend to dinner. At dessert the much-praised and long-cared-for melon was brought in, and the host, knife in hand, was about to cut it open when it fell apart of itself. One of Erin's daughters, who had been serving us for several days with muskmelons, and had never seen a watermelon, had kept the edible portion in the kitchen and had sent in to us the rind! General surprise was followed by as general a laugh, and your father, turning to his guest, asked: "Bascom,[4] why am I at this moment like that melon? We are equally crusty."

⫸ Chicago *Inter-Ocean*, 6 February 1887. Not in *Film* from this source.

1. This letter was written after Henry Stanton died on 14 January 1887 in New York City. Theodore Stanton included it in his dispatch to the Chicago *Inter-Ocean*, dateline "Paris, Jan. 21," along with tributes to his father by Theodore Tilton and Frederick Douglass. Stanton died with his sons Henry and Robert at his side, while ECS was in England. His illness was not considered serious until shortly before his death, when a cold developed into pneumonia. Obituaries praised Stanton for his journalistic work, oratorical skills, and physical and intellectual vigor. Reports disagreed whether Stanton's body was to be cremated or held until ECS's return to the United States. (New York *Sun*, 15 January 1887; *New York Times*, 15 January 1887; *New York Tribune*, 15 January 1887.)

2. The text reads inexcustable; inexhaustible was substituted when the letter was reprinted in William A. Stanton, *A Record, Genealogical, Biographical, Statistical, of Thomas Stanton* (Albany, N.Y., 1891), 459–61.

3. John Gough (1817–1886) was a reformed drunkard whose temperance lectures moved countless people to sign a pledge of abstinence.

4. Probably a reference to Ansel Bascom (1802–1862), a lawyer, reformer, and local political leader in Seneca Falls, who was a close friend of the Stantons. In 1848, he was, as the Free Soil party candidate for Congress, a political ally of Henry Stanton, and as a member of the legislature that passed New York's Married Women's Property Act of 1848, he shared some of ECS's goals. He attended the woman's rights convention of 1848 but did not sign the Declaration of Sentiments. (Harris, *Genealogical Record of Thomas Bascom*, 61–62; Judith Wellman, "The Seneca Falls Women's Rights Convention: A Study of Social Networks," *Journal of Women's History* 3 [Spring 1991]: 9–37. See also *Papers* 1.)

249 ~ SBA TO RACHEL G. FOSTER

On Cars—Jan. 15—1887—[1]

My Darling Rachael

Among the letters my dear sister Mary forwarded to Lincoln I find the enclosed from E. M. Davis—[2] I am sorry you didn't at once go to him & consult about the Phila meetings—[3] But I have written him on this giggling car—that he & I could safely trust Rachel not be sold, or to sell out us of the National—to the Mary Grew Party— He evidently forgets—for my sister wrote him a long time ago [a]bout <u>Mary & Henry Jones</u>—& he returned her card—↑his clerk,↓ saying on it—Mr Davis knows nothing of them—while now you see he writes as if it was <u>my failure</u>—<u>he sold</u> the first Vols. I & II to them— I remember it perfectly well—

I have written him too—that after the Jubilee of 1888—<u>I</u> shall leave the helm of the good National ship to Rachel—Mrs Sewall—Shattuck Colby & others—and that we older one's must learn to surrender our wills to those who <u>do</u> <u>the</u> <u>work</u>— He evidently feels sore—about something—so coax him & all of us <u>old</u> <u>fellows</u> up—& keep us good-natured as possible—& get out of us all the help & cash you possibly can— Lovingly yours

~ *Susan B. Anthony*

I can't bear to think that you wont be at the Wash. Con. Ex. meetings—

~ ALS, on NWSA letterhead, Anthony-Avery Papers, NRU. Letter in square brackets torn at margin.

1. On 14 January 1887, SBA attended a meeting of the Michigan Equal Suffrage Association in Lansing. She then headed east, arriving in Washington on January 20.

2. Enclosure missing.

3. Rachel Foster organized a meeting in Philadelphia to be held on January 31 and February 1. The press referred to it as a meeting of the National Woman Suffrage Association, and SBA and others traveled from the Washington convention to speak. But the presence of several Philadelphians with a history of opposition to the National association and ties to the American association,

most notably Charles G. Ames, suggests that Foster sought to build new collaboration in Pennsylvania between the two suffrage camps. SBA's comments in this letter indicate that Edward Davis, as leader of the Citizens' Suffrage Association and opponent of Mary Grew's state association, objected to Rachel Foster's plan. (*Film*, 25:219–20.)

250 ⇒ HENRY W. BLAIR TO SBA

Washington, D.C., Jany 25, 1887.

My Dear Miss Anthony,

The vote stood 16 yeas—34 nays—7 pairs which would have made the suffrage vote 23.—[1] Mr Plumb lost his vote by accident[2] & there are several names not voting which I think would have voted yea if at they had voted at all—

You will see the list tomorrow in the Record.

I think we have at least one third of the Senate—all Republicans. I do not know of a Democratic vote. Resply Yours

⇒ *H. W. Blair.*

⇒ ALS, on letterhead of U.S. Senate, Clara B. Colby Papers, WHi.

1. Henry Blair moved again to take up Senate Resolution No. 5 on January 25, and a majority of senators, including Joseph Brown, voted to do so. The press estimated that one hundred women sat in the Senate gallery to hear the debate. As Blair reports to SBA, the vote on the resolution was sixteen yeas and thirty-four nays, with twenty-six senators counted as absent. As he goes on to say, many of the "absences" were accounted for by the seven pairs of senators who did not vote. Pairing allows a senator to be absent during a vote without tipping the political balance: in the pair a colleague of the opposing view promises not to vote during the absence of the other. Blair assumes that one out of every pair would have voted yes. Senator John Ingalls, who voted nay, thought Blair was shocked by the results. He wrote to his wife the next morning, "Blair looked at the result, like one who had been struck over the head with the tailboard of a wagon. It was some time before he recovered his breath. The galleries soon cleared silently, and the delegates from the Suffrage Convention departed, to denounce the Senate, and especially me." (*Congressional Record*, 49th Cong., 2d sess., 978–1003; J. J. Ingalls to A. L. C. Ingalls, 26 January 1887, John James Ingalls Papers, KHi.)

2. Preston Bierce Plumb (1837–1891) of Kansas had a long history of opposition to woman suffrage, dating back to the Kansas constitutional amendment

campaign of 1867, when he stumped the state on behalf of the anti-female suffrage movement. He brought this opposition to the Senate when he arrived in 1877. Immediately after the vote on Senate Resolution No. 5, however, he stated for the record that he "was unexpectedly called out of the Senate just before the vote was taken on the constitutional amendment," and that had he been there he would have voted in its favor. (*BDAC*; *Leavenworth Daily Conservative*, 7 September 1867; *Western Home Journal*, 26 September 1867; *Congressional Record*, 49th Cong., 2d sess., 1003.)

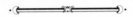

251 ⮞ INTERVIEW WITH SBA IN WASHINGTON, DISTRICT OF COLUMBIA

[*26 January 1887*]

The ladies of the suffrage convention were in high spirits to-day over the vote in the Senate yesterday on the suffrage amendment. Miss Anthony was radiant. "A defeat!" she exclaimed, in reply to a *Star* reporter's inquiry. "Why no. It was a triumph for us. You see we have on our side one-third of the United States Senate. At the first time such an important question as this—a question involving an entire revolution, one that proposes to change the very base of our government—comes before the Senate, to have one-third of the Senators with us is most encouraging. How do I figure out that we have one-third!" said Miss Anthony, taking up the printed record of the vote in the Senate. "Well, there were sixteen Senators who voted for the bill. Of the absentees or Senators paired we count on Allison, Aldrich, Cameron, Chace, Dawes, Frye, Harrison (I have some doubts about Harrison), Miller, Plumb, Sabin and Stanford as our friends.[1] There are eleven of them, who, with the sixteen that voted, make in all twenty-seven Senators on our side. It is my intention to interview every Senator who did not vote and find out just how he would have voted. Our plan of action will be in the case of Senators such as Ingalls and Hawley,[2] who are known as our opponents, when they come up again for election to prevent their return to the Senate if possible. Now, in Kansas the women there will work for the election of members of the legislature who will promise to support for the United States Senate only some man pledged to vote for our amendment. We can accomplish this. We have women enough at our back, and these women are an immense power. Why, we have five hundred women making speeches through-out the country. Miss Frances Willard, who will have a reception here Friday, is at the head of half a million women, all of them pledged to suffrage.[3] These women have discovered that their tears and prayers were ineffectual to get rid of saloons when the man's vote brought the saloon into existence. So they are with us because they want to vote on this one question. In other movements for good, earnest women, who are striving for better conditions of living, have learned that they are powerless against the voting of men, and they are with us."

"This is the first time," continued Miss Anthony, "that we ever got a vote on our amendment. We have accomplished a great deal in securing recognition. Our bill is now on the calendar of the House,[4] and my first work now will be to have it brought before the House so we can get an expression there. We will ask our leader there, Hon. Ezra B. Taylor, of Ohio, to make a motion to lift the bill out of the calendar. In the Senate, you see, new men are for us. The new Senator in the place of Mr. Fair is on our side,[5] and you see Mr. Farwell[6] is for us. He cast his first vote for us."

"Any one who knows Mrs. Stanton's jolly nature," said Miss Anthony, speaking of the letter from Mrs. Stanton published in yesterday's *Star*, "would of course read her letter and see her laughter under it. She seemed to be scolding about matters, but I have no doubt when she had written that letter and read it over, she lay back and laughed heartily over it for half an hour. Fighting!" continued Miss Anthony, referring to one of Mrs. Stanton's suggestions. "Why, of course, in days when success in warfare depends more upon military sagacity and discipline than upon physical strength, women might go to war, but that is not what we look to. The time is coming when there will be no fighting."

⤳ Washington *Evening Star*, 26 January 1887.

1. In SBA's list of Republican senators, one group was recorded as absent during the vote but not paired. These were William Boyd Allison (1829–1908) of Iowa; Nelson Aldrich; Preston Plumb; and Dwight May Sabin (1843–1902) of Minnesota. The paired senators not voting were James Donald Cameron (1833–1918) of Pennsylvania; Jonathan Chace; Henry Laurens Dawes (1816–1903) of Massachusetts; William Pierce Frye (1830–1911) of Maine; Benjamin Harrison (1833–1901) of Indiana; Warner Miller; and Leland Stanford (1824–1893) of California. Chace, Dawes, and Stanford announced that theirs would have been yea votes. (*BDAC*.)

2. Republicans John James Ingalls (1833–1900) of Kansas and Joseph Roswell Hawley (1826–1905) of Connecticut voted nay, to no one's surprise. Both men had stood in the way of woman suffragists for more than a decade. Ingalls served in the Senate from 1873 to 1891. Hawley, who represented Connecticut in the House from 1872 to 1875 and 1879 to 1881, won election to the Senate in 1881 and served until 1905. (*BDAC*; *Papers*, 3:36, 230n, 241–42, 243n.)

3. This reception for Frances Willard on January 28 followed the first in a series of meetings in local churches planned by the Woman's Christian Temperance Union. During the Senate debate, Henry Blair presented a petition from the officers of the temperance union, "on behalf of the hundreds of thousands of Christian women engaged in philanthropic effort," seeking passage of the amendment for woman suffrage. (*Washington Post*, 29 January 1887; *Congressional Record*, 49th Cong., 2d sess., 25 January 1887, p. 991.)

4. See above at 23 May 1886.

5. James Fair of Nevada, a consistent opponent of woman suffrage, lost his bid for reelection in 1886 and was about to be replaced by William Morris Stewart (1827–1909). Stewart had served in the Senate from 1864 to 1875 and then retired. Upon reelection he served from 1887 to 1905. (*BDAC*.)

6. Charles Benjamin Farwell (1823–1903), a former member of the House of Representatives from Illinois, entered the Senate on 19 January 1887 to replace John A. Logan, who died in office. He voted for the amendment. (*BDAC*.)

·❮————❯·

252 ⮜ RESOLUTIONS OF THE NATIONAL WOMAN
SUFFRAGE ASSOCIATION

[27 January 1887]

Whereas, The disfranchisement of women citizens of this country is a denial of its claim as a republic and of its fundamental principles of citizenship, as set forth in the original constitution and reiterated in the fourteenth amendment; and,

Whereas, The supreme court has nevertheless decided that the federal constitution does not confer upon women the right to the ballot; therefore,

Resolved, That the National Woman Suffrage Association demand the passage of a sixteenth amendment, which shall secure the lawful and constitutional right of suffrage to the women citizens of the United States.

Whereas, For the first time a vote has been taken in the senate of the

United States on an amendment to the national constitution enfranchising women; and,

Whereas, One-third of the senators voted for the amendment; therefore,

Resolved, That we rejoice in this evidence that our demand is forcing itself upon the attention and action of congress, and that when a new congress shall have assembled, with new men and new ideas, we may hope to change this minority into a majority.

Whereas, On the vote in the United States senate to admit Washington territory as a state, thirteen senators voted to deprive the women of the proposed state of elective franchise;[1] and,

Whereas, The anti-polygamy bill passed by both houses of congress provides for the disfranchisement of the non-polygamous women of Utah;[2] and,

Whereas, The women thus sought to be disfranchised have been for years in the peaceable exercise of the ballot, and no charge is made against them of any crime by reason of which they should lose their vested rights; therefore,

Resolved, That this association recognizes in these measures a disregard of individual rights which is dangerous to the liberties of all; and, while we rejoice in the majority vote by which the women of Washington territory were protected, we would urge upon congress that the rights of women of Utah should be equally sacred; since to establish the precedent that the ballot may be taken away is to threaten the permanency of our republican form of government;

Resolved, That we call the attention of the working women of the country to the fact that a disfranchised class is always an oppressed class, and that only through the protection of the ballot can they secure equal pay for equal work;

Resolved, That the fact that in New York a woman is under arrest for casting a ballot—an act held to be commendable when performed by a man—is a proof of the inconsistency and injustice of the present position of women;[3]

Resolved, That the fact that there are now several women under sentence of death in this country is a proof of the monstrous injustice which ranks women with idiots and minors, as incapable of making the laws, and yet holds them amenable, without a trial by a jury of their peers, to penalties from which idiots and minors are always exempt;[4]

Resolved, That we recognize as hopeful signs of the times the endorsement of woman suffrage by the Knights of Labor in the national assembly,[5] and by the National Woman's Christian Temperance Union, and that we congratulate these organizations upon their recognition of the fact that the ballot in the hands of woman is necessary for their success;

Resolved, That in view of these wrongs perpetrated and the rights imperiled by the disfranchisement of one-half of the citizens of these United States, it becomes our sacred duty to work for the defeat of the legislators who, by their votes, continue to obstruct the progress of liberty;

Resolved, That the alarming frequency of criminal assaults upon women and children reveal the vital need of the enfranchisement of woman, in order that she may protect herself and her children.

Resolved, That we thank Senators Blair, of New Hampshire; Dolph, of Oregon;[6] and Hoar, of Massachusetts, for their support of the resolution providing for a 16th amendment, and Senators Blair, of New Hampshire; Bowen, of Colorado; Cheney, of Illinois; Dolph, of Oregon; Farwell, of Illinois; Hoar, of Massachusetts; Manderson, of Nebraska; Mitchell, of Oregon; Mitchell, of Pennsylvania; Palmer, of Michigan; Platt, of Connecticut; Sherman, of Ohio; Teller, of Colorado; Wilson, of Iowa, for voting in its favor,[7] and also Senators Dawes, of Massachusetts; Stanford, of California; and Chace, of Rhode Island, who openly announced in the Senate their allegiance to the amendment.

Resolved, That we have reason to rejoice in the prospect of the speedy success of municipal suffrage in several of the western states,[8] in the remarkable vote in the New York assembly by which, if three assemblymen had not, at a most critical moment changed their minds, the women of New York would have municipal suffrage today; and in the action of the Rhode Island Legislature, in taking the first step towards submitting to the voters an amendment to the state constitution conferring full suffrage on the women of Rhode Island.[9]

Resolved, That in the death of Abby Kelley Foster, of Massachusetts, we recognize the loss to our cause of one of its earliest and most fearless pioneers.[10]

Resolved, That we extend our sympathy to our beloved president, Elizabeth Cady Stanton, in the recent death of her husband; and we recall with gratitude the fact that he was one of the earliest and most consistent advocates of human liberty.

Resolved, That we hereby express the loss to our association in the death of its earnest co-workers, Mary Bayard Clarke of North Carolina,[11] Sarah H. Hallock of New York[12] and Mary Olney Brown[13] of Washington Territory, and that we express to their families and friends our sympathy in their bereavement.

Resolved, That the *Woman's Tribune*, edited by Clara B. Colby of Beatrice, Nebraska, while not in a formal sense the organ of the National Woman Suffrage Association, is yet the present medium of communication between the association, its members and the community; and that we desire thus publicly to recognize its value as the only newspaper in the country which gives full or adequate reports of national work and methods.

᪥ *Woman's Tribune*, March 1887.

1. On this vote, see note at 3 June 1886.

2. Clara Colby edited this resolution for publication to reflect the passage of a single bill by Congress. The original text, published on January 28, referred to bills. A congressional conference committee was then at work reconciling the Senate's antipolygamy bill, Senate 10 or Edmunds bill, passed in 1886, with an amended bill, authored by John Randolph Tucker and passed by the House of Representatives on 12 January 1887. The Edmunds-Tucker Act, enacted on 3 March 1887, retained the language on the disfranchisement of women offered by Edmunds in 1886, with only minor revision. (*Film*, 25:213; Edward Leo Lyman, *Political Deliverance: The Mormon Quest for Utah Statehood* [Urbana, Ill., 1986], 34–35, 42–44; chap. 397, sec. 20, *U.S. Statutes at Large* 24 [1887]: 639.)

3. Lucy Sweet Barber (1833–1901), of Alfred, New York, voted for a congressman in the elections of November 1886, and for that she was arrested by a federal marshal on 3 January 1887, while attending a meeting of the local Woman's Christian Temperance Union. Responding to Lillie Blake's pleas in 1885 for women to vote, Barber was turned away from the polls by the inspectors of election, but a year later, she prevailed. Although originally charged with a federal crime, she was ultimately tried in state court and sentenced to spend twenty-four hours in jail. (Ilou M. Sanford, *First Alfred Seventh Day Baptist Church Membership Records: Alfred, N.Y.* [Bowie, Md., 1995], 6; *Woman's Journal*, 11 December 1886, 1, 15, 22 January, 31 December 1887; *New York Times*, 16 December 1887.)

4. This resolution was likely inspired by the New York State and New York City suffrage societies. At its convention in March 1886, the state association protested the sentencing of two women to the death penalty in New York,

calling their sentences "evidence of the cruel absurdity of the position of women." In December 1886, members of the city suffrage league signed a petition to the governor asking him to commute the sentence of Roxalana Druse, an allegedly abused wife who murdered her husband. The governor replied that those who urged women's exemption from laws they had no voice in making should address their complaint to the legislature. Druse was hanged on 28 February 1887, the fifth woman in the state's history and the first one in thirty-nine years to be hung. (New York *Evening Telegram*, 24 March 1886; *Woman's Journal*, 11 December 1886; *New York Times*, 23 December 1886, 1 March 1887.)

5. This resolution credits the Knights of Labor with deeds not done. The order's tenth General Assembly in October 1886 received a resolution from District Assembly 30 in Massachusetts about recognizing "the right of the female portion of our membership to exercise the franchise and better their social condition by use of the ballot." The newly formed Committee on Woman's Work, to which it was referred, reported back to the General Assembly "that there is more important work for women to do before they are prepared to vote in the affairs of the Nation." (Knights of Labor, *Record of the Proceedings of the Tenth Regular Session of the General Assembly, Held at Richmond, Va., Oct. 4–20, 1886* [Reading, Pa., n.d.], 211, 288.)

6. Joseph Norton Dolph (1835–1897), Republican of Oregon, served in the Senate from 1883 to 1895. (*BDAC*.)

7. Those not previously identified, all Republicans, are: Person Colby Cheney (1828–1901) of New Hampshire, not Illinois, who served only from November 1886 to June 1887; Charles Frederick Manderson (1837–1911), senator from 1883 to 1895; John Hipple Mitchell (1835–1905), senator from 1873 to 1879, 1885 to 1897, and 1901 until his death; John Inscho Mitchell (1838–1907), senator from 1881 to 1887; John Sherman (1823–1900), senator from 1861 to 1877 and 1881 to 1897; Henry Moore Teller (1830–1914), senator from 1876 to 1882 and 1885 to 1909; and James Falconer Wilson (1828–1895), senator from 1883 to 1895. (*BDAC*.)

8. The chief example was the bill pending in Kansas, but legislatures in Nebraska, California, and Michigan were presented with bills for municipal suffrage in 1887. None of those passed. (*Woman's Tribune*, January, May, June 1887; *History*, 4:494, 633, 760–61, 805.)

9. In 1886, the Rhode Island legislature passed a constitutional amendment to allow women to vote for all civil officers and in all meetings of local government. By constitutional requirement, the measure needed another favorable vote in the legislative session of 1887. In the months ahead, the legislature again passed the amendment by substantial majorities and sent it to the voters in April. The amendment suffered a major defeat, described as "the largest defeat woman suffrage ever received." (*History*, 4:909–11; *Woman's Journal*, 27 March 1886, 29 January 1887.)

10. Abby Kelly Foster died on 14 January 1887.

11. Mary Bayard Devereux Clarke (1827–1886), a poet and editor, died on March 30. A first cousin of Lillie Devereux Blake, Clarke represented North Carolina as a vice president of the National Woman Suffrage Association. (*NAW*; *ANB*.)

12. Sarah Hull Hallock (1813–1886) died on June 11. A Quaker who joined the Friends of Human Progress in the late 1840s, she was an abolitionist and an ally of ECS and SBA through the Women's Loyal National League, the American Equal Rights Association, and the National Woman Suffrage Association. She farmed and ran a summer boarding house in Milton, New York, along the Hudson River. (Shirley V. Anson and Laura M. Jenkins, comp., *Quaker History and Genealogy of the Marlborough Monthly Meeting, Ulster County, N.Y., 1804–1900* [Baltimore, Md., 1980], 60, 128, 131; *Woman's Journal*, 19 June 1886; *Papers*, 1:340, 342n, 492.)

13. Mary Olney Brown (c. 1820–1886) died on November 17 in Olympia, Washington Territory. She went west with her husband, Benjamin F. Brown, in 1846, settling first in Portland, Oregon, and moving to Thurston County, Washington, early in the 1850s. With her sister, Martha Olney French, she agitated in 1869 and 1870 for women to claim their voting rights as citizens under territorial law that defined eligible voters as "white American citizens twenty-one years of age," but her own attempts to vote were rebuffed. She became the first president of the Washington Territorial Woman Suffrage Association in 1871 and later the National association's vice president for Washington. (Mrs. George E. Blankenship, ed., *Early History of Thurston County, Washington, Together with Biographies and Reminiscences of Those Identified with Pioneer Days* [Olympia, Wash., 1914], 116–21; *History*, 3:780–86; Pearce, "Suffrage in the Pacific Northwest"; Federal Census, 1880.)

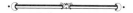

253　⤙　REMARKS BY SBA TO THE NATIONAL WOMAN SUFFRAGE ASSOCIATION

EDITORIAL NOTE: For the final, evening session of the Washington convention, the audience filled the Metropolitan Methodist Episcopal Church. After Hannah Smith offered prayers, Mary Eastman, Lillie Blake, and Wyoming's congressional representative, Joseph M. Carey, addressed the gathering. Then SBA offered these remarks to close the convention.

[27 January 1887]

After three days of such argument and such appeal from these young women, what can I say. I am proud as I listen to them. What they bring to you are the results of this agitation. They are graduates of colleges.

Forty years ago when we began there was but one college which admitted women. Today the young women who are flocking to the platform of all reforms, are the educated women, are the fruit of the demand that has been made for equality in all the departments of life. The vote in the senate is granting that it is a question before the people. It is the test question of this age. I wish I had ten thousand dollars to send copies of history to educate congressmen and our legislators. A man does not blush to say he has not thought about it. What business has he to be in congress if he has not thought about the foundation principles of government and their practical application to the people?

❧ *Woman's Tribune*, March 1887.

254 ❧ ELIZA ROXEY SNOW[1] ET AL. TO SBA

[*Salt Lake City, Utah Territory, after 28 January 1887*]

Miss Susan B. Anthony, Riggs House, Washington, D.C.:

In behalf of the women of Utah, we, the undersigned, respectfully tender our grateful acknowledgements to the officers and members of the National Woman's Suffrage Convention for the able and timely effort made in exercising their influence with the President and the people of the United States in opposing the disfranchisement of the legal woman voters of Utah and the obnoxious Edmunds-Tucker Bill.[2]

[Signed]

❧ *Eliza R. Snow Smith,*
❧ *Zina D. H. Young,*
❧ *M. Isabella Horne,*
❧ *Sarah M. Kimball,*
❧ *Jane S. Richards,*
❧ *Emily S. Richards,*
❧ *Josephine R. West,*
❧ *Ellen B. Ferguson, M.D.,*
❧ *Zina Y. Williams,*
❧ *Romania B. Pratt, M.D.,*
❧ *Emmeline B. Wells.*[3]

⨴ *Woman's Exponent*, 1 February 1887. Originally sent as telegram.

1. Eliza Roxcy (or Roxey) Snow (1804–1887), who here used the name of her first husband, Joseph Smith, and was also one of the wives of Brigham Young, was the leading woman among the Mormons, not only for her obvious connections to the church's leaders but also for her early convictions about women's equality and ideas about their organized contributions to public life. (*NAW*; *ANB*.)

2. At the National's executive session on January 26, Lillie Blake was appointed chairman of a committee to visit President Cleveland and urge him to veto whichever antipolygamy bill came out of the congressional conference committee. In a memorial presented to Cleveland on January 28, the committee argued that "disfranchisement is reserved by the United States government for arch traitors," and the precedent of disfranchising the women of Utah would be "subversive of the fundamental principles of our government, and threatening the security of all citizens." When news reached Salt Lake City, this telegram was sent to Washington. (*Washington Critic*, 26 January 1887, and Washington *Evening Star*, 26 January 1887, in *Film*, 25:208, 211–12; *Woman's Tribune*, March 1887.)

3. Joining Snow in signing the telegram were some of the most accomplished women in Utah, many of them familiar to members of the National Woman Suffrage Association. Zina Diantha Huntington Young (1821–1901), a wife of Brigham Young and earlier married to Henry Jacobs and Joseph Smith, Jr., worked closely with Eliza Snow and, after Snow's death in 1887, she became president of Snow's Women's Relief Society. In 1881, she was sent east to make connections with woman suffragists and defend the church. (Augusta Joyce Crocheron, *Representative Women of Deseret, A Book of Biographical Sketches* [Salt Lake City, Utah, 1884], 10–16, 69; Daniel H. Ludlow, ed., *Encyclopedia of Mormonism*, 5 vols. [New York, 1992], 4:1611–13.) Mary Isabella Hales Horne (1818–1905), who migrated to Salt Lake in 1847, was a prominent leader in numerous Mormon social service organizations and an advocate of woman suffrage. (Crocheron, *Representative Women of Deseret*, 17–23; *Encyclopedia of Mormonism*, 2:657–59.) Sarah Melissa Granger Kimball (1818–1898), well known in Utah for her advocacy of woman's rights, was president of the Fifteenth Ward Relief Society in Salt Lake City from 1857 until her death. She became president of the Utah Woman Suffrage Association in 1890. (Jill C. Mulway, "The Liberal Shall be Blessed: Sarah M. Kimball," *Utah Historical Quarterly* 44 [Summer 1976]: 205–21; *Encyclopedia of Mormonism*, 2:784–85.) Jane Snyder Richards (1823–1912), a leader in relief societies, met with members of the National association in 1884 in Washington, where she helped to lobby against the Edmunds bill. (Connie Duncan Cannon, "Jane S. Richards," in Vicky Burgess-Olson, *Sister Saints* [Provo, Utah, 1978], 175–98; research assistance from Leigh Hutchinson, Church History Library, Salt Lake City.) Emily Sophia Tanner Richards (1850–1929),

daughter-in-law of Jane Richards, was a leader in many women's organizations and became active in the National Woman Suffrage Association and the International Council of Women. (*Woman's Who's Who 1914*; *WWW1*.) Josephine Richards West (1853-1933), a daughter of Jane Richards, was a part of a Mormon mission sent to Washington in 1886 to lobby against the Edmunds bill. (Cannon, "Jane S. Richards," 184; Constance L. Lieber and John Sillito, eds., *Letters from Exile: The Correspondence of Martha Hughes Cannon and Angus M. Cannon, 1886-1888* [Salt Lake City, Utah, 1989], xl, xix, 8-9.) Ellen Brooke Ferguson (1844-1920), a physician born in England, became a suffragist before she became a Mormon, holding office in the Indiana and Northwestern suffrage associations in 1870. She moved to Salt Lake City in 1876 and was a loyal defender of polygamy and leader among physicians until her excommunication in 1896. (Ann Gardner Stone, "Ellen B. Ferguson," in Burgess-Olsen, *Sister Saints*, 327-39; *History*, 3:572n, 4:947. See also *Papers* 2.) Zina Priscenda Young Williams (1850-1931), the daughter of Brigham and Zina Young and a teacher at Brigham Young Academy, attended the National Woman Suffrage Association meeting in 1879 to counter the lobby against polygamy. Though she here identified herself with the surname of her deceased husband, she had in fact already entered into a polygamous marriage with Charles Ora Card. In the spring of 1887, she followed him to Canada and a new Mormon settlement to escape federal prosecution. (Crocheron, *Representative Women of Deseret*, 121-25; Martha Sonntag Bradley and Mary Brown Firmage Woodward, *4 Zinas: A Story of Mothers and Daughters on the Mormon Frontier* [Salt Lake City, Utah, 2000], passim.) Romania Bunnell Pratt (1839-1932) received her medical education at the Woman's Medical College of Philadelphia and returned to Utah to practice, teach midwifery, and serve the Deseret Hospital, opened in 1882. Though she used the surname of a husband she had divorced, Parley Pratt, she had recently become the third wife of the prominent Mormon leader and editor Charles W. Penrose. (Crocheron, *Representative Women of Deseret*, 72-75; Cristine Croft Waters, "Romania B. Penrose," in Burgess-Olsen, *Sister Saints*, 343-60.) Emmeline Blanche Woodward Wells (1828-1921), editor of the Salt Lake City *Woman's Exponent*, joined Zina Williams at the National Woman Suffrage Association meeting in 1879 and reported on Utah at the meeting in Omaha in 1882. (*NAW*; *ANB*; *Film*, 22:637-43; *History*, 4:939. See also *Papers* 3.)

255 ❧ SBA TO RICHARD W. BLUE[1]

Washington, D.C., January 29, 1887.

Senator Blue: The National Woman Suffrage Association, in executive session, rejoice in the passage of the municipal suffrage bill by the Kansas Senate.

❧ *Susan B. Anthony,*
Vice President.

❧ *Lincoln Beacon*, n.d., in SBA scrapbook 12, Rare Books, DLC. Originally sent as telegram.

1. Richard Whiting Blue (1841–1907) was the manager of the municipal suffrage bill and chair of the judiciary committee in the Kansas senate, where he served from 1880 to 1888. The senate passed the bill on January 28 by a vote of twenty-five to fifteen. By consent of the senate, this telegram was read on the senate floor. (*BDAC*; *History*, 3:422, 649–50.)

AS A MOTHER

Tenafly, New Jersey, Oct. 1st [*1885*].

Editor New Era:

Your letter was read aloud to us, in which you said that you intended to devote the November number of your *New Era* to my mother, in honor of her seventieth birthday; and that you desired to have a pen picture of our family life, and I, being the only child at home, was thereupon delegated to be the special artist for the work.

As my mother could not set forth in glowing colors her own domestic virtues, and as Miss Anthony, who is a part of our household, is now in the agonies of Vol. III. of *The History of Woman Suffrage*, buried under mountains of illegible manuscripts, I, with much hesitancy, undertake the task. To write of a mother loved, honored, worshiped, as mine is by me, is so like viewing one's self subjectively and unveiling to others what is most sacred in the solitude of individual life, that I will leave the recording angel to write down all that is best of her as he did for the good Abou Ben Adhem.

So many sketches have been given of mother in *Eminent Women, Famous Women,* and in the press of our nation, that there is nothing new, from an objective point of view, that can be told, except what the children think of her, and what she has been doing among the hills of Jersey the last six months.

We children, two girls and five boys (take notice I put the girls first, because we belong to the superior sex?) have only pleasant memories of a happy home, of a sunny, cheerful, indulgent mother, whose great effort was to save us from all the fears that shadow the lives of most children. God, was to us sunshine, flowers, affection, all that is grand and beautiful in nature. The devil had no place at our fireside, nor the Inferno in our dreams of the future.

Our father was never held up to us as Justice with a flaming sword, but as the man bountiful who brought us presents from the metropolis. Mother had too much self respect to recognize a superior court, so was never heard to say, "I'll tell your father when he comes home."

We heard nothing under our roof of "original sin," total depravity, but of the great possibilities bound up in us all to be grand men and women. The absurd dogmas we gathered from others in the outside world were promptly placed in such a ridiculous light, that we have all grown up comparatively free from the popular superstitions, and from the conceit that would attempt to explore the mysteries of the unknown world.

Your reporter is a bright, young woman, residing in Council Bluffs, Iowa, though much of the time on the wing between her husband and mother. I have no remarkable genius in any direction, but I have some practical talent in the ordinary affairs of life. My friends say I am grand in emergencies. I suppose I would shine in floods, fires, shipwrecks or earthquakes! I have sufficient aesthetic taste to dress well, decorate my house with fall leaves and golden rod, and supply my table with appetizing food. My sister, who married an Englishman and lives near London, may be said to have a good deal of genius; she is an eloquent speaker, a fine writer, talks well, and recites with great effect, and added to all this she has rare physical beauty. Our brothers are quite equal to the ordinary sons of Adam,—two are rising young lawyers in New York city, with more causes than effects; one is solving the problem of life in the rigid analysis of pig iron in Pittsburg; another is a gentleman of leisure; while the fifth is Theodore, who lives in France, and has strong sympathy with the movement for woman's enfranchisement, and has recently published a book, "The Woman Question in Europe," full of interesting facts.

But to return to my picture of mother and Susan. They are busy all day and far into the night on said Volume III. As our house faces the south the sunshine streams in all day. In the centre of a large room, 20 by 22, with an immense bay window, hard wood floor and open fire, beside a substantial office desk with innumerable drawers and doors, filled with documents,—there *vis-a-vis* sit our historians, surrounded with manuscripts and letters from Maine to Louisiana. In one drawer are engravings of some of the leading advocates, fifteen in number, all waiting to take their places in this last volume. *Entre nous*, I am

fearfully tired of this History. It has stood in the way of everything we
have wanted mother to do for the last seven years. We all feel towards
these volumes as a family of children would to some favorite adopted
child, that filled their places in a mother's heart. Well, if this volume is
to linger as long as the others did, I fear we shall not see the end of it
before the Fourth of July, the day when all questions of freedom seem
to culminate. But it is of little interest to you to know what I, a
lukewarm suffrage saint, may think.

To return again to our historians, in the centre of their desk are two
ink stands and two bottles of mucilage, to say nothing of divers pens,
pencils, scissors, knives, etc., etc. As these famous women grow intense in working up some glowing sentence, or pasting some thrilling
quotation from John Stuart Mill, Dumas or Secrétan, I have seen them
again and again dip their pens in the mucilage and their brushes in the
ink. Either of these blunders brings them back to the facts of history,
where they should be if that blessed word *finis* is ever to be written. *Sub
rosa*, it is as good as a comedy to watch these souls from day to day.
They start off pretty well in the morning, fresh and amiable. They write
page after page with alacrity, they laugh and talk, poke the fire by turn,
and admire the flowers I place on their desk each morning. Everything
is harmonious for a season, but after straining their eyes over the most
illegible, disorderly manuscripts I ever beheld, suddenly the whole sky
is overspread with dark and threatening clouds, and from the adjoining
room I hear a hot dispute about something. The dictionary, the encyclopedia, the *Woman's Journal, Our Herald, The National Citizen,
The Revolution, The Woman's Tribune, The New Northwest, The New
Era*—all piled on the floor in one corner—are overhauled, tossed about
in an emphatic manner for some date, fact, or some point of law or
constitution. Susan is punctilious on dates, mother on philosophy, but
each contends as stoutly in the other's domain as if equally strong at all
points. Sometimes these disputes run so high that down go the pens,
one sails out of one door and one out of the other, walking in opposite
directions around the estate, and just as I have made up my mind that
this beautiful friendship of forty years has at last terminated, I see them
walking down the hill, arm in arm, to a seat where we often go to see the
distant hills and lovely valleys, and to watch the sun go down in all his
glory. When they return they go straight to work where they left off, as
if nothing happened. I never hear another word on that point—the one

that was unquestionably right assumes it, and the other silently concedes the fact. They never explain, nor apologize, nor shed tears, nor make up, as other people do; but, figuratively speaking, jump over a stone wall at one bound and leave the past behind them, seemingly with no memory of the hour before. These ebullitions of weariness and impatience are really quite pardonable. In fact, I wonder with all they have encountered, that they have one ray of hope or tenderness left. These two women are worthy to be canonized as saints, not the weeping, fasting, passive kind, nor angels with folded wings, waiting at the doors of the temples. No! no, mother and Susan are what Luther called "fighting saints" and "angels with a will."

In the evenings, with a bright wood fire on the hearth, they plot and plan, in their easy chairs, work enough ahead to keep them busy, if they should live to be the age of Methuselah. I notice they never contend in the evenings. Sometimes we have an interesting novel on hand, which Susan reads aloud. We have just finished "Bart Sinister," and are wondering whether it was written by a man or a woman. Often we read aloud the scourgings and criticisms they get in letters and papers, at which they cooly laugh, no matter from what quarter they come. So long as they are at peace with each other, what others think or say seems to trouble them very little. And why should they care for the opinions of a heedless world in regard to the grand movement they have inaugurated for freedom to women, knowing that they are strongly intrenched on eternal principles, and that the position of their opponents is clearly untenable and to the last degree contemptible, their determined self assertion is as grand as it is remarkable.

They have fought a hard battle and opened to the young women of coming generations paths of usefulness and happiness, and secured for them positions of honor and emolument such as they will never attain for themselves. Let us then who enter into this glorious inheritance sing our divinest songs of praise to those who through much tribulation shall have won for us an equal place everywhere on this green earth.

⇝ *Margaret Stanton Lawrence.*

⇝ *New Era*, November 1885.

INDEX

Abbett, Leon, 517, *518n*
Adams, Abigail Smith, 250, *263n*
Adams, Franklin George, *22n*; and *History*, 21, 32, 125, 127; letter from SBA, 127; letters to SBA, 125, 432
Adams, Mass., 107
Adams, N.Y., 472
Address of Gov. John W. Hoyt upon Woman Suffrage in Wyoming, 163, 163–64n
Adler, Felix, *94n*, 469; ECS hears, 93, 330; SBA reads, 241
African Americans: and Colo. campaign, 423; equality of, 84
aging: A. B. Blackwell on, 450–51; ECS on, 445, 451–61, 451–61; SBA on, 108, 280. *See also* menopause
Albani, Dame Emma, 250, *263n*
Alcott, Louisa May, 250, *263n*
Alderly Edge, England: ECS and SBA in, 299
Aldrich, Nelson Wilmarth, *404n*; and amendment, 546; letter from SBA, 404; letter to SBA, 405
Allegheny City, Pa.: conservatory for, 499–501
Allen, Charles, *335n*; and Eddy will, 334, 335n
Allen, Mary Henrietta Swisshelm, 210, *211n*
Allison, William Boyd, *547n*; and Senate vote, 546
Amalfi, Italy: SBA in, 228–29
American Anti-Slavery Society: Declaration of Sentiments of, 303–4, 304–5n; fiftieth anniversary of, 302–4; SBA's remarks to, 302–4; thirtieth anniversary of, 304–5n
American Exchange (London), 223
American Exchange (Paris), 236, 238, 241
American history: and women, 249–50
American Red Cross: Monroe County chapter of, 112, 113nn, 115
American Woman Suffrage Association, 53; affiliates of, 156–58, 313; annual meetings of, 6–7, 42, 45n, 521; constitution of, 10n; and federal amendment, xx, 380, 387; in *History*, 118, 162n; and National association, 156, 521; and Neb. campaign, 139n, 177n, 182–83n; petitions Congress, 387n; SBA speaks to, 176–77
Anderson, Mary, 310, *311n*
Andrews, Alexander Edward, *208–9n*; and N.Y. campaign, 207–8
Anglo-American history: and women's progress, 248
Anthony, Abram, 108, *110n*

Anthony, Anna Wadsworth, 109, *110n*
Anthony, Anne E. Osborne, 231, *232n*
Anthony, Charles, 107, *109n*
Anthony, Daniel, 108–9, *109n*, 279, 302
Anthony, Daniel Read, 107, *110n*, 410; attempted murder of, 99; letters from SBA, 228–31, 232–34; SBA visits, 506
Anthony, Elizabeth Wadsworth, *109n*; letter from SBA, 107–9
Anthony, Frances Brown, 236, *236–37n*, 238
Anthony, Henry Bowen, *133–34n*, 404n; death of, 374, 375n, 376; letters to SBA, 169, 377; and Senate committee, 133–34n, 305, 377; and suffrage in D.C., 376
Anthony, Horace G., 107, *109n*
Anthony, Humphrey (cousin), 107, *109–10n*
Anthony, Humphrey (grandfather), 107, 108, *109n*
Anthony, Humphrey, Jr. (uncle), 108, *110n*
Anthony, Jacob Merritt, *201–2n*, 410; SBA visits, 201, 506
Anthony, Jessie, 107, 109, *109n*
Anthony, John, 107–8, *109n*
Anthony, Joseph, 107, *109n*
Anthony, Joseph, Jr., 107, *109n*
Anthony, Joshua, 107, *109–10n*
Anthony, Lucy Elmina, *110n*, 287, 288; in Kan., 107
Anthony, Lucy Read, 12, *13n*, 108–9, 279
Anthony, Mary Stafford, *51n*; letter from SBA, 243; mentioned, 51, 104, 107, 112, 237, 280, 285, 288, 544; and N.Y. campaign, 439; at suffrage meeting, 476
Anthony, Maude, 243, *243n*, 288
Anthony, Samuel, 107, *109–10n*
Anthony, Scott J., 236, *236–37n*, 238
Anthony, Susan B.: ECS describes, 225–26; and foreign languages, 231, 233, 237, 238; gifts for, 225, 227nn; letters from ECS, 169–70, 281, 339–40, 382, 501–2, 537–39; letters to ECS, 323–26, 371–72, 381; pictures of, 321; religious views of, 52, 229, 491; substitutes for ECS, 9n, 17, 17n
Anti-Monopoly party: in 1884 election, 362, 365nn; and woman suffrage, 362, 365n
appeals: "Stand by the Republican Party" (ECS and SBA), 361–64; "To the Governors of the Thirteen Colonial States" (ECS), 515–17
Ariosto, Ludovico, 82–83, *88n*
aristocracy of sex, 90–91
Armstrong, James M., 378, *379n*
Arthur, Chester Alan, 115, *116n*; annual

(Arthur, Chester Alan, *continued*)
message of, 123; and National association, 123; quoted, 122; SBA meets with, 117n
articles: "Has Christianity Benefited Woman?" (ECS), 433–36; "The Politics of Reformers" (ECS), 1–3; On SBA's arrival in London (ECS), 224–26; "The Woman's Bible" (ECS), 510–11
"As a Mother" (Lawrence), 447, 558–61
Auclert, Marie Anne Hubertine, *240n*; letter to SBA, 335–36, 336n; SBA visits, 240, 241
Augustine of Hippo, Saint, *401n*, 412; and women, 396

Bacon, Eliza F. Merriam, *131n*; and Eddy will, 129–30, 132n
Bacon, Jerome Augustus, *164n*; and Eddy will, 164, 178, 179n
Baldwin, Charles Hume, 52, *53n*
Baldwin, Elizabeth McMartin, 52, *53n*
Baptist church: and women, 392, 414
Barber, Lucy Sweet, *551n*; jailed for voting, 549
Barnes, Mrs. (of Hartford, Conn.), 414
Barnes, Sarah Jane Allen, 142, *144n*
Barrau de Muratel, Caroline Françoise Coulomb de, *119n*; and *History*, 118; hosts SBA, 236, 238–42, 243–44; letter to ECS, 530; and *Woman's Bible*, 530
Bartol, Cyrus Augustus, 369, *370n*
Barton, Clara, *50n*, 117n; and *History*, 49–50; letters from SBA, 49–50, 112–13, 115; SBA hears, 104
Bascom, Ansel, 543, *543n*
Basingstoke, England: ECS describes, 215; ECS in, 212, 215–16, 276–77, 281, 291–92, 525–26, 528–29, 537–39, 541–43; SBA in, 295–96
Baxter, Richard, 74, *86n*; *The Saints Everlasting Rest*, 458
Bayard, Thomas Francis, *141n*; and Senate committee, 140
Bayard, Tryphena Cady, 166, *167n*, 406; and ECS birthday, 463
Beach, Lewis, *365n*; and House Committee, 362
Beck, James Burnie, *141n*; and Senate committee, 140
Becker, Lydia Ernestine, *199n*, 273, 299; in Glasgow, 197; letter to ECS, 294–95; letter to SBA, 332–33; and married women's suffrage, 284; and National Society for Women's Suffrage, 285; and parliamentary petitions, 225; in U.S., *372n*; with SBA in Paris, 239, 240; and *Women's Suffrage Journal*, 469
Beecher, Henry Ward, *386n*; and 1884 election, 385, 386n

Belfast, Ireland: SBA in, 286–88
Belford, James Burns, *316n*; and House committee, 316, 316n
Bennett, Sarah Lewis Clay, *159–60n*, 312, 314; and National association, 157; at suffrage meeting, 478
Berlin, Germany, 230; Sargent family in, 232n; SBA in, 233
Berridge, Edward William, 212, *213n*, 291
Berry, Mme. (mother of Marguerite), 238, 238–39n
Berry, Marguerite Marie, *62–63n*; letter from ECS, 61–62; marries T. W. Stanton, 62–63n. *See also* Stanton, Marguerite Marie Berry
Besant, Annie Wood, *290n*; SBA hears, 290
Bible: as historical text, 412; used for and against reform, 394; and women's oppression, 511; women's revisions needed, 396–97, 399, 474, 491, 510–11, 513–15, 518–20, 528–29
"The Bible and Woman Suffrage" (ECS): quoted, 77
biblical quotations and references, 75, 426; to Cain, 187; chosen people in, 147; to covered heads, 310; creation in, 72, 73, 252, 395, 396; equality in, 392; to Golden Calf, 147; to Golden Rule, 395; to Gospels, 412; to Lord's Prayer, 77; love in, 81; love of man in, 363; male superiority in, 3; to Moses, 147, 538; to Paul's views of women, 3, 369, 413–14, 424, 484; to Pharaoh, 538; to Pharisees, 42; polygamy in, 369, 370n, 519; praise in, 342; social distinctions in, 73; teachings of Jesus in, 369, 398, 413, 481; wandering in, 468
Bickerdyke, Mary Ann Ball, 187, *190–91n*
Bickersteth, Edward, *462n*; *A Treatise on Prayer*, 458
Biggs, Caroline Ashurst, *226–27n*; and parliamentary petitions, 225
Billings, Frederick, 251, *264n*
Bird Club (Boston), 93
Birney, James Gillespie, 27, *28n*
birth: of E. C. Stanton, Jr., 164–65; of N. S. Blatch, 291; of Z. Wilkeson, 165
Bismarck, Otto Eduard Leopold von, 234, *235n*
Black, George Robison, *365n*; and House committee, 362
Blackwell, Antoinette Louisa Brown, 449, *449–50n*; books by, 470, 471n; and ECS birthday, 450–51; letters from ECS, 470, 504–5; letters to ECS, 450–51, 524; and *Woman's Bible*, 524
Blackwell, Henry Browne, 6, *10n*, 42; in Ill., 522n; in Kan., 521; and National association, 156, 159n; and Neb.

campaign, 177n, 181; and presidential suffrage, 209n; at R.I. meeting, 376

Blackwell, Samuel Charles, 470, *471n*, 505

Blaine, James Gillespie, 115, *116n*; and 1884 election, 363–64, 366n, 372, 385; and woman suffrage, 364

Blair, Henry William, *133–34n*, 142; and amendment, 205, 208, 535, 536n, 537, 538; letter to SBA, 545; and Senate committee, 133–34n, 305; and Senate report, 471–72, 490; and Senate vote, 545, 550

Blake, Grinfill, 99, *100n*

Blake, Katherine Muhlenbergh Devereux Umsted, 99, *100n*

Blake, Lillie Devereux, *59n*; and Dix's lectures, 310–11; and ECS birthday, 440, 444, 445, 459–60; and *History*, 99; and H. Willcox, 465–66, 467n; letter from ECS, 445; letters from SBA, 99, 207–8, 217, 431, 438–39, 444, 465–67, 492, 495; and National association, 466–67; and Neb. campaign, 183; and New England tour, 57; and newspaper, 380; and N.Y. campaign, 217, 217–18n, 431, 438–39, 492, 495; at Senate hearing, 344; at suffrage meetings, 134, 553; *Woman's Place To-Day*, 310–11

Blanchard, Mrs. (in London), 284

Blatch, Alice, 221, *222n*; travels with SBA, 226, 228

Blatch, Harriot Eaton Stanton, *xxvii*, 559; and ECS's London speech, 245–46; and English suffrage movement, 406; health of, 296; letters from ECS, 301n, 520n; in London, 218–19, 273; marriage of, 464; mentioned, 221, 239, 277, 291, 292, 301, 330, 447, 463, 469; pregnancy of, 215; travels of, 371; in U.S., 506–7; and *Woman's Bible*, 515n, 519. *See also* Stanton, Harriot Eaton

Blatch, Nora Stanton, 295, 406, 469; birth of, 291

Blatch, William Henry, Jr., xxvii, *192–93n*; ECS describes, 277; letter from ECS, 296–97; marriage of, 200, 200n, 202

Bliss, Archibald Meserole, *365n*; and House committee, 362

Bloomer, Amelia Jenks, *13n*; and *History*, xxv, 12–13, 23–24, 29–30, 31, 101, 102–4, 429–30, 437–38, 448–49; letters from ECS, 29–30, 31, 101, 448–49; letters from SBA, 12–13, 23–24, 102–4, 429–30, 437–38, 438n

Bloomer, Dexter Chamberlain, 12, 13, *13n*, 101

Bloomfield, Iowa: SBA in, 410

Blue, Richard Whiting, *557n*; telegram from SBA, 557

Book of Common Prayer: quoted, 102–3

Booth, Mary Louise, *68n*, 371; and ECS birthday, 447; letter from SBA, 447–48; letter to SBA, 67–68

Borg, Selma Josefina, 104–5, *106n*

Bowditch, William Ingersoll, *384n*; and "Woman's Realm," 383

Bowen, Thomas Mead, *491n*; and Senate report, 490; and Senate vote, 550

Bowles, Ada Chastina Burpee, 69, *70n*

Bowring, John, *260–61n*; at World's Anti-Slavery Convention, 246

Boyd's Opera House (Omaha), 183

Boyles, Hannah Dickinson, 108, *110n*

Boyles, Margaret Louise, 108, *110n*

Bradlaugh, Charles, *291n*; SBA hears, 290

Breitung, Edward, *365n*; and House committee, 362

Bridge of Sighs (Venice), 78

Briggs, Emily Pomona Edson, 506, *507n*

Bright, Esther, 299, *299n*

Bright, Jacob, 245, *263–64n*, 272; hosts ECS and SBA, 299; and international plans, 299–300n; and married women's suffrage, 310; and parliamentary franchise, 274; and property rights, 250

Bright, John, 197, *204n*; ECS visits, 203–4, 204n

Bright, John Gratton, 299, *299n*

Bright, Ursula Mellor, *263–64n*, 464; hosts ECS and SBA, 299; letter to ECS, 272; in Liverpool, 300; and married women's suffrage, 272, 279, 282, 283n, 284, 285, 309–10; and property rights, 250

Bristol, England: ECS recalls visit to, 291–92

Broadhead, James Overton, *319n*; and House committee, 318–19; and Judiciary Committee, 318

Brontë, Charlotte, 83, *89n*

Brooks, Harriet Sophia Brewer, 61n, *489n*; and resolutions on religion, 482; at suffrage meeting, 482

Broomall, John Martin, 358, *359n*; and "Woman's Realm," 383

Brown, Alexander, 277, *278n*

Brown, Harriet Eaton, 277, *278n*; and ECS birthday, 463

Brown, Joseph Emerson, *307–8n*; minority report of, 535, 535–36n, 537, 538–39; and Senate committee, 305

Brown, Martha McClellan, *43n*; at suffrage meetings, 40, 142–43

Brown, Mary Olney, 551, *553n*

Brown, Olympia, *59n*, 531; and *History*, 145–46; letter from ECS, 145–46; and New England tour, 57, 95–96; and school suffrage, 526; at suffrage meeting, 89; in Wis., 533; and *Woman's Bible*, 515n

Brown, Ryland Thomas, 176, *178n*

Brown, Susan Anthony, 108, *110n*
Browne, Martha Griffith, 371, *372–73n*
Browne, Thomas McLelland, *319n*; and House committee, 318–19; and Judiciary Committee, 318
Buckle, Henry Thomas, 454, *461n*
Buddha, 435, *436n*
Buddhism, 433
Bull, Mary Sherwood Bascom, 30, *31n*
Bullard, Laura J. Curtis, 239, *240n*; letter from ECS, 385; and menopause, 463
Burchard, Samuel Dickinson, *386n*, 393; and 1884 election, 385, 386n
Burns, Robert, 194, *195n*
Burr, Frances Ellen, *399n*; at equal rights club, 411, 414; letters from ECS, 411–13, 496–98; at suffrage meetings, 392, 480; and *Woman's Bible*, 515n
Burrows, Julius Caesar, *151n*; and Dakota statehood, 151, 153, 154; letter from SBA, 153; and woman suffrage, 154
Butler, Alban: *Lives of the Saints*, 458
Butler, Benjamin Franklin, *19–20*; and 14th Amendment, 205, 214–15; and 15th Amendment, 214; and 1884 election, 362, 364n, 367, 368, 368–69n, 370, 370–71n; and amendment, 208, 214–15; and declaratory act, 18; and Eddy will, 163, 179, 334, 350, 352, 367, 381; inauguration of, 205, 206n; letters from ECS, 367, 370; letters from SBA, 213–14, 350, 367, 368; letters to SBA, 214–15, 352; minority report of, 18, 121, 362, 367, 370; and National association, 214–15; visits ECS, 370–71n; and woman suffrage, 368, 368–69n
Butler, Josephine Elizabeth Grey, 192, *193n*, 295
Byron, Lady (Anna Isabella Milbanke), 247, *261n*

Cabot, Frederick Samuel, 55, *56n*, 369
Cady, Daniel, 458, *462n*
Cady, Margaret Livingston, 62, *63n*
Caird, Alice Mona Alison Henryson, 296, *296n*
Caird, Edward, 197, *198n*
California Woman Suffrage Association: and National association, 158
Calvin, John, 412, *415n*
Cameron, Angus, *375n*; and Senate committee, 375
Cameron, James Donald, *547n*; and Senate vote, 546
Camp, John Henry, *167n*; and House committee, 167
Canada: woman suffrage in, 332, 333n
Canning, Hubert George De Burgh (earl of Clanricarde), 539, *540n*

canon law: and women, 73–75, 397, 413, 416, 473
Carey, Francis King: and common law, 373n
Carey, Joseph Maull: at suffrage meeting, 553
Carlisle, John Griffin, *218n*; and House Committee, 217, 312
Carpenter, Aurelius Ormando, 32, *33n*, 127
Carpenter, Matthew Hale, 361, *364–65n*
Carpenters' Hall (Philadelphia), 515–16
Cato, Publius Valerius, 457, *462n*
Centennial Exhibition (1876), 25; in *History*, 166–67; and women, 516
Cervantes, Miguel de, 84, *89n*; quoted, 114
Chace, Elizabeth Buffum, 55, *56n*; and *History*, 148; letter from SBA, 404–5
Chace, Jonathan, *405n*; and amendment, 546; letter to SBA, 404–5; and Senate report, 490
Chaillé, Stanford Emerson, 408, *409n*
Chain, Helen Henderson, *231n*; in Paris, 242; travels with SBA, 228
Chain, James Albert, *231n*; in Paris, 242; travels with SBA, 228
Chalmers, Thomas, 194, *195n*
Chandler, Lucinda Banister, *488n*; and National association, 477
Channing, Grace Ellery, 301, *301n*, 519
Channing, Mary Jane Tarr, 55, *55–56n*, 301; letter to ECS, 518–19; and *Woman's Bible*, 518–19
Channing, William Ellery, 63, *64n*
Channing, William Francis, *53n*, 55, 519; ECS visits, 93; letters to ECS, 301, 360, 369; quoted, 79; religious views of, 52, 63, 369; visits ECS, 52
Channing, William Henry, 6, *9n*, 248; and *History*, 145, 146n; and wedding of H. E. Stanton, 200n
Chapin, Sarah Flournoy Moore, 418, *419n*
Charles, Emily Thornton, *43–44n*; at suffrage meeting, 40
Chaucer, Geoffrey, 457, *462n*
Cheney, Person Colby, *552n*; and Senate vote, 550
Cheney Brothers, 227
Chevallie, M. R. (of New Orleans), 408, 409n
Chicago *Inter-Ocean*, 161. *See also* "Woman's Kingdom"
Chicago Sanitary Fair, 506
Child, Lydia Maria Francis, 70, *71n*, 250; *Progress of Religious Ideas*, 518; quoted, 74–75
children: rearing of, 165
Christianity: and poverty, 434; and slavery, 434–35; and women, 73–85, 369, 391–92, 396–97, 433, 497, 498
Christlieb, Theodor, 252, *264n*

Chrysostom, Saint John, 412, *415n*
churches: exclude women, 435; and secular state, 398; sustained by women, 79–80; and temperance, 394; and woman suffrage, 394–95, 480–84, 496–98; and women, 73–85, 369, 412, 416, 473–74, 504–5; women as teachers in, 413; women to come out from, 391–92
Church of Our Father (Washington), 391
Cincinnati Commercial Gazette: letter from SBA, 321
citizenship: in 14th Amendment, 69; national protection of, 69, 70, 477–79, 484
Citizens' Suffrage Association (Philadelphia), 225, 227n; in *History*, 358–59, 359n; honors SBA, 222; and National association, 157; and "Woman's Realm," 383
La Citoyenne (Paris), 240
Civil War: in *History*, 49, 162; role of women in, 49, 186–87
Clanricarde, earl of. *See* Canning, Hubert George De Burgh
Claremont Hall (London), 290
Clark, Charles Benjamin, 527, *528n*
Clark, Emily, 449, *449–50n*
Clark, Helen Priestman Bright, *204n*; and Liberal party, 291, 292–93n; mentioned, 203, 215, 292, 295; SBA visits, 297–98
Clarke, Adam, *85–86n*, 260; and creation, 73, 85–86n; *Holy Bible, with a Commentary*, 73, 514
Clarke, James Freeman, 363, *366n*
Clarke, Mary Bayard Devereux, 551, *553n*
Clay, Anne Warfield, *159–60n*, 314; and National association, 157
Clay, Francis Warfield Herrick, 314, *315n*
Clay, Green, 314, *315n*
Clay, Laura, *159–60n*, 314; and National association, 157
Clay, Mary Barr, *159–60n*; and American association, 312–13; letter from SBA, 312–14; and National association, 157
Clay, Mary Jane Warfield, *159–60n*, 314; and National association, 157
clergy: as allies, 394–95; and woman suffrage, 473–74, 480–84, 496–98; and women, 2–3, 391–92, 396, 442, 497–99, 504–5
Cleveland, Grover, *366n*; and 1884 election, 363, 375, 385; annual message of, 465, 466; letter from SBA, 465
Clifton, England: SBA in, 297–98
Cobbe, Frances Power, *87n*; and ECS birthday, 463; ECS describes, 218–19; letter to ECS, 220–21; *The Peak in Darien*, 219; quoted, 78
Cobden, Emma Jane Catherine, *292n*; letter to SBA, 328–29; and Liberal party, 291, 292–93n
Cobden, Richard, 309, *311n*; quoted, 329

Cobleigh, Mr. (of N.Y.), 460, 463n
Cockrell, Francis Marion, *468n*; and amendment, 404n; minority report of, 535, 535–36n, 537, 538–39; and Senate committee, 305, 466, 468n; at Senate hearing, 344
coeducation, 248, 253–56
Colby, Clara Dorothy Bewick, 60, *61n*, 151, 531; and ECS birthday, 440; in Kan., 521, 522–23; and National association, xxiii, 441, 535, 544; and Neb. association, 105–6, 157; and Neb. campaign, 136, 139n, 142; in New Orleans, 408; and resolutions on religion, 395, 401n, 481–82, 498; at suffrage meetings, 142, 395, 476, 477, 478–79, 481–82; in Wis., 533; and *Woman's Tribune*, xxiii, 306, 308n, 379, 441, 492, 521
Collins, Emily Parmley Peltier, 411, 414, *415n*
Collins, Patrick Andrew, *319n*; and House committee, 318–19; and Judiciary Committee, 318
Collyer, Robert, *29n*; and L. C. Mott, 28
Colorado: school suffrage in, 248
Colorado amendment campaign, 1877, 96–97, 176, 185, 186n, 422–24
Colorado Woman Suffrage Association: and National association, 158
Columbus, Christopher, 509, *509n*
common law: and women, 373n, 388–89
Commonwealth (Boston), 58
The Complaint; or, Night-Thoughts (Young), 458
Comte, Auguste, 87n, 88n, 454, *461n*
Concord, N.H., 57; SBA speaks in, 95–97
Confucius, 435, *436n*
Congregational church: and women, 414
Conkling, Roscoe, *43n*; and 14th Amendment, 210, 211nn; and Senate committee, 39, 43n
Connecticut: divorce in, 251; property rights in, 517
Connecticut Woman Suffrage Association: and National association, 157
constitutional amendment for woman suffrage, 226; action urged on, 18–19, 111, 140, 154, 347–48, 465, 484, 548–49; advocated, 69, 70, 89–93, 95–97, 161, 345–48, 491; B. F. Butler's views of, 214–15; campaign for, 205, 307, 312, 317, 376–77, 380, 427; in Congress, 524–25, 527; defeated in Senate, xxi, 545, 546–47; in House, 18–19, 312, 314n, 547; and National association, xx; and Republican party, 362; in Senate, 18–19, 205, 206–7n, 208, 312, 314n, 375, 380, 404, 404n, 405–6, 537–38; and state legislatures, 95, 97n, 208

Contagious Diseases Acts, 192, 193n, 238, 239n

Converse, George Leroy, *365n*; and House committee, 362

Conway, Dana, 469, *469n*

Conway, Ellen Davis Dana, *469n*; letter from ECS, 468–69

Conway, Eustace, 469, *469n*

Conway, Mildred E., 469, *469n*

Conway, Moncure Daniel, *278n*, 529; ECS to preach for, 277, 278n; returns to U.S., 469; and wedding of H. E. Stanton, 200n

Cook, Francis, 526, *526n*

Cook, Tennessee Celeste Claflin, 525, *526n*

Cook County Woman Suffrage Association, 531

Corbin, Caroline Elizabeth Fairfield, *535-36n*; *Letters from a Chimney Corner*, 535, 538–39

Corbin, Hannah Lee, 250, *263n*

Cornell University, 255, 256

Correll, Erasmus Michael, 61n, 139n, 176

corruption: ECS condemns, 91–92

Couzins, Phoebe Wilson, 35, *35-36n*; at Mott memorial, 36; and National association, 48, 466; in Neb. campaign, 183, 187, 207n; as speaker, 310; substitutes for SBA, 48

Craigen, Jessie Hannah, *197-98n*; at Glasgow meeting, 196–97; and married women's suffrage, 272, 272n

Crawford, Mrs. (of Belfast, Ire.), 288

Crawford, Francis Marion: *Mr. Isaacs. A Tale of Modern India*, 330

Crawford, Samuel Johnson, 21, *22n*

crimes: against women, 259; by women, 184–85

Croly, Jane Cunningham, 445, *446n*

Culberson, David Browning, *319n*; and House committee, 318–19; and Judiciary Committee, 318

Curtis, George William, 363, *366n*; and N.Y. constitutional convention, 421; quoted, 421

Curtis, Lucy W., 385, *386n*

Cushing, Sarah Lamb, 431, *432n*

Cushman, Charlotte Saunders, 249, *262n*

Cuthbert, Mrs. (of Belle Plaine, Kan.), 523

Dakota Territory: school suffrage in, 248; statehood proposed, 140, 141n, 142, 151, 153, 153n, 154, 379, 379n; and woman suffrage, 140, 142, 151, 153, 153n, 154, 379

Dall, Caroline Wells Healey, 317, *317n*; letter from SBA, 536–37

Dall, Charles Henry Appleton, 536–37, *537n*

Dall, William Healey, 537, *537n*

Daniels, Hattie, *228n*; travels with SBA, 226

Dansville Water-Cure (N.Y.), 50; SBA visits, 104–5

Dante, 230, 231, *232n*

D. Appleton & Company, 24n

Darwin, Charles Robert, 454, *461n*

Davis, David, *365n*; and Senate committee, 362

Davis, Edward Morris, *17n*, 25; and *History*, 358–59; letter from SBA, 358–59; letters from ECS, 16–17, 27–28, 358–59; letter to ECS, 41–42; at Mott memorial, 37–38; and resolutions on religion, 395, 482, 483; and suffrage factions, 544; at suffrage meetings, 39, 395, 478, 479, 482, 483

Davis, Henry Gassaway, *43n*; and Senate committee, 39, 43n

Davis, Maria Mott, *17n*, 28; letter from ECS, 16–17

Davis, Martha Ann Powell, 125, *126n*

Davis, Mary Fenn Robinson Love, *316n*, 316–17

Davis, Paulina Kellogg Wright, 7, *10-11n*, 376

Davitt, Michael, *294n*; SBA hears, 293

Dawes, Henry Laurens, *547n*; and Senate vote, 546

death: of C. I. H. Nichols, 433n; ECS on, 170–71; of H. B. Anthony, 375, 376n; of H. B. Stanton, 541–43; of J. Mott, 298; of L. C. Mott, 16–17; of P. H. Jones, 102; SBA on, 108–9; of S. Pugh, 376; of W. R. Hallowell, 170–71

deceased wife's sister bill, 250, 260

declaratory act for woman suffrage, 18

Democratic party: in 1884 election, 362; in Congress, xxi; and House majority, 312

Denison, Ruth Carr, *327-28n*; and F. Douglass, 324; at suffrage meeting, 476

Desraimes, Maria, *237-38n*; SBA visits, 237

Devil: capitalization of, 494; and women, 74

Dickinson, Anna Elizabeth, 119, *119n*, 250; and 15th Amendment, 150, 152

Dickinson, Ann Eliza Anthony, 107, *109n*

Dickinson, Charles, *293-94n*; in England, 293, 295, 297, 299, 300

Dickinson, Frances, 107, *109n*; in England, 293, 295, 297, 299, 300

disfranchisement: degradation of, 187; of rebels, 187

District of Columbia: Senate vote on suffrage in, 376, 378

divorce, 251

Dix, Morgan, *311-12n*, 397; Lenten lectures of, xxii, 311, 311–12n

Dodge, Mary Elizabeth Mapes, 447, *448n*

Dolley, Sarah Read Adamson, 115, *115-16n*

Dolph, Joseph Norton, *552n*; and amendment, 550; and Senate vote, 550

domestic science: and National association, 485–86

Don Quixote de la Mancha (Cervantes): quoted, 114

Dorsheimer, William, *319n*; and 1884 election, 372, 374n; and House committee, 318–19; and Judiciary Committee, 318

Douglass, Anna Murray, 147, *147–48n*

Douglass, Charles Remond, 147, *147–48n*

Douglass, Frederick: and 15th Amendment, 152; and D.C. women's movement, 324; feted in Washington, 212; and *History*, 147, 150, 152; letters from ECS, 147, 152, 353–55; letters to ECS, 150, 356–57; *Life and Times of*, 150, 150n, 152; and manhood suffrage, 325–26; marriage of, 323–26, 326n, 353–55, 356–57; at Mott memorial, 37; at R.I. meeting, 376; at suffrage meeting, 39

Douglass, Frederick, Jr., 147, *147–48n*

Douglass, Helen Pitts, 323, 325, *326n*, 354, 355, 356–57

Douglass, Lewis Henry, 147, *147–48n*

Dover, N.H., 57; suffragists in, 158

dress reform: in *History*, 449; and Lady Harberton, 215, 218

Dundore, Lavinia C., *489n*; and resolutions on religion, 482; at suffrage meeting, 482

Duniway, Abigail Jane Scott, *139n*; and 1884 election, 378; in Boston, 348; and National association, 441; and *New Northwest*, 314, 422, 441; and Ore. campaign, 136, 142, 307, 348, 422; at Senate hearing, 344, 355; and Wash. campaign, 307

The Duties of Man (Mazzini), 454

Eastman, Mary F., *384n*; at suffrage meeting, 553; and "Woman's Realm," 383

Eaton, Daniel Cady (1834–1895), 406, *408n*

Eaton, Daniel Cady (1837–1912), 277, *278–79n*, 406

Eaton, Ellen Dwight, 277, *278n*

Eaton, Harriet Eliza Cady, *277n*, 461n; and ECS birthday, 463; letter from ECS, 276–77

Eddy, Amy, 130, *132n*

Eddy, Eliza F. Jackson Merriam, *131n*; will of, xxv, 129–31, 131–32n, 132–33

Eddy, Sarah James, 130, *132n*

Eddy will case, 163, 164n, 178–79, 179n, 314, 334, 348–49, 350, 352, 381, 390; and *History*, 367; settled, 410, 410–11n

Edinburgh, Scotland: ECS in, 197; ECS plans visit to, 202–3, 212, 213n, 215, 218; SBA visits, 284, 286

Edinburgh National Society for Women's Suffrage, 212

Edmunds, George Franklin, 122, 123, *124n*, 374; and 14th Amendment, 210, 211nn; and Utah suffrage, 141–42n, 490n, 491, 551n

Edmunds Act, 141–42n, 485, 490n, 491

Edmunds-Tucker Act, 549, 551n, 554

Edson, Susan Ann, *327–28n*; and F. Douglass, 324

Egypt: women in, 258

election of 1880, xxi, xxiv; ECS attempts to vote in, 14; and reformers, 1–3, 3–4n

election of 1882: Republican losses in, 205

election of 1884, 371–72, 385, 385; and B. A. Lockwood, 372; and B. F. Butler, 368, 370; and National association, 341, 361–64; in Washington Terr., 378–79, 379n

Eliot, George, 83–84, *89n*, 248, 403

Ellsworth, Bertha H., 492, *493n*

Emerson, Ralph Waldo, 7, *11n*, 248; quoted, 253

Eminent Women of the Age (Parton), 24, 558

Encyclopaedia Britannica—American Reprint, 381, 381–82n

"The Enfranchisement of Women" (H. T. Mill), 248, 417

England, Isaac W., 330, *330–31n*

England, Mary, *330–31n*; letter from ECS, 330

Episcopal church, 12–13; and women, 393

Equal Rights for All (Curtis), 421

Estlin, Mary Anne, *298n*; SBA visits, 297–98

Evans, Mary Ann. *See* Eliot, George

Evarts, William Maxwell, 406, *407n*

Ewing, Emma Pike, *487n*; at suffrage meeting, 477, 486

Exeter Hall (London), 219

Fair, James Graham, *133–34n*, 547; and Senate committee, 133–34n, 305

Fall, the: and woman's curse, 74, 75–76

Farrar, Frederic William, *475n*; quoted, 474

Farwell, Charles Benjamin, *548n*; and amendment, 547; and Senate vote, 550

Fawcett, Henry, *297n*; ECS and SBA hear, 297

Fawcett, Millicent Garrett, *274n*, 297; letter to SBA, 331–32; SBA hears, 273

feminine element, 73, 75, 79–81, 90, 92, 195, 252–53, 392, 396, 413, 458–59

Ferguson, Ellen Brooke, *555–56n*; telegram to SBA, 554–55

Ferry, Thomas White, *133–34n*; and amendment, 19n; and Senate committee, 133–34n

Field, Cyrus West, 120, *121n*

Field, Martha Reinhard Smallwood, 418, *420n*; at suffrage meeting, 476

Fifteenth Amendment, 96; in *History*, 147, 150, 152; and woman suffrage, 426, 491

Finley, Jesse Johnson, *365n*; and House committee, 362

Flower, Frank, 284

Flower, Roswell Pettibone, *365n*; and House committee, 362

Fort Scott, Kan.: SBA in, 201, 506–7; suffragists in, 157

Fort Scott Monitor (Kan.): interviews SBA, 201

Forum: ECS writes for, 499

Foster, Abigail Kelley, 302, 303, *304n*, 550

Foster, Emory Miller, 287, *289n*

Foster, Judith Ellen Horton Avery, 287, *289n*, 306; in Washington, 320

Foster, Julia Manuel, 48, *48–49n*; death of, 470, 471n; in Europe, 279

Foster, Julia T., *48n*, 57, 66, 67; in Europe, 279; letter from SBA, 51; minutes by, 142–43; and National association, 16n, 48; at suffrage meetings, 142–43, 476

Foster, Rachel G., *44n*; and death of mother, 470; in Europe, 279; and *History*, 358; leaves London, 275; leaves SBA, 238, 243; letter from ECS, 48; letters from SBA, 51, 116, 163, 180, 284–85, 544; mentioned, 24, 28, 64, 66, 67, 148, 217, 239, 273, 285; and National association, xxiii–xxiv, 16n, 48, 54, 56–58; and Neb. campaign, 139n, 163, 180, 182–83n; and New England tour, 57; speaks in London, 275; at suffrage meetings, 40, 135, 136, 142–43; travels with SBA, 223, 226, 231, 236, 237

Foster, Stephen Symonds, 302, 303, *304n*

Foster, William Horton, 287, *289n*

Fourteenth Amendment, 96; B. F. Butler's views of, 214–15; reinterpreted by Supreme Court, 210, 211nn; and woman suffrage, 205, 210, 211n, 214, 361, 426, 491

Fowler & Wells (publishers), xxv, 23, 68n, 115, 371, 372, 507

France: ECS describes, 169, 171–72; education in, 530; religion in, 81, 530; woman question in, 92; and woman suffrage, 237–38n, 240, 240–41nn, 242. *See also* Paris

Francis, John, 125, *125n*

Franklin, Mich.: suffragists in, 157

Frederick II (king of Prussia), 233, *235n*

Frederick William I (king of Prussia), 233, *235n*

free love, 156, 159n

Free Religious Association, 93; ECS addresses, 72–85

free thought: in National association, xxiv; and woman suffrage, 2–3

"Free Trade" (Cobden): quoted, 329

Friend, Mary A., 295, *295n*

Friends, Society of (Quakers): and abolitionists, 25; and L. C. Mott, 24–25, 27

frontier, American: and education, 253–54; effects on women, 251–52; and manners, 252

Fry, Elizabeth Gurney, 24, *26n*, 27, 78, 247

Frye, William Pierce, *547n*; and Senate vote, 546

Fuller, Margaret, *102n*, 250, 357; in *History*, 101

Furness, William Henry, 302, *304n*

Gage, Frances Dana Barker, *11n*; and *History*, 8

Gage, Matilda Joslyn, *5n*, 57, 66, 99; and amendment, 161; and *History*, xxv, 8, 9n, 30, 101, 150, 162, 503; letters from SBA, 4–5, 503; and National association, 54; and *National Citizen*, 3–4n, 4–5, 5nn, 21, 135, 137, 139n; and New England tour, 57; as speaker, 310; at suffrage meetings, 89, 134–35; in Tenafly, 54; "Woman, Church, and State," 74–75, 76, 83–84, 93, 146n, 277

Galton, Francis, *175n*; quoted, 174, 259

Gardner, Frank, 495, *495–96n*

Garfield, James Abram, *100n*, 183, 184; and 1880 election, xxi; assassination of, 99

Garrison, Agnes, 334, *335n*

Garrison, Charles, 334, *335n*

Garrison, Eleanor, 334, *335n*

Garrison, Ellen Wright, *182n*, 333–34; letter to SBA, 181–82; and National association, 181–82

Garrison, Francis Jackson, 333, 334, *334–35n*

Garrison, Frank Wright, 334, *335n*

Garrison, Gertrude, *445–46n*, 452; and "Pleasures of Age," 445

Garrison, Wendell Phillips, 333, *334–35n*

Garrison, William Lloyd, *34n*, 286, 303; quoted, 33, 247; and U.S. Constitution, 502; at World's Anti-Slavery Convention, 247; as writer, 541

Garrison, William Lloyd, III, 334, *335n*

Garrison, William Lloyd, Jr., 181, *182n*; letter from SBA, 333–34; at R.I. meeting, 376; SBA visits, 333–34, 334–35n; and suffrage factions, xxiv, 182–83n, 334, 335n

Gay, Elizabeth Johns Neall, 246, *260n*

Geddes, George Washington, *365n*; and House committee, 362

Geneva, N.Y.: ECS in, 309–11

Geneva, Treaty of, 50n, 104, 115

George, James Zachariah, *133–34n*; and Senate committee, 133–34n

George Blogg & Co. (jewellers), 284

Germany: SBA travels in, 232–34; woman question in, 92. *See also* Berlin, Heidelberg

Gillig, Henry F., 241, *241n*

girls: rearing of, 453–54

Girton College, 258

Gladstone, William Ewart, *266n*, 537; and Catholic church, 258; quoted, 258; resignation of, 469

Glasgow, Scotland: ECS in, 196–97; ECS speaks in, 194–95

God: as feminine and masculine, 76, 80; as masculine, 75, 76, 79–80, 81–82; as tyrannical, 81

Goethe, Johann Wolfgang von, 84, *89n*, 458

Gordon, Laura De Force, *401–2n*; and resolutions on religion, 398; at suffrage meeting, 398

Gougar, Helen Mar Jackson, *138–39n*, 151, 167; and Kan. association, 493–94n; and National association, xxiii, 441; and N.Y. association, 492, 492, 493n; and *Our Herald*, 136, 205, 306, 313, 379, 441–42n; and presidential suffrage, 209n; and prohibition, 493n; and resolutions on religion, 480, 483, 496–97; at Senate hearing, 344, 345; as speaker, 310; at suffrage meeting, 476, 477, 478–79, 480, 483

Gough, John, 542, *543n*

G. P. Putnam & Son, 371

Grand Rapids, Mich.: suffragists in, 157

Grand Traverse County, Mich.: suffragists in, 157

Granville, earl. *See* Leveson-Gower, Granville George

Gray, Barzillai, 21, *21–22n*

Gray, Jessie M., 21, *21–22n*

Gray, Lawrence T., 21, *21–22n*

Gray, Mary Tenney, *21–22n*; and *History*, 125, 127; letter from SBA, 20–21

Gray, Mary Theodosia, 21, *21–22n*

Great Britain: woman question in, 92. *See also* municipal suffrage, parliamentary franchise, married women's property rights, Scotland

Greeley, Horace, *190n*; and military service, 186, 188

Greenback National party: in 1884 election, 362, 365n; and woman suffrage, 362, 365n

Greenback party, 188, 191n

Greenleaf, Halbert Stevens, *314–15n*; and woman suffrage, 312

Greenwood, Grace, *242n*; SBA visits, 242

Grew, Mary, 246, *260n*; and *History*, 358, 359n; and suffrage factions, 544; and "Woman's Realm," 383

Grimké, Angelina Emily. *See* Weld, Angelina Emily Grimké

Grimké, Sarah Moore, *47n*; in *History*, 46

Guenther, Richard William, *365n*, 527; and House committee, 362; letter from SBA, 524–25

Gurney, Samuel, 24, *26n*

Hackensack Cemetery Co. (N.J.): and racial discrimination, 353, 355n

Haggart, Mary E. Rothwell, 176, *177n*

Hale, Sir Matthew, 74, *86n*

Hall, Mary, 412, *415n*

Hall, Mary J., 297

Hallett, Lilias Sophia Ashworth, 275, *276n*

Hallock, Sarah Hull, 551, *553n*

Hall of Science (London), 290

Hallowell, Mary H. Post, *172n*, 302; letter from ECS, 170–72; SBA visits, 171

Hallowell, William R., *172n*, 302; death of, 170–71; ECS recalls, 170–71

Halstead, Murat, *321n*; letter from SBA, 321

Hamilton, Sarah Grimké Weld, 46, *47n*

Hammond, Nathaniel Job, *319n*; and House committee, 318–19; and Judiciary Committee, 318

Hanaford, Phebe Ann Coffin: and *Woman's Bible*, 515n

Harbert, Arthur Boynton, 151, *151n*, 161, 307

Harbert, Corinne Boynton, 151, *151n*, 161, 307

Harbert, Elizabeth Boynton, 151, *151n*, 161, 307

Harbert, Elizabeth Morrison Boynton, *54n*; and ECS birthday, 440, 441–42n, 446–47; and *History*, 54, 161–62, 166–67; letters from ECS, 309–11, 446–47, 513–15; letters from SBA, 53–54, 150–51, 161–62, 166–67, 305–7, 318–19, 379–80, 384n, 440–41, 506–7, 521, 531, 535; and National association, 53–54, 143; and *New Era*, 440, 441–42n, 446–47, 558; at Senate hearing, 344; and *Woman's Bible*, 513–15; and "Woman's Kingdom," 53–54, 161, 166–67, 311, 318; and "Woman's Realm," 307

Harbert, William Soesbe, 307, *308n*, 447; and ECS birthday, 446; and *History*, 446

Harberton, Florence Wallace Legge Pomeroy (viscountess), *216n*; and dress reform, 215, 216n, 218; ECS visits, 218–19

Hardenbergh, Augustus Albert, *365n*; and House committee, 362

Harper's Bazar (New York), 68

Harriet Martineau's Autobiography, 452–53, 459

Harris, Henry Schenck, *365n*; and House committee, 362

Harrison, Benjamin, *547n*; and Senate vote, 546

Hartford, Conn., 57

Hartford Equal Rights Club: debates ECS's views of religion, 411–14; letters from ECS, 411–13, 496–98

Harvard University, 147; and women's education, 256, 266n

"Has Christianity Benefited Woman?" in Boston *Index* (ECS), 433–36

"Has Christianity Benefited Woman?" in *North American Review* (ECS): critics of, 416, 417n, 433; mentioned, 369, 369–70n, 416

Hastings, Selina (countess of Huntington), 78, *87n*

hats: for women, 310–11

Hawley, Joseph Roswell, *548n*; and Senate vote, 546

Hayes, Lucy Ware Webb, *35n*; hosts National association, 41; letter from SBA, 35; at Mott memorial, 36

Hayes, Rutherford Birchard, *19n*; annual messages of, 18–19; letter from SBA, 18–19

Hayford, James Henry, *189n*; and Wyoming suffrage, 185

Heidelberg, Germany: SBA in, 232–34

Henderson, David Bremner, *365n*; and House committee, 362

Henry, Emma Gertrude, *352n*; hosts SBA, 350–51

Henry, Jane Akin, *352n*; hosts SBA, 350–51

Hereditary Genius (Galton): quoted, 174, 259

Herrick, Clay, 314, *315n*

Hervey, James, *462n*; *Meditations among the Tombs*, 458

Higginson, Thomas Wentworth, *10n*, 248; and 1884 election, 363, 366n, 372, 373n, 385, 386n; and American association, 6; quoted, 83, 394

Hinckley, Elizabeth Shepard Carter, 55, *56n*, 148

Hinckley, Frederic Allen, 6, *9n*; and *History*, 148; letters from ECS, 54–55, 148; and National association, 54–55; and Progressive Friends, 421; at suffrage meeting, 148, 148–49n

Hindman, Matilda, *189–90n*; and *History*, 429; letter from ECS, 388–89; letter to SBA, 383–84; and National association, 383; and suffrage factions, xxiv; and "Woman's Realm," 383–84, 384n; and Wyoming suffrage, 185

Hines, Mr., 241

Hinton, Richard Josiah, 36

History of the Christian Religion (Waite): ECS recommends, 40

History of the Condition of Women, in Various Ages and Nations (Child): quoted, 74–75

History of Woman Suffrage, xxiv–xxv, 63, 171; as a wedding present, 431; distribution of, 110–11, 123, 127, 128, 145, 154, 191–92, 200, 205, 408, 440, 468, 507, 521, 525, 544; European distribution of, 118; financing of, 8, 12, 20–21, 23, 51, 51–52n, 99, 127, 367; index for, 167, 440, 506, 508–9; portraits for, 20–21, 23, 28, 32, 50, 58, 99, 125, 127, 145, 149, 151, 448–49; publisher for, 371–72, 429; volumes needed for, 7–8, 145, 162, 166–67

The History of Woman Suffrage. A Review (W. H. Channing), 145, 146n

History of Woman Suffrage volume 1, 50, 54, 55, 58, 212; C. I. H. Nichols' contributions to, 8, 13, 21, 32; F. D. B. Gage's contributions to, 8; Grimké sisters in, 46; Ind. in, 33, 34n, 46; L. C. Mott in, 46; Mass. in, 7–8, 58; M. Fuller in, 101; N.Y. in, 101, 102; Pa. in, 28; R. D. Owen in, 33, 46; reviews of, 67–68, 98, 99, 120, 121n, 145, 146n, 169–70

History of Woman Suffrage volume 2, 93, 103, 112, 161, 166, 181, 210; 15th Amendment in, 147, 150, 152; Civil War in, 49, 162; Kan. in, 145; O. Brown's contributions to, 145; opening of, 49, 50–51n

History of Woman Suffrage volume 3, 210, 223, 277, 307, 349, 440, 442, 443, 467, 468–69, 495, 506, 520, 521, 525, 529, 558–61; Centennial Exposition in, 166–67; Europe in, 118, 119n; Ill. in, 54, 161, 166–67, 446; Ind. in, 161; Iowa in, 429, 437, 438n, 449; La. in, 418; Mass. in, 58, 118, 351; Neb. in, 101, 105; Pa. in, 358–59; preface to, 501–2, 503; R.I. in, 148; state chapters for, 161–62, 166–67, 439; Wis. in, 145

Hoar, George Frisbie, *20n*; and amendment, 18, 550; letter from ECS, 550; letters from SBA, 128, 133, 154–55; and National association, 140; and Senate committee, 124, 124n, 128, 128–29n, 133, 133–34n, 140, 154, 375, 466; and Senate vote, 550; and Utah suffrage, 490n, 491

Holley, Marietta, *472n*; letter from SBA, 471–72; *Sweet Cicely*, 471

Holloway, Laura Carter, *121n*; letter from SBA, 120

Holy Bible, with a Commentary and Critical Notes (Clarke), 73, 514

Holy Ghost: as feminine, 79

Homer, 84, *89n*

Hooker, Isabella Beecher, *10n*; and amendment, 161; and New England tour, 57; and suffrage factions, 6; at suffrage meetings, 69, 135

Hoover, Hattie, *231–32n*; travels with SBA, 228

Horne, Mary Isabella Hales, *555–56n*; telegram to SBA, 554–55

Horticultural Hall (Philadelphia), 302

Hôtel de la Place du Palais Royal (Paris), 236, 237, 238

House of Commons: Ladies' Gallery in, 224–25, 257; SBA attends, 274

House of Lords: and deceased wife's sister bill, 250, 260; and divorce, 250–51; ECS and SBA visit, 225

Howard University: gift to, 41–42

Howe, Julia Ward, *419n*, 450; and Louisiana exposition, 418; and *Woman's Bible*, 528

Howell, Mary Catherine Seymour: at Senate hearing, 344

Howitt, Mary Botham, 247, *261n*

Hoyt, John Wesley, *163–64n*; *Address upon Woman Suffrage in Wyoming*, 163; and Wyoming suffrage, 417

Hubbard, Richard Dudley, 517, *518n*

Hubbs, Emma M. Leavitt, 125, *126n*

Hugo, Victor Marie, *166n*; quoted, 165

Humboldt, Alexander von, 455, *461n*

Hunt, Harriot Kezia, 57, *58n*

Hurlbut, Elisha Powell, 442, *443–44n*

Hutchins, Waldo, *365n*; and House committee, 362

Illingworth, Alfred, 388, *390n*

Illinois: in *History*, 54, 161, 166–67, 446

Illinois Equal Suffrage Association: meeting of, 521

Illinois Woman Suffrage Association: and National association, 157

immigrants: and manhood suffrage, 91; and voting rights, 111; and woman suffrage, 202n, 423

Independence Hall (Philadelphia), 516

Index (Boston), 1, 58, 412, 512; and ECS's birthday, 442, 443n; ends, 529, 529n

India: women's medical education in, 290; women's movement in, 221

Indiana: divorce in, 251; in *History*, 33, 34n, 46, 161; suffrage campaign in, 69, 71n, 136, 139n, 141, 176–77, 178n

Indianapolis Equal Suffrage Society: and National association, 157

Indiana Woman Suffrage Association: and National association, 157

Inferno (Dante), 231

Ingalls, John James, *548n*; and Senate vote, 546

Ingersoll, Robert Green, 461n

In Memory of Angelina Grimké Weld (Weld): ECS praises, 46

Institute of Heredity, 65n, 67n; and ECS, 66, 72; and M. J. Gage, 66; and SBA, 66

International Association of Artists (Rome), 231

International Council of Women: plans for, xxvi, 299–300n

international suffrage association: proposed, xxvi, 299–300n, 335–36, 339, 349, 349–50n, 520

interracial marriage, 323–26, 353–55, 356–57

interviews: ECS on W. W. Patton's sermon, 402–3; SBA on congressional committees, 34–35; SBA on her travel plans, 222–23; SBA on Neb. campaign, 201; SBA on Senate vote, 546–47; SBA on Wis. tour, 526–27

Iolanthe (Gilbert & Sullivan), 297

Iowa: in *History*, 12–13, 29–30, 31, 103,

429–30, 437–38, 438n; school suffrage in, 104; woman suffrage in, 320, 320n

Iowa Woman Suffrage Association: and National association, 158, 160n

Ireland: SBA visits, 288; women's violence in, xxiii, 539

Irving, Henry, 225, *227n*

Irving, Washington, 354, *356n*

Islam: and women, 79

Italics. Brief Notes on Politics, People, and Places (Cobbe): quoted, 78

Italy: SBA travels in, 228–31; woman question in, 92

Jackson, Francis, 129, *131n*, 179n; and woman's rights funds, 131–32n, 132

Jackson, Howell Edmunds, *133–34n*; and Senate committee, 133–34n

Jackson, James, 130, *132n*

Jackson, James Caleb, 50, *50n*, 104; on women, 105

Jacournassy, 165, 166n, 169, 172

jails: matrons for, 186, 317, 317n

James and Lucretia Mott. Life and Letters (Hallowell), 27–28

Jerrold, Douglas: *Mrs. Caudle's Curtain Lectures*, 83

Jesus Christ, 79, 435; and women, 369

Joan of Arc, 231

Johns, Laura Lucretia Mitchell, *523–24n*; at suffrage meeting, 522–23

Johns Hopkins University, 256

Johnson, Nancy Maria Donaldson, 317, *318n*

Johnson (ECS), 93–94n

Johnstown, N.Y., 494; ECS in, 339, 340–43, 349, 353–54, 361–64, 367, 370, 382, 385, 405–7; ECS moves to, 330, 331n; ECS recalls, 276–77; effects of on ECS, 371, 382; and glovemaking, 351; SBA in, 350–51, 358–59, 361–64, 367, 368, 374–75

Joint Committee on Reconstruction, 210

Joly, Nicolas, 169–70, *170n*

Jones, Mr. (of Germantown, Pa.), 286, 288

Jones, Mrs. (of Germantown, Pa.), 286, 288, 319

Jones, Charles William, *307–8n*; and Senate committee, 305, 362

Jones, Henry, 544

Jones, Jane Grahame, *122n*; and National association, 121

Jones, John Percival, 116, *117n*

Jones, Mary, 544

Jones, Phebe Hoag, *104n*; death of, 102

Jordan, Marsh & Company (Boston), 93

Joy, Jerusha G., *327–28n*; and F. Douglass, 324

Judaism, 391, 392, 393, 398, 433; and male divinity, 79

Julius, 93–94n

Junction City, Kan.: suffragists in, 157
juries: women on, 185–86
Justice, Helen Mary Cobb, 283, *283n*
Justice, Philip Syng, 283, *283n*

Kaley, Timothy, 95, *97n*
Kansas: congressional district meetings in,
    521–23, 535; constitutional convention of,
    32, 32–33n; in *History*, 20–21, 125, 145;
    municipal suffrage in, 492, 493–94n,
    521–22n; municipal suffrage won in, 557;
    prohibition in, 111, 111–12n; SBA in, 521;
    school suffrage in, 111, 248
Kansas, University of, 233
Kansas amendment campaign, 1867, 96–97,
    111, 176, 422
Kansas Equal Suffrage Association, 493–
    94n; meeting of, 531; and National
    association, 521–23; and nonpartisanship,
    522
Kansas State Historical Society, 125
Keartland, Fanny, *228n*; travels with SBA,
    226, 228
Keatinge, Harriette Charlotte Harned
    Veazie, 418, *419–20n*
Keene, N.H., 57; suffragists in, 158
Keifer, Joseph Warren, *122n*; and House
    committee, 121–22, 315, 316, 316n; letter
    from SBA, 121–22; quoted, 124
Kelley, Florence, *139n*; and National
    association, 136
Kellogg, Day Otis, 381, *381–82n*
Kennard, Coleridge John, 388, *390n*
Kent, John H., 371, *373n*
Kentucky: school suffrage in, 248; suffragists
    in, 157
Kimball, Emily O. Richardson, 413–14, *415n*
Kimball, Sarah Melissa Granger, *555–56n*;
    telegram to SBA, 554–55
Kimber, Abby, 246, *260n*
kindergarten: and coeducation, 254
King, Susan Ann: controversies about, 5n
King Lear (Shakespeare): quoted, 449
Kingman, Samuel Austin, *32–33n*; at Kan.
    constitutional convention, 32
Kingsley, Charles, *86n*, 248; quoted, 74
Knights of Labor: and woman suffrage, 550,
    552n
Knox-Little, William John, 252, *264–65n*,
    397
Kossuth, Louis, 472, *472n*

Laboulaye, Edouard René Lefebvre de,
    244n; funeral of, 244
Ladd, Christine, 256, *266n*
Ladies' National Association for Repeal,
    192, 193n
Lafayette, marquis de, 335, *336n*
Lake Geneva, Wis., 506

Langston, John Mercer, 96, *98n*
Lapham, Elbridge Gerry, *133–34n*; and
    amendment, 167, 205, 208, 314n, 381; and
    Senate committee, 133–34n, 305; at
    Senate hearing, 347
law: as woman's occupation, 186
Lawes Resolutions of Womens Rights, 76
Lawrence, Frank Eugene, 13, *14n*
Lawrence, Margaret Livingston Stanton,
    14n; and "As a Mother," 447, 558–61;
    letter from ECS, 463–64; marriage of, 13;
    mentioned, xxvii, 62, 277, 326, 406;
    travels of, 447, 463, 464n
Lawrence, Mass., 57
Lawrence, Samuel B., *527n*; hosts SBA, 526
laws of nature, 455, 456
Lease, Mary Elizabeth Clyens, *523n*; at
    suffrage meeting, 522–23
Leavenworth, Kan.: SBA in, 505–6;
    suffragists in, 157
Letters from a Chimney Corner (Corbin),
    535, 538–39
Leveson-Gower, Granville George (earl
    Granville), 225, *226n*
Liberal party (Great Britain): Conference on
    Parliamentary Reform, 291, 292–93n, 329;
    and woman suffrage, 537
"The Liberals in Religion Afraid of Us"
    (ECS): mentioned, 266n
*Life and Times of Frederick Douglass,
    Written by Himself*, 150, 150n, 152
Life of Louis Adolphe Thiers (LeGoff), 115n
Lily (Seneca Falls, N.Y.): and *History*, 12,
    30, 102, 104
Lincoln, Abraham, 19, *20n*
Lincoln, Neb.: SBA in, 180
Lincoln Center, Kan.: suffragists in, 157
Lincoln Hall (Washington), 35, 35n, 36, 214
Lindsay, Thomas Martin, 197, *198n*
Lippincott, Sara Jane Clarke. *See* Green-
    wood, Grace
Livermore, Mary Ashton Rice, 55, *55n*; in
    London, 105, 106–7n; and *Woman's Bible*,
    515n; and "Woman's Realm," 383
Liverpool, England, 224; ECS and SBA in,
    299, 300, 300n
Lives of the Saints (Butler), 458
Lockwood, Belva Ann Bennett McNall, 96,
    97–98n, 317; and 1884 election, 372,
    374n; and National association, 16n, 122,
    320; SBA hears, 372
Loder, Helen M., *138n*; at suffrage meeting,
    135
Logan, John Alexander, *129n*; and Senate
    committee, 128, 375
Logan, Mary Simmerson Cunningham, 320,
    320n
Loizillon, Marie Célestine, *244n*; visits SBA,
    243

London, England: ECS in, 202–3, 218–19,
224–26, 273, 296–97; ECS speaks in, 245–
60, 272n; SBA arrives in, 224–26; SBA in,
273–76, 279–80, 283–86, 290, 293, 295,
296, 297; SBA speaks in, 245
Long, John Davis, 93, *94n*
Longfellow, Henry Wadsworth, *461n*;
quoted, 452, 457–58, 461
Longfellow, Samuel, 288, *289n*
Longwood, Pa.: SBA speaks in, 420–27
Lord, Mrs. (in Washington, D.C.), 319
Lord, Henrietta Frances, *512n*; and Chicago,
515, 529; and *Woman's Bible*, 512, 512n,
514, 519
Loring, George Bailey: and amendment, 19n
Loughridge, William, 19n
Louisiana: in *History*, 418; suffragists in, 158
"Love" (Emerson), 253
Lowell, Mass., 57
Lozier, Clemence Sophia Harned, *100n*;
and ECS birthday, 444, 445, 447, 451, 459;
and *History*, 99; and N.Y. campaign, 444;
at Senate hearing, 344; and state
association, 495
Lucas, Margaret Bright, *193n*; hosts SBA,
275–76; in Liverpool, 300; and married
women's suffrage, 281n; mentioned, 192,
197, 273, 280, 285, 286, 297, 299; at
suffrage meeting, 299; travels with ECS,
200, 201n
Luise (grand duchess of Baden), 234, *235n*
Luther, Martin, 74, *86n*, 342, 412; quoted, 74

Macaulay, Thomas Babington, *87n*, 88n;
quoted, 77–78, 82–83
McCoid, Moses Ayers, *319n*; and House
committee, 318–19; and Judiciary
Committee, 318
MacConnell, John Gilmore, *501n*; letter to
ECS, 499–501
McCormick, Mrs. (of Manchester, Eng.),
275–76, 276n
McDonald, Joseph Ewing, *43n*; and Senate
committee, 20n, 39, 41, 43n
McDowell, Anne Elizabeth, *472n*; and
National association, 159n; reviews M.
Holley, 471
McGrigor, Alexander Bennett, 197, *198n*
McGrigor, Elizabeth Robertson, 197, *198n*
McKinney, Jane C. Amy, *438n*; and *History*,
437
McLaren, Charles Benjamin Bright, 196,
197, *197n*; hosts SBA, 279–80
McLaren, Duncan, *198–99n*, 200; hosts ECS,
197
McLaren, Eva Maria Müller, 274, *275n*
McLaren, Laura Elizabeth Pochin, *195–96n*,
196, 197; at Glasgow meeting, 195; hosts
SBA, 279–80

McLaren, Priscilla Bright, *192n*; escorts SBA,
274; hosts ECS, 197; and international
plans, 299–300n; letters to ECS, 191–92,
199–200, 282–83; in Liverpool, 300; and
married women's suffrage, 281n;
mentioned, 196, 212, 273, 275, 279–80,
299; political views of, 282–83; at suffrage
meeting, 299
McLaren, Walter Stowe Bright, 274, *275n*
McMartin, Margaret Chinn Cady, 62, *63n*,
461n
McMurdy, Robert, *400n*; and resolutions on
religion, 483–84; at suffrage meetings,
393, 483–84
McPherson, Mary E., *400n*; and resolutions
on religion, 483; at suffrage meetings,
392, 483
Madison, Wis.: SBA in, 531, 534; SBA speaks
in, 533
"Maiden Tribute of the Modern Babylon"
(Stead), 435, *436n*
Manchester National Society for Women's
Suffrage: ECS attends, 201n; ECS invited
to, 294–95; SBA attends, 299
Manderson, Charles Frederick, *552n*; and
Senate vote, 550
Manhattan, Kan.: suffragists in, 157
Manhattan Hotel (Wichita), 522
Manistee, Mich.: suffragists in, 157
Mansfield, earl of. *See* Murray, William
Mariolatry, 369
Mariology, 77–79
marriage: and republican government, 251
married women: and suffrage, 272, 272n,
276, 279, 281, 281n, 282, 283, 284, 285,
388–89
married women's property rights: in Conn.,
517; in England, 227n, 248, 250, 262n,
389; and joint earnings, 345; in N.Y., 250
Martin, Charles, 279, 290
Martin, John Biddulph, 525, *526n*
Martin, Victoria Claflin Woodhull: letter
from ECS, 525–26. *See also* Woodhull,
Victoria Claflin
Martineau, Harriet, 248, *262n*, 403; quoted,
452–53, 459
Mary (mother of Jesus), 77–79
masculine element, 73, 75, 76, 79–81, 90,
195, 252–53, 413
Mason, Hugh, *274–75n*; and married
women's suffrage, 274–75n, 275–76; and
parliamentary franchise, 274
Massachusetts: in *History*, 7–8, 58, 118, 351;
municipal suffrage in, 349; school suffrage
in, 248
*Massachusetts in the Woman Suffrage
Movement* (Robinson), 8, 58, 118, 205
Massachusetts Reformatory Prison for
Women, 93

Massachusetts Woman Suffrage Association, 159n; celebration in Worcester, 6

Mather, Cotton, 74, *86n*

May, Abigail Williams, *206n*; and National association, 204

May, Samuel Joseph, *13n*; and temperance work, 12

Mazzini, Giuseppe, *461n*; quoted, 454

Meditations among the Tombs (Hervey), 458

Meionaon Hall (Boston), 7, 56

Mellen, Ellen Seymour Clarke, *273n*, 296; entertains ECS and SBA, 273

Mellen, Helen S., 297, *297n*

menopause: and ECS, 463–64; and L. C. Bullard, 463

Merchant of Venice (Shakespeare): characters in, 4

Meriwether, Elizabeth Avery, *59n*; and National association, 158; and New England tour, 57; and resolutions on religion, 481; and states' rights, 477–79; at suffrage meetings, 89, 477–79, 481

Merrick, Caroline Elizabeth Thomas, *418–19n*; and *History*, 418; letter from SBA, 417–18

Merrick, Edwin Thomas, 418, *418–19n*

Merrick, Edwin Thomas, Jr., 418, *418–19n*

Merrick, Richard Thomas, *373–74n*; and 1884 election, 372, 374n

Methodist church: and women, 393, 394, 414; women as teachers in, 392, 399–400n

Mexican Americans: and Colo. campaign, 423

Michel, Louise, 406, *408n*

Michigan: disaster relief for, 112, 113n; school suffrage in, 248

Michigan, University of, 256

Michigan amendment campaign, 1874, 96–97, 176, 422–23; votes cast, 346

Michigan Equal Suffrage Association, 531; plans for, 307, 308n, 313

military service: for women, 186–87

Mill, Harriet Hardy Taylor, *261n*; "Enfranchisement of Women," 248, 417

Mill, John Stuart, 74, *86n*, 454; and married women's suffrage, 310; quoted, 389; and woman suffrage, 248, 261n

Miller, Anne Fitzhugh, *465n*; and ECS birthday, 464

Miller, Charles Dudley, 93, *94n*

Miller, Elizabeth Smith, *93–94n*, 452; and ECS birthday, 464; ECS visits, 309–11; letters from ECS, 93, 218–19; letter to ECS, 513; and *Woman's Bible*, 513

Miller, Mary Millicent Garretson, *355–56n*; and pilot's license, 353, 355, 355–56n

Miller, Warner, *382n*; and amendment, 381, 546

Mills, Mr. (in Paris), 236, 237, 238

Mills, Mrs. (in Paris), 236, 237

Mills, Ella, 236, 237, 238

Mind Cure, 529, 529n

ministry: women enter, 252

Minnesota: school suffrage in, 248

Minnesota Woman Suffrage Association: and National association, 157

Minor, Francis, 319, *319n*, 361, 365n

Minor, Virginia Louisa Minor, *160n*, 319; and resolutions on religion, 481; and St. Louis association, 158; at suffrage meeting, 476, 477, 481

Minor v. Happersett, 18

Mitchell, Mrs. (of Clifton, Eng.), 298

Mitchell, John Hipple, *552n*; and Senate vote, 550

Mitchell, John Inscho, *552n*; and Senate vote, 550

Mitchell, Maria, 255–56, *266n*, 450

Moltke, Helmuth Karl Bernhard von, 234, *235n*

monopolies: of men over women, xxii, 188

Moody, Dwight Lyman, 385, *386n*

Moody, Loring, 66, *67n*

Moore, Rebecca Fisher, *285n*; travels with SBA, 284, 286; in U.S., 371, 372n

Moral Education Association of Massachusetts, 72

"Moral Influence vs. Political Power" (SBA), 533

moral standards: inequality of, 184–85

Morgan, John Shepard, 112, *113n*

Morgan, John Tyler, *141n*; and Senate committee, 140; and Utah suffrage, 141, 141–142n

"Morituri Salutamus" (Longfellow): quoted, 452, 457–58, 461

Mormons: and polygamy, 396

Mosher, Arthur Anthony, 286, *288–89n*

Mosher, Frank Merritt, 286, *288–89n*

Mosher, Hannah Lapham Anthony, 286, *288–89n*

Mosher, Helen Louise, *110n*, 319; in Kan., 107; letter from SBA, 286–88

Mosher, Wendell Phillips, 286, 288, *288–89n*

Moss, Mrs. (of Hyde, Eng.), 275–76, 276n

mothers: influence of, 114

Mott, James, 36–37, *38n*

Mott, Jane, *298n*, 299; death of, 298

Mott, Lucretia Coffin, *17n*; death of, 16–17, 17n; ECS remembers, 16–17, 27–28; in Eng., 24–25, 27–28; in *History*, 23, 27–28, 46; memorial service for, 35, 36–38, 41–42, 46; mentioned, 21, 50, 99, 249, 287, 303, 304, 376, 403, 491; plans Seneca Falls convention, 247; SBA remembers, 24–25; at World's Anti-Slavery Convention, 246, 247

Mott, Lydia, 298, *298n*
Moulton, Samuel Wheeler, *315n*; and House
  committee, 318–19, 362; and Judiciary
  Committee, 318; and woman suffrage, 312
Mr. Isaacs. A Tale of Modern India
  (Crawford): ECS recommends, 330
Mrs. Caudle's Curtain Lectures (Jerrold), 83
Much Ado about Nothing (Shakespeare): SBA
  sees, 225
Mugwumps: in 1884 election, 363, 385
Muhammad, 435, *436n*
Müller, Frances Henrietta, *278n*, 469; ECS
  visits, 277, 291; escorts SBA, 293; SBA
  visits, 279, 290, 296, 297; single life of,
  277, 279, 284
municipal suffrage, 205, 550; defeated in
  Mass., 349; defeated in N.Y., 495,
  495–96n; in Eng., 193n, 248, 262n, 277,
  341; in Kan., 492, 493–94n, 521–22n, 557;
  in N.Y., 493n, 504–5; in power of
  legislatures, 425; in Scotland, 193n, 194,
  248; uses of, 424–26
Munro, Sarah Keene Healey Dall, 537, *537n*
Murray, William (earl of Mansfield), 502,
  503n
Murray Hill Hotel (New York), 405
music, 454

Napoléon I (emperor of France), 77, *87n*
Nason, Mary C. Snow, 116, *117n*; and M.
  Holley, 471
Nason, William, 316, *316n*
National Citizen and Ballot Box (Syracuse),
  4n, 5n, 5nn, 24, 27, 53, 60, 135, 136, 139n;
  and 1880 election, 3–4n; and *History*, 21
nationalization of land: H. Taylor on, 296;
  M. Davitt on, 293
The "National" Method (Shattuck), 479, *479*
National Prohibition Alliance, 143, 144n
"National Protection for National Citizens"
  (ECS): quoted, xx
National Society for Women's Suffrage, 222,
  223n, 310; demonstrations of, 272, 272n,
  273; and married women's suffrage, 272,
  281, 284, 285; meetings of Central
  Committee, 275, 284, 285; office of, 273,
  274, 275, 284; and parliamentary
  franchise, 275; welcomes ECS and SBA, 245
National Woman Suffrage Association: and
  14th Amendment, 18; and 15th Amendment, 18; and 1884 election, 341, 361–64,
  364n; affiliates of, 156–58, 313; and
  amendment, xx, 18–19; basis of
  representation in, 143, 476–77, 487n;
  committees of, 121–22, 122n, 136, 143, 151,
  485–86; and domestic science, 485–86;
  executive committee of, 53–54, 54n, 54–
  55, 485–86; executive sessions of, 134–37,
  142–43, 476–85; incorporation of, 486;

leaders for, xxiii–xxiv; lecture bureau of,
  485, 531; to meet in New Orleans, 383,
  384n; meets in Philadelphia, 142–43, 145,
  147; and membership of men, 143, 144–
  45n; memorial service for L. C. Mott,
  36–38; memorials to Congress, 153n; and
  national citizenship, 53, 55, 69; and Neb.
  campaign, 163, 180, 182–83n; New
  England tour of, 53, 54, 57, 89–93, 95–97;
  and newspaper for, 135, 306–7, 313–14,
  379–80; petitions Congress, 18–19; and
  political parties, 306; and Prohibition
  party, 306; reporting of meetings, 135,
  333, 334n, 479; and state campaigns,
  202n; and temperance movement, 305–6;
  and Third Decade Celebration, 287; and
  tour of Kan., 521–23, 535; and working
  women, 485–86, 549
National Woman Suffrage Association of
  Massachusetts, xxiii, 479; founding of,
  158–59n; and L. Stone, 158–59n; meeting
  of, 204–5; and National association, 157;
  and suffrage factions, 204–5
National Woman Suffrage Association of St.
  Louis: and National association, 158
National Woman Suffrage Association's
  annual meetings: of 1881, 68–70; actions in
  1881, 69–70; ECS describes, 93; letter from
  ECS, 173–75; plans for 1881, xxiv, 7, 53–54,
  54–55, 56–58, 64–65, 66–67; plans for
  1882, 136, 151, 175; postponed in 1882, 136
National Woman Suffrage Association's
  Washington conventions, 42–43n; of
  1881, 36–38; of 1882, 134–37, 140–41; of
  1885, 391–99; of 1886, 476–86; of 1887,
  548–51, 553–54; actions in 1881, 43n;
  actions in 1882, 140–41; actions in 1886,
  477, 479, 483–85, 485–86; actions in
  1887, 548–51; debate resolutions on
  religion, 391–98, 402–3, 479–84; ECS
  attends, 36–38, 134–35, 391–99; ECS
  describes, 39–42; ECS misses, 339–40,
  473–75; ECS speaks to, 391–92, 395–97,
  398–99; foreign letters to, 328–29,
  331–33, 335–39; letters from ECS, 340–43,
  473–75, 537–39; plans for 1881, 7, 15;
  plans for 1882, 118–19, 120; plans for
  1883, 205, 210, 213–14; plans for 1884,
  305, 307, 320, 324, 333–34; plans for
  1885, 382, 390; plans for 1886, 471–72;
  plans for 1887, 534, 535; SBA attends, 36–
  38, 134–37, 391–99, 476–86; SBA speaks
  to, 553–54; telegram to Kan. senate, 557
National Women's Rights Convention, First
  (1850): commemorated, 6, 9n
Neall, Elizabeth Johns. *See* Gay, Elizabeth
  Johns Neall
Nebraska: in *History*, 101, 105; school
  suffrage in, 248

Nebraska amendment campaign, 61n, 69, 161, 163, 422; ECS encourages, 173–75; and National association, 136, 139n, 141, 142, 180, 182–83n; plans for, 59–60, 176–77, 177n; SBA describes, 201; SBA joins, 176–77, 180, 180–81n, 183–89; suffrage factions in, 181, 182–83n; votes cast, 201, 202n, 208

Nebraska Woman Suffrage Association, 61n; meeting of, 104; and National association, 105–6, 157

"The Need of Liberal Divorce Laws" (ECS): mentioned, 370n

Nekrasov, Nikolay Alekseyevich, 88n; quoted, 83

Nelson, Horatio (viscount), 27, 29n

Nelson, Julia Bullard, 489–90n; and resolutions on religion, 483; at suffrage meeting, 483

Nevada: suffragists in, 158

Newbury Woman Suffrage Political Club (South Newbury, Ohio): and National association, 157

New Century Club (Philadelphia), 222

New England Woman Suffrage Association: annual meeting of, 7

New England Women's Club, 204, 206

New Era (Chicago), 441–42n, 521; and ECS birthday, 440, 441–42n, 446–47, 449, 558

New Hampshire: school suffrage in, 248

New Haven, Conn., 57

New Jersey: and woman suffrage, 517

New Northwest (Portland, Ore.), 314, 422, 441

New Orleans: Bienville School, 408; Girls' Central High School, 408; McDonogh School, 408; National association to meet in, 383, 384n; SBA in, 408–9; Tulane Hall, 408; Webster School, 408; World's Industrial and Cotton Centennial Exposition in, 384n. See also Woman's Club of New Orleans

Newport, R.I., 414

newspapers, women's: need for, 306–7, 313–14, 441, 441–42

Newton, Richard Heber, 394, 400–401n

New York (city): ECS in, 164–65, 330, 354–55; SBA in, 166–67

New York (state): capital punishment in, 549; constitutional convention plans, 495, 496n; divorce in, 251; in History, 101, 102; municipal suffrage defeated, 537, 550; property laws in, 250, 263; school suffrage in, 248; women voting in, 549

New York Assembly: defeats Andrews bill, 208–9n

New York Constitutional Convention (1867), 70n, 186, 421

New York legislative campaign: in 1880, 208–9n; in 1881, 208–9n; in 1882, 208–9n; in 1883, 217, 217–18n; in 1885, 407n, 428n, 467n; in 1886, 493n, 495; Andrews bill, 207, 208–9n; and attempts to vote, 431, 431–32n, 438–39, 444, 444–45n, 549, 551n; divisions in, 465–66, 467n; ECS joins, 405, 407n; for constitutional amendment, 217–18n; for municipal suffrage, 492, 493n, 495, 495–96n, 504–5; SBA describes, 424–25

New York Observer: criticizes ECS, 416, 417n

New York State Freethinkers Association: and ECS, 442, 443n

New York State Temperance Society: bars women, 12, 13n

New York State Woman Suffrage Association: and Andrews bill, 208–9n; ECS joins campaign of, 405–6, 407n; ECS speaks to, 414; meetings of, 146, 495; and National association, 157; reception for ECS, 405–6, 407n; and state amendment, 217–18n; and Woman Suffrage party, 208–9n, 465–66, 467n

New York Sun: endorses B. F. Butler, 371n; and H. B. Stanton, 370; letter from ECS, 122–24

New York Times: quoted, xxii

New York Tribune: and ECS's name, 463

New York World, 185

Neymann, Clara Low, 486n, 528; and resolutions on religion, 482; at suffrage meeting, 476, 477, 478, 482, 483

Nichol, Elizabeth Pease, 203n, 247, 287, 371; letters from ECS, 202–3, 212; SBA visits, 286

Nichols, Clarina Irene Howard, 11n; death of, 432; and History, 8, 13, 20–21, 23, 32, 125; at Kan. constitutional convention, 32, 32–33n; letters from SBA, 33–34, 174; letter to SBA, 32

Nichols, George Bainbridge, 127, 127n

Nichols, Helen Clarina, 432, 433n

Nicholson, Eliza Jane Poitevent Holbrook, 418, 420n

nihilists, 81, 82, 104–5

Nolan, Michael Nicholas, 365n; and House committee, 362

nonpartisanship, 523; of suffrage societies, 306

Normandy Hotel (Paris), 236, 241

Norris, Juliet G., 464, 464n

Norris, William, 464, 464n

North American Review, 433, 434, 443, 474, 480; ECS writes for, 360n, 369, 369n, 370n

Northern Pacific Railroad, 251

Norton, Caroline Elizabeth Sarah Sheridan, 83, 89n

O'Brien, George, 288

O'Brien, Mary, 288
occupations: opened to women, 248
O'Connell, Daniel, *260–61n*; at World's
   Anti-Slavery Convention, 246
O'Connor, Ellen M. Tarr, *137–38n*; and F.
   Douglass, 324; at suffrage meeting, 135
O'Connor, Jean, 341–42, *344n*
Oeuvre des libéreés de Saint-Lazare: SBA
   visits, 244
Ohio Woman Suffrage Association: SBA
   attends, 417
Omaha, Neb.: SBA speaks in, xxii, 176–77,
   183–89
"On the Position of Woman in America"
   (ECS), 245–60
Opie, Amelia Alderson, 247, *261n*
Oregon: school suffrage in, 248; suffrage
   campaign in, 69, 70–71n, 136, 141, 142,
   176–77, 308–9n, 314, 332, 345, 346;
   suffrage defeated in, 422, 425, 428n
Oregon State Woman Suffrage Association:
   and National association, 158
original sin, 76
Orthodox church, 433–34
Osborne, Eliza Wright, 359, *359n*
Oshkosh, Wis.: SBA in, 526–27
Oshkosh *Daily Northwestern*: interviews
   SBA, 526–27
Ouida. *See* Ramée, Marie Louise de la.
"Our Boys on Sunday" (ECS): mentioned,
   499, *499–501*
Our Famous Women, 558; ECS in, 240n; SBA
   in, 239, 240n
Our Herald (Lafayette, Ind.), 136, 205, 306,
   313, 379, *441–42n*
Owen, Mary Jane Robinson, *34n*, 46
Owen, Robert Dale, 33, *34n*, 46
Owen, Rosamund Dale, *34n*; and *History*,
   33, 46

Painter, Hettie Kersey, 180, *181n*
Pall Mall Gazette (London), 435, *436n*
Palmer, Roundell (earl of Selborne), 225,
   226n
Palmer, Thomas Witherell, *307–8n*; and
   amendment, 381, 427, 429n; letters from
   SBA, 374–75, 378–79; and Senate
   committee, 305, 466, 467; at Senate
   hearing, 346; and Senate report, 490; and
   Senate vote, 550
Pan-Presbyterian Council of 1880, 397
Papyrus Club (Boston), 83
Paris, France: SBA in, 236–44
Paris Commune, 244
Parker, Harvey D., 64, *65n*
Parker, Jane Marsh, 351, *352n*; *Rochester. A
   Story Historical*, 351
Parker, Margaret Eleanor Walker, *298n*; and
   international plans, 299–300n; letter to

SBA, 338–39; in Liverpool, 300; SBA visits,
   298–99
Parker, Mary, 298, *298n*; in Liverpool, 300
Parker, Theodore, *88n*, 248, 435; quoted,
   78
Parker House (Boston), 58, 64, 410
Parker Memorial Hall (Boston), 72
Parliament. *See* House of Commons, House
   of Lords
parliamentary franchise: debated in
   Parliament, 274, 275–76; and married
   women, 227n, 272, 272n, 274–75n,
   275–76, 279, 281, 281n, 282, 283, 284,
   285, 309–10, 388–89; petitions for, 225;
   women's need for, 259. *See also* Reform
   Act of 1884
Parnell, Charles Stewart, 466, *468n*
Parsons, Cornelius R., 112, *113n*
Patton, Francis Landey, 42, *45n*
Patton, William Weston, *45n*; antisuffragism
   of, 402–3; ECS and SBA hear, 402–3; and
   National association, 42
Paul (the apostle), 73, 310, 369, 413–14
Payne, Sereno Elisha, *365n*; and House
   committee, 362
The Peak in Darien (Cobbe): ECS recom-
   mends, 219
Pease, Elizabeth. *See* Nichol, Elizabeth
   Pease
Pell, Mary Rodman Howland, *490n*; and
   resolutions on religion, 484; at suffrage
   meeting, 484
Penketh, England: SBA in, 298
Pennsylvania: in *History*, 28, 358–59;
   organizing in, 383–84, 544; school
   suffrage in, 223, 223–24n; suffrage factions
   in, 544
Pennsylvania Hall (Philadelphia), 46
Pennsylvania Woman Suffrage Association:
   in *History*, 358, 359n; and "Woman's
   Realm," 383
Pennsylvania Yearly Meeting of Progressive
   Friends: SBA speaks to, 420–27
Pépin III (king of the Franks), 77, *87n*
Perkins, Sarah Maria Clinton, *401n*; and
   resolutions on religion, 480–81; at
   suffrage meetings, 397, 477–78, 479,
   480–81
Perry, N.Y.: SBA to speak in, 112
petitions to Congress, 140, 363; for
   constitutional amendment, 134, 427; for
   relief from political disabilities, 134, 137n;
   for woman suffrage in Dakota, 142
Peyton, Jesse Enlows, 516, *518n*
Phelps, Elizabeth B., 371, *373n*
Philadelphia: ECS in, 142–43; Girls Normal
   School of, 222; National association meets
   in, 142–43, 145, 147; SBA in, 142–43,
   302–4; SBA sails from, 222–23

Philadelphia *Call*, 321
Philadelphia *Evening News*: interviews SBA, 222–23
philanthropy: of women, 147
Phillips, Ann Terry Greene, 246, *260n*, 343
Phillips, Ellen, 297; boarding house of, 203n; in Liverpool, 300
Phillips, Wendell, *9n*, 248; death of, 330, 331n; ECS's tribute to, 342–43; and Eddy will, 129–31, 132–33, 163, 178–79; funeral of, 334–35n; letter from SBA, 132–33; letters to SBA, 129–31, 178–79; mentioned, 6, 25, 302, 303, 368; quoted, 18; "Scholar in a Republic," 280, 342–43; as speaker, 541; *Speech . . . Oct., 1851*, 417; at World's Anti-Slavery Convention, 246
Phipps, Henry, Jr., 499–500, *501n*
Pittsburgh, Pa.: suffragists in, 157
Pittsburgh Commercial Gazette, 383–84
Platt, Orville Hitchcock, *375n*; and Senate committee, 375; and Senate vote, 550
"The Pleasures of Age" (ECS), 451–61; mentioned, 445, 447, 463
Plumb, Preston Bierce, *545–46n*; and Senate vote, 545, 546
Poland, Luke Potter, *319n*; and House committee, 318–19, 322; and Judiciary Committee, 318; letter to SBA, 322; and woman suffrage, 322
political parties: women's loyalty to, 345–46
"The Politics of Reformers" (ECS), 1–3
polygamy, 396, 491, 519; attacks on, 141, 485, 490n; in Bible, 369, 370n; and National association, 485
Pomeroy, Samuel Clarke, 36
Porter, Albert Gallatin, 40–41, *44–45n*
Porter, Cornelia Stone, 41, *44–45n*
Portland Hall (London), 296
positivists, 80, 88n; ECS meets in London, 219
Post, Amy Kirby, 171–72, *172n*, 302
Post, Issac, 302, *304n*
Potter, Henry Codman, 393, *400n*
poverty: and Christianity, 434
Pratt, Charles R., 495, *495–96n*
Pratt, Romania Bunnell, *555–56n*; telegram to SBA, 554–55
pregnancy: of H. S. Blatch, 215; of M. B. Stanton, 114
Presbyterian church: and women preaching, 467, 468n
presidential suffrage, 207, 209n
Priestman, Anna Maria, *216n*; letters from ECS, 215–16, 291–92; SBA visits, 297–98
Priestman, Mary, 215, *216n*; letter from ECS, 291–92; SBA visits, 297–98
Prince, Frederick Octavius, 93, *94n*
Prince's Hall (London), 245
"The Princess" (Tennyson), 248, 460

Princess Napraxine (Ouida), 360
Princeton Review, 372, 373n
Princeton University, 147
The Progress of Religious Ideas (Child), 518
prohibition: and Republican party, 205; and woman suffrage, 493n
Prohibition party: in 1884 election, 362–63, 366n; and woman suffrage, 306, 362–63, 366n
prostitution: control of, 238, 239n; in London, 435; in Sioux City, 185
Protestant churches, 413
Providence, R.I., 57; ECS speaks in, xxi–xxii, 89–93; SBA in, 89; SBA speaks in, 376–79; suffrage meeting in, 89–93
Providence Free Religious Society (Rhode Island): SBA speaks to, 17n
Pugh, Sarah, *98n*, 246, 260n, 287; death of, 376; and *History*, 98; letter to ECS, 98
Purvis, Charles Burleigh, *38n*; at Mott memorial, 37–38
Purvis, Robert, 28, *29n*, 38n, 222, 383; at antislavery anniversary, 302, 304; ECS visits, 46; remarriage of, 324; at suffrage meeting, 39
Purvis, Tacy Townsend, *29n*; and *History*, 28
Putnam, George Haven, 371, *373n*

Radical Club (Philadelphia): in *History*, 358–59, 359n
Ramée, Marie Louise de la, 360, *360n*
Ransom, Chandler R., *131n*; and Eddy will, 129–30, 132–33, 178–79, 334, 348, 390, 410
Ransom, Matt Whitaker, *365n*; and Senate Committee, 362
Raphael, 77, *87n*
Rational Dress Society (London): ECS attends, 215
Rayner, Kenneth, *356n*; and M. Miller, 355
Read, Daniel, 108, *110n*
reading, 454, 458
Reagan, John Henninger, *316n*; and amendment, 316n; and House committee, 316
Reconstruction: in *History*, 147, 150, 152
Reed, Samuel Rockwell, 4, *5n*
Reed, Thomas Brackett, *155n*; and amendment, 490–91, 491–92n; and House committee, 318–19, 467; and Judiciary Committee, 318, 427, 429n; letter to SBA, 155
Reform Act of 1884, xxi, 292–93n, 339, 339n, 388–89, 389–90n, 537
Reid, Elizabeth Jesser, *261n*
Reid, Mrs. Hugo. *See* Reid, Marion Kirkland
Reid, Marion Kirkland, 247, *261n*
religion: and preparation for death, 458–59;

and social classes, 434–35; and women, 2–3, 188, 257–59, 412–13, 435–36
"Religion for Women and Children" (ECS): mentioned, 494
religion of humanity: and A. Comte, 87n; and Free Religious Association, 77
republican government: imperfect, 434–35; and marriage, 251; and religion, 81; and secularism, 398–99
Republican party: in 1882 election, 205; in 1884 election, 363–64; in Congress, xxi; convention of 1884, 357; ECS and SBA support, 361–64; and federal amendment, 361; in Iowa, 176–77, 178n; in Kan., 176–77, 178n, 201, 202n; in Neb., 178n; and prohibition, 205; and woman suffrage, 375. *See also* Mugwumps
Revels, Hiram Rhoades, 96, 98n
Rhode Island: in *History*, 148; restricted suffrage in, 210, 211n; and woman suffrage, 550, 552n
Rhode Island Woman Suffrage Association, 372; and National association, 157; SBA speaks to, 17n, 376–78; and suffrage factions, xxiv
Rhodes, Georgine M., 220, 221n
Richards, Emily Sophia Tanner, 555–56n; telegram to SBA, 554–55
Richards, Jane Snyder, 555–56n; telegram to SBA, 554–55
Richardson, Abby Sage McFarland, 447, 448n
Richer, Léon, 240–41n; letter to SBA, 337, 338n; SBA visits, 240
Ricker, Marilla Marks Young, 487n; at suffrage meeting, 476, 479
Riggs House (Washington), xxvi, 15n, 41–42, 134, 135, 391, 466, 476
Ripon, Wis.: SBA in, 524–25
Ristori, Adelaide, 232n; SBA hears, 231
Ritchie, John, 125, 126n, 127
Robinson, Charles, 21, 22n
Robinson, Charles Edward, 112, 113n
Robinson, Elizabeth Johnson Devereux Umsted. *See* Umsted, Elizabeth Johnson Devereux
Robinson, Elizabeth Osborne, 206, 207n
Robinson, Harriet Jane Hanson, 8–9n, 55; and *History*, xxv, 8, 58, 118, 351; letters from ECS, 118–19, 512, 519–20; letters from SBA, 6–8, 56–58, 66–67, 156–58, 204–6, 350–51, 408–9, 410; letter to SBA, 64–65; and L. Stone, 156, 158, 158–59nn; *Massachusetts in the Woman Suffrage Movement*, 8, 58, 118, 205; and National association, 6–8, 56–58, 64–65, 66–67; at suffrage meetings, 68, 70, 135, 136, 142–43, 477; and *Woman's Bible*, 512, 519–20

Robinson, Lucius: gubernatorial campaign of, 5n
Roby, Ida Hall, 531, 532n
Rochester, N.Y.: Red Cross in, 115
Rochester. A Story Historical (Parker), 351
Rockland, Me.: suffragists in, 158
Rogers, Caroline Gilkey, 138n; at Senate hearing, 344; at suffrage meetings, 135, 142
Roland, Jeanne Marie Philipon, 402, 403n
Roman Catholic church, 433; and Mariology, 77–79; and women, 392, 393
Rome, Italy: SBA describes, 228, 230–31
Root, Frances Eveline Alden, 21, 22n
Root, Joseph Pomeroy, 21, 22n
Rose, Ernestine Louise Siismondi Potowski, 21, 24n, 282; in *History*, 23; SBA visits, 280, 283, 293, 296, 297
Rose, William Ela, 283, 283n
Rosewater, Edward, 189n; debates SBA, 183–89; at suffrage meeting, 183
Routt, John Long, 423, 428n
Russell, Elizabeth, 317, 317n
Russia: and religion, 81

Sabin, Dwight May, 547n; and Senate vote, 546
St. Augustine's Church (Washington), 36, 38n
St. James Hall (London), 272n, 273, 293
St. John, John Pierce, 111n; and 1884 election, 362; letter to SBA, 110–11; suffrage views of, 110–11
The Saints Everlasting Rest (Baxter), 458
Salvation Army, 219, 385
Sancho Panza, 114
San Mateo County v. Southern Pacific R.R., 210, 211n
Sargent, Aaron Augustus, 26n; and *History*, 25; hosts SBA, 233–34
Sargent, Elizabeth, 25, 26n
Sargent, Ellen Clark (1826–1911), 26n, 461n; and *History*, 25; hosts SBA, 230, 233–34
Sargent, Ellen Clark (1854–1908), 25n; hosts SBA, 233–34; letter from SBA, 24–25
Sargent, George Clark, 25, 26n
Savage, Minot Judson, 536, 537n
Savile, Sylvia, 310, 311n
Savoy Theatre (London), 290
Sawyer, Philetus, 527, 528n
Saxon, Elizabeth Lyle, 144n; and *History*, 418; in Kan., 521, 522; and National association, 158; at suffrage meetings, 89, 142
Scatcherd, Alice Cliff, 274n, 299; in Liverpool, 300; SBA hears, 273
Schenck, Elizabeth T., 341, 343–44n
Schmucker, Martha, 125, 126n
"The Scholar in a Republic" (Phillips), 280, 342–43; quoted, 343

school suffrage, 248, 262n; in Eng., 277, 279, 282; limited value of, 425; in Pa., 223; in Wis., 526–27, 527n
science: and religion, 81–82
Scoble, John, 27, 28n
Scotland: municipal suffrage in, 193n, 194. *See also* Edinburgh, Glasgow
Scott, Thomas, 260, 267n
Scott, Sir Walter, 84, 89n, 194, 195n
Scottish National Demonstration, 191, 193n, 200; ECS describes, 196–97; ECS speaks to, 194–95
"A Secular View of Moral Training" (Adler): SBA reads, 241
See, Isaac McBride, 468n; in *History*, 467
Selborne, earl of. *See* Palmer, Roundell
Selden, Henry Rogers, 361, 364–65n
"Self-Government the Best Means of Self-Development" (ECS): mentioned, 339, 340n
Seneca Falls convention, 1848, 105, 247; response to, 247–48
Seney, George Ebbert, 319n; and House committee, 318–19; and Judiciary Committee, 318
Sewall, May Eliza Wright Thompson, 44n; and amendment, 161; and ECS birthday, 440; and *History*, 161; and Ind. campaign, 136; and *Indianapolis Times*, 307; mentioned, 42, 151, 167, 241, 285, 515; and National association, xxiv, 48, 205, 320, 441, 535, 544; in New Orleans, 408, 409n; at Senate hearing, 344; at suffrage meetings, 40–41, 134–37, 142, 476, 477, 482, 483
Seward, William Henry, 248–49, 262n
Shakespeare, William, 84, 89n; *King Lear*, 449; *Merchant of Venice*, 4; *Much Ado about Nothing*, 225; *Taming of the Shrew*, 83
Sharpstein, Mrs. (in Paris), 236, 241
Shattuck, Harriette Lucy Robinson, 9n; and *History*, 118, 149; letter from ECS, 149; mentioned, 6, 58, 64, 205, 206; and National association, xxiii, 57, 66, 118–19, 544; rebuts ECS, 433; and resolutions on religion, 394–95, 481, 482–83; at Senate hearing, 344; at suffrage meetings, 135, 142–43, 394–95, 476, 477, 478, 479, 481, 482–83; and *The "National" Method*, 479; and *Woman's Bible*, 512, 519–20, 520n
Shattuck, Sidney Doane, 206, 207n
Shaw, Mme. (of Sioux City), 185
Sheffield, William Paine, 375n; and Senate Committee, 375
Sheldon, Ellen Harriet, 138n; hears House debate, 316; minutes by, 134–37; and National association, 16n, 217; at suffrage meetings, 134–37, 476

Sherman, Caroline A., 486–87n; at suffrage meeting, 476
Sherman, John, 552n; and Senate vote, 550
Sherman, William Tecumseh, 187, 191n
Siddons, Sarah Kemble, 83, 89n
Sime, George W., 495, 495–96n
Simonides of Ceos, 457, 462n
Simpson, Matthew, 358, 359n, 376
Sioux City, Iowa: and prostitution, 185
sleep: importance of, 114
Smith, Miss (of Hyde, Eng.), 275–76, 276n
Smith, Abby Hadassah, 520, 520n
Smith, Alys, 287, 289n
Smith, Elizabeth Oakes Prince, 7, 11n
Smith, Gerrit, 309, 311n; and Bible, 513; as speaker, 541
Smith, Hannah Whitall, 149n, 287–88; and National association, 148, 149; at suffrage meeting, 553; and *Woman's Bible*, 515
Smith, Joseph, 491, 492n
Smith, Julia Evalina, 520, 520n
Smith, Lewia C. Hannibal, 439, 439n
Smith, Mary, 287, 289n
Smith, Robert Pearsall, 149n; and National association, 148; and Neb. campaign, 149n
Smith, William Robertson, 197, 198n
Smith College, 256
Snow, Eliza Roxey, 555n; telegram to SBA, 554–55
Snow, Sophronia C., 116, 117n, 466, 471; and National association, 121; and resolutions on religion, 482; at suffrage meeting, 482
social science: and woman question, 92
Socrates, 342, 344n, 414
Solitude (Zimmermann), 458
solitude of self, 85
Somerville Club (London), 275
Sophocles, 457, 462n
Sorèze, France: ECS in, 169–72
South Carolina: divorce in, 251, 264n
South Place Chapel (London): ECS to preach in, 277
Southworth, Louisa Stark, 487–88n; at suffrage meeting, 477, 478
Spalding, John Lancaster, 370n, 417n, 480; rebuts ECS, 416, 417n
speeches: ECS, "On the Position of Woman in America," 245–60; ECS to Free Religious Association, 72–85; ECS to meeting in Providence, 89–93; ECS to Mott memorial, 36–37; ECS to National Woman Suffrage Association, 391–92, 395–97, 398–99; ECS to Scottish National Demonstration, 194–95; "Moral Influence vs. Political Power" (SBA), 533; "The Pleasures of Age" (ECS), 451–61; SBA debates E. Rosewater, 183–89; SBA in

Concord, N.H., 95–97; SBA to American Anti-Slavery Society, 302–4; SBA to Mott memorial, 37; SBA to National Woman Suffrage Association, 490–91; SBA to Progressive Friends, 420–27; SBA to Rhode Island Woman Suffrage Association, 376–78; SBA to Senate Suffrage Committee, 344–48

Speech of Wendell Phillips, Oct., 1851, 417

Spencer, Anna Carpenter Garlin, 55, *55n*

Spencer, Herbert, 369, *370n*, 454, 481; quoted, 455

Spofford, Caleb Wheeler, xxvi, 42, *45n*

Spofford, Jane H. Snow, xxvi, *15n*; and F. Douglass, 324; hears House debate, 316; hears W. W. Patton, 402; letters from SBA, 15, 534; mentioned, 38, 41, 116, 241, 315, 317, 319, 320, 418, 466; and M. Holley, 471; and National association, 534; at suffrage meetings, 135, 136, 476, 477, 486

Sprague, Rosetta Douglass, 147, *147–48n*

"Stand by the Republican Party" (ECS and SBA), 361–64

Stanford, Leland, *547n*; and Senate vote, 546

Stanley, Arthur Penrhyn, 397, *401n*

Stansfeld, James, 238, *239n*

Stanton, Daniel Cady, *xxvii*, 165, 559; in Johnstown, 370, 406–7; marriage of, 407n

Stanton, Elizabeth Cady: on aging, 406; attempts to vote, 14; birthday of, 440, 441–42n, 444, 445, 446–48, 450–51, 451–61, 463–64; complains about meetings, 15; on death, 170–71; grand-children of, 164–65, 168, 295; health of, 17, 66, 118, 212, 215, 330, 339–40, 340n, 442, 443n, 463–64, 475n; leaves for Europe, 166n, 524; letters from SBA, 323–26, 371–72, 381; letters to SBA, 169–70, 281, 339–40, 382, 501–2, 537–39; on marriage, 63–64; medical advice of, 52, 296, 460; pictures of, 321; religious initiative of, 391–98, 411–13, 433–36, 442, 473–75, 479–80, 496–99, 504–5, 510–11, 520; returns to Tenafly house, 416; wedding of, 168; weight of, 359

Stanton, Elizabeth Cady, Jr., *166n*, 405, 406; letters from ECS, 164–65, 168

Stanton, Florence Lanyon, 407n

Stanton, Frederika F. Anthony, xxvii, 407n

Stanton, Gerrit Smith, *xxvii*, 559

Stanton, Harriot Eaton, 62; ECS describes, 46; and *History*, 118, 162, 162n; letters from ECS, 52, 196–97, 201n; marriage of, 200, 200n, 202; travels of, 52. *See also* Blatch, Harriot Eaton Stanton

Stanton, Henry Brewster, *xxvii*, 62, 558–59; and B. F. Butler, 370; death of, 541–43,

543n, 550–51; ECS describes, 46; ECS recalls, 541–43; in Johnstown, 370, 406–7; tours Great Britain, 27; at World's Anti-Slavery Convention, 246

Stanton, Henry Brewster, Jr., *xxvii*, 559; ECS visits, 405, 406

Stanton, Marguerite Marie Berry, xxvii, 168; letters from ECS, 114–15, 405–7; in U.S., 93; with SBA in Paris, 236, 238, 239, 241, 242, 244. *See also* Berry, Marguerite Marie

Stanton, Robert Livingston (1859–1920), *xxvii*, 444, 559; ECS visits, 405, 406

Stanton, Theodore Weld, *xxvii*, 559; childhood of, 542; ECS describes, 442–43; and *History*, 118; and *Index*, 443, 444n; letters from ECS, 14, 63–64, 374n, 541–43; marries M. M. Berry, 62–63n; mentioned, 52, 165, 168, 277, 405, 406, 469; as translator, 115n, 118, 336n; travels of, 201n; in U.S., 93, 506–7; with SBA in Paris, 236, 237, 238, 239, 241, 242, 244; *Woman Question in Europe*, 119n, 173, 371

Star Route Cases, 372

state action for woman suffrage: objections to, 154, 161, 201, 345–47, 422–23

state legislatures: and federal amendment, 95, 97n, 208

states' rights: and citizenship, 477–79

Stead, William Thomas, 436n

Stebbins, Catharine Ann Fish, *71n*; and Mich. association, 307; at suffrage meeting, 70

Stephens, Alexander Hamilton, *365n*; and House committee, 362

Stephens, Kate, *235n*; travels with SBA, 233–34

Stephens, Nannie A., *523n*; hosts SBA, 522–23

Stewart, William Morris, 547, *548n*

Stone, Lucy, *10n*, 505; and 1884 election, 385; age of, 450; and American association, 6–7; and ECS birthday, 463, 464; and ECS invitation, 470, 471n; and Eddy will, 129–31, 163, 178, 348, 390; in Ill., 522n; in Kan., 521; letters to SBA, 348–49, 387, 390; and National association, xxiv, 6, 58, 156, 158, 158–59nn, 312–13, 334, 387, 390; and Neb. campaign, 176, 177n, 181; and polygamy, 159n; at R.I. meeting, 376; and SBA, 6–7, 335n, 351, 411n; and suffrage factions, 205, 207; and "Woman's Realm," 383

Straight University: SBA visits, 408

suffrage, African-American: effects of, 96

suffrage, manhood: ECS objects to, 89–93, 91; for blacks, 303; for immigrants, 91

suffrage, woman: acceptance of, 257; effects of, 4–5; importance of, 173–75; need for,

(suffrage, woman, *continued*)
194–95, 303; objections to answered, 184–87; and other reforms, 1–3, 65, 66, 323–25, 480, 481; and religion, 2–3; resistance to, 257–58; and social progress, 174
Le Suffrage des femmes: SBA attends meeting of, 242
Sullivan, Margaret Frances Buchanan, 311, *312n*
Sunday closing, 499–501
Sun Jiaku, 248–49, *262n*
Surbiton, England: SBA in, 295
Swain, Adeline Morrison, *488n*; and National association, 477
Swedenborg, Emanuel, 77, *87n*
Sweet Cicely (Holley): SBA reads, 471
Swing, David, 42, *45n*, 458
Swisshelm, Jane Grey Cannon, *210–11n*; letter from SBA, 210

Tacitus, Cornelius, *344n*; quoted, 343
The Taming of the Shrew (Shakespeare): characters in, 83
Tanner, Margaret Priestman Wheeler, *292n*; letter from ECS, 291–92; and Liberal party, 292
Taylor, Clementia Doughty, *227n*; entertains ECS and SBA, 225
Taylor, Emily Annette Winslow, 246, *260n*
Taylor, Ezra Booth, *319n*; and amendment, 547; and House committee, 318–19; and Judiciary Committee, 318; minority report of, 505–6
Taylor, Helen, *294n*; ECS hears, 296, 296n; SBA hears, 293, 296
Taylor, Peter Alfred, *227n*; entertains ECS and SBA, 225
Taylor, Rachel Ann Broadhead, 20–21, *22n*
Teller, Henry Moore, *552n*; and Senate vote, 550
temperance: in antebellum N.Y., 101, 102; and churches, 394; and woman suffrage, 1, 111, 305–6
Temple Café (Washington), 320
Tenafly, N.J.: ECS attempts to vote in, 14; SBA in, 6–8, 12–13, 14, 15, 20–21, 23, 24–25, 30, 33–34, 46, 49–50, 52, 56–58, 120, 128, 132–33, 148, 150–51, 153, 154, 161, 438–39, 440–41, 444, 447, 465–67, 558–61
Tennessee: suffragists in, 158
Tennyson, Alfred Lord, 248, *262n*; quoted, 460
territories: and woman suffrage, xxi, 134, 140, 151, 153, 154
Terry, Ellen, 225, *227n*
Texas: woman suffrage in, 69, 71n
Theophrastus, 457, *462n*
Thiers, Louis-Adolphe, 114, *115n*
third parties: and woman suffrage, 362

Thirteenth Amendment, 96
Thomas, Julia Josephine, 255, *265n*
Thomas, Mary Frame Myers, *488n*; and National association, 477
Thomasson, Katharine Lucas, *199n*, 200, 274, 285; in Edinburgh, 197; entertains ECS and SBA, 273; letter to ECS, 203–4
Thompson, Barbara J. Binks, *60–61n*; letters from SBA, 59–60, 104–6
Thompson, Elizabeth Rowell, *11n*; and *History*, 8, 11n, 12, 13
Thompson, George, 27, *29n*; at World's Anti-Slavery Convention, 246
Thompson, May Eliza Wright. *See* Sewall, May Eliza Wright Thompson
Thomson, Anna, 48, *49n*
Thomson, Mary Adeline, 48, *49n*, 383; hosts SBA, 217; at suffrage meeting, 142; in Tenafly, 54; travels with SBA, 409n
Tilton, Theodore, *150n*, 385; and 15th Amendment, 150, 152
Tippecanoe Club (Indianapolis), 176, 177n
Tod, Isabella Maria Susan, 197, *198n*, 273, 285; at Glasgow meeting, 196; SBA visits, 288
Toledo Woman Suffrage Association: and National association, 157
"To the Governors of the Thirteen Colonial States" (ECS), 515–17
Toulouse, France: ECS in, 168, 173–75
Toulouse, University of, 168n, 170
A Treatise on Prayer (Bickersteth), 458
Tremont Temple (Boston), 56, 68
Trinity, the, 75, 79, 80
Tucker, John Randolph, *319n*; and House committee, 318–19; and Judiciary Committee, 318, 426
Tunbridge Wells, England: SBA in, 280, 283

umbrellas, 220, 295
Umsted, Elizabeth Johnson Devereux, 99, *100n*; marriage of, 431
Una (Providence), 104, 104n
Underwood, Benjamin Franklin, *3–4n*, *443n*, 529; letters from ECS, 442–43, 494, 498–99
Underwood, Sara A. Francis, *409n*, 442, 499; letters from ECS, 416, 528–29; and National association, 408; and *Woman's Bible*, 528–29
Union Club (New York), 406
Union Pacific Railroad, 187
Union Signal (Chicago), 380
Unitarian church: and women, 392
Universal Franchise Association (Washington): and National association, 157
Universalist church: and women, 392
Universal Suffrage. Speech of Hon. Thomas W. Palmer, 427

Upton, Harriet Taylor, *506n*; letter from SBA, 505–6
U.S. Congress: and 1884 election, 361–64. *See also* Joint Committee on Reconstruction
U.S. Constitution: attempts to put God in, 2; centennial of, 515–17
U.S. House of Representatives: amendment in, 18, 19n, 167, 167n, 312, 314n, 491, 491–92n; Committee on Territories, 151, 153, 153n, 154; hearings of, 426, 429n; Judiciary Committee, 121, 318, 319n, 426–27; Judiciary Committee, reports of, 426–27, 429n, 505–6, 506n; proposed women's committee in, 18, 20n, 34–35, 121–22, 134, 136, 137, 312, 315, 316, 318, 322, 361–62, 378, 466; Rules Committee, 315; Suffrage Committee, xx, 137n, 155, 163, 205, 361–62, 426; Suffrage Committee, renewal of, 217; Suffrage Committee, reports of, 217, 218n, 426, 428–29n
U.S. Senate: amendment in, 18, 19n, 167, 205, 206–7n, 312, 314n, 375, 380, 381, 404, 404n, 405–6, 507, 508n, 535, 536n; Committee on Privileges and Elections, 96, 97n; hearings of, 145, 146n, 147, 344–48, 426; proposed women's committee in, 18, 20n, 34–35, 39, 43n, 123, 124, 124n, 128, 128–29n; Suffrage Committee, xx, 133, 133–34n, 134, 136, 140, 154, 161, 163, 217, 305, 361–62, 374–75, 375n, 379, 426, 466; Suffrage Committee, reports of, 169, 347–48, 348n, 377, 426, 428–29n, 429n, 471–72, 472n, 490, 535, 535–36n, 537, 538–39; and Utah suffrage, 485, 490n; vote on amendment, 545, 545n, 546–47, 548–49, 550, 554
U.S. Supreme Court: and *Minor v. Happersett*, 18; and *San Mateo County v. Southern Pacific R.R.*, 210, 211n
Utah Territory: disfranchisement in, xxi, 141, 141–142n, 485, 490n, 549, 554; woman suffrage in, 248
Utah Territory Woman Suffrage Association: and National association, 158
Utica, N.Y.: SBA in, 437–38

Vanderbilt, William Henry, *331n*; art gallery of, 330
Van Lew, Elizabeth L., 319, *320n*
Vassar College, 255–56
The Vatican Decrees (Gladstone), 258
Vermillion, A. Martha, *106n*; and *History*, 105
Vermont: school suffrage in, 248
Vest, George Graham, *141n*; and Senate committee, 140
Victor, Miss (of Ohio), 317
Victoria (queen of England), 92, *93n*, 226

Victoria Adelaide Mary Louisa (crown princess of Prussia), 234, *235n*
Vigil, Agapito, 423, *428n*
Villard, Henry, 330, *331n*
Vineland, N.J.: suffragists in, 157
violence: against women, 92
Voorhees, Charles Stewart, 378, *379n*

Wadleigh, Bainbridge, 96, *97n*
Wait, Anna Amelia Churchill, *126n*; and *History*, 125
Waite, Catherine Van Valkenburg, *44n*; and National association, 143; at suffrage meeting, 40
Waite, Charles Burlingame, *44n*; *History of the Christian Religion*, 40; at suffrage meeting, 40
Waite, Jessie Fremont, *44n*; at suffrage meeting, 40
Walker, Mary Edwards, 323, *327n*
Wall, Sarah E.: at Senate hearing, 344
Wallace, Zerelda Gray Sanders, 306, *308n*; and *Woman's Bible*, 515
Walton, Genevieve Maria Julia, *231–32n*; in Paris, 242; travels with SBA, 228
Ward, Eliza Titus, 236, *237n*
Warren, Mercy Otis, 250, *263n*
Washburn, William Drew, *365n*; and House committee, 362
Washington, D.C.: ECS in, 391–99, 402–3; SBA in, 34–35, 116, 204–6, 207–8, 213–14, 217, 305–7, 312–14, 315–20, 323–26, 379–80, 381, 391–99, 402, 404–5, 471–72, 492, 535, 546–47, 553–54
Washington, George, 317, *317n*, 516
Washington, Martha Dandridge Custis, 372, *374n*
Washington *Evening Star*: interviews SBA, 546–47
Washington Post: interviews ECS, 402–3
Washington Territory: statehood proposed, 507, 508n, 549; suffrage campaign in, 308–9n, 314; suffrage victory in, 335; woman suffrage in, xxi; women voting in, 378–79
Washington Territory Woman Suffrage Association: and National association, 158
Waterloo House (London), 273
Weaver, Archibald Jerard, *365n*; and House committee, 362
Weinheimer, John L., 506, *508n*; and *History*, 508–9; letter from SBA, 508–9
Weld, Angelina Emily Grimké, *47n*, 70, 250; in *History*, 46
Weld, Charles Stuart, 46, *47n*
Weld, Theodore Dwight, *47n*; letter from ECS, 46–47; *In Memory of Angelina Grimké Weld*, 46
Weld, Theodore Grimké, 46, *47n*

Wellesley College, 256
Wells, Emmeline Blanche Woodward, *555–56n*; telegram to SBA, 554–55
Wellstood, Jessie Morrison, *373n*; in U.S., 371
Wendt, Mathilde F., 99, *100n*
Wesley, John, 74, *86n*, 412
West, Josephine Richards, *555–56n*; telegram to SBA, 554–55
Westminster, Palace of, 224–25
Westminster Palace Hotel (London), 284, 285
Westminster Review, 248
Whipple, Edwin Percy, *89n*; quoted, 83–84
White, Andrew Dickson, *265n*; quoted, 255
White, John Daugherty, *137n*; and amendment, 167n; and House committee, 134–35, 217
Whittle, Ewing, 299, *299n*
Whittle, Laura, 300, *300n*
Whittle, Margaret, 300, *300n*
Wichita, Kan.: SBA in, 522–23
Wichita Equal Suffrage Association: founded, 522–23
Wigham, John, Jr., 27, *29n*
Wilbour, Charles Edwin, *241–42n*; SBA visits, 241
Wilbour, Charlotte Beebe, *241–42n*; SBA visits, 241
Wilkeson, Catharine Henry Cady, 461n
Wilkeson, Zelma, 165, *166n*
Wilkie, Dr. (in Paris), 241
Willard, Amelia, 12, *14n*
Willard, Frances Elizabeth Caroline, *106n*, 287, 306; in Dansville, N.Y., 104; and *Our Famous Women*, 239, 240n; and *Woman's Bible*, 514, 515; and woman suffrage, 116, 117n, 547
Willcox, Albert Oliver, *489n*; at suffrage meeting, 478
Willcox, John Keappock Hamilton, *467n*; and L. D. Blake, 465–66; and N.Y. campaign, 208–9n, 465–66
William I (emperor of Germany), 234, *235n*
Williams, Zina Priscenda Young, *555–56n*; telegram to SBA, 554–55
Willis, Catharine, 171, *172n*
Willis, Edmund P., 171, *172n*
Willis, Gwendolen Brown, 146, *146n*
Willis, Henry Parker, 146, *146n*
Willis, John Henry, 146, *146n*
Willis, Sarah L. Kirby Hallowell, 171, *172n*
Wilson, David, 212, *213n*
Wilson, James Falconer, *552n*; and Senate vote, 550
Winchester, England: SBA in, 295
Winslow, Caroline Brown, 323, *326–27n*
Winslow, Emily Annette. *See* Taylor, Emily Annette Winslow

Winthrop House (Boston), 66
Wisconsin: congressional district meetings in, 524–25, 526–27, 535; in *History*, 145; school suffrage in, 526–27, 527–28n
Wisconsin Woman Suffrage Association: and National association, 157
Wise, Anne, 182, *183n*
Wise, William G., 182, *183n*
witchcraft, 74, 86n
Wittenmyer, Annie Turner, 116, *117n*
wives: violence against, 389
Wolfe, John B., *400n*; at suffrage meeting, 393–94
Wollstonecraft, Mary, 403, *403n*
"Woman, Church, and State" (Gage), 93, 146n, 277; quoted, 74–75, 76, 83–84
The Woman Question in Europe (Stanton), 119n, 371, 559; and ECS, 173
Woman's Bible, xxiii; committee for, 510–11, 512, 513–15, 519–20, 528–29
"The Woman's Bible" (ECS), 510–11
Woman's Christian Temperance Union: annual meeting of, 116, 117n; and federal amendment, xx, 380; and National association, xxiv; and *Union Signal*, 380; and woman suffrage, 116, 117n, 306, 550
Woman's Club of New Orleans: SBA speaks to, 408, 409n
Woman's Journal (Boston), 10n; and 1884 election, 364n, 372, 373n, 385; funding of, 313–14; and *History*, 351, 358; mentioned, 6, 118, 301, 387; and National association, 5n, 58, 156, 159n
"Woman's Kingdom" (Chicago), 53, 54, 54n, 311, 318
Woman's Place To-Day. Four Lectures (Blake): ECS reads, 310–11
"Woman's Realm" (Pittsburgh), 383–84; letter from ECS, 388–89
"The Woman's Rights Movement and Its Champions in the United States" (ECS): mentioned, 24
Woman's Tribune (Beatrice, Neb.), xxiii, 379, 408, 441, 492, 521; founded, 306, 308n; and National association, 479
Woman Suffrage party (N.Y.), 208–9n; and state association, 465–66, 467n
"Woman Wants Bread, Not the Ballot" (SBA): mentioned, 183, 527
women, single, 277, 279, 284–85; and suffrage, 388–89
women as writers, 83–84
Women's Loyal National League, 7
Women's Suffrage Journal (Manchester, Eng.), 332, 469
Wood, Margaret Walker Lyon, 125, *125–126n*
Woodall, William, *389–90n*; and married women's suffrage, 388

Woodhull, Victoria Claflin, 323, *327n*; in *History*, 430, 430n; and National association, 403, 403n. *See also* Martin, Victoria Claflin Woodhull
working women: and B. F. Butler's campaign, 368, 368–69n; and National association, 485–86; and suffrage, 549
World's Anti-Slavery Convention: ECS describes, 246–47; female delegates to, 246–47, 260n; L. C. Mott delegate to, 24–25
World's Industrial and Cotton Centennial Exposition, 384n; SBA attends, 408–9
Wormley, James, 38n
Worms, Henry De, 388, *390n*
Worthington, Alfred D., 239, *240n*
Wright, Anne W., *448n*; and ECS birthday, 447; letter from SBA, 447–48
Wright, Edith Livingston, *464n*; and ECS birthday, 463
Wright, Flora McMartin, *17n*, 359; and ECS birthday, 463

Wright, Frances, 403, *403n*
Wright, Martha Coffin Pelham, 16, *17n*, 99, 286
Wright, William Pelham, *17n*
Wyoming Territory: opposition to suffrage in, 185, 189n; suffragists in, 158; support for suffrage in, 163, 185, 189n, 417; woman suffrage in, 248

Xanthippe, 414

Yale University, 147
Yorke, John Reginald, 388, *390n*
Young, Edward, *462n*; *The Complaint; or Night-Thoughts*, 458
Young, Zina Diantha Huntington, *555–56n*; telegram to SBA, 554–55

Zhi Kang, 248–49, *262n*
Zimmermann, Johann Georg, *462n*; *Solitude*, 458